XML Applications

Frank Boumphrey, Olivia Direnzo, Jon Duckett, Joe Graf, Dave Hollander, Paul Houle, Trevor Jenkins, Peter Jones, Adrian Kingsley-Hughes, Kathy Kingsley-Hughes, Craig McQueen and Stephen Mohr

Wrox Press Ltd. ®

XML Applications

Arden House, 1102 Warwick Road, Acock's Green, Birmingham, B27 6BH, UK
Printed in the United States
ISBN 1-861001-9-08

Trademark Acknowledgements

Credits

Authors
Frank Boumphrey
Olivia Direnzo
Jon Duckett
Joe Graf
Dave Hollander
Paul Houle
Trevor Jenkins
Peter Jones
Adrian Kingsley-Hughes
Kathy Kingsley-Hughes
Craig McQueen
Stephen Mohr

Managing Editor
Anthea Elston

Editors
Jon Duckett
Peter Jones

Technical Reviewers
Andrew Enfield
David Bostock
Dave Hollander
Jim Johnson
Benoît Marchal
Craig McQueen
Boyd Nolan

Design/Layout
Frances Olesch

Cover
Andrew Guillaume

Index
Marilyn Rowland

About the Authors

Frank Boumphrey currently works for Cormorant Consulting, a firm that specializes in medical and legal documentation. He started programming in the dark ages of punch cards and machine language. One of his first projects was to help write a program that differentiated between an incoming Soviet ICBM and a flock of geese. The fact that we are reading this is evidence that it probably worked!

Burnt out by thinking in Hexadecimals, he left programming and became a medical doctor, ending up as a Professor and the chief of spine surgery at a large American Midwest institution. Along the way he was involved with the introduction of the MRI to the medical world.

Semi-retirement returned him to his first interest of computing and now he tries to get medical institutions to organize their medical records in a semi rational fashion, and on the side lectures to medical personal and healthcare executives on documentation issues.

Interestingly he is most in demand by legal firms that want to rationalize their medical databases! His main objective at the present is to help XML to become the language of choice in Web documents.

Olivia Direnzo is an artist who adores plants and animals. Olivia graduated from Cornell with a degree in Animal Science. She and Paul Houle are Honeylocust Media Systems, which does research into web-based hypermedia, since that seems to be the most interesting thing going on right now.

Jon Duckett. Having graduated from Brunel University, London, with a degree in Psychology, Jon took a change of direction, coming back to his home town, to work for Wrox in their Birmingham offices. Thanks to the lovely people at Wrox, he isn't missing London too much, and has found a new base for his endeavours in single-handedly supporting the economies of several tea-producing nations.

Joe Graf was a consultant developing large-scale client/server systems for six years before founding the e-comm group inc., a software company focussed on the emergence of XML as a medium for performing transactions on the Internet. Recently, he lead the design and development of one of the first XML Application Severs, OFX Script, that enables financial institutions to support financial transactions via the Internet.

Dave Hollander. After graduating from Michigan Tech, Dave worked at Bell Labs, several computer graphics companies and Phillips DuPont Optical. Dave joined Hewlett-Packard in '88. At HP Dave has led the development of information publishing tools, processes, production DTDs and systems. Dave created and managed `www.HP.com` as it went from under a thousand to over a million hits a day. Currently, Dave is developing XML based content management systems targeted at channel communications.

During this time Dave has been husband, father, cub-scout leader, school committee chairman and active in formal and informal standards activities, including the Rock Ridge format (CD-ROM), Davenport, and the OSF DTD effort. Dave is an original member of the XML Working Group, co-author of the XML Namespace specification and Co-Chair of the W3C XML Schema Working Group.

Paul Houle recently got a PhD in Physics from Cornell and now works at the Max Plank Institute for the Physics of Complex Systems in Germany.
An avid Linux user, he likes to program in C, Perl and Java.

Trevor Jenkins is a free-lance consultant working on document and text management systems. His recent clients have included a major STM publisher and a fast food chain. Previously, he has undertaken work for major accountancy and telecommunication companies. SGML is in his blood; he participates in the work of the BSI and ISO on SGML and related standards, which includes technical evaluation of XML. He has contributed to several technical reports on SGML that have been published by ISO ("Techniques for Using SGML" and "Text Entry Systems").

Peter Jones is a technical editor and in-house author with Wrox Press. He has a diverse range of interests, few of which he has had time to pursue since joining Wrox. Whenever he gets the opportunity he likes to relax by hurtling around on a large, ludicrously fast motorcycle just for the hell of it. He would like to express his thanks to his family, friends, all the people at Wrox and all those on the XML-Dev mailing list, who were so supportive throughout the production of this book.

Adrian Kingsley-Hughes (awkh@khd.co.uk) has been Technical Director of Kingsley-Hughes Development Ltd, a Training and Consultancy firm specialising in Web dev and visual programming languages, since starting the company in 1996 whilst studying chemistry at Bangor University. He is a consultant in Internet Development and Windows platform programming, writing educational software in such diverse areas as chemistry, astronomy and the Welsh language. He also writes horror novels and is learning to play the didgeridoo.

Kathie Kingsley-Hughes (kkh@khd.co.uk) is the MD of Kingsley-Hughes Development Ltd, a Training and Consultancy firm specialising in web dev and visual programming languages, first going into CDF channels with The Dragon Channel, a popular animated magazine written in dynamic HTML, which was among the first active channels in the UK. Before that she was a trainer in IT for almost 6 years before studying chemistry and computing at Bangor and the Open University. Her interests include home-based education and the Internet classroom. She also tutors in chemistry, physics and mathematics.

Craig McQueen is a Principal Consultant with Sage Information Consultants Inc. His area of expertise is developing middle-tier COM components for e-commerce. He has worked with Wrox Press on a number of projects. He also writes articles monthly for Visual C++ Developer newsletter. Craig led development of two retail Internet software products, InContext FlashSite and InContext WebAnalyzer.
Craig has a Master of Science degree from the University of Toronto where he specialized in Human-Computer Interaction in the Computer Science department. He has five publications and presented at three International conferences as a result of his research. Craig can be reached at cmcqueen@sageconsultants.com.

Stephen Mohr began programming in high school, back when that was somewhat unusual. Over the last ten years, he has specialized in the PC computing platform. A senior software systems architect with Omicron Consulting, he designs and develops systems using C++, Java, JavaScript, COM, and various internet working standards and protocols. Stephen holds BS and MS degrees in computer science from Rensselaer Polytechnic Institute. His research interests include distributed object-based computing and the practical applications of artificial intelligence.

Table of Contents

An Introduction to XML

XML, or **Extensible Markup Language**, has widely been touted as the most exciting new development in Web technology. After reading this book, we hope that you too will share this enthusiasm. If you already have an understanding of HTML you will be amazed by the flexibility of XML. Not only will you be writing XML applications in no time at all, you will also see the potential that XML can offer you as a Web developer.

In this book we aim to give you a thorough grounding in what XML is and the different processes you'll need to master to create an XML application. We then go on to look at how XML links with some of the most recent developments in Internet technology, such as ActiveX Data Objects (ADO) and Active Server Pages, giving you examples of many working XML applications.

Who Should Read This Book?

This book assumes a basic knowledge of the Web and a familiarity with HTML. However, no experience of XML is assumed. After building a foundation for understanding what XML is and how it is used, we will go into enough depth to allow you to create powerful XML applications. In the later chapters there are applications which use Active Server Pages and SQL scripts, Java and C++. While an understanding of these would be useful for working through the examples in some of the later chapters, even if you are not familiar with these topics you will still be able to follow the architecture of the XML solution.

You should read this book if:

- You want to know all about XML
- You have ever wished for more tags than HTML offers
- You have wished you could create your own tags
- You would like your markup to actually mean something

- You have wanted to separate a document's styling from its content
- You want a more powerful way to create Web applications
- You just don't want to be left behind while one of the most exciting revolutions in the ever-changing world of the Web takes place

What You Need to Use this Book

There's nothing to stop you creating your first XML application today. While there are various HTML and XML editors that can help you to author XML, all you really need is a simple text editor such as Windows Notepad. Providing you have a computer, a browser such as Netscape Communicator 4+ or Internet Explorer 4+ running on your computer, and Internet access to download the components you need to work through the examples, you'll be writing XML in no time at all.

Rather than diving straight into the topic of XML, it would be helpful to take a look at markup and its history in the context of SGML and HTML.

What is a Markup Language?

While you may not realize it, we come across markup every day. Quite simply, markup refers to anything put on a document which adds special meaning or provides extra information. For example, highlighted text is markup.

But, unless others understand our markup it is of little use, so we need a set of rules encompassing the following points for it to be understood:

- To declare what constitutes markup
- To declare exactly what our markup means

A markup language is any such set of rules. It is possible to classify markup as one of three types, stylistic, structural or semantic:

Stylistic Markup

This indicates how the document is to be presented. When we use bolding or italics on a word processor, it is stylistic markup. In HTML the `<FONT>`, `<I>`, `<B>`, and `<U>` tags are all stylistic markup.

Structural Markup

This informs us of how the document is to be structured. The `<Hn>`, `<P>` and the `<DIV>` tags are examples of structural markup, which indicate a heading, paragraph and container section respectively.

Semantic Markup

This tells us something about the content of the data. As such `<TITLE>` and `<CODE>` are examples of semantic markup in HTML.

Markup languages define the markup rules which add meaning to the structure and content of documents. They are the grammar and the syntax which specify how a language should be 'spoken'.

Tags and Elements

Even those who are familiar with HTML still often get the meaning of **tags** and **elements** mixed up. Just to clarify, tags are the angled brackets (known as delimiters) and the text between them. Here are some examples of tags used in HTML:

`<P>` is a tag that marks the beginning of a new paragraph
`<I>` is a tag indicating that the following text should be rendered in italic type
`</I>` is a tag indicating that this is the end of the text to be rendered in italic

Elements, however, usually refer to tags plus their content, so the following is an example of an element:

```
<B> This is bold text </B>
```

In general terms tags are a label that tells a user agent (such as a browser) to do something to whatever is encased in the tags.

> *A **user agent** is anything which acts on behalf of a user. You are a user agent working for your boss, your computer is a user agent working for you, your browser is a user agent working for your computer, and so it goes on.*

Empty elements (which don't have closing tags), such as the `<IMG>` tag in HTML, have to be treated a little differently in XML, for now don't worry about this – we will come back to it later.

The following diagram illustrates the parts of an element:

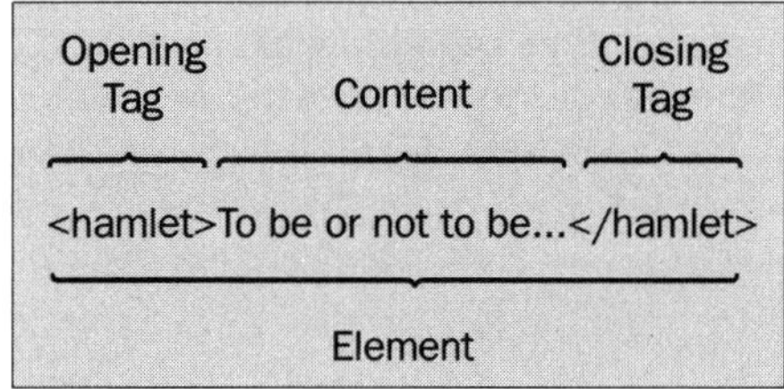

Attributes

Any tag can have an attribute as long as it is defined. They take the form of **name/value pairs** (also referred to as **attribute/value pairs**), in that the element can be given an attribute (with a name), and the attribute must then carry a value. They take the form:

```
<tagname attribute="value">
```

For example, in HTML 4.0 the `<BODY>` element can take the following attributes:

CLASS	ID	DIR	LANG	STYLE	TITLE
BACKGROUND	BGCOLOR	ALINK	LINK	VLINK	TEXT

So, for example, in HTML BODY could take the following attributes:

```
<BODY BGCOLOR="#000000" ALINK="#999999" LINK="#990099" VLINK=#"888888"
TEXT="#999999">
```

Markup languages

In this section we'll be looking at three markup languages, SGML, HTML and, of course, XML. **SGML** is a markup language that is used to create other markup languages. The most famous language written in SGML is HTML, which we all know and love from its use on the Web. Because HTML is written according to the rules of SGML, it is known as an **SGML application**. The problem with SGML is that it is a highly complex language, which is why we're interested in XML - XML was designed especially for the Web as a simpler version of SGML, although it retains much of SGML's functionality. Let's take a closer look at each of these markup languages in turn:

SGML

Back in 1986, **Standardized Generalized Markup Language** (**SGML**) became an international standard (ISO 8879) for defining markup languages - long before the Web was thought of - although SGML had been in existence since the late 1960's. Its purpose was to describe markup languages, by allowing the author to provide formal definitions for each of the elements and attributes in the language, thus allowing authors to create their own tags which relate to their content. At the time it was one of several such competing languages, however it was its popular offspring, HTML, which gave SGML prominence over the others.

As a language SGML is very powerful, but with its power came complexity, and many of its features are rarely used. It is also difficult to interpret an SGML document without the definition of the markup language – kept in the **Document Type Definition** (**DTD**). The DTD is where all the rules for the language are kept in SGML. The DTD has to be sent with, or included in, the SGML document so that the custom created tags can be understood. Markup languages created in SGML are known as SGML applications.

HTML

HTML was originally an SGML application. It describes how information is to be prepared for the World Wide Web. HTML is just a set of SGML rules, in a DTD – the rules that explain what the tags and elements mean. In HTML's case the DTD is stored in the browser, and is covered in many books and on several Web sites. Being a fraction of the size of SGML and far simpler HTML is very easy to learn, a factor which quickly made it very popular and widely adopted by all sorts of people.

HTML was created by Tim Berners-Lee in 1991 as a way of marking up technical papers so that they could be easily organized and transferred across different platforms for the scientific community. The idea was to create a set of tags that could be used to mark up a document. The use of these tags would then enable documents to be transferred between computers so that others could render the document in a usable format. For example:

```
<H1> This is a primary heading </H1>
<H2> This is a secondary heading </H2>
<PRE> This is text where formatting is important </PRE>
<P> The text between these two tags is a paragraph </P>
```

Back then, the scientific community had little concern over the appearance of their documents. What mattered to them was that the meaning was preserved. They weren't worried about the color of their fonts or the exact size of their primary heading!

HTML uses a protocol called **HTTP** (**Hypertext Transfer Protocol**) to transfer information across the Internet. It is one of a number of protocols used on the Internet, which are collectively known as the Internet Protocol Suite, or more commonly as **TCP/IP**. Several of the other TCP/IP protocols are still widely used, and before HTML came along the most popular was **FTP** (**File Transfer Protocol**).

The ease with which HTTP could be used to connect to another document gave it an edge over other protocols. And the combination of this with a language that is simple to learn ensured the rapid spread of systems implementing HTML and HTTP.

However, as HTML usage exploded and Web browsers started to become readily available, the non-scientific users soon started to create their own pages *en masse*. These non-scientific users became increasingly concerned about the presentation of their material. Manufacturers of the browsers used to view Web sites were all too ready to offer different tags that would allow Web page authors to display their documents with more creativity than just using plain ASCII text. Netscape were first, adding the familiar `<FONT>` tag which allowed users to change the fonts themselves, as well as their size and weighting. This triggered a rapid expansion in the number of tags that browsers would support.

With the new tags came new problems. Different browsers' implementation of new tags was inconsistent. Today we have sites that display signs saying that they are Best viewed through Netscape Navigator, or Designed for Internet Explorer, and we expect to be able to produce Web pages that resemble documents created on the most sophisticated Desk Top Publishing systems.

Meanwhile, the browser's potential as a new application platform was quickly recognized, and Web developers started creating distributed applications for businesses using the Internet as a medium for information and financial transactions.

Drawbacks of HTML

While the widespread adoption of HTML propelled the rise in numbers of people on the Web, users wanted to do an ever-increasing variety of new and more complex things, and weaknesses with HTML became apparent:

- **HTML has a fixed tag set**. You cannot create your own tags that can be interpreted by others.
- **HTML is a presentation technology**. It doesn't carry information about the meaning of the content held within its tags.
- **HTML is "flat"**. You cannot specify the importance of tags, so a hierarchy of data cannot be represented.
- **Browsers are being used as an application platform**. HTML does not provide the power needed for creating advanced Web applications at a level which developers are currently aiming for. For example, it does not readily offer the ability for advanced processing and retrieval upon documents.
- **High traffic volumes**. Existing HTML documents that are used as applications clog up the Internet with high volumes of client-server traffic, for example sending large general recordsets across networks when only a small amount of information is required.

Over time, the Web has become more and more fragmented as individuals have attempted to display information in different ways, not only using differing implementations of HTML, but also using scripting languages, Dynamic HTML, Channels etc. that are not compatible with all browsers.

While HTML has proven to be very useful as a way of marking up documents for use over the Web, a document marked up in HTML tells us very little about the content. For most documents to be useful in a business situation there is a need to know about the document's content. If a document does contain details about its contents then it is possible to perform generalized processing and retrieval upon that file with ease. SGML fulfills this requirement for carrying information about a document; however, because it is such a complex language it has never really taken off in the way in which HTML has. As an example of why carrying information about the data you are storing can be useful on the Web consider the following scenario:

Imagine you had a library of CD's marked up in HTML stored on a Web server. If you wanted to find a track by a certain artist, you would have to download the whole recordset then do a search through the all the records in their entirety.

On the other hand, imagine that your library had been marked up with tags that held information about the data. For instance, you used `<artist>` to indicate performers, `<title>` to indicate CD titles, and so on. You would then be able to send a request to the server for just the relevant part of the document, rather than the document as a whole. This would result in smaller faster searches and less network traffic.

Think about the possibilities. If you could mark up all your documents in tags which described their contents, contacts' details could then have tags such as `<firstname>` and `<email>`, catalogs could use tags such as `<price>` and `<partnumber>`. This was possible with SGML, but it was never been widely used, and now it is possible with XML...

How XML Came About

The major players in the browser market made it clear that they had no intention of fully supporting SGML. And its complexity prevented many people from learning it. So moves were made to create a simplified version of SGML for use on the Web, signaling a return to documents being marked up according to their content. The World Wide Web Consortium (W3C) saw it's worth and agreed to sponsor the project. A group of SGML experts, led by Jon Bosak of Sun Microsystems, began work on creating a subset of SGML that could be adopted by the Web community. When SGML was put under the knife, several of the non-essential aspects were cut, re-modeling it into a new language to be called XML. This lean alternative is far more accessible, its specification running to just 26 pages, compared with the 500+ pages that defined SGML.

What is XML?

XML got the name Extensible Markup Language because it is not a fixed format like HTML. While HTML is limited to a fixed set of tags that the author can use, XML users can create their own tags (or take tags created by others), which actually relate to their content. As such it is a metalanguage – a language that describes other languages. Let's go back to the example of the CD library, in XML we could have CDs marked up like this:

```
<cd>
<artist>Arnold Schwarzenegger</artist>
<title>I'll Be Bach</title>
<format>album</format>
```

```
<description>Arnie plays Bach's Brandenburg Concertos 1-3 on the Hammond
     Organ</description>
</cd>
```

Here you can see that the tags contain information about their contents. The <artist> tag tells you that the element's contents relate to the artist, <format> tells you that the content is about the CD's format. So this XML file actually contains information about a CD marked up with tags that describe their contents.

Alternatively, if you wanted to make a document that contained details about customers you could create one like this, which contains contact and ordering information. See how the tags actually describe contents:

```
<customer id="1023">
     <company-name>Groovydesign</company-name>
     <first-name>Alex</first-name>
     <last-name>Homer</last-name>
          <house-number>10</house-number>
          <street-name>North Greenside Avenue</street-name>
          <town>Sunnytown</town>
          <state>CA</state>
          <zip-code>94026</zip-code>
          <tel-no>408-725-0975</tel-no>
          <fax-no>408-725-0976</fax-no>
          <email>alexh@groovydesign.com</email>
     <on-order>Professional ASP Techniques for Webmasters</on-order>
          <qty>3</qty>
          <date-ordered>09-11-98</date-ordered>
          <delivery-date>09-14-98</delivery-date>
     <US$balance>-149.97</US$balance>
          <previous-purchases>
               <purchase qty=2>Pro ASP 2.0</purchase>
               <purchase qty=5>Instant HTML 2nd edit</purchase>
               <purchase qty=3>Pro MTS MSMQ with VB and ASP</purchase>
          </previous-purchases>
</customer>
```

As you can see, this contains a lot more detail. And, even though you have never seen it before, you can understand its contents. If there were entries like this for each customer it could be used in a number of ways, including:

- As a list of contacts
- The accounts department could see how much is owed
- A marketing department could see what areas a customer is interested in for direct marketing purposes
- To produce sales figures from each item purchased

> **It is very important to note that XML is case sensitive, unlike HTML, so the tags <artist> <Artist> and <ARTIST> are all different tag names.**

But, how do we know what these tags are supposed to do and how they are supposed to be displayed? Unfortunately if you were intending to learn *one* new language that would revolutionize your Web authoring, there's bad news. Creating XML applications is a little bit more complicated than that – there are several pieces which go together to create a coherent picture rather like a jigsaw puzzle. We'll take a quick look at the other pieces next, including:

- Document Type Definitions
- Style Sheets
- Extensible Linking Language
- Viewing XML
- Parsers

As if these weren't enough, there are moves to create even more technologies to use with XML – including Namespaces, XML-Data and Document Content Definitions. We will come back to these in the next chapter, but for the moment let's stick to the basics.

Document Type Definition

It is all very well being able to create our own tags which have special meaning and help explain the contents of a document, but if everyone is merrily creating their own tags we need a way for the tags to be understood. The original XML specification uses Document Type Definitions (DTDs) as a way of defining these tags. As we said earlier we have to incorporate the following rules when we create our new application of a metalanguage:

- Declare what constitutes markup
- Declare exactly what our markup means

So, it is necessary to declare each of the specific elements' tags. In the CD library example we need to declare `<cd>`, `<artist>`, `<title>`, `<format>` and `<description>`. The attributes that the elements can take also have to be declared in the DTD.

Style Sheets

Neither the XML document, nor the DTD contain anything that declares how the XML is to be displayed, but we can use a style sheet with a document to control its presentation. Style sheets contain the rules that declare how the document should appear and can be written in several languages including **Extensible Stylesheet Language (XSL)** and the **Cascading Style Sheets** mechanism **(CSS)**, both of which we cover. The style sheet is used when the data has to be displayed for human interpretation, be it a screen, paper, braille or an audio user agent. The style sheet simply tells the user agent how to display the information contained in the tags. Because the style sheet and the XML are kept separate it is possible to use different style sheets to display the same XML file in different contexts, and the same style sheet to display several XML documents in a similar format. We cover style sheets in detail in Chapters 7 and 8.

Viewing XML

Because XML is such a new technology the current version 4 browsers to not offer much support for viewing XML directly. Don't panic, this doesn't mean that you cannot use your XML and XSL/CSS files over the Web yet. All it means is that you need to convert the XML and its style sheet to HTML (or some other viewable format) so that the XML source can be viewed in a browser. There are several ways in which this can be done and we explore many of them in different sections of this book. Luckily it is unlikely that this measure will be required for too long as both Netscape and Microsoft have plan to offer far greater support for XML in their Communicator 5 and Internet Explorer 5 releases.

Parsers

For a system to use XML it requires two components:

- XML Processor
- The Application

The first part, known as the **XML processor**, has the job of checking that the XML file follows the specification. Then, so that the computer can interpret the XML files, the XML processor creates what is known as a **document tree**. It is this tree which the computer uses to follow processing instructions. The **parser** takes up the role of the XML processor. The **application** is the part which then processes the data in the tree.

Parsers also have another use, as tool for checking your XML document's syntax and structure. As the main browser manufacturers brought out new versions of their browsers during HTML's development, they included increasing amounts of code that allowed their browser to display HTML pages that had been written incorrectly – or not exactly according to the HTML specifications. It is intended that XML should be authored more accurately, and parsers are used to check that the XML document conforms to the rules of XML.

Linking

The simple links used in HTML have helped make it possible to surf around and between Web sites written in HTML with great ease and have certainly added greatly to the experience of using the Web as a hypertext medium. However, HTML's linking mechanism is only limited, and some developers have been looking for a new, more powerful way of linking their documents. XML doesn't actually change the way links are provided at a basic level; the basic HTML link structure has been preserved. However, it does add to it rather spectacularly. The linking specification for XML is comprised of two parts: **XLinks** and **XPointers**. XLinks can be used to link between documents with many-to-one and one-to-many relationships, while XPointers allow linking to specific parts of documents. We find out more about linking in XML in Chapter 5.

Why XML Is So Exciting

XML is very versatile, and the key to its flexibility is that the XML file is marked up in a way that describes its contents. It's not like HTML, which is a particular application for the display of content. XML is able to do this for two reasons. Firstly, because XML authors can create their own tags which relate to their content. Secondly, because it only contains information about the structure and meaning of the document, leaving the formatting of the elements to the style sheet. So, not only do XML tags mean something and say something about the content of elements allowing processing instructions to be carried out upon an XML file. The data can then be used and re-used across different platforms and in different applications.

XML as Data

Originally SGML was designed for use in marking up documents and as such is still widely used in the printing industry. In turn HTML has become a ubiquitous format for marking up documents for transmission across the Web. XML can be seen in a similar light to both of these languages – basically as a way of marking up documents – however, it is gaining wider interest in other fields not only as a way of marking up documents. Because its markup actually describes its contents, XML can be used as a universal format for any number of applications. Therefore, an XML file will not only be able to be displayed in your Web browser, as XML is integrated into a number of other applications it will also be possible to use the same file to supply data for a number of uses. Furthermore, it is gaining popularity as a data storage format as well as a document markup language. We look at an application which stores technical papers in XML format on the server in Chapter 10. However, because you have to store the tags as well, it may not always be suitable for large sets of records – developers may prefer to use a traditional database, and convert its contents into XML on the fly. We develop an application which stores data in a SQL database, and uses this to generate XML from this on the fly in Chapter 9.

So, as XML becomes more popular we are likely to see it creeping into a number of applications. Your accounts in your spreadsheet would be able to be used to display sales figures on your corporate intranet. Your customers database could be written in XML so that your email program could use it when you need to send a bulk mail out at the same time as your accounts department are checking on payments of individual orders. And at the same time the whole recordset is human readable.

Merging Multiple Documents

Another great strength of XML is that it is possible to merge several XML document instances into one big one. For example, if you had several documents or sets of records, they could all be merged into one master document. If our CD library represented the stocks of one retail outlet in a chain, it would be possible to create regional and national reports of stock. If we use this in conjunction with the ability to turn database content into XML we can also then create one XML document instance that includes data from several data sources.

Non-human Interaction

We shouldn't always assume that it will just be humans looking at XML pages in browsers over the Web. HTML authors have already had to get used to using `<META>` tags with keywords that describe their Web sites' contents so that the small programs sent out by search engines can index their sites more effectively. Because XML files describe their contents it is possible for a number of non-human user agents, such as the programs sent out by search engines, to process the information in the file. In the specific case of search engines, it will mean that they can provide far more accurate results to queries. While HTML has become a presentation format, XML acts as a common syntax so that many more non-human user agents will be able to use the data stored in XML files for different purposes. However, XML is just part of a movement towards describing contents of documents, as the Internet grows there is an increasing need for metadata.

Metadata

At the present time, we largely expect our Web pages to be rendered in browsers that visually display their contents on computer monitors. While mechanisms such as Cascading Style Sheets provide display rules for outputting to braille and audio based user agents, there is also a move towards making data machine-readable. Behind this move is a vision that the Internet will become populated by machine-based user agents which will be able to act on behalf of humans. For example, user agents that would be able to go and find a book on XML, or find the cheapest copy of Arnie's CD where he plays Bach on the Hammond organ for you. It is **metadata** which provides this type of information, describing the contents of documents. So metadata is, in fact, data about data, or more specifically in this case data describing Web resources. This will in turn enable, amongst other things, machines to perform far more accurate searches. Other areas where it will have an impact include:

- Document content rating
- Describing collections of pages that represent a single logical "document"
- Describing intellectual property rights of pages
- Expressing the privacy preferences of documents and of sites

It is the W3C's interest in metadata that has initiated the development of the **Resource Description Framework** (**RDF**) – which is a language for representing metadata. It has also spawned **PICS** – the **Platform for Internet Content Selection** – something we regularly hear about on the Web regarding rating of content.

RDF is the W3C's chosen language for expressing metadata that machines will be able to process simply. It is expected to play a large role in the automation of a wide variety of tasks.

Resource Description Format

Resource Description Framework (RDF) can be seen as a foundation for processing metadata, providing application independent exchange of machine-understandable information on the Web, emphasizing and facilitating automated processing of Web resources.

There are two main areas of RDF:

- The RDF Data Model
- The RDF syntax

The RDF data model is an abstract, conceptual framework for representing metadata. It is a syntax-neutral way of representing RDF expressions. The data model representation is used to evaluate equivalence in meaning. Data models can then be compared, and if the representations are the same, the RDF expressions can be seen as equivalent.

The RDF syntax is the concrete syntax for creating and exchanging metadata. Currently the syntax proposed is XML, although others may appear in time. RDF also requires the XML namespace facility (which we meet in Chapter 4) to precisely associate each property with the domain in which the property is defined.

RDF and XML are therefore complementary.

RDF allows authors to choose the vocabulary they desire; they just have to define the allowed use of the vocabulary. Imagine an application that organises CDs, marked up as we saw in our earlier example. Then imagine a similar application used as a library of paintings. The vocabulary is likely to be application-specific. As such, they both may have an `<artist>` tag, however, unlike the `<format>` tag we met in the CD library example, the art library may have a `<medium>` tag describing whether it is a watercolour, oil or pastel painting for example. RDF allows you to make it clear which vocabulary is being used. This is done by assigning a Web address to each particular vocabulary – by employing the namespace mechanism.

It also means that the operations we are used to performing with a database –is such as queries – we will be able to perform on data marked up according to the RDF. You would be able to filter and sort the information you require.

Of course, there is more to RDF than this, and you can find out further information by going to

`http://www.w3.org/Metadata/`

The motivation for this work is clear to see. As the Web increasingly grows in size, and more data is being accessed and maintained through the use of the Internet, there is an increasing need for it to be formally described. We have all tried to find information using a search engine, only to have it return large numbers of irrelevant URLs. Now, when metadata comes of age it will be possible for non-human agents to perform greatly improved processing and retrieval on our behalf. It will also help the meta-analysis of data in assessing business trends and performance, using RDF as a way of preparing analyses.

The World Wide Web Consortium

The World Wide Web Consortium (W3C) helps the creation and development of standards on the Web. It is supported by various grants and the fees paid by its members. There are about 300 members, but they comprise an enormous pool of wealth and, more importantly, expertise.

When a new standard is first submitted to the W3C it is as a **proposal** which then becomes a **note** when accepted by the W3C. The note for XSL was introduced in August 1997. This note then became a draft that was mulled over and altered by the members, usually on closed mailing lists of members and invited experts. This draft has since been made public in August 1998, and public discussion took place on the public mailing lists. Anyone can join these. Some of the lists are owned by W3C and others, such as the DSSSL list (hosted by ArborText), are outside. There is every indication that the members listen to non-members' views.

Finally the members come up with a proposed recommendation which the members vote on over a 6 week period. Depending on the result of the vote it either becomes an official standard, or it goes back to the draft stage.

Microsoft, Netscape, and the W3C

When it boils down to it, it doesn't really matter what we write in this book, what protocols are issued by bodies such as the W3C, what international standards we promulgate, if they are ignored by the majority of the world. And realistically 95% of the world uses Netscape or Microsoft browsers. So if the major players don't support XML what then?

As far as XML is concerned, the evolution of the Web is something that is needed by industry, and as such will be driven by the marketplace rather than by the marketing efforts of the major players. You can take it as a given that XML is here to stay.

The next generation of browsers will provide much greater support for XML with CSS type style sheets. Internet Explorer will use ActiveX to support XSL and the final implementation will support both XSL and CSS. You can keep up to date with XML support in IE5 by looking at:

`http://www.Microsoft.com/XML/`

Netscape have also pledged to support XML, their final intended implementation was less than clear at the time of writing, although it is expected to include XML and CSS, with support for XSL via Java Applets and JavaScript. You can keep an eye out for their progress at:

`http://home.netscape.com/browsers/`

As with so many things, there is a time when you have to stop watching from the sidelines and just jump in and get involved. Admittedly, it may seem a little bit daunting, learning about XML before there is widespread support for it and while the standards are changing. However, XML is rapidly gaining support, and now is the time to be learning about it. As we have said IE5 will provide support for XML, CSS and XSL, and, if the final release is not out when you come to read this, you can download a beta version from:

`http://www.microsoft.com/sitebuilder/ie/ieonsbn.htm`

There are examples in this book and on our Web site that show XML in action in the IE5 beta. Why not give it a go? The only related difficulty with IE5 is in running the application developed in Chapter 10, which requires a DLL from IE5 running in IE4 – don't worry, there's more information on this in the Chapter. Of course, as this is just a beta version there may be bugs in the program.

A Little Bit of Terminology

When we come to talk about how to define the new tags we will be creating in XML we will be talking about **schemas**. Generally speaking schemas are a generalized plan or diagram, however in computer science, schemas define the characteristics of classes of objects. So, what are **classes** and **objects**?

Well, objects are all around us. You can think of `computer` as a class of object. Then my computer, called `bobbin`, is an instance of `computer`. In fact your computer, my computer, Auntie Mable's computer could all be known as instances of the class `computer`. So a class is a collection of objects with common properties. The particular set of properties of an object defines what makes that object a member of a particular class. And a schema defines which properties (and their interrelations) a particular class should have. In effect a schema defines the internal structure of a class.

So, a class defines the parameters you need to define for an object to be a member of that class - for our purposes at least. Of course, the parameters chosen to define an object are subjective - different people may use different parameters to define the same thing. When you come to defining your tags it will be up to you to decide what aspects of the object you need to include. Of course this will in turn depend upon the problem you are addressing. This may all sound a little abstract, so let's think about a specific example - how about books?

`Book` could well be a **class** of object that we need to define. In order to describe your books you may just want to include the title of the books and the names of their authors. This could be done using two strings of characters such as `"Professional Style Sheets for HTML and XML"` for the title and `"Frank Boumphrey"` as the author. So the book 'Professional Style Sheets for HTML and XML' is the particular object (of class `book`) that we are describing in this case. The parameters that define the object of a class are known as **attributes**. So here the attributes are the `title` and `author`.

And, why did you need to know this again? Because a schema is a definition of the set of properties (and their interrelations) of a particular class of objects. And the schemas we are concerned with in XML are those defining the properties and structure of a class of documents.

XML-Dev

XML-Dev is a mailing list for XML developers. You will find references to this mailing list in a number of the chapters in this book. It is a list for people actively involved in developing resources for XML. While it is not restricted to members of the working group (WG) many subscribers to XML-Dev are actively working on implementing some part of the specification. XML-Dev is an informal unmoderated list to support those who are interested in the implementation and development of XML. You can subscribe by sending an email to:

majordomo@ic.ac.uk

You only need to enter the following message:

subscribe xml-dev

As this can be quite a busy mailing list, you may prefer to subscribe to the digests, which contain the major threads of the discussions in one daily email, rather than filling your inbox with lots of messages. To subscribe to the digest enter the following message instead (mailed to the same address):

subscribe xml-dev-digest

An archive of the mailing list is maintained at:

`http://www.lists.ic.ac.uk/hypermail/xml-dev/`

They have the following to say regarding what is discussed on the mailing list:

> Examples of what might be discussed:
>
> - the detailed implementation of the specification
> - resources such as documentation, test data, test results
> - XMLification of components (DTDS, entity sets, catalogs, etc.)
> - APIs for software developers
> - problems in implementation, and queries for XML-related resources
> - the use of existing SGML tools in creating XML resources
>
> It is NOT appropriate to:
>
> - request general information on XML (use the FAQ)
> - discuss non-XML topics in SGML (use comp.text.sgml)
> - discuss revision of the specification (use the WG)

The XML FAQ is maintained by Peter Flynn, and can be viewed at:

http://www.ucc.ie/xml/

Are You Convinced Yet?

Hopefully you will already have started to see the potential XML has to offer. Let's just recap on a few of the advantages there are in using XML:

- For widespread use across the Internet there needs to be a standard –because of its complexity SGML isn't that popular – and XML looks like it should gain far greater usage
- XML separates the syntax and structure from the presentation of a document
- You can create your own tags that relate to content of the document
- By defining your own markup language, information can be encoded much more precisely than is possible with HTML
- It is human-readable
- We cannot assume that it will just be browsers that consume structured info; XML allows non-human agents easy access to files, providing far greater functionality
- It's a relatively easy language to learn, allowing HTML programmers to get into structured markup
- XML doesn't need a DTD unlike SGML
- XML tags can be used to drive searches
- XML can be used as an exchange format for transaction protocols
- It encodes data not just documents
- It's designed to be easy to implement
- It allows you to bring multiple files together to form compound documents
- Interoperable, unlike HTML which has become browser specific

Keep Your Eyes Peeled

Because XML is such a rapidly evolving technology, we cannot guarantee that all the information contained is strictly up to date. Any publisher that made such a rash promise would be foolish (and, before long lying). However, as with any technology there is a time when you have to take the plunge and get stuck in, or be left behind. So, to help your new experience be as painless as possible, throughout the book we have provided information on where you can keep up to date with any changes. What's more, as we all wish there were more hours in the day, we'll keep our eyes out fo you - the XML Center on our Web site will provide news of major developments in the XML field. Its URL is:

`http://Webdev.wrox.co.uk/XML/`

At the time of writing we were receiving beta versions of Microsoft's Internet Explorer 5. Early indications have lead us to fully expect that the publicly available parser components are likely to change in line with updates to XML standards. For example, the method and property names are expected to change in some of the applications developed in later chapters. While the theory behind these applications is still sound, we anticipate some changes will be required for the code to work. So, to avoid disappointment, we will be providing updates to the chapters where necessary on our Web site. These updates, along with all the code for the book, will be available at:

`http://webdev.wrox.co.uk/books/1525/`

Conventions (How This Book is Marked Up)

We have used a number of different styles of text and layout in the book to help differentiate between the different kinds of information. The following conventions are a perfect example of markup. Here are examples of the styles we use and an explanation of what they mean:

Advice, hints, or background information comes in this type of font.

> **Important pieces of information come in boxes like this**

Important Words are in a bold type font

Words that appear on the screen in menus like the File or Window are in a similar font to the one that you see on screen

Keys that you press on the keyboard, like *Ctrl* and *Enter*, are in italics

Code has several fonts. If it's a word that we're talking about in the text, for example, when discussing the `For...Next` loop, it's in a bold font. If it's a block of code that you can type in as a program and run, then it's also in a gray box:

```
<SCRIPT>
… Some VBScript …
</SCRIPT>
```

Sometimes you'll see code in a mixture of styles, like this:

```
<HTML>
<HEAD>
<TITLE>Cascading Style Sheet Example</TITLE>
<STYLE>
style1 {color: red;
     font-size: 25}
</STYLE>
</HEAD>
```

The code with a white background is code we've already looked at and that we don't wish to examine further.

Quotes from sources such as official specifications come in boxes like this

Quotes from specifications are used in accordance with permissions from W3C. Copyright © 1995-1998 World Wide Web Consortium, (Massachusetts Institute of Technology, Institut National de Recherche en Informatique et en Automatique, Keio University). All Rights Reserved. **http://www.w3.org/Consortium/Legal/**

Where the pages of this book are not wide enough to hold a long line of code, we often use an underscore character to indicate that your code should continue on the same line.

These formats are designed to make sure that you know what it is you're looking at - hence they are a form of markup. We hope they make life easier.

Tell Us What You Think

We've worked hard on this book to make it enjoyable and useful. Our best reward would be to hear from you that you liked it and that it was worth your money. We've done our best to try to understand and match your expectations.

Please let us know what you think about it. Tell us what you have liked best and what aspects have made you regret spending your hard-earned money. If you think this is just a marketing gimmick, then test us out –drop us a line!

We'll answer, and we'll take whatever you say on board for future editions. The easiest way is to use email:

`feedback@wrox.com`

You can also find more details about Wrox Press on our Web site. There, you'll find the code from our latest books, sneak previews of forthcoming titles, and information about the authors and the editors. You can order Wrox titles directly from the site, or find out where your nearest local bookstore with Wrox titles is located. The address of our site is:

`http://www.wrox.com`

Customer Support

If you find a mistake, please have a look at the errata page for this book on our Web site first. Appendix H outlines how can you can submit an errata in much greater detail, if you are unsure.

The full URL for the errata page is:

`http://www.wrox.com/Scripts/Errata.idc?Code=1525`

If you can't find an answer there, tell us about the problem and we'll do everything we can to answer promptly! But please remember to let us know the book your query relates to, and if possible the page number as well. This will help us get a reply to you quicker.

Just send us an email to `support@wrox.com`.

Piecing Together the XML Jigsaw

As XML is only just coming of age, it is a very interesting time to be learning about it. However, it can also be quite a challenging time to come to XML as the standards are being argued over and new proposals are being made. Hopefully we will guide you towards what can sometimes appear to be a moving target. In this chapter we will show you how the various pieces of the XML jigsaw fit together to create a working XML application.

We also give you a taste of some of the new proposals, so you know which areas are the ones to keep your eyes on. In this chapter we will discuss:

- Document Type Definitions (DTDs)
- The difference between well-formed and valid documents
- Style Sheets for adding formatting to your XML documents
- Parsers
- Linking in XML
- Displaying XML in a browser
- The emerging proposals for Namespaces
- The new emerging proposals for XML Schemas including XML-Data and DCDs
- Why you should be getting so excited about XML

Bits and Pieces

As we saw in the introduction, to use XML practically and to be able to view it over the Web we need a number of pieces that together make up the XML jigsaw. We will give you an overview of these pieces, so that when we come to look at them in detail in the following chapters you will know how they all fit together. To demonstrate them we will keep coming back to the CD Library example we met earlier. Here it is again to remind you, remember that the full XML file would contain many more CDs between the <cdlib> root tags marked up in exactly the same way:

```
<cdlib>

      <cd>
      <artist>Arnold Schwarzenegger</artist>
      <title>I'll Be Bach</title>
      <format>album</format>
      <description>Arnie plays Bach's Brandenburg Concertos 1-3 on the Hammond
      Organ</description>
      </cd>

      <cd>
          ...
      </cd>

</cdlib>
```

Document Type Definition (DTD)

So, we have seen that you can have your XML document nicely marked up with handy tags that you can understand and which provide information about their content. But we need to declare the rules for the language we have created somewhere. We referred to this as having to:

- Declare what constitutes markup
- Declare exactly what our markup means

Practically speaking, this means that we have to give details of each of the elements, their order and say what attributes they can take. The XML specification defines these rules using a DTD, or Document Type Definition. When a DTD is sent with an XML file the user agent can then expect a document that conforms to the DTD.

However, as XML keeps changing we need to be aware of the other proposals put in for alternative ways of providing this information, which all come under the banner of **XML Schemas**. We will cover DTDs first, as they are part of the original core XML 1.0 specification, before coming back to these other options, which are just at the proposal stage, later in this chapter.

The DTD can either be an external file or it can be declared internally within the **document type declaration**. If the DTD is in an external file we link it to our document in the following way:

```
<!DOCTYPE cdlib SYSTEM "cdlib.dtd">
```

HTML has a DTD, but you don't get to see it every day because it is contained within most popular Web browsers. You can view it at `http://www.w3.org/TR/REC-html40/loose.dtd`. According to the HTML standard, when authoring HTML documents you are supposed to include the following line of code:

```
<!DOCTYPE HTML PUBLIC "-//W3C//DTD HTML 4.0 //EN">
```

It tells the user agent the location of HTML's DTD, however it is often left out because, practically speaking, it is not necessary and if you are using browser specific tags which deviate from the specification it may cause unpredictable results.

Creating your own markup language using a DTD need not be excessively complicated. Here is the internal DTD for the CD Library example. As you can see, it is a very simple DTD. We go into more detail in the next chapter, however this is enough to make our library example functional.

```
<!DOCTYPE cdlib [
<!ELEMENT cdlib (cd+)

<!ELEMENT cd (artist+, title+, format?, description?)>
<!ELEMENT artist (#PCDATA)>
<!ELEMENT title (#PCDATA)>
<!ELEMENT format (#PCDATA)>
<!ELEMENT description(#PCDATA)>

]>
```

Briefly, the `<!DOCTYPE cdlib [` line is used to distinguish it from other DOC types. It also gives the same name as the root element of the document. While `<!ELEMENT>` is used to declare elements in the format:

```
<!ELEMENT name (contents)>
```

where `name` gives the name of the element, and `contents` describes what type of data can be included and which elements are allowed to be nested inside that element. The element <cd> has to include the elements <artist> and <title> (they are forced to be included by the use of the `+` symbol which means one-or-more), while the <format> and <description> elements are optional (denoted by the `?` symbol).

The elements included in <cd> are then defined. These can take almost any ordinary text without markup (we explain the exceptions in the next chapter).

> **It's very easy to get confused between Document Type Definitions and Document Type Declarations... To clarify, just remember that a document type declaration either refers to an external document type definition, or else it contains one in the form of markup declarations as in the example we have just seen.**

As XML grows it is likely that there will be an ever increasing number of popular DTDs that we will be able to download and use, without always having to go to the trouble of writing our own. It is widely expected that industry standards for marking up certain types of document will soon appear. You can see this happening already with examples like Channel Definition Format (CDF) and Chemical Markup Language (CML) which we look at later in this chapter. But even if you are not planning to write your own DTDs an understanding of how they work will still be very important when writing XML applications.

Well-formed and Valid Documents

The XML specification defines two types of document, **well-formed** and **valid** ones. To be well-formed a document must conform to the following three rules:

- The document must contain at least one element
- The document must contain a root element, that is a unique opening and closing tag that surrounds the whole document
- All other elements contained within the document must be nested with no overlap between elements

So, looking again at our example of a record library, the following is a well-formed XML document:

```
<cdlib>
      <cd>
            <artist>Arnold Schwarzenegger</artist>
            <title >I'll Be Bach</title>
            <format>album</format>
            <description>Arnie plays Bach's Brandenburg Concertos 1-3 on the
            Hammond Organ</description>
      </cd>
</cdlib>
```

It contains more than the one required element. It has a root element in the form of the `<cdlib>` element – this can be compared to the opening `<HTML>` and closing `</HTML>` tags in HTML documents. And its sub-elements, or child elements, nest without any overlap. So it meets the criteria for being well-formed.

Valid documents on the other hand should not only be well-formed, they should also have a Document Type Definition which the well-formed document conforms to. This means that it must only use elements that have been declared in the order specified, and take the allowed types of content defined in the DTD.

The concept of a valid document is borrowed from SGML, however documents in SGML *must* be valid – there is no concept of SGML documents just being well-formed. We go into the area of well-formed and valid documents in detail in Chapter 2. However, simply put, XML was designed for the Web, and as long as the well-formed document can be meaningfully used - whether displayed on the browser or used by some other user agent - there is no need to send a DTD, it's just extra traffic. It may sound strange, but it is possible to make use of an XML document even without its DTD in certain instances, despite the user agent not knowing exactly what the tags you created mean.

Although XML is far simpler than SGML it is actually stricter, which is why you don't *need* a DTD with an XML file. This is the case because XML's strictness allows an XML processor to infer what rules apply from a well-formed document. It does this by constructing a tree of all the nested elements, and establishing the relationships between all of the various parts. As SGML doesn't require closing tags it would be impossible to do this with an SGML document if there wasn't a DTD. But, as long as the XML document can be used/displayed with functionality it is not always necessary to use the extra bandwidth by sending a DTD.

This doesn't mean that you should skip the DTD section of Chapter 2 too quickly, it's still advisable for a set of tags created in XML to conform to a DTD. This is because, if several people are creating or using documents that need to be compatible, the DTD sets out the rules that have to be obeyed. This helps maintain the structure and feel of a multi-author project. DTDs also allow you to use a piece of software called a validating parser to make sure that they are not violating the rules of the DTD. And if that means less work for you, and the other authors, then all the better.

Having seen the DTD, the following diagram shows how it can link to the XML document, and how the document can then be formatted for a browser when linked to a style sheet. It is to style sheets that we will turn next.

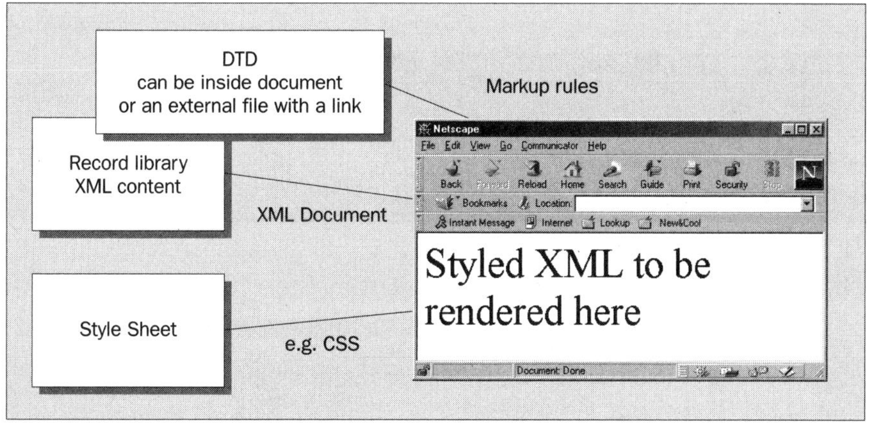

Remember that, at the time of writing, the main browsers had very little support for XML. Although it is likely that both Netscape Communicator 5 and Microsoft IE 5 will feature a high degree of support for XML, there are ways we can display XML in non-compliant browsers - which we come back to after our discussion of style sheets.

Style Sheets

Unlike most of the things we have talked about so far, style sheets are by no means a recent invention. They are as old as printing. Style sheets are made up of rules that declare how a document should be displayed. Even in the days of manual typesetting, book publishers would have a written set of instructions that told the printer how their house style was to be represented. The printer would then use this to mark up the publisher's manuscript. As our XML documents do not contain details of how the contents are to be displayed (maintaining the distinction between content and presentation), we use style sheets when displaying our documents to a Web browser so that we can present them in an attractive or practical manner.

Advantages of Using Style Sheets

As we have seen, style sheets are needed when we want to specify how our XML documents are to be presented. Apart from being a necessary addition, they offer a number of general advantages:

- Improve the clarity of documents
- Can help reduce download time, network traffic and server load
- Allow you to present the same source in different ways for different purposes
- Allow you to change the presentation of several files by just altering the one file that contains the rules of how it is to be displayed

As we saw in the introduction, when the non-scientific crowd began to create Web pages, their concern over the appearance of their pages led to the creation of many new and heavily used stylistic tags and attributes. As a result the size of files soared - known as **page bloat** - which made it harder to read the documents' code, thus making maintenance of pages more difficult. Take the following pages for example:

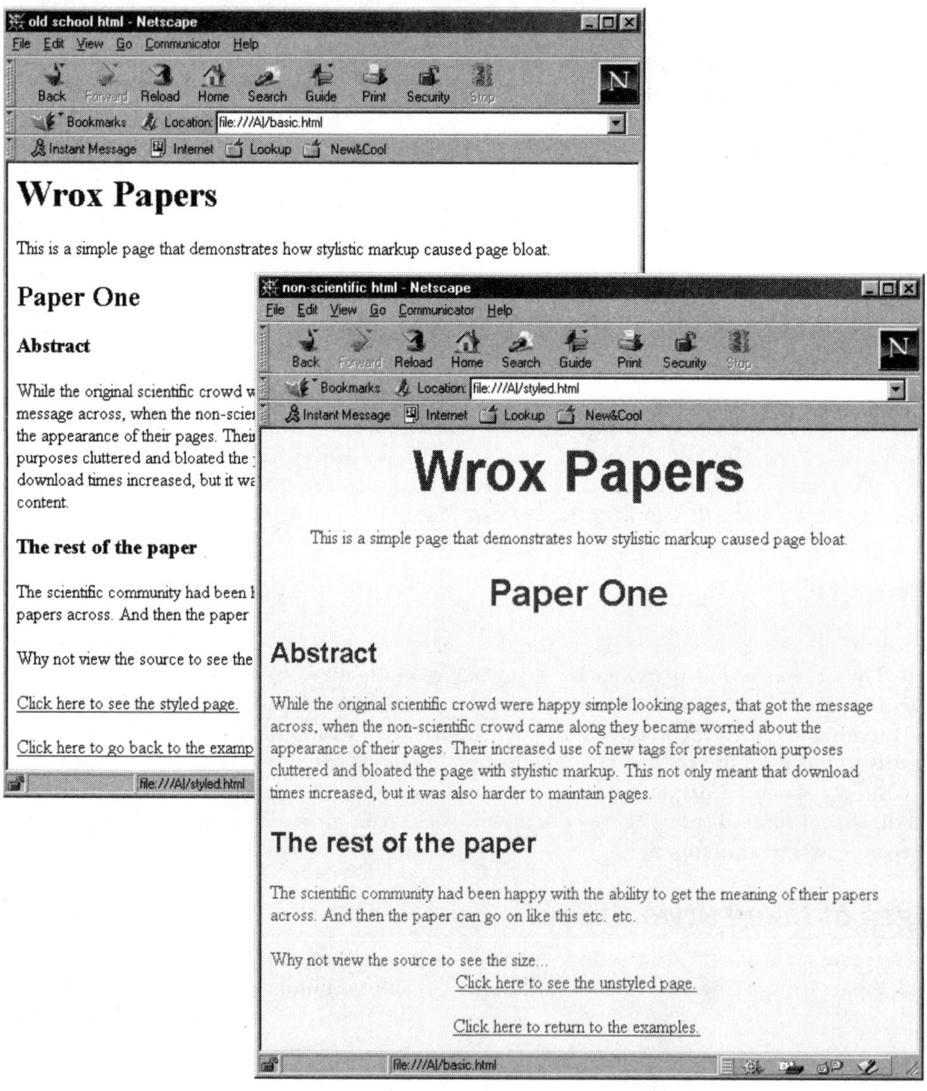

The use of stylistic markup in the second page increases the file size and decreases legibility of code. You can view the full pages and their source on our Web site at:

```
http://webdev.wrox.co.uk/books/1525
```

But here is the code so that you can see the difference in file size:

<HTML> <HEAD> <TITLE>old school html</TITLE> </HEAD>	<HTML> <HEAD> <TITLE>non-scientific html</TITLE> </HEAD>
<BODY>	<BODY BGCOLOR="#F5FFFA" ALINK="#F4A460" LINK="#993200" VLINK="#556B2F" TEXT="#556B2F">
<H1>Wrox Papers</H1>	<H1 ALIGN=CENTER><FONT FACE=ARIAL SIZE=7>Wrox Papers</FONT></H1>
This is a simple page that demonstrates how stylistic markup caused page bloat.	<DIV ALIGN=CENTER><FONT COLOR="#993200">This is a simple page that demonstrates how stylistic markup caused page bloat.</FONT></DIV>
<H2>Paper One</H2>	<H2 ALIGN=CENTER><FONT FACE=ARIAL SIZE=6>Paper One</FONT></H2>
<H3>Abstract</H3>	<H3><FONT FACE=ARIAL SIZE=5 COLOR="#993200">Abstract</FONT></H3>
While the original scientific crowd... ...see their content.	While the original scientific crowd... ...see their content.
<H3>The rest of the paper</H3>	<H3><FONT FACE=ARIAL SIZE=5 COLOR="#993200">The rest of the paper</FONT></H3>
The scientific community had been ...	The scientific community had been ...

Any Web site or company intranet that spans several pages, while maintaining a consistent appearance, requires the same style rules to be repeatedly sent to the browser with each page. Because browsers cache the data they receive from Web pages, this repeated sending of the same rules is a waste of bandwidth, download time and server load. Style sheets put all the style rules in one separate document so that they only need to be sent once, then each of the site's pages can link to the same style sheet which is stored in the browser's cache – how net-environmentally friendly.

In addition, because all the style rules are kept in one file, it is then possible to change the appearance of the whole site by just altering the style sheet rather than the individual style rules on each page.

If you use the same data in several pages, each of which present the data in different ways, all you have to change is the line which links to different style sheets. An example of where this may be useful could be where your site has different sections, but has common information that has to be presented in a style relevant to that section. Alternatively, if you wanted to provide a large text version for people with sight difficulties, you could offer the same page styled with bigger fonts for those who would have trouble reading the normal size font.

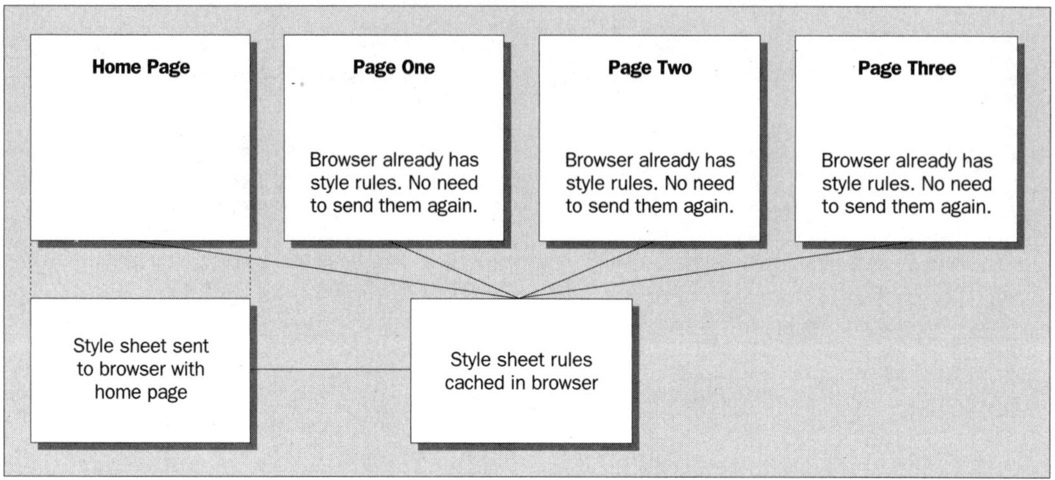

The content pages contain a reference to the style sheet, so that the user agent knows where to get it from - rather like the way links to an image are used. There are several style sheet languages including:

- CSS Cascading Style Sheets
- XSL Extensible Stylesheet Language
- DSSSL Document Style Semantics and Specification Language
- XS also known as DSSSL-0

The two that really concern us here are CSS and XSL. DSSSL was the official styling language for SGML and is extremely powerful, however it is also extremely complicated and has not been widely adopted. XS or DSSSL-0 was intended to be a simplified form of DSSSL, although it was still seen as too complicated to ever become a success on the Internet. So let's take a quick look at the other two.

Cascading Style Sheets

The Cascading Style Sheets Level 1 specification was released by the W3C in late 1996. It was supported to a degree in both Communicator 4 and IE4, although both of the main browser manufacturers have pledged to fully support CSS1 in their forthcoming Communicator 5 and IE5 browsers.

CSS Level 1 will eventually be superceded by CSS Level 2 (the recommendation was released May 1998). However, it may be some time before the browser manufacturers fully support CSS Level 2 seeing how they haven't fully implemented Level 1 yet.

Cascading Style Sheets are already finding their way onto the Web and got their name because, when several style sheets are present, a cascade is formed with properties being taken from all of the sheets, any conflicts being resolved according to a set of rules. CSS are simple to construct, and once they have been created there is no limit to the number of pages that can use them. HTML documents just need one simple line of code to link to a CSS:

```
<LINK REL="stylesheet" TYPE="text/css" HREF="example.css">
```

The W3C are currently addressing the way in which XML documents will link to CSS. There is a note on the subject available from:

http://www.w3.org/TR/NOTE-xml-stylesheet

Although one popular way to do this at the moment is:

```
<?xml-stylesheet href="cdlib.css" type="text/css"?>
```

Here is an example of a cascading style sheet that could be used with the CD library we have been looking at:

```
artist {
      display: block;
      font-family: Arial, Helvetica;
      font-weight:bold;
      font-size: 20pt;
      color: #9370db;
      text-align: center;
      }

title {
      display: block;
      font-family: Arial, Helvetica;
      font-size: 20pt;
      color: #c71585;
      }

format {
      display: block;
      font-family: Arial, Helvetica;
      font-size: 16pt;
      color: #9370db;
      }

description {
      display: block;
      font-family: Arial, Helvetica;
      font-style: italic;
      font-size: 16pt;
      color: #FF1010;
      }
```

When eventually viewed through a browser our CD Library with this style sheet would present a list of CDs as shown in the following screen shot. This was taken using a beta version of IE5, if you have a copy of IE5 you can try it from our Web site at: `http://webdev.wrox.co.uk/books/1525`

There are many advantages to using CSS, and such style sheets are discussed further in Chapter 7. However, CSS uses a fixed set of markup, you cannot create your own new tags – it is not extensible. While CSS can be used for presentation of XML documents, there is another more powerful option – XSL.

Extensible Stylesheet Language

While many XML authors will be content with the functionality of Cascading Style Sheets to display simply structured XML documents, XSL offers all the same advantages that CSS offers with additional functionality, and is likely to be used where more powerful formatting capabilities are required.

XSL draws on both DSSSL and CSS, (and DSSSL-0). It also uses ECMAScript, which was derived from JavaScript.

XSL is made up of two parts:

- An XML vocabulary for specifying formatting semantics
- A language for transforming XML documents

XSL not only allows the user to specify how parts of a document should look (font, size, color, alignment, borders etc.) just like CSS, but is also extensible, so it allows users to create their own new formatting tags and properties.

XSL also offers users further control over the presentation of their documents. For example, it can add rules that order the presentation of sections. If you go back to the CD library example, these rules would allow you to specify different orders for the presentation of the data, so you could have either `<artist>` first, or `<title>`. The order of the data doesn't matter, because the tags can be interpreted and re-ordered.

At the time of writing XSL was at the First Draft stage of the W3C process. It was originally a joint proposal from Microsoft, Inso Corporation and ArborText, however the Working Draft 1.0 supercedes the proposal. To keep up to date with the development of XSL, keep an eye on the W3C site's XSL page, located at

`http://www.w3.org/Style/XSL/`

CSS vs. XSL

It is likely that both CSS and XSL will be present on the Web for the foreseeable future because they address different needs. XSL allows the author control over complex formatting where the contents of a document might be displayed in multiple places; for example the singer of a track in our CD library example might also appear in a dynamically generated table displaying their back catalog, or used as a page header. Meanwhile, CSS is intended for dynamic formatting of online documents for multiple media not just visual browsers, but also audio, braille, hand-held devices etc.

	CSS	XSL
Can be used with HTML	Yes	No
Can be used with XML	Yes	Yes
Is a transformation language	No	Yes
Syntax	CSS	XML

For more information on Style Sheets, see Professional Style Sheets for HTML and XML from Wrox Press (ISBN 1-861001-65-7).

Parsers

I don't want to get embroiled in philosophical rambling here. But, when we have stored our XML in a plain text format that we consider to be human-readable, we can't really say that computers can 'read' the file - they interpret it. It is the job of a parser to help the computer interpret the XML file by putting it in a format they can use. XML applications in turn help both us and parsers interpret the file because of the information they contain on the nature of the text chunks within the tags.

The XML specification refers to two components for practical use of XML: the **XML processor** and the **application**. Parsers fulfil the role of the XML processor, they load the XML and related files, check that the XML is either well-formed or valid (depending on the type of parser), and build a document tree structure that can be passed on to the application. It is this tree structure which can then be practically used by the computer. The application is the part which processes the data that is in the document tree created by the processor.

In practice the parser is generally just a component for programmers to call upon when building their application. As such IE5 integrates an XML parser called MSXML.

Remember that we said XML documents do not always need a DTD? It is the ability of parsers to form a document tree without a DTD that allows XML files to be functional on their own.

HTML browsers combine the role of the processor and the application. Because HTML is the set of rules for how the document is to be displayed, there are strict rules that say how the files can be interpreted. However, by separating the DTD and the style sheet from the XML file, applications can use the same document for different purposes. So the type of application is not just restricted to being a browser, it could be a word-processor, braille printer etc. It may not even be an application that is used directly by humans; it may be an automated tool, for example a system which creates letters when certain events happen – such as when you go over your overdraft limit. It could even add a charge for the letter to your account.

While this is a central use for parsers, they also perform another very useful function. We have already seen that, because XML is a far stricter language than SGML, parsers can be used as a tool to help XML authors check their documents, and to help XML editing software to make sure that they produce compliant documents. While it may seem that authoring XML is a lot more demanding than writing HTML, XML's advantages in processing ability and flexibility outweigh the disadvantages of its rigidity – closing tags and carefully watching syntax. When you have just finished writing a long and complicated XML document, only to find that it doesn't work, the task of going through the code to find out where the error is can seem daunting. So before you actually use an XML document it is wise to run it through a parser, which checks the document for you and points out mistakes – such as the absence of a closing tag.

Although, as we have seen declining numbers of people writing HTML "by hand" with just Notepad, turning instead to authoring programs, so too can we expect a number of XML editors to appear in the near future.

Primarily there are two types of parser. The simpler **non-validating** parsers just check for well-formedness and can be as small as 30-40 Kb, while the more complicated **validating** parsers also check for validity using the DTD.

There are several parsers freely available across the Internet, and you are strongly advised to download at least one. If you can, download more than one, as different parsers handle the reporting of errors in different ways. Let's take a quick look at some of the parsers that are available.

An added advantage of making sure that the document accurately follows the specification is that there is no need to put lots of code into the user agent so that they can handle poorly written documents. The current major Web browsers are notorious for including code that allows them to display HTML that is not directly compliant with the HTML specification.

Lark by Tim Bray

Lark, written by Tim Bray (one of the editors of the XML specification), was one of the best of the early tools for checking your work. It is a non-validating XML processor written in the Java programming language - to use it you need a Java Virtual Machine.

You get a Java Virtual Machine in Microsoft Visual J++ for Windows, the Macintosh Runtime for Java SDK, OS/2 Warp version 4, or you can download the Sun Java Development Kit (JDK) or the lighter Java Runtime Environment (JRE) from `http://java.sun.com/`

Although Lark does not have a visual user interface it is compact and does a reliable job. It efficiently builds document trees and matches tags, however it doesn't check that the document is valid – by comparing the document to its DTD. Tim has also written a validating XML parser, based on the same code as Lark, it is called Larval. You can download a free copy of both from:

```
http://www.textuality.com/Lark/
```

XP by James Clark

XP is a non-validating XML 1.0 parser written in Java. It can check for a document's well-formedness. XP can be downloaded from:

```
ftp://ftp.jclark.com/pub/xml/xp.zip
```

Microsoft XML Parser in Java

Microsoft's XML parser written in Java is a parser which checks for well-formedness of documents and optionally permits checking of the documents' validity. Once parsed, the XML document is exposed as a tree through a simple set of Java methods, which Microsoft are working with the World Wide Web Consortium (W3C) to standardize. If you use this parser it is worth keeping up to date with its development as Microsoft are constantly updating it. For more details and to download a version visit:

http://www.microsoft.com/xml/

There are, of course, many more parsers available on the Internet and we haven't enough space here to cover them all. To find out more why not have a look on your favorite search engine?

Linking in XML

With all the new things you'll have to learn, you'll be glad to know that the type of linking you learnt in HTML is still effective in XML. You can still use a link such as:

```
<a href= "http://webdev.wrox.co.uk">Wrox Web Developer</a>
```

Of course, because we're writing XML now, the `<a>` element has to be declared in the DTD, as does the attribute `href`, even though `href` and `HREF` are reserved keywords in the linking specification. However, as we're using XML we might as well use a more descriptive tag, such as:

```
<webdevlink href="http://webdev.wrox.co.uk">Wrox Web Developer</webdevlink>
```

This would then be declared in the DTD like so:

```
<!ELEMENT webdevlink (#PCDATA)>
<!ATTLIST webdevlink
     xml:link CDATA #FIXED "simple"
     href CDATA #REQUIRED
>
```

`xml:link` is a reserved XML keyword used as an attribute to define links; it can take the value `"simple"` or `"extended"`. Because the `xml:link` attribute's value is `#FIXED`, `xml:link` does not need to be included in each instance of the element; it is implied in each `<webdevlink>` tag, which is why we can use:

```
<webdevlink href="http://webdev.wrox.co.uk">Wrox Web Developer</webdevlink>
```

instead of having to put:

```
<webdevlink xml:link="simple" href="http://webdev.wrox.co.uk">Wrox Web
Developer</webdevlink>
```

The proposals for linking in XML reached working draft status in March 1998, and as you may have already worked out, they are expressed in XML. Originally known as XLink, then XML-Link, **Extensible Linking Language (XLL)** is the current term for the linking languages under development. XLL is based upon on SGML, HyTime and the Text Encoding Initiative (TEI) – the latter two are used as linking methods in SGML.

If you are happy with plain links, like those in HTML, there will be little more to learn on this topic. However, the linking capabilities in XML are far more powerful. Beware, you will probably find that you will see lots of uses for the new types of link and will want to learn all about it. Using XLL you can:

- Create your own link elements
- Use any element as a linking element
- Create bi-directional links with one-to-many and many-to-one relationships
- Specify traversal behavior – how users get between links
- Create link databases to specify and manage links outside of the documents to which they apply
- Aggregate links
- Transclusion – the link target appears to be part of the link's source document

There are two basic link types:

- **Inline links** that are specified at the point where the link is initiated
- **Out-of-line links** that are stored in an intermediary file – a link database

Linking is not covered in the XML specification. Instead there are two separate specifications for linking in XML:

- **XLinks** for linking separate XML documents to other XML documents
- **XPointers** are to be used for addressing the internal structures of XML documents providing specific references to elements, character strings, and other parts of XML documents, even those without an explicit ID attribute

Any element can be an XLink, and elements including links are referred to as **linking elements**. Because the linking specifications are written in XML, you can create your own tags for links that describe the link as shown in the `webdevlink` example. The link then describes the relationship between the objects or parts of data objects.

The specification for XLinks is available from:

`http://www.w3.org/TR/1998/WD-xlink-19980303`

XPointers are used in conjunction with URIs to specify a part of a document (or a sub-resource). They can be used to link to a specific part in the whole of a document, or create a link that just takes part of the document (as opposed to all of it). Any link that addresses part of a document must be in the form of an XPointer. However, it is not necessary to include explicit ID attributes in the XPointer language in the same way that they are needed in HTML and they can provide for specific reference to elements, character strings, and other parts of XML documents.

The XPointers specification is available from:

`http://www.w3.org/TR/1998/WD-xptr-19980303`

Using HTML, if you wanted to link to a specific part of a document the document itself has to be changed using named anchors. This is not necessary using XLL with XPointers. XLL will also allow custom applications – without a human user being present – to establish connections between documents, and parts of documents.

XML Comments

Comments in XML are the same as they are in HTML. They are placed inside these tags:

```
<!-- comment -->
```

Good use of comments is almost an art form. You develop your ability to use them as you develop as a programmer. They are absolutely essential – when you go back to a document after a couple of months, what seemed so obvious then suddenly is not so clear. Good use of comments also means that others can use your documents with greater ease. This is particularly important when creating DTDs because you may want others to use your DTD. The correct placing of comments in XML documents is covered in Chapter 2.

The New Kids on the Block

By now, you'll have got the idea that XML and the other related specifications are far from being stable and finished. In this section we introduce some of the new specifications that are creating a stir in the XML community. This doesn't mean that any of the things they claim to be improvements on will disappear, far from it. Once you have built a solid understanding of building XML applications with this book, you will be in a strong position to watch for the development of these specifications. We shall be looking at proposals for:

- XML Namespaces
- XML-Data
- Document Content Declarations

XML Namespaces

One of the advantages of XML that we mentioned in the introduction was that it is possible to create compound documents from several separate sources. To save us the work it is likely that software modules will be used to create these compound documents. There are, however, two problems these software modules must overcome in order to create compound documents:

- Recognizing the markup they are to process (tags and attributes)
- Coping with name 'collisions' in markup

The first problem is self-explanatory; the tools have to know what part of the document they are addressing. The second problem is less obvious. While the ability to use documents from multiple sources can be very useful, there is the risk that, with everyone creating their own tags, there will be a collision of names used for tags or attributes. If some people are merrily creating their own tags while others are following a standard, it will not be long before two files use the same tagname, for example, to describe different things. In our CD Library example we used the element `<format>` to describe whether the CD was an album or a single. It could be equally possible that another similar document uses a `<format>` tag to describe whether the recording was on CD, vinyl, cassette, DVD, MiniDisc, etc. The **XML namespaces** proposal was designed to counter these two problems.

To get over these hurdles the document constructs must have globally unique names. One way of doing this is by defining a unique namespace for element types and element attributes.

Here is the W3C definition of XML namespaces:

> An XML namespace is a collection of names, identified by a URI, which are used in XML documents as element types and attribute names. XML namespaces differ from the "namespaces" conventionally used in computing disciplines in that the XML version has internal structure and is not, mathematically speaking, a set.

Namespaces associate a prefix with a URI using the following syntax:

```
xmlns:[prefix]= "[URI of namespace]"
```

So we could use:

```
xmlns:wroxcds="http://webdev.wrox.co.uk/books/1525"
```

to declare the `wroxcds` prefix, with elements from that domain uniquely identifying those tags within the compound document.

Now this may all sound like a lot of extra work, so let me put your mind at rest. Without going into too much detail at this early stage, once the namespace has been defined earlier in the document instance, the `format` element doesn't become much more complicated and will end up looking like this:

```
<wroxcds:format>album</wroxcds:format>
```

As you may have guessed, the namespaces proposal is still subject to change in the W3C process.

The XML Namespaces Working Draft came out on August 2nd 1998. We come back to the topic of namespaces in Chapter 4, you can also keep an eye out at:

`http://w3.org/TR/1998/WD-xml-names`

XML Schemas

Schemas define the characteristics of classes of objects. So in XML, a schema is simply a definition of the way that the document is marked up. The DTD is actually a good example of a schema in that the DTD defines a class of documents and the element and attribute types in that class.

At the time of writing the following **XML Schema** proposals were still at the Note stage of the W3C proceedings, although they were generating a lot of interest in XML circles:

- XML-Data
- Document Content Description for XML

An XML Schema Work Group has since been formed by the W3C, whose job will be to look at and review the various XML Schema proposals, though it is too early to tell what they will decide to do with them. Their first step is to create a requirements document which will be used to drive the following discussion. So it is unlikely that these schemas will stay in their present form. However, we have covered them in this book to introduce the concept of schemas written using XML syntax, which as you will see have several advantages over traditional DTDs.

As this suggests, XML Schemas have arisen because of weaknesses in the traditional DTD that we saw earlier (and come back to in the next chapter). The criticisms of traditional DTDs circle around the following characteristics:

- It uses a different syntax to XML
- It is difficult to write good DTDs
- It is limited in its descriptive powers
- They are not extensible
- They do not describe XML as data well
- There is no support for the Namespaces proposal

We come back to discussion of this subject in Chapter 3, for the moment let's just take a quick look at what XML-Data and DCDs are.

XML-Data

XML-Data was a proposal submitted to the W3C on 11th December 1997 as a way of describing schemas using XML syntax. As you'll see in the next chapter DTDs use a modified form of a notation called **Extended Backus-Naur Form** notation (**EBNF**), and simplicity is *not* one of its strong points. So the idea of declaring schemas in XML (as XML-Data does) has been gratefully received.

When we have relatively simple documents, the DTD may seem like a perfectly adequate way of representing schemas. However, there is also a move on the Web to see XML as data, not just a way of marking up documents, and when doing so, we benefit from the ability to relate different types of schemas to our data.

`http://www.w3.org/TR/xml-data`

or the Microsoft site at:

`http://www.microsoft.com/xml`

Document Content Description for XML – DCD

This schema for XML documents is even more recent and was only submitted in July 1998. DCD also uses XML syntax. The basic syntax is introduced in Chapter 3, along with references of where you can find out more information on XML Schemas. It uses a modified Resource Description Framework (RDF) syntax for its description and includes a subset of the XML-Data submission in an RDF compliant way.

You can find the note at:

`http://www.w3.org/TR/NOTE-dcd`

Learning XML-Data and DCD syntax will provide a solid basis for understanding alternative XML Schemas written in XML syntax. So, you will be equipped to watch out for their progression if you so desire.

Displaying XML

This is one area of XML development where newcomers often get confused, so we're going to spend a little time here making your options clear. Hopefully, you will already be excited about the possibilities that XML can offer you, but you still need to know how XML files can be displayed over the Web. In looking at style sheets we have already covered half of the ground, so you know a little about how style rules are applied to the XML file – this section focuses on displaying the XML file in a browser.

Viewing HTML files over the Web is something we have all got very used to, it seems so simple. All you need to do is type in a URL and press *enter*, or click on a hyperlink and up comes your page. So that we can understand the process of outputting XML, let's just have a quick look at how it's done in HTML.

Outputting HTML

This is a simplified description of how the browser gets and displays the page, however it should suffice for our purposes:

- An HTML document is requested and returned to the client by HTTP (or the file system if it is not requested over the Internet).
- The browser strips the document of its tags and makes an array of the element's contents.
- The browser must work out what each tag means, look for styling associated with it – remember that the browser already has a knowledge of HTML (its DTD).
- It must then display the contents on the screen.

XML Browsers

Unfortunately things are not so simple with XML. At the time of writing the major browser manufacturers' products (up to version 4) did not allow direct viewing of XML in the same way you could view HTML – you couldn't just open an XML file in your browser and view the contents as you intended. Netscape and Microsoft have promised XML support in their Communicator 5 and IE5 browsers, but the level of support is still a little unclear – we discuss this in more detail in the later chapters. (Early beta versions of IE5 show strong support for the core XML 1.0 Specification, the Document Object Model, Namespaces, CSS and XSL.) In the mean time, don't panic, this does not mean that the `.xml` and `.xsl/.css` files you create cannot be viewed in Communicator 4 and IE4. What it means is that they have to be converted into HTML to be viewed - either statically (before the document is viewed), or dynamically (as it is being requested). But, if browsers could display XML a similar process would need to be undertaken.

- The browser would have to get the XML file, strip it of its tags and make an array of the elements' content.
- Because the tags in XML are not predefined, the browser would then have to look for information on how to style each element in a style sheet.
- To display the document, the HTML browser has a display window. However, an XML browser may be able to convert the document into a different format for display in another application – such as a rich text format displayed in a word processor – as well or instead.

Because an XML browser would not have any built-in knowledge of how the XML document is to be displayed, the styling process is – as we have seen – absolutely necessary. For now let's focus on how XML can be converted to HTML for viewing in a normal Web browser.

Static Conversion

Static conversion takes place before the file is put on the Web server. It involves using a program that takes the XML file and style sheet, then marries them to create an HTML file that can be viewed through the browser. It is the HTML file which is then put on the server for viewers to request.

One example of this type of tool is the Microsoft MSXSL Command Line Utility, this marries XML and XSL files, creating an HTML file. Unfortunately this only works with Windows 95/98 and Windows NT (x86 only) and IE4. It can be downloaded from:

```
http://www.microsoft.com/xml/xsl/downloads/msxsl.asp
```

Briefly here's what it does. From the command line you type:

```
C:\xslproc\msxsl -i xmlfile.xml -s xslfile.xsl -o result.htm
```

For those blissfully unaware of what the command-line is (and sometimes ignorance is bliss!), in Windows 9x go to Start | Run and type in exactly the above, substituting the correct file names and the directory the files are in. You have to make sure that the `.xml` and `.xsl` files are in the same folder as the processor for this to work.

The `-i` is the input XML file, `-s` is the XSL style sheet and `-o` is the output in HTML. The resulting HTML file can then be put on the Web server or opened in an HTML browser and the style rules will have been applied.

A less common approach is to run a special program, load in your XML file, then manually apply style rules to it. An example of this is the Cormorant XML Parser, written by one of our authors – Frank 'Boomer' Boumphrey. It is freely available from our Web site at:

```
http://webdev.wrox.co.uk/books/1525
```

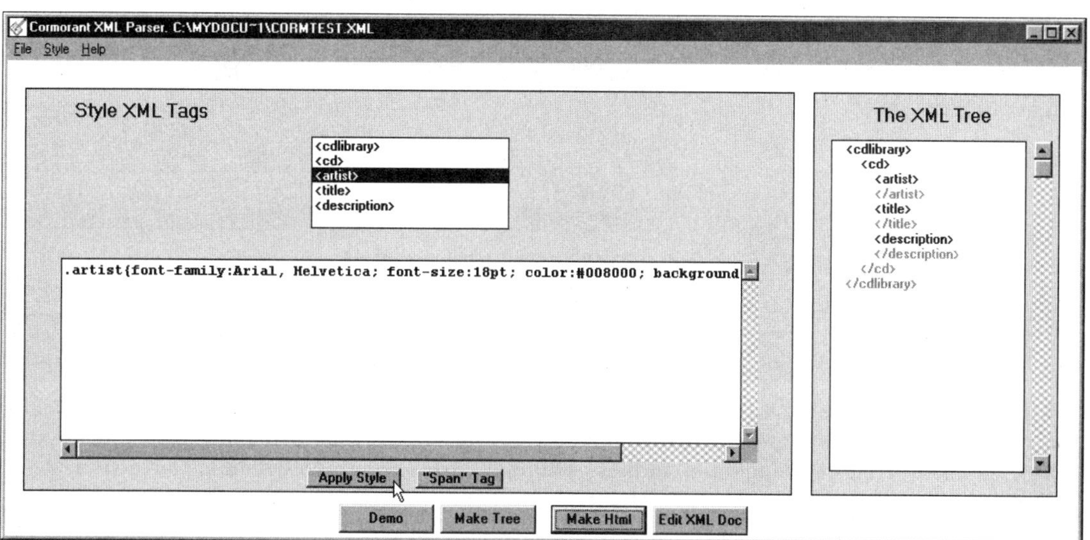

After opening an XML file (shown in the right-hand pane – The XML Tree), style rules can be applied to each tag in the left-hand pane, by clicking on the appropriate tag and typing in the style rules between the empty brackets. Then you click on the Apply Style button to make your amendments. Finally clicking the Make HTML button opens Notepad with the HTML file in it.

Saving this as an `.html` file allows you to view the original XML in an HTML browser.

```
testttcc - Notepad
File  Edit  Search  Help
<HTML>
<HEAD>
<!--Created using Cormorant XML Styler-->
<!-- Use "save as"  to permenantly save this file-->
<TITLE>
 HTML equiv. of XML document <cdlibrary>
</TITLE>
<STYLE>
        DIV{
        font-size:12pt;
        color:black;
        background-color:white;
        }

<!-- special formatting for the XML tag "<artist>" -->
.artist{font-family:Arial, Helvetica; font-size:18pt; color:#008000; background-color:#f0fff0}


<!-- special formatting for the XML tag "<title>" -->
.title{font-size:14pt; color:#483d8b; background-color:#f0f8ff}

</STYLE>
</HEAD>
<BODY>
<DIV><DIV CLASS="cdlibrary">
        <DIV CLASS="cd">
                <DIV CLASS="artist">Arnie Schwarzenneger</DIV>
                <DIV CLASS="title">I'll Be Bach</DIV>
                <DIV CLASS="description"></DIV>
        </DIV>
</DIV>
</DIV></BODY>
</HTML>
```

And here we see the displayed HTML document:

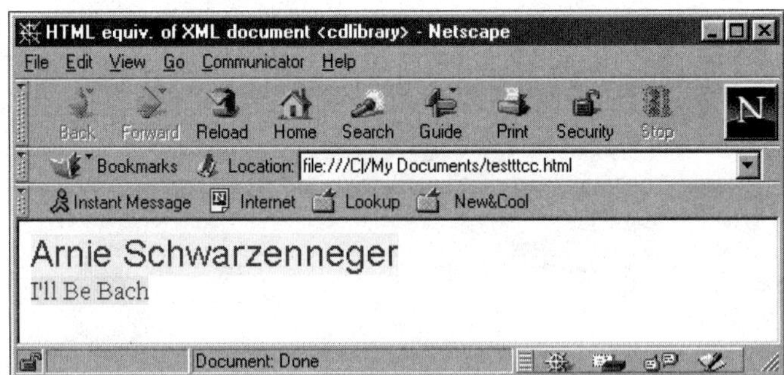

While the static approach is fine if you just want to prepare static XML documents for the Web, it is not very helpful if you want to harness the full power of XML. Creating dynamic pages, that use the data in your XML files, serving different files to different users requires a dynamic conversion technique.

Dynamic Conversion

The dynamic conversion of XML files allows you to serve different pages to different users. There are a number of dynamic conversion techniques available that can use:

- MSXSL Command Line Utility
- ActiveX Control
- Java Applet
- JavaScript program

to convert the `.xml` and `.css/.xsl` files to HTML on the fly. Again, these options are freely available. Rather than cover them all here, we will just give you an idea how one of these options works - we will take a quick look at the MSXSL ActiveX Control.

MSXSL ActiveX Control

The MSXSL ActiveX Control is based on the same code as the MSXSL command-line utility that we have already seen. Again, it carries the disadvantage that it can only be used with Windows 9x/NT and IE4+. However, the advantage is that you don't have to know a lot about Java or JavaScript to get it to work.

Simply put, the ActiveX Control can be embedded into a basic HTML page. The ActiveX Control then downloads the XML file and its style sheet and converts them into HTML. Some simple JavaScript holds the result of the parsing in the HTML page. So the HTML page is really just a holder for the ActiveX Control and a wrapper for the returned code. The same ActiveX Control can be used on the Web server.

You can download the MSXSL ActiveX Control from:

`http://www.microsoft.com/workshop/c-frame.htm#/xml/default.asp`

While this may be the easiest option, if you want cross-browser compatibility, you'll have to look further into the other two options (JavaScript and Java Applets). Or dip into the possibility of creating the HTML server-side, something we look at in Chapter 9.

XML in the Real World

So far we have been talking about XML in rather general terms, so let's have a look at some examples where XML is already in use.

Channel Definition Format

When push technologies started to take off, browser manufacturers needed a way to describe the content of what was being pushed at your machine. Channel Definition Format (CDF) is an XML-based markup language which allows Web site authors to let subscribers know when the Web site changes, to varying degrees. CDF was introduced in IE4 and has significantly helped boost the profile of XML. Documents sent in the CDF format follow the CDF DTD.

CDF files are just linked to the `.html` or `.asp` files in a site. They remain separate, so there is no need to re-write your site in order to add CDF.

Note that CDF is different to the method that Netscape use. Here is our WebDev Channel in IE4. We explore channels further in Chapter 13.

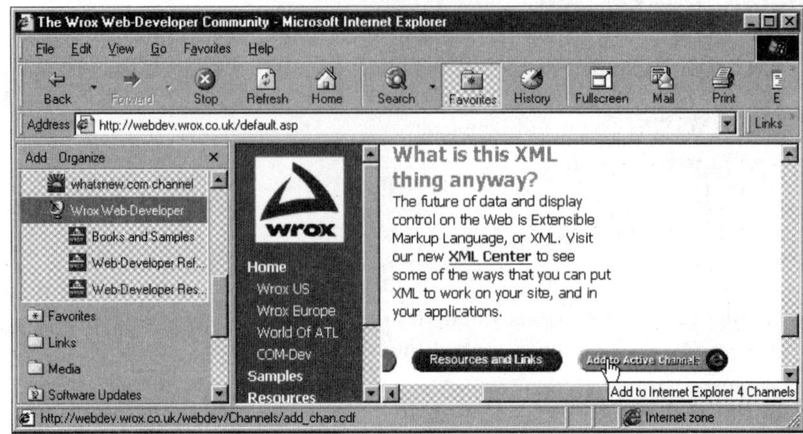

Chemical Markup Language

The Chemical Markup Language (CML) was designed by Peter Murray-Rust as a way of supporting the management of molecular information. Because of the subject area's complexity, the information could not adequately be rendered using normal HTML. Although CML was originally an SGML application, it has moved onto XML as a standard for its development.

CML is the nearest thing to an industry standard in the XML community so far. It allows researchers to capture chemical data in a form that can be reused. By using terms that are common in chemistry such as molecules, atoms, bonds, crystals, formulas, sequences, symmetries, reactions, etc., it makes the use of the XML application very straightforward for chemists. The way it handles objects means that documents can easily be worked on by a computer – searched and indexed. And because CML is written in XML it is platform independent, unlike the common binary formats used in the molecular sciences.

Professor Murray-Rust also created JUMBO, which was the first general-purpose XML browser, written in Java (although it is not suitable for displaying XML pages in the same way that the more popular Web browsers do). Jumbo is shown here demonstrating a document in CML:

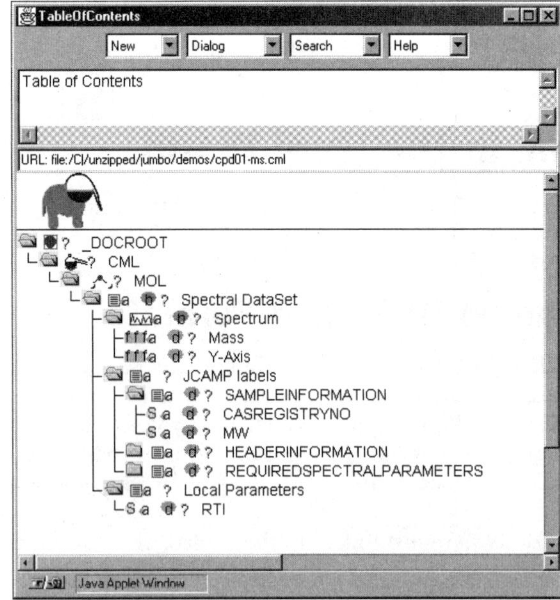

JUMBO can be downloaded from:

```
http://www.vsms.nottingham.ac.uk/vsms/java/jumbo/
```

Open Financial eXchange

Open Financial eXchange (OFX) is the result of a collaboration between CheckFree, Intuit and Microsoft to develop a language that allows financial transactions to take place securely over the Web using the OFX DTD. Again it was originally an SGML application, although it now uses XML syntax. The proposal also includes security considerations to give peace of mind when sending credit card numbers over the Internet supporting Secure Sockets Layer (SSL) and the public/private encryption methods underlying SSL. It is designed so that it can be embedded in larger applications.

Among the activities which it supports are: consumer and small business banking, consumer and small business bill payment, bill presentment, and investments, including stocks, bonds and mutual funds. At the time of OFX was at version 1.5. It is intended to encourage the provision of online financial services. You can find out more about OFX at their Web site:

```
http://www.ofx.net/ofx/ab_main.asp
```

Summary

In this chapter we have taken a closer look at the pieces which go together to make up the XML jigsaw. We should have prepared you for the coming chapters that address these sections in more detail, after which we go on to creating some more complex XML applications. We have looked at:

- Well-formed and Valid Documents
- Document Type Definitions
- Document Type Declarations
- Cascading Style Sheets
- Extensible Stylesheet Language
- Parsers
- Namespaces
- XML Schemas
- How to view XML documents
- Some existing XML applications

Hopefully you will already be convinced of the advantages XML can offer. While XML may still be changing, the following chapters should give you a solid grounding in creating XML applications of your own. The later chapters will also encourage you that it is not too soon to be writing XML, and the examples will prove that it is possible to create significant XML applications despite a slight feeling of instability due to the evolving nature of such a new language.

2

Well-Formed and Valid Documents

In this chapter we will look at how to write well-formed and valid XML documents that conform to the XML 1.0 specification; the distinction between valid and well-formed being that valid XML documents have, and must conform to, DTDs (Document Type Definitions). In discussing the syntax used in such XML documents we hope to equip you with the core information you will need to be able to create your own XML documents.

Well-formed Documents

In this section we will take you through the various aspects of XML markup needed to produce a well-formed document. But what does it mean to say that a document is well formed? Well, the XML 1.0 specification defines the syntax for XML. If a programmer understands the specification properly, then he can construct a program that will be able to 'look' at a document which is supposed to be XML, and if the document conforms to the specification for XML, then the program can do further processing upon it. The idea underlying the specification for XML is therefore that XML documents should be intelligible as such, either to people or processing applications. 'Well-formedness' is the minimum set of requirements (defined in the specification) that a document needs to satisfy in order for it to be considered to be an XML document. These requirements are a mixture of ensuring that the correct language terms are employed, and ensuring that the document is logically coherent in the manner defined by the XML specification (i.e. that the terms of the language are used in the right way). If a document fails to meet any one of the requirements for well-formedness it is considered to be a **fatal error**, and the processor *must* stop and inform the application using it.

Valid documents go a stage further than well-formed documents. By definition a valid document is also a well-formed one. But valid XML documents also conform to the standards for SGML documents, and can be used as such, whereas documents which are well-formed but not valid can't.

The principal feature of a valid document is that it has, and conforms to, a document type definition (which we'll cover in the second part of the chapter) containing declarations that specify the overall structure of a document and the acceptable **types** of data content values.

So, (combining the premises above) well-formed XML documents don't necessarily conform to the SGML standard, as they might not have a document type definition (DTD).

Validation also includes checking to make sure that the data within the document is suitable for being passed across to the application using it; that none of the values for data segments are outside the range of acceptable or expected values. XML validation itself (checking the document against a DTD) really only includes mechanisms for checking that values are of the right type though, and only a very limited capacity to check whether they fall within some required range (as we shall see in the second part of the chapter).

In this first section we'll only be covering what is required to produce a well-formed document. It is inevitable that in doing so we will be covering material that will reappear (albeit in a slightly different form) in the second part of the chapter, because, as we've already said, valid documents are also well-formed, and so have to conform to all the constraints upon document formation that we'll be dealing with here. But initially we won't be directly covering anything relating to the declarations required in the DTD to make the document suitable for validation.

So in this diagram, although we will cover some of the declarations which must reside within the DTD section, these are only declarations required for basic well-formedness.

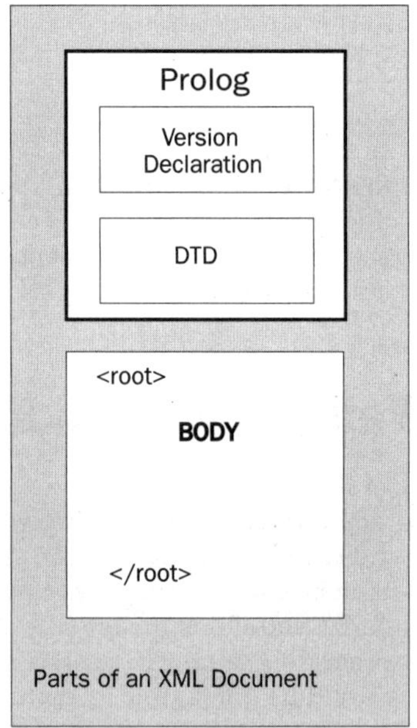

Parts of an XML Document

Starting the Document: The XML Declaration

The XML declaration is actually optional, but the W3C specification suggests that you should include it to indicate the version of XML used to construct the document so that an appropriate parser, or parsing process, can be matched to the document. When you include the declaration it must be placed at the very beginning of the document file without preceding characters (not even white space).

The basic format of an XML declaration is the same as that for a **processing instruction**, `<?name...?>`, which we will look at in detail later in the chapter. A processing instruction contains the name of the application for which the instructions are intended, followed by those instructions. Here the XML declaration is intended to inform parsers and other applications about the way in which the data in the file (the XML document) should be treated.

The minimum content of an XML declaration is the reserved name, `xml`, and a version number. At the time this book was written the version number was 1.0, indicating the number of the specification to which our documents conform. So, our documents could begin:

```
<?xml version="1.0"?>
```

Within the XML declaration itself the version number can be followed by the (optional) encoding details, and the (optional) standalone declaration (both of which we will treat in the second part of the chapter). Only the version number is mandatory.

Elements

As we have already seen in the introductory chapter the XML document essentially consists of data marked up using tags. Each start-tag/end-tag pair, with the data that may lie between them, constitutes an element.

```
<mytag>Here is some notable text data</mytag>
```

The names in the start and end tags for an element *must* be the same. Since XML is case sensitive care must be taken to ensure that the names match in letter case. For example `<mytag>` and `<Mytag>` are two distinct names in XML.

Text typically consists of character data and markup, as we saw in the introductory chapter. The XML 1.0 specification defines the sentence, "`Here is some notable text data`", between the tags to be **character data**. The two tags either side of the character data are the **markup**.

For the purposes of our discussion all we need to know at this stage is that character data between element tags can consist of any sequence of legal characters (conforming to the Unicode standard which we'll discuss later) *except* the element start character <. The < character is not permitted because the parser might mistake it as the start of a new tag and, when it fails to find the tag name that ought to follow the < according to its rules of operation, generate an error.

> *You might be wondering why we can't just write a program which is smart enough to deal with this possibility. One of the goals of the XML specification is that it should be (comparatively) easy to write programs which process XML documents. It makes it much easier to code a parsing application if it isn't required to cope with certain problems in the first place.*

End tags contain a forward slash character in front of the tag name, `</tagname>`, to distinguish them from the start tags, `<tagname>`. However, there is also a shorthand notation for an element that does not contain any content consisting of one tag with a forward slash character after the tag name, `<my_empty_element/>`. You needn't worry too much about how these empty tags are used just yet as we'll deal with this in more detail later; for now just note the syntax.

You will notice that in the earlier example above I have simply given the tags the name 'mytag'. XML allows you to give the tags any name you desire, so you could (if you wanted) have the following perfectly legitimate tag.

```
<Wop-bop-a-loo-bop-a-lop-bam-boom_Tutti-frutti>
      As sung by Little Richard
</Wop-bop-a-loo-bop-a-lop-bam-boom_Tutti-frutti>
```

A word of warning however: individual parsing programs may set limits on the length of names even though the XML specification makes no mention of such. So consult the literature for the particular program before writing enormously long tag names.

Legitimate names begin with a letter, an underscore _, or a colon character :, followed by any combination of letters, digits, hyphens, underscores, colons, or periods. Names must not begin with the three characters 'xml' in any combination of upper or lower case letters as this set of letters is reserved for use in special standardized XML instructions. It is also recommended that you avoid starting any names with a colon, as this is likely to cause confusion later on when you begin to construct more complex documents (in particular those using namespaces: see Chapter 4).

This freedom in the naming of tags is where the power of XML lies. You can give your tags names that *describe* the content of the element. Suppose for example, that we were constructing a taxonomic database for South American wildlife. We might have the following general entry for llamas:

```
<taxonomy>
  <class>Mammalia
    <order>Artiodactyla
      <suborder>Tylopoda
        <family>Camelidae
          <genus>Lama</genus>
        </family>
      </suborder>
    </order>
  </class>
</taxonomy>
```

The above is a well-formed document. For well-formed documents nearly everything we need to know about how to markup correctly (in accordance with the W3C specification) is contained in three simple rules:

- The document must contain one or more elements.
- It must contain a uniquely named element, no part of which appears in the content of any other element, known as the **root element**.
- All other elements within the root element must be correctly nested.

So, according to these rules the following are examples of well-formed documents:

```
<my_document></my_document>
```

```
<?xml version="1.0"?>
<class>Mammalia</class>
```

```
<root>
   <class>Mammalia</class>
</root>
```

Even this, strictly speaking, is a well-formed document:

```
<emptytag/>
```

For tags to be correctly nested there cannot be any overlap between the start and end tags of two different elements. So this is correct:

```
<parent>
   <child>Some info</child>
</parent>
```

with the child element starting and finishing within the parent element, but this is not

```
<badparent>
     <naughtychild>
        Some text info
</badparent>
     </naughtychild>
```

because the `naughtychild` element overshoots the end of the `badparent` element, which should encapsulate the `naughtychild` element completely.

So we are now in a position to construct a well-formed document which completes our taxonomic database entry for the humble llama:

```
<taxonomy>
 <class>Mammalia
  <order>Artiodactyla
   <suborder>Tylopoda
    <family>Camelidae
     <genus>Lama
      <species>glama
        <common_name>Llama</common_name>
      </species>
      <species>pacos
        <common_name>Alpaca</common_name>
      </species>
      <species>guanicoe
        <common_name>Guanaco</common_name>
      </species>
      <species>vicugna
        <common_name>Vicuna</common_name>
      </species>
     </genus>
    </family>
   </suborder>
  </order>
 </class>
</taxonomy>
```

Note that a <species> element contains both character data and the sub-element <common_name>, and that the <genus> element contains both character data and the <species> elements. This pattern of element nesting alongside character data is permissible, as the sub-elements in both cases start and end within the containing element.

Nesting elements in the way shown above allows us to represent the overall structure of the relations between the various pieces of information in our (in this case) database. In our complete taxonomic database we will undoubtedly have more than one 'class', e.g. Mammalia, Chondrichthyes, Myxini..., but each of these classes might have the same level of importance in the database. Classes hold orders, and orders in turn contain sub-orders. Nesting is a powerful means of representing these relations. So the final structure might be something more like:

```
<taxonomy>
   <class>Mammalia
      <order>...</order>
      <order>...</order>
      ...
   </class>
   <class>Chondrichthyes
      <order>...</order>
      <order>...</order>
      <order>...</order>
      ...
   </class>
   <class>Myxini
   ...
   </class>
</taxonomy>
```

Attributes

Elements can have attributes. These are values that are passed to the application by the XML parser but which do not constitute part of the content of the element. Attributes are given as part of the element's start tag. Consider this example:

```
<trousers   areJeans = "No">
     Sportif multi-coloured spandex flares
</trousers>
```

In the above, areJeans is an attribute of the trousers tag. For this particular instance of the element trousers the areJeans attribute has been assigned the value "No". Attributes can also be part of an empty element. So we might have an empty element that looked like this:

```
<has_surfboard     cansurfwell = "Yes"/>
```

Elements can have as many attributes as you want. So you could have:

```
<BigElement  attrib_1="one" attrib_2="two" attrib_3="three" .... />
```

For well-formedness no attribute name can be repeated in the same start tag for an element. So the following tags are not permissible because the NastyCloneAttrib appears twice:

```
<BadElement   NastycloneAttrib="ugh!" NastycloneAttrib="sicky!">
  Blah blah blah
</BadElement>

<BadEmptyElement   NastycloneAttrib="pew!" NastycloneAttrib="yet more ugh!"/>
```

For the merely well-formed, but not valid, document, there will be no markup declarations in the DTD (because strictly speaking such documents don't have DTDs) which dictate what types of data the attribute values can contain. In this case all attribute values will be treated as having the data type CDATA (ordinary character data). The string values of the attributes between the quote marks, e.g. `pew!` in the above, should not contain the characters <, &, or a single ' or ".

There are additional constraints on the values that well-formed attributes can contain, but these concern...

Entities

We will deal with these in greater detail in the second half of the chapter (see DTD: the Valid Document), but in order to deal thoroughly with the issue of well-formed documents we must make mention of them here. There are two categories of entities: **general** entities and **parameter** entities.

Entities are usually used within a document as a way of avoiding having to type out long pieces of text many times within a document. It provides a mechanism whereby you can associate a name with the long piece of text, and then, wherever you need to place that text within the document you just mention the name instead. When the document is processed the name is replaced by the text specified, saving a lot of time and effort. This in turn entails that if any modifications have to be made to the replacement text, that you only have to make one set of changes to one piece of text, rather than having to make a large number of alterations within the document.

All entities have two parts, a **declaration** and an **entity reference**. We will return to the subject of entity references shortly, but we'll start with entity declaration.

General Entities

For general entities the declaration is of the form

```
<!ENTITY  entityname  "some lengthy ... replacement text">
```

for an **internal** entity, or

```
<!ENTITY entityname  SYSTEM "http://www.someserver.com/dir/somefile.xml" >
```

for an **external** entity. For an external entity, as opposed to the internal type, the contents of the replacement text for the entity resides in a text file separate from the XML document. The `SYSTEM` keyword directs the parser to look for a file at the specified Uniform Resource Identifier (URI) address, in this case `http://www.someserver.com/dir/somefile.xml`.
Note that the description of these entities as internal or external really only indicates that the **replacement text** for the entity is given inside the declaration or lies in an external file outside the declaration. It does not indicate whether the declaration itself is within the document instance or not. It is helpful in this context, then, to think of the words 'internal' and 'external' as indicating the type of entity, *not* the location of the declaration or its parts.

So I can declare an entity which is of the internal type, in a file which is outside the document instance. And likewise an entity of the external type can be declared inside the document. This issue becomes more important when dealing with valid documents (and we explore it in the second half of the chapter).

As the writers and editors of the XML specification realized, it is useful when talking about entities and their declarations to draw a distinction between the **literal value** of the entity in the declaration, and the **replacement text** after an entity reference has been resolved. In the example above, the text string "`some replacement text`" is known as the literal entity value when it occurs in the declaration, but the same string is known as the replacement text after a reference to the entity (see Entity References below) has been processed and resolved.

Parameter Entities

As we shall see later, in the second half of the chapter, parameter entities have a special purpose, and their declarations are similar except that they contain an extra `%` character thus:

```
<!ENTITY  %  entityname  "Some replacement text">
```

Parameter entities can also be either internal or external type.

Entity Declarations and the <!DOCTYPE [...]> Declaration

The `<!DOCTYPE [...]>` declaration follows the XML declaration in the prolog of the document, and is used to indicate a section containing any declarations needed by the document. We need to include the `DOCTYPE` declaration in our well-formed documents if we want to declare entities. A very simple XML document containing the `DOCTYPE` declaration would have the following general syntax:

```
<?xml version="1.0" ?>
<!DOCTYPE mydocname [
...declarations go in here...
]>

<mydocname></mydocname>
```

For now, we will stipulate that for the well-formed document all entity declarations must occur between the square brackets of a `<!DOCTYPE [...]>` declaration at the beginning of the document. As it stands this stipulation is actually a gross simplification, as a distinction can be drawn between the **physical** location of the declaration and its **logical** (or syntactic) location within the document instance. Declarations might be referred to within the `DOCTYPE` declaration but actually reside in an external file. Logically these declarations are still 'within' the `DOCTYPE` declaration even though they reside in an external file.

Declarations that are within the `DOCTYPE` declaration and also physically within the document entity are said to be in the **internal subset** of the DTD. Those that are logically 'within' the `DOCTYPE` declaration, but which are external to the document entity are said to be in the **external subset** of the DTD.

So the stipulation that all entity declarations lie within the square brackets of the DOCTYPE declaration is basically correct, but hides complexities. A further set of complexities concerns the differences between the ways in which validating and non-validating (those which only check for well-formedness but not validity) parsers process the document. Although some declarations may be logically within the DTD but not physically, non-validating parsers tend to focus more on the issue of physical location when considering the processing of entity declarations or references. Non-validating parsers are *not obliged* to read any entity declarations physically outside the document entity, so if you only require well-formed but not valid documents it makes sense to keep all entity declarations in the internal subset.

Opting for merely well-formed documents containing general entities and using a non-validating parser carries with it the implication that projects, and documents' entity sets, must be fairly small, otherwise the costs (in time, money, energy,...) of inserting all the relevant entity declarations into each of the documents soon becomes prohibitively expensive. Upgrading to validation and a validating parser enables you scale up to larger projects more easily, by allowing you to move useful declarations of entities to external files which can be referenced by each document instance. Alternatively, if you wish to take advantage of the faster processing of merely well-formed documents (if these are suitable for your needs) by a non-validating parser, avoid using any entities in the documents.

We will deal with the DOCTYPE declaration in more detail later in the chapter, but for now we will stick to following syntax:

```
<!DOCTYPE mydocname [
<!ENTITY  entityname  "Some replacement text">
]>

<mydocname></mydocname>
```

Note that the document name (whatever name you substitute for mydocname **in the above) must be the same as the name of the root element of the document.**

The entity name can be anything you want it to be as long as it conforms to the rules about the construction of names given earlier in the section on Elements. If the entity is of the external type then it must only contain either text (character data plus markup) or character data.

Entity References

After the declaration has been made the entity can be referred to using the entity name in the following way within the document.

```
&entityname;
```

As the parser runs through the XML file it must encounter the declaration for an entity before any reference to that entity otherwise it will flag an error. References to undeclared entities within the document are also not permitted (and would be useless anyway).

There must not be any white space between the &, the entity's name, and the trailing semi-colon. So the following would-be references do **not** work because of the inserted spaces:

```
& entityname;
&entityname ;
& entityname ;
```

In the case of the general entity the reference to the entity is usually made within the text content of an element. Thus:

```
<myElement>I am reminded of the Gettysburg address in
 which Abe said, "&gettysburg;"
</myElement>
```

This mechanism of text replacement can be very useful if you have to include a chunk of text several times in the document and want to avoid typing it out in full every time – for example, the copyright statements at the bottom of documents.

A non-validating parser must only check that internal-type entities are well-formed, and will not necessarily read and include the contents of any external entities, let alone check them for well-formedness. It seems sensible therefore, to only include internal entity declarations and references to such in a document that only conforms to the minimum requirements for well-formedness. This will ensure that the data that you wish to pass to the application has the desired form after parsing.

While internal entities can be referred to within the value of an attribute of an element, external entities cannot. (The reason for this is that external entities can be in a variety of character encodings, and that placing data with a character encoding different from that of the root document entity within an attribute value is considered to give rise to more trouble than it's worth. If it were allowed the complexity of the parsers required would be vastly increased.)

And also, while we're on the subject....

References to general entities cannot be made anywhere within the DOCTYPE declaration.

Note that all such internal or external entities declared in the way we have shown are known as **parsed** entities in the XML 1.0 specification. By definition such entities can only contain character data or XML markup.

The replacement text of all entities is required to be well-formed in accordance with the stipulations of the XML specification. This means that no start-tag, end-tag, element, or entity reference can begin in one entity and end in another. So, for example, the following is **not** allowed:

```
<!ENTITY  myent     "<mytag>The text of the element..." >
```

Lastly, entities must not contain references to themselves, either directly or indirectly. So the following declarations are not allowed.

```
<!ENTITY net   "Talk about the &net;" >

<!ENTITY one   "refer to &two;" >
<!ENTITY two   "refer to &one;" >
```

But entities can refer to other entities as long as there is no direct or indirect self-reference of the type above. So we can have:

```
<!ENTITY    where      "the mat" >
<!ENTITY    didwhat    "sat on &where;" >
<!ENTITY    who        "The cat &didwhat;" >
```

If we then used the reference `&who;` within the content of an element, the entity references would be expanded by the parser, and the replacement text formed to give "The cat sat on the mat."

Referring to Parameter Entities

Parameter entities are referenced using the syntax

```
%param_ent;
```

Parameter entity references can **only** occur within the `DOCTYPE` declaration between the square brackets.

> **Within the internal subset of declarations parameter entity references can only be made *between* the other declarations in the subset, but *not* used within the declarations.**

In the external subset parameter references may be used *within* other declarations.

We will discuss parameter entities in more detail in the sections on the valid document, as they are not really of much use in the merely well-formed document entity. The reason for this comes in two stages.

Stage one is that although non-validating parsers process any information within the DOCTYPE declaration, checking to make sure it is well-formed, they don't necessarily read and expand external-type parameter entities and their references. So we cannot safely use external-type parameter entities in our merely well-formed documents.

Stage two is that the logical form of internal-type parameter entities, and the fact that they can only be referenced between declarations in the internal subset, means that they really don't have any possible usage which is relevant to the merely well-formed, but not valid, document. (This will become clear later when we discuss them in the context of valid documents.)

Entity References in Attribute Values

You will have seen above in the discussion of element attributes that the values that attributes can accept include character data. With some key limitations you can also have general entity references as attribute values. So you might want to include in your document an element that looks like this:

```
<Llama     DNAsequence="&llama_DNA;">
```

There are a few constraints upon this usage that must be noted though. Firstly the attribute value cannot contain a reference, directly or indirectly, to an *external*-type entity. So `llama_DNA` must not be an external entity (as described earlier), as the reference to it in the attribute value in the above example would be a direct reference to an external entity.

But let's assume that our `&llama_DNA;` entity reference refers to an internal entity that we'd declared earlier:

```
<!ENTITY  llama_DNA   "CAGTCAGTCAGT- &base_sequence;">
```

but that `&base_sequence;` was an external entity that we declared earlier in the document thus:

```
<!ENTITY base_sequence  SYSTEM "http://www.someserver.com/dir/bases.txt" >
```

Then, our reference to `llama_DNA` in the value for the `DNAsequence` attribute would contain a reference to an external entity, and thus the use of `&llama_DNA;` as the value of `DNAsequence` constitutes an indirect reference to an external entity, which is illegal.

Which brings us to the second well-formedness constraint on attribute values. The replacement text of any entity referred to directly or indirectly in the attribute value must not contain the < (less-than) symbol. (There is one exception to this rule that we will deal with shortly.)

This is because, assuming the replacement text of our `llama_DNA` internal entity were something like, "blah blah CAGT<CAGTCAGT", then the parser would replace this in the `<Llama>` element to give:

```
<Llama     DNAsequence=" blah blah CAGT<CAGTCAGT ">
```

Our parser, checking for well-formedness, would flag an error as it would interpret the presence of the < character as the start of a new tag, and would 'infer' that this new tag was not correctly nested (a very bad thing indeed!).

The exception to this rule is that you can include the character entity reference `<` in an attribute value, which is a reference to a pre-defined entity which has the < character as its replacement text. We will discuss how this exception works as we discuss...

Character Entities

Character references are also entity references. There are two main reasons for their use:

- To make reference to a character that is in the ISO/IEC 10646 character set (see the section on Character References below) but which is not directly accessible from the keyboard or the operating system.
- Or, to '**escape**' a character which might otherwise be considered to be markup from being processed by the parser prior to the data being passed to the client application.

The ISO/IEC 10646 character set is an International Standards Organization standard defining the way in which certain characters, e.g. the letters in these words, are encoded in binary within your computer. Each distinct letter or symbol is matched to a unique binary code.

Character references

For the first case reference to the character would take either the form `&#decimal_character_code;` or `&#xhexadecimal_character_code;` where the character code is the number of the character according to the ISO/IEC 10646 standard. The Unicode character encoding standard is the equivalent of the ISO standard and the character codes can be readily accessed (at the time of writing) at the following URL: `ftp://ftp.unicode.org/Public/UNIDATA/UnicodeData-Latest.txt`. So examples of character codes for the same character for the Bengali 'tt' consonant would be:

- `ট` with a hexadecimal code, or
- `ট` using a decimal code

Escaping characters

In the second case, there are some characters that we might want to appear in a section of character data, but which cannot appear there in their literal form as the parser will generate an error. For well-formed documents the XML specification defines a set of pre-defined character entities that can be used in place of the character's literal form should this be required. In well-formed documents we don't have to declare these character entities explicitly, but we do in valid documents. However, we'll look at the declarations as an aid to explaining how these entities work in the well-formed document. Here are the declarations that are implicitly included for every well-formed document showing the Unicode character codes for the characters we wish to escape (ASCII character codes match the first 256 Unicode codes).

```
<!ENTITY   lt        "&#38;#60;" >
<!ENTITY   gt        "&#40;" >
<!ENTITY   amp       "&#38;#38;" >
<!ENTITY   apos      "&#39;" >
<!ENTITY   quot      "&#34;" >
```

And the table below shows the resultant symbols which replace the entity references after parsing:

Entity Name	Name	Symbol
<	less than	<
>	greater than	>
&	ampersand	&
"	quote	"
'	apostrophe	'

You will notice that in the set of declarations for the entities for the `<` and `&` symbols there are two character references, e.g `"<"` for `lt`. This means that these entities are doubly escaped. The reason for this is that these characters are only permitted to occur in their literal form, i.e. as `&` and `<`, when they occur as markup delimiters. That is, they can only occur in their literal form when they are present as part of markup: `<` in `<tags>` including those which occur at the start of entity declarations and so forth; the ampersand, `&`, in an entity reference, `&ent;`. As character references in the declared entity values are expanded immediately (`&` is replaced by `&`) this means that the would-be replacement text for a reference to `lt` is then `<` and upon a reference, `<`, being parsed this becomes `<`. If `lt` wasn't doubly escaped then the entity value itself would be `<` and this would cause a parser checking for well-formedness to flag an error.

There are two exceptions to this rule:

- They can occur in their literal form in the contents of comments, XML processing instructions, and CDATA sections, which we'll treat later. For now all you need to know is that the reason that these are exceptional is that the parser ignores their contents at parse time.
- And they can appear in the literal entity value (the replacement text for an entity) in the declaration of an internal entity.

BUT... in the case of the second exception the following would ***not*** in fact be advisable:

```
<!ENTITY   ampsign    "&" >
<!ENTITY   ltsign     "<" >
```

This is because when *writing* the declaration it is in fact permissible to insert the & or < character into the literal value for the entity, as at this point the characters are not treated as markup delimiters. However, when the entity is referenced the result would not be well-formed, as the character would be treated as markup contravening the well-formedness rules we gave earlier. A non-validating parser would then reject the document.

Doubly escaping the character solves the problem. But how does double escapement work? And why is it needed? We can answer both these questions by looking at an example given in Appendix D of the XML 1.0 specification. In our document we have the following declaration:

```
<!ENTITY example  "<p> An ampersand (&#38;#38;) may be escaped numerically
&#38;#38;#38;) or with a general entity (&amp;amp;).</p>" >
```

When the XML processor parses this it will recognize the character references, and replace the references to give the following string, which it will then store as the value for '`example`'.

```
<p> An ampersand (&#38;) may be escaped numerically (&#38;#38;) or with a
general entity (&amp;amp;).</p>
```

If the document contains a reference to the entity, `&example;` , this will cause the text above to be re-parsed, and, in the words of the specification's authors, "the start- and end-tags of the 'p' element will be recognized and the three [entity] references will be recognized and expanded, resulting in a 'p' element with the following content (all data, no delimiters or markup)":

```
An ampersand (&) may be escaped numerically (&#38;) or with a general
entity (&amp;).
```

You might now be wondering why in order to arrive at a piece of text which contains `&` we need to put `&` in our original entity declaration, but for `&` we only need to insert `&`.

The reason is that the XML specification defines a set of rules as to how the parser should process entities depending on their context within the document. The specification authors have given a table that describes how the rules apply in section 4.4 of the specification. Below is a table that reproduces three of the columns. The omitted columns concern external unparsed entities, which can only occur in valid documents, and parameter entities.

Context	Entity Type			Character
	Internal General	External Parsed General		
Reference in Content	Included	Included if validating		Included
Reference in Attribute Value	Included in literal	Forbidden		Included
Occurs as Attribute Value	Forbidden	Forbidden		Not recognized
Reference in Entity Value	Bypassed	Bypassed		Included
Reference in DTD	Forbidden	Forbidden		Forbidden

The table concerns the way in which the XML parser treats the references to entities as they occur in their various contexts within the document.

So if we take the second column in the table above concerning internal entities then we find that the non-validating parser will accept the following:

```
<?xml version="1.0" ?>
<!DOCTYPE col2 [
<!ENTITY ent "textInEntity" >
<!ENTITY otherent "yes" >

<!ENTITY doodah   "Big Bob's &amp;ent;" >
]>

<col2  attrib="&otherent;"> some text including &ent; or &doodah;</col2>
```

In which case, after parsing we would have:

```
<col2 attrib="yes"> some text including textInEntity or Big Bob's &ent;
</col2>
```

The reference to the `amp` character entity is bypassed by the parser as it reads the declaration, because it is a reference to an internal general entity within `doodah`'s entity value. Then when `doodah` is referred to within the document the substitution of the ampersand sign is made, but this does not result in the substitution for `ent` as the inserted `&` is automatically treated as character data and not markup.

We can ignore the third column above here as the non-validating parser is not required to include the replacement text of an external parsed entity, so it isn't worth giving examples.

As far as the fourth column above is concerned, it is more revealing to talk about the two contexts in which character references aren't recognized or permitted. In the case of attribute values it is important to distinguish between

```
<Element   attrib="&#60;" />
```

where the replacement character for the reference is included at parse time, and

```
<Element   BadRefattrib="#60" />
```

where the character entity is simply no longer recognized since it doesn't conform to the syntax for entity references.

When the above table states that character entity references in the DTD are not allowed it means that such character references can only be made within the string literal value for an entity declaration (or that of an attribute value for a valid document).

So while

```
<!ENTITY doodah   "text including &#38;textInEntity;" >
```

is O.K., the following is not:

```
&#60;!ENTITY doodah   "text including &#38;textInEntity;" >
```

Nor is just `<` between other declarations.

Escaping data chunks

We will now discuss various methods for escaping chunks of character data from the document entity. It will become clear as to why we should want to do this as we discuss each method in turn.

CDATA sections

CDATA sections can be used, wherever character data can appear within a document, to escape blocks of text that contain characters that would otherwise be considered to be markup. So let's imagine that we wanted the final output of our document to be thus:

```
<DisplayedElem> "Time for bed," said Zebedee </DisplayedElem>
```

How would we go about arranging things so that the `DisplayedElem` was not actually considered to be a piece of markup? Answer: a CDATA section in our document as follows:

```
<NotDisplayed>
<![CDATA[ <DisplayedElem> "Time for bed," said Zebedee </DisplayedElem> ]]>
</NotDisplayed>
```

Comments

It is always good practice in programming to put comments in code which explain, remind about, or simply point out, salient sections of code as an aid to future understanding and interpretation. Most of the time the ability within XML to give your elements any name that you choose will relieve you of much of the burden of commenting code. However, in those cases where tag names just aren't explanatory enough XML provides a mechanism for commenting. It has the same syntax as for HTML comments:

```
<!-- Put any old text you want in here -->
```

Your text should not include the character '-' or the sequence '--' to avoid the parser confusing it with the end delimiter of the comment section.

Comments can appear in a document in positions outside the other markup, or at places within the DOCTYPE declaration permitted by the grammar. So, if we recycle one of the earlier examples, we can insert comments in the following ways:

```
<?xml version="1.0" ?>
                     <!-- A document to demonstrate entity replacements -->
<!DOCTYPE col2 [
                     <!-- We have now entered the DOCTYPE declaration -->
<!ENTITY ent "textInEntity" >
                     <!-- And declared an entity -->
<!ENTITY otherent "yes" >
                     <!-- And another -->
<!ENTITY doodah   "Big Bob's &amp;ent;" >
]>
                     <!-- And now we leave the DOCTYPE declaration -->

<col2  attrib="&otherent;"> some text including &ent; or &doodah;
                     <!-- We can even put comments here -->
</col2>
                     <!-- And here -->
```

Comments should **not** occur within declarations or inside element tags. So this is wrong:

```
<!ENTITY  speech
     <!-- This is Big Bob's Oscar acceptance speech  -->
"I would just like to thank my Ma and Pa, my sister Frank, my
     _nasal hair sculptor,..." >
```

and so is this

```
<Arnie     <!-- with menace -- >    >
 Arl be bok
</Arnie>
```

Lastly we come to...

Processing Instructions

These allow documents to contain instructions for applications using the XML data. They take the form:

```
<?NameOfTargetApp    Instructions for App ?>
```

Processing instructions do not constitute part of the character data of the application, but must be passed on to the application unchanged. To expand: the parser processes the document and passes these instructions unchanged through to the application using the parser. The processing instruction might be directly for use by the application using the parser. But it can also contain instructions for another target application that the processing application can call in order to do the processing. The instructions should be in a format appropriate for the target application. The target name cannot be 'xml', in any combination of upper- or lowercase letter, as the 'xml' name is reserved for other uses.

You can place processing instructions anywhere in the document that a comment will go (see the example in the previous section on Comments).

DTD: The Valid Document

When we read a book, manual or magazine article we rarely notice its structure; if it is well written then the structure will be transparent. Yet, without that structure there would be no communication. We might notice the headings and paragraphs but many other aspects usually pass us by. For one thing this structuring makes the information in the document intelligible, either to us or to an application using it. But it also entails that when a document is **parsed**, by an application for example, that the presence of required portions can be checked and any missing ones reported.

Assuming that we have planned the structure of our documents well in the first instance, then the resultant document instances should be logically complete because they conform to that structure. The process of **validation** for XML documents is that of checking that the document instance is logically complete with respect to its predefined structure (the syntax of which is in turn defined by the W3C specification). This predefined structure against which the document instance is checked can be given in a DTD, or Document Type Definition. (The notion of a DTD is contained in the original XML 1.0 specification, whereas ideas like XML-Data and DCDs are later suggestions for alternative ways of producing defined data schemas for XML documents.) The DTD can either reside in the same file as the rest of the document, or can be in a separate file that is referred to by each document instance that is supposed to conform to it.

Earlier in the chapter we mentioned the difference between a well-formed document and a valid document, and examined the details of well-formedness. In this section we will look at how to define the structure of our valid documents. As a database is described in a formal way, with a schema declaration, so XML has a formal method for describing document structures.

As XML does not have a logical structure that is well suited to linear explanations, early sections below regrettably have to presuppose some information which can only really be revealed later in the chapter. I can only beseech the reader to persevere, as the interrelations between the various aspects of the language will become clearer as we progress.

The XML Declaration

We saw at the beginning of the chapter that each XML document has a prolog that can contain an XML declaration followed by a document type declaration. The XML declaration controls how the parser will interpret the document.

If you recall, the format of an XML declaration is the same as that for a processing instruction. The minimum content of an XML declaration is a version number. At the time this book was written the version number was 1.0. So our documents should begin:

```
<?xml version="1.0"?>
```

The XML declaration is actually optional, but the W3C specification suggests that you should include it to indicate the version of XML used to construct the document so that an appropriate parser, or parsing process, can be matched to the document. When you include the declaration then the mandatory version number must be first, followed by the (optional) encoding details and (optional) standalone declarations (see below).

The encoding of the character set used in the document can if necessary be inferred from the encoding of the document instance itself. Every XML parser is required to support at least the 8 bit encoding of Unicode that corresponds to the ASCII character set. It can also support the 16 bit encoding which contains more characters than ASCII permits. The 8 bit encoding would be specified in the following manner:

```
<?xml version="1.0" encoding="UTF-8" ?>
```

Other possible values for the encoding are given in section 4.3.3 of the XML specification (see Appendix C of this book).

Lastly, the `standalone` attribute of the document declaration indicates whether the document has any **markup declarations** (see the following sections) that are external to the document entity that *would affect* the values passed to the surrounding application. If the value of `standalone` is '`yes`' then the document is effectively self-contained and there are no extra markup declarations in external DTDs and no internally declared external parameter entities containing such declarations (see later). We saw examples of external entity declarations in the DOCTYPE declaration earlier. If necessary, it should be possible to process such a document using only a non-validating parser.

The value '`no`' for `standalone` indicates that there might be markup declarations external to the document, in a DTD external subset or in an external type parameter entity. However, provided that the markup declaration for an external general entity is *internally* declared then references to such an entity within the body of the document do not affect its being able to be considered for `standalone='yes'` status.

The validity constraints that apply to the standalone declaration are given in the specification as follows:

> The standalone document declaration must have the value '`no`' if any external markup declarations **contain declarations** of:
>
> - attributes with default values, if elements to which these attributes apply appear in the document without specifications of values for these attributes, or
> - entities (other than `amp`, `lt`, `gt`, `apos`, `quot`), if references to those entities appear in the document, or
> - attributes with values subject to *normalization*, where the attribute appears in the document with a value which will change as a result of normalization, or
> - element types with element content, if white space occurs directly within any instance of those types.

Assuming our document is not 'standalone' the full XML processing declaration might then look like this:

```
<?xml version="1.0" encoding="UTF-8" standalone="no">
```

If the value for standalone is '`no`', it should only be processed using a validating parser, otherwise the data passed to the application will not be correct.

Document Type Declaration

As we saw before, we need a starting point for our document instance. This is the root element of our document, and for a valid document it must be defined within the document type declaration.

Yes, there is a document type **definition** and a document type **declaration**. It can be confusing especially as the declaration includes the definition. A document type definition (the DTD) comprises all the declarations of the document's elements together with any associated attribute declarations. The document type definition may also require one or more entity declarations (either internal to the document type declaration or as external entities). The document type **declaration** is the `<!DOCTYPE somename [ ... ]>` statement, and all the DTD declarations are placed between the square brackets.

```
<!DOCTYPE arootname
[ <!ELEMENT arootname ...>

<!--Other element declarations and associated attributes -->
] >

<arootname>
        ...    <!-- the rest of the document goes here -->
</arootname>
```

Note that `arootname` is mentioned in both the document type declaration and in an element declaration, `<!ELEMENT ...>`. We *must* include within the document type declaration an element declaration corresponding to the root element. The name of the document type must be the same as that of the root element of the document.

Within the body of the document type declaration we can declare all the elements and their attributes, and any entities and notations that define the form of our document. It is permissible to include declarations that a document instance does not need. The parser will take longer to read the document type declaration and may require additional resources while it processes the instance but it's not an error to include them.

Document Type Definition

A document type definition consists of the declarations within the DOCTYPE declaration, which includes entity, element and attribute declarations, and any other declarations required for describing our documents. Conveniently though, we don't need to include all of our DTD in each document of a set of documents with the same structure. It would be very tiresome if we had to copy the same DTD into every document we are working with. What we need is a way to reference a hard won DTD stored in a separate file. XML provides a mechanism for doing this. Within each document instance we can refer to the external DTD file using the following syntax:

```
<!DOCTYPE wrox SYSTEM "wrox-book.dtd">
```

Easy isn't it? If the `DOCTYPE` statement contains the `SYSTEM` keyword followed by a URI address as its value, the processor will read the DTD for us from the URI and then start validating the rest of the document against it. The DTD referred to in this way does not have to be one that we have written, we can (with their permission) use DTDs written by others that may have been prepared for common document formats.

Visit `http://www.schema.net` *to find some examples of freely distributed DTDs for popular XML document formats*

As we mentioned in the context of well-formed documents the `DOCTYPE` declaration has two portions – the internal subset, and the external subset. We can place declarations in both:

```
<!DOCTYPE  full.structure SYSTEM "wrox-book.dtd"
[
<!ELEMENT  para  ( em | quote | blah )>
]>
```

The `[ ]` brackets surround the internal subset portion of the DTD. The `SYSTEM` identifier names the external subset. If we are using a standard DTD then we could provide the name of a public identifier as well (just as we do for an external entity – more on this later).

For some regular set of documents which all conform to a particular schema the provision in XML for external DTDs means that we only have to write one DTD which can then be referred to by all of them. Providing these document instances all conform to the schema defined in the external DTD they will all be valid (and not merely well-formed) documents.

An XML parser reads the internal subset first. If any "conflicting" declarations occur in the external subset then they are read but ignored. Indeed the parser will use the first declaration that it encounters while reading the document type declaration. This would allow you to override certain definitions given in the external DTD for a particular document should you need to do so.

Element Declarations

Every document consists of one or more pieces, for example there are chapters and paragraphs in this book. In XML we refer to these pieces as **elements**. We can define as many elements as we need for the documents that we will deal with. An element can consist of other elements or of **character data**. As we shall see later in the chapter in the section on '`ENTITY` Attributes' some elements serve as place holders for other types of (non-XML) content and are otherwise empty.

We might define a chapter of this book like this,

```
<!ELEMENT chapter (title, text) >
```

This says that every chapter element consists of two further elements called title and text, which we will have to define in their own element declarations. Every element is defined in the same way: a < character followed immediately by `!ELEMENT`, the name of the new element, the content of this element and finally by a > character. In our actual document instance we would then use the chapter tag in the following way.

```
<chapter>
      <title>...</title>
      <text>...</text>
</chapter>
```

There are rules governing the elements' **names**. Some of the characters that we might like to use in element names are reserved for other purposes within XML, others were left out in order to maintain compatibility with SGML.

> **For XML names we can use letters, digits and the punctuation symbols underscore, hyphen and period; although names cannot begin with a digit. But we cannot use the question mark and quotation mark symbols as these are reserved for other purposes within XML.**

The notion of letters in XML is much larger than you might imagine. If your native tongue includes more than just the English alphabet's *a* through *z* as letters then you're in luck. As long as you use a character deemed to be a "letter" in Unicode then it's considered a letter in XML too. So you can write XML names in any tongue that you want (as long as its character set is supported in Unicode).

Obviously, if you have a well-formed occurrence of an element within the body of the document but you don't provide a declaration for the element's type (and any of its associated attributes) then the element cannot be validated. An element is valid if:

- there is a declaration for an element type in the DTD which has a name matching that of the element itself
- there are declarations for all of the element type's attributes and their value types in the DTD
- and the data type of the content of the element matches that of the content schema defined in the declaration.

There is a validity constraint on the declaration of elements in that no element *type* can be declared more than once for the same document. This means that you cannot have more than one declaration with the same element-type name within the same document (including any part of the document DTD physically outside the document entity). So we cannot have both of the following declarations within the same DTD because the elements have the same name, `chapter`:

```
<!ELEMENT chapter (title, text) >
<!ELEMENT chapter (religious_order, number_of_nuns) >
```

However, if we really wanted to have both these elements in our document, since XML names are case sensitive we could avoid the name collision by simply calling our elements `chapter` and `CHAPTER`. A word of warning though: some older parsers fold the case of tags to uppercase before processing, reinstating the name collision. And should you wish to pass the same document through an SGML parser, be aware that the default in SGML is case-*in*sensitivity (no case-sensitivity).

Element Content Models

Each element is described by a **content model** within the declaration that lists the subsidiary elements it can contain, with some elements defined as being optional or repeated. The content model is part of the element declaration and is (with two exceptions covered later) enclosed in parenthesis. The model describes what lower level elements make up the current element. There are no restrictions upon what you name these subsidiary elements provided that you follow the rules for naming.

```
<!ELEMENT   sample            (date.taken, volume, substance) >
```

The element `sample` consists of three lower elements `date.taken`, `volume`, and `substance` in that order. In the document instance these would appear as:

```
<sample>
      <date.taken>...</date.taken>
      <volume>     ...</volume>
      <substance>...</substance>
</sample>
```

The "language" used for content models is similar to that of the Unix regular expressions used for search and replace operations on documents viewed under that operating system. We won't assume that you're familiar with Unix regular expressions here, but if you are then you ought to be able to adjust easily to reading content models. However, in XML content models it is not actual text that is to be matched but elements. The symbols used for XML content models are the same as a subset of those for regular expressions. For example, parentheses are used for grouping; a question mark is used to signal optional elements; asterisk and plus symbols are used to signal repetition. We'll also find a symbol to denote the sequencing of elements; in regular expressions we rely upon the adjacency of the sub-expressions for that idea.

Below is a table that shows all the content model operators and their usages:

Symbol	**Usage**
,	Strict ordering
|	Selection
+	Repetition (minimum 1)
*	Repetition
?	Optional
()	Grouping

Let's look at an example content model for the element `test`:

```
<!ELEMENT  test        (sample+, conclusion)  >
```

Our `sample` element is now part of a higher level element's (`test`) content model. The + means that there must be at least one `sample` but there can be more. After the last `sample` there must be one `conclusion` element. So this would appear in the document as:

```
<test>
      <sample> ...</sample>
      <sample> ...</sample>
      ...
      <sample> ...</sample>
      <conclusion>...</conclusion>
</test>
```

If we altered the model to `(sample, conclusion)+` then each sample element would have to be followed by a conclusion element, and there would have to be at least one sample–conclusion pair within the `<test>` element. The use of the comma symbol in a content model means that the content elements must occur in that order. So, for this altered model we would have something like:

```
<test>
        <sample> ...</sample>
        <conclusion>...</conclusion>
        ...
        <sample> ...</sample>
        <conclusion>...</conclusion>
</test>
```

Where all but the first sample–conclusion pair are optional.

If we replace the comma by a pipe-stem character `|` then it becomes 'either...or'. So `(sample | conclusion)` means that we expect either one `sample` or one `conclusion` element but not both. So in the document, we get either

```
<test>
        <sample> ...</sample>
</test>
```

or

```
<test>
        <conclusion> ...</conclusion>
</test>
```

You should exercise a little caution when you think about the `|` or **selection connector**. It is wrong to think that both elements can be included; rather it is strictly either...or. Don't be mislead by the use of the `|` character that is commonly used in programming languages to signify Bitwise-Or operations on binary data.

Adding a `?` to the end, as in `(sample|conclusion)?`, would make inclusion of either one of these two elements optional. So in addition to the previous two examples we could also have:

```
<test>
</test>
```

And if we used a wildcard symbol `*` then we can have the elements there but it's okay to leave them out. The result is different to what the `(sample|conclusion)?` model allows; with the `(sample | conclusion)*` we are allowing any number of `sample` or `conclusion` elements to appear including none at all. So we could have:

```
<test>
        <sample> ...</sample>
        <sample> ...</sample>
        ...
        <sample> ...</sample>
</test>
```

or an unordered mix of both,

```
<test>
        <sample> ...</sample>
        <conclusion> ...</conclusion>
```

```
        <conclusion> ...</conclusion>
        <sample> ...</sample>
        ...
        <sample> ...</sample>
        <conclusion> ...</conclusion>
        <sample> ...</sample>
</test>
```

or,

```
<test>
        <conclusion> ...</conclusion>
        <conclusion> ...</conclusion>
        ...
        <conclusion> ...</conclusion>
</test>
```

or,

```
<test>
</test>
```

Within a group `(...)` the connector symbols (the `,` and `|`) must be the same. We cannot mix them like this, `(sample+, test | conclusion)`, within a content model unless we introduce more parenthesis, `(sample+, (test | conclusion))`. Unlike arithmetic expressions there is no implied precedence between the connectors.

When a validating parser reads an XML document it uses the content models to verify that each element in the document has been keyed-in correctly.

The following table demonstrates the syntax of various element content declarations:

Content Model	Comments
x	Single element (x) expected
x | y	Single element (either x or y expected)
x, y	Two elements (x and y) expected; in that order
x, y?	Two elements allowed; x expected y optional
(x, y , z)	Three elements expected; x, followed by y followed by z
x, (y | z)	Two elements allowed; x expected, followed by either y or z
x, (y | z)*	Two elements allowed; x expected followed by any number of y and z including none
x, (y | z)+	At least two elements expected. x followed by at least one of y or z. Any number of y and z may follow

Table Continued on Following Page

Content Model	Comments
x | (y ,z)	Either a single x element expected or a y element followed by a z element expected

Complex models may be constructed by replacing parenthesized groups for x, y and z

Below is a document with a mock internal DTD, using what we've learnt so far. Please note that many of the tags are not defined with a declaration (e.g. subA, myA, myB,...), so strictly speaking this document is not valid, but it does provide an example of the use of content models:

```
<?xml version ="1.0">
     <!DOCTYPE  exampledoc [
     <!ELEMENT  TopOne        (subA | subB)>
     <!ELEMENT  subB          (myA, myB, myC)>
     <!ELEMENT  Another       (First, Gorilla?)>
     <!ELEMENT  Gorilla       (Y)+>
     <!ELEMENT  almostLast    (giraffe, Zebra)*>
     ]>

<exampledoc>
     <TopOne>
           <subA>...</subA>
     </TopOne>
     <TopOne>
           <subB>
                 <myA> ...</myA>
                 <myB> ...</myB>
                 <myC> ...</myC>
           </subB>
     </TopOne>
     <Another>
           <First> ... </First>
     </Another>
     <Another>
           <First> ...</First>
           <Gorilla>
                 <Y> ...</Y>   <!-- at least one Y must be present -->
                 ...
                 <Y> ...</Y>   <!-- others are optional -->
           </Gorilla>
     </Another>
     <almostLast>
           <giraffe> ... </giraffe>    <!-- zero or more giraffe_ -->
           <Zebra>  ...  </Zebra>      <!-- _followed_by_Zebra pairs -->
           ...
           <giraffe> ... </giraffe>
           <Zebra>  ...  </Zebra>
     </almostLast>
</exampledoc>
```

Ambiguous Content Models (and how to avoid creating them)

It is possible using the operators above to create ambiguous content models. Ambiguity happens when there are two or more possible interpretations of the current content model. The XML developers use a very restrictive definition of "unambiguous". At any point they expect there to be only one applicable element. However, good validating parsers should show an error when encountering ambiguous declarations.

You'll notice that all the examples we've looked at in this chapter have been unambiguous. When the same element appears more than once in a model you introduce the possibility of ambiguity. Take the following example:

```
<!ELEMENT ambig ((date.taken, volume, substance) |
                                        (date.taken, stolen.article))>
```

When the parser encounters a date.taken element in the document instance should the following one be a volume or stolen.article? Basically, the parser does not know at this stage in the process which of the two possible content models it should apply to the <ambig> element. Unless the parser is equipped to test whether the element following date.taken is volume or stolen.article and then backtrack if it encounters an incompatability, it will be unable to parse the document appropriately. However, the content model can be altered so that there is no ambiguity:

```
<!ELEMENT  ambig  (date.taken, ( (volume, substance) |  stolen.article))>
```

With the first version when a start tag for ambig was encountered we did not know whether to expect a volume or a stolen.article element after the date.taken. As the choice had to be made *before* the element following date.taken was even seen, because it concerned the ambig element, we have an ambiguous content model. In the second version when a start tag for ambig is seen we know that it is to be followed by a date.taken element. Only after that do we have to make a choice, but by then we can see whether a volume or a stolen.article occurs. The difference between the two versions being that in the first the parser has to simultaneously look two levels ahead along two logical paths in its construction of the logical tree for the <ambig> element before reaching a decision. Whereas in the second it only has to test one step at a time. Most parsers currently available are unlikely to have the sophistication built in to cope with the first version and are likely to flag an error on attempting to parse such documents.

And in fact, the XML specification says that content models must be such that the parser only has to move one step at a time.

We can also introduce ambiguity using the optional occurrence indicators (i.e. asterisk and question mark – * and ?).

```
<!ELEMENT  ambig2      (date.taken?, (date.taken, volume, substance) ) >
```

When we create a content model such as this the parser cannot decide whether the first date.taken tag satisfies the optional element or not. There is a simple correction for this model:

```
<!ELEMENT  ambig2      (date.taken, (date.taken?, volume, substance) ) >
```

#PCDATA

Eventually we reach an element that will have character content. When we have such an element then its content model will include the special element name `#PCDATA`. We can use `#PCDATA` on its own in a content model:

```
<!ELEMENT pname (#PCDATA) >
```

We call it `#PCDATA` as a reminder that what we are dealing with at this point in the document is **parsed character data**. All other elements will have been dealt with (i.e. parsed) and what we are left with is character data. The # symbol is there to prevent PCDATA from being interpreted as an element name. It is the **reserved name indicator**.

There is nothing to prevent you from having a content model of `(#PCDATA | pcdata)`. Users of your document type definition might not appreciate it if you did though.

There are often occasions when we need to construct element content models which include `#PCDATA` together with other sub-elements.

```
<!ELEMENT pname (#PCDATA | TweetyElem | SylvesterElem )*>
```

This should be done carefully, especially if our documents are to be parsed by an SGML parser later rather than just an XML parser you are using now, as SGML parsers throw out whitespace and some other formatting characters within elements in their parsing process, which may compromise record ends. If you need to use **mixed content** like this then you will have to consider how record ends are to be dealt with by using the `xml:space` (whitespace preservation, covered later) attribute with various elements in your document.

When you create a mixed content declaration like this the `#PCDATA` and any other elements in the content group must be separated using the `|` character. The `,` character must not be used to separate the terms in mixed content groups.

Any `#PCDATA` content is implicitly optional. So

```
<pname></pname>
```

is acceptable to an XML parser i `pname` is declared to have `#PCDATA` content.

> **Declarations for mixed content models must not contain the same name twice.**

So the following content model is **not** valid because the `evil_clone` sub-element occurs twice:

```
<!ELEMENT    BadMixedRepeater    (#PCDATA | evil_clone |
                                       Dolly | sheep | evil_clone)*>
```

EMPTY

Sometimes the content of an element is not textual at all. We need the element name to act as a placeholder in the document structure but we do not want the XML parser to interpret the content itself. A graphic might need to be inserted when this element is processed but as far as the parser is concerned this element is empty. (We'll see an example of this later in the section on attributes.) If we have this requirement then we can use `EMPTY` as the content model for the element.

```
<!ELEMENT  artwork     EMPTY>
```

Note that there are no parentheses and therefore no reserved name indicator, `#`, is required here. EMPTY elements do not require the presence of a completing end tag in the document, but they require a forward slash at the end of the single tag. So the `artwork` element could then have the following form in the document instance:

```
<artwork />
```

ANY

You may see content models of ANY; it isn't used very often and is discussed even less frequently in the SGML/XML community. The consensus amongst that community is that it's useful as a temporary measure when developing a document type definition; particularly if you are having to construct a DTD by working back from an existing XML document.

It lets us put *any* type of content (even `#PCDATA`) within the element. There will be situations where it would be appropriate to let any type of content appear. If that need arises then the content model becomes:

```
<!ELEMENT  ElemName     ANY >
```

Again, we do not need the parentheses or the reserved name indicator.

Attribute List Declaration

An element can have attributes associated with it. Attribute declarations begin with the `<!ATTLIST...` instruction and contain: the element name to which the attributes belong; the names of the attributes in the element; the data types or possible values for the attributes' contents; and default values for the attributes. As an example:

```
<!ELEMENT  mycar         EMPTY >
<!ATTLIST  mycar
                is_blue     (yes|no)          "yes"
                brandname   ID                #REQUIRED
                descripton  CDATA             #IMPLIED
>
```

Each attribute has 3 components: a name (e.g. `is_blue`), which follows the same rules as element names do; the type of information to be passed; and how default values are to be handled. (For more on the significance of the keywords `#REQUIRED`, `#IMPLIED`, and `#FIXED` (used later) see the section on Default Values of Attributes later in this chapter.)

The `mycar` element would then be used in the following way within the document:

```
<root>
 <mycar  isblue="no"  brandname="68Studebaker"  description="My second home" />
</root>
```

An element can have any number of attributes associated with it. You will get bored typing them before your parser is likely to report an error.

With DTDs we can control how the attribute's value is interpreted. In well-formed documents the value is always seen as containing character data for there are no attribute declarations to tell us otherwise. However, for valid documents we can have attributes that have different properties.

For an attribute to be valid the attribute type must have been declared in an `ATTLIST` declaration and the value for the attribute must match the data type declared for its type.

One last thing before we move on to discussing the various attribute types: the value of an attribute specified in the `ATTLIST` declaration must not contain any one of the characters, <, &, ", or ', in literal form as these will be interpreted as markup at parse time, the result being a document that is not well-formed. However, attribute values in the `ATTLIST` declaration can contain the & character if it is part of an entity reference for an internal entity that has been declared above the `ATTLIST` declaration. So none of the following attribute values are permissible:

```
<!ATTLIST   elementName
           Bad_attrib1      #FIXED    " 10 < 15"
           Bad_attrib2      #FIXED    " Custard & French fries"
           Bad_attrib3      #FIXED    " Thus " spoke Zoomer"
           Bad_attrib4      #FIXED    " Hooray ' said Dan"           >
```

But we can have this:

```
<!ENTITY    longdescription
                "yadayadayadayadayadayadayadayadayadayadayada......." >
<!ENTITY    lt    "&#38;#60;" >
<!ATTLIST   elementName
               okAttrib     #FIXED       "&longdescription; 10 &lt; 15"      >
```

(See the section on Entities later for more on entity declarations.)

CDATA Attributes

How the parser deals with attribute values depends upon what you declared them to be. For well-formed documents attribute values are assumed to consist of nothing but character data. If you wished to retain that interpretation in a valid document then you would have to declare the attributes as `CDATA`.

```
<!ELEMENT  with.attributes   (#PCDATA)>
<!ATTLIST  with.attributes
                sample         CDATA   #IMPLIED
>
```

Using this element in a document we could set the attribute as

```
<with.attributes sample="Any old text provided that it isn't meant to have
                         markup in it">
```

Whenever you pass a value to a CDATA attribute the parser will do very little with it. You're assumed to know what you're doing and that the application using the parser can make the necessary decisions about what to do with the value.

ID and IDREF Attributes

Once you start dealing with valid documents though, there are several things that you can do with attribute values that increase the power of the concept. You're probably used to using the internal links within Web pages, where you click on a "hot spot" and you're shown some other portion of the page. There's a similar mechanism available in XML where you can define these intra-document links. (There's no mechanism available in the main XML 1.0 specification for inter-document links but we shall be looking at an additional specification which provides such a mechanism in Chapter 5 on Linking in XML.)

Before we can refer to a position within the document we need some way to define it. This is provided with the ID type attribute.

```
<!ELEMENT   Intralink   EMPTY>
<!ATTLIST   Intralink
                 arrive_at    ID         #REQUIRED
>
```

Each element can only have one attribute of type ID.

With the use of the #REQUIRED keyword we stipulate that every occurrence of the Intralink element must contain an accompanying arrive_at attribute.

ID type attributes must have default values of either #REQUIRED or #IMPLIED.

Our Intralink element would appear in the document instance as:

```
<Intralink  arrive_at="ReferToThisName"/>
```

There is no separate end tag as we defined Intralink as an EMPTY element.

Each occurrence of an Intralink element can only have one ID attribute (in this case named arrive_at), and each instance of the attribute must have a unique value.

> **An ID value for the ID attribute of an element must have a name value that is unique over the entire document in which it occurs.**

So in the example above, 'ReferToThisName' can only be used as a value for that one particular element within the document, and for no other element. So the following is **not** allowed:

```
<Intralink  arrive_at="ReferToThisName"/>
<Intralink  arrive_at="ReferToThisName"/>
```

But we can have:

```
<Intralink  arrive_at="ReferToUniqueOne"/>
<Intralink  arrive_at="ReferToUniqueTwo"/>
<Intralink  arrive_at="ReferToUniqueThree"/>
<Intralink  arrive_at="ReferToUniqueFour"/>
```

Once we have defined the elements we want to refer to, we can then use IDREF attributes to refer to them (from other elements).

```
<!ELEMENT  refIntralink        (#PCDATA)>
<!ATTLIST       refIntralink
                      link_to        IDREF   #IMPLIED
>
```

Notice that we don't have to make the IDREF a required attribute as we made the one for ID. Even though we've defined a link_to attribute for refIntralink we might not need to use it with every occurrence of the refIntralink tag in the document instance, so we make its use optional with the #IMPLIED keyword.

If we need a tag to make multiple references to other locations in the document we can use the IDREFS type.

```
<!ELEMENT  Manyrefs            (#PCDATA)>
<!ATTLIST  Manyrefs
                link_to_many    IDREFS        #IMPLIED
>
```

IDs referred to in the IDREFS statement are separated by a single whitespace character.

When we come to use the attributes we get:

```
<Intralink  arrive_at ="Figure_1"/>
<Intralink  arrive_at ="Figure_2"/>
<Intralink  arrive_at ="Figure_3"/>
<refIntralink   link_to="Figure_1">This element refers to Figure 1
  </refIntralink>
<Manyrefs  link_to_many="Figure_1 Figure_2 Figure_3">
 This tag refers to all three figures.
  </Manyrefs>
```

To be valid the value of an IDREF attribute must match the name of some ID attribute value on some element within the document. The names in an IDREFS value must conform to the same rule.

ENTITY Attributes

Content models are a useful mechanism for describing the structure of our documents but they do not provide us with a way to control the type of data passed as #PCDATA. This is particularly the case when we deal with binary data. We can solve the problem by including an ENTITY **attribute** for the appropriate elements.

Ordinary general entities referred to in the document using the `&entity;` syntax can only contain text (parsed character data or XML markup). If we want to include other types of data (e.g. binary data formats like `.zip` files or Java `.class` files) with our documents then we have to use entity-type attributes.

We can "name" a single entity by declaring the attribute as type `ENTITY` in the `ATTLIST` declaration for the element concerned. It is possible to declare the attribute to accept multiple entities by using the type `ENTITIES`, which works in the same way as the `IDREFS` type in the section above. Here's an example:

```
<!ELEMENT  illustration        (#PCDATA) >
<!ATTLIST  illustration
                external.artwork      ENTITY         #IMPLIED
>
<!ENTITY        sune.logo   SYSTEM "Macintosh HD:XML Book:Chapter 2:entity
                      example"      NDATA          PICT
>
<!ENTITY    WROX.logo    SYSTEM "http://www.wrox.com/images/smallogo.gif"
                                    NDATA          gif
>
<illustration external.artwork="sune.logo" ></illustration>
<illustration external.artwork="WROX.logo"></illustration>
```

Note also that the two external entity declarations for `sune.logo` and `WROX.logo` have `NDATA` data types. These should have been declared earlier using the `<!NOTATION ... >` declaration (see the following section).

Entities with an `NDATA` term are **unparsed** external entities. This means that the data contained within these entities may or may not be text, and if it is text, this may or may not be XML code; in any case the parser skips over the details of the contents of such entities. So there are no constraints upon the type of data that an unparsed entity may contain. In the example above our unparsed external entities are image files, but unparsed entities can be any format. However,...

> **The only way to include unparsed entities as part of the document is through the use of ENTITY type attributes for some element. Such attributes can *only* accept unparsed entities as values.**

That is, a freestanding reference with the normal `&some_entity;` syntax is not permitted for an unparsed entity. For unparsed entities you should always follow the model given in the example above.

Once again, for the attribute to be valid its value must match the name of an unparsed (external) entity declared in the DTD.

Notation Attributes

It might be the case that you would want to define certain terms to have particular consequences. You might perhaps want to have the mention of file formats within the document instance trigger the application processing the document to perform certain actions or call up other appropriate applications for processing such files.

We can do this using a combination of NOTATION declarations and notation-type attributes. First we provide our NOTATION declarations like this:

```
<!NOTATION  PICT    SYSTEM   "PikEdit1.exe">
<!NOTATION  jpg     SYSTEM   "file://myserver/myfolder/JPEGEdit.exe">
<!NOTATION  gif     PUBLIC   "http://www.server.com/somedir/GifEditor.exe">
```

And we could then use them in the content model for an attribute:

```
<!ATTLIST   clipart
            file.format    NOTATION     ( jpg | gif )
>
```

Note that we don't have to include all the defined NOTATION values in our content model for the attribute.

In effect we have used the NOTATION declarations to define a data type, any subset of values of which we can then use in attribute content models. Typically the data values for NOTATION attributes are external, non-XML data formats.

If we couple NOTATION attributes with ENTITY attributes then we can make sure that nothing is forgotten or misinterpreted. Indeed as we saw earlier, the only way that you can include such unparsed data in the document is by using such attributes.

```
<!ELEMENT   graphic      EMPTY >
<!NOTATION  gif      PUBLIC    "_//Wrox//NOTATION WroxGifs format//EN">
<!ATTLIST   graphic
            file.name    ENTITY    #REQUIRED
            file.format NOTATION  gif
>


<!ENTITY    LOGO.entity   SYSTEM   "C:\IMAGES\LOGO.gif"   NDATA   gif>

<graphic  file.name="LOGO.entity" file.format="gif" />
```

You will notice that the LOGO.entity is both external to the document and declares its data type to be 'NDATA gif'. The use of the keyword NDATA indicates that the entity has a data type that was declared earlier with a NOTATION declaration, and that it is an unparsed entity.

For validity all the notation names must have been declared first using NOTATION declarations, and then the value of the notation-type attribute must match one of the notation names declared in the ATTLIST declaration for the element.

Name Token (NMTOKEN) Attributes

Often we do not need attributes that are treated as character data, refer to other locations within the document, or cause the inclusion of binary data, but we do want a name value. Such names might be used for the security level of the document, or a language name or a code. In XML we can declare an attribute to be a NMTOKEN. The values of such attributes must follow the same rules as other names in XML, e.g. those of elements and attributes, except that Name Tokens do not have to start with a letter, underscore, or colon.

```
<!ELEMENT  para  (#PCDATA | ... )*>
<!ATTLIST  para
                 security   NMTOKEN  #IMPLIED
>
...
<para>This paragraph has whatever the application's default security level
is.</para>
<para security="confidential">Whereas this paragraph is assumed to be confidential
because we used a NMTOKEN attribute.</para>
```

The `NMTOKEN` attribute can then be used by an application that, for example, could select which people should see which pieces of information within the document.

We have to take care in our use of `NMTOKEN` values as no check is made upon the spelling but only upon whether the value satisfies the requirement of an XML name.

We may need to include several name values with an attribute. If we tried to do that with a `NMTOKEN` attribute we would get an error. What we must do is use a `NMTOKENS` attribute, as this allows us to include more than one value. However, we can still provide a single value there if we wish. If there are to be several values then each one is separated from its neighbors by a single whitespace character. The difference between `NMTOKEN` and `NMTOKENS` is the number of values that may be included in the start tag.

```
<!ATTLIST  para
                       secure.users   NMTOKENS     #IMPLIED
>
<para security="confidential" secure.users="JONSOND dj BOUMPHREYF fb">...
```

Since the change to the specification that makes XML case-sensitive the letter case of each value will be preserved when it is passed to the application. For the example above, where I've used login names, the case might be significant. Unlike inconsistencies with the case of element and entity names, which the parser will report on, any similar inconsistencies in the case of NMTOKEN values depend upon an application (and its programmer) being smart enough to cope with them.

Enumerated Attributes

We can use `NMTOKEN` attributes for any purpose we like. So long as it's recognized as a name any value is acceptable to the XML parser. However, this might not be acceptable to us. The application code surrounding the parser may require name values to be spelt a particular way. For whatever reason the application has been coded to accept a name value of `"millennium"` but sadly there are some people who write the incorrect `"millenium"` (*sic*). We can stop them misspelling it by enumerating all the acceptable values.

```
<!ATTLIST  para
                 epoch.name  (millennium)     #IMPLIED
>
```

If we tried to use `<para epoch.name="millenium">...` then the parser will produce an error message, as it would if we used `<para epoch.name="LotusYr1900">`.

When there is more than one value we list them all and separate each one with a | character. In SGML we are allowed to use any of the connectors (SEQUENCE, AND and OR) but there is merit in the XML approach as it reminds us that we have to select one of the allowed values. All we have to do is list out the possible values that are acceptable, one of which must occur if the `choices` attribute (below) is used.

```
<!ATTLIST  para
                choices      (this | that | other) #REQUIRED
>
```

In order for the `choices` attribute to be valid, values for the attribute given when it occurs in the `para` element start tag must match one of the group of values given in the `ATTLIST` declaration.

As with `NMTOKEN` values we need to consider letter case for these enumerated values. The parser will report errors for any values that are not in the appropriate case. Should you have a requirement for different cases of the same value then you must accommodate that within the attribute declarations you write and within any supporting application code.

```
<!-- The following values are all seen as distinct in XML parsers -->
<!ATTLIST  para
                case.choices  (this | This | tHis)   #REQUIRED
>
```

We need to be careful with attribute list declarations containing enumerated values that are to be used later with an SGML parser. Until a pending technical correction is ratified for SGML all enumerated values for an element must be unique. This is an interoperability issue between XML and SGML parsers. It is seen as an unfortunate restriction within SGML. Until such time as the correction is made you should be wary of declaring attributes like this if you want your documents to double as SGML documents:

```
<!ATTLIST  para
                lockable     (yes | no)
                printable    (yes | no)
>
```

This is acceptable to XML parsers but will be rejected by existing SGML parsers. XML users will expect that the values of the `lockable` and `printable` attributes should be considered unique (e.g. lockable-yes and printable-yes). But SGML treats all values as globally unique, and will consider the two instances of, for example, the `yes` value to be a name collision – an error.

Default Values of Attributes

At the back of our minds should have been thoughts about how we provide a default value, and how we can leave off attributes that are inapplicable to the current element. XML allows us some control over the answers to these important questions. You will have noticed that each attribute declaration in this chapter included `#REQUIRED` or `#IMPLIED` or `#FIXED` but that we glossed over what they meant.

#REQUIRED or #IMPLIED

The #REQUIRED flag forces the attribute to appear in each start-tag for this element. That is, there is no default value for any attribute with this mark against it. Whereas the #IMPLIED flag indicates that the application supplies the default value if one isn't supplied in the document instance. A possible flaw in this #IMPLIED approach is that it means that different applications can provide different defaults even when the same document instance is processed. Although it has worked in SGML for years it still seems to go against the foundation that everything is spelt out in the markup. If the document designer is competent though, those attributes for which the presence of supplied values is crucial will be marked #REQUIRED, and those for which user supplied values are not essential (where the use of any default value whatever will make little or no difference for the application) should be marked #IMPLIED.

#FIXED

Any attribute that has #FIXED attached to it means that it can only have the one value when the attribute is used in that element. In the example below, if the attribute spelling appears in the word element it can only have the value that is #FIXED: millennium.

```
<!ELEMENT  word  (#PCDATA)>
<!ATTLIST  word
                spelling   CDATA  #FIXED    "millennium"
>
<word spelling="millennium"></word>
```

When the word element appears in the document it doesn't have to include the spelling attribute explicitly as the declaration means that in the absence of an actual instance of the attribute for the element the default 'millennium' is assumed. So in the case where we have:

```
<word> A little bit of text </word>
```

the parser actually assumes

```
<word  spelling="millennium"> A little bit of text </word>
```

Enumerated Defaults

Suppose we want to have an attribute that accepts two or three possible values, and provides a default value when the attribute doesn't appear in the element. Here we might be acknowledging that other people spell 'millennium' incorrectly even though their intentions were good. In this case we would have a declaration as follows:

```
<!ELEMENT  word  (#PCDATA)>
<!ATTLIST  word
                spelling   ( millenium | milenium | millennium )
                                                        "millennium"
>
<word spelling="millennium"></word>
```

This declaration states that any of the three spellings of 'millennium' are acceptable values, and in the absence of a supplied value for the attribute (like in the case for #FIXED) the parser will assume that of 'millennium'. You can explicitly declare as many acceptable values in the group as you like.

E.g.

```
<!ATTLIST    counting
              numbers     (one |two | three | four |and | so | on | ...)
                                                                    "ten"
>
```

One last thing to mention before we leave the subject of attribute default values: for validity declared default values must be of the correct data type for the attribute declared.

To help, the table below lists all the possible content data types for an attribute:

Attribute "type"	Attribute value content
CDATA	Character data
ID	A name that is unique over all other ID attribute values
IDREF	A name that is defined by some other ID type attribute
IDREFS	A series of names that are defined by ID type attributes and are separated by white space
ENTITY	A name of a pre-existing external entity. The entity is assumed to contain binary data
ENTITIES	A series of names of pre-existing external entities that are separated by white space. The entities are assumed to contain binary data
NMTOKEN	A name, which cannot begin with the characters _ or :
NMTOKENS	A series of NMTOKEN values separated by white space
NOTATION	A series of NMTOKEN values separated by white space that have been named in NOTATION declarations
Enumeration	A series of NMTOKEN values that you explicitly listed in the attribute declaration

Multiple Declarations of Attributes

Occasionally you will need to declare the attribute in several pieces, for example, you might be extending the attributes for an element defined in the external subset of your document type declaration. When that occurs the XML parser will take the first occurrence of the attribute and ignore the rest. You can override any attribute with your own declaration because the internal subset is read first.

```
<!ELEMENT   over.ride.sample  (#PCDATA) >
<!ATTLIST   over.ride.sample
                       attr.to.over.ride      CDATA   #IMPLIED
>
<!-- The following declaration will be ignored by the parser -->
<!ATTLIST   over.ride.sample
                       attr.to.over.ride      NOTATION       (gif)
                                                        #FIXED "gif"
>
```

When we come to put all the declarations together to construct a document type definition we can exploit the ordering of portions within the DOCTYPE declaration when overriding attribute definitions. Although the external subset is named ahead of the internal subset it is the latter that is *read* first.

```
<!DOCTYPE  book  PUBLIC "-//BigBook Press//DTD Easyreader Series//EN"      [
      <!--  Here's the internal subset where we can introduce declarations
            that over ride any others          -->
      <!ATTLIST  artwork
                   format    NOTATION  (TeX | PostScript |
                                              Private)    #IMPLIED
      >
]>
```

In this example we're assuming that the external declaration for the artwork element has a format attribute associated with it that does not include the Private notation.

Normalization of Attribute Values

By default an XML parser does not pass the original attribute values to the surrounding application. Instead it transfers a **normalized** version so as to save memory and to stop misinterpretation. The parser replaces all **record ends** (commonly return and/or newlines) by spaces, thereafter multiple whitespace characters are reduced down to a single space character. If you happen to be using an old XML parser that has not yet implemented the case-sensitivity change then all NMTOKEN values are case folded to upper case letters.

xml:space Reserved Attribute

When we deal with text like poetry set in-line we will probably require an additional attribute to control the insertion of line-end marks; this is typically a '/' where the original author wrote on a new-line.

However, by convention, there is a **reserved attribute name** (xml:space) that we can associate with any element wherever whitespace is important. When this attribute is included in an element's tag with the value 'preserve' then the parser has to maintain the whitespace and pass it to the surrounding application to deal with.

```
<!ELEMENT  poetry      (#PCDATA | %emphasis;)*>
<!ATTLIST  poetry
                xml:space   (default | preserve) 'preserve'
>
```

The root element itself does not have any implicit default for whitespace preservation or non-preservation. So unless you explicitly declare this attribute for the root element and provide a default value, the surrounding application will process the root element (and hence all those parts of the document for which whitespace handling has not been given an explicit default) according to the application's defaults.

Entity Declaration

We talk about saving our documents as files. XML uses a more general concept of entities, which we touched upon briefly earlier in the context of attributes.

Like the C or C++ pre-processor, the entity mechanism allows us to include "files" and to define macros. There are some restrictions about where certain types of entities are allowed to be referenced or declared within a document, as we shall see below. They also have to be complete, for example: if an entity contains a start tag it must also contain the corresponding end tag; or if it contains the start of a declaration then the declaration end must be there too.

There are two distinct sorts of entity we can declare. We have **parameter entities** that are only applied in the scope of the document type declaration. The other entities (**general entities,** which we divided into internal and external types earlier) are declared in the document type declaration but are only for use in the document content.

To begin with we will note one general consideration about the validation of entities:

> **For the valid document the name used in an entity reference (`&entityname;` or `%entityname;`) within the document entity must match that given in an entity declaration in the DTD.**

That is, for each entity reference that occurs in the document there must be a declaration for its type somewhere in the DTD.

Parameter Entities

Parameter entities are used solely within the DTD. Suppose that you have a long list of parameters that will occur in the content models of several elements. By using a parameter entity declaration such as the following,

```
<!ENTITY % lotsoftags "V1|V2|V3|V4|V5|X1|X2|X3|X4|X5|X6" >
```

you can then shorten the declarations for the other elements or attributes. The `%` sign marks the entity as a parameter entity. For example, using the above parameter entity, we might have these declarations:

```
<!ELEMENT   BigElem  (value1, value2, (%lotsoftags;|#PCDATA)*)>
<!ELEMENT   SmallElem    (goat|sheep|wolf|bear|%lotsoftags;)?>
```

> **However, you can only refer to parameter entities in this way (within other declarations) in the external subset of the DTD. In the internal subset you are only allowed to refer to parameter entities *between* declarations.**

So the above example must be declarations that reside in the external subset, whereas in the internal subset we are only allowed

```
<!ELEMENT   BigElem  (value1, value2, (#PCDATA))*>
%xternParamEnt;
<!ELEMENT   SmallElem    (goat|sheep|wolf|bear)?>
%anotherXternParamEnt;
```

The declarations for parameter entities must precede any reference to them in the DTD.

Since the internal subset of a DTD for a document is read first you cannot refer to parameter entities declared in the external subset within the internal subset. The parser will give an error. You can refer to internally declared ones within the external subset though.

There is a validity constraint on the use of parameter entity references within element content model declarations as in the example above. The replacement text of the parameter entity referred to in a parenthesized group cannot contain a text string that would cause the element declaration to cease to be well-formed when that text is inserted. So if the replacement text for the parameter entity contains an opening bracket it must also contain a closing bracket. It is also strongly recommended that its replacement text should not be empty, and that the first or last characters of the string must not be a pipe-stem or a comma.

The data that will replace the occurrence of an entity reference does not have to be given within the DTD, as in the first example above. It can reside in a file that is external to the document. The declaration for such an entity would be of the form:

```
<!ENTITY  %  ExtEntities  SYSTEM
     "http://www.someserver.com/somedir/extentity.txt " >
%ExtEntities;
```

In the internal subset of a valid document it is good practice to reference such external entities immediately after the declaration. Until they are referenced the data or declarations they contain do not constitute part of the DTD.

Such external parameter entities referred to in the internal subset should contain replacement text that will be well-formed when it replaces the entity reference in the DTD. So the markup in the replacement text should be comprised of complete markup declarations.

The validity constraint in the specification simply says that:

Parameter entity replacement text must be properly nested with markup declarations.

And this applies to parameter entities in both the internal and external subsets of the DTD.

General Entities

In contrast to parameter entities we use **general entities** to reduce the complexity of document instances rather than that of our document type definitions. We have already seen the form that declarations for general entities take:

```
<!ENTITY      artworkmodel                "Jean Jacques Rousseau">
<!ENTITY      bigtext      SYSTEM         "http://www.server.com/dir/bigfile.txt" >
```

For our valid document there are more rules to follow concerning general entities.

Internal Entities and Attribute Defaults

You will recall a table we showed earlier about the processor's treatment of entities according to their context; and hopefully you will also recall that we are allowed to have references to internal-type entities in the values of attributes. For the purposes of validation this in turn means that a reference to an internal-type entity can also occur in a default value in the ATTLIST declaration for the attribute. If this is the case then the declaration for the entity must precede that for the attribute. So the following is correct:

```
<!ELEMENT   secret_info    EMPTY >
<!ENTITY  access_pass_no      "094850157132857-13097310987309457147" >
<!ATTLIST   secret_info
           password    CDATA  #FIXED  "Access Permitted: &access_pass_no;" >
```

but the following declarations are in the wrong order as the validating parser won't know how to interpret the reference to `&access_pass_no;`

```
<!ELEMENT   secret_info    EMPTY >
<!ATTLIST   secret_info
           password    CDATA  #FIXED  "Access Permitted: &access_pass_no;"  >
<!ENTITY  access_pass_no      "094850157132857-13097310987309457147" >
```

Required Entities

In XML we can assume that our well-formed documents can use the entities corresponding to <, >, &, " and ' without us declaring them. However, for valid documents they need to be declared in the DTD in the following way:

```
<!ENTITY   lt            "&#38;#60;" >
<!ENTITY   gt            "&#40;" >
<!ENTITY   amp           "&#38;#38;" >
<!ENTITY   apos          "&#39;" >
<!ENTITY   quot          "&#34;" >
```

Recall that the `lt` and `amp` entities are doubly escaped to meet the stipulation in the W3C XML specification that entity declarations themselves be well-formed.

External Entities

Eventually the number of entities we deal with will become too large to cut-and-paste between DTD files. Or perhaps we'll have entities with very long replacement texts. When the entities are intended to be shared between many document instances it *might* be acceptable to copy them into the DTD, but when the entities are to be shared between many document type definitions such copying is not acceptable. We can save ourselves time and effort if we store the replacement text in entities separate from the document instance or any external DTD. In XML these are known as **external entities,** which are almost identical to the unparsed entities that we use with the `ENTITY` attributes, except that they can contain only text or XML.

An external entity can be included (**referenced**) in exactly the same fashion as internal entities are referenced.

```
<!ENTITY    copyright.statement   SYSTEM "Macintosh HD:XML Book:Copyright Text">
...
&copyright.statement;
```

When the parser encounters the entity reference it looks up the definition and determines where the external entity is located. In this example it is stored in a file on my Macintosh's hard drive. But what if the external entity were archived somewhere on the Internet or on a separate machine? Perhaps the entity is stored as a file on my Unix workstation, which has a different convention for naming files from that used in Mac OS.

When you declare external entities you can specify a **public identifier** for the entity. The parser will first try to resolve the identifier and only when it cannot will it try to use a specific file reference.

```
<!ENTITY   public.statement
           PUBLIC      "-//Suneidesis//TEXT  Mission Statement //EN "
           "http://localhost/~tfj/company.mission.statement.xml"
>
```

If you can see a hole in this scheme – well done! How do we (and the parser) know where to go to get an entity from the `PUBLIC` identifier? The solution adopted by programmers of SGML parsers is to use a "catalog" file. Many of the programmers producing XML parsers have also adopted their use. You will need to check the specifics of the parser you are using for details.

The catalog approach hides the system identifiers from you and, more importantly, from your documents. You include entries for each entity in the catalog. Indeed you can stash away the identifiers for anything: document type definitions, entity declarations, etc. This will aid you when you come to exchange document instances with other people. They do not have to edit your document but only update their catalog.

You should consult the documentation for the XML parser that you are using for details of whether and how it implements the catalog feature.

```
     -- ISO latin 1 entity set for HTML --
PUBLIC      "ISO 8879-1986//ENTITIES Added Latin 1//EN//HTML" ISOlat1.sgm

DOCTYPE   wrox   wrox.dtd
```

The bottom line in this extract from a catalog file on my PC names the actual file that will be used by my XML parser to locate the DTD I wish to use. Similarly I've also given the location for some character entities.

Entity Sets

It is common practice within the SGML and XML community to collect together entity declarations and save them in a file (i.e. an external entity). Unless you do introduce recursion (where an entity declaration refers to the entity containing that declaration) there is no problem with this approach. Indeed when you are dealing with several documents it is a boon to have such **entity sets** available.

There is nothing to prevent you from extending this idea so as to keep element declarations and attribute list declarations in entities. Most of the publicly available DTDs are defined this way. Of course, they are then referred to as element and attribute sets rather than entity sets.

One frequent use of such entity sets is the inclusion of standard character entities. The ISO has specified a number of entity sets for various categories (related to their own character set standards). A number of sites like

`http://www.schema.net/entities/`

have made XML-compliant copies of these entity sets freely available so we could create a single (external) entity of our own that references them.

```
<!-- This is our own external entity that references external entity sets that
eclare character entities -->
<!ENTITY    ISOsets    SYSTEM  "/home/XML/Entities/all.entities">
```

Now to reference our entity set we say `&ISOsets;` and let the parser look up the PUBLIC identifier or read the operating system file. Whereupon it might find the following:

```
<!-- Declare entities corresponding to each of the ISO cntity sets -->
<!ENTITY ISOlat1 PUBLIC  "ISO 8879-1986//ENTITIES Added Latin 1//EN"  "">
<!ENTITY ISOlat2 PUBLIC  "ISO 8879-1986//ENTITIES Added Latin 2//EN"  "">
<!ENTITY ISOnum  PUBLIC  "ISO 8879-1986//ENTITIES  Numeric and Special
          Graphics//EN"     "">
...
<!-- Now reference them so that the (character) entities they in turn declare are
available to us -->
&ISOlat1;
&ISOlat2;
&ISOnum;
...
```

The complete collection of ISO characters is described by 21 entity sets. The actual content of these entity sets is based on lists given in the original SGML standard and associated technical reports.

Entity Set Name	Character Entities Defined
ISOlat1	Latin letters (similar to ASCII)
ISOlat2	Latin letters (additional)
ISOgrk1	Modern Greek letters
ISOgrk2	Modern Greek letters
ISOgrk3	Greek symbols for Mathematics
ISOgrk4	Greek symbols for Mathematics
ISOcyr1	Modern Russian (Cyrillic) letters
ISOcyr2	Modern non-Russian (Cyrillic) letters
ISOdia	Diacritical marks (accents, etc.)
ISOpub	Publication symbols
ISOtech	Technical symbols

Entity Set Name	Character Entities Defined
ISObox	Box-drawing symbols
ISOnum	Mathematics symbols (Numerical)
ISOamsa	Mathematical symbols
ISOamsb	Mathematical symbols
ISOamsn	Mathematical symbols
ISOamso	Mathematical symbols
ISOamsr	Mathematical symbols
ISOmfrk	Mathematical symbols
ISOmopf	Mathematical symbols
ISOmscr	Mathematical symbols
ISOchem	Chemical symbols

Processing Instructions

If we are honest we must admit that there are occasions when pure XML cannot provide us with the power or flexibility that we require our documents to have. However, XML has a mechanism that allows us to extend its functionality to take advantage of the capabilities of other applications. We can activate these applications' capabilities using processing instructions (PIs), which are distinguished from tags or markup declarations by the use of `<?` and `?>` around them.

> *Software companies developing applications that use XML often use PIs to include information or instructions specific to their applications. Other people can then use these XML documents in other contexts without that vendor specific information affecting their capacity to use the document and view its contents, as the vendor specific PIs are meaningless without the appropriate application being present on their system.*

They take the form:

```
<?PITarget  processing instructions ?>
```

`PITarget` is the name of the application that is to perform whatever actions are specified in the processing instructions. This name can be formally declared beforehand using a `NOTATION` declaration, but it must not begin with the character sequence '`xml`' in any combination of upper or lower case letters. For example, we could make this `NOTATION` declaration in the DTD:

```
<!NOTATION  MyFabApp  SYSTEM "file://mydir/FabApp.exe" >
```

and then use the following processing instruction at some point within the document to pass instructions to `FabApp.exe` as the document is processed.

```
<?MyFabApp     Do_this   ?>
```

FabApp.exe might be the application using the XML processor/parser to access the data in the XML file, or it can be another application which will do some processing relating to the document being processed.

The processing instruction lets us pass additional data to this application. The XML standard assumes that this will be command line options and other "instructions" relevant to the application.

The format of the PI data is not specified within the XML standard except for the one predefined PI <?xml ... ?> and that uses an attribute–value–like style. The instructions (PI data) for the PITarget application should be in a format that the application shall be able to interpret. However, different XML parsers may deal with PI data in different ways, so you must check the documentation for the parser you are using as to how the processing instruction is manipulated.

Strictly speaking it is never an error to declare a NOTATION and to use the corresponding PI but not have a suitable processor available – the PI will simply not cause anything to happen. It is up to you to make sure that a suitable application is available on the system.

There is a small but significant difference between the processing of PIs in XML and SGML. In XML the PI data is enclosed in the character pairs <? and ?>, by default in SGML it is <? and only a >. If your documents are to be processed by both an XML and an SGML parser then you should make sure that the extra ? is not going to cause problems for the SGML-based application. The SGML parser will see that question mark as data to be passed to the application, whereas the XML parser will consume it for itself. (If you change the system declaration for your SGML parser so that the SGML Processing Instruction Close (PIC) symbol becomes ?> then you can ignore this problem.)

The XML Text Declaration

We have already encountered the XML declaration, <?xml version="1.0"?>, which appears at the start of documents. There is an XML **text declaration** as well. At the moment it is reserved for future expansion but one usage has already been defined.

Any external entities we reference from our document instance might have a different character set encoding; this is also true for a DTD external subset. We might be conscientious and always create our external entities (separate XML or text data files) according to Unicode's UCS-2 (16 bit) encoding, but we cannot guarantee that other people will follow our example. The XML text declaration provides us with a way to signal what encoding we have used.

```
<?xml encoding="ISO-10646-UCS-2" ?>
```

This instruction should be placed at the top of the file containing the external entities' declarations.

If we include the encoding attribute in the XML declaration for the main document, like so

```
<?xml version="1.0"? encoding="UTF-8" standalone="no">
<!DOCTYPE rootname SYSTEM "mydtd.dtd" [
<!ENTITY % xTypeParameterEntity SYSTEM "entdeclars.ent" >
%xTypeParameterEntity;
]>
```

then it affects the complete document instance, and every external entity with a different encoding is required to have an XML text declaration. So for the example above, if the file of entity declarations, entdeclars.ent, had a different encoding, it must contain the XML text declaration at the beginning

```
<?xml encoding="EncodingName"?>
<!ENTITY ...>
<!ENTITY ...>
```

There are many different encoding names we can include in the encoding clause. The XML standard specifically mentions those corresponding to Unicode and its equivalent ISO standard (ISO 10646). These encodings will control whether 8 or 16 bit character codes are to be recognized, and whether any Unicode transformation rules are to be applied. The standard even allows us to use other character encoding schemes. If the encoding is registered with the Internet Assigned Naming Authority then we are advised to use the IANA names (see below). You might even have to deal with documents that have been prepared using EBCDIC character codes.

For more information about the IANA and character set names go to `http://www.iana.org/numbers.html` *and look at the information on 'Character Sets'.*

When we prepare entities in a peculiar encoding then the XML text declaration encoding name must match the encoding of the content. The text declaration itself must also be in the same encoding as the encoding it names.

Conditional Sections

Things change. Over time we will amend DTDs or use them for several different purposes. Some of the declarations will be appropriate to one purpose but not to another. We can introduce conditional sections so that we can activate or de-activate the correct portions.

Conditional sections can only be used in the external subset of the DTD.

First we'll take a look at the two types of conditional section, `INCLUDE` and `IGNORE` sections, and then we'll look at how these can be used.

INCLUDE Sections

An `INCLUDE` section contains declarations in the following way:

```
<![INCLUDE[
<!-- As this is a public document include all the ISO entity sets -->
%ISOsets;
<!ELEMENT  included.element  (...)>
<!ATTLIST  included.element  ...>
]]>
```

Note that the declarations with the `INCLUDE` section are of the same syntax as those that would be made within a DTD.

IGNORE Sections

`IGNORE` sections are parsed but no action is taken with respect to markup declarations in their contents.

```
<![IGNORE[
<!-- Let's not bother with the ISO sets we'll do our own thing later -->
%ISOsets;
<!ELEMENT  ignored.element   (...)>
<!ATTLIST  ignored.element   ...>
]]>
```

Now let's look at how these declarations can be used.

Parameter Entities in Conditional Section Declarations

One common practice within the SGML and XML communities is to use parameter entities to enable or disable the `INCLUDE` and `IGNORE` sections. The XML standard permits us to use a parameter entity reference where the words `INCLUDE` and `IGNORE` appear.

```
<!ENTITY % confidential"IGNORE">
<!ENTITY % public      "INCLUDE">
```

```
<![%confidential;[
<!-- These element, attribute and other declarations are only used when we have
confidential material in the document -->
<!ELEMENT  sec.level   (#PCDATA, secret_stuff)>
]]>
```

```
<![%public;[
<!-- Whereas these are only included for truly public documents -->
<!ELEMENT  kick.back.rate    (#PCDATA) >
]]>
```

Now, when we come to process a set of XML documents and we want to process them according to the schema of definitions within the `%public` section (but not according to the schema within the `%confidential` section), we set the value of the `%public` entity declaration to "`INCLUDE`" and that of the `%confidential` entity to "`IGNORE`". If at some later date we wish to process documents according to the schema in the `%confidential` section rather than that of the `%public` section we simply switch around the values of the two entity declarations. Assuming we planned our two versions of the parts of the DTD well, then this should save our having to edit and rewrite key portions of the overall DTD.

Declaration Style

Before we finish with the declarations we ought to look at them one more time. Not for their purpose or usage but for how we are going to lay them out so that anyone who reads our DTD later will be able to figure out what the structures are. We do not want to obfuscate the declarations just as we don't want to obfuscate the markup of the document instance itself.

Throughout this chapter you'll have seen my preferences for typing up a series of XML declarations. It works for me and I trust that it has worked for you as you followed along with the examples.

After working with XML for a while you may wish to adopt a different set of conventions. Remember that an XML parser doesn't care about the amount of whitespace between words in the declarations. But you might when you come back to a DTD in six months time. Here are my basic rules, which might help:

- Each declaration is presented on a separate line

```
<!ELEMENT e1      (...)>
<!ELEMENT e2      (...)>
```

rather than

```
<!ELEMENT    e1     (...)><!ELEMENT     e2     (...)>
```

- Element declaration precedes any attribute list associated with it

```
<!ELEMENT e1      (...)>
<!ATTLIST e1      ...>
```

rather than

```
<!ATTLIST e1      ...>
<!ELEMENT e1      (...)>
```

- Comment declarations to be included copiously

```
<!-- There's no such thing as too many comments -->
```

- Comment declarations describing the purpose of a DTD to be included at the start

- Do not use multiple characters to surround long comments; use the `<!--` and `-->` symbols and generous amounts of white space only

```
<!--

Preferred long comment format

-->
```

rather than

```
<!-- ------------------------------------------------
--                                                 --
--          Nasty layout of long comments          --
--                                                 --
---------------------------------------------------->
```

The most important rule of all is:

- Be consistent!

Summary

In this chapter we've looked at the core XML 1.0 specification, and the difference between merely well-formed and valid documents as defined in that standard. Most of this chapter has dealt primarily with the syntax of XML, but hopefully we have also provided enticing glimpses of the power of XML. You should now be aware of:

- how to mark up your documents using XML
- the flexibility of being able to create your own tags
- how elements, attributes, entities, and other aspects of valid documents are declared in the DTD

In the chapters that follow we expand upon the knowledge gained in this chapter to provide you with significant expertise in this fast growing and exciting area of Internet technology.

3
XML Schemas

As a general definition, schemas are a generalized plan or diagram. In computer science, schemas define the characteristics of classes of objects. In XML this means that schemas also describe the way that data is marked up, and as such the classical DTD is a schema.

In this chapter we will start by taking a look at the use of schemas in a very general way, and some limitations with the XML DTD before moving on to look at two proposals that use XML syntax to describe a document's structure.

The two schemas we will look at are called **XML-Data**, and **Document Content Definition for XML** (**DCD** for short). At the time of writing both were still Notes in the W3C process. There is also another schema being proposed on the XML-DEV list, called **Schema for Object-oriented XML (SOX)**, but we will not be looking at that, although there is already partial implementation of it in some of the XML freeware that is available. The references for all these are given in Appendix B.

At the time of going to press (October 1998), the W3CC XML-Schema Working Group had just been established. Its purpose being to work on a schema written in XML syntax. It is likely that their efforts will start with a review of XML-Data and DCD, along with any other XML based schema submissions. Their first step is to create a requirements document and that will be used to drive the following discussion. So it is unlikely that either of the two Notes in this chapter will become widely supported. However their contents will give you an excellent introduction to the principles of an XML based schema, which, when it arrives, is anticipated to help with the advancement of new applications using XML. (Note that the plural terms 'schemas' and 'schemata' are both acceptable.)

Before we discuss the various schemas, let's discuss their purpose. Schemas directly impact the first four design goals of XML itself:

- XML shall be straightforwardly usable over the Internet.
- XML shall support a wide variety of applications.
- XML shall be compatible with SGML.
- It shall be easy to write programs which process XML documents.

In essence, to make XML a language for interchanging information between applications. From an application developer's perspective, a schema sets constraints on what is allowable in an XML document. This allows you to develop software that can anticipate specific information and make design assumptions that add features to the application. Validation, the checking of a document instance against its schema, gives you confidence that the document will comply with the design assumptions.

From an application user's perspective, validation against a schema increases the chances that the interchanged information will be understood and useful. The sender can check the correctness of a message before it is sent and the receiver can validate that message before having to process it.

Much of the interest in new schemas is driven by the needs of new kinds of applications that XML is being used for. The SGML/XML DTD met many of the needs of document interchange, although some limitations have been discovered over the years of its use. Document interchange is mostly concerned with document structure and hierarchy, which the XML DTD describes well. However, data interchange between processing applications requires more rigorous validation; the ability to constrain data types, provide easy extensions and easy processing are just a few we will look at in more detail.

The XML DTD as a Schema

As we have already stated, in an XML document, a schema is a description of the way that the document is marked up: its grammar, vocabulary, structure, datatypes, etc. As a schema for XML, the classical DTD has some advantages, and several disadvantages.

You have already seen how to write an XML DTD, and you probably realize already that one disadvantage of such a schema is that it uses a different syntax (a simplified form of EBNF) to XML in order to describe itself.

The DTD type schema has several other less obvious disadvantages. Here are just a few of them (we will come back to look at them in turn shortly):

- Good DTDs are difficult to write.
- DTDs are not extensible.
- DTDs do not describe XML as data well.
- There is no provision for inheritance from one DTD to another.
- DTDs do not provide support for namespaces.
- It is limited in its descriptive powers.
- There is no provision for default element content.
- You need two separate pieces of authoring software, one to write your DTD, and another to write your XML document. And two parsers to process the document.

For these reasons there has been a large amount of interest in using alternative schemas instead of DTDs, particularly in schemas based on XML type syntax.

One such proposal to the W3CC is contained in the XML-Data note of January 1998 which is available from:

```
http://www.W3C.org/TR/1998/NOTE-XML-data
```

Another such proposal is found in the Document Content Definition for XML note of July 1998:

```
http://www.W3C.org/TR/NOTE-dcd
```

The syntax in the DCD note is similar in concept to the XML-Data note, but incorporates some of the RDF syntax.

Another proposal which was submitted in October 1998, too late to be discussed here, is "Schema for Object-oriented XML (SOX)"which can be found at:

```
http://www.W3C.org/Submission/1998/15/
```

Unfortunately there is no guarantee that the final forms for schemas using XML based syntax will look like either of these two notes. However, it is almost certain that some new form of XML based schema will be forthcoming, and the principles it will be based on will be similar to the principles used in these two notes. They should allow you, the reader, to easily prepare for any new syntax.

The following chapter is offered as an analysis of the XML based schemas XML-Data and DCD for XML. We will look at some of the general issues concerning schemas, then we will look at XML-Data in some detail, followed by a look at DCDs.

XML Schema: General Issues

Before moving on to the detailed study of the XML-Data syntax, let's study some of the general issues involved.

Good DTDs are Difficult to Write

DTDs are difficult to write. Rather, a *good* DTD is difficult to write (as we saw in Chapter 2) and that is why, when we are starting a new project using a markup language, for the most part we look around for a ready-made DTD to use. Wouldn't it be nice if we could just take what we want out of a DTD and leave the rest of it? Although Namespaces allow us to refer to individual elements, there is no way in classical DTD theory that I could, say, take the `<Author>` section out of a `Book` DTD, and the `<content>` section out of the (hypothetical) `Wrox` DTD, then roll them together and validate the results, to produce exactly what I want.

The fact that DTDs do not use the XML syntax adds to the difficulty level when writing them. As we saw in the last chapter, DTDs use a form of notation called EBNF - which used to drive fear into my heart. Every time I saw EBNF syntax my mouth turned dry and my eyes glazed over. Over the years with forced usage, I have actually got an acquired taste for EBNF and I am close to liking it and even occasionally extol its virtues. But for those of you who would prefer an easier syntax XML-Data or DCDs are for you.

DTDs Are Not Extensible

If I had already written a Book DTD to catalog my books and I wanted to add a new section to the code, specifically for ASP books, I would have to re-write the whole DTD. This is because DTDs are not extensible. I would then have to make sure that my original and new documents were still valid.

DTDs Do Not Explain XML As Data Well

Originally XML and DTDs, like SGML, were envisioned as a structured syntax for documents. Increasingly XML is seen as a repository for data and objects. To understand this further let's look at a simple example.

Here is a simple XML file that marks up a class of objects called hat.

```
<class name= "hat">

      <hat id="h1">
            <style>Baseball</style>
            <size>8</size>
            <color>red</color>
      </hat>

      <hat id="h2">
            <style>Stetson</style>
            <size>7</size>
            <color>gray</color>
      </hat>

      <hat id="h3">
            <style>Bowler</style>
            <size>6</size>
            <color>Black</color>
      </hat>

</class>
```

If you remember the brief introduction to classes and objects in Chapter 1, what we have here are three object instances (referred to by their id number as 1, 2 and 3), of the class hat with their various properties (style, size and color) and values.

In Java terminology the class name is hat, and each <hat> element is an instance of the hat class, it is a hat object. The sub-elements <style>, <size> and <color> are class attributes with their respective values between the tags.

Or, from another point of view, each hat object is an instance of the hat class, and each hat object has properties defined by the classes attributes.

The above document may have the following schema (a classical DTD) to describe it:

```
<!DOCTYPE class [

<!--element declarations-->

<!ELEMENT class (hat)>
<!ELEMENT hat (style,size,color)>
```

```
<!ELEMENT style (#PCDATA)>
<!ELEMENT size (#PCDATA)>
<!ELEMENT color (#PCDATA)>

<!--attribute declarations-->
<!ATTLIST hat id ID #REQUIRED>

<!--pre-defined entities-->

<!ENTITY lt"&#38;#60;">
<!ENTITY gt"#62;">
<!ENTITY amp     "&#38;#38;">
<!ENTITY apos    "&#39;">
<!ENTITY quot    "&#34;">
<!--end of DTD-->
```

As a schema for a document it is perfectly adequate, however as a schema to mark up data it has some serious limitations. Here are some of the more obvious:

- There is no way to easily extend the class. A new DTD must be written.
- There is no way that the hat class can inherit from other classes such as say the clothes class.
- There is no way a sub-class, say the female-hat class, can inherit from the hat class.
- There is no data typing. Hat size is not an integer, it is a string in this document, and will remain a string for ever, as long as we use a DTD to describe it.

DTDs Do Not Provide Support For Namespaces

I can use a Namespace to introduce an element type into my document, however I can't use a Namespace to refer to an element declaration or an entity declaration in my DTD. And, if I do use Namespaces, I must modify the DTD to include any elements taken from the other Namespaces. Namespaces are covered in detail in the next chapter.

DTDs are Limited in their Descriptive Powers.

DTDs have a very fixed format, which is good for defining document structures. For other applications though, we may want to add more information about an element. The `description` element in DCD is an example of this.

DTDs Have No Provision For Default Element Content

Although neither of the schemas we look at in this chapter make provision for default element content (XSL does, see Chapter 8) it is possible to imagine a schema that could add default content to an element, such as some boiler plate text, or a legal disclaimer.

Testing your DTDs

If you have IE5, we have built a simple HTML file that you can use to parse and check for accuracy all your XML files and DTDs. It can be found at `http://webdev.wrox.com/books/1525/` and is called `xmltest.htm`. Open the source code:

```
<HTML>
<HEAD>
<TITLE>Checking XML Files for Errors</TITLE>
<STYLE TYPE="text/css">
BODY {font-family:Tahoma,Arial,sans-serif; font-size:10pt;}
</STYLE>

<SCRIPT>

function startTest(strXMLFile) {

//create an activeX object
var myDocument = new ActiveXObject("microsoft.xmldom");

//load an xml file into the activex object and name it myDocument
myDocument.async=false;
myDocument.load(strXMLFile);

//build the error details string
strErr = new String();

strErr = 'Source URL : <B>'
       + myDocument.parseError.url
       + '</B><P>';

strErr += 'Error Description: <B>'
       + myDocument.parseError.reason
       + '</B><BR>';

strErr += 'Error Number: <B>'
       + myDocument.parseError.errorCode
       + '</B><BR>';

strErr += 'Error File Position: <B>'
       + myDocument.parseError.filepos
       + '</B><BR>';

strErr += 'Error Line Number: <B>'
       + myDocument.parseError.line
       + '</B><BR>';

strErr += 'Error Line Character: <B>'
       + myDocument.parseError.linepos
       + '</B><BR>';

//build the error pointer strings
strShow = new String();
strShow = myDocument.parseError.srcText;

strPoint = new String();
for (i = 1; i < myDocument.parseError.linepos; i++)
  strPoint += '-';
strPoint += '^';

//display the strings in the page
document.all['errText'].innerHTML = strErr;
document.all['errLine'].innerText = strShow;
document.all['errPoint'].innerText = strPoint;
myDocument = null;
```

```
}
</SCRIPT>

</HEAD>
<BODY>

<H4>Checking XML Files for Errors</H4>
<SPAN ID="errText"></SPAN><P>

<PRE>
<SPAN ID="errLine"></SPAN>
<SPAN ID="errPoint"></SPAN>
</PRE>

<DIV STYLE="position:absolute; top=250">
<HR>
<INPUT TYPE="BUTTON" VALUE="   "
ONCLICK="startTest('wroxdb1.xml')">
  Push the button to test your file.
</DIV>

</BODY>

</HTML>
```

and at the fifth line from the bottom where we have:

```
myDocument.load("wroxdb1.xml");
```

simply substitute the URL of the XML document that you want to test. The HTML file uses a Microsoft XML parser to test your document for errors. The errors will be displayed in an alert box, and each error must be corrected individually.

XML as a Database

Although XML as a database is described more fully in Chapter 10, we need to say just a little bit about it here to understand why schemas other than classical DTDs are necessary when we use XML as a storage system in a relational database.

Simply put, a database is any collection of information. In common computer usage however, a database is a collection of related information that is stored in a defined way. Here is some of the jargon surrounding databases:

Tables	A collection of information that has some kind of logical reason to be collected together, such as an inventory of parts, or a list of customer names and addresses as in the example below.
Records	A record is an individual entry in a table. Also known as a row.
Fields	The individual items that make up a complete record. Also known as a column.
Index	A field, or collection of fields that is used to sort the table into some logical order. In the example below the field `customer name` is the index.

Table Continued on Following Page

Primary key	A field, or collection of fields, in the table that uniquely identifies the record. It is often a number. In the example below it is given as `customer id`. Sometimes the Primary key and the index are identical.
Database engine	The program that files, organizes and retrieves all the information contained in our database.
Query	The process of getting the information we want out of our database.
Recordset	A collection of different records or tables.

Here is a simple table, and one way it could be expressed in an XML document:

Customer Name	Customer id	Customer Address	Customer Phone number
Bloggs, Joan	001	24 Hemlock Place	216-222-3333
Smith, John	004	5 Maple street	440-123-4567
Smith, John	003	144 Elm	406-765-4321
Williams, Hugh	002	27 Chestnut	257-757-5757

In the above table we have four records or rows, and four fields or columns.

The index field is (sensibly) the customer's name, so that we can organize the names in alphabetical order, and the primary key field is (sensibly, because we can have several names that are the same) a unique integer, in this case the customer id.

One way this database could be written up in XML is as follows. I am sure you can think of others.

```
<customer-table>

     <customer-id id= "a001">
          <customer-name>Bloggs,Joan</customer-name>
          <customer-address>24 Hemlock Place </customer-address>
          <customer-phone>216-222-3333</customer-phone>
     </customer-id>

     <customer-id id= "a004">
          <customer-name> Smith, John </customer-name>
          <customer-address>5 Maple street </customer-address>
          <customer-phone>440-123-4567</customer-phone>
     </customer-id>

     <customer-id id= "a003">
          <customer-name> Smith, John </customer-name>
          <customer-address>144 Elm </customer-address>
          <customer-phone>406-765-4321</customer-phone>
     </customer-id>

     <customer-id id= "a002">
```

```
            <customer-name> Williams, Hugh </customer-name>
            <customer-address>27 Chestnut </customer-address>
            <customer-phone>257-757-5757</customer-phone>
      </customer-id>

</customer-table>
```

Note that we have had to put a letter in front of the id. The reason for this is that in XML `id` *attribute values are not allowed to start with a number, they must start with a letter or an underscore (_).*

In this XML file we have made the index field the `customer-id` (instead of the customer name as it was in the table). I'm sure that now you would have no difficulty writing a DTD for this XML file.

The difficulty arises, however, when we have a set of tables, such as a table of orders.

```
<customer-order>
      <customer-id id= "a002">

      etc.…….

</customer-order>
```

Obviously this table is going to use the same data as in the table above, particularly the unique id. But how is the DTD of the orders table going to express the idea that the id in the customer order table is identical to the id in the customer-table table?

The answer is it can't, there is no way of relating the two documents and letting the XML software know that they are part of a record set.

Enter XML-Data and DCDs, which are schemata that can express these relationships.

The drawbacks of the DTD as a schema may appear trivial when dealing with small databases, but when dealing with databases with millions of records and thousands of different kind's of queries, the problems posed by the inability of DTD *x* to relate to DTD *y* can be overwhelming.

XML Data: A Proposed Solution

Note that we have used the term a proposed solution, because at present it is not even in the form of a W3C working draft.

XML-Data solves the above problems, and as a bonus it can also be used as a DTD. When wearing its 'DTD' hat, XML-Data (or any other schema) is known as a **syntactic schema** i.e. a schema that describes the syntax of a document. When it is wearing its 'data object' hat it is known as a **conceptual schema**, i.e. a schema that describes relationships between concepts or objects.

However, don't worry – you are not going to have to learn two sets of syntax. Whichever hat is worn the syntax is the same, it's just the mindset that needs to be different.

XML-Data: A Simple Start

Let's start off simply, and because we are already familiar with the concept of a DTD, show you how a simple DTD can be transferred to XML-Data. Tradition mandates that we start off with "Hello World!"

Here is the complete well-formed and valid `Hello World` document.

```
<?xml version= "1.0" ?>
<!--DTD-->
<!DOCTYPE greeting [
<!ELEMENT greeting (#PCDATA)>
]>

<greeting> Hello World! </greeting>
```

Now, let's convert this DTD into XML-Data.

The work-horse of the XML-Data schema is the `elementType` declaration, which defines the type of element in XML terminology. (Or class object in a conceptual schema.) It takes an attribute `id`, which has the dual purpose of not only identifying the definition, but also naming the specific class.

So the following:

```
<elementType id= "greeting"/>
```

identifies the element type `<greeting>`, and is identical in purpose to:

```
<!ELEMENT greeting... >
```

in the DTD in a syntactic schema.

> *It also identifies the class* `greeting` *if we are using our DTD with documents that store data i.e. if we are using the schema as a conceptual schema. The syntax is the same, and the document looks the same even though the purpose of the document is different.*

Now the second part of our element declaration in the DTD is:

```
<!ELEMENT greeting (#PCDATA)>
```

which tells the processor that the element greeting can have parsed character data (i.e. unmarked-up text) as content, but no elements.

How do we express this concept in XML-Data? Simply by adding the element `<string/>`, so we have:

```
<elementType id= "greeting">
<string/>
</elementType>
```

Which expresses exactly the same thing as our element declaration in the DTD.

So the final document with its prolog should look like this:

```
<?xml version= "1.0" ?>
<schema  xmlns="urn:W3C.org:xmlschema"
      xmlns:dt="urn:W3C.org:xmldatatypes">
<elementType id= "greeting">
<string/>
</elementType>
</schema>

<greeting> Hello World! </greeting>
```

We have already seen the first line, the XML Declaration, but you may be wondering what the other parts are. In XML-Data, all element declarations must be contained within `schema` elements. To define the type of schema that is being used, in this case XML-Data, we have to include a namespace in the opening `<schema>` tag. This is what the second line is for:

```
<schema xmlns="urn:W3C.org:xmlschema"
```

It declares an XML namespace identified by the URN that must be included in order to signal to the validating user agent that we are using a schema called `xmlschema` to define our document. Chapter 4 deals with namespaces. As for:

```
xmlns:dt="urn:W3C.org:xmldatatypes">
```

this is for the schema that defines datatypes, and obviously in this simple document it could be omitted as there is no question as to the correct data type of the `<greeting>` element. I just put it there for the purposes of completeness. It should not cause the validator any extra work, because the validator should not contact the URN unless the prescribed prefix is associated with an element.

The closing `</schema>` tag must then be put at the end of the element and attribute declarations. We must use this element exactly as it is if the document is to be an XML-Data compliant document.

> **These examples uses the namespaces syntax of the August 2nd 1998 Working Draft (see `http://www.W3C.org/TR/` for updates), as opposed to the syntax shown in the XML-Data specification.**

The syntax in the example uses **scoping** (which will be explained in the following chapter on namespaces) to include all the children elements in the namespace. Some users may be more comfortable with the following syntax, which is also perfectly valid.

```
<?xml version= "1.0" ?>
<schema xmlns:s="urn:W3C.org:xmlschema"
     xmlns:dt="urn:W3C.org:xmldatatypes">
<s:elementType id= "greeting">
<s:string/>
</s:elementType>
</schema>

<greeting> Hello World! </greeting>
```

It should be noted that if you run either of the above through an XML parser that does not support XML-Data you will generate an error as the document is not well-formed. There isn't a unique opening and closing tag. To make it well-formed you would simply need to add the following two lines as an opening and closing tag. You could remove them as soon as you have finished running the sample through your non-XML-Data compliant parser. An XML-Data compliant browser of course would recognize that the namespace represents a schema.

```
<?xml version= "1.0" ?>

<root>

< s:schema xmlns:s="urn:W3C.org:xmlschema"
     xmlns:dt="urn:W3C.org:xmldatatypes">
 <s:elementType id= "greeting">
<s:string/>
 </s:elementType>
 </s:schema>

<greeting> Hello World! </greeting>

</root>
```

Now that we've been introduced to the concept let's look at a slightly more complex example.

XML-Data: Adding Complexity

We are going to build a simple database in XML that simply lists the books that Wrox Press publishes, then we will look at a DTD for this database, and how it would be expressed in XML-Data.

The XML template `ch03_books.xml` looks like this:

```
<wrox-books-table>

     <book id="">
          <title></title>
          <author rank=""></author>
          <isbn></isbn>
          <publication-date></publication-date>
          <book-type></book-type>
          <book-family></book-family>
     </book>

</wrox-books-table>
```

Here is the DTD for the books XML template:

```
<?xml version="1.0"?>
<!DOCTYPE  wrox-books-table [
<!ELEMENT wrox-books-table (book)+>
<!ELEMENT book (title,author+,isbn,publication-date,book-type,book-family+)>
<!ELEMENT title (#PCDATA)>
<!ELEMENT author (#PCDATA)>
<!ELEMENT isbn (#PCDATA)>
<!ELEMENT publication-date (#PCDATA)>
<!ELEMENT book-type (#PCDATA)>
<!ELEMENT book-family (#PCDATA)>
```

```
<!--attribute list-->

<!ATTLIST book
     id ID #REQUIRED>
<!ATTLIST author
     rank CDATA #IMPLIED>
]>
```

If we run this example above in the `xmltest.htm` test page we introduced earlier, we will be prompted to put in a value for `id` because the DTD declares that a value is required.

The version of `ch03_books.xml` on the site contains the DTD, if you are typing it in manually you will need to include the DTD for this test to work. Remember, you can get the `xmltest.htm` page and all the samples for this chapter (and the book) from our Web site at `http://webdev.wrox.co.uk/books/1525`

Let's examine how we would express the above DTD in XML-Data.

Declaring Elements in XML-Data

For a start we need to declare the element types that we have. We do this with the `elementType` declaration and use the `id` attribute to name our XML document element.

```
<?xml version= "1.0" ?>
< schema  xmlns="urn:W3C.org:xmlschema"
     xmlns:dt="urn:W3C.org:xmldatatypes">
<elementType id= "wrox-books-table"/>
<elementType id= "book"/>
<elementType id= "title"/>
<elementType id= "author"/>
<elementType id= "isbn"/>
<elementType id= "publication-date"/>
<elementType id= "book-type"/>
<elementType id= "book-family"/>

</schema>
```

In our DTD the element declaration for `wrox-books-table` indicates that this element can take one or more book elements. Namely:

```
<!ELEMENT wrox-books-table (book)+>
```

How do we indicate this using XML-Data?

Declaring Element Content in XML-Data

We have already seen an example of declaring `PCDATA` in our `Hello World` example namely:

```
<elementType id= "greeting">
<string/>
</elementType>
```

To declare an element inclusion we use the element element as a child of elementType.

```
<elementType id= "wrox-books-table">
     <element type="#book" occurs="ONEORMORE"/>
</elementType>
```

Note the syntax of this example. The element element has two attributes: the type attribute and the occurs attribute. The type attribute takes a value of a hash mark (#) followed by the name of the element (in this case the <book> element).

The book element is a child of <elementType id= "wrox-book-table"> and thus its type (in this case the <book> element) should be included as children in the XML document.

book of course also has its own children, and the inclusion of book under wrox-books-table also implies inclusion of all the book descendants.

The occurs attribute takes a value of a string, in this case the string "ONEORMORE", which is the equivalent of the plus (+) mark in classical EBNF notation. The other notations translate as follows:

EBNF notation	XML-Data notation	Remarks
[nothing]	REQUIRED	As in classical DTD syntax, REQUIRED is the default. I.e. if nothing is mentioned there must be one and only one instance of the element.
?	OPTIONAL	
*	ZEROORMORE	
+	ONEORMORE	

Here are the declarations for the book element. Note that although occurs="REQUIRED" has been specified for title by way of example, because it is the default it has not been specified for the other elements.

```
<elementType id= "book">
     <element type="#title" occurs="REQUIRED"/>
     <element type="#author" occurs="ONEORMORE"/>
     <element type="#isbn"/>
     <element type="#publication-date"/>
     <element type="#book-type"/>
     <element type="#book-family" occurs="ONEORMORE/>
</elementType>
```

Specifying Element Order

In the DTD, because we have used a comma as an operator, the elements must appear in the same order as they are defined. In XML-Data the order they appear as children under the elementType element serves the same purpose.

We can relax the order in the classical DTD by using a | as a tokenizer followed by the * indicator.

For example, we could have written:

```
<!ELEMENT book (title | author | isbn | publication-date | book-type | book-
amily)*>
```

Which would have allowed for the inclusion of as many of the elements we wanted in any order.

In XML-Data we can relax the order, and accomplish things not possible in DTDs, by using the `group` element.

```
<elementType id= "book">
     <group occurs= "OPTIONAL">
            <element type="#title" occurs="REQUIRED"/>
            <element type="#author" occurs="ONEORMORE"/>
            <element type="#isbn"/>
            <element type="#publication-date"/>
            <element type="#book-type"/>
            <element type="#book-family" occurs="ONEORMORE"/>
     </group>
</elementType>
```

This means that if one of the elements appears they must ALL appear, i.e. either none or all of them must appear. The order they appear in is not relaxed.

We can relax the order using the `group` element's attribute `groupOrder` which can take the values of `"SEQ"`, `"AND"` or `"OR"`.

`"SEQ"`	The default and merely maintains that the order the elements are listed in is the order in which they must occur. It is usually left out.
`"AND"`	Relaxes ordering among elements, and allows them to appear in any order
`"OR"`	Allows any one of a list of elements (or groups) to occur

If included the above example would begin:

```
<elementType id= "book">
     <group groupOrder="SEQ" occurs="OPTIONAL">
        ...etc.
```

To specify optional ordering use the following:

```
<elementType id= "book">
     <group groupOrder="AND" occurs="OPTIONAL">
            <element type="#title" occurs="REQUIRED"/>
            <element type="#author" occurs="ONEORMORE"/>
            <element type="#isbn"/>
            <element type="#publication-date"/>
            <element type="#book-type"/>
            <element type="#book-family" occurs="ONEORMORE"/>
     </group>
</elementType
```

This indicates that all the elements must occur, but their ordering is optional. Of course if one of the individual elements took the attribute-value pair of `occurs = "ZEROORMORE"`, it would not have to appear.

The following code indicates that only one of the elements need appear, with of course the requirements imposed upon them by their own `occurs` attribute.

```
<elementType id="book">
     <group groupOrder="OR">
          <element type="#title" occurs="REQUIRED"/>
          <element type="#author" occurs="ONEORMORE"/>
          <element type="#isbn"/>
          <element type="#publication-date"/>
          <element type="#book-type"/>
          <element type="#book-family" occurs="ONEORMORE"/>
     </group>
</elementType
```

Content Other Than Element Content

In our example all the other elements just take `PCDATA` as their content. We have seen that we declare this using the `string` element. Here is what it looks like:

```
<elementType id= "title">
     <string/>
</elementType>
<elementType id= "author">
     <string/>
</elementType>
<elementType id= "isbn">
     <string/>
</elementType>
<elementType id= "publication-date">
     <string/>
</elementType>
<elementType id= "book-type">
     <string/>
</elementType>
<elementType id= "book-family">
     <string/>
</elementType>
```

The other element keywords allowed are for mixed data are `ANY` and `EMPTY`. They are expressed in a classical DTD as:

```
<!ELEMENT mega-element (#PCDATA|[list of allowed elements])*>
```

and their use is very similar to that in the classical DTD.

In XML-Data we declare `mixed` data as follows:

```
<elementType id= "mega-element">
     <mixed>
          <element type= "#a">
          <element type= "#b">
```

```
            <element type= "#etc">
        </mixed>
</elementType>
```

Where the sub-elements have already been declared, as so:

```
<elementType id="#a">
        </string>
</elementType>
etc...
```

Here is how we infer the keyword of ANY.

```
<elementType id= "mega-element2">
        <any/>
</elementType>
```

which means that mega-element2 can contain any number of elements but NO strings.

An empty element can be declared as follows:

```
<elementType id= "mini-element">
        <empty/>
</elementType>
```

Although just putting an empty elementType would suffice just as well.

```
<elementType id= "mini-element"/>
```

Defining Attributes in XML-Data

In the classical DTD attributes are defined in the ATTLIST namely in our example:

```
<!ATTLIST book
        id ID #REQUIRED>
<!ATTLIST author
        rank CDATA #IMPLIED>
```

In XML-Data we use the attribute element to assign an attribute to a definition. The attribute element has its own attributes:

atttype	Which defines the type of attribute. The default is CDATA, so there is no need to include atttype if CDATA is the value.
values	Has to be included if and only if atttype takes a value of ENUMERATION or NOTATION. See next section for example.
default	A default can be specified for ENUMERATION. It must be one of the specified values.

In our example the book element becomes:

```
<elementType id= "book">
     <element type="#title" occurs= "REQUIRED"/>
     <element type="#author" occurs= "ONEORMORE"/>
     <element type="#isbn"/>
     <element type="#publication-date"/>
     <element type="#book-type"/>
     <element type="#book-family" occurs= "ONEORMORE"/>

     <!--define book attribute here-->

     <attribute name="id" atttype="ID">

</elementType>
```

and the attribute for author is slipped in here:

```
     <element type="#author" occurs="ONEORMORE"/>
           <!--define author attribute here-->
           <attribute name="rank" atttype="CDATA"/>
```

Because CDATA is the default type there is no need to include an atttype attribute for book.

The other values that atttype can take are the same as in the classical DTD namely:

```
(URIREF | ID | IDREF | IDREFS | ENTITY | ENTITIES | NMTOKEN | NMTOKENS |
ENUMERATION | NOTATION | CDATA)
```

with a default of CDATA. See the specification for further details.

http://www.W3C.org/TR/1998/NOTE-XML-data/

Example of an Enumeration

Our example has no instance of an enumerated attribute. The following example is taken from Chapter 3 of *Professional Style Sheets*, Wrox Press, ISBN 1-861001-65-7. To recap, an enumerated attribute is one that provides a list of values and can also supply a default value.

```
<!ATTLIST attitude
     interest(hot|warm|cool|unknown) "unknown">
```

In a classical DTD we don't have to specify that we are providing enumerated values, the syntax makes this obvious. In XML-Data we do have to specify the type using the atttype attribute.

The above example would be rendered in XML-Data as follows:

```
<elementType id="attidude">

     <!—-element types would go here -->

     <!--define attidudes attribute here with enumerated values and the default-
>
```

```
        <attribute name="interest" atttype="ENUMERATION" values= "hot warm cool
_unknown" default= "unknown">
    </elementType>
```

That just about wraps up our look at how a classical DTD should be rendered in XML-Data. Remember it is an XML file itself, and should validate in an XML parser. Here is the completed schema of our example, before we go on to look at how XML-Data expands on the abilities of DTDs.

```
<?xml version= "1.0" ?>
<schema  xmlns="urn:W3C.org:xmlschema"
     xmlns:dt="urn:W3C.org:xmldatatypes">
<elementType id="wrox-books-table">
     <element type="#book" occurs="ONEORMORE"/>
</elementType>

<elementType id= "book">
     <element type="#title" occurs="REQUIRED"/>
     <element type="#author" occurs="ONEORMORE"/>
          <!--define author attribute here-->
          <attribute name="rank" atttype="CDATA"/>
     <element type="#isbn"/>
     <element type="#publication-date"/>
     <element type="#book-type"/>
     <element type="#book-family" occurs="ONEORMORE"/>

     <!--define book attribute here-->
     <attribute name="id" atttype="ID">

</elementType>

<elementType id= "title">
     <string/>
</elementType>

<elementType id= "author">
     <string/>
</elementType>

<elementType id= "isbn">
     <string/>
</elementType>

<elementType id= "publication-date">
     <string/>
</elementType>

<elementType id= "book-type">
     <string/>
</elementType>

<elementType id= "book-family">
     <string/>
</elementType>

</schema>
```

Before going on to look at some of the more specialized aspects of XML-Data, let's look at two of its other aspects that enhance the classical DTD.

Open Content Models

If I have an XML document with a DTD and I want to add an extra element called <author-biog> to the content part of my document in our example, so that we have:

```
<wrox-books-table>

      <book id="b1">
            <title></title>
            <author rank=""></author>
            <author-biog></author-biog>
            <isbn></isbn>
            <publication-date></publication-date>
            <book-type></book-type>
            <book-family></book-family>

      </book>

</wrox-books-table>
```

the parser won't understand it. However, in XML-Data we can use the content attribute to permit element types that aren't explicitly listed to still be valid. We declare this using an OPEN or CLOSED content model thus.

```
<elementType id="book" content="CLOSED">
```

If I declare the value of the content attribute to be "CLOSED" my XML-Data compliant browser should still get confused if I add this extra element, but if I declare it "OPEN"

```
<elementType id="book" content="OPEN">
```

or leave it undeclared (the default is OPEN) then it will accept an undeclared element without protest.

It is impossible to emphasize how important this aspect of XML-Data is. With a classical DTD if I want to add one element, I must modify the whole DTD. With XML-Data I can choose to be either very strict (and there are several advantages of being strict in document work) and enforce the schema, or I can take a looser attitude and allow new elements. Although the looser approach means that the document can only be well-formed if it contains undeclared elements; the new elements cannot be validated. Taking a looser approach is particularly important if we are building Database Tables from a Database 'on the fly'.

Default Element Content

If an element has an occurs value of "REQUIRED" or "OPTIONAL", i.e. there can only be one of them per group, then we can specify a <default> value for the content of the element.

In our example above we might want to provide a default content for <book-type> as "Computer Related".

We would do this as follows:

```
<element type="#book-type"occurs="REQUIRED" >
       <default> Computer Related </default>
<element>
```

Now whenever no content is provided our browser will fill in the element content of "Computer Related".

To ensure that this is the only content allowed we could use the presence = "FIXED" attribute/value pair as follows.

```
<element type="#book-type" occurs= "REQUIRED" presence = "FIXED">
  <default> Computer Related </default>
    </element>
```

This will ensure that our XML-Data compliant parser would register an error each time we attempted to add content other than "Computer Related" to this element.

XML-Data: Adding Complexity II

XML-Data has several other features, which can not only add extra functionality to our DTD, but can also be useful when using XML as a Database or as a repository for objects. Let's look at some of these now.

Aliases and Correlatives.

Sometimes we have different words that mean the same thing. This is quite common in bilingual documents.

For example, we might want to alter our tags to French for the Franco-phone branch of Wrox books. To do this we would use the schema element elementTypeEquivalent as follows:

```
<elementTypeEquivalent id= "livre" type= "book"/>
<elementTypeEquivalent id= "auteur" type= "author"/>
```

Other times we have groups of words that describe the same object. For example, in our Wrox database we could have the following snippet in the wrox-books-table:

```
<book>
     <title>Professional style Sheets for HTML and XML</title>
     <author>Frank Boumphrey</author>
...etc.
</book>
```

Later on, if we extend the database we could have:

```
<person>
     Frank Boumphrey
     <works> Professional style Sheets for HTML and XML</works>
...etc.
</person>
```

How do we express the idea that <title> and <works> describe identical objects? The answer is we use the schema element <correlative> as follows:

```
<elementType id="title">
     <string/>
</elementType>

<elementType id= "works">
     <correlative type= "#title"/>
     <string/>
</elementType>
```

Note the syntax using a hash mark before the element name we wish to correlate with.

Class Hierarchies

Element types can be organized into categories using the `superType` element.

In the following example the use of the `superType` element in the following manner indicates that `last-name`, and `first-name` are both related to name.

```
<elementType id= "author">
     <string/>
</elementType>

<elementType id= "name">
     <element type= "#author"/>
</elementType>

<elementType id= "last-name">
     <superType type= "#name"/>
     <element type= "#author"/>
</elementType>

<elementType id= "first-name">
     <superType type= "#name"/>
     <element type= "#author"/>
</elementType>
```

So `last-name` and `first-name` are subsets of the superset type `name`. Note that the superset type (`name`) must have a `content = "OPEN"` model.

Key References

Using XML-Data we can also make elements act as references to other references using **key references**. Look again at our example where we have objects referred to in two different ways:

```
<book>
     <title>Professional style sheets for HTML and XML</title>
     <author> Frank Boumphrey</author>
</book>

<!-- and later on in the same document -->

<person>
   <name>Frank Boumphrey</name>
     <works>Professional style sheets for HTML and XML</works>
</person>
```

Frank Boumphrey is the value of the <author> sub-element in the <book> element, and he is also the value of the <name> sub-element in the <person> element. We can express this relationship using the key, keyPart and the foreignKey elements.

First we announce the element:

```
<elementType id="name">
      <string/>
</elementType>
```

Next we announce that name is a child of person, and assign it an id of a_person1. Using the key element we create an id of a_key1, which announces that a person can be uniquely identified by their name, and using the keyPart element announce that it is associated with the element with the id a_person1, i.e. the name element.

```
<elementType id="person">
      <element id="a_person1" type="#name"/>
      <key id="a_key1"><keyPart href="#a_person1"/></key>
      <string/>
</elementType>
```

The following informs the user agent that the content of the author element is a string with a foreign key identifying the author by name.

```
<elementType id="author">
      <string/>
      <foreignKey range="#person" key="#a_key1"/>
</elementType>
```

These schema declarations may seem rather cumbersome, and the concepts are a little difficult to grasp, and you will probably never have a need to use them unless you are manipulating a database.

You are referred to the specification for further discussion of one-to-many relationships, using attributes as references, and Multipart Keys. They would have been of use if XML-Data was ever going to get implemented in its present form, but they only refine the concept that it is possible to describe relationships between different elements and objects.

Constraints

Another aspect of XML-Data that is useful is the concept of constraints. It is possible to put limits on what an element can contain. For example, we may want to limit the amount of a withdrawal from a bank account. To do this we use the <max> and <min> elements to restrict ranges.

Obviously we would not want to allow a negative withdrawal (this would be the same as crediting our account!), and let's put the maximum withdrawal amount at $500. This is how we would do it.

```
<elementType  id= "withdrawal">
      </string>
</elementType>

<elementType  id= "account">
      <element href= "#withdrawal"><min>0</min><max>500</max>
</elementType>
```

The withdrawal would, however, need to be converted into a form other than a string, which brings us to the another major advantage of XML based schemas, the ability to define datatypes. Here's how XML-Data proposes to do it.

Datatypes

The problem with a classical DTD is that we can only define element content as either another element, or PCDATA which is a string. There is no way to stipulate that our content should be a date, a signed or an unsigned integer, a float, a boolean or a URL. Obviously if we are going to use elements to define objects, or as part of a database, that can be interpreted then this is important.

Going back to our Hat class:

```
<hat id="h2">
            <style>Stetson</style>
            <size>7</size>
            <color>gray</color>
</hat>
```

What we really need is to be able to specify the nature of the content of our sub-elements or properties. For example:

```
<hat id="h2">
            <style dataType= "string">Stetson</style>
            <size dataType= "integer">7</size>
            <color dataType= "string">gray</color>
</hat>
```

Of course we could put this attribute in the classical DTD, and this would describe how the data is meant to be interpreted, but the content would still be a string and a parser would not throw an error if we put in the information <size dataType="integer">large</size>. Obviously here large is not an integer!

We can get around this by declaring a namespace for datatypes as we did in our first simple example (slightly modified). To recap:

```
<?xml version= "1.0" ?>
<schema  xmlns="urn:W3C.org:xmlschema"
      xmlns:dt="urn:W3C.org:xmldatatypes">

      <elementType id= "xdoc">
            <element type="#greeting"/>
            <element type="# days-taken-for-creation "/>
      </elementType>

      <elementType id= "greeting">
            <string/>
      </elementType>

      <elementType id= "days-taken-for-creation">
            <int/>
      </elementType>
</schema>
```

```
<xdoc>
    <greeting> Hello World! </greeting>
    <days-taken-for-creation dt:dt= "int">7</days-taken-for-creation>
<xdoc>
```

How the user agent uses the information is, of course, up to the user agent, but at least we have told it "Hey stupid, the `days-taken-for-creation` element is meant to be an integer, please ensure that it is one". The datatypes recognized by both XML-Data and DCD are given in Appendix D.

That more or less wraps up our coverage of XML-Data. We haven't covered some of the more obscure aspects of it but we have covered enough to hopefully give you an understanding of the advantages of such a schema over the classical DTD.

Of course, there are no applications as of yet which support such a schema, and indeed such an application is probably more than a year away. IE5, however, does support the datatypes namespaces. In other words you can label an instance with a particular datatype. For example:

```
<price dt:dt="fixed.14.4">1.95</price>
```

We can be sure however, that as soon as a standard schema is decided upon, applications will support it! Now let's turn our attention to the other schema proposal we mentioned earlier – DCD for XML.

The Document Content Description Proposal

This proposal for an XML document schema was submitted to the W3C in July 1998. Just like XML-Data it is in Note form. It uses a modified Resource Description Framework (RDF) syntax for its description and includes a subset of the XML-Data submission in an RDF compliant way. You may remember that we briefly introduced RDF and its implications in the Introduction.

DCD takes the approach of describing **constraints** that apply to the structure and contents of XML documents. We will not be going into the same depth as we did with XML-Data. However, we will provide an overview that shows you enough to gain an understanding of the DCD's potential. The DCD note is surprisingly readable and well written, so feel free to download it to get more detailed insight into the syntax. You can find it at:

`http://www.W3C.org/TR/NOTE-dcd`

The specification is built upon the following design principles:

1.2 Design Principles

1.DCD semantics shall be a superset of those provided by XML DTDs.

2.The DCD data model and syntax shall be conformant with that of RDF.

3.The constraints in a DCD shall be straightforwardly usable by authoring tools and other applications which wish to retrieve information about a document's content and structure.

4.DCD shall use mechanisms from other W3CC working groups wherever they are appropriate and efficient.

5.DCDs should be human-readable and reasonably clear.

So that DCDs can conform to Design Principle 2, the authors require a modification in the RDF syntax as follows:

2.1.1 Proposed Simplification of RDF Syntax

As stated earlier, it is intended that DCD be conformant to the RDF Model and Syntax Specification. However, it assumes certain simplifications in the RDF syntax which we intend to propose to the RDF working group. This syntax will be adopted only if ratified by the RDF working group. These syntactic simplifications are:

RDF:li

The `RDF:li` should not be required if typed nodes are being inserted into a collection.

Collection type

The collection type for properties can be specified as an attribute of the node.

For more information on RDF visit the following site:

`http://www.W3C.org/RDF/Overview.html`

This includes a link to the RDF syntax, which is at:

`http://www.W3C.org/TR/WD-rdf-syntax/`

What follows is a brief overview of DCD, however, the principles are similar to XML-Data. So, if you have followed the arguments so far, you will have no difficulty following our discussion of DCD. You will see that in most places DCD is an improvement and simplification of XML-Data.

To highlight the syntactic differences between XML-Data and DCD let's repeat our simple XML-Data example using DCD!

DCD - A Simple Start

Here is our simple `Hello World` example again in XML-Data:

```
<?xml version= "1.0" ?>
<schema  xmlns="urn:W3C.org:xmlschema"
     xmlns:dt="urn:W3C.org:xmldatatypes">
<elementType id= "greeting">
     <string/>
</elementType>
</schema>

<greeting> Hello World! </greeting>
```

And here is one way it can be rendered in DCD:

```
<DCD>
     <ElementDef>
          <type>greeting</type>
          <model>Data</model>
     </ElementDef>
</DCD>

<greeting> Hello World </greeting>
```

In this first example, allowable properties of the `greeting` element are expressed as sub-elements of `ElementDef` which is short for Element Definition.

Using Elements and Attributes Interchangeably

One of the strengths of the DCD proposal is that, when using RDF syntax, non-repeatable properties can be expressed as attributes of the parent element rather than as sub-elements. This is exactly what we do in the following second example – the properties are expressed as attributes. So, in this example, `Type` and `Model` can be used as either elements or attributes (but, obviously, not both).

```
<DCD>
     <ElementDef Type="greeting" Model="Data">
          <Description>Our first simple example</Description>
     </ElementDef>
</DCD>
<greeting> Hello World! </greeting>
```

Note that our element `greeting` is defined by `ElementDef` in the DCD (c.f. `elementType` in XML-Data), and is identified by the `Type` attribute (cf. `id` in XML-Data). The `Model` property of the `ElementDef` is `Data` which indicates that it will contain a single data value. The default datatype for this value is equivalent to the XML-Data `<string/>`.

Note also, the use of the `Description` element in the second example. This may seem to be the same as a comment - you can of course use XML comments as well, however `Description` allows you to describe semantics in the markup, which can then be used by tools or agents to support human operations.

Remember that XML is case sensitive; so be sure to get those uppercase letters correct!

Limiting the Syntax

Before we get on with taking a closer look at the specification, it is worth explaining an optional processing instruction (PI), which is defined near the beginning of the specification as it can be a source of confusion. In Section 2.1.2, an optional PI:

```
<?DCD syntax="explicit"?>
```

is introduced. When this, strictly optional, PI is included it is to be placed directly after the opening <DCD> tag. Its inclusion means that the following properties *must* be specified using attribute syntax:

```
Type            Model        Occurs       RDF:Order    Content      Root
Fixed           Datatype
```

We will meet these properties shortly. But what the specification does not tell you is why the PI is there. During the development of DCD some developers believed that the ability to specify properties either as attributes or as elements was too general and would make parsers bigger and slower. The PI is included as a way to limit the flexibility of the syntax. This would allow developers to build a smaller, faster parser. Knowing that this is strictly optional (and why you would consider using it), the rest of the specification is very clear.

DCD Nodes and Resource Types

The following types of nodes (or keyword element types) are defined at the DCD namespace (note that you cannot view this namespace in a browser, its contents are described in the specification). You do not need to include this namespace because it is implied by the `<DCD>` tag.

```
DCD         ElementDef          Group          AttributeDef
ExternalEntityDef                     InternalEntityDef
```

Again remember that XML is case sensitive; so be sure to get those uppercase letters correct!

Referring to Elements and Attributes

Apart from declaring what element types, attributes and values can be used in a document instance, the DCD specification emphasizes the point that a DCD constrains the structure and contents of a document that uses it. This may seem redundant, as all schemas can do a similar job, however this is a conceptual design point. It is also possible for documents to be constrained by more than one DCD.

We have already seen in our simple example that element types are declared using `ElementDef`. Constraints are then made upon these elements by assigning properties to them. Element definitions also declare that elements may have children, and may have attributes provided with certain names and properties. Where child elements are defined, they must be collected together into `Groups`, which require `Order` and `Occurs` properties. Each `ElementDef` must have a `Type` property – which serves the same purpose as `id` in XML-Data – giving the name of the element type. Of course, `Type` has to be unique within the DCD to conform to the requirements of valid XML. We shall see an example of `Group` when we cover it in more detail shortly.

The DCD specification also permits attributes and elements that are not from the same DCD, others can be referenced by namespaces (we cover namespaces in detail in the following chapter). Briefly though, an XML namespace is a collection of names, identified by a URI, which are used in XML documents as element types and attribute names. If the elements are from the same DCD, they are referred to by their `Type` property. While, if they use namespaces to refer to another DCD the `Type` might be a qualified name, where the prefix identifies the namespace.

Attributes are declared using `AttributeDef`. They can either be used on their own, or within an element definition. Every attribute must have a `Name` property. It may also have a `Global` property whose value is a Boolean. This indicates whether the name of the attribute must be unique to that DCD. If the value of `Global` is `True` the `Name` property must be unique in the DCD. If it is `False` then other elements can take an attribute of the same name.

You can use a global attribute anywhere in any element definition within a DCD just by using its name. While global attributes in other namespaces must be referred to using qualified names. (Qualified names are covered in more detail in Chapter 4 on Namespaces.) Local attributes, for which the value of the `Global` property is `False`, can only be used within the `ElementDef` they are declared in.

We have already seen `DCD` and `ElementDef` in action in our example, let's briefly look at these and the others before moving on to our other Wrox database example.

DCD

The `DCD` element acts as a container for the DCD. The types of elements that can appear within it correspond to RDF's property types. Here are the properties which apply to DCDs:

```
ElementDef        AttributeDef        Description        InternalEntityDef
ExternalEntityDef        Content              Namespace
```

We come to ElementDef shortly, however here are the others:

AttributeDef

As we have seen, attributes can be defined as properties of a DCD. We shall see later that attributes can also be defined within an `ElementDef`.

Description

This property is used to provide a human-readable description of the semantics and usage of the DCD.

InternalEntityDef and ExternalEntityDef

We will come back to these later, but they identify entities that may be invoked via reference in such documents. They are equivalent to the DTD declarations for these entity types.

Content

`Content` can be used to allow elements that have not been defined using `ElementDef` to appear in a document instance, when it takes a value of `Open`. Although this would mean that documents using elements that haven't been defined would not be able to be validated, unless the parser could handle external entities which may contain further entity definitions and that the element types were defined there. The other value `Content` can take is `Closed`, which means that all elements used must have been declared using `ElementDef`.

Namespace

This property is required for every DCD and provides the namespace for the DCD. Its value must be a URN which identifies a namespace. Because it applies to all elements and attributes attached by properties to the DCD, it allows the elements and attributes in a document instance to be referenced from more than one DCD. Again, we will cover namespaces in more detail in the next chapter.

ElementDef

`ElementDef` is like an element type declaration. Here are the properties that `ElementDef` can take, either as sub-elements or using attribute syntax:

```
Type          Model      Attribute    AttributeDef    Group
RDF:Order     Content    Description  Root            Default
Fixed         Min        Max          Datatype
```

Type

Each `ElementDef` in a DCD must have a `Type` property, which describes the element it is defining. When `Type` is used in conjunction with `ElementDef` it may not start with a prefix or colon.

> *This is because it is possible to refer to elements and attributes in another DCD using namespaces. Element definitions which come from another DCD may have a qualified name as the property of* `Type`*, the prefix indicating the namespace. If a prefix or colon was used as a value of* `Type` *in an internal element definition, it could cause the parser to look for a matching namespace – which would cause an error.*

Model

Defines the type of content the element may have. It takes the values:

Value	Content
`Empty`	No content
`Any`	Anything within general XML rules
`Data`	A single data value
`Elements`	Only child elements, the type of element being controlled by `Group` and `Element` properties
`Mixed`	Text and embedded child elements, the type of element being controlled by the `Element` property

The default is `Data`.

> *Note that the DCD definition of* `Any` *is like the classical DTD definition of* `ANY`*. The XML-Data definition of element restricts content to elements and not text although it is not clear why!*

AttributeDef

An `AttributeDef` that can also appear as a property of an `ElementDef`.

Attribute

This identifies the attributes which an element may take. `Attribute` properties must be unique for each element definition. So a `<greeting>` element could not take two attributes that are both called `friendly`. However, different element definitions may use the same (global) attribute property name. So, both `<greeting>` and `<salutations>` elements could take an attribute of `friendly`.

Group, Occurs and Order

If an `ElementDef` takes a value of `"Elements"` for its `Model`, it must also take a `Group` property. This specifies the elements and groups which can occur as children of elements of this type.

Group can in turn take a property called `Occurs` which will have values of `Required`, `Optional`, `OneOrMore`, or `ZeroOrMore`. The default is `Required`.

The order of occurrence of the children is defined by the `RDF:collection` attribute. Permitted values are `Seq` when the sequence must be followed or `Alt` where only one of the specified children may occur. A value of `Bag` may also be allowed at a later date, which will allow appearance of the children in any order. Here's an example culled from the proposal:

```
<ElementDef Type="employee" Model="Elements" Content="Closed">

     <AttributeDef Name="employment" Occurs="Required" Datatype="enumeration">
          <Values>Temporary Permanent Retired</Values>
     </AttributeDef>

<Group RDF:Order="Seq">

     <Element>FirstName</Element>
     <Group Occurs="Optional"><Element>MI</Element></Group>

     <Element>LastName</Element>
     <Group Occurs="OneOrMore" RDF:Order="Alt">
     <Element>Street</Element><Element>PO-Box</Element>
     </Group>

     <Group RDF:Order="Seq">

     <Element>Telephone</Element>
     <Element>Salary</Element>

     </Group>

</Group>
</ElementDef>
```

This was included for use with the RDF Model and Syntax Specification, which DCDs were intended to be compliant with. However, it assumes certain simplifications in the RDF syntax which the authors of the specification are proposing to the RDF working group.

Content

Declares whether this element type can include child elements not explicitly defined with its `Group`. It takes the values `Open` or `Closed`. `Open` permits the inclusion of element types not included in the `Group` element. `Closed` only allows children of types that have been declared in the `Group` element. The default was missed out of the specification, but its authors say that it is `Closed`.

Root

This property declares whether the element type it is used with can be used as a root of a conforming document. It is a Boolean. The default is `False`. If no element type has this property, then any element can serve as a root. If several element types have the `Root` property with a value of `True`, any of these element types may serve as the root element of the conforming document.

Default

Provides a default value as in XML-Data, e.g.

```
<ElementDef Type="AirTicketClass">
     <Default>Y</Default>
</ElementDef>
```

Fixed

Specifies that the default value is the only one allowed, `Fixed` can take a value of `True` or `False` e.g.

```
<ElementDef Type="Namespace" Model= "Data" Fixed="True">
     <Default>http://www.wrox.com/namedefs</Default>
</ElementDef>
```

Min and Max

Constrain the legal values of the element type. If no datatype is specified or if the datatype is `string` then the `Min` and `Max` values are treated as strings and upper and lower bounding is performed during validation.

Datatype

The datatypes are very similar (but not identical!) to the XML-Data datatypes. See the two specifications (XML-Data and DCD) for details. The default is `string`.

AttributeDef

Unsurprisingly `AttributeDef` defines attributes. Remember that these can be used as properties of the DCD or as properties of an Element Definition. Here is an example that will doubtless be familiar to you:

```
<ElementDef Type="IMG">
     <AttributeDef Name="SRC" DataType="URI">
</ElementDef>
```

`AttributeDef` can take the following properties:

```
Name          Global          ID-Role          Occurs
Min      Max
```

Name

This property is required with each attribute and gives the name of an attribute. It may not start with a prefix or colon, unless the prefix and colon are referring to a namespace.

Global

This indicates whether the `Name` has to be unique in that DCD. It can take the values `True` and `False`, where `True` means that the `Name` must be unique. `False` is the default.

For example, in HTML nearly all elements can take the attributes `class`, `style`, `name`, `id`, `type` etc. If we were using DCD to define the HTML 4 schema we could do the following:

```
<DCD>
<AttributeDef Name="class" DataType="Data" Global="True">
<AttributeDef Name="style" DataType="Data" Global="True">

etc...
```

Which means that the attributes would apply to all the `ElementDef`'s declared in the `<DCD>` element simply by adding `Attribute= "class"`.

For example:

```
<ElementDef Type="DIV" Attribute = "class style etc">
```

with the attributes name separated by whitespace.

ID-Role

This is used to signify that the attribute has a unique identifier or unique ID pointer semantics. It takes the values `ID`, `IDREF` and `IDREFS`. Each of these are the same as they are in DTDs.

Occurs

This defines whether the presence of the attribute is required, taking the values `Required`, where it occurs exactly once, and `Optional`, where it may occur zero or one times. The default being `Optional`.

Min and Max

Constrain the legal values of the attribute type exactly as they constrained the legal values of an element type covered earlier.

InternalEntityDef And ExternalEntityDef

These work like entity declarations in a classical DTD. Here is an example:

```
<InternalEntityDef Name="www" Value="World Wide Web"/>
<ExternalEntityDef
Name="boilerplate"SystemId="http://www.legalese.com/boiler.htm"/>
```

`InternalEntityDef` can take the properties `Name` and `Value`. While `ExternalEntityDef` can take the properties `Name`, `PublicID` and `SystemID`.

In both cases `Name` gives the name by which the entity can be invoked, and is required. `Value` gives the replacement text for the internal entity. `PublicID` and `SystemID` are the same as they are for DTDs.

Datatypes

The datatypes in the DCD specification are based upon those supported by SQL and modern programming languages. We cover them in greater detail in Appendix D.

That wraps up our brief look at DCD. Both DCD and XML-Data have easy-to-learn syntaxes which have all the advantages and none of the disadvantages of the traditional DTD.

Summary

In this chapter we had a look at two propositions for XML based schemas: XML-Data and Document Content Description for XML. By looking at these proposals, you will see that their work is important in making XML a language for interchanging information between applications. Specifically, we looked at:

- What a schema is and does
- The advantages and disadvantages of the Classical DTD
- The XML based schema XML-Data in detail
- The more recent schema proposal Document Content Description for XML

And, having seen the advantages XML based schemas hold over DTDs, you will now have a solid foundation of knowledge which will be helpful in following the progress of the XML-Schema Working Group.

Namespaces

Markup is only valuable if we know what the markup means. Consider this piece of code:

```
<bzx>14.2</bzx>
```

Without any clues to guide us this is patent gibberish. It could be the time taken to run the 100 meters hurdles, the average age of puberty, the average life span of a cat, or Bill Gates' wealth in billions of dollars (No it's much too small for that, but it could be his annual income!). The fact is that any user agent needs to know what markup means for it to be of any use.

Now consider the second piece of code:

```
<hemoglobin>14.2</hemoglobin>
```

An educated person may guess that it has something to do with blood. To any medical person though it is immediately obvious that this is the concentration of hemoglobin measured in mg/%.

This illustrates the fact that markup may have special meaning to an educated user agent. Wouldn't it be nice if we could educate any user agent so that it had knowledge of the meaning of the markup? Consider this markup:

```
<title>Big Sur</title>
```

Every one knows what a title is, but in this particular case is it the title of a book? A job title? Or an honorific? (The Mudville Moose lodge never could spell.) Without guidance it is difficult to say.

Wouldn't it be wonderful if we could indicate to an intelligent user agent what kind of title it was dealing with?

If we were writing a document, wouldn't it be great if we could take a chunk of markup, and say to the user agent, "Make sure that this corresponds to a book title." And take another chunk, put it in the same document and say, "Make sure that this corresponds with a job title"?

In fact there is a way we can accomplish all of these objectives. It involves the use of namespaces.

As we will see namespaces allow us to do two very important things:

- Blend documents from two or more different sources while being able to identify what element or attribute comes from which source.
- Possibly allow the user agent to access further material such as a DTD or other description of the elements and attributes.

What We'll Cover

This chapter essentially covers the current Namespaces specification of the 16th September 1998, which can be found at `http://www.w3.org/TR/WD-xml-names`. Unlike most W3C Working Drafts, this is actually quite a readable document with some excellent examples, and you are encouraged to read it.

In what follows we will look at:

- What a namespace is
- How to identify and declare namespaces, including the syntax employed
- What is meant by scope in namespaces
- Expected user agent behavior
- Some current applications.

What is a Namespace?

A namespace is a collection of names that can be used in XML documents as element or attribute names, which are used to identify that name with a particular domain. Namespaces in XML are identified by a URI (Uniform Resource Identifier)(see note 1 following). This allows each namespace to be universally unique, as it must be if we are looking at element and attribute names from all over the Internet.

> *(1) URI is a super-class that includes both URNs (Uniform Resource Number) and URLs (Uniform Resource Locator). Although in the future it is expected that URNs will become numerous, for the present a URI means a URL in nearly all cases. The point is that we have a universally unique number or name that can identify an element or attribute in a universally unique way. Why do we use an URI? Quite simply because this gives us a number, or string, managed by others, that is designed to be universally unique.*

For example we can have four elements all called '`class`'. The first one refers to the academic classes in Mudville High School; the second to the type of seat on an airplane; the third identifies a class of compounds in chemistry; and the last refers to the social standing of an English gentleman.

We can identify these different classes with a different, and appropriate, URI. The first can be associated with Mudville's URI, the second with the FAA's URI, the third with a 'chem-lang' domain's URI, and the last with the URI of 'baronage' peerage. We could put the following in the document to associate the element with the namespace:

```
<http://www.mudville-schools.org.class>

<http://www.faa.gov.class>

<http://www.chem-lang.org.class>

<http://www.baronage.co.uk.class>
```

or

```
<class namespace="http://www.mudville-schools.org">

<class namespace="http://www.faa.gov/">

<class namespace="http://www.chem-lang.org">

<class namespace="http://www.baronage.co.uk/">
```

etc., but these present a few problems.

- Obviously we would very quickly get tired of doing this for each and every element.
- Suppose I wanted to use two attributes of the same name in the same element (illegal in XML).
- URIs often contain characters that are illegal in XML names.

The W3C Namespaces specification gives us a much better way of associating elements and attributes with their URIs, and we will have a look at this next.

Identifying and Declaring Namespaces

Let's look at how the W3C specification allows us to declare and identify namespaces.

Namespace Syntax

Essentially, in any given document, one associates a prefix with the URI we want to use as a namespace using the syntax:

```
xmlns:[prefix]= "[URI of namespace]"
```

Where `xmlns:` is a reserved attribute. The prefix can be any of the characters allowed in an XML tag, provided it does not start with any form of the string '`xml`'. (Such strings are reserved.)

What we have done is to declare the prefix as an alias for the namespace.

Now when we want to associate a given local element or attribute with a namespace, we just prefix it with the declared prefix. So if we have declared the namespace for Mudville High School `class` elements as follows

```
xmlns:sch= "http://www.mudville-schools.org"
```

then

```
<sch:class>Advanced Basket Weaving</sch:class>
```

tells the user agent that we are using the class element in the manner defined somehow, and somewhere, as the http://www.mudville-schools.org:class element and not a class element from some other domain.

Just because a URI is used to define a namespace does not mean that the user agent can find information about the use of the namespace at that site. Another separate method must be provided to educate the user agent. This fact can be a tremendous source of confusion when one initially reads the Namespaces specification.

Declaring the Namespace

The namespace is often declared in the root element of the document, but it can be in any other element. However the namespace cannot be used before it is declared. We will look at this in a little more detail when we look at scoping below.

An example will make this clearer:

```
<xdoc xmlns:sch="http://www.mudville-schools.org">
      <sch:class-list>
            <sch:class>Advanced Basket Weaving</sch:class>
            <sch:class>3D Art</sch:class>
            <sch:class>Remedial Reading</sch:class>
      </sch:class-list>
</xdoc>
```

Looking at this document both we and the user agent can tell that all the elements with the prefix of sch:, i.e. all the elements within this document, belong to the http://www.mudville-schools.org namespace. The declaring element xdoc is also assumed to be in the same namespace as a result of being the element containing the xmlns:[prefix] namespace declaration attribute.

For practical purposes, in an XML document an element or attribute employing the use of a namespace can be identified by the presence of a colon ":" in the tag name. XML keywords, such as the xml:space *attribute, tell both the carbon-based human reader and the intelligent silicon-based user agent that the attribute space belongs to the* 'xml' *namespace and is to be treated as such.*

Now what if we want to add a chemistry class, one about the class of compounds called "esters", and a second about a class of compounds called "benzenes". Here is what the revised document might look like:

```
<xdoc
      xmlns:sch="http://www.mudville-schools.org"
      xmlns:chem="http://www.chem-lang.org">
      <sch:class-list>
```

```
            <sch:class>Advanced Basket Weaving</sch:class>
            <sch:class>3D Art</sch:class>
            <sch:class>Remedial Reading</sch:class>
            <sch:class>
                  OrganicChemistryI <chem:class>Esters</chem:class>
            </sch:class>

            <sch:class>
                  OrganicChemistryII <chem:class> Benzenes</chem:class>
            </sch:class>
      </sch:class-list>
</xdoc>
```

Now both the human reader and the user agent know that the second type of "class", that with the 'chem:' prefix belongs to the "http://www.chem-lang.org" namespace. We would emphasize again that the prefix is not the namespace, it is merely the alias that the document writer has chosen to represent the namespace.

There is in fact a different (and better) way to write the above examples as we will see when we look at scoping below.

Namespaces and Scope

Let us have a look at the first example from the previous section again.

```
<!-- This document does not use scoping -->
<xdoc xmlns:sch="http://www.mudville-schools.org">
      <sch:class-list>
            <sch:class>Advanced Basket Weaving</sch:class>
            <sch:class>3D Art</sch:class>
            <sch:class>Remedial Reading</sch:class>
      </sch:class-list>
</xdoc>
```

There is really only one namespace, so why should we go through all the trouble of prefixing every element?

In fact, using scoping, we can write the above as follows:

```
<xdoc xmlns="http://www.mudville-schools.org">
      <class-list>
            <class>Advanced Basket Weaving</class>
            <class>3D Art</class>
            <class>Remedial Reading</class>
      </class-list>
</xdoc>
```

What we have done is simply declare a default namespace of http://www.mudville-schools.org. The scoping rules state that everything within the content of that element is considered to be in its namespace UNLESS the attribute or sub-element has a prefix. As you can see, with scoping the xdoc element and all its descendants are considered to be in the http://www.mudville-schools.org namespace.

But what about those elements and attributes that we DO NOT want to be in the `http://www.mudville-schools.org` namespace?

Let's look at the second example and rewrite it as follows:

```
<xdoc
      xmlns="http://www.mudville-schools.org"
      xmlns:chem="http://www.chem-lang.org">
      <class-list>
            <class>Advanced Basket Weaving</class>
            <class>3D Art</class>
            <class>Remedial Reading</class>
            <class>
                  OrganicChemistryI <chem:class>Esters</chem:class>
            </class>

            <class>
                  OrganicChemistryII <chem:class>Benzenes</chem:class>
            </class>
      </class-list>
</xdoc>
```

Now everything is within the `http://www.mudville-schools.org` namespace except those elements prefixed with `chem:` which are in the `http://www.chem-lang.org` namespace. Note the difference between the two namespace declaration attributes:

```
<xdoc
      xmlns="http://www.mudville-schools.org"
      xmlns:chem="http://www.chem-lang.org">
```

The `xdoc` element is considered to be in the `http://www.mudville-schools.org` namespace rather than the `http://www.chem-lang.org` namespace because the declaration:

```
xmlns="http://www.mudville-schools.org"
```

lacks an explicit prefix, and is therefore assumed to declare the default namespace, which takes precedence over the `xmlns:chem` declaration for the `xdoc` element and its dependants.

Attributes and Namespaces

Attributes are considered to be within the namespace of their element unless they are prefixed otherwise. So in a slightly modified version of the first example of the section above

```
<!--Note: scoping is prefered to this syntax-->
<xdoc xmlns:sch="http://www.mudville-schools.org">
      <sch:class-list>
            <sch:class sch:type="simple">Advanced Basket Weaving</sch:class>
            <sch:class type="simplest">3D Art</sch:class>
            <sch:class>Remedial Reading</sch:class>
      </sch:class-list>
</xdoc>
```

both the first and the second `type` attributes are correct and are considered to be within the same namespace, namely `http://www.mudville-schools.org`.

Problems can arise with the use of "global attributes" in XML and SGML. The second '`type`*' attribute could be a global or be a* `class` *attribute, and there is just no way to tell.*

We could have had:

```
<xdoc
      xmlns="http://www.mudville-schools.org"
      xmlns:chem="http://www.chem-lang.org">
      <class-list>
            <class type="simple">Advanced Basket Weaving</class>
            <class chem:type="simple">Esters II</class>
            <class>Remedial Reading</class>
      </class-list>
</xdoc>
```

where the Mudville `class` element 'inherits' the `chem:type` attribute from the 'chem-lang' domain. Even the following is legitimate

```
<class type="simple" chem:type="simple">Esters II</class>
```

because the namespace represented in the `chem:` prefix prevents the confusion of the two different `type` attributes. This inheritance does not change the fact that the `class` element concerned is a Mudville `class` element.

'Un'scoping Elements

It is only necessary to provide a namespace if we want the user agent to do something with select elements. (See the section 'Why the Need for Namespaces?' further on.) Presumably in our above examples we wanted the user agent to check that our elements were either conforming to some schema, or to see if they were otherwise associated with some behavior. And this can be a lot of work for the user agent. What if we want to use some namespace, for example the HTML namespace, and in the middle of it we want to drop in some simple well-formed XML which doesn't need to conform to any namespace.

Namespaces and scoping allow us to do this. If the URI in the default namespace declaration is empty, e.g.

```
<mydoc xmlns="">
      <class> Some Class </class>
</mydoc>
```

then the prefix-less elements are not in any namespace . In other words, neither the element `<mydoc>` nor the element `<class>` is in any namespace.

The following example is taken from the specification.

```
<?xml version="1.0"?>
<Beers>
<!-- the default namespace is now that of HTML -->
```

```
    <table xmlns="http://www.w3.org/TR/REC-html40">
        <tr>
            <td>Name</td>
            <td>Origin</td>
            <td>Description</td>
        </tr>
        <tr>
  <!-- drop the HTML namespace inside table cells -->

            <td>
                 <brandName xmlns="">Huntsman</brandName>
              </td>
              <td>
                 <origin xmlns="">Bath, UK</origin>
              </td>
              <td>
                 <details xmlns="">
                    <class>Bitter</class>
                    <hop>Fuggles</hop>
                    <pro>Wonderful hop, light alcohol, good summer beer</pro>
                    <con>Fragile; excessive variance pub to pub</con>
                 </details>
              </td>
          </tr>
    </table>
  </Beers>
```

Within this document we have made use of the HTML namespace. This will be useful if our user agent knows how to do something useful with HTML table elements, perhaps applying styles from a style sheet or converting to a spreadsheet. Inside the table however we have just gone back to our well-formed XML, which is represented by the italics in the example.

Why the Need for Namespaces?

In the introduction we touched on some of the ways namespaces could be useful. Let's expand on these now.

Uniquely Branding Elements and Attributes

This is the core purpose of a namespace. All that the present specification really sets out to do is to provide us with a means to do this. The specification sets out to allow us to uniquely identify elements and attributes using a URI. Whatever an application cares to do with this unique URI is up to the software. We will look at a couple of ways we could make use of namespaces below.

Reuse of Schemas

We have purposely used the word 'schema' here, although the only 'official' schema at present is the DTD.

As we have seen, good schemas are difficult to write, so it would be great if we could make use of those already written.

If we have an element or an attribute that is in the namespace of a certain schema, then the validating parser will be able to check that the element is in conformance with the appropriate schema.

However note that the URI in the namespace is NOT necessarily the URI that the user-agent should go to in order find the DTD against which the elements' validity should be checked, even though it might well be. There needs to be some further, as yet not worked out, mechanism to enable the user-agent to do this. Proprietary software applications will probably have the means to do this built into them.

Indeed it is likely that a Web browser of the future will have several 'schemas' built into it, allowing it to check out for example the HTML, the MATH, the CHEM, the MUSIC, DTDs of the next generation of XML-based HTML. Ultimately, browsers and other user software will be able to check your document against user-defined schemas. (See `http://www.w3.org/MarkUp/Activity.html`)

Educating User Agents

As we saw in the introduction, markup may have some real meaning to a user agent (or human) that understands it. To expand on our `<hemoglobin>14.2</hemoglobin>` example, we could identify this with a namespace that provides the means to interpret this information, say, `www.hypermedic.com/results/hemoglobin`. Somewhere at this URI would be the following table:

Hemoglobin ranges	Meaning	Expected user agent behavior
>17	Possibly dehydrated. In serious danger of stroke or death	0
16.1 - 17	Possibly dangerously high	1
13.1 - 16	Normal range	3
11.1 - 13	Anemia type=mild	3
9.1 - 11	Anemia type=moderate	3
7 - 9	Anemia type=severe	2
<7	Possibly life threatening	1
<4	EMERGENCY	0

Of course the strings are for human convenience only. The user agent would look at the integer in the final column that would trigger explicit responses.

A lab could then store all its hemoglobin results as an XML document as follows:

```
<meddoc xmlns= "www.hypermedic.com/results/hemoglobin">
      <hemoglogin date= "Sept2" id= "h001">14.2</hemoglobin>
      <hemoglogin date= "Sept2" id= "h002">12.2</hemoglobin>
      <hemoglogin date= "Sept2" id= "h003">16.2</hemoglobin>
...
</meddoc>
```

Now a compliant user agent could read through this document, access the relevant URI (remember it would have to have a mechanism for doing this) and use the information there to interpret a list of hemoglobin readings.

This hypothetical user agent would cross-reference the `id` values against patient records to get all the relevant details. It would then directly contact the patients' doctors about all the dangerous results (User Agent behavior = 1), and print out all the rather abnormal results (User Agent behavior = 2) for review by a technician. All the patients with life threatening results could be directly referred to an emergency center for immediate action.

Namespaces would have thus allowed the user agent to be 'educated' by sending it to a source where it can be 'taught' the meanings of the results.

With a little imagination I am sure that you can see all kinds of applications along these lines.

What a Namespace Isn't

Although a namespace employs a URI in its signature, that does not imply that information about how the elements are to be interpreted can be obtained from that site. Obviously for a namespace to be really useful, the user agent should have some knowledge on either how to use the namespace, or where to obtain that information.

However the present specification has as its object the purpose of merely identifying certain elements and attributes as belonging to a certain namespace. It leaves it up to the individual user agents to decide how to associate the namespace with a site where information can be obtained, how to interpret the information at that site, and how to act on that information. We have speculated a little below on some of the ways that this could be done, but we would emphasize that this is purely our speculation. Future standards will hopefully define the specific mechanisms.

Expected User Agent Behavior

It is important to realize that the new namespace specification merely represents the first step in a many step process. In this section we will look at what behavior is expected from a user agent in order to conform to the current specification, and we will speculate a little about what may be expected of a user agent in the future.

Presently a user agent is merely expected to associate each element or attribute with a namespace in order to make it unique. In the future a user agent may be expected to acquire a 'knowledge' of its expected behavior. This may be built-in, as is the case for HTML in the present browsers, or a 'protocol of learning' may be established.

In the future a user agent may be able to go to a named authority to see how it should behave (as for the hemoglobin example above). In this case the user agent will probably go to that authority to acquire a set of 'learning behaviors' to exhibit when it comes across an element in the `http://www.hypermedic.com/results/hemoglobin` namespace, another when it comes across an element belonging to the `http://www.hypermedic.com/results/electrolytes` namespace, and perhaps a third when it came across the `http://www.harvardlabs.org/hemoglobin` namespace.

Another example may be when an XSL (Extensible Style Language) enabled browser may go to a site and find out how the tags should be rendered as flow objects.

Namespace Applications

Namespaces are already being used by several XML applications. Here are just three of the many.

Internet Explorer 5 (Style Sheets)

The Beta1 release of IE5 makes use of namespaces in the application of styling to XML tags in an HTML document. This is covered in detail in Chapters 7 and 8. We will just show another quick example here.

The W3C namespaces draft specification was changed often during the development of Microsoft's Beta1 release of IE5. In the Beta1 release Microsoft have used their own version of a namespace declaration using an empty tag as is seen below. It is probable that by the time you read this the namespace will be declared in a way compatible with the specification.

The following example shows how to apply CSS (Cascading Style Sheets) styling to an XML tag incorporated in an HTML document. Another example can be found in Chapter 8. Don't worry too much about the details of the code at this point; all we're really interested are those elements that utilize the namespaces syntax.

```
<HTML>

<xml:namespace prefix="myns"/>

<STYLE TYPE="text/css">

      .wroxstyle1{
            display:block;
            padding-top:36pt;
            font-size:56pt;
            font-weight:bold;
            text-align:center;
            background-color:red;
            color:yellow;
            }


      .wroxstyle2{
            display:block;
            padding-bottom:36pt;
            font-size:30pt;
            font-weight:bold;
            text-align:center;
            background-color:red;
            color:yellow;
            }
</STYLE>

<BODY BGCOLOR="white" id="body">
      <P>An example of an using a namespace to apply style to an XML tag</P>

      <xtag1>The default display property for an unknown tag is inline.</xtag1>
      <xtag2>As is demonstrated here</xtag2>
```

```
        <myns:xtag class="wroxstyle1">Style Sheets</myns:xtag>
        <myns:xtag class="wroxstyle2">for HTML and XML</myns:xtag>

    </BODY>
    </HTML>
```

Note how the application recognizes that the `myns:xtag` element is in the Microsoft `xml:namespace`, and so is able to apply the CSS styling to them. This is an example of a 'educated' user agent.

If you run the above in IE5 this is what you will see:

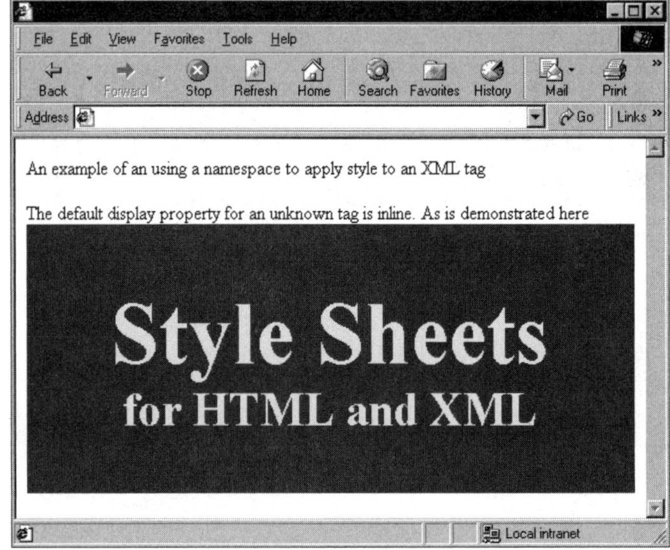

XSL

The new XSL (Extensible Style Language) syntax is described in Chapter 8. XSL makes use of namespaces to identify both its own tags, and also the formatting vocabulary tags.

Here is our first full XSL example taken from Chapter 8. Again, don't worry too much about the specifics of the code – just observe how the namespaces are used.

```
<stylesheet
     xmlns:xsl="http//www.w3.org/TR/WD-xsl"
     xmlns:fo="http//www.w3.org/TR/WD-xsl/FO"
     result-ns="fo">

     <xsl:template match="/">
          <fo:page-sequence
               font-family="times new roman,serif"
               font-size="12pt">
               <xsl:apply-templates/>
          </fo:page-sequence>
     </xsl:template>
```

```
    <xsl:template match="*">
        <fo:block
            font-family="times new roman,serif"
            font-size="12pt">
            <xsl:apply-templates/>
        </fo:block>
    </xsl:template>

    <xsl:template match="sheepobject">
        <fo:block
            font-size="16pt">
            <xsl:text>YES I CAN!</xsl:text>
            <xsl:apply-templates/>
            <xsl:apply-templates/>
            <xsl:apply-templates/>
            <xsl:apply-templates/>
        </fo:block>
    </xsl:template>
</stylesheet>
```

Note how all the tags with the `xsl:` prefix are in the `http//www.w3.org/TR/WD-xsl` namespace, and all those with the `fo:` prefix are in the `http//www.w3.org/TR/WD-xsl/FO` namespace.

Now the intelligent and educated user agent, the XSL/XML browser/styler, will know what set of rules and actions to apply to which element.

We could of course take advantage of scoping to write the document in a more elegant manner! Here is what the example looks like using `http//www.w3.org/TR/WD-xsl` as the default namespace. The rendering of the document should be exactly the same!

```
<stylesheet
    xmlns ="http//www.w3.org/TR/WD-xsl"
    xmlns:fo="http//www.w3.org/TR/WD-xsl/FO"
    result-ns="fo">

    <template match="/">
        <fo:page-sequence
            font-family="times new roman,serif"
            font-size="12pt">
            <xsl:apply-templates/>
        </fo:page-sequence>
    </template>

    <template match="*">
        <fo:block
            font-family="times new roman,serif"
            font-size="12pt">
            <apply-templates/>
        </fo:block>
    </template>

    <template match="sheepobject">
        <fo:block
            font-size="16pt">
            <text>YES I CAN!</text>
```

```
                    <apply-templates/>
                    <apply-templates/>
                    <apply-templates/>
                    <apply-templates/>
               </fo:block>
          </template>
     </stylesheet>
```

The use of namespaces in the style sheets allows the user agent to determine which elements carry which type of instruction.

Now we move on to look at the importance of namespaces in metadata.

RDF

Resource Description Framework is a 'standard in the making' that makes very heavy use of namespaces. Although everything on the Web is machine readable, the machines can't understand what they are reading. RDF is the first step in allowing machines to 'understand' Web-content, in that it provides interoperability between applications that exchange machine understandable information.

The latest RDF specification can be found at `http://www.w3.org/TR/WD-rdf-syntax`

Basic RDF

We won't attempt to show you RDF in great detail here; we will just look at enough to show how and why namespaces are necessary.

RDF is about metadata, or structured data about data, describing named properties and property values, and their relationship to each other. The goal of RDF is to improve the discovery of and access to information.

Take the following sentence that describes the relationship between Wrox Press and their Web page.

"Wrox Press is the creator of `http://www.wrox.com`"

In RDF terminology any Web object such as the above URI is a resource, and resources can be described by a set of tags that are included in the RDF namespace. Here is how the above resource would be defined

```
<RDF xmlns="http://www.w3.org/TR/WD-rdf-syntax">
     <description about="http://wrox.com"/>
</RDF>
```

This of course tells us that both the element `description` and its attribute `about` are in the `http://www.w3.org/TR/WD-rdf-syntax` namespace, so that an intelligent user agent educated about RDF will know how to interpret the results. To be meaningful to the users of RDF data, the description needs to use markup from the namespace associated with the resource that is being described.

Now of course we may want to include information about "Wrox Press" so that a user agent searching the Web would be able to find out something about Wrox Press.

Furthermore, we may want to describe Wrox Press and a few of its books to user agents that know the Dublin Core standard metadata element set; or describe them to a publishers' association that provides some standard elements for publishers' Web sites.

> *For more information on Dublin Core Metadata Standards visit* `http://purl.org/metadata/dublin_core`

The namespace for the publisher's association could be `http://www.bigpublishers.org`. Wrox Press could then use their elements to say a little about their own Web site.

The XML document below illustrates matters more clearly. It could be the case that two or more organizations constructing metadata resources describing the contents of their 'archives' are likely to use similar tag names but conceivably with different intent. Thus namespaces prevent confusion of interpretation when multi-source (meta-) metadata files are composed (e.g. by a search engine searching over many domains.) The following RDF metadata file contains information about Wrox relevant to both a Dublin Core compatible catalog and the publishers' association.

```
<RDF xmlns= "http://www.w3.org/TR/WD-rdf-syntax"
     xmlns:dc=http://purl.org/metadata/dublin_core#
     xmlns:pub="http://www.publishers.org">
     <!-- this tag is in the rdf namespace-->
     <description about="http://wrox.com">
          <!--these tags are in the publishers namespace-->
          <pub:webpage>
               <pub:url>www.wrox.com</pub:url>
               <pub:sitetitle>Wrox Press</pub:sitetitle>
               <pub:sitecontent type="computer">Computer Books
              </pub:sitecontent>
          </pub:webpage>
          <pub:booktitles>
            <pub:book authors="multiple" isbn="1525">
               <pub:title>Professional XML Applications</pub:title>
               <pub:description>How to make XML work for you</pub:description>
               <dc:Creator>
                    <rdf:Seq ID="CreatorsAlphabeticalBySurname">
                    <rdf:li> Boumphrey, Frank </rdf:li>
                    <rdf:li> Hollander, Dave </rdf:li>
                    <rdf:li> others</rdf:li>
                    </rdf:Seq>
               </dc:Creator>
            </pub:book>
            <pub:book authors="Frank Boumphrey" isbn="1657">
               <pub:title>Professional Style Sheets for HTML and XML
               </pub:title>
               <pub:description>How to make your Web pages look great.
               </pub:description>
            </pub:book>
          </pub:booktitles>
     </description>
</RDF>
```

Without namespaces most useful metadata descriptions would be impossible. Namespaces have allowed us to create a single document that contains description information that is understandable to both carbon and silicon based agents trained in RDF, the particulars of the Dublin Core or the publishers' association.

Summary

In this chapter we have looked at what is potentially one of the most important specifications in the XML family. We have seen how namespaces give us the opportunity to reuse schemas, and how they have the potential to enrich Web applications by allowing them to be 'educated'.

We examined the syntax of the current specification, and saw how scoping made for ease of use in XML documents. We saw how it was possible to switch back and forth from one namespace to the other, and even go to a 'null' namespace.

Even though the present specification has a modest goal of allowing attributes and elements to be uniquely identified across the web, we saw how this could lead to important applications.

Lastly we looked at three areas that are making use of namespaces right now.

5

XML Links and Pointers

In this chapter we will have a look at how to use links in XML, and how XML links differ from the links in HTML. The linking standard is being designed separately from the present core XML 1.0 specification, but is intended to be fully part of the overall suite of standards for XML. There are two specifications, both of which are working drafts, which define links in XML:

- The **XLink** specification sets the standard as to how separate documents should link into one another. You can find it at `http://www.w3.org/TR/WD-xlink`

- The **XPointer** language is to be used in conjunction with XLink for addressing the structures within XML documents. It can been seen at `http://www.w3.org/TR/WD-xptr`

In this chapter we will look at:

- Simple links
- Extended linking
- How we can use pointers to define parts of a document

XLink and XPointer used to be combined in one standard as XLL (XML Linking Language), and this TLA (Three Letter Acronym!) is still widely used as an umbrella term, so if you see it you now know that it is referring to these two standards. Indeed, you will see the term XLL used several times in this chapter!

In addition a note outlining the design principles, also from March 1998 can be found at:

`http://www.w3.org/TR/NOTE-xlink-principles`

While these specifications have a tendency to alter as they develop along the W3C process, it is expected that the final proposed recommendation will be similar to the March Working Draft document. An XML Linking Working Group has now been formed to work on the Linking standards.

Unfortunately, as with much of XML there is no implementation of the W3C standard as yet, so much of what we will be writing about will be abstract, and falls into the "won't this be cool when they implement it" category. However, before you consider skipping this chapter, it will provide an important background to the different methods of linking in XML. While it may not be of practical use today, it could well affect your design considerations when it comes to implementing an XML application.

Having said a little about the standard, let's take a brief look at linking in HTML so that we can then see how linking in XML differs from it.

Linking in HTML

It can be plausibly argued that the initial success of the HTTP format, over, say, the FTP format, was largely due to the ease with which one could link to another document.

In HTML, we link to another document with the `<A>` tag. The type of link used in HTML is referred to in XML as a simple link.

Simple links

Here are two minimal HTML documents, which should be located in the same folder or directory.

ch05_docA.htm

```
<HTML>
<A HREF= "ch05_docB.htm">This hyperlink will take you to ch05_docB.htm</A>
</HTML>
```

ch05_docB.htm

```
<HTML>
<A HREF= "ch05_docA.htm">This hyperlink will take you to ch05_docA.htm</A>
</HTML>
```

Load these up in the same directory, open one of them, and then click on the hyperlink. You can have endless hours of fun just going from one to another!

Some Terminology

The following paragraph will serve to introduce you to some of the jargon surrounding links. We will go into more detail, and give more formal definitions later on, but because we are all familiar with the HTML link this will serve as a good starting point.

The links we have just seen are **simple** links. The **link** is what you click on. When you click on a link the user agent looks for the **locator** or **address**, which is the URL (e.g. ch05_docA.htm). Clicking on the link takes you from one **resource** to another **resource**. A document or part of a document is a resource. Note that both ch05_docA and ch05_docB are **participating resources**. When I click on the link in ch05_docA, ch05_docA is acting as the **source**, and ch05_docB is acting as the **destination**. This is an **inline** link because it serves as one of its own resources. (We will see what an out-of-line link is when we study XML extended links later in this chapter.)

Note that there is a difference between linking and addressing that we will look at next.

Difference Between Linking and Addressing

At this point we need to distinguish between linking and addressing, two terms which are often confused and used interchangeably, but which are in fact subtly different.

If I say that two items are linked, all I am doing is establishing a relationship between the two. For example, Wrox Press and Frank Boumphrey are linked in that Frank Boumphrey writes books for Wrox Press.

Addressing on the other hand is about how to find the objects being linked. Both Frank Boumphrey and Wrox Press have e-mail and snail (postal) mail addresses, and they also have Web sites with their own domains and URLs. If we have this information we know *how* to make a connection between the two.

In our simple example above ch05_docA and ch05_docB are linked. They also have addresses, their URIs. Because ch05_docA contains the address of ch05_docB, and vice-versa the link between them is a simple one, if we had to refer to another document or resource to get this information, then the link would be an extended link. In HTML there is no direct mechanism for creating an extended link.

Pointers in HTML

As stated pointer is used for addressing *into* a document. The pointer identifies a specific area inside the document using some means or another, in the case of the following example, which works in IE4+, the id of an individual element is used.

Here is another minimal HTML document, note how the paragraphs are identified using an id. It is called ch05_docD.htm

```
<HTML>
<A HREF= "ch05_docC.htm">This hyperlink will take you to ch05_docC.htm</A><BR>
"Lorem ipsum etc"
<P ID="a1">Here is the first paragraph with an id of a1</P>
"Lorem ipsum dolor  etc"
<P ID="a2">Here is the second paragraph with an id of a2</P>
"Lorem ipsum dolor sit etc."
<P ID="a3">Here is the third paragraph with an id of a3</P>
"Lorem ipsum dolor sit amet, etc"
</HTML>
```

(Please don't try to translate the "Lorem ipsum...", it is mock text used in the publishing industry to fill in parts of a document during an initial layout process but before the real copy has arrived.)

And here is a minimalist document with links and pointers that point into the document using the ids as identifiers. This is ch05_docC.htm

```
<HTML>
<BR><A HREF= "ch05_docD.htm#a1">This hyperlink will take you to the first
paragraph of      ch05_docD.htm</A>
<BR><A HREF= "ch05_docD.htm#a2">This hyperlink will take you to the second
paragraph  of ch05_docD.htm</A>
<BR><A HREF= "ch05_docD.htm#a3">This hyperlink will take you to the third
paragraph of      ch05_docD.htm</A>
</HTML>
```

Now when you click on the link, the link will point into the target document, and should take you to the relevant paragraph.

In fact this document is so small you would not see this effect, because the whole document can be displayed on one page. To see the effect clearly, add in some 'junk' text.

The part of the URL beginning with a hash mark (#) is the fragment identifier, which in this case is the id of the element.

In XML the syntax would have to be written `<A HREF= "ch05_docD.htm#id(a1)">`, (note the addition of id telling us the type of pointer). The use of id as a pointer only works in IE 4+ browsers.

Note, however, that using this XML syntax I require nothing special to get to a place in ch05_docD; "ch05_docD.htm#id(a1)" has all the information necessary to find the required place. I can point into a document, and it can be any document provided it has elements with id attributes. I do not have to have physical access to ch05_docD in order to insert a special place to link to.

Note how this is very different from using the familiar syntax:

```
<A NAME= "a1"></A>
```

Here I have to have physical access to ch05_docD in order to place the other end of my link. This is not a pointer because you have to put something unique and special into the document in order to get to the place you want to go.

With XML-style syntax when you point to the id you are pointing to a place in the document with a certain id, a property that has many other uses. Provided ch05_docD has tags with ids, I do not need access to ch05_docD in order to point into it.

We can make this clearer with a simple analogy. The unique thing about a pointer is that it points. If I am out for a walk with my child I can point to a leaf on the ground and say pick up that red leaf. If I was using some thing like the NAME method of location I would say, "There is a leaf over there, I am going to go over and mark it with this special tag, then I want you to go over and pick it up".

As we shall see XPointers for XML carries this concept, the concept of being able to point into a document to which we have no access, much further.

Having briefly reviewed the familiar and got used to some of the jargon surrounding XLL, let's move on to Links and Pointers in XML. We will look at the terminology in more detail as we go. If you are more comfortable with a full explanation of the terminology you can read the section entitled *A Review of Terminology* now?

Simple Links in XML

Simple links in XML are very similar to HTML links. However, whereas in HTML the HTML-aware user agent knows that an <A> tag is a link (technically an anchor in HTML terminology) tag, in XML we have to let the XML user agent know that the tag is a linking tag. We also have to let it know what type of link it is.

Specifying 'Link' Tags

Consider the following well-formed XML document.

```
<linkdoc>
      <para>Comment can be found at <mylink href="DocumentA.htm">Document
      </mylink>where all
               is explained
        </para>
      <para>
              <mylink href="DocumentB.htm">Document B</mylink> can be found here
        </para>
</linkdoc>
```

This document obviously contains links to both `DocumentA` and `DocumentB`. It is also obvious to us (because of our understanding of English and of HTML), that the `<mylink>` tag is indeed a link tag, and the value of the `href` attribute is the address, or more specifically the URL, of the resource that we want to link to.

However, the XML user agent, can't see this. For all it is concerned we might have called the tag `<wroxlink>`, `<address>`, or even `<timbuctoo>`! We therefore need to have a way to inform the user agent that this link should indeed be treated as a link.

In an XLink compliant browser we would be able to do this by using the XML reserved and designated attribute `xml:link`. This can take the following values:

`simple` `extended` `group` `locator` `document`

> `simple` *describes a link similar to that employed by the* <A> *element in HTML. The others will be new concepts to HTML folk and will be described in some detail below.*

By adding the XML reserved attribute `xml:link = "simple"` we now have the following:

```
<linkdoc>
     <para>Comment can be found at
           <mylink xml:link="simple" href="DocumentA.htm">Document A</mylink>
where all is explained
       </para>
```

```
        <para>
              <mylink xml:link="simple" href="DocumentB.htm">Document B</mylink> can
be found here
        </para>
</linkdoc>
```

So, now an XLink aware browser would be able to tell that when we click on the text we are meant to be taken to the relevant address.

For a document to be valid, of course, we would need to define our attributes in the DTD. We would do this as follows:

```
<!ELEMENT mylink (#PCDATA)>
<!ATTLIST mylink
      xml:link    CDATA          #FIXED          "simple"
      href        CDATA          #REQUIRED
>
```

The advantage of this, of course, is that by making the `xml:link` attribute `#FIXED`, we no longer have to include it in our tag, its presence is always assumed.

The astute may have been asking the question, "But what about the `href` attribute? I don't see any XML prefix with this!"

The XLink specification in fact provides several predefined names for attributes and these are laid out in the specification. These attributes extend the role of even a simple link to much more than is possible in HTML with the `<A>` element. We will have a look at these next.

Suggested XLink Attributes

The following is a list of the suggested attributes with their permitted values. Taken together they can expand the usefulness of even a simple link. Remember that XML is case sensitive.

```
xml:link       (simple|extended|group|locator|document)       'simple'
```

```
href      CDATA                    #REQUIRED
```

```
inline      (true|false)          'true'
```

```
role         CDATA                #IMPLIED
```

```
title        CDATA                #IMPLIED
```

```
show         (embed|replace|new)           #IMPLIED
```

```
actuate      (auto|user)          #IMPLIED
```

```
behavior        CDATA                      #IMPLIED
```

Let's have a look at each in turn.

xml:link

As we have noted already the behavior of the simple link is very similar to the HTML link. We will be having a look at the other values in some detail later on in this chapter.

href

This is a locator, which essentially consists of an address. In practice this consists of an URI plus or minus an XPointer. We will be looking at XPointers in detail in the second part of this chapter. For now here are a couple of examples of acceptable values which should be familiar to you.

Same Directory Resource:	`"documentB.htm"`
Same Directory Resource + XPointer	`"documentB.htm#a1"`
Distant Resource	`"http://www.hypermedic.com/documentC.htm"`
Distant Resource + XPointer	`"http://www.hypermedic.com/documentC.htm#a1"`

inline

All simple links must take the value of `true`. Most other links are also inline. We will look at an out-of-line link, whose value is `false`, later on.

role

This is a utility attribute to signal to the user agent the meaning of the link. The string value of the `role` attribute is most likely to be used by the user agent as a means of providing the user with further information about the destination link before she 'clicks' on the link.

title

This is self-explanatory; it is the title of the link. One suggested use of the `title` attribute is to have the user agent display it (the title) when there is a mouse-over or such event.

show

If the value of `replace` is taken then the new resource replaces the old. This is the traditional method in HTML.

If the value of `new` is taken then a new window is opened. This can also be achieved in HTML using a simple script.

If the value of `embed` is taken the new resource will be embedded in the old. This is also possible with a LOT of scripting in HTML and an IE4+ browser.

In the following example:

```
<linkdoc>
      <para>Comment can be found at
               <mylink xml:link="simple" href="DocumentA.htm" show="embed">document
A</mylink>
               where all is explained
          </para>
</linkdoc>
```

DocumentA would be embedded in the source document, presumably at the location of the 'clickable hotspot' (link) in the source document.

actuate

This is used with extended links. Upon retrieving one resource of an extended link, the resource attached to the link with the value of auto will also be retrieved. If the value of the link is user some user action is required to retrieve the resource. This should become clear to you when you have read about extended links.

behavior

behavior describes what can happen when the link is traversed. The user may be presented with a fresh window, a drop down list etc. The behaviors that are possible are dictated by the user agent, however behavior can indicate suggested values. The behavior attribute provides a handy receptacle for indicating the behavior required.

Presumably an XLink compliant user agent will have a built in understanding of these attributes, but they should still be declared in the DTD for the document to be valid.

The only absolutely essential attributes that a link must have are xml:link and href.

xml:attribute

It is possible that we may want to use an element as a link element that already has an attribute with the same name as those which we have just met. title is the most obvious candidate for this scenario, for example we may have a book element which already has a title attribute. In this case XLink gives us a means to map the "known" attribute using the xml:attribute attribute in a process called attribute remapping.

The following example is taken from the March specification.

I have a <text-book> element that I want to have take the attributes title and role. title of course being the title of the text book, and role being type of use it will be put to. Its role could be either a primary book in the course I am teaching, or it will play a supporting role.

Here's what the element and attribute declaration might look like:

```
<!ELEMENT text-book ANY>
<!ATTLIST text-book
     title       CDATA                          #IMPLIED
     role        (PRIMARY|SUPPORTING)           #IMPLIED
>
```

I now want to make this a link element, but the attributes `title` and `role` have already been assigned. What do I do?

This is where the `xml:attribute` attribute comes to the rescue. By taking the default XLink name (`role`, `href`, `title`, `show`, `inline`, `actuate`, `behavior`, `steps`) and the replacement name (separated by whitespace) as the value, it is possible to then reference the XLink name using the replacement name. If more than one replacement is required, the value of the `xml:attribute` attribute can be several of these pairs separated by whitespace.

The second name can now be used in place of the default XLink name. The user agent when it sees the second name will automatically map it to the first.

The attribute list would now look like the following:

```
<!ATTLIST text-book
     title            CDATA                         #IMPLIED
     role             (PRIMARY|SUPPORTING)          #IMPLIED
     xml:link         CDATA                         #FIXED "simple"
     xml:attributes   CDATA
                            #FIXED "title xl-title role xl-role"
>
```

Now when the XLink compliant user agent comes across the following code:

```
     <text-book  title="Professional Style Sheets"
           role="PRIMARY"
           xl-title="Primary text book for the course"
           xl-role="ONLINE-PURCHASE"
           href="http://www.wrox.com"/>
```

it will recognize `xl-title` and `xl-role` as playing the parts of `role` and `title` as described in the XLink specification.

Summary of XML Simple Links

At its simplest the XML simple link is an inline link very similar to the linking `A` element of HTML. It is identified to the user agent by the reserved attribute of `xml:link`. If this link just took the `href` attribute it would be just the same as an `A` link. The other XLink attributes, however, give it added functionality, especially the `show` attribute that can specify how the resource at the other end of the link should be displayed.

XLink Compatible User Agents

The trouble with what we have seen so far and what is to follow, indeed the problem with most 'bleeding-edge' specifications, is that there is no user agent which implements the specification. The use of the XLink specification in a document does not preclude the use of other linking specifications and any implementation is left up to the user agent.

As we do not yet even have an XML compliant browser, we certainly don't have an XLink or an XPointer compliant one!

A Review of Terminology.

Before going on to a discussion of extended links, let us review some of the terminology in a more formal manner than we have to date.

The following is taken from the March specification. Our comments and clarifications have been put in italics.

1.3 Terminology

The following basic terms apply in this document.

element tree

A representation of the relevant structure specified by the tags and attributes in an XML document, based on "groves" as defined in the ISO DSSSL standard.

A full explanation of trees can be found in Chapter 6, which is on the DOM. We will also cover this in somewhat less detail when we cover pointers further in this chapter.

inline link

Abstractly, a link which serves as one of its own resources. Concretely, a link where the content of the linking element serves as a participating resource. HTML `A`, HyTime `clink`, and TEI `XREF` are all examples of inline links.

If the link is actually embedded in a document that you can read, and if you can click on something and get somewhere we are talking about an inline link. If the links and addresses are contained in a separate resource then we are talking about an out-of-line link. The examples given under extended links will hopefully clarify this definition.

link

An explicit relationship between two or more data objects or portions of data objects.

Note that a link is different from an address. A link is just the declaration of a relationship between two resources.

linking element

An element that asserts the existence and describes the characteristics of a link.

local resource

The content of an inline linking element. Note that the content of the linking element could be explicitly pointed to by means of a regular locator in the same linking element, in which case the resource is considered remote, not local.
In the following code:

```
<P> Click <A HREF= "somedoc.htm"> here </A> to link to some doc.
```

`'here'` is the local resource.

locator

Data, provided as part of a link, which identifies a resource.

The locator is usually a URL or a fragment identifier.

multidirectional link

A link whose traversal can be initiated from more than one of its participating resources. Note that being able to "go back" after following a one-directional link does not make the link multidirectional.

out-of-line link

A link whose content does not serve as one of the link's participating resources . Such links presuppose a notion like extended link groups, which indicate to application software where to look for links. Out-of-line links are generally required for supporting multidirectional traversal and for allowing read-only resources to have outgoing links.

participating resource

A resource that belongs to a link. All resources are potential contributors to a link; participating resources are the actual contributors to a particular link.

remote resource

Any participating resource of a link that is pointed to with a locator.

resource

In the abstract sense, an addressable service or unit of information that participates in a link. Examples include files, images, documents, programs, and query results. Concretely, anything reachable by the use of a locator in some linking element. Note that this term and its definition are taken from the basic specifications governing the World Wide Web.

If it has an address that you can use to locate it by clicking on a hotspot then it is a resource. This could be an image, a database, another document, or even code that can be used to construct some kind of display. A 'hotspot' is an old multi-media term. In a document it is any place that reacts in some way when the cursor isolates it in some way, either with a click, a mouse-over, etc.

sub-resource

A portion of a resource, pointed to as the precise destination of a link. As one example, a link might specify that an entire document be retrieved and displayed, but that some specific part(s) of it is the specific linked data, to be treated in an application-appropriate manner such as indication by highlighting, scrolling, etc.

We may in fact just want to retrieve part of a document. This part would be termed a sub-resource. See the first of the later XPointer examples.

traversal

The action of using a link; that is, of accessing a resource. Traversal may be initiated by a user action (for example, clicking on the displayed content of a linking element) or occur under program control.

In other words the act of going from one resource to another.

Extended Links

Simple links are indeed simple. We start off in one resource, click on a link, and usually end up either in or with another resource. They are extremely versatile, and as we have already stated they are probably the reason that the Web really caught the popular imagination and took off.

They do, however, have their limitations. Consider the following snippet from an HTML document.

```
<P>This is the report of a debate on the origins of the cold war.</P>
<P>
      <BR><A HREF="intro.htm">Introduction</A>
      <BR><A HREF="propos.htm">Proposal</A>
      <BR><A HREF="rebut.htm" >Rebuttal</A>
      <BR><A HREF="comment.htm">Commentary</A>
      <BR><A HREF="summary.htm">Summary</A>
</P>
```

Here is what the same might look like in an XML document fragment:

```
<para>This is the report of a debate on the origins of the cold war.</para>
<para>
      <debate-link xml:link="simple" href="intro.xml">Introduction</debate-link>
      <debate-link xml:link="simple" href="propos.xml">Proposal</debate-link>
      <debate-link xml:link="simple" href="rebut.xml" >Rebuttal</debate-link>
      <debate-link xml:link="simple" href="comment.xml">Commentary</debate-link>
      <debate-link xml:link="simple" href="summary.xml">Summary</debate-link>
</para>
```

The following screen shot shows how a browser may display either of the above.

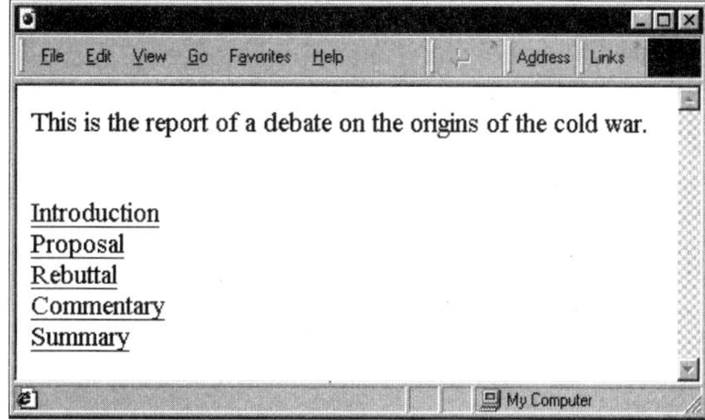

This is certainly serviceable, and achieves what we want, but the XLink specification provides a better way to handle affairs by allowing extended links.

Inline Extended Links

Here is what the above code would look like expressed as an inline extended link.

```
<xdoc>
<para>
This is the report of

      <mylink xml:link="extended" inline="true" title="Debate">
            <locator xml:link="locator" href="intro.xml" title="Introduction"/>
            <locator xml:link="locator" href="propos.xml" title="Proposal"/>
            <locator xml:link="locator" href="rebut.xml" title="Rebuttal"/>
            <locator xml:link="locator" href="comment.xml" title="Commentary"/>
            <locator xml:link="locator" href="summary.xml" title="Summary"/>

      a debate

      </mylink>

  on the origins of the cold war.

</para>
</xdoc>
```

Note the following:

- We now have a single link `mylink` which takes the attribute values of `xml:link = 'extended'`, `inline = 'true'`, and `title = 'debate'`.
- This element by itself is pretty useless, it's rather like an empty office building, it looks pretty, but it can't accomplish much without office equipment and workers. All it does is provide a housing for the working elements. In this case the working element is the `locator` element which gives the address and information about our links.
- The `locator` elements in this example take the attributes `xml:link = "locator"`, `href = [URI]`, `title = [CDATA]`.
- The `locator` element could have been called anything we wanted, such as `debate-link` that we used in the example of the simple link. We just called it `locator` to make the point that that is what it is.

- Note that this is an inline link, because it acts as one of the resources, namely the clickable text 'a debate'.
- The extended link element can also house other elements, namely the group and the document elements, which we will look at shortly.
- The extended link element can take other attributes and we will have a look at these later on.
- The locator link element can also take other attributes, and we will also have a look at these.

How the XML aware browser handles an extended element when it comes across one is entirely up to the browser. It is possible that it may just display the links when it loads the page, which would produce a result very similar to the last simple example. It is possible it may display them when the user clicks on the extended element's contents, and simply re-flow the document round them.

More likely it will create some kind of drop down box allowing the user to make a further selection as in the following screen shot. (Note this is a 'rigged' shot, no XML browser with these capabilities exists yet!)

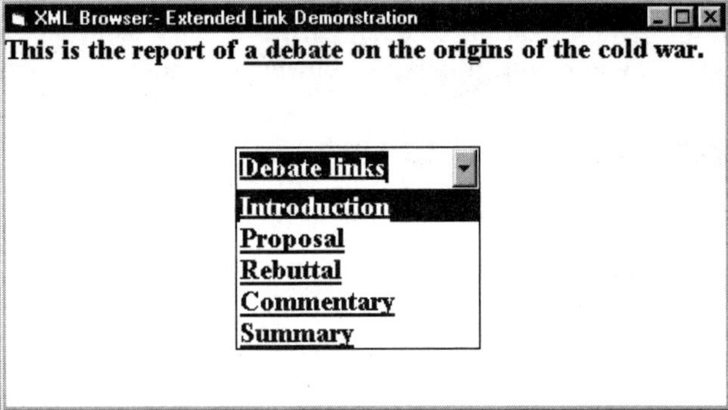

Note especially that, in this example, the header displays the mylink element title value, and the dropdown list displays the titles of the respective locator elements.

If we had added a role attribute, when we hovered our pointer over the link the role text might appear, for example in a small yellow box, but such details are of course up to the user agent. The specification merely makes these refinements possible.

Out-of-line Extended Links

In the last example the link is inline because there is something that can be clicked on, namely the string 'a debate'. It is quite possible though for the links to reside in a completely different document as is shown below.

Note that although this is a valid XML file, it is not meant for display, indeed there is nothing in the file that can be displayed. All the file does is define links between the various documents and provide their addresses.

```
<xdoc>

<!--The following is an example of an out-of-line, extended link.-->

      <mylink xml:link="extended" inline="false" title="Out-of-line example">
            <locator xml:link="locator" href="DocA.htm" title="Document A"/>
            <locator xml:link="locator" href="DocA.htm" title="Document B"/>
            <locator xml:link="locator" href="DocA.htm" title="Document C"/>
```

```
        </mylink>

    <!-- Note that this link is NOT a resource. It is merely a file establishing links
    between the various documents.-->

    </xdoc>
```

Also note that the documents that this link document refers to are probably not even aware they are being referred to, or perhaps that they are being linked together.

A similar situation exists in real life. My daughter is referring to Leonardo DiCaprio all the time, and I say "Yes when I was a lad we used to refer to Sean Connery in the same way".

Our statements link Leo and Shawn, but I am sure that neither is aware of our interest in them. I am sure, however, that both are very much aware that there is a considerable general interest in them, and they may also be aware in a general way that comparisons may be made.

I happen to have a Web site (`www.hypermedic.com`, never miss an opportunity to advertise!), and I am sure that several other sites link to it, but unless I stumble upon one I am not aware of it.

The following diagram illustrates this point.

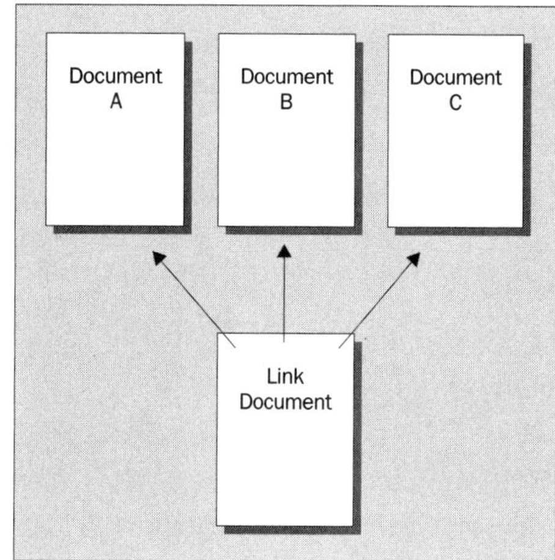

Note that the flow of information is entirely one way! There is no 'flow' back from the document that is being linked to, neither do any of the documents have any 'awareness' that they are linked in any way.

"Alright" you may ask, "and what good does this do? How does this further our cause?"

As the specification puts it:

> A key issue with out-of-line extended links is how linking application software can manage and find them, particularly when they are stored in completely separate documents from those in which their participating resources appear.

The fact is that by itself an out-of-line link is pretty useless. However, if it is combined with a suitable user agent, all kinds of wonderful things are possible, and that is the subject of our next section.

Uses For Extended Out-of-line Links

Of course it goes without saying that there is no user agent available that does all the wonderful things we are going to describe, but then you might be reading this book because you are going to create this software! Lets look at various scenarios where software might employ out of line links.

A Small Intranet

In this scenario we have several documents, `doc 1`, `doc 2`, `doc 3...` `doc n`, none of which have a single link in them, however they are all linked together by out-of-line links contained in several documents, `link1`, `link 2`, `link 3....` `link n`.

Let us assume that we want to be able to access any of the document's links by right clicking on the document. (Sorry we have a PC. I suppose you could accuse us of being platformist! Well for you Mac users click and hold down *shift* at the same time.)

The software needs to maintain a database with all the links in it (and it will have to create this, see below). Suppose the user right clicks on `doc m`. There happen to be two out-of-line links documents with references to the following links:

The first reference is in a group of documents called `Annual Report` contained in `report-links.xml`:

```
<xdoc>

      <mylink xml:link="extended" inline="false" title="annual report">
            <locator xml:link="locator" href="docM.xml" title="Document M"/>
            <locator xml:link="locator" href="sales.htm" title="Quarterly sales
            _reports"/>
            <locator xml:link="locator" href="production.htm" title="Quarterly
            _Production output"/>
      </mylink>

</xdoc>
```

The second reference is contained in a group of documents called `Think Tank` contained in `think-tank-links.xml`:

```
<xdoc>

      <mylink xml:link="extended" inline="false" title="Think Tank">
            <locator xml:link="locator" href="docM.xml" title="Document M"/>
            <locator xml:link="locator" href="predict.htm" title="Future Widget
            _needs"/>
            <locator xml:link="locator" href="market.xml" title= "Marketing
            _stratergies for widgets."/>
      </mylink>

</xdoc>
```

In the intranet, which probably contains both XML and HTML documents my software has already looked through all the documents looking for links, indeed it does so whenever a new document is added. It will find every reference to `Document M` and it will list it in the `Document M` field.

If the reference to Document M is from a simple link, then the database will merely list the file that references it.

For example, here is a snippet from Document C, an HTML document:

```
<P> Comments on company progress can be found in <A HREF= "docM.xml">Document
</A> where future trends are discussed. </P>
```

The database would then contain the following link information (in some form) about Document M links.

Document M Links

Title	URI	Type	Associated links
Document C	docC.htm	Simple	Null
Think Tank	think-tank-links.xml	Extended	Sales.htm, production.htm
Annual Report	report-links.xml	Extended	predict.htm, market.xml

When a user right clicks on Document M she may very well be presented with a table very similar to the above, and links could be made by clicking on the appropriate URI.

While this approach is suitable for a small intranet, for a large intranet the number could soon get out of hand, and of course for the whole Web, who is going to maintain a suitable database? This leads us to our next example of a large intranet.

A Large Intranet

For a large intranet although it is obvious that link management is made much easier by extended out-of-line links, it is also obvious that a user may be presented with an overwhelming number of links when he right clicks the document.

Luckily the XLink specification provides a group and a document element to handle this situation.

In this scenario we still need a central database of all the links, and indeed this is added to each time a new document is added to the intranet collection. However, in the large intranet scenario each document also includes a group type of link. For example, Document J may have the following link element:

```
<docgroup xml:link="group">
      <doc xml:link="document" href="links1.xml"/>
      <doc xml:link="document" href="links2.xml"/>
      <doc xml:link="document" href="links3.xml"/>
</docgroup>
```

Note that this is very similar to the extended/location setup. Here group *is the containing element, and* document *is the element that contains the URI.*

This would tell the user agent that the links we are interested in are contained in these (presumably) out-of-line link documents.

What happens is that when we now right-click on our document, instead of going to the database, the user agent will just display the links in the `docgroup` element and then use the paths specified in the group statement to locate the files. Now we may have our user agent set up to follow up a whole line of links.

For example, `links1.xml` may contain a reference to `report.htm`, which has several references to URIs that have even more references, and very soon we would have more links than we would know how to deal with. In fact it is highly likely that if we followed link after link after link, we would lock up our computer, or even form a loop. To prevent this the XML specification provides the designated attribute `steps`, which tells the user agent how many levels to go to. Thus in the above example, if we wrote:

```
<docgroup xml:link="group" steps= "2">
        <doc xml:link="document" href="links1.xml"/>
        <doc xml:link="document" href="links2.xml"/>
        <doc xml:link="document" href="links3.xml"/>
</docgroup>
```

The user agent would know that it should not go further than two levels in its exploration of links. In this case we have access to the documents involved, after all they are on our own intranet. But what if we have no access to the documents at all? How can extended links help us? We will look into this shortly.

Some Notes on User Agent Behavior

Although it is not part of the specification, perhaps it is as well to say a little about user agent behavior here.

All the specification does is give a standard set of tools for user agents to employ, and a standard language that we can embed in the document that should trigger user agent behavior. For example the specification makes no recommendation about how the user agent manages group links, all it says are that these links are some how grouped together.

One user agent may make provide a drop down list box of the links, another may provide a short synopsis.

Again the specification says nothing about how a user agent should treat an out-of-line link. All the document says is that these documents are related. Again different user agents may convey this information in different ways. One may provide a drop down list when we right click on the document, another may provide a status bar with that information.

Adding to Remote Documents

Supposing a rival company (Rival Inc.) has put up a document on the Internet and we want our executives to read it and post comments about it that can be accessed by other people in our company (Acme Ltd.). How can we go about this?

Here is the document that we want our exec's to read.

```
<rivaldoc>

     <para>Our company is the greatest.</para>
     <para>Acme company is the worst.</para>
     <para>We float like a butterfly and sting like a bee.</para>
     <para>Acme is ugly.</para>
     <para>We are going to bury Acme.</para>
     <para>Our widgets are the greatest!</para>

</rivaldoc>
```

We, of course, have no access to Rival Inc.'s source documents, even though we can of course view their outputted documents. Here is what the above looks like when we load it into our browser.

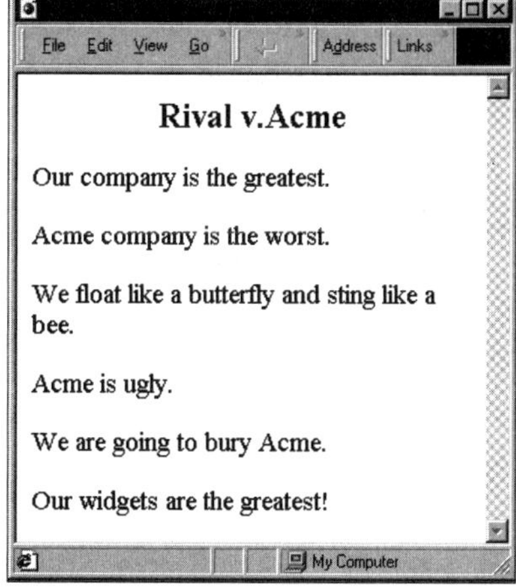

In fact, we have special user software that allows us to post comments on the above document. When the Rival document is downloaded, our user agent substitutes a version that will record the various comments of our executives on it. We have assigned various symbols to our executives. All they have to do is click on the document and record their comments, rather like the 'comment' feature in Word. The symbol then becomes part of the document in our data source. Of course if Rival is really smart they will change their document at regular intervals, thereby frustrating our efforts! The fellow executives can read these comments just by clicking on the symbols.

Here is what the document may look like after our executives have finished with it:

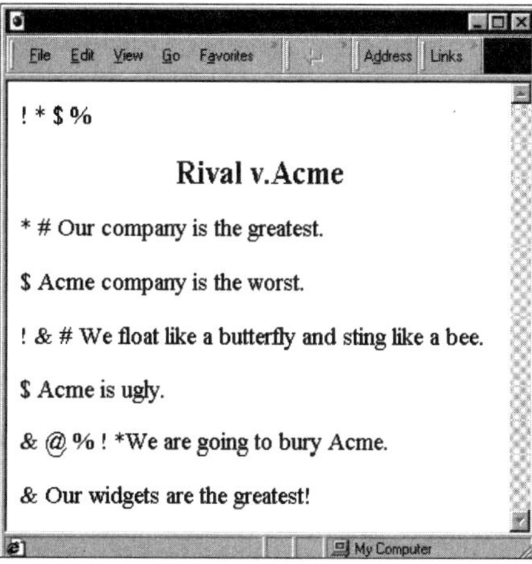

Each symbol represents a link to the comments of one of our executives. The dollar sign represents the comments from Bob Rich and the hash mark the comments from Joe Sycophant, then by clicking on a dollar sign we would be able to see the comments of Bob Rich, on the hash mark those of Joe Sycophant, etc.

How the user agent stores and organizes the comments is of course up to the user agent. However one way it could do this would be to keep each separate comment as a document that is accessed when the viewer clicks on the appropriate symbol. This comment could either be embedded in the original document, and have the whole document reflow, or it could appear in a separate popup window

Maintaining Links

One of the biggest headaches of any Webmaster is broken links. If we have a thousand pages on our Web site, 300 of which have a link to Widget Manufacturers Association, if Widget Manufacturers Association changes its URL then we have to manually change every one of the 300 pages.

There are of course several software programs that automate this task.

By placing all the links in an out-of-line link document and referencing them from our pages we need only change one document. This is very similar in concept to Style Sheets, DTDs or other Schema, and Scriptlets where we have several pages referencing a single source. The following diagram illustrates the concept.

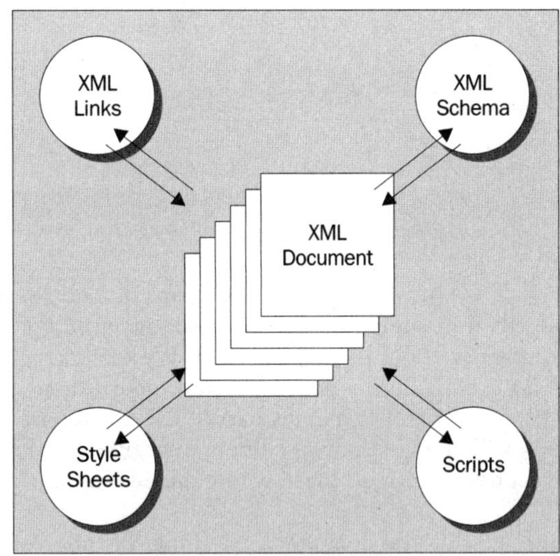

These are just a few examples of what a user agent may be capable of accomplishing using XLink methods. I'm sure that you can think of more.

Let's now look at the expanded versatility that the XPointer specification makes available to us.

XPointers

As we have already seen above, the XLink specification is for linking between various documents, the XPointer specification gives us means for pointing into the document. We have already seen how IE4+ uses the robust `id` attribute to point into a document, and this can be used equally well in an XML document. Indeed its use is even encouraged by the specification.

Here is an example which, although very simple, demonstrates some of the power of the pointing capabilities as defined in the XLL specifications, and also illustrates the similarity and differences between HTML links and those available for XML:

```
<xDocA>
      <para id="p1">This is the first paragraph.</para>
      <para id="p2">This is the second paragraph.</para>
      <para id="p3">This is the third paragraph.</para>
      <para id="p4">This is the fourth paragraph.</para>
</xDocA>
```

We are going to use `DocB` to embed the third paragraph of `DocA` into `DocB`.

Here is what the code for `DocB` looks like:

```
<xDocB>
      <para>Click on the hash marks to embed the third paragraph of Document A in
      _this document

            <mylink
                  xml:link="simple"
                  show="embed"
                  href="DocA.htm|id(p3)">
            [####]
            </mylink>
      </para>

</xDocB>
```

Note that in XML we need to tell the user agent what kind of pointer we are employing. In this case we are employing an element's `id` as an identifier. So we need to put `|id(p3)` after the URL. Actually if we leave out the `id` bit and just put `|p3`, the specification requires the user agent to imply the presence of `id`, so the syntax that is used in the IE4+ version of HTML is perfectly acceptable. (See the following section on locator syntax.)

Note that we are using the pipestem (`|`) instead of the hash mark (#) as a fragment identifier. This could be used to tell the user agent that we don't want to retrieve the whole document, just the part identified by the fragment identifier, the element with the `id` of `p3`.

> *This would, of course, be dependant on how the user agent was programmed to react to the pipestem. A similar result would also be possible with the use of a* `span` *pointer. This is discussed below. It's just that we didn't want to complicate this 'simple' example!*

Here is our hypothetical user agent again displaying what this would look like before we click on the hash marks:

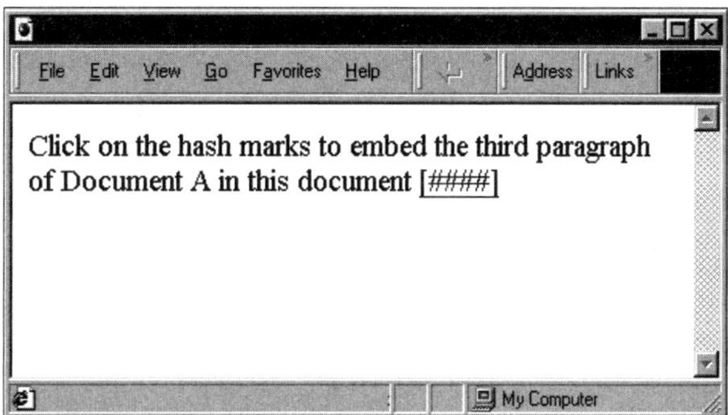

And here is what it would look like after:

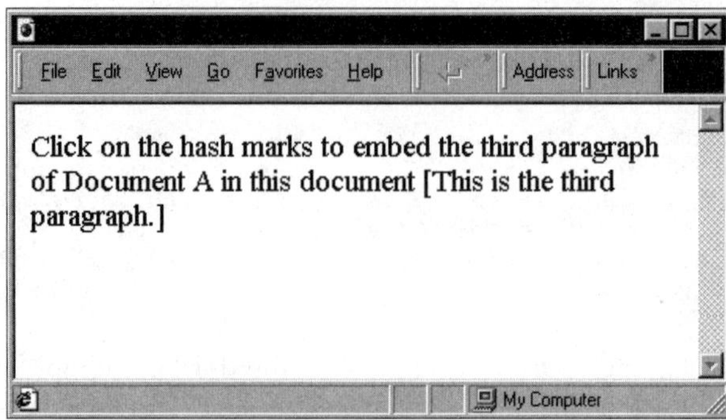

This simple example demonstrates in a very clear way some of the advantages of the XLL specification:

- We have linked to a document
- We have indicated to the user agent what action we want it to take
- We have pointed into a remote document using a pointer. `[ |id(p3) ]`
- The pointer is what comes after the hash mark (#) or the pipestem (|)
- We have identified the fragment as an element with an `id`
- We have indicated the remote sub-resource that we want to embed also using the same pointer
- Our user-agent has then fetched the fragment and embedded it in our current document

This is the basis of the XPointer specification, but as the pitchman says "Wait there is much, much more". Let's now have a look at the "much, much more".

Locator Syntax

The locator is the value of the `href` attribute. i.e. `href=[locator]`.

It takes the form of a URL followed by a connector – either the pipestem, (|), or the hash mark (#) followed by an XPointer or a name.

As the XLink specification puts it more formally:

```
[1] Locator::= URI
| Connector ( XPointer | Name)
| URI Connector (XPointer | Name)
[2] Connector ::= '#' | '|'
```

The hash mark, is used as a signal to the user agent that the whole document is to be retrieved, the pipestem, is used as a signal that only part of the document needs to be retrieved as in our example above, or as the specification puts it:

> If the connector is "|", no intent is signaled as to what processing model is to be used for accessing the designated resource.

The URI of course is the familiar URL.

We will be discussing XPointer syntax in some detail below, but if as already mentioned the connector is followed by a Name e.g. `#p3`, this is assumed to be shorthand for an `id`, i.e. shorthand for `#id(p3)`. As the specification puts it:

> If the Connector is followed directly by a Name, the Name is shorthand for the XPointer `"id(Name)"`; that is, the sub-resource is the element in the containing resource that has an XML ID attribute whose value matches the Name. This shorthand is to encourage use of the robust `id` addressing mode.

Name of course is any allowed XML name, see Chapter 2.

Here are some examples of valid locators.

```
DocA.htm#id(p3)
```

```
DocA.htm#p3
```

```
http://www.someserver.com/DocA.htm#p3.
```

The above are all equivalent except the full address was given in the last example, and indicates that the whole of Document A is to be retrieved from the server, but somehow the element with the id = "p3" is to be highlighted. In an HTML document this is usually accomplished by automatically scrolling the element to the top of the page. Here are some more examples:

```
DocA.htm|id(p3)
```

```
DocA.htm|p3
```

```
http://www.someserver.com/docA.htm|p3.
```

This locator points to the same place in the document, but there is no need for the server to supply the whole document, probably it will just send the element as in our first simple example.

The astute may have noticed that for this to happen there must be some server side recognition of the XLL specification. Somehow the client must signal to the server that only a partial piece of the document is required, and the server of course must be able to recognize this request, and more importantly act on it. It is probably unlikely that this part of the specification will be implemented for some time. Attractive as it is to save bandwidth by only sending part of a requested document, my guess is that this will be one of the last parts of the spec to be implemented.

Here are some more examples:

```
DocA.htm#root().child(2,para)
```

```
DocA.htm#child(2,para)
```

This is in fact a pointer, and tells the user agent to point to the second child of the root element of the document that is also of the type `para`. These two locators are similar.

In other words it would point to where we have placed the asterisk in the following document. (The asterisk is of course not part of the document, it's just there to illustrate our point.)

```
<xdoc>
     <para>This is paragraph 1.</para>
     *<para>This is paragraph 2.</para>
     <para>This is paragraph 3.</para>
</xdoc>
```

> **Note that in most computer practice the numbering process starts from zero, 0. For some reason in the XLink specification it starts from 1. As the DOM would call the second paragraph** `para` **[1] this is obviously a potential source of tremendous confusion.**

Having had a look at one XPointer, let's take a more detailed look at XPointer syntax.

XPointer Syntax

An XPointer consists of a series of location terms separated by a period, each of which specifies a location in the document usually in terms of the previous location. These locations are expressed in terms of the document tree. See Chapter 6 on the DOM for a full description of a document tree if you are not familiar with this concept. We have then a series of location terms, which are either absolute locations or relative to an absolute location.

Absolute locations.

There are four forms of absolute location in a document:

- The root
- The origin
- An element with an id
- An HTML type location

Here is a document that contains all four kinds of location. Let's look at each of these in turn using the following simple document, `simpledoc.xml`.

```
<xdoc>
     <para>This is paragraph 1.</para>
     <para>This is paragraph 2 which contains <mylink xml:link="simple"
     _href="#p3">a link</mylink>.</para>
     <para id="p3">This is paragraph 3.</para>
     <A NAME= "bottom"/>
</xdoc>
```

The Root

This, of course, is the root element of the document, which in the above simple document is the `<xdoc>` element.

An outside link pointing to the root of this document would use the following syntax:

```
"href=simpledoc.xml#root()"
```

In fact there would be no need to do this, because if no pointer is added, the root of the document is implied.

Mimicking our simple example above and getting a little ahead of ourselves:

```
href= "simpledoc.xml#root().child(2,para)"
```

```
href= "simpledoc.xml#child(2,para)"
```

Both point to the same place, the second paragraph.

The Origin

This absolute location is only good for a pointer pointing to somewhere in the same document. It refers to the sub-resource from which the traversal begins. In the example above, <mylink> is pointing to the <para> element with an id of "p3".

In fact if <mylink> had the href value as follows:

```
href =#origin().following(1,#element)
```

it would select the same place, namely the first element following the origin!

Obviously the origin absolute location can only be used for pointing to a place in the same document, so its use is limited. However, it is ideal for pointing to abstract items, such as the next chapter of the same document.

An Element with an id

We have already used this in our examples, and an id is certainly the most robust method (and the least demanding of resources) for pointing into a document. To recap, in our example document above:

```
<mylink xml:link="simple" href="#p3">a link</mylink>
```

Is pointing to the next paragraph.

If the locator was outside the document the link might appear as follows:

```
<mylink xml:link="simple" href="simpledoc.xml#p3">a link</mylink>
```

An HTML Type Location

There are obviously going to be a lot of HTML documents around for a long time to come, and this absolute locator is designed to make use of the <A NAME = ".."> syntax that they employ.

A document that wanted to point to the `<A NAME = "bottom"/>` element in our example would employ the following syntax:

```
<mylink xml:link="simple" href="simpledoc.htm#html(bottom)">a link</mylink>
```

As the specification puts it:

> ***3.2.4 The html Keyword***
>
> If an XPointer begins with `html(NAMEVALUE)`, the location source is the first element whose type is `A` and which has an attribute called `NAME` whose value is the same as the supplied `NAMEVALUE`. This is exactly the function performed by the "#" fragment identifier in the context of an HTML document.

Having had a look at the absolute locators let's have a look at the relative locators. For reasons of space we will not be looking at them all but will just provide enough examples so that you can see the methodology, and be able to understand the specification, which is relatively clearly written and straight forward.

Relative Locations

The XPointer always begins with an absolute locator. If none is given, root is implied. There is then a period and any number of relative locators all separated by a period.

So, for example, the following identifies the 29th paragraph of the fourth sub-division of the third major division of the location source, which happens to be the root:

```
href= "somedoc.htm#root().child(3,DIV1).child(4,DIV2).child(29,P)"
```

Note in passing that this is the same as:

```
href= "somedoc.htm# child(3,DIV1).(4,DIV2).(29,P)"
```

because when the keyword is omitted it is assumed to be the same as the preceding keyword. But we are getting a little ahead of ourselves. Let's have a look at what these keywords are.

Relative Keywords

This is a little confusing because the words employed are similar to, but not quite the same as the DOM keywords. We have already looked at the other potential source of confusion; namely that in the XLL spec the numbering starts from 1 and not 0.

Here are the keywords taken from the specification, which really require no elaboration:

> Each of these keywords identifies a sequence of elements or other XML node types from which the resulting location source will be chosen. The arguments passed to the keyword determine which node types from that sequence are in fact chosen. Each keyword summarized here is described in detail in the following sections.

child

Identifies direct child nodes of the location source.

descendant

Identifies nodes appearing anywhere within the content of the location source.

ancestor

Identifies element nodes containing the location source.

preceding

Identifies nodes that appear before (preceding) the location source.

following

Identifies nodes that appear after (following) the location source.

psibling

Identifies sibling nodes (sharing their parent with the location source) that appear before (preceding) the location source.

fsibling

Identifies sibling nodes (sharing their parent with the location source) that appear after (following) the location source.

If the keyword is omitted, it is treated as equivalent to the immediately preceding keyword; the keyword must not be omitted from the first location term of any XPointer (including embedded ones).

Let's look at how to use these keywords to pinpoint a location inside the document.

Using Keywords

The general notation for a pointer is:

```
#[absolute location].Keyword ([integer],[Node Type])
```

For a full discussion of nodes see Chapter 6 on the DOM.

In other words we use one of the keywords, then as the first argument to the keyword we pass the numeric instance of that keyword and the type of node. A couple of examples will make it clear. The examples will be taken from the following XML document (almost the same one as is used in the specification).

```
<?xml version= "1.0"?>
<!DOCTYPE SPEECH [
<!ELEMENT SPEECH (#PCDATA|SPEAKER|DIRECTION)*>
<!ATTLIST SPEECH
ID ID #IMPLIED>
```

```
<!ELEMENT SPEAKER (#PCDATA)>
<!ELEMENT DIRECTION (#PCDATA)>
]>

<SPEECH ID="a27">
<SPEAKER>Polonius</SPEAKER>

<DIRECTION>crossing downstage</DIRECTION>

Fare you well,my lord.

<DIRECTION>To Ros.</DIRECTION>

You go to seek Lord Hamlet? There he is.

</SPEECH>
```

First, however, let's look at the type of nodes recognized by the XLL specification.

Node Types

The node type can be one of the following types. Here is the syntax taken from the specification (3.3.3)

```
NodeType ::= Name|'#element' | '#pi' | '#comment' | '#text' | '#cdata' |
'#all'
```

Note that with the exception of `Name`, the syntax requires a hash mark before the node type.

Name

The `Name` applies to the name of an element. From our snippet of Hamlet above here is an example of an XPointer using a Name.

```
Id(a27).child(2,DIRECTION)
```

This will select the second node with the name `DIRECTION`, i.e. the node containing the text `"To Ros"`. Note that as XML is case sensitive the name must match exactly.

Note also how we use the robust `id` as an absolute locator for our relative syntax.

#element

These count the XML elements. Here is an example:

```
Id(a27).child(2,#element)
```

This will match the second child element of the element with an `id` of `'a27'`, namely the first direction which has the content "`crossing down stage`".

Note again the difference between the XLL and the DOM in numbering the children, i.e. XLL numbers from 1 not from 0.

#pi

There are no processing instructions in the above example, but if there were the selection would work the same way as for an element.

#comment

There are no comments in the above example, but if there were the selection would work the same way as for an element.

#text

For a definition of what a text child is see the Chapter 6 on the DOM. Briefly it is any section just containing unmarked up text. Can you see how many "text" children there are in the element SPEECH ID="a27" in the above example?

The answer is 4! The line breaks between SPEECH and SPEAKER, and between SPEAKER and DIRECTION both count as a text child!

```
Id(a27).child(3,#text)
```

Therefore points to the text child with the string value:

```
"

Fare you well,my lord.

"
```

Note the inclusion of the line breaks in the string. This is XML!

#cdata

There are no cdata nodes in the above example. Note how the pointer specification (somewhat confusingly) uses lowercase for the cdata node whereas the DOM specification refers to a CDATA section. Expect this to change in the final recommendation!

#all

This selects all nodes, so:

```
Id(a27).child(3,#all)
```

would select the third child node, which is the second line break!

Before concluding our brief review of XPointers let's have a look at selection by attribute, and selection using the string keyword, and the span key word.

Selection by Attribute

The XLink specification allows us to point into a document using an attribute and its value. The general syntax of the pointer for doing this is:

```
[keyword]([integer],[#element | name], [attribute name],[attribute value])
```

In our examples we will use the `child` keyword, although of course any of the keywords could be used.

Note also that, as only an element can take an attribute, the only valid node types are either an element or a name.

Here is an example:

```
child(1,#element,title, "Professional XML Applications")
```

This would then point to the first element that had an attribute called title with a value of `"Professional XML Applications"`.

Note in passing that the following two XPointers are equivalent:

```
html(top)
```

and

```
root().descendant(1,A,NAME, "top")
```

Wildcards

We can also use wildcards for either attributes or for their values, so:

```
child(1,#element,title, *)
```

Would point to the first element with a title attribute that had any value, and:

```
child(1,#element,*, *)
```

Would point to the first element that had any form of attribute.

Spanning Location Term

Because XPointers allow us to return just part of a document (as when we use `"show='embed' "`) we need a means of isolating just part of the document. The `span` keyword allows us to do this.

The general syntax is:

`span([XPointer], [XPointer])`.

Here is an example. In our Hamlet snippet above:

```
Id(a23).span(child(1),child(5))
```

Would return everything from the first child through to the fifth child i.e.

[1st child type = element]

[2nd child type = text]

```
<SPEAKER>Polonius</SPEAKER>
```

[3rd child type = element]

[4th child type = text]

```
<DIRECTION>crossing downstage</DIRECTION>
```

[5th child type = text]

```
Fare you well,my lord
```

We have added the child number and node type to make it clearer.

String Location Term.

The XPointer specification also allows us to select specific strings using the `string` keyword.

Here is the general syntax:

```
[absolute locator].string([integer:- which instance of the string to be
used | all], [string to be searched for],[integer:-where to start the
return,[integer:-number of characters to be returned]
```

This rather long syntax string is confusing, but essentially we select the string to be searched, the string to search for, what part of that string to start returning, and how much to return.

A few examples should clarify the matter. Here is a simple XML document with a familiar nursery rhyme.

```
<xdoc>
     <verse id= "v1">
     Here we go gathering nuts in May,
           nuts in may,
           nuts in may,
     Here we go gathering nuts in May,
           nuts in may,
           nuts in may,
     All on a frosty morning.
     </verse>
</xdoc>
```

This XPointer:

```
id(v1).string(3, "")
```

identifies the position just before the third character, in this case `e`. Remember that in XML a line break is considered a single character. (Actually we also have some tabs which we would have to take into account, so I am really over simplifying it.)

This XPointer:

```
id(v1).string(2, "nuts in may")
```

identifies the position just before the second `nuts in may`.

This XPointer:

```
id(v1).string(2, "nuts in may",9)
```

identifies the position just before `may` in the second `nuts in may`.

This XPointer:

```
id(v1).string(2, "nuts in may",9,3)
```

Identifies the position just before `may` in the second `nuts in may`, and returns three characters, in other words it returns the string `may`.

That really wraps up our very brief summary of XPointers.

We have really only looked at examples that mainly use the `child` keyword, but using the other keywords are very similar in concept. You are referred to the specification for more detailed usage. With this section under your belt you should have very little difficulty understanding and interpreting the specification.

Before we leave the subject of pointer lets just say a few words about the syntax of XPointers and the DTD.

XPointers and the DTD

In our explanations we have really just been using well-formed examples. However, in any valid XML document all special attributes have to be declared in the DTD.

Luckily for us XPointers are just part of the value of the `href` attribute, so a simple attribute declaration of the `href` value of `CDATA` is all that is required!

All the other link attributes we use in our document must of course be declared. Here is an example of a simple link attribute declaration for the `mylink` element.

```
<!ATTLIST mylink
xml:link  CDATA #FIXED "simple"

     href CDATA #REQUIRED
>
```

Summary

In this chapter we have had a look at the XML linking language and seen how much more powerful these specifications are compared with the simple links of HTML. We have looked at:

- Simple HTML links
- Simple XML links, and how they can do more than the simple HTML links
- Extended links and how they can be used either inline, or out-of-line
- Some of the software requirements to support extended links
- Pointers in XML and saw how they could do much, much more than the simple fragment identifiers and rudimentary pointers of HTML

You should now have an understanding of what it will be possible to do using the linking specifications when user agents employ them. And as we mentioned the XML Linking Working Group has now been formed, so we can expect to see Working Drafts of the linking specifications before too long.

6

The XML Document Object Model

One of the great problems with any standard such as XML is that applications that make use of it all tend to develop their own proprietary methods to handle the document. This is very evident in DHTML where in order to carry out a given task, quite different methods and syntax have been developed by both the major browsers.

The W3C XML DOM is potentially one of the most important standards since the XML specification, because it gives implementers a common vocabulary to use in manipulating the XML document. Whether the application was written in C, in Java, Perl, Python, or in Visual Basic, exactly the same methods can be used. Or rather, exactly the same commands can be given to accomplish the task even though what is going on 'under the hood' is likely to be vastly different. After all when I am driving a road vehicle, stepping on the brake should do the same thing no matter whether I am driving a Mack truck, a Porsche 911, or a Yugo.

Again on the client side it doesn't matter whether my viewers are browsing with Netscape Communicator or with Microsoft Internet Explorer 5 (IE5) or with 'brandX'. Provided they all implement the same DOM I can be assured that my script will work. (At the time of writing IE5 was almost 100% compliant.)

What We Will Look At

In this chapter we will be looking at the concept of the DOM as applied to XML documents, and specifically we will be looking at the 'Core' model proposed by the World Wide Web Consortium (W3C). This consists of a suggested API (Application Program Interface) for various different applications. We will first look at some general concepts.

- An XML document as a tree model.
- An XML document as an object model
- We will discuss the importance of a common API
- We will then explore in some detail the suggested interface, and use IE5 to show examples of the ECMAScript bindings, using examples that will both analyze and rebuild a document

In this chapter we will confine ourselves almost exclusively to the W3C DOM Level 1 Core API, and examples using the ECMAScript (JavaScript) binding.

The specification can be found at `http://www.w3.org/TR/REC-DOM-Level-1`

General Concepts of Document Models

Before looking at the W3C's model, let's look in a general way at the various models available, and some of their requirements.

Whether we realize it or not we are all very familiar with the concept of a Document Object Model, because we use one model or another every day of our lives to find our way around books, magazines or other kinds of documents.

Linear Model of a Document

If I told you to go to the book "Professional Style Sheets for HTML and XML, page 243, line 18", you would have no difficulty in following my instructions, and would find that you were at a section entitled "The Document Object Model".

What I have done is use a linear model to describe a book document, and I could indeed go further and tell you to go to the second word and the third character. I can't go any further than this, because the character, like the atom of pre-subatomic physics, is the smallest element allowed.

In computing terms using some fictional programming language I might write:

```
Var myBook= Professional Style Sheets for HTML and XML

X=myBook.page(243).line(18)

Print X
```

And this would print out the string "`The Document Object Model`".

This linear model works pretty well for a static document object like a book, but consider what would happen if the book were to be revised, or republished in another format, then this description would no longer work.

Take this chapter I am writing. How do I reference this when the book has not even been printed? Obviously another type of model is required, and again we are already familiar with it.

Tree Model of a Document

I could say, "Go to 'Professional XML Applications', the fifth chapter, and the first paragraph".

For documents that are dynamic this is a much better model, and should work fine unless the editor decides to put in an extra chapter or change their order! So to make this model work I would really need to keep a chapter list, and update it every time the chapter order changed.

This model is used quite extensively in document work and is called a 'tree' model. In this type of model, each chapter and paragraph is considered a 'node' in the tree. Starting from any single point we can get to any part of the tree by walking the tree – e.g. "Go back three paragraphs, and then forward two sentences".

In biology each node is a branch in a tree or plant (OED: "The point of a stem from which the leaves spring"). So we start with our 'root' node and work towards the 'leaves' which would correspond to an individual character in our document. Each node has a parent node, and a series of child nodes (not counting the leaves at the tips of the branches, of course). Nodes originating from the same branch are called siblings.

This is a much better model for a dynamic document, but again it has a big drawback that each time a change is made to the document, much of the tree must be redrawn.

Object Model

This brings us to the third type of model with which we are familiar, the object model. Here each part of the book is considered as an object. The book is an object with properties, each chapter is an object with properties, and each section in a chapter is an object with its own properties.

The advantage of this model is that all I have to do is call the object that I want to access by name. So I could say, "Get 'XML Applications', go to the 'XML DOM' chapter, and the 'Object Model' subsection", which would bring you to the section that you are reading right now regardless of how the chapter or section order was manipulated.

Because the objects have name properties, I can still find my way to a section of the book even though the editor may decide to cut out or reverse the order.

XML documents are usually dynamic, so if we want a good way to model an XML document, we need a model that can not only describe the intrinsic document parts, but also can alter and add to them! The W3C Document Object Model does do this, and in fact uses both the 'tree' and the 'object' concepts rolled into a single model.

Factory Methods

When we were younger and some of us bought a kit of a model airplane or ship, it came with a nice set of plans. It was certainly exciting to study the plans, but the real fun came from building the model.

This is also true of XML document models. It's all very well to have a way to describe a document in great detail, but we also need a way to build up a document. We need to be able to say, "Put an element here," "Add text there," and, "Put a comment there."

The set of 'methods' that allow us to do this are known collectively in the DOM specification as 'factory methods', and a good DOM will allow us to build a complex document from scratch. The W3C DOM API provides an excellent set of such methods that we will look at as we progress through the chapter.

An XML Document as a Tree

Let's look at a simple well-formed XML document and draw a tree representing it. Here is the document:

```
<xdoc>
     <greeting>Hello XML</greeting>
     <farewell>Goodbye HTML</farewell>
</xdoc>
```

And here is the tree representing it:
This document has one child node, the so-called root node, and the root node has two child nodes, greeting and farewell, which happen to be element nodes. Each of these has a text node child.

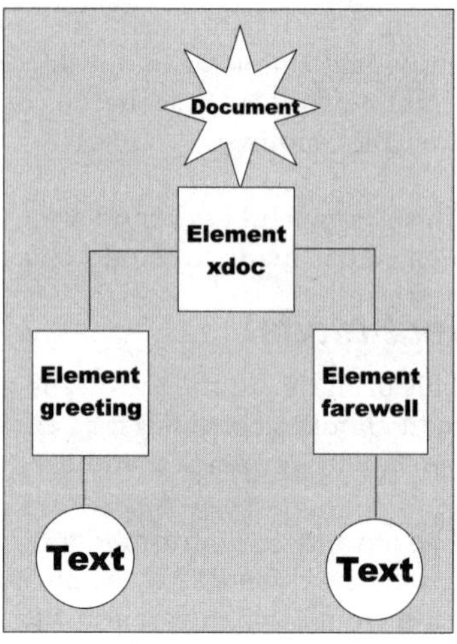

(We could of course say that the text nodes have word children that have character children, but in our dissection of the document we will only go as far as text string nodes (as does the W3C DOM).)

Let's make one small addition to our XML document:

```
<xdoc>
      <greeting>Hello XML</greeting>
      <farewell>Goodbye <emph>(no way!)</emph> HTML</farewell>
</xdoc>
```

We have added an emph element, but as you can see in the following diagram this has produced more than one extra node! The text string that it was inserted into, which was a single node, has been split into two nodes. Even though we have made what seems like a small addition to our document, the tree has become considerably more complicated, but the basic relationships stay the same.

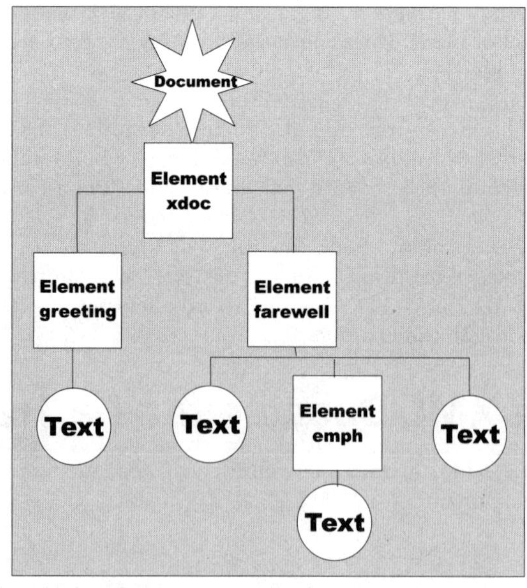

An XML Document as an Object Collection

Let's consider our basic document again. How many objects do we see here, and what are their properties?

```
<xdoc>
      <greeting>Hello XML</greeting>
      <farewell>Goodbye HTML</farewell>
</xdoc>
```

Of course we could atomize the document so that each word and character would have its own property (an ASCII number perhaps), but for this exercise we will only go down as far as blocks of text.

XML Objects

Here is a list of the objects of the above simple XML document:

- The `Document` object – this of course includes the whole document.
- The `xdoc` object – this is an element object that has two element children, `greeting`, and `farewell`.
- The `greeting` object – this is another element object, which has a sibling element object, `farewell`, and a child text object.
- The '`Hello XML`' text object – the child of `greeting`.
- The `farewell` object – this is another element object, which has a sibling element object, `greeting`, and a child text object.
- '`Goodbye HTML`' text object – the child of `farewell`.

Let's now look at some of the properties that we may want to assign to each object.

Possible Properties

Now that we have looked at the objects that this well-formed XML document can be divided into, let's look at the properties that each object should have to enable us to build an exact replica of the original document from the model. It should be obvious that if each object knew its own name, its parent, and its position in a list of siblings, it should be possible to build up an entire document from its component parts.

The chroniclers of English aristocracy have used this system for centuries. "John Blueblood, the third son of the fifth Duke of Barchester", very accurately describes John's position in the Barchester family tree. If we had similar information about all the members it would obviously be an easy job to reconstruct the whole tree.

Extending our analogy to the nodes of XML documents, here are some of the properties we might want to include. Even though we have not yet looked at the W3C DOM in any detail, we make reference in places to their suggested object properties. Obviously, not all the properties are needed by all types of node. For example, a text node will not have an attribute property, so the attribute property of a text node would always be `null`.

- Node type

Is it a comment, an element, a processing instruction, a CDATA section, a text node, etc.?

- Name

The name of an element node can be its tag name. For a text node the name suggested by the W3C DOM specification, is the generic reserved name `#text`.

- Value

In the W3C specification, the element value is '`null`', for a text node it is the text string.

- Parent

The parent of the current node. A document root node of course has no parent.

- Child list

A list of all the node's children, from first to last.

- Siblings

A knowledge of its position in a list of siblings, or a knowledge of who its elder and younger siblings are. While not necessary for accurate positioning in the whole tree (we could go to the parent and ask the parent for a list of their children), it is certainly a convenience.

- Attributes

A list of the attribute/value pairs of the element. In XML their order is not important. Attributes could be treated as child nodes, and it would be quite legitimate for a Document Object Model to take this approach. However the W3C DOM chooses to treat them as properties of the element node rather than as children.

Other Types of Node Objects

The astute reader may have noticed that although we have looked at element and text nodes we have not mentioned other types of objects common in XML documents, such as comments, processing instructions, XML declarations and DTDs. Obviously the DTD would need a complete set of node types of its own.

We have omitted these because we have been talking about DOMs in general terms, but obviously if any DOM is going to be a complete model it will have to provide means of describing these nodes. It should come as no surprise to you that the W3C DOM does in fact address this issue, and we will look at the W3C's DOM implementation later on in this chapter. However we can note right now that the Core W3C DOM does not give a very full treatment for the DTD.

Now that we have had a look in a general way at DOMs, and what information they should contain to allow dismantling and reconstruction of an XML document, let's specifically explore the recommended W3C API for a DOM.

The W3C DOM API

With the advent of the W3C DOM, Web builders may finally have reached the Promised Land: a standard, vendor-neutral API that allows them to manipulate Web pages without worrying about the quirks of a particular browser or scripting language. Is the DOM really a milestone in Web development, or yet another false hope in the search for meaningful standards? Below we will explain what the standard means for Web builders, and how to put it to work today. We will then look a little at what the future may hold.

Importance of a Common API

At the present time if I want to use script in an HTML page to do anything but the most trivial task, I have a problem. I will have to query the browser, ask it what type it is, and then write different code to accomplish the same task depending on whether the browser is a Netscape Communicator, or a Microsoft Internet Explorer.

Similarly if I have a program written in C, or a program written in VB, or even two programs written in the same language by different vendors, I will probably have to use a different set of methods to accomplish the same task.

What a common API would do, always provided the different vendors agreed to stick with it, is allow me to use the same commands to accomplish the same tasks in any collaborating application.

Gosh, wouldn't that make a poor programmer's life simple!

It almost looks as if with XML we have reached that 'Holy Grail', because all the major vendors have promised to adhere to the W3 DOM interface, and IE5 has already implemented the majority of it.

Before looking at the W3C DOM specifics, let's take a quick look at the interface that the W3C DOM uses, the Common Object Request Broker Architecture (or CORBA) interface, as this can be a source of confusion if not understood.

The Object Management Group Interface Definition Language

Before going any further it is probably best to say a little about the syntax used to define the properties and methods of the DOM in the W3C specification. Many people are confused by the specification, and this is partly because they are not used to concepts of distributed objects. Java gurus familiar with Java's Remote Method Invocation (RMI) will have no problems with the terminology and can safely skip this section.

> *Those interested in learning more about RMI are directed to Ivor Horton's 'Beginning Java' (Wrox Press, ISBN 1861002238).*

The Object Management Group's (OMG) Interface Definition Language (IDL) is a language that allows applications and their objects to communicate with each other even though they are written in different languages.

Most readers will be familiar with the client/server model. Whenever I am using my browser and click on a link, my browser, the client, is requesting the server to retrieve a document object. In any network the machine doing the asking is the client, and the machine providing the service is the server.

The OMG IDL is a language for defining object interfaces. If I have a Java program that wants to communicate over a network with a C++ program I can do so using a CORBA conforming broker which will translate between the two languages. This broker is constructed in accordance with the Common Object Request Broker Architecture defined by the OMG using IDL.

An Analogy

Probably the easiest way to understand this is with a simple analogy.

Suppose I have an investment portfolio with several stocks and bonds in it (I wish!). I could have Government Bonds, Municipal Bonds, and shares on the London Stock Exchange, the New York Stock Exchange (NYSE), and the Tokyo Stock Exchange.

If I wanted to buy some Microsoft shares on the New York Stock Exchange, I would have two options: I could buy them directly, or I could go to a broker.

If I decided to buy them directly I would first of all have to purchase a seat on the NYSE, which would probably cost me several millions of dollars! Next I would have to learn all the customs and rules necessary to complete the transaction, make the transaction, and then complete all the paper work necessary for the transaction. If I wanted to trade in Japan I would of course have to learn, among other things, how to speak Japanese!

Or I could go to my broker and ask him to purchase the shares, obviously much simpler!

Before using my broker, though, I would have to negotiate a set of protocols; in other words we would have to agree to the terms of business between us. Next we would agree on how we would communicate, or in computing terms we would have to agree on some kind of 'interface'.

Now to communicate with my broker I would use this 'interface', which for the sake of argument could be a simple form (although it could just as easily be a phone call or a Web site).

The first interface he gives me is a portfolio interface, which could have some 'attributes' that would lead me to another interface, and some methods that would allow me to get things done.

The attributes may be bonds, stocks, etc. which would lead me to the bonds, stocks, etc. interfaces.

The methods could include `ShowInvestmentList()`, which would give me a list of my investments.

If I requested the stocks interface it may have methods on it such as `GetShareList()` or `GetSharePrice([sharename])` or `SellShare([sharename],[number])`, etc.

The main point is that using these simple methods I would not have to worry about the nuts and bolts of any of the transactions – I can just leave that to the broker. I would just have to call up a suitable interface, and then use the methods provided.

IDL Syntax

The OMG IDL works on similar principles. Instead of worrying about the type of document or the language that a processor is written in, I can just use the IDL definitions and the ORB (Object Request Broker), will do all the work for me.

When I access a document, in computing terms I am in fact accessing a document object, which contains node objects, which may be element objects, type objects, comment objects, etc., etc.

However in the IDL syntax I am using an interface between my client and those objects, and I address all my requests and methods to the interface ORB, which passes on my request.

In order to avoid confusion between the fields that an interface must have and an XML element's attributes the specification distinguishes between the '`attribute`'s of an interface and `Attr` interface nodes representing XML attributes.

The `Document` interface has a `documentElement` attribute, so using the syntax:

```
X=Document.documentElement
```

will directly load the node object that is the root element of the document into my variable `X`. The original object may have been defined in C++, and I may be using Java, but the interface will ensure that the properties can be accessed and changed using requests made in whatever language.

Status of the DOM

The DOM may well be one of the more important Internet documents to be written, so it would be a good idea to look at the aims of the DOM's W3C Working Group, what they have accomplished to date, and what they hope to accomplish in the future.

The initial DOM is a minimal set of objects and interfaces for accessing and manipulating XML (and other) document objects. It does not provide a way to create or save an XML document. Creating or saving an XML document is left up to the user agent.

Although the Core model gives excellent functionality in document manipulation, it does not cover certain areas and these will be left to the Level II implementation.

Specifically the present Level I DOM does not cover:

- A structure model for the internal and external subsets of a DTD or other schema
- Validation against such a schema
- Control for rendering documents via style sheets

Support for these topics is expected in Level II of the DOM.

The DOM Interfaces

The DOM presents documents as a hierarchy of node objects that implement interfaces. The following is a list of XML node interfaces supported by the DOM together with the children that each interface supports. We have also listed the node names and node values for each node type, as well as a short explanation of the chief properties each node can take. A more detailed analysis is given with the 'Examples of DOM Interfaces' section later.

For now note that each interface represents an object, which can be assigned the following properties:

- A **Type**: this as we will see later is indicated by an integer or a string constant. All interfaces have a type value.
- A **Name**: this may be different for each individual object, for example an element's name will be its tag name, or it may just be a generic name. For example a comment's name is always `#comment`, and a document's name is always `#document`. When a generic version is used it is always preceded by a hash mark.
- A **Value**: many of the interfaces do not take a value in which case the value is always `null`, otherwise the value is related to the node's content, for example the value of a text node is the string it contains.
- **Attributes**: actually the only interface that returns a value for the '`attributes`' property is the element interface.

Here are the types of interface specified by the DOM:

Document

`Element` (maximum of one), `ProcessingInstruction`, `Comment`, `DocumentType`

The document, of course, is the whole thing. There are no methods given to create a document, it is left up to the user agent to create a document object. The document created can of course be minimal. `<xroot></xroot>` is a perfectly well-formed document, and can be used as a basis to build up an increasingly complicated document.

Again the DOM does not provide the means to save the built-up document, this is left up to the user agent. As we will see, because client scripts (such as ECMAScript) used in browsers cannot access the platform's hard drive, most documents built up via script die with the termination of the browser window.

A document's name value is `#document`, and it has a `null` value.

> *As I'm sure you know already, a* `null` *value is different from a 0 (zero) value. Zero implies that there has been or can be a value.* `null` *means that no value has ever been assigned, and in terms of the DOM when an interface has a null value it means that it is never meant to have a value assigned to it.'*

A document can only have one element node, the root node. Here is a diagram showing the Document node and the types of child nodes it can have:

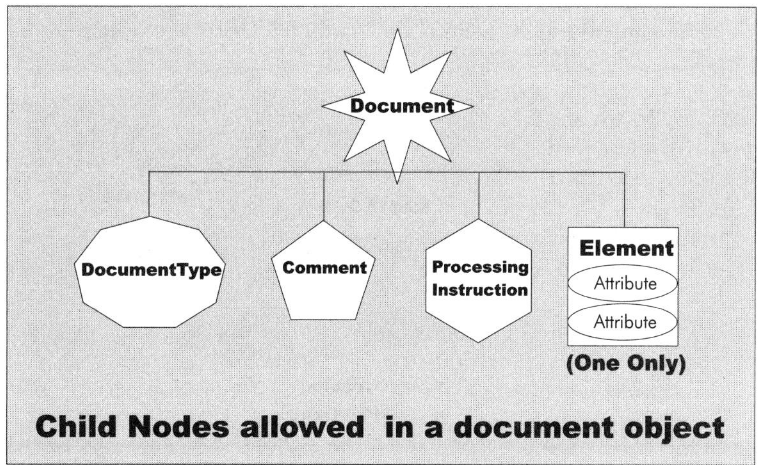

DocumentFragment

`Element`, `ProcessingInstruction`, `Comment`, `Text`, `CDATASection`, `EntityReference`

A document fragment is a very useful concept. We can create a document fragment, build it up with various nodes, and then insert it into the document. The only consideration is that the document must remain well-formed after the fragment has been placed in its final position.

A document fragment's name is '`#document-fragment`', and it has a `null` value.

DocumentType

`Notation`, `Entity`

The W3C DOM makes no effort to support a complete DTD. `DocumentType` gives access to the entities and notations contained in the DTD, but in the Level I Core DOM there is no attempt to support element and attribute declarations.

A `DocumentType`'s name is the string that immediately follows `<!DOCTYPE`; as in the declaration `<!DOCTYPE xdoc SYSTEM= "somedoc.dtd">`, the name is '`xdoc`'. This is the same name as that of the root element, of course. `DocumentType`s have a `null` value.

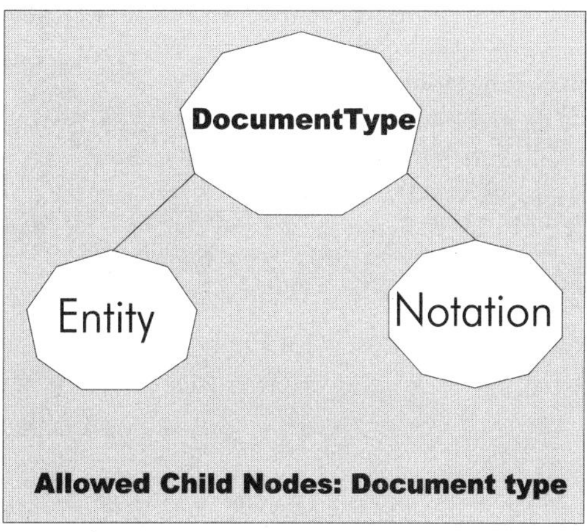

EntityReference

Element, ProcessingInstruction, Comment, Text, CDATASection, EntityReference

An EntityReference can have as its child node a complete document fragment, including other EntityReferences.

The name of an EntityReference is the name of the entity referenced. E.g. with the entity reference &dom;, the name is dom. An EntityReference has a null value.

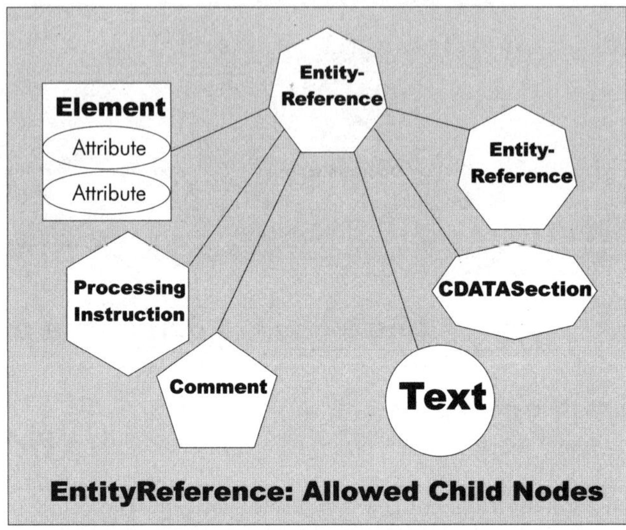

Element

Element, Text, Comment, ProcessingInstruction, CDATASection, EntityReference

The majority of nodes in a typical document are probably going to be text and element nodes. An element's attributes are not really considered children, but are considered properties of the Element node. See below under the discussion of the Attr node.

An Element's name is its tag name, and it has a null value. It also has an attributes property that is a NamedNodeMap. This will be discussed later when we examine accessing an element's attribute/value pairs through code.

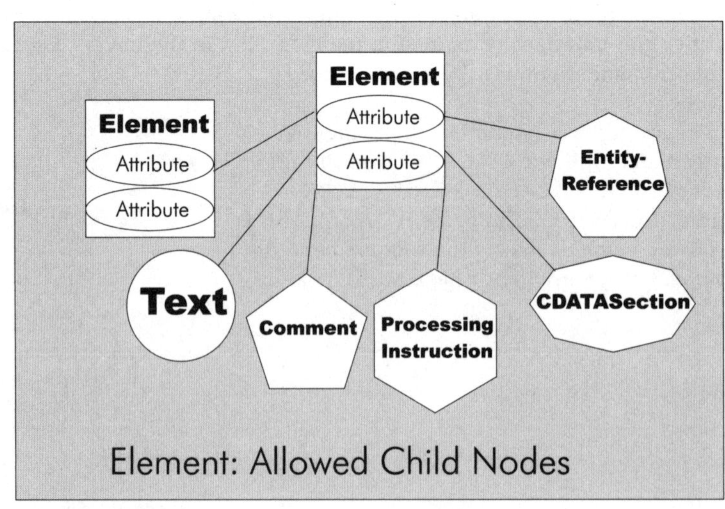

Attr

`Text, EntityReference`

In the DOM the attribute interface name has been shortened to `Attr` to avoid confusion with the `attribute` keyword in the IDL interface. `Attrs` are not considered to be children of elements in the sense that there is an 'oldest' and 'youngest' child. The order that the `Attrs` appear in is unimportant. The attribute/value pair is best visualized as a property of the element contained in an `Attr` node.

In an attempt to dispel any possible confusion you might have:

- `Attr` is a type of DOM node representing an XML element's attribute
- '`attributes`' is a specific interface field of type `NamedNodeMap` (see later)
- Interfaces defined using IDL terminology have properties (fields) of type 'attribute' (no 's')

So '`attributes`' is an IDL interface attribute of type `NamedNodeMap`.

In XML of course, an internal entity reference is a valid attribute value.

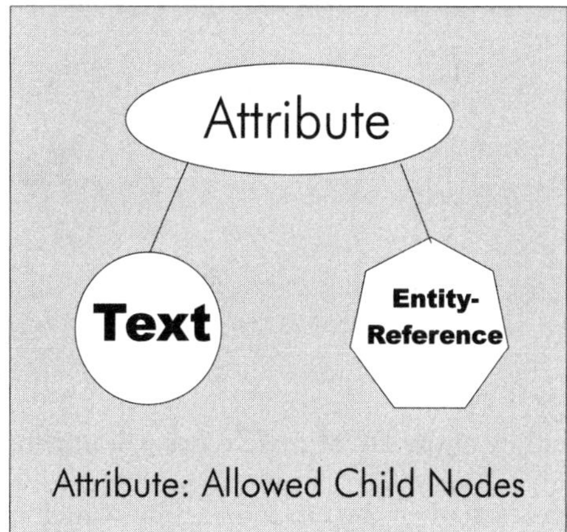

Attribute: Allowed Child Nodes

ProcessingInstruction

No other nodes

A `ProcessingInstruction`'s name is its target. Its value is its entire content, i.e. everything between `<?` and `?>`.

Comment

No other nodes

A `Comment` node's name is `#comment`, and its value is its content, i.e. everything between `<!--` and `-->`.

Text

No other nodes

A `Text` node's name is '`#text`', and its content is its string value.

CDATASection

No other nodes

A CDATA section's value is the content of the CATA section, and its name is #cdata-section.

Entity

No other nodes

An Entity's name is the entity name. It has no value.

Notation

No other nodes

A Notation's name is the NOTATION name. It has no value.

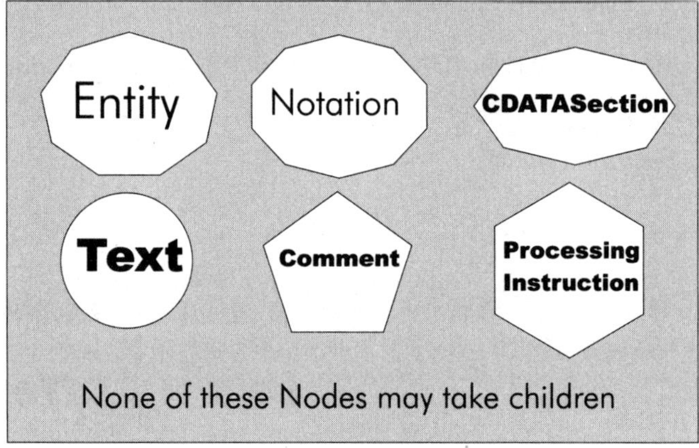

This outline of the DOM node types will hopefully become more significant as we move on.

Let's have a look at the DOM in action, which in practice at the time of writing means using an IE5 beta as this is the only implementation. Hopefully by the time you read this there will be several other implementations of the DOM.

XML in IE5

As we will be using IE5 to illustrate our examples, it is well to say a little about how an XML document is created in IE5. There are two basic methods, via an XML Island, and via an ActiveX Control.

XML Islands

The simplest way to create an XML document object in IE5 is to use the HTML tag <XML>. Imagine that we have created a very simple XML file called myxmlfile.xml containing the following: <greeting>Hello World!</greeting>. The following code uses the ID of the <XML> tag, and its SRC attribute to create an XML document object.

```
<XML ID="island" SRC="myxmlfile.xml"></XML>
```

The XML must be well-formed, and if it has a DTD it must also be valid, otherwise the built in MSXML parser will refuse to load it!

It is well to check that it is valid using the `parseError` method. Note that the `parseError` method is specific to IE5, and is not part of the DOM. In the document below we have included the `parseError` method in a conditional statement so that the viewer will know that in case of an error the document has not been loaded, and will know the reason why it has not been loaded.

> *One of the great 'selling points' of XML is that it requires syntactical correctness. This means that an application or user agent can be sure it is getting a well-formed document.*

This is what the code looks like:

```
<HTML>
      <XML ID="island" SRC="myxmlfile.xml"></XML>
<SCRIPT>
      myDoc=island;
      if(myDoc.parseError.reason !="")
            {
            alert(myDoc.parseError.reason)
            }
</SCRIPT>
</HTML>
```

If we want we can also put our XML file between the tags thus:

```
<HTML>
      <XML ID="island" >
      <Greeting>Hello IE5 XML</greeting>

      </XML>
<SCRIPT>
      myDoc=island;
      if(myDoc.parseError.reason !="")
            {
            alert(myDoc.parseError.reason)
            }
</SCRIPT>
</HTML>
```

and provided that our XML is well formed it will load as a document object. Here is a screen shot of what happens when we run the last file.

Whoops! Our beginning and end tags don't match, we were careless about the case. Change 'Greeting' to 'greeting', and we are fine.

Just to be sure that we have loaded the file let's add the following line of code:

```
alert(myDoc.documentElement.nodeName);
```

We will look at this more later, but for now note that documentElement.nodeName should return the name of the root element, i.e. the string 'greeting'.

And it does!

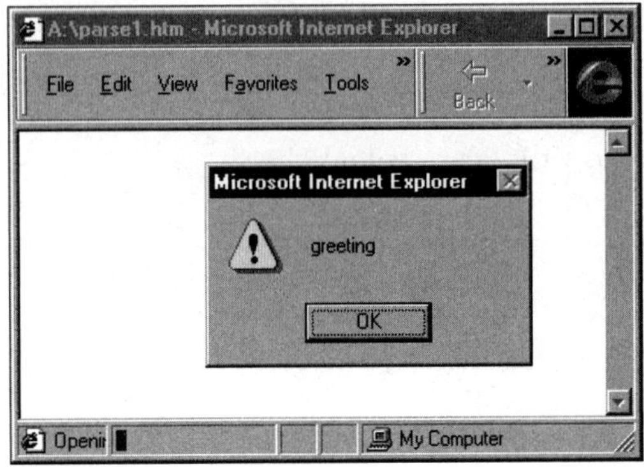

IE5 XML ActiveX Control

The ActiveX Control that comes with IE5 can also be used to create an XML document object.

Here is the code to do this:

```
<HTML>

<SCRIPT>
  //create an activeX object and assign it to the myDocument variable

  var myDocument = new ActiveXObject("microsoft.XMLDOM");

  //load an xml file into the activex object named myDocument

  myDocument.load("myxmlfile.xml");


      if(myDocument.parseError.reason !="")
            {
            alert(myDocument.parseError.reason);
            }

      alert(myDocument.documentElement.nodeName);

</SCRIPT>
</HTML>
```

Again we have carried out some rudimentary error checking, and have made sure that the file is indeed loaded.

It doesn't really matter which method is used to load our XML document as an object; the author's purely personal preference is to use an Island, and that is what is used in the examples below.

Having seen how to load an XML document into our IE5 browser, let's look at some examples from the W3C DOM using IE5.

Examples of DOM Interfaces

This section does not attempt to explain the significance of the interfaces, it just shows you what tools are available for manipulating the document. We will just try to show you how to use the tools provided, not what you can build from them, that is left up to the reader's imagination and ingenuity.

We will however show you a couple of complete examples at the end.

The Document and Node Interfaces

We will look at these two interfaces together, because they constitute the foundations of the DOM "Tree" model.

We will not look at examples of all the methods and attributes, but we will look at enough to enable us to understand how to manipulate our XML document. We will also look in a little more detail at those methods or attributes that may seem a little obscure.

Here is the basic XML document that we will be dissecting in our study of the `Document` and the `Node` interfaces:

```
<?xml version="1.0"?>

      <!DOCTYPE xdoc [
      <!ELEMENT xdoc (greeting)*>
      <!ELEMENT greeting (#PCDATA)>
      <!ENTITY dom "document object model">
      <!ATTLIST greeting
            type  CDATA #IMPLIED
            position CDATA #IMPLIED
      >

      ]>
      <!--a first comment-->
<xdoc>

      <greeting type="cordial" position="first">&amp; Hello &dom;</greeting>
      <greeting> Hello XML</greeting>
      <!--a comment-->
      <?pi do this and that ?>
</xdoc>
```

And here is how we will include it in our HTML document. Note again how we create a document object by the syntax `myDoc=xisle;`. Once we have created our document object we can manipulate it using the DOM.

At this point in the chapter we would advise you to type the following HTML code into a text editor and save it as `DOMmain.htm`:

```
<HTML>
<P>Below is an XML island</P>
<XML ID="xisle">
     <?xml version="1.0"?>

     <!DOCTYPE xdoc [
     <!ELEMENT xdoc (greeting)*>
     <!ELEMENT greeting (#PCDATA)>
     <!ENTITY dom "document object model">
     <!ATTLIST greeting
           type  CDATA #IMPLIED
           position CDATA #IMPLIED
     >

     ]>
     <!--a first comment-->
 <xdoc>

     <greeting type="cordial" position="first">&amp; Hello &dom;</greeting>
     <greeting> Hello XML</greeting>
     <!--a comment-->
     <?pi do this and that ?>
 </xdoc>
</XML>
<SCRIPT>
     //create an XML document object
     var myDoc=xisle;
     var rootEl=myDoc.documentElement;

</SCRIPT>
</HTML>
```

In the discussion of the methods and attributes of the `Document` and `Node` interfaces that follows the snippets of code are examples of lines of code that would be inserted into the `<SCRIPT>` section of `DOMmain.htm` demonstrating the manipulation of the properties of the `myDoc` XML document. We will be referring back to the code above as we go.

The Node Interface

All the node types in the DOM inherit a basic set of properties and methods from the Node interface. We will divide the Node interface properties up into attributes and factory methods.

Node Read-only Attributes.

Here is a list of the `Node` interface's read-only attributes:

Attribute	**Type**	**Comments**
`nodeName`	A string	The name a node has varies with its type. The name of an element is its tag name, that of a text node is `#text`, etc. The table later in 'Summary of Names and Values of Node Types' shows the names and values of the various node types

Attribute	Type	Comments
nodeValue	A string	In many cases, e.g. an element there is no value and a 'null' is returned. Again, the 'Summary of Names and Values...' table shows the values of the various nodes
nodeType	An unsigned short	The table in the section on the nodeType attribute later on shows the values returned for each different type of node.
parentNode	A Node object	Will return 'null' if there is no parent, i.e. if it is the document node.
childNodes	A NodeList object	The node list produced is an indexed list of children nodes
firstChild	A Node object	Will return 'null' if there is no first child
lastChild	A Node object	Will return 'null' if there is no last child
previousSibling	A Node object	Will return 'null' if there is no previous sibling
nextSibling	A Node object	Will return 'null' if there is no next sibling
attributes	A NamedNodeMap	Obviously only an element node will return a NamedNodeMap; all other types of node will return 'null'. Although a NamedNodeMap (see 'The NamedNodeMap Interface' below) has an index, the order is of no significance (unlike a NodeList), and is merely a convenience for accessing the map. The list is usually manipulated using the attribute name as an argument.
ownerDocument	A Document node	Every node has to be owned by a document. This property is of use in applications where several document are being manipulated at the same time

The 'NodeList' Interface

NodeList nodes can be accessed via an item method that takes the index as an argument. Its length can be obtained using the length method. We will see it in action right away in the next section when we have a look at the childNodes attribute. The NodeList interface essentially keeps a record of the node's child nodes and their positions. It is the basis for the maintenance of the 'tree' structure for a document in the computer's memory.

The'childNodes' Attribute

The childNodes attribute returns a NodeList object of all the children of any given node.

In our example DOMmain.htm code the use of:

```
var x=myDoc.childNodes;
```

in the <SCRIPT> section would assign a NodeList of all myDoc's children to x.

Inserting the code:

```
var  x=myDoc.childNodes;
   var  z=x.length;
for(var i=0; i < z; i++)
      {
      document.write(x(i).nodeType+ " | ");
      document.write(x(i).nodeName+ " | ");
      document.write(x(i).nodeValue + "<BR>");
         }
```

will produce the following screen output:

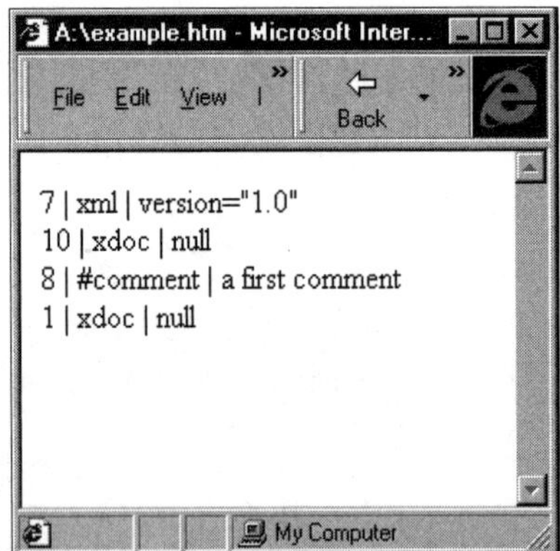

We will explain what the values mean when we look at nodeType, nodeName, and nodeValue attributes in the following sections. For now just note that what we did was to create a NodeList x holding the properties of four objects, that we were able to access using an index.

The 'nodeType' Attribute

The nodeType attribute of the Node interface returns an integer value indicating what type of node we are dealing with. Here is a list of the various types of nodes with their defined constants, and their integer value.

Integer value	Defined Constants
1	ELEMENT_NODE
2	ATTRIBUTE_NODE
3	TEXT_NODE
4	CDATA_SECTION_NODE
5	ENTITY_REFERENCE_NODE
6	ENTITY_NODE
7	PROCESSING_INSTRUCTION_NODE
8	COMMENT_NODE
9	DOCUMENT_NODE
10	DOCUMENT_TYPE_NODE
11	DOCUMENT_FRAGMENT_NODE
12	NOTATION_NODE

In our example code for the `childNodes` attribute we saw that '`myDoc`' had four children. The integer values tell us that the first was a version declaration, which happens to be a form of processing instruction, the second was a `DocumentType` node, the third was a comment, and the fourth was an element.

'nodeName' and 'nodeValue' Attributes

Every different type of node has a name. Several of the nodes also have a value. These can be accessed using the `nodeName` and `nodeValue` attributes of the `Node` interface.

If we ask for the value of a node that does not have one, `null` is returned. The table in the next section entitled 'Summary of the Name and Values of the Various Types of Nodes' shows the different types of nodes, and their names and values. The values of `nodeName`, `nodeValue`, and `attributes` vary according to the node type.

Summary of the Names and Values of the Various Types of Nodes

The values of `nodeName`, `nodeValue`, and `attributes` (note that this is an interface field and not the IDL data type `attribute`) vary according to the node type as follows:

Node Type	nodeName	nodeValue	attributes
`Element`	tagName	`null`	`NamedNodeMap`
`Attr`	name of attribute	value of attribute	`null`
`Text`	`#text`	content of the text node	`null`

Table Continued on Following Page

Node Type	nodeName	nodeValue	attributes
CDATASection	#cdata-section	content of the CDATA Section	null
EntityReference	name of entity referenced	null	null
Entity	entity name	null	null
Processing Instruction	target	entire content excluding the target	null
Comment	#comment	content of the comment	null
Document	#document	null	null
DocumentType	document type name	null	null
DocumentFragment	#document-fragment	null	null
Notation	notation name	null	null

Relational Attributes

All the following Node interface attributes hold the relevant node.

```
parentNode
firstChild
lastChild
previousSibling
nextSibling
```

For example, in our `DOMmain.htm` file above, as we saw we can use the `documentElement` interface attribute to assign the root element node of the document to `rootEl`:

```
rootEl=myDoc.documentElement;
```

This code will create an object `rootEl` that contains all of `xdoc`'s properties.

So the code:

`alert(rootEl.parentNode.nodeName);`	will display	`#document`
`alert(rootEl.firstChild.nodeName);`	will display	`greeting`
`alert(rootEl.lastChild.nodeName);`	will display	`pi` (The target of the processing instruction)
`alert(rootEl.previousSibling.nodeName);`	will display	`#comment`
`alert(rootEl.nextSibling.nodeName);`	will display	Nothing, there is no `nextSibling`

The 'attributes' Attribute

The `attributes` attribute can only be applied to an `Element` node type. The attribute holds a `NamedNodeMap` object containing the attributes of the XML element.

In our example we can assign the node of the first `greeting` element with the following code in the `SCRIPT` section of `DOMmain.htm`:

```
var rootEl=myDoc.documentElement;
var anEl=rootEl.firstChild;
```

We can now create a `NamedNodeMap` of its elements.

The NamedNodeMap Interface

The `NamedNodeMap` has the following methods and attributes:

Method or attribute	Parameters accepted	Comments
`getNamedItem`	The name of the attribute to be accessed	Returns an `Attr` node object
`setNamedItem`	The node to be added to the `NamedNodeMap`	(Not implemented in the early betas of IE5)
`removeNamedItem`	The name of the attribute to be removed	If the `Attr` to be removed is a required attribute, an error should be registered. If the removed node is an `Attr` with a default value it is immediately replaced.

Table Continued on Following Page

Method or attribute	Parameters accepted	Comments
item	An index integer	Returns an Attr node object at that index. If there is no attribute at that position, null is returned
length (attribute)	No parameters	Holds the length of the NamedNodeMap

First, in the SCRIPT section of DOMmain.htm we have the code:

```
var rootEl=myDoc.documentElement;
var anEl=rootEl.firstChild;
```

Recall that the attributes property of the Node interface returned a NamedNodeMap interface. The following code fragments illustrate the ways in which the existence of a NamedNodeMap for the node anEl allows us to access various properties:

```
alert(anEl.attributes.getNamedItem("position").nodeValue);
alert(anEl.attributes(1).nodeValue);
alert(anEl.attributes.item(1).nodeValue);
```

All these code lines will return the value of the position attribute of the first greeting element: first.

If we now add the code

```
var x=anEl.attributes.removeNamedItem("position");
alert(anEl.attributes.item(1));
```

the alert will show 'null', as the attribute has been removed.

However, if instead we add:

```
var x=anEl.attributes.removeNamedItem("type");
alert(anEl.attributes.item(1));
```

the alert will register 'first', indicating that the NamedNodeMap has not been updated with respect to position; thus showing its difference from a NodeList where position is updated.

Node Factory Methods

The Node factory methods allow us to insert the nodes we have already created with the Document factory methods (see the section on 'The Document Interface' later) into the relevant place in the document.

Here is a table of them:

Method	Parameters	Returned values	Comments
`insertBefore`	Takes two parameters: 1.The node object to insert 2.The node to insert it before	The node being inserted.	
`replaceChild`	Takes two parameters: 1.The node object to insert in the child list 2.The node to be replaced	The node replaced	
`removeChild`	The node being removed	The removed node	
`appendChild`	The node to add	The node added	Adds the node to the end of the node list
`hasChildNodes` (a boolean)	No parameters	Returns true if the node has child nodes otherwise returns false	Not supported in the early betas of IE5. Test for child node's length instead
`cloneNode`	deep = (true | false)	The duplicate node	If clone node takes the parameter 'deep=true' then all the children of the node are cloned. Otherwise just the node object, together with its attributes, (if it is an element) are cloned

We show an example that will make these methods easier to understand in the next section on 'The Document Interface'.

Let's now move on and look at the `Document` interface supplied by the DOM.

The Document Interface

Document Read-only Attributes

Here is a list of the read-only attributes of the `Document` interface.

Attribute	Type	Comments
`doctype`	`DocumentType`	This provides access to the DTD of the XML document.
`implementation`	`DOMImplementation`	This has a method `hasFeature()` which returns a Boolean. It is passed two arguments, a `'feature'` argument, and a `'version'` argument.
`documentElement`	`Element`	This returns the root element of the document.

The 'doctype' Attribute

This attribute provides access to the *'internal'* DTD of the document. In our `DOMmain.htm` file placing the following line of code in the `SCRIPT` section:

```
alert(MyDoc.doctype);
```

produces the following:

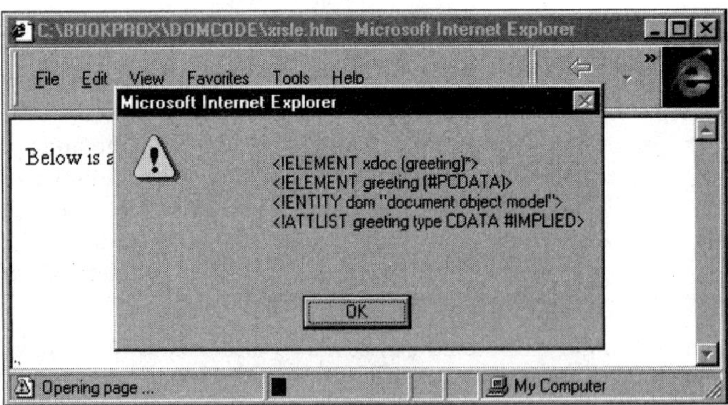

If we change the XML part of `DOMmain.htm` to read as follows:

```
<XML ID="xisle">
     <?xml version="1.0"?>

     <!DOCTYPE xdoc SYSTEM "xisle.dtd"
```

```
        [
        <!ENTITY dom "document object model">
        ]>
        <!--a first comment-->
        <xdoc>

        <greeting type="cordial">&amp; Hello &dom;</greeting>
        <greeting> Hello XML</greeting>
        <!--a comment-->
        <?pi do this and that ?>
    </xdoc>
</XML>
```

with a separate xisle.dtd file (in the same directory) reading as follows.

```
<!ELEMENT xdoc (greeting)+ >
<!ELEMENT greeting (#PCDATA) >
<!ENTITY amp "&#38;#38;">
<!ATTLIST greeting
   type CDATA #IMPLIED
>
```

we have for all intents and purposes exactly the same document. However now the same code

```
alert(MyDoc.doctype);
```

produces the following result:

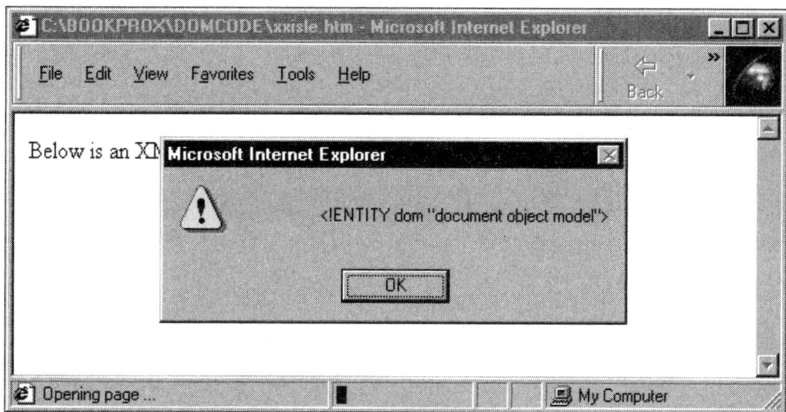

In other words all that this attribute holds is the internal subset of the DTD. When we look at entities later we will see the significance of this.

There are some occasions when we may want access to the full DTD of a document, for example when we may want to change element content on the fly. Level I of the DOM does not give us the interfaces to do this though.

The 'implementation' Attribute

This attribute returns a `DOMImplementation` interface representing the type of document implementation. The `DOMImplementation` interface provides a method `hasFeatures()` that returns a Boolean. It takes two arguments, a `feature`, and a `version`.

The `feature` argument can be either '`XML`' or '`HTML`' (letter case immaterial). In the case of XML the version number has to be the same as that specified in the version declaration.

In the `SCRIPT` section for `DOMmain.htm`, the code:

```
MyDoc.implementation.hasFeature("XML", "1.0");
```

would return `true`, anything else, including:

```
MyDoc.implementation.hasFeature("XML", "1");
```

would return `false`, because it is the string value that is tested not the numerical value.

Again, version checking is important in document management, and although we probably would not have much use for version checking in a simple HTML page, it is important in other cases. For example we may wish to run through our whole bank of documents and sort them into HTML documents and XML documents.

The 'documentElement' Attribute

This attribute holds the root element of the document. Access to the root element is obviously important as it contains all the actual content of the document, so with a root element object we can access the rest of the document.

So if we use this code in our `DOMmain.htm SCRIPT` section:

```
var rootEl=myDoc.documentElement;
```

This would create a variable `rootEl` containing all the document nodes after the XML prolog. We can then use the `childNodes` attribute of the interface (recall that a `Document` interface inherits this from the basic `Node` interface) to start accessing every other node in the document.

Document Interface Factory Methods

If we create a node it in fact belongs to the document, even though it is an orphan at the time of creation. We have to use the factory methods inherited from the `Node` interface to place the node we have created within the document structure. Anything we create is however an object in its own right.

The `Document` interface methods are all factory methods, and we use them to create each and every kind of node. Here is a list:

Method	**Parameters accepted**	**Node type returned**	**Comments**
`createElement`	A string that is the tag name of the element	`Element`	

Method	Parameters accepted	Node type returned	Comments
createDocument Fragment	none	Document Fragment	This just creates a document fragment node. Elements etc. can be added to it by the node methods
createTextNode	A string	Text	The string is the value of the text node, or in plain English, it's the stuff you want written
createComment	A string	Comment	The <!-- and --> will be added automatically. The parameter should be what goes between the delimiters
createCDATA Section	A string	CDATASection	
createProcessing Instruction	Two strings, the first being the processing instruction's target, the second being the data for the node.	Processing Instruction	The <? and ?> are added as for comments
createAttribute	A string	Attr	It is probably better to create an attribute and value using the element interface's setAttribute method.(see the section on the 'Element Interface' later)
createEntity Reference	A string of the name of the entity	Entity Reference	The & and ; are added automatically
getElementsBy TagName	A tag name	A NodeList of all the elements of the given name	This node list can be accessed by index

Let's see an example of how these work.

Document and Node Interface Methods in Action

The following example demonstrates the scripting code to be inserted in our **DOMmain.htm** file for manipulating the DOM. Please note that this example has no purpose other than to demonstrate the mechanics of the syntax.

Essentially we'll create three new nodes, `greeting`, `other`, and a comment node, then:

- We'll append one of the nodes: the `comment` node.
- We'll clone the `comment` node, and append that.
- And we'll insert our `other` element at the beginning of the document.
- Then we'll replace a processing instruction node with a `greeting` node.

Here's the script containing comments that indicate what's happening:

```
<SCRIPT>
  //create an XML document object
     myDoc=xisle;          //'xisle' is the XML Island in the original HTML document
                           //shown in the section 'The Document and Node Interfaces'

     rootEl=myDoc.documentElement;
     anEl=rootEl.firstChild;

  //document and node factory methods
    document.write("<H1 align='center'>Demonstration of factory methods</H1>");

  //create the new elements
     x=myDoc.createElement("greeting");
     y=myDoc.createElement("other");
     z=myDoc.createComment("A created comment");

  //make a node list
     nlist=rootEl.childnodes;

  //write out the starting node list
     writechildnodes(nlist);

  //put in the new nodes
     rootEl.appendChild(z);

  //write out the new node list
     writechildnodes(nlist);

  //clone a node and insert it put in the new nodes
     var zz=z.cloneNode(false);
     rootEl.appendChild(zz);

  //write out the new node list
     writechildnodes(nlist);

  //insert the 'other' element
     rootEl.insertBefore(y,anEl);

  //write out the new node list
     writechildnodes(nlist);
```

```
    //replace pi with x
       rootEl.replaceChild(x,nlist(4));

    //write out the new node list
       writechildnodes(nlist);

    //-----function write nodes------

       function writechildnodes(nlist2)
       {
             len=nlist2.length;
             document.write("<BR>");
             for(var i=0;i<len;i++)
             {
             document.write(nlist(i).nodeName + " | ");
             }
       }
    //---------end function------------------
  </SCRIPT>
```

We get this screen output:

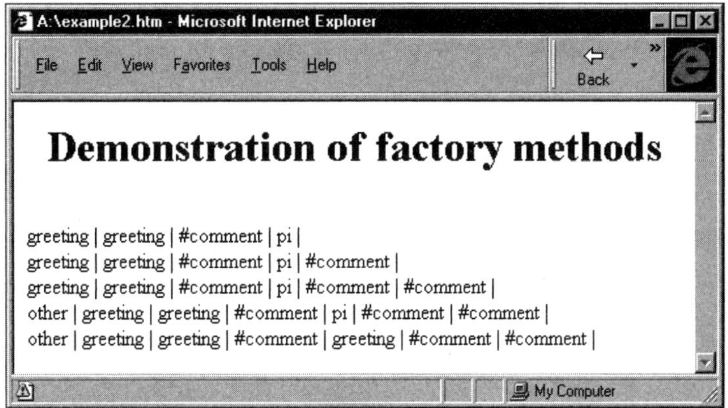

Note the following:

- How we use a simple function `writechildnodes` which uses the JavaScript `for` statement to show the names of the nodes on the screen.

- How the node list `nlist` is automatically updated each time we add a node to the list. There is no need for us to write code to update it.

- How the `cloneNode()` method takes a parameter of '`true`' or '`false`'. This applies to the depth of the cloning, i.e. deep = '`true`', or deep = '`false`'. In this example we have just cloned a comment which can have no children, but if this had been an element then deep = '`true`' would have cloned all its child objects. With deep = '`false`' just its attributes and their values would have been cloned.

We have only looked at examples of some of the methods and attributes of the `Document` and `Node` interfaces, but hopefully you will have no difficulty with using some of their other properties.

The CharacterData Interface

The `CharacterData` interface provides a whole series of methods and two attributes for manipulating strings in any nodes that take character data, such as a text node or a comment node. The table below shows the methods and attributes available. Attributes are indicated.

Method or attribute	Parameters accepted	Value returned	Comments
`data` (attribute)	none	The string content of the node	In a PI it returns everything between `<?` and `?>`, in a comment every thing between `<!--` and `-->`, and in a text node it returns the text
`length` (attribute)	none	The number of string characters in the node	
`substring-Data`	Two integers: 1: the start of the offset of the substring to extract. 2: The number of characters to extract	A string starting from the offset, of length equivalent to the second parameter.	If the count to be extracted extends beyond the end of the string, the string is returned to its termination
`appendData`	The string to append to the end of the node.	Returns nothing	
`insertData`	Two parameters, the offset at which to begin the string insertion , and the string to insert.	Returns nothing	An exception is raised if the offset is negative, or is greater than the length of the node.
`deleteData`	Two parameters, the offset at which to begin the deletion, and a count of the number of characters to delete.	Returns nothing	An exception is raised if the offset is negative, or is greater than the length of the node, or if the specified count is negative.
`replaceData`	Three parameters, the offset at which to begin the replacement, a count of the number of characters to delete, and the string with which to replace the deleted characters.	Returns nothing	If the count extends beyond the end of the string, then all the characters starting from the offset are replaced.

Again we'll try to bring the above to life with the help of a few examples. Insert the following script into `DOMmain.htm` from the 'Document and Node Interfaces' section earlier. In this example we take our second `greeting` element, and make an object of its child `text` node.

We then

- measure its length
- print out its data
- extract a substring
- append it
- then insert some text
- replace some text
- and finally delete some text.

Again we stress that this example has no purpose other than to demonstrate the mechanics of the DOM syntax.

```
<SCRIPT>

  //create an XML document object
     myDoc=xisle;

     rootEl=myDoc.documentElement;

  //make an object of the text node Hello XML
     anEl=rootEl.firstChild.nextSibling.firstchild;

  //characterData

     document.write("<H1 ALIGN ='center'>Examples CharacterData Interface
     _</H1>");
     document.write("<BR><SPAN STYLE='font-size:14pt;'>Example of length :-
     _</SPAN>")
     document.write(anEl.length);

     document.write("<BR><SPAN STYLE='font-size:14pt;'>Example of data :-
     _</SPAN>");
     document.write(anEl.data);

     document.write("<BR><SPAN STYLE='font-size:14pt;'>Example of a substring :-
     _</SPAN>");
     document.write(anEl.substringData(6,3));

     document.write("<BR><SPAN STYLE='font-size:14pt;'>Example of appendData :-
     _</SPAN>");
     anEl.appendData(" More Text!!");
     document.write(anEl.data);

     document.write("<BR><SPAN STYLE='font-size:14pt;'>Example of insertData :-
     _</SPAN>");
     anEl.insertData(5," Inserted Text!! ");
     document.write(anEl.data);
     document.write("<BR><SPAN STYLE='font-size:14pt;'>Example of replaceData :-
     _</SPAN>");
     anEl.replaceData(21,4,"Core1 level XML DOM!!");
     document.write(anEl.data);
```

```
        document.write("<BR><SPAN STYLE='font-size:14pt;'>Example of deleteData :-
         _</SPAN>");
        anEl.deleteData(21,11)
        document.write(anEl.data);

    </SCRIPT>
```

There are really no catches in the above code; it is all quite straightforward.

The result of this code is shown in the screen shot below.

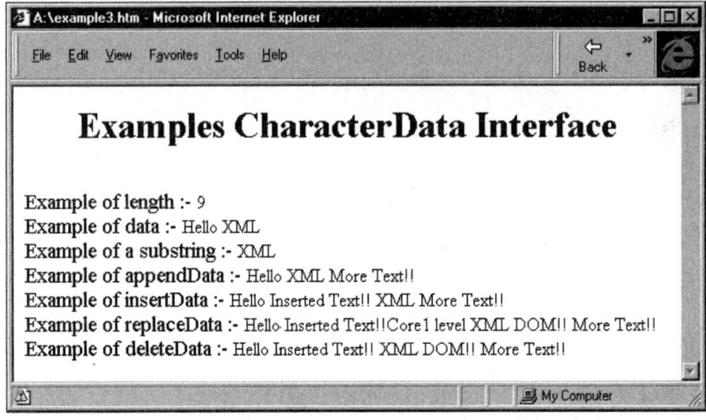

Let's move on to the `Attr` interface.

The Attr Interface

In the W3C DOM the element's attributes (see note 1 below) are not considered to be a part of the document tree, but rather are considered to be an integral part of the element.

(1)The `Attr` interface (which represents an XML attribute) was the 'attribute' interface in earlier versions of the DOM. It was changed to `Attr` to prevent confusion with the IDL keyword 'attribute', which is used to indicate fields of the interfaces.

Because they are part of the element, the methods such as `parentNode`, and `nextSibling` will return a `null` value when used with this interface.

Here are the attributes of the `Attr` interface.

Attributes	Returned values	Comments
name	The attribute's name	
specified	true or false	This is true if the attribute was explicitly given a value in the original document. If the attribute is a default value, then the returned value will be false.
value	The attribute's value	

In our DOMmain.htm document, if we write in our SCRIPT the code:

```
myDoc=xisle;
rootEl=myDoc.documentElement;
anEl=rootEl.firstChild;
x=anEl.attributes(0);

document.write(x.specified+ "<BR>");
document.write(x.nodeValue +"<BR>");
document.write(x.nodeName + "<BR>");
alert(x.parentNode);
alert(x.nextSibling);
```

both the alerts will return 'null', and the browser will show:

true
cordial
type

Let's now look at the Element interface.

The Element Interface

The majority of nodes in a document are going to be text and element nodes. Because the Node interface methods can be used for all elements, the only methods associated directly with the Element interface are concerned with attributes and their values.

We have already seen how the code syntax:

```
X=[nodeobject].attributes;
```

will create a NamedNodeObject X, and we have also seen how the code syntax:

```
[document object].createAttribute("[tag name]");
```

can create an orphan Attr node that can be assigned to an element by one of the methods we are about to look at.

Here are the methods and attributes associated with the Element interface.

Method or attribute	Parameters accepted	Value returned	Comments
tagName (attribute)	none	The tagName of the element	Will return the same value as if the node interface method [nodeobject].nodeName was used

Table Continued on Following Page

Method or attribute	Parameters accepted	Value returned	Comments
getAttribute	The attribute's name	The attribute's value	Note that this is the only way in the current DOM to get the attribute's value, unless you isolate an Attr node (see getAttributeNode below), or use NamedNodeList
setAttribute	Two parameters: 1: the name of the attribute 2: a string, which will be the attribute's value.	nothing	Note that if the attribute is already present, this method will merely change the attribute's value. However if there is no attribute present with the supplied name, then it will create an attribute of that name and give it the prescribed value If the attribute name is not allowed by the DTD an error will be raised
remove Attribute	The name of the attribute to remove	nothing	
getAttribute Node	The name of the attribute to retrieve	The Attr node named	nodeType, nodeName, and nodeValue can be applied to the returned object
setAttribute Node	The attribute node to be added to the attribute list	If the attribute replaces an Attr of the same name, then the old attribute object is returned, otherwise null is returned	If the attribute name is not allowed by the DTD an error should be raised
remove Attribute Node	The Attr node to be removed from the list	The removed node	
getElements ByTagName	The name of the tag to match on	A Nodelist of all the elements of that name	The individual nodes can be accessed by index
normalize	none	none	This will combine all adjacent text children under the element. See note below

Again we have provided a few examples to try and make this clearer. We emphasize again that the following example is purely to demonstrate the mechanics of the DOM. Insert the following pieces of code into `DOMmain.htm`:

```
<SCRIPT>
     //create an XML document object
     var myDoc=xisle;

     var rootEl=myDoc.documentElement;

    //make object of the first greeting element
     var anEl=rootEl.firstChild;

     document.write("<DIV STYLE='font-size:22pt;'>");
     document.write("<SPAN STYLE='font-size:14pt;'>We use getAttribute to get the
                    _first 'greeting' type attribute value </SPAN><BR>");
     ...
```

The following block of code merely gets the value of an attribute and writes it:

```
     ...
     document.write(anEl.getAttribute("type")+"<BR>");
     ...
```

The following block uses the `setAttribute` method to change the value of `type`, and then writes it:

```
     ...
     anEl.setAttribute("type","cold");
     document.write("<SPAN STYLE='font-size:14pt;'>We have used setAttribute to
      _change cordial to cold </SPAN><BR>");
     document.write(anEl.getAttribute("type")+"<BR>");
     ...
```

Next we have created a new attribute named `class` with a value of `simple`:

```
     ...
     anEl.setAttribute("class","simple");
        document.write("<SPAN STYLE='font-size:14pt;'>We use setAttribute to make
          _a new attribute with a value of 'simple' </SPAN><BR>");
     document.write(anEl.getAttribute("class")+"<BR>");
     ...
```

Here we create a new element using the `Document` interface's `createElement` method. We then append this element to the end of `xdoc`'s children:

```
     ...
     x=myDoc.createElement("other");
     document.write("<SPAN STYLE='font-size:14pt;'>We have created an element
      _called other </SPAN><BR>");
     rootEl.appendChild(x);
     document.write(rootEl.lastChild.nodeName+"<BR>")
     ...
```

Now we create an attribute called `junk` using the `Document` interface's `createAttribute` method. We use the `setAttributeNode` method to add this attribute to `other` which we had earlier read into the variable `x`. We use `getAttribute` to demonstrate that at this time it has no value assigned to it. Then we use `setAttribute` to add a value to it, and use `getAttribute` again to confirm that we have indeed done this.

```
        ...
        var y=myDoc.createAttribute("junk");
        x.setAttributeNode(y);
        document.write("<SPAN STYLE='font-size:14pt;'>We are getting the value of
        _ the 'junk' attribute we created and set in the other element
        _(should be null)</SPAN><BR>");


        document.write(x.getAttribute("junk")+"<BR>");
        document.write("<SPAN STYLE='font-size:14pt;'>We give it a value of
        _'junkvalue'</SPAN><BR>");
        x.setAttribute("junk","junkvalue");

        document.write(x.getAttribute("junk")+"<BR>");
        document.write("</DIV>")

    </SCRIPT>
```

Here is what the screen output looks like:

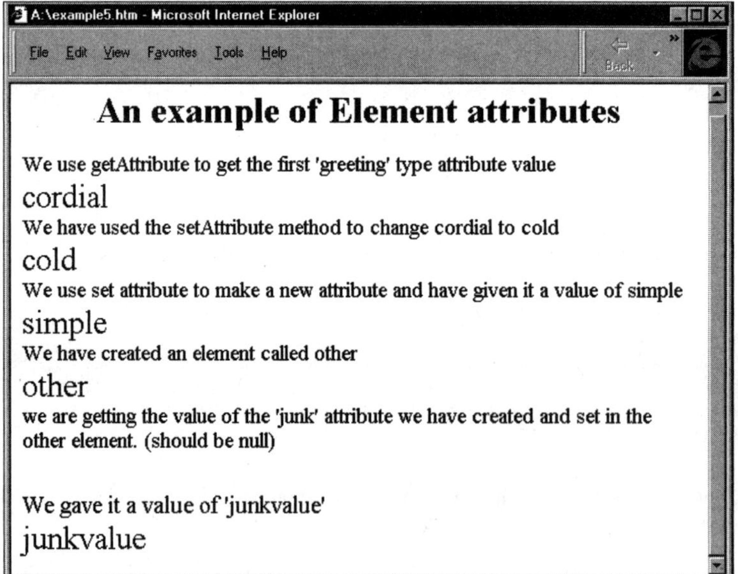

Here we cover the remaining two methods in the `Element` interface.

getElementsByTagName

This method will make a node list of all the elements of a given name. The individual nodes can then be accessed by index.

The code:

```
var greetlist=myDoc.getElementsByTagName("greeting");
```

would produce an indexed `Nodelist` of all the `greeting` elements.

normalize

In the course of writing a document with factory methods it is possible that a text string may have been built up by several different `createTextNode`, and `appendChild` methods.

It is thus quite possible that the string in the `<macbeth>` element

```
<macbeth> "Tomorrow, and tomorrow, and tomorrow creeps on our petty pace from day
o day" </macbeth>
```

is not one node but several!

```
<macbeth> "tomorrow, | and tomorrow, | and tomorrow | creeps on our petty pace |
rom day to day" </macbeth>
```

This could play havoc with, for example, any XPointer system that we might be using. To merge all these children into a single child of `macbeth` we would put (assuming that this was the four hundred and thirty second `macbeth` element):

```
maclist=shakedoc.getElementsByTagName('macbeth');
macbeth(432).normalize;
```

Now instead of five child nodes we would have one! All we have done is roll adjacent text nodes into a single node.

It should be noted that if a document created by a factory method is saved repeatedly, then we would not expect these child nodes to persist between edits, as saving should force normalization to occur anyway.

Now we move on to the text node interface.

The Text Node Interface

The `Text` node interface inherits all the methods and attributes of the `CharacterData` interface, which basically means that all the methods that we have looked at under the `CharacterData` interface can be used to manipulate any text nodes.

In addition the `Text` interface has one method of its own, the `splitText` method.

The 'splitText' Method

This method will divide a single text node into two separate nodes. It takes a single parameter, an integer, which is an offset from the beginning of the text string. So if `txtObj` represents the following string:

```
"There is a time to be born and a time to die"
```

the code:

```
newTxtObj=txtObj.splitText(26);
```

would create two text objects, `newTxtObj` which would have a value of "`and a time to die`", and `txtObj` which now has a value of "`There is a time to be born`".

It is difficult for me to imagine under what circumstances this method might be used, but there it is if you want it!

The Comment Interface

The `Comment` interface inherits all the methods of the `CharacterData` interface, but has none of its own.

All the methods that we have looked at under the `CharacterData` interface can be used to manipulate any text string in the comment between `<!--` and `-->`.

The Processing Instruction Interface

A processing instruction is a way to keep processing specific information in the text of a document. They consist of a target and data. The PI that will be encountered most frequently is the one linking a document to a style sheet.

```
<?xml:stylesheet type="text/css" href="myxml_style.css"?>
```

In this PI, the target is '`xml:stylesheet`', and everything after the first white space is data.

The PI interface has two read-only attributes, `target` and `data`. They can then be manipulated using the `CharacterData` interface methods.

Assuming we had the style sheet PI in our XML document then our script code:

```
var targetStr=myPI.target;
```

would produce a text object `targetStr` with the content '`xml:stylesheet`', and

```
var dataStr=myPI.data;
```

would produce a text object `dataStr` with the content '`href="myxml_style.css" type="text/css"`'.

The DocumentType Interface

We have already seen how when we use the `Document` interface the attribute:

```
X=myDoc.doctype;
```

assigns a `DocumentType` object to `X`.

The DocumentType interface has the following read-only attributes.

Attributes	Returned values	Comment
name	The name of the document	This is the string immediately following <!DOCTYPE, i.e. xdoc in our example Note that the same value is returned if we use the Node attribute nodeName
entities	A NamedNodeMap of all the entities	This map can be accessed by index, although the order is of no significance. C.f. The NamedNodeMap interface earlier
notations	A NamedNodeMap of all the notations	

Let's add the following to our DTD for the XML Island in DOMmain.htm:

```
<!ATTLIST greeting
      type CDATA #IMPLIED
      class CDATA #IMPLIED
      position CDATA #IMPLIED
>
<!ENTITY dom "document object model">
<!ENTITY htm SYSTEM "core2.xml">

<!NOTATION gif SYSTEM "http://someserver.com/gwswin/gws.exe">
```

And see how we can use the DocumentType, the Entities and the Notation interfaces to access the information.

In our example the following code in the SCRIPT section of DOMmain.htm would make a NamedNodeMap of all the entities:

```
document.write(docObj.entities(0).nodeName);
document.write(docObj.entities(1).nodeName);
```

would print out 'dom', and 'htm' respectively. The code:

```
document.write(docObj.notations(0).nodeName);
```

would print out 'gif'.

The Notation Interface

The Notation interface just has two read-only attributes, publicId, and systemId.

Used with the code in the previous section:

```
document.write(docObj.notations(0).systemId);
```

would print out "http://someserver.com/gwswin/gws.exe".

The Entity Interface

The `Entity` interface has three read-only attributes, `publicId`, `systemId`, and `notationName`.

Used with the changes we made to the DTD of the XML of `DOMmain.htm` in the earlier 'DocumentType Interface' section, the code:

```
document.write(docObj.entities(1).systemId);
```

would print out "`core2.xml`".

`notationName` would give the name of the notation for an unparsed entity, in this case as both entities are parsed, it would return '`null`'.

The EntityReference Interface

How user agents deal with entity references that they come across is, to a large extent, up to them. User agents must expand all the pre-defined entities (&, ", ', < and >) and usually expand all the character entities.

For example this is how IE5 expands the following script code:

```
for(i=930;i<976;i++)
      {
      document.write("&#"+ i +";");
      }
```

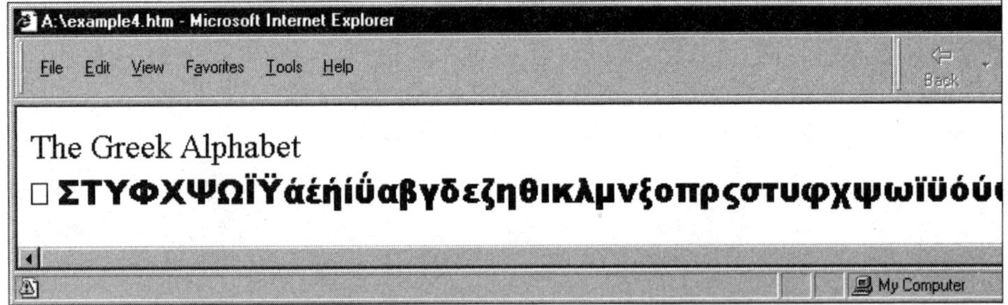

The expansion of the entity, if available, will appear as a child of the entity reference. So in our example code in `DOMmain.htm`:

```
      x=anEl.lastChild;
```

creates an object of our entity reference `&dom;`, and:

```
      alert(x.firstChild);
```

would display the expansion of the entity "`document object model`".

W3C DOM Conclusions.

That wraps up our look at the W3C DOM, and its implementation in IE5. The DOM gives us a tremendous, cross-platform, application independent way to manipulate our XML documents.

Hopefully there will soon be applications that allow us to persistently save the document that we have manipulated. Even though we obviously cannot do this with a browser, we can use the browser to do some fairly advanced things with XML and the DOM. Next we will just have a look a couple of simple things we can do using the DOM and IE5.

All the rather sterile examples in the above have been to illustrate the mechanics of the DOM. Lets have a look at some simple implementations which could have some real life advantage.

Some Simple Implementations

A workable DOM gives us tremendous power to manipulate and display our documents. The following three very simple examples are offered as examples of what is possible right now with XML and a DOM compliant browser.

The Basic Recursion Loop

The basis of most XML tree manipulation is a simple recursive loop which will loop through all the nodes in order. Such a loop is shown here.

The function `getchildren` in the code below takes a node as a parameter, makes a node list of the children, loops through the node list testing to see if each child has children of its own, and if it does it calls itself. The `nest1.xml` file it uses for the XML Island is given after this HTML code:

```
<HTML>
<!-- this simple progam loads an XML document into an IE5 browser, and loops
through the nodes using a recursive function-->

      <!--load a well formed document into an island-->

      <XML ID="island1" SRC="nest1.xml"></XML>

      <SCRIPT>
      //create a document object and a node list


            var myDoc=island1;
            var myDocNodeList=myDoc.childNodes;
      if(myDoc.parseError.reason!="")
            {
            alert(myDoc.parseError.reason);
            }
      else
            {
            alert("valid XML document");
            }
      //create a root element object
```

```
        var rootEl=myDoc.documentElement;

    //loop through it's content

        x=getchildren(myDoc);

//================begin recursive function 'getchildren'=========================

    function getchildren(node)
    {
    //create a child list
    var x=node.childNodes;
    var z=x.length;

    if(z!=0)
        {
        for(var i=0;i<z;i++)
            {
    //all manipulations to XML elements go here
            document.write("Node Type=" + x(i).nodeType);
            document.write(" Node Name=" + x(i).nodeName);
            document.write("Node Value=" + x(i).nodeValue + "<BR>");
            getchildren(x(i));
            }
        }

    }
//==========end function 'getchildren'===================
    </SCRIPT>

</HTML>
```

In this example we have chosen the following file to loop through, and as you can see we have chosen to display details about each node.

Here is the file we loop through:

```
<xdoc>a
    <nest1>b<nonnest1/>
        <nest2>c<nonnest2/>
            <nest3>d<nonnest3/>
            </nest3>
        </nest2>
    </nest1>
    <nonnest1/>
    <nonnest2/>
    <nonnest3/>
</xdoc>
```

As you can see it is rather unexciting, but is just designed to show how the recursion works.

Here is a screen shot of the file output:

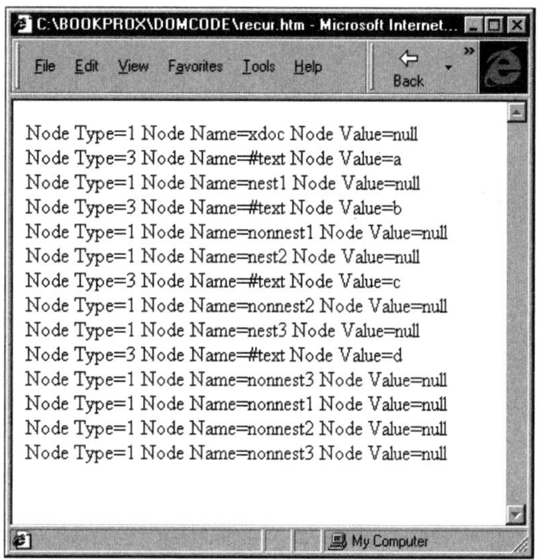

As you can see the recursive function calls all the children in order. We can now use this or a similar type of function to carry out some manipulations of real use on our XML document. We will use variations on this function to display and style an XML document, and to display some simple data in the form of a table.

Simple Styling

Using a variation of the recursion scheme, here is how we style a simple document. We modify the recursive function as follows:

```
function getchildren(node)

    {
    //create a child list
    var x=node.childNodes;
    var z=x.length;

    if(z!=0)
        {
        for(var i=0;i<z;i++)
            {
            if(x(i).nodeType==3)
                {
                document.write(x(i).nodeValue);
                getchildren(x(i));
                }
            else if(x(i).nodeType==1 && x(i).nodeName=="farewell" )
                {
                document.write(" <DIV STYLE='font-size:20pt;color:red'> ");
                getchildren(x(i));
                document.write(" </DIV> ");
                }
            else if(x(i).nodeType==1 && x(i).nodeName=="greeting" )
                {
```

```
                    document.write(" <DIV STYLE='font-size:16pt;color:green'>
                    _");
                    getchildren(x(i));
                    document.write(" </DIV> ");
                    }
                else
                    {
                    getchildren(x(i));
                    }
            }
        }

    }
```

Note how:

- We write an opening HTML tag with appropriate styling.
- We look at the tagName, and apply the appropriate style to the tag.
- We call `getchildren` to see if there are any children to be dealt with.
- We close the HTML tag after calling `getchildren`.

When applied to this simple file:

```
<?xml version="1.0" encoding="UTF-8" ?>
<xdoc>
    <greeting>Hello DOM</greeting>
    <greeting>Hello XML</greeting>
    <farewell>Goodbye HTML</farewell>
</xdoc>
```

Here is what the output looks like:

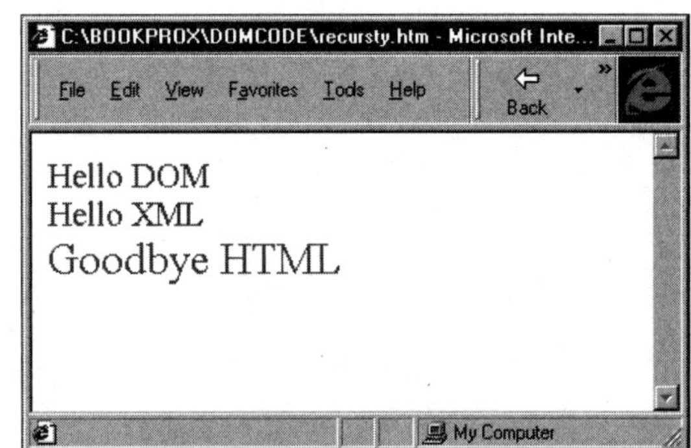

Obviously with a bit more work, we could design a function to read an external style sheet that we could import as a second XML island.

This exercise is left up to the reader.

Simple Tables

Again we can display data in an XML file as a simple table.

Here is a simple XML file used as a database:

```
<inventory>

     <item>
          <name>Name of item</name>
          <qty>Quantity in '000's</qty>
          <cost>$'s for 10</cost>
          <sell>recommended price each item </sell>
     </item>
     <item>
          <name>Knife </name>
          <qty>100</qty>
          <cost>50</cost>
          <sell>10</sell>
     </item>

     <item>
          <name>Fork </name>
          <qty>200</qty>
          <cost>60 dollars</cost>
          <sell>10</sell>
     </item>

     <item>
          <name>Spoon </name>
          <qty>150</qty>
          <cost>70</cost>
          <sell>10 </sell>
     </item>
</inventory>
```

And here is how we would modify our function to display it:

```
function getchildren(node)
     {
     //create a child list
     var x=node.childNodes;
     var z=x.length;

     if(z!=0)
          {
          for(var i=0;i<z;i++)
               {
               if(x(i).nodeType==3)
                 {
                 document.write(x(i).nodeValue);
                 getchildren(x(i));
                 }
               else if(x(i).nodeType==1 && x(i).nodeName=="inventory" )
                 {
                 document.write(" <TABLE BORDER=1 WIDTH=75% ALIGN='center'> ")
                 getchildren(x(i));
                 document.write(" </TABLE> ")
                 }
               else if(x(i).nodeType==1 && x(i).nodeName=="item" )
                 {
                 document.write(" <TR> ")
                 getchildren(x(i));
```

```
                    document.write(" </TR> ")
                    }
                  else if(x(i).nodeType==1)
                    {
                    document.write(" <TD ALIGN='center'> ")
                    getchildren(x(i));
                    document.write(" </TD> ")
                    }
                  else
                    {
                    getchildren(x(i));
                    }
                  }
            }

      }
  //==========end function 'getchildren'=================
```

And here is what the output looks like:

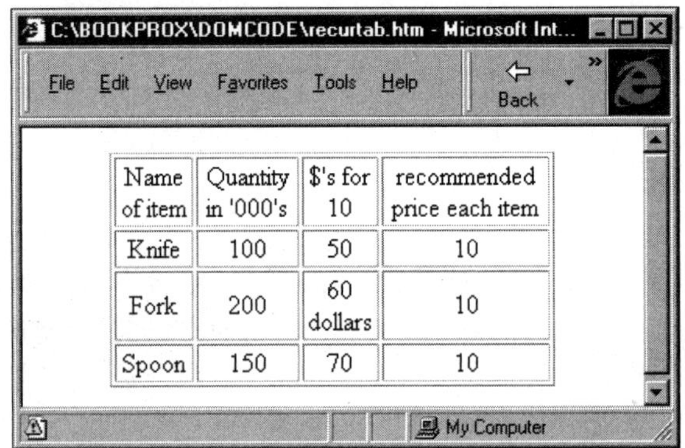

Name of item	Quantity in '000's	$'s for 10	recommended price each item
Knife	100	50	10
Fork	200	60 dollars	10
Spoon	150	70	10

Again although this script is especially designed for this type of data file, with a little work we could write a generic script that used a style sheet, and displayed any data in any form.

The Slide Example - a Real Life Application

Like many lecturers I have literally thousands of slides, and I have had difficulty organizing my slides in the past. For some time now I have been keeping the content of my slides as XML documents, which allows me to organize and categorize my slides. Until recently I have been using a simple Visual Basic program to convert them for display, either by creating a bitmap, or by converting them to HTML.

It struck me that they could in fact be shown 'on the fly' using the DOM. This is how it was done.

The Slide Template

As with any new XML project the first thing to do is to figure out what needs to be in the document. I figured out that at least 99% of my slides consisted of the following types:

- A bulleted list of points
- A statement, such as a string of text or a quotation

- An announcement, which needed to be put in large text, an example would be a title slide
- I also realized that by projecting an HTML page I could make use of the object tag to show 'live' code and text

This is what the XML template looks like:

```
<?xml version="1.0" ?>
<!DOCTYPE slide SYSTEM "slide.dtd">

<slide>

<header>
<line></line>          <!--line is used for simple formatting.-->
</header>

<slidebody>
     <!--only one of these per slide-->
     <object></object>
     <image></image>
     <statement><line></line></statement>
     <announcement><line></line></announcement>


     <bullet-list>
           <bullet_title></bullet_title>
           <item>
           </item>
           <item>
           </item>
     </bullet-list>
</slidebody>
<footer>
</footer>
</slide>
```

Save this file as `slide.xml`. Or download it from `http://webdev.wrox.co.uk/books/1525/`

Even the simplest XML application benefits from a DTD. Every time we make a new slide document we can run it through the validator to make sure that we are following the rules we set for ourselves.

The DTD for the `slide.xml` is very simple, but it makes sure that out slide follows certain rules. In particular note the element content of `body`. It ensures that we cannot accidentally add two different types of slide to the same slide document.

```
<?xml version="1.0" ?>

<!ELEMENT slide (header,slidebody,footer)>

<!ELEMENT header       (#PCDATA|line)*>
<!ELEMENT slidebody (object | image | statement | announcement | bullet-list) >

<!ELEMENT object       (#PCDATA)>
<!ELEMENT image        (#PCDATA)>
<!ELEMENT statement    (#PCDATA|line)*>
<!ELEMENT announcement (#PCDATA|line)*>
<!ELEMENT line         (#PCDATA)>
```

```
<!ELEMENT bullet-list  (bullet_title?,item)+>
<!ELEMENT bullet_title (#PCDATA)>
<!ELEMENT item         (#PCDATA)>

<!ELEMENT footer       (#PCDATA)>

<!ATTLIST slide  type  CDATA   #IMPLIED>
```

Save this file as `slide.dtd`. This can also be obtained from the Wrox Web site `http://webdev.wrox.co.uk/books/1525/`.

Before the advent of the DOM, I used this template either to generate a bitmap slide using a simple VB program, or used another simple program to generate an HTML document.

Now however, I can use the DOM to create my slides on the fly directly from the XML document. The code used to do this follows. As you can see it is a variation of the recursion file used in the first three examples.

Essentially the code does the following:

- Creates an XML `documentObject`
- Loops through the document converting the XML to HTML on the fly
- Displays the HTML using a style sheet

The first part of the code creates an XML document object out of the XML file and also associates the file with a style sheet. Save this as `slides.htm`:

```
<HTML>
<!-- this simple progam loads an XML document into an IE5 browser, and loops
through the
 nodes using a recursive function-->
<LINK REL=STYLESHEET TYPE="text/css" HREF="slide1.css" TITLE="Cnet">

     <!--load a well formed document into an island-->

     <XML ID="island1" SRC="s_cnet5.xml"></XML>

     <SCRIPT>
     //create a document object and a node list

           var myDoc=island1;
           var myDocNodeList=myDoc.childNodes;
     if(myDoc.parseError.reason!="")
           {
           alert(myDoc.parseError.reason);
           }
     else
           {
           alert("valid XML document");
           }
     //create a root element object

           var rootEl=myDoc.documentElement;
...
```

In order to change the content of the slide we have to change the value of the SRC attribute in the following line of code:

```
<XML ID="island1" SRC="s_cnet5.xml"></XML>
```

to the name of whatever XML slide file is required.

The second part of the code loops through the XML file, converts the XML tag to an appropriate HTML tag, and displays it.

```
...
    //loop through it's content

          x=getchildren(myDoc);

//================begin recursive function 'getchildren'========================

    function getchildren(node)
    {
    //create a child list
    var x=node.childNodes;
    var z=x.length;
          if(z!=0)
          {
          for(var i=0;i<z;i++)
                {
                if(x(i).nodeType==3)
                      {
                      document.write(x(i).nodeValue);
                      getchildren(x(i));
                      }
                else if(x(i).nodeType==1 && x(i).nodeName=="title" )
                      {
                      document.write(" <TITLE> ");
                      getchildren(x(i));
                      document.write(" </TITLE> ");
                      }

                else if(x(i).nodeType==1 && x(i).nodeName=="header" )
                      {
                      document.write(" <DIV CLASS='header'>");
                      getchildren(x(i));
                      document.write(" <HR></DIV> ");
                      }

                else if(x(i).nodeType==1 && x(i).nodeName=="slidebody" )
                      {
                      document.write(" <DIV CLASS='container'>");
                      getchildren(x(i));
                      document.write(" </DIV> ");
                      }

                else if(x(i).nodeType==1 && x(i).nodeName=="announcement" )
                      {
                      document.write(" <DIV CLASS='announcement'>");
                      getchildren(x(i));
                      document.write(" </DIV> ");
                      }
```

```
                else if(x(i).nodeType==1 && x(i).nodeName=="statement" )
                        {
                        document.write(" <DIV CLASS='statement'>");
                        getchildren(x(i));
                        document.write(" </DIV> ");
                        }

                else if(x(i).nodeType==1 && x(i).nodeName=="line" )
                        {
                        getchildren(x(i));
                        document.write(" <BR>");
                        }

                else if(x(i).nodeType==1 && x(i).nodeName=="footer" )
                        {
                        document.write(" <HR><DIV CLASS='footer'>");
                        getchildren(x(i));
                        document.write(" </DIV> ");
                        }

                else if(x(i).nodeType==1 && x(i).nodeName=="footer2" )
                        {
                        document.write(" <HR><DIV CLASS='footer2'>");
                        getchildren(x(i));
                        document.write(" </DIV> ");
                        }

                else if(x(i).nodeType==1 && x(i).nodeName=="footer3" )
                        {
                        document.write(" <HR><DIV CLASS='footer3'>");
                        getchildren(x(i));
                        document.write(" </DIV> ");
                        }

                else if(x(i).nodeType==1 && x(i).nodeName=="object" )
                        {
                        document.write("<OBJECT data=" +
x(i).getAttribute('source')+">");
                        getchildren(x(i));
                        document.write(" </OBJECT> ");
                        }

                else if(x(i).nodeType==1 && x(i).nodeName=="image" )
                        {
                        document.write("<DIV ALIGN='center'><IMG SRC=" +
                                       _x(i).getAttribute('source')+">");
                        getchildren(x(i));
                        document.write(" </DIV> ");
                        }

                else if(x(i).nodeType==1 && x(i).nodeName=="bullet_title" )
                        {
                        document.write(" <DIV CLASS='bullet_title'>");
                        getchildren(x(i));
                        document.write(" </DIV> ");
                        }
                else if(x(i).nodeType==1 && x(i).nodeName=="bullet-list" )
                        {
                        document.write(" <UL>");
                        getchildren(x(i));
```

```
                        document.write(" </UL> ");
                        }

                  else if(x(i).nodeType==1 && x(i).nodeName=="item" )
                        {
                        document.write(" <LI>");
                        getchildren(x(i));
                        document.write(" </LI> ");
                        }

                  else
                        {
                        getchildren(x(i));
                        }
                  }
            }

      }
//==========end function 'getchildren'==================
      </SCRIPT>

</HTML>
```

Of course, one of the advantages of this is that we can change the 'look' of a slide simply by changing the style sheet, and indeed it is my practice to maintain several different style sheets for several different looks.

> *This doesn't mean that you should employ several different looks in a single presentation. One of the golden rules of speaking with slides is to maintain a consistent look, and that is what CSS plus XML allows us to do very easily.*

Here is the style sheet, `slide1.css`, employed in the screen shots we will meet shortly:

```
      BODY{
            background-color:#000080;
            color:yellow;
      }

      UL{
            margin-top:.5cm;
            margin-left:2cm;
            font-size:18pt;
            height:60%;
            width:70%;
      }

      LI{
            line-height:36pt;
      }

      OBJECT{
            width:80%;
            height:80%;
            margin-left:10%;
            margin-right:10%;
      }
```

```
.container{

      background-color:#804000;
      border-style:solid;
      border-color:#FFFF00;
      border-width:2px;
      margin-top:.5cm;
      margin-right:15%;
      margin-bottom:.5cm;
      padding-bottom:.5cm;
      margin-left:15%;
      height:60%;
      width:70%;
}

.header{
      text-align:center;
      font-family:arial, sans-serif;
      font-size:36pt;
      text-decoration:underline;

}

.statement{
      text-align:center;
      font-family:Times new Roman,Times,Serif;
      font-size:24pt;
      padding-top:5%;
      height:60%;

}

.announcement{
      text-align:center;
      font-family:Times new Roman,Times,Serif;
      font-size:30pt;
      line-height:42pt;
      padding-top:5%;
      height:60%;
}

.footer{
      color:#AAAA00;
      text-align:right;
      padding-right:.25cm;
      padding-top:.2cm;
}
```

Here is one of the slides from a recent talk I gave. It should be kept in the same path as the style sheet, DTD and `slides.htm` file. As you can see this is a slide, `sl_cnet5.xml`, where I took advantage of HTML's object to show 'live' code:

```
<slide>

<title>XML</title>

<slidebody>
     <header>XML: A Brief Review </header>
```

```
<main>

<object source="sl_cnet5.txt"></object>

</main>

<footer>Frank Boumphrey</footer>
</slidebody>

</slide>
```

Also save a second version of this code as a text file, `sl_cnet5.txt`, for it to be displayed as shown in the following screen shot:

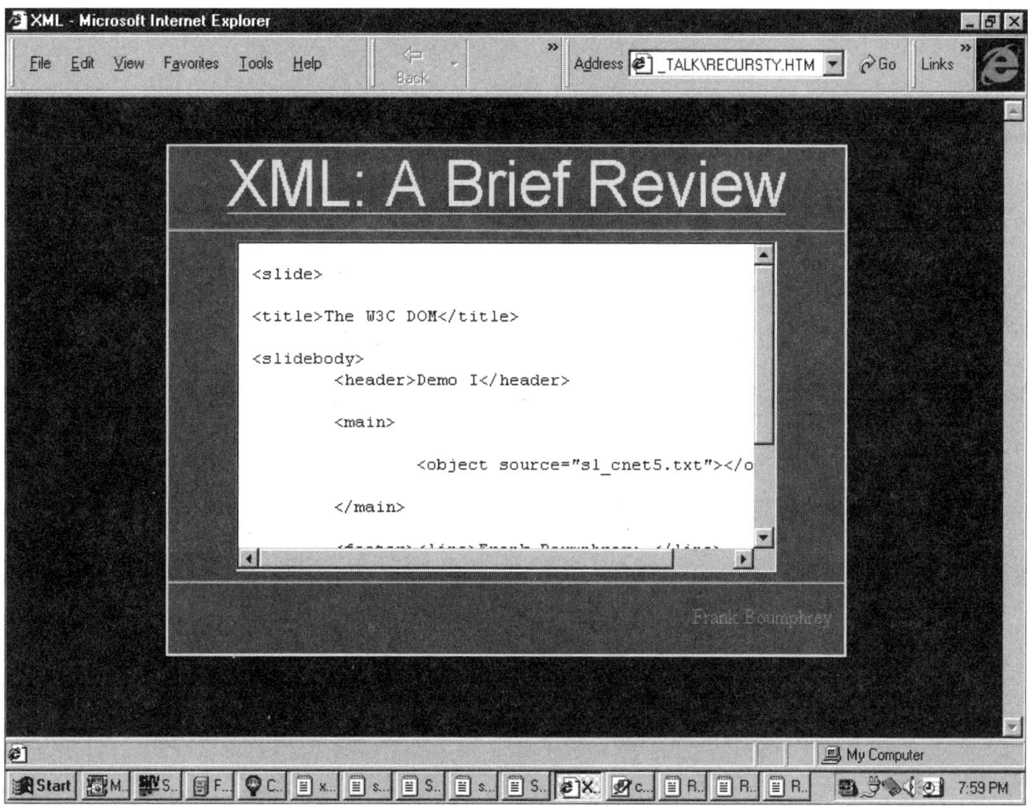

As you can see the slide is actually showing its own source code!

Here is the XML for an announcement type slide:

```
<slide>

<title>XML</title>

<slidebody>
     <header>XML: A Brief Review </header>
```

```
        <main>


        <announcement>
              <line>XML</line>
              <line></line>
              <line>The 'Well-Formed and Valid' document</line>
        </announcement>

        </main>

        <footer>Frank Boumphrey</footer>
   </slidebody>

   </slide>
```

Save this file as sl_cnet6.xml, and change the line of code in the HTML page slides.htm for the XML Island to:

```
   <XML ID="island1" SRC="s_cnet6.xml"></XML>
```

to correspond with the name of the slide we want to display. Here is a shot of the slide as it appears on the screen:

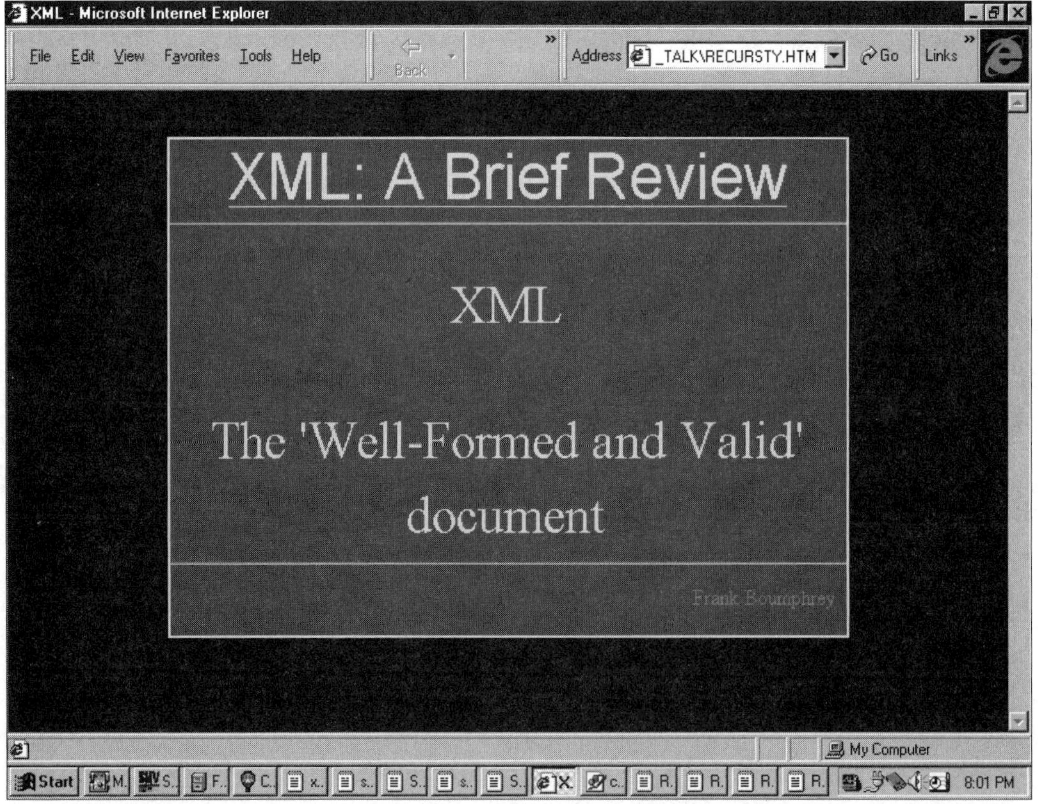

Here is a slide of a bulleted list:

```
<slide>

<title>XML</title>

<slidebody>
      <header>XML: A Brief Review </header>

      <main>

      <line/>
      <bullet-list>
            <bullet_title>The valid document:</bullet_title>
            <item>Is well formed</item>
            <item>Conforms to its DTD</item>
      </bullet-list>

      </main>

      <footer>Frank Boumphrey</footer>
</slidebody>

</slide>
```

Save this file as `sl_cnet7.xml`, and again change the line of code in the HTML page `slides.htm` for the XML Island to:

```
<XML ID="island1" SRC="s_cnet7.xml"></XML>
```

to correspond with the name of the slide we want to display. Here is the screen shot of the slide:

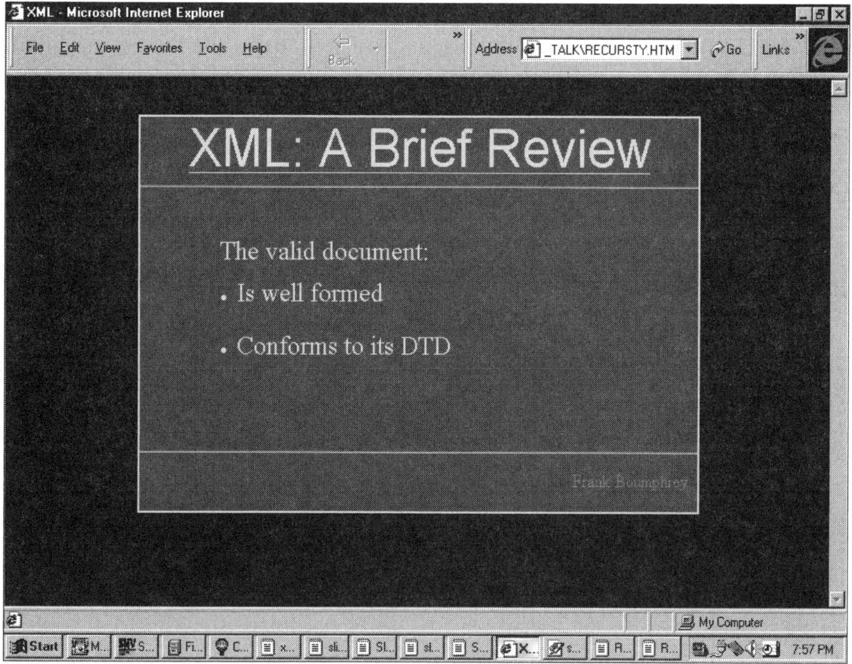

Although this is a very simple example, it is a real one and one that has been put to the test already in two talks I have given.

Using the DOM I have been able to lift my talks to a whole new level of interactivity. The audience can actually see the change being made to the XML slide, and then see the results immediately on the screen.

Other Examples

Although these are very simple examples I think they show the potential for the DOM to revolutionize the way we use XML, both on the client, and on the server side. Only the ingenuity of the user will limit its use.

XML and Data Engines

You may ask, "But I can already accomplish things like this using a database. My scripts just go through the database and provide information on the fly. Why should I bother to have all my data in XML files?"

The answer to this is that a search engine or a robot visiting your site has no access to your data, and so can't do anything meaningful or useful. But if I have all my data marked up in XML, it is exposed to the robot, and the robot can sort through it.

For example, suppose I run a restaurant, I may choose to mark up offerings according to a special DTD put out by a restaurant association. A 'bot' (search robot) could be instructed to look for such DTDs, use the DOM to extract required information, and put on a meaningful display for the client.

For example, say I am visiting Chicago, and want to entertain a client who likes Indian food, near the downtown area. I would instruct my 'bot' to look for such restaurants while I sleep on the flight. When I arrive, I plug in my laptop, and there will be a list of such restaurants.

However for this to work there must be sufficient restaurants willing to mark up their data according to such a DTD.

This is all quite feasible right now. The fact that no-one is doing is because there is no data to work on; i.e. no data marked up in XML. There is thus no incentive to develop an intelligent search 'bot'. Thus there is no incentive to mark up data in XML. Thus there is no incentive to develop an intelligent search 'bot' ...which is a chicken and egg situation.

Now that we have a simple universal DOM we will no longer have to have proprietary software to manipulate XML documents. Expect to see uses like the above gain momentum.

Summary

In this chapter we explored the use of a Document Object Model with XML.

After looking at some general concepts of the DOM, we concentrated on the W3C DOM recommendation and looked at why a common interface for XML document manipulations is important.

We studied this in some detail and used the IE5 Beta implementation to provide examples of factory methods.

Lastly we looked at a couple of simple implementations of the DOM that demonstrate the potential for much, much more.

7

Displaying XML

Although XML was originally designed for improved document storage, distribution, and display on the Web, it is more than that. It is rapidly being regarded as a means to store data, in a cross platform, non-proprietary manner.

In order for us to view the document or data, we must somehow display it. This chapter describes how this is done. In the rest of this first section we will look at:

- The different needs of XML and HTML
- What style sheets are
- The nature of flow objects
- Other means of displaying XML content

Then in the rest of the chapter we will look at:

- CSS in sufficient detail to allow you to write a CSS type style sheet
- The current situation in the 'big two' browsers
- A little about transformations, and custom processors
- Spice – a new styling language proposal

In the next chapter we will go on to take an introductory look at XSL.

HTML v. XML

As we saw in the introduction, HTML 4 is an application of SGML, and the next generation of HTML will be an application of XML (see `http://www.w3.org/MarkUp/Activity`). As such HTML consists of a limited number of tags, all of which can have meaning to the relevant user agent, in most cases this is a Web browser. When a browser sees an `<H1>` element, it 'knows' it is a heading element which is to be displayed as a 'block' flow object. When it sees an `<I>` element it 'knows' that this element is to be displayed as an 'inline' flow object with the text styled in an italic font. When it sees a `<P>` tag it 'knows' that all the content up to the next 'block', whether a `<P>` or another block element is to be to be treated as a single block element.

We will discuss flow objects shortly, but briefly a flow object is what is flowed on to the page when a document is displayed. Each individual character is a flow object with it's own styling, but we usually deal in larger sizes of flow object, like a phrase, a sentence or a paragraph. There are two basic flavors of flow object, the **block** flow object, that has a line-break before and after it, and the **inline** flow object which doesn't.

Here is the relevant section dealing with P from the strict HTML 4. DTD:

```
<!ELEMENT P - O (%inline;)*              -- paragraph -->
```

In SGML end tags are optional. That is what the O means (two hyphens - - would mean that both an opening and a closing tag are required). When HTML moves to XML all <P> elements, for example, will have to have a closing tag!

XML, of course, can be used to generate such a wide variety of tags that it is impossible for any one application to 'know' how to display them. In order to display them a style sheet of some kind is absolutely essential. It is likely that an XML aware user agent, when it comes across an XML document, will first look for a style sheet, and if it doesn't find one will inform the human user and then display all the elements as inline flow objects.

Style Sheets

A style sheet is, quite simply, a set of instructions mandating how a flow object is to be displayed. It is a machine readable instruction to the user agent that says for example, "Take this chunk of text, and display it in a red, 18 point 'Arial' font".

Human Readable Style Sheets

There are several varieties of style sheets available to us, and in this chapter we will look at CSS (Cascading Style Sheets), in some detail, and also look at Spice. In the next chapter we will look at XSL, Extensible Stylesheet Language. One thing they all have in common is that they are not only machine readable, but also human readable. Their other advantage, when they are used in conjunction with XML (or HTML), is that a single style sheet can be applied to several documents allowing for modularity.

Machine Readable Style Sheets

There are, of course, style sheets that are not human readable, they are in binary format, and most word processing programs employ such a style sheet. All the user sees is the output. But when, for example in Word 97, I select a style, the word processor consults its binary style sheet for instructions on how to format the text. The drawbacks of a binary style sheet are:

- They are not human readable
- There are problems transporting it across platforms and applications

RTF

We should probably make a quick mention of Rich Text Format, which is a style language in ASCII format that is embedded in the document. It is readable across platforms and applications, but is very difficult for humans to read and, because it is embedded in the document, it can only be applied to the single document in which it is embedded.

Flow Objects

When my computer or I display or write any text or graphics, we are in fact creating a series of flow objects. The smallest flow object could be considered to be a single character or an image (although we couldn't go smaller than a single pixel image), but these can be grouped together into larger flow objects, such as a phrase, a paragraph, a page, or even a whole document.

Styling Flow Objects

Each flow object is styled with a certain style, and the smaller flow objects contained within it are usually styled in the same style unless instructed to do otherwise. So, if I took a paragraph flow object, and styled it in a 12 point, black, Times New Roman font (a reasonable choice), every word and every letter contained in it, would appear with the same styling. However, I could choose to take a chunk of text in that paragraph and apply a different style, say italic text. If I did this I would have divided my original flow object into four flow objects, the original paragraph, and three child flow objects, these are the flow object before my italic chunk of text, the italic chunk of text, and another flow object after the italic chunk of text.

The flow object before and the flow object after the italic chunk of text are usually referred to as **anonymous** flow objects.

Block and Inline Flow Objects

As we mentioned earlier, flow objects are usually divided into two fundamental classes: block and inline flow objects. A block flow object is a flow object that has a line break before and after it. A main heading, or a paragraph, are both examples of this. In HTML `<P>`, `<DIV>`, and `<H1>` are all usually formatted as block flow objects.

The following illustration demonstrates three paragraph flow objects, all with different styling, on a single page.

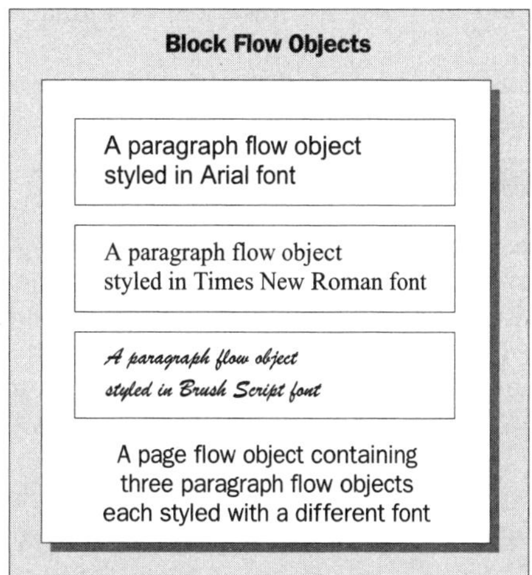

An inline flow object is an object that appears in a line of text. A single word in a sentence is an inline flow object. A phrase of emphasized text is an inline flow object. In HTML `<I>`, `<B>`, and `<SPAN>` elements are all usually formatted as inline flow objects.

In the following figure note how we start off with a single block flow object, and how, by making some of the text italic, we create three child inline flow objects, as described in the last section.

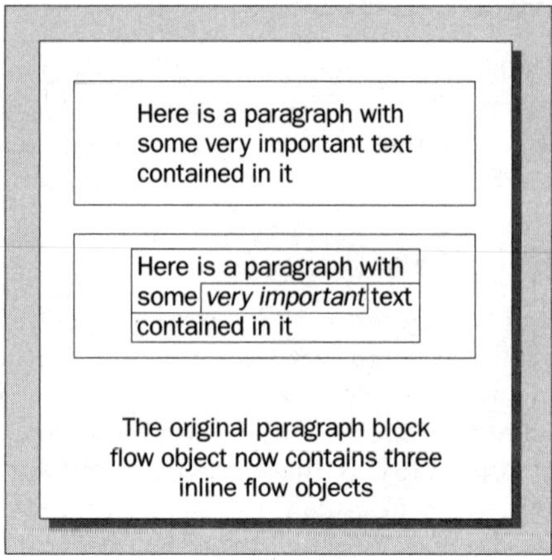

Here is a paragraph with
some very important text
contained in it
Here is a paragraph with
some *very important* text
contained in it
The original paragraph block
flow object now contains three
inline flow objects

Displaying XML in a Browser

At the time of writing Netscape's Mozilla 5 source code, and Microsoft's Internet Explorer 5 still hadn't been released.

The Betas of the IE5 browser show good support for XML included in an HTML document. We will have had a look a little more at this in Chapter 6 on the DOM.

Mozilla promises full support for XML with a CSS type style sheet. However, the early Beta's have given no clue as to what form this may take. In the absence of specifics we can only assume that its support for CSS with XML will be similar to the support it gives HTML.

Rumor has it though that we are going to be pleasantly surprised!

Other Means of Displaying XML

If we do not have a browser that displays XML, we can convert it into another format that we can display, such as HTML. It is likely that the high percentage of Web denizens will have browsers that fall into this category up until the year 2000. So it may be advisable to convert our XML documents into HTML for display purposes. Doing this manually is fairly easy, but the process can be a bit tedious using a search and replace function, or by using a simple script. So later in this chapter we will look at a simple Visual Basic application that does HTML conversion for us.

However we output XML, we need some kind of style sheet that tells the software how to style our document objects, and turn them into flow objects.

Displaying XML in Other Media

One of the beauties of XML is that, unlike HTML it makes no assumptions about the structure of the document. This makes it particularly well suited for displaying in media other than scrollable or print media. Using an appropriate style sheet and suitable software it should be just as easy to display XML in Braille, or through a voice synthesizer. For the same reasons XML is particularly well suited for display on low-resolution appliances.

Displaying XML on Custom Applications

Particularly with the increased use of XML to store data, we will see a number of XML applications designed to extract data from the XML document and display it as a record or a field. These applications are surprisingly easy to write using a language such as Visual Basic 5 which front ends for databases.

Having had a brief introduction to the generalities of displaying XML let's get down to specifics, and have a look at a style sheet language that is being increasingly employed on the Web: CSS.

Cascading Style Sheets

This section does not try to be exhaustive, it is only designed to introduce you to the subject, but you should be able to write a useful style sheet for HTML or XML after reading it. For a more exhaustive treatment you are refered to *Professional Style Sheets for HTML and XML*, from Wrox Press (ISBN 1-861001-65-7).

Most of the examples are given in both XML and HTML, because we know that the HTML works and can demonstrate it in action. Hopefully it won't be long before both types of example will work in the version 5 browsers.

What is a CSS Type Style Sheet?

A CSS type style sheet is nothing more than a whole series of styling rules. The rules first of all select the document object (in practice an element) to be styled, and then declare what these style properties are. A style sheet should contain nothing but style rules, white space, and comments. So let's look at a style rule and then see how we can associate it with our XML or HTML document.

A Simple CSS Style Rule

Let's start by styling a simple XML document and its HTML equivalent. Here is the simple `Hello_XML.xml` document:

```
<xdoc>
<greeting> Hello XML ! </greeting>
</xdoc>
```

The following style sheet just has a single rule in it. Note that the rule has two parts:

- A **selector** part which selects the element to be styled, in this case `greeting`
- A **declaration** part, that declares what properties to associate with our element to make a flow object

This style sheet will be contained in a separate file called `myxml_style.css`, which in our example needs to be in the same path. We shall show you how to link the two shortly. But for now here is the sole content of that file:

In the writers view the best tool to write a CSS style sheet with is NotePad, or some similar text editor. Once you have written your CSS style sheet you save it with a `.css` *extension.*

```
greeting{
      display:block;
      font-size:16pt;
      color:red;
}
```

This rule quite simply states that the contents of all <greeting> elements need to be displayed as block flow objects styled in a red, 16 point font. (We will discuss the syntax in a moment, however using CSS with XML we need to tell the user agent when it is dealing with a block flow object).

Now let's look at the HTML equivalent:

```
<HTML>
<DIV> Hello XML!</DIV>
</HTML>
```

Here is the style rule which will be contained in a separate file called myhtm_style.css, which in our example needs to be in the same path. Here is the sole content of that file:

```
DIV{
      font-size:16pt;
      color:red;
}
```

Note that we did not tell the HTML processor how to display the element, as it 'knows' that all <DIV> elements need to be displayed as block flow objects. However, it would not be a mistake to include display:block;, it will not cause an error. And if it was included in the Style Sheet then the HTML file could also be displayed in an XML browser. So it is probably best to get into the habit of putting in the formatting on all style sheets designed for HTML.

Note that if we had put in DIV{display:inline;} *the HTML browser would probably ignore it, as it is entitled to, but if we then displayed the document on an XML browser, the* DIV *element would indeed be formatted to an inline flow object.*

Having written the XML and HTML files and a style sheet for each, how do we associate the two? In other words how do we let the document know where to find the style sheet that contains rules for its presentation? Once we have effected the connection, the greeting/DIV flow object will be styled in red, 16 point font, which will be the user agent's default font.

The user agent usually has a default style sheet, certainly all the HTML browsers do for HTML documents. If a style is not specified, the default styling is applied.

Linking the Style Sheet and the Document

Having created our style sheet, we will need a way to link it to our document so that the user agent knows where to go to collect the style rules.

Linking an HTML Document

There are two main ways to link an HTML document to a style sheet, the style sheet can either be included in the document, or the <LINK> element can be used.

To include the style sheet in the document, the style rules are enclosed as content in the <STYLE> element thus:

```
<HTML>
<STYLE TYPE="text/css">
     DIV{
           font-size:16pt;
           color:red;
     }
</STYLE>
<DIV> Hello XML!</DIV>
</HTML>
```

To link the document externally to its style sheet the <LINK> element is employed.

```
<LINK HREF="myhtml_style.css" REL="stylesheet" TYPE="text/css">
```

So the completed document with an external CSS style sheet would look like this:

```
<HTML>

<LINK href="myhtml_style.css" rel="stylesheet" type="text/css">

<DIV> Hello XML!</DIV>
</HTML>
```

The output should be identical in both cases.

Documents can also be linked in other ways using the @import rule. You are referred to the specification or a specialist text, such as *Professional Style Sheets for HTML and XML* from Wrox Press (ISBN 1-861001-65-7), for details.

Linking an HTML document is discussed in the CSS specification found at:

http://www.w3.org/TR/REC-CSS2

Linking an XML Document

With an XML document we do not have the option of using an internal style tag, and the only way we can put the link information in a classical Prolog is to use a processing instruction thus:

```
<?xml:stylesheet href="myxml_style.css" type="text/css"?>
```

This is not quite true, it is possible to use a namespace tag, and if we were using a schema such as DCD we could also put the style instructions in the schema, but for the purposes of this chapter we will use a processing instruction.

The complete XML document will look as follows:

```
<?xml version= "1.0"?>

<?xml-stylesheet href="myxml_style.css" type="text/css"?>
```

```
<xdoc>
<greeting> Hello XML ! </greeting>
</xdoc>
```

The output should be the same in all three cases, HTML and XML.

Linking an XML document to a style sheet is discussed in a note found at:

http://www.w3.org/TR/NOTE-xml-stylesheet

Talking about how to apply styling to the XML and HTML document object, in order to create a flow object, we got a little ahead of ourselves. Let's have a look at the CSS style rule and its syntax in a little more detail.

Anatomy of a Style Rule

The CSS style sheet is nothing more than a collection of CSS style rules. These take the same basic form whether they are referring to an HTML or an XML element object.

The basic syntax is the object or objects to be styled, followed by an opening curly bracket, followed by a style property, followed by a colon, followed by a property value followed by a semi-colon, with different properties repeated. Or formally put:

```
[object(s) to be styled]{([property name]:[property value];)+}
```

The first part of the rule is called the selector, as it selects the document object that is to be styled. The second part, the part inside the curly brackets, is called the declaration, as it declares what properties are to be applied. The following diagram clarifies the syntax.

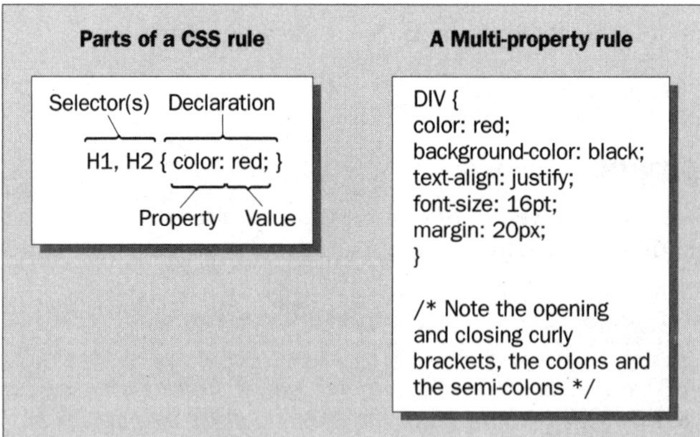

It should be noted that the last semi-colon is optional, but in practice you are always advised to put it in. It is never wrong to include it, because experience shows that we often add to the style rules, and if we omit the semi colon, it may cause the whole of our styling to be rejected.

Upper Case v. Lower Case

In HTML when defining our selector `DIV`, `div` and `Div` would all be the same, as case is immaterial. As we have seen, however, XML is case sensitive, so `Greeting` and `greeting` would be two different elements. In other words:

```
Greeting{font-size:16pt}
```

and

```
greeting{font-size:16pt}
```

are two different rules in XML.

Comments and White Space in CSS

CSS sheets use the old C style comments:

```
/*everything between the opening slash star and the closing star slash is a
omment*/
```

Comments, of course, cannot be nested.

For the most part **white space** is ignored by the browser. Formatting is only important from the point of view of clarity. For considerations of space the single line version will be used quite often in this book, but I urge you to always expand your code for maximum clarity

> **Anyone who has done any programming will tell you that clarity is probably the most important thing in writing code. What seems abundantly clear to you today will seem a complete mystery when you review it in the weeks ahead. Also remember that someone else is likely to be reviewing your efforts and they will have no insight into your thinking. The important thing is to develop your own clear style and stick to it. If you have any doubts at all as to the clarity of what you have done, or if the reason for doing it is not abundantly clear, comment it. It will save endless headaches.**

As mentioned above, the semi-colon, which is used to separate multiple properties, is optional if you have just one value. However, it's always best to put it in as experience tells us that we are going to be adding to and subtracting from the properties, and the absence of a single semi-colon can cause your whole page not to display. When it comes to style sheets browsers are very finicky about the correct syntax. The most commonly overlooked errors are getting a colon or semi-colon wrong, or leaving out a unit designation such as `pt` in `font-size:12pt`. The browser is just meant to ignore the incorrect property, but often it skips over the whole rule, sometimes the whole sheet and occasionally the whole page.

Properties and Values

The styling properties and the values they can take are all laid out in the CSS specifications. We will make no attempt to familiarize you with them in this chapter. However, we have included CSS1 properties in Appendix F and CSS2 properties in Appendix G; these appendices list the properties, values taken, syntax and inheritance.

You have already seen the syntax in the brief example above, namely:

```
[property name]:[property value];
```

The property is any of the CSS styling properties. The value may be a string, a number with a unit attached to it, an integer, or a color value. Values may also be absolute or relative, inheritable or not.

Let's have a brief look at some of these:

Units

The following relative units are available:

em	The height of the elements font
ex	The height of the letter 'x'
px	Pixel. Relative to the resolution, although in fact the CSS specification defines the suggested size of a pixel, and so makes it into almost an absolute unit
%	Percentage

The following absolute units are available:

in	Inches
cm	Centimeters
mm	Millimeters
pt	Point defined as 1/72 of an inch
pc	Pica defined as 12 points

Absolute v. Relative Units

An example of this may be a width of a margin:

```
DIV{margin-left:2cm;}
```

would ensure a two centimeter margin regardless of the size of the screen or the page. While

```
DIV{margin-left:15%;}
```

would ensure that the margin was always 15% of the width of the page.

Inheritable v. Non-inheritable

Some properties are inherited by their child flow objects, others are not. For example, the following minimal HTML document demonstrates some of the issues involved. The `font-size` property is inherited by the child `<P>` from the `<DIV>`, but the other two (`margin-left` and `background-color`) are not. Here is an example `ch07_inherit.htm`:

```
<HTML>
<STYLE TYPE="text/css">
     DIV{
          margin-left:2cm;
          font-size:16pt;
          border-style:solid;
          background-color:white;
     }
     P{
          border-style:solid;
     }
</STYLE>
<DIV>This text in a DIV is two centimeters from the left and 16 points.
     <P>
     So is this , there is no 'extra' margin for the P flow object. The font size
     is inherited, but the margin isn't
     </P>
</DIV>
</HTML>
```

Here is what ch07_inherit.htm looks like in IE5:

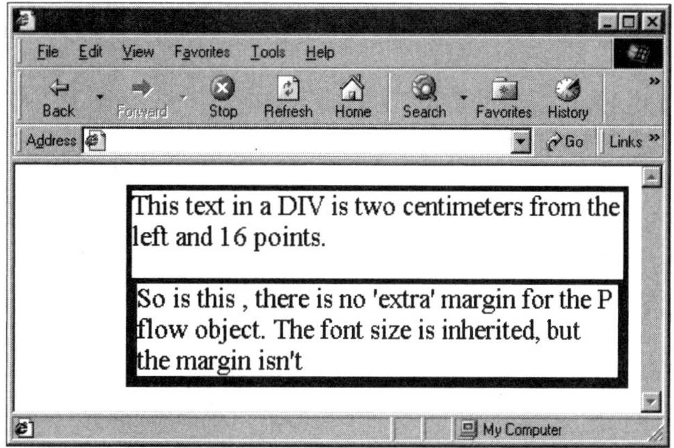

Here you can see how font-size has been inherited, but the left-margin property has not. The left-margin of <P> is 0, in other words it is flush up against the border of <DIV>. What about the background-color property? Has that not been inherited? No, because the default value for background-color is transparent and all that is happening is that the color of the <DIV> is shining through!

Color Values

Color values are expressed the same way as they are in HTML, as follows:

```
#[hexadecimal value for red] [hexadecimal value for green] [hexadecimal
value for blue]
```

So, #888888 represents light gray, #FFFFFF is white, and #FF0000 is bright red. CSS also allows the color values to be expressed in other ways:

	Gray	White	Red
In short form	#888	#FFF	#F00
As a decimal integer	rgb(136,136,136)	rgb(255,255,255)	rgb(255,0,0)
As a percentage	Rgb(55%,55%,55%)	rgb(100%,100%,100%)	rgb(100%,0,0)

Forms of Cascading Style Sheet Rules

There are four basic forms a CSS rule can take, but they all follow the same structure of `selector{property:value;}`. Here is a table that shows the four types followed by an example of each one:

Type	Syntax	Example
Simple Selector, single declaration	SELECTOR1{property1:value1;}	BODY{color:red;}
Multiple or grouped selectors, multiple declarations	SELECTOR2,SELECTOR3{property1: value1;property2:value1;}	H1,H2{ font-size:32pt; color:#FF0000; text-align:center;}
Property with multiple values	SELECTOR4{property1:value1 value2 value3;}	P{ font: italic bold 12pt Arial, sans-serif;}
Contextual selector	SELECTOR5 SELECTOR6 {property1:value1;}	DIV EM{font-style:italic;}

Let's briefly look at these four different types of rules.

Simple Selector

This was the type we looked at in our first example. Such as:

```
greeting{
      color:red;
}
```

The `greeting` element would be displayed in a red font.

Multiple Selectors

By separating our elements with a comma, it is possible to group together several elements so in the example below:

```
greeting, farewell{
      display:block;
      color:red;
      font-family: 'times new roman',serif;
      font-size:16pt;
}
```

both the `greeting` and the `farewell` elements would be rendered as block flow objects styled in a 16 point, red, Times New Roman font.

Properties with Multiple Values

Some properties can take multiple values. This can sometimes be a convenience, but in this author's view is usually more trouble than it is worth.

The `font` property, is a shorthand property for `font-style`, `font-variant`, `font-weight`, `font-size`, `line-height`, and `font-family`. Here is an example

```
DIV{font:italic bold 12pt/24pt Times, serif}
```

(The `font-variant` value has been omitted. If we had included it we could have had italic bold smallcaps.) The `font-size` property is separated from the `line-height` property by a forward slash. So this would produce italic, bold, double-spaced 12 point Times font. (Or a suitable serif font if 'Times' was not available.)

Other properties that can take multiple values include `font`, `border`, `background`, `margin`, and `padding`. You are referred to the specification or a specialized text for details.

Contextual Selectors

Consider the following XML document:

```
<xdoc>

      <heading>An <emphasis>Important</emphasis> subject</heading>

      <para>
            The speaker raised several <emphasis>important</emphasis> points.
      </para>

      <para>
            The speaker is a native of Rome
            <background>Roman citizenship is <emphasis>important</emphasis> to any
            Orator.</background>
      </para>

</xdoc>
```

We have three occurrences of the `<emphasis>` element, once it is a child of `<heading>`, once a child of `<para>`, and once a grandchild of `<para>` and a child of `<background>`. **Contextual selectors** allow us to differentiate between the different occurrences of `<emphasis>`. For this example:

`emphasis{[declarations]}`	Would select out the all the emphasis elements
`heading emphasis{[declarations]}`	Would select out the first emphasis elemen
`para emphasis{[declarations]}`	Would select out the second emphasis element
`background emphasis{[declarations]}`	Would select out the third emphasis element
`para background emphasis{[declarations]}`	Would also select out the third emphasis element, but with more specificity than the previous one

Conflicting Rules

What happens when there are a set of conflicting rules all applying to the same element as is the case above? There is in fact a complex set of rules that can be found in section 6.4.3 (on Calculating a Selector's Specificity) of the CSS2 specification. However, if you just remember that as a rule of thumb the most specific selector wins, you will be right 99% of the time! In the selectors above we go from least specific to most specific.

Other Selectors

There are in fact many other ways that we can employ selector syntax, but they are beyond the scope of this chapter. You are referred to the specification for details.

Cascading and Inheritance

We have already taken a brief look at inheritance in contextual selectors. What inheritance means is that, by and large, a child flow object inherits its ancestors' properties. As we saw certain properties are inherited and others aren't. The only way to be sure is to look at Appendices F and G or reference the specification, but again as a rule of thumb if it makes sense for a property to be inherited, it probably is!

What do we mean by **Cascading** in Cascading Style Sheets? Consider the following XML document:

```
<?xml version= "1.0"?>

<?xml-stylesheet href="myxml_style.css" type="text/css"?>
<?xml-stylesheet href="yourxml_style.css" type="text/css"?>
<?xml-stylesheet href="hisxml_style.css" type="text/css"?>
<?xml-stylesheet href="herxml_style.css" type="text/css"?>
<?xml-stylesheet href="itsxml_style.css" type="text/css"?>
<?xml-stylesheet href="ourxml_style.css" type="text/css"?>
<?xml-stylesheet href="theirxml_style.css" type="text/css"?>

<xdoc>
<greeting> Hello XML ! </greeting>
</xdoc>
```

We have no less than seven style sheets, all of which may contain a reference to the `<greeting>` element! Which style wins?

Again there is a complex algorithm, which can be found in the specification (section 6.4.1 - *Cascading Order*) and again there's a simple rule of thumb. If it isn't marked with the `!important` attribute (which we come to next) the last style sheet mentioned wins. In other words, the rule 'cascades' from top to bottom.

!important Declarations

It is possible to declare a property as being `!important`. This is how you do it:

```
P{font-weight:bold !important}
```

When this is used an `!important` property takes precedence over any non-important properties.

Generally speaking, in CSS2 the author's style rules take precedence over the user's style rules, but if both author and user declare the same property `!important`, the user wins.

> *The user can declare his own style sheet in IE5 go to* tools / internetoptions / general / accessibility. *In IE4* internetoptions *was under* view.

This is a conceptual change from CSS1 to CSS2. It used to be the other way round. A moments thought will show the correctness of this change, because the user may have some handicap (for example color-blindness) that requires different styling.

Having had a quick look at inheritance and the cascade let us have a brief look at how CSS treats block flow objects.

Boxes

Boxes is the word CSS uses to describe their flow objects. They are indeed containers for text and elements. We referred to 'containers' above implying that they were containers for text and elements, and in fact they are, but in CSS they go by the much more plebeian name of boxes. And boxes, as I am sure you are not surprised to learn, have numerous properties.

Any block of text can be contained in a box, and this box is then placed on the 'canvas' i.e. your browser desktop. The three basic properties that apply to the box are `margins`, `border`, and `padding`.

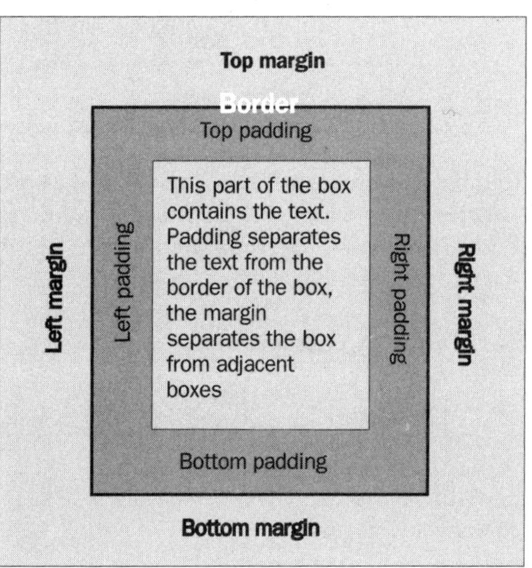

First, every box has a border – even if it is not visible – which separates it from the edge of the canvas, or from adjacent boxes. The distance between the border and the outer edge of the adjacent box, or between the border and its containing box, is called its margin. The distance between the contents of the box and its border, e.g. text, images, etc., is called its padding.

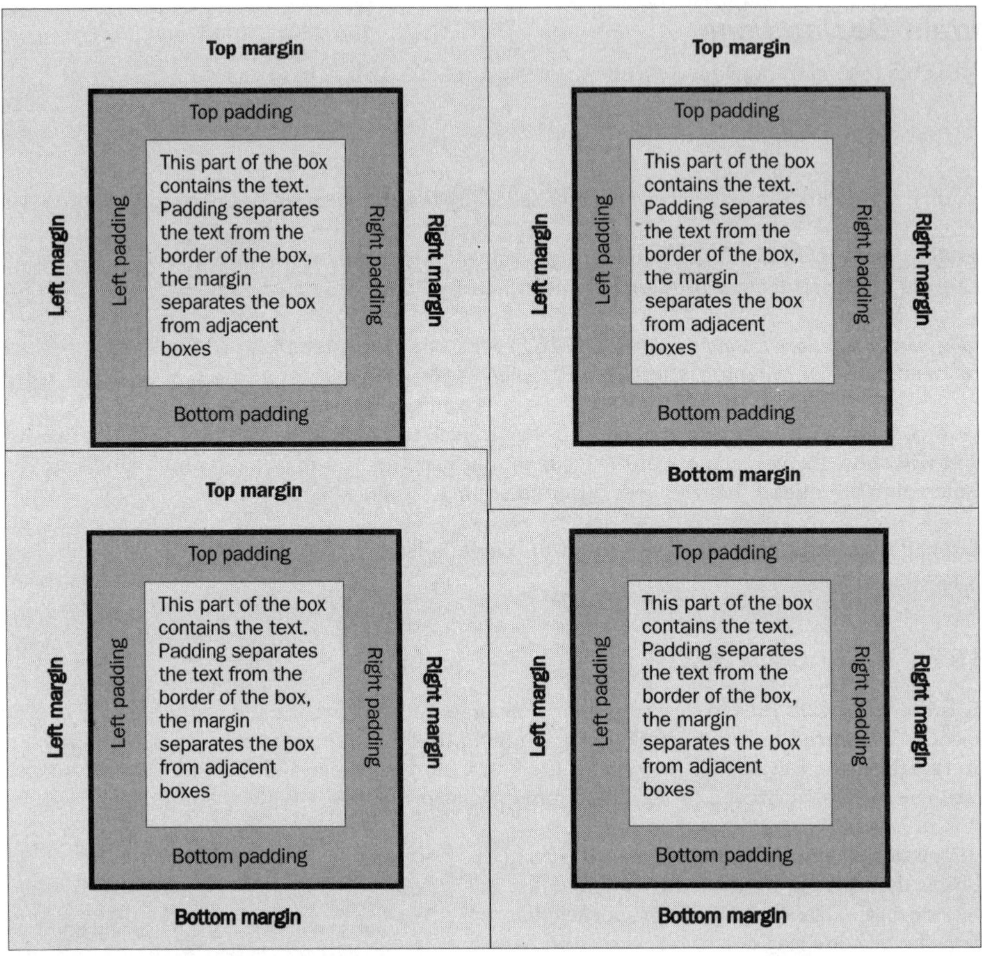

Note that in this example, in the vertical axis the margins are collapsed so that only the larger margin is displayed. In other words instead of adding the margins together to give a large distance between the boxes, they are just separated by the larger of the two margins. However in the horizontal axis, both margins are maintained.

Here is a simple example of boxes `ch07_box.htm` which can be downloaded or run from our Web site at `http://webdev.wrox.co.uk/books/1525`:

```
<HTML>
<HEAD>
<TITLE>Boxes</TITLE>

<STYLE TYPE="text/css">
```

```
    P{
            font: 14pt 'Times New Roman',serif;
            color:black;
            margin:0.5in;
            padding:0.25in;
            border:solid blue;
    }

    DIV{
            font:  italic bold 12pt  Arial,sans-serif;
            color:red;
            margin:0.25in;
            padding:0.25in;
            border:solid green;
    }

    EM{
            color:red;
    }

    DIV EM{
            color:green;
            font-style:normal;
    }

</STYLE>
</HEAD>

<BODY>
This text is just in the body.

<P>
This text is in a &lt;P&gt;.
</P>

<DIV>
This text is in a &lt;DIV&gt;.
</DIV>

Here's a line of text, in the body.

<DIV>
This text is again in a &lt;DIV&gt;.
</DIV>

</BODY>
</HTML>
```

This example highlights one of the major problems with style sheets at the present moment in time. The fact that Communicator 4 and IE4 give very different interpretations of this code, as shown in the following screenshot:

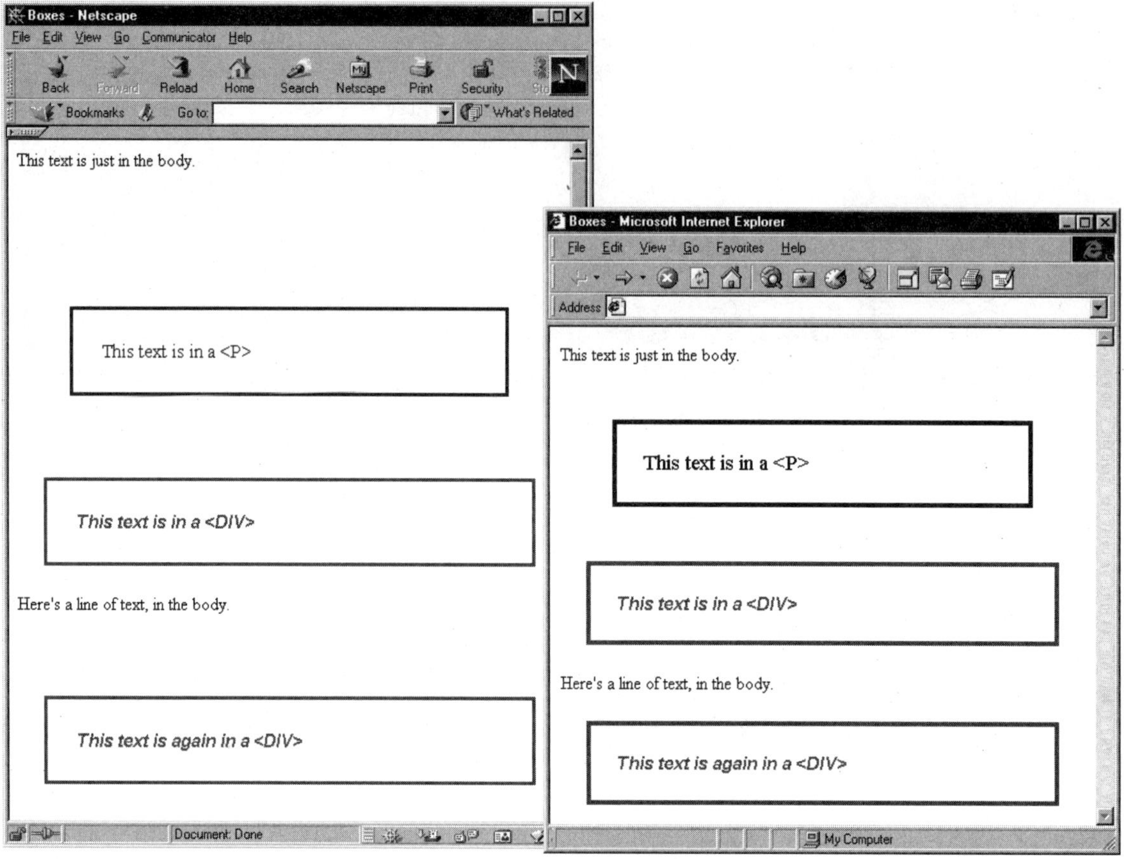

The (almost) correct presentation is that of IE4. A neat box is made around the text. There is a logical quarter inch padding between the text and the border, and there is a quarter inch margin all round the box. In Communicator 4 the margins are not collapsed.

Where boxes abut from top to bottom (in a vertical orientation), the margins are collapsed on each other so that the space between the `<P>` and the `<DIV>` is .5 inches not .5 + .25 inches.

> *A word of warning: If you paste text from a word processor to a text editor, sometimes the text editor will put in a different opening and closing quotation, i.e. other than the upright double quotes – ASCII 34. When this happens, your code will not work. So if you have used a word processor, look very carefully at the nature of your single and double quotes.*

Classes

One of the great things about CSS is that it allows you to define your own classes of style (actually classes of selectors). This can be quite a complex subject but the basics are simple enough, and we will just look at enough here to allow you to start using them. Classes can be very important in HTML because they allow software to distinguish between various structures.

Take this dialog from A Midsummer Night's Dream:

Hermia. I frown upon him, yet he loves me still
Helena. O that your frowns would teach my smiles such skill!
Hermia. I give him curses, yet he gives me love.
Helena. O that my prayers could such affection move!
Hermia. The more I hate, the more he follows me.
Helena. The more I love the more he hateth me.
Hermia. His folly, Helena, is no fault of mine.
Helena. None, but your beauty: would that fault were mine!

If you wanted to distinguish between the two in your HTML document you could assign both Hermia and Helena a class and make their dialog different in your HTML document.

```
DIV.hermia{font-style:italic; color:blue;}

DIV.helena{font-style:normal; color:black;}
```

Note how this was done – simply by adding a period followed by a name. The name must contain alpha-numeric content. Hyphens (-) are also allowed, but the name cannot begin with a number or a hyphen.

Now when we write our HTML we can use the `CLASS` attribute:

```
<DIV CLASS="hermia">Hermia. I frown upon him, yet he loves me still </DIV>
<DIV CLASS="helena">Helena.O that your frowns would teach my smiles such
skill!</DIV>
```

Look at the sample `ch07_play.htm` on our Web site (`http://webdev.wrox.co.uk`) to see what it looks like in practice.

Note that the class name was semantically marked up i.e. the class didn't just give us a description of the style, which would be a stylistic markup, but rather gave us a description of the content viz. Hermia's words, Helena's words. Although this is not necessary, it is good practice because you can now use your `CLASS` attribute to do meaningful searches on your HTML document. For example, return all of Hermia's lines by looking for `CLASS="hermia"`.

Thus you can give HTML some of the semantic advantages of XML.

One other thing, HTML is case insensitive, but XML is case sensitive, so start getting into the habit of putting all your HTML tags in upper case, and all your XML tags in lower case. (This is a suggested convention in XSL and XML.)

How would we accomplish the same thing in XML? Here is the XML version of the above as marked up by Jon Bosak.

```
<SPEECH>
<SPEAKER>HERMIA</SPEAKER>
<LINE>I frown upon him, yet he loves me still.</LINE>
</SPEECH>
```

```
<SPEECH>
<SPEAKER>HELENA</SPEAKER>
<LINE>O that your frowns would teach my smiles such skill!</LINE>
</SPEECH>

<SPEECH>
<SPEAKER>HERMIA</SPEAKER>
<LINE>I give him curses, yet he gives me love.</LINE>
</SPEECH>

<SPEECH>
<SPEAKER>HELENA</SPEAKER>
<LINE>O that my prayers could such affection move!</LINE>
</SPEECH>
```

One way to do it would be to use an attribute selector (we will not be discussing all the types of selectors, here we just show the syntax without comment – see the specification or a specialist text for full details). We could alter (using a script perhaps) the XML to read:

```
<SPEECH>
<SPEAKER NAME="HERMIA"/>
<LINE>I frown upon him, yet he loves me still.</LINE>
</SPEECH>

<SPEECH>
<SPEAKER NAME="HELENA"/>
<LINE>O that your frowns would teach my smiles such skill!</LINE>
</SPEECH>
```

and then write the following contextual style sheet:

```
SPEAKER [NAME=HELENA] LINE{color:blue;}

SPEAKER [NAME=HERMIA] LINE{color:black;}
```

Note that the attribute values are NOT quoted in CSS!

The other way we could do it is to use the HTML `CLASS` attribute, and namespaces. This would have the added benefit of also allowing us to use the HTML `STYLE` attribute.

Namespaces and CLASS and STYLE Attributes

We have already discussed Namespaces in Chapter 4. If we declare the HTML namespace in our Shakespeare document, say in the root element thus:

```
<PLAY xmlns:HTML="http://www.w3.org/HTML">
<TITLE>A Midsummer Night's Dream</TITLE>
```

we can use the `CLASS` and `STYLE` elements just as they can be used in HTML thus:

```
<SPEECH>
<SPEAKER>HERMIA</SPEAKER>
<LINE HTML:STYLE="color:blue;">I frown upon him, yet he loves me still.</LINE>
</SPEECH>
```

```
<SPEECH>
<SPEAKER>HELENA</SPEAKER>
<LINE HTML:STYLE="color:black;">O that your frowns would teach my smiles such
skill!</LINE>
</SPEECH>
```

This could be particularly useful if we wanted to use the same style sheet to display our XML version and our HTML version in an identical manner. Of course, this assumes that our user agent recognizes the HTML namespace. (None do up to version 4!)

Using Namespaces and XML in an HTML Document

In the early beta release of IE5 we could demonstrate the use of namespaces in an HTML document. The following example shows how to apply styling to an XML tag incorporated in an HTML document:

```
<HTML>

<xml:namespace prefix="myns"/>

<STYLE>
.mystyle1{font-size:24pt;display:block;}
</STYLE>

<BODY BGCOLOR="white" id="body">
      <P>An example of an using a namespace to apply style to an XML tag</P>

      <xtag1>The default display property for an unknown tag is inline.</xtag1>
      <xtag2>As is demonstrated here</xtag2>

      <myns:xtag class="mystyle1">An XML tag with style applied.</myns:xtag>
      <myns:xtag class="mystyle1">A display='block' property has been
      applied</myns:xtag>

<P>The following script demonstrates that the 'namespaced tag' is treated as a
known HTML tag.</P>
<SCRIPT>
      var x=document.all.length
      for(var i=0;i<x;i++)
            {
            document.write(document.all[i].tagName+ " ... ");
            }
</SCRIPT>
</BODY>
</HTML>
```

If you run this example in IE5 you will see the following. Note that the XML tags with the namespaces applied are treated as HTML tags, whereas those that aren't are treated as unknowns, as evidenced that the closing tags are included in the tree. You can download the code, or run the example, from our Web site at `http://webdev.wrox.co.uk/books/1525`. It is called `ch07_names.html`.

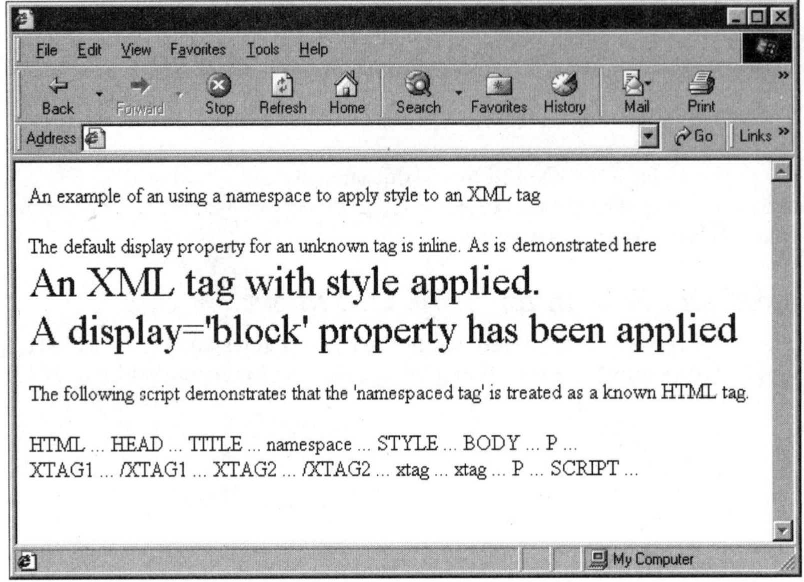

As a matter of interest note how the `<HEAD>` and `<TITLE>` tags are 'assumed' by the HTML document model.

That really wraps up our look at CSS. It has been brief, but hopefully detailed enough for you to realize that we can use CSS for most of our styling needs. CSS also has the advantage that most of the CSS1, and a large amount of the CSS2 specifications are well implemented, and more will probably be implemented for XML in both the version 5 browsers.

Let's now look at some backend transformations of XML so that it can be displayed in non-XML compliant user agents.

Transforming XML

Apart from displaying XML documents on a browser, it is possible to transform our well-formed XML document into another DTD such as HTML, and then use the transformed document for display. This process is illustrated in the diagram below.

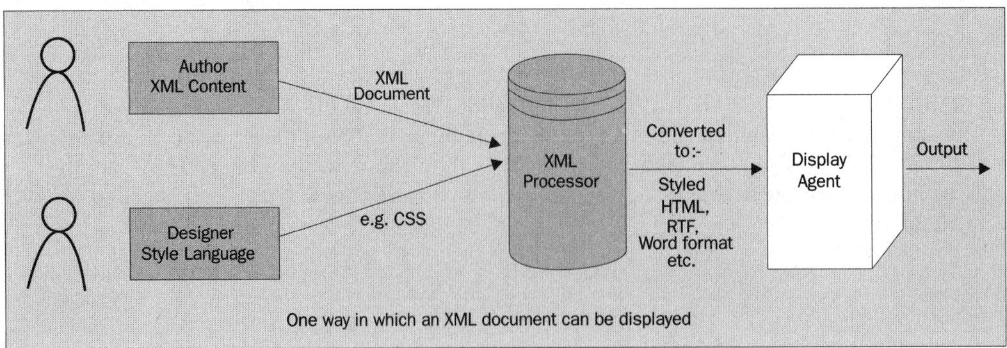

One way in which an XML document can be displayed

Manual Transformation

This is mentioned because it is not often thought about, but is extremely useful if we just have one or two documents that we want to display. The document is manually transformed to HTML, then married to a style sheet for display. We will demonstrate how to do this with Shakespeare's *Midsummer Night's Dream.*

The document is loaded into a text editor with a good search and replace function, such as Windows WordPad. We then systematically go through the tags, replacing the opening tag called `<SPEECH>` with `<DIV CLASS= "SPEECH">`, and each closing tag `</SPEECH>` with `</DIV>`.

Here is a picture of the process in action:

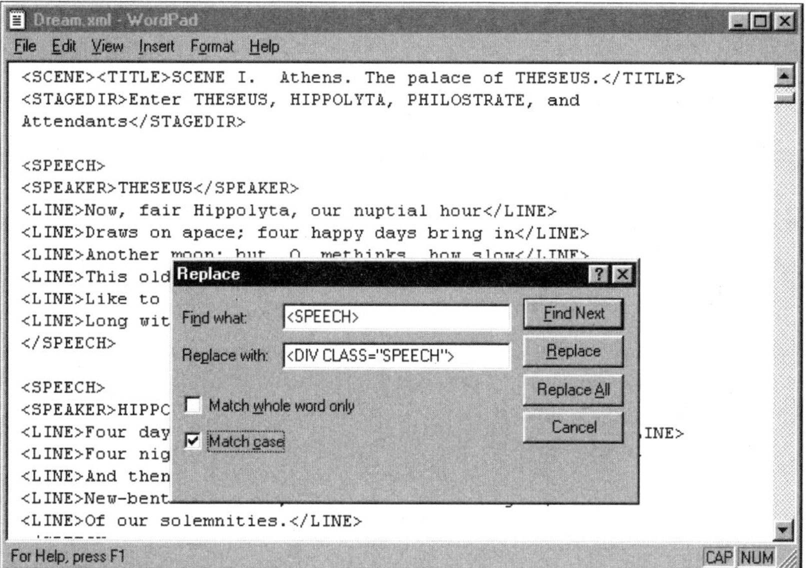

Here is a fragment from `dream.xml`:

```
<SPEECH>
<SPEAKER>HELENA</SPEAKER>
<LINE>O that your frowns would teach my smiles such skill!</LINE>
</SPEECH>

<SPEECH>
<SPEAKER>HERMIA</SPEAKER>
<LINE>I give him curses, yet he gives me love.</LINE>
</SPEECH>
```

And here is what it looks like transformed into `dream.htm`:

```
<DIV CLASS="SPEECH">
<DIV CLASS="SPEAKER">HELENA</DIV >
<DIV CLASS="LINE">O that your frowns would teach my smiles such skill!</DIV >
</DIV>
```

```
<DIV  CLASS="SPEECH">
<DIV CLASS="SPEAKER">HERMIA</DIV >
<DIV CLASS="LINE">I give him curses, yet he gives me love.</DIV >
</DIV>
```

The whole process takes about 5 minutes, which definitely makes it cost effective for the occasional document.

Using XMLparse.exe

`XMLparse.exe` is a simple tool developed in Visual Basic by the author for teaching purposes. It allows you to open up an XML document, check that its structure is valid, style it and then convert it to HTML for display purposes. To run it, download it from the Wrox web site at `http://rapid.wrox.co.uk/books/1525` and place it in the same directory as the XML files you want to use it with. It comes complete with a `Readme.txt` file which gives more details on installation.

> *It should be made quite clear up front that this is just a simple teaching tool, and* ***not*** *suitable for any heavy manipulation of XML documents.*

The utility looks like this:

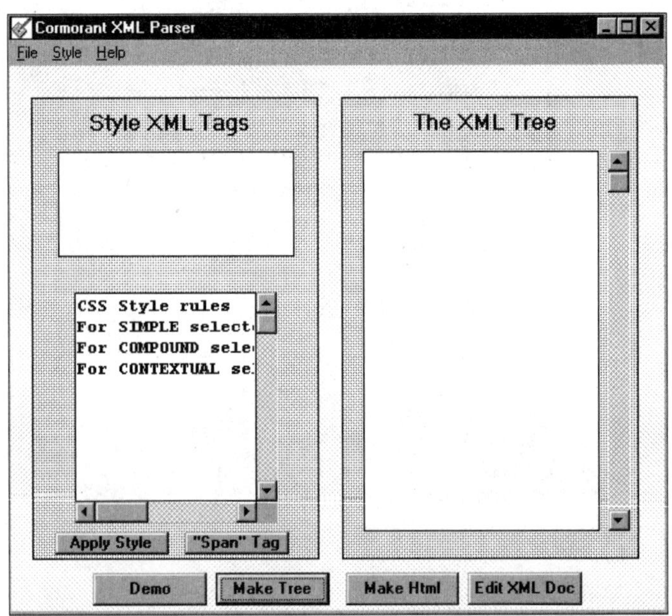

As a file to work with we will use one of the contacts which we developed a DTD for in the previous chapter. All the files used in this example can be downloaded from the Wrox site at `http://rapid.wrox.co.uk/books/1525`.

Here is the XML file, `ch7_contacts.xml`.

```
<client>
   <name id="CPQ142">
      <honorific> Dr.</honorific>
      <first> Pierre</first>
      <middle> R. </middle>
      <last> LeBlanc </last>
      <nickname> Butch</nickname>
   </name>
   <phone> 440-123-4567</phone>
   <company lang="french"></company>
   <contact type="first" ><date> Jan 1992</date></contact>
   <contact type="last"><date> Dec 19 1997</date></contact>

   <attitude interest="warm"/>
   <personal> Baby Girl b. <date> Nov 1997</date>, golf mad!, handicap 7, likes
   _Mexican food, completely bi-lingual French and English</personal>
</client>
```

First of all we open the document in the parser, using the Open command off the File dropdown menu:

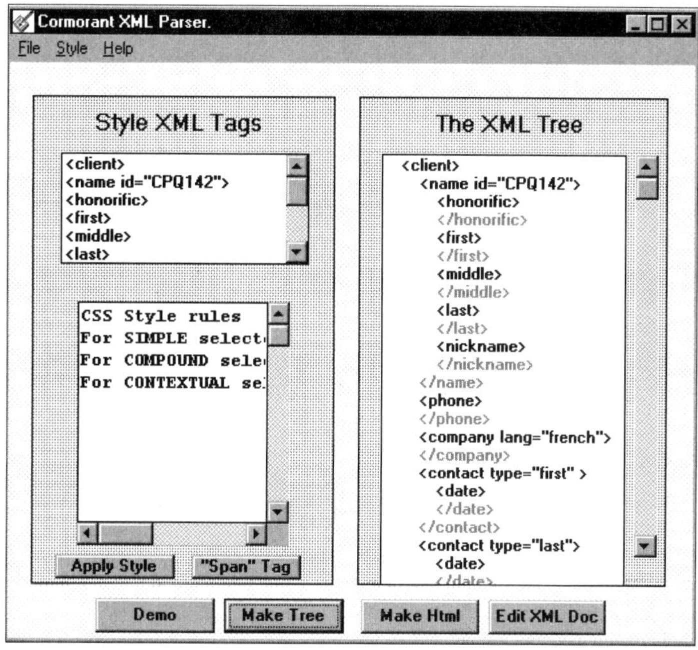

As you can see, the document is automatically parsed and a tree of the document is presented in the right hand XML Tree window.

In the upper left window a list of all the tags appear, plus simple instructions on how to make compound (multiple) or contextual selectors.

Right-clicking anywhere on an opening tag in the tree will open the XML file in a window with the relevant tag highlighted.

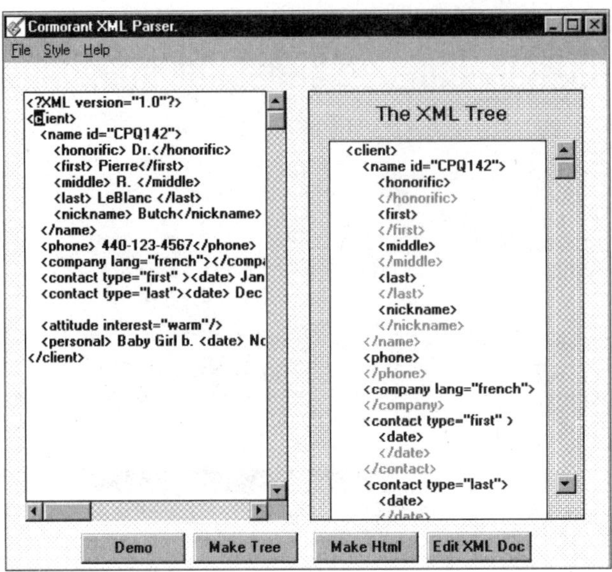

To style the document we first of all decide which of the elements should be inline elements. To make an element inline, we simply click on the name in the list box and then click on the "Span" Tag button. Note that the default is to make the element a block element.

We decide that all the name tags and the date tag should be inline.

To apply styling to a tag we left click on the appropriate element in the Style XML Tags list box and a selector with an empty declaration will appear in the window below the box. The next screenshot shows `personal` being assigned a declaration of:

```
{font-size:16pt;color:navy;}
```

Once the rule has been entered in the empty declaration, you must click the Apply Style button to apply it. This should mean that when we convert the XML document to HTML anything contained within the `<personal>` tags will be displayed in 16point navy blue font.

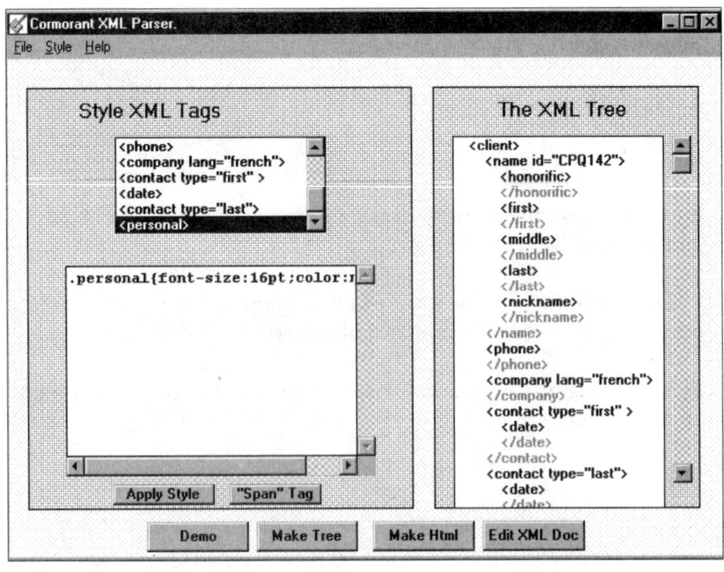

We repeat the process outlined above to apply the following styles:

- Make the last name display in bold type
- Make the nickname display in red
- Make the phone number and personal display in 16pt type
- Make a contextual selector out of the `<date>` in `<personal>`, highlighting that date in red

To convert our XML document into HTML we simply click the Make HTML button. The parser creates a `temp.htm` file containing the HTML code. A Notepad window will open up with our code in it. We can "tweak" our code any way we want, and then we use the Save As from the menu to save it as an HTML file. We'll save this file as `ch7_contacts.htm`.

Temp.htm - Notepad

File Edit Search Help

```
<!-- special formatting for the XML tag "<date>" -->
.personal .date{color:red;}


<!-- special formatting for the XML tag "<date>" -->
.personal{font-size:16pt;color:navy}

</STYLE>
</HEAD>
<BODY>
<DIV>
<DIV CLASS="client">
   <DIV CLASS="name">
      <SPAN CLASS="honorific"> Dr.</SPAN>
      <SPAN CLASS="first"> Pierre</SPAN>
      <SPAN CLASS="middle"> R. </SPAN>
      <SPAN CLASS="last"> LeBlanc </SPAN>
      <SPAN CLASS="nickname"> Butch</SPAN>
   </DIV>
   <DIV CLASS="phone"> 440-123-4567</DIV>
```

This screenshot of Notepad shows some of the style sheet, and how the XML tags have been converted into HTML `<DIV>` and `<SPAN>` tags with appropriate `CLASS` attributes. The screenshot below shows what the converted XML file looks like opened in Communicator.

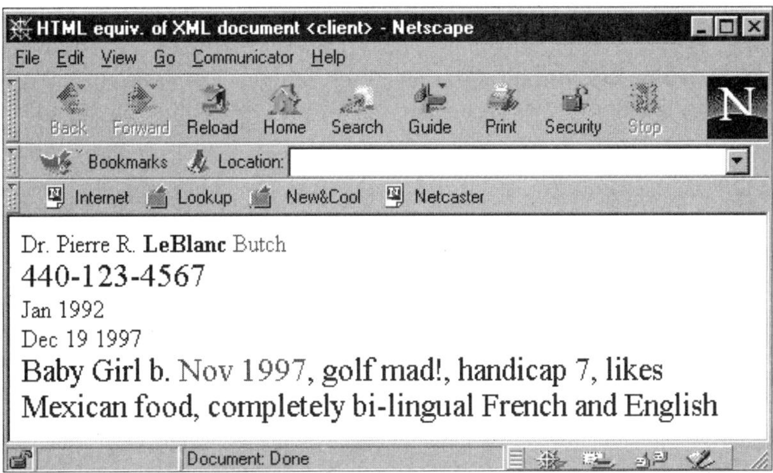

This is obviously a very simple example, but is typical of how XML is being used at the present time.

Transforming XML with 'old' XSL

Microsoft had an interesting command line parser that would transform an XML document and an 'old style' xsl style sheet to styled HTML.

The parser is still available (as of October 1998) at:

`http://www.microsoft.com/xml/xsl/downloads/msxsl.asp`

and a tutorial on how to use it can be found at:

`http://www.hypermedic.com/style/xsl/xsl_tut1.txt`

This tool, which was essentially a 'technology preview', has been used to transform countless XML documents and is probably the main reason for the popularity of XSL! This tool is indeed used in Chapter 11 to style the 'Travel Broker'.

Spice

Spice is a new styling language written by Dave Raggett and Robert Stevahn of Hewlett Packard. It leverages user's knowledge of CSS and JavaScript, which can be used to style both XML and HTML documents. Like XSL and DSSSL – but unlike CSS – it allows manipulation of the flow objects, and even allows the user to write his own kind of flow object in the form of a macro. Although there are no tools available at the time of writing, a browser will probably be available in the fall of 1998, as well as plug-ins to enable the mainstream browsers to read Spice style sheets.

We will look at it here in some detail as there is little other information readily available. However, please note that this language is only in its formative stage, so the following may well change. This is only offered as an introduction to the Spice.

Spice in Concept

For such a powerful language, the concepts are remarkably simple. The basic construct is a style rule, which has been written utilizing CSS type properties. Here is an example of such a rule:

```
style H1
{
      fontFamily: "Arial";
      fontSize: 12pt;
      display: block;
}
```

There are some important points to note here:

- The hyphens have been removed from `font-family` and `font-size` and have been replaced with a camelBack notation, (capitalizing the first letter of the second word in a hump like fashion) in order to avoid confusion with the JavaScript subtraction operator.
- The type of flow object, `block`, has been declared. `block` is derived from a library of flow objects maintained by the Spice engine or referenced from a URL (see later).
- The flow object definitions have to be specifically imported (see next section).

Here is a simple HTML document showing one way that Spice rules can be included in it:

```
<HTML>
<STYLE TYPE= "text/spice">

import document, block, inline;
      import wroxheader from "http://www.wrox.com/Spice/std.lib"
      /*the above is hypothetical!*/
      import "Mystyle.css"
      import "Hisstyle.spi"
      style HTML
            {
                  fontFamily: "Times New Roman";
                  fontSize: 12pt;
                  display: block;
            }
      style H1
            {
                  fontFamily: "Arial";
                  fontSize: 1.5em;
                  display: wroxheader;
            }
      style H2
            {
                  fontFamily: "Arial";
                  fontSize: 1.5em;
                  textAlign: center;
                  display: block;
            }
      style P
            {
                  textAlign: left;
                  display: block;
            }
      style EM
            {
                  fontStyle: italic;
                  display: inline;
            }
      </STYLE>
            <H1> 15 Spice and XS</H1>
            <H2> Spice</H2>
            <P> Hello Spice!</P>
            <P> This is a<EM> really cool</EM> language.</P>
      </HTML>
```

Here is what this file would look like in a browser that supported Spice. Note that this screenshot has been rigged, just to show you how the file would appear.

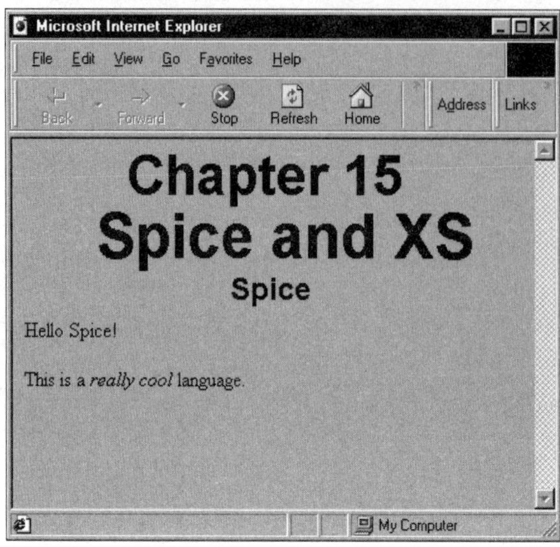

Spice Points to Note

We have included the rules in <STYLE> tags here, but it is probable that they will also be able to be included in <SCRIPT> tags. This will have several advantages as <SCRIPT> allows an `SRC` attribute, which we can use to include any modifying code that we might write. (See later under the heading *Spice Flow Objects.*)

Just like CSS, Spice style sheets cascade. This example has imported both a CSS and a Spice type style sheet. (In a CSS type style sheet we would use `@import`, here we just use `import`.) We will discuss this in more detail in a moment.

Just like Cascading Style Sheets, Spice style sheets inherit. In addition to the stated style of `textAlign:left;` our <P> will also be rendered with the `document` styles – `fontFamily: "Times New Roman"; fontSize:12pt;` – as `P` is contained in the `document` block.

Note at the head of the document the `import` statement. This is completely analogous to the Java language `import` or the C language `include`, and imports a library of functions. In this case they are functions that tell the rendering engine how to display the flow objects. We will discuss this in more detail in a moment.

This simple example will create 6 flow objects, an `HTML`, an `H1`, an `H2`, two `P`s and an `EM`. They will be displayed according to the definitions given in the imported libraries.

So far Spice may just seem to be a slightly more complex way of writing CSS type style sheets. However, the real power of Spice can be seen both in the way that it manipulates flow objects, and also in the way that it allows for creation of new flow objects. First, however, it would be helpful to understand a little about the way that the Spice engine renders documents.

Document Rendering

When the user agent receives a Spice style sheet it iterates through the parent document and examines each element in turn. It then looks for a rule that it can apply to it and creates a flow object based on that rule. If it finds no rule it will apply a `default` rule.

Spice Flow Objects

Spice can use any kind of flow objects at all as long as they are included in a library. This library may be hard wired into the user agent itself, it may be cached, or it may be referenced in an outside URL.

In our sample above the `<H1>` tag is to be rendered as a `wroxheader` flow object. But the user agent needs to find the code describing how this kind of flow object is to be rendered. First it will look in its hard-wired library, then in its cache to see whether it has been recently downloaded, then it will look at the URL and import the necessary code. If all this fails – the user may be off-line – it will use a default rendering.

To not display an item we must use the property `display:none;`.

Modifying a Flow Object

Spice also allows us to create our own flow objects. This can either be from scratch, or by modifying an existing flow object. To do this we can use Java, JavaScript, Spice itself or even create an ActiveX object.

Here is how we would go about modifying the block object to create a `wroxheader` flow object using Spice:

```
//note similarity to java 'extends' keyword

      prototype wroxheader extends block
            {
                  function layout(element)
                  {
                        this.style.borderStyle=solid;
                        this.style.backgroundColor=black;
                        this.style.color=white;
                        this.style.position=absolute;
                        this.style.top=0;
                        this.style.left=0;
                        this.append (new Text("Chapter "));
                        processChildren(element,this);
                  }
            }
```

Note the use of the keyword `prototype` that tells the Spice engine that we are creating a new prototype and calling it `wroxheader`.

Note also the use of the keyword `extends` which tells the Spice engine what object we are modifying to create our prototype `wroxheader`. This is very similar to its use in Java.

Now, whenever we use the `display:wroxheader;` property/value pair we will produce white text on a black background at the top left hand corner of the page, and the text will be prefixed with Chapter. So in our earlier example:

```
<H1> 13 Spice and XS</H1>
```

would appear in Arial 1.5*12=18pts (our base font size is 12) from the style sheet instructions. From the display instructions it would be at the top left corner of the page, with white text on a black background.

As a reminder here is the relevant part of the style sheet:

```
style H1
            {
                    fontFamily: "Arial";
                    fontSize: 1.5em;
                    display: wroxheader;
            }
```

and here's what it would look like:

Chapter 13 Spice and XS

We would put this code in our file `std.lib` which, as we saw, was referenced from the head of the style sheet.

There are a few Spice keywords here. The `layout` function is passed the name of the element that the layout is to be applied to (i.e. `H1`). The `append` keyword is used to append a new child to the sequence, in this case a `text` type child `"Chapter"`, and `processChildren` is a built-in method that iterates through the flow tree processing the children of the element. (In our example there are no children.) As well as appending text, Spice allows us to append graphics from a standard library. (See the section on *Graphics* below.)

Next let's look at how Spice will let us manipulate the order and sequence of our document.

Modes and Out of Sequence Rendering

Just as in XSL, Spice allows us to do modes and out of sequence renderings. Consider the following simple XML document:

```
<document>

      <contents></contents>
      <chapter> Introduction</chapter>
      <chapter_text> In this chapter....</chapter_text>
      <chapter> CSS</chapter>
      <chapter_text> Cascading Style....</chapter_text>
      <chapter> Spice </chapter>
      <chapter_text> Spice is a new...</chapter_text>

</document>
```

I would like to pull out all the chapter headings and print them in my `contents` tag, using a different style to the one I use at the top of each chapter. How do I go about this?

In CSS you would have to rewrite the parent document and use separate style rules to accomplish this. For example:

```
<document>

<contents>
      <chapter class="toc"> Introduction</chapter>
      <chapter class="toc"> CSS</chapter>
      etc, etc
</contents>
      <chapter class= "heading"> Introduction</chapter>
      <chapter_text> In this chapter     </chapter_text>
      etc, etc
```

Here I've had to include all of the chapter headings within the `<contents>` element, and give them a class of `toc` when used in this element, then a style of `heading` when I use them at the beginning of each chapter. So, I have to reference a CSS style sheet that would contain the following rules:

```
.toc{font-size:10pt}
.heading{font-size:18pt}
```

In Spice there is a better way to do it using the `mode` rule. The first step is to create a style rule for the `<chapter>` element as a whole:

```
style chapter
      {
      fontSize:18pt;
      }
```

The next thing is to create a special mode to display the chapters as a table of contents:

```
mode toc
      {style*
      {
            display:none;
      }

      style chapter
      {
            fontSize:10pt;
      }
}
```

Note what we have done. The asterisk * tells the processor to apply this rule to every element, so none will be displayed except the `<chapter>` element, which will be displayed using a font size of 10 points. Now to display this in our `<contents>` we just give our tag a unique `id` as an attribute. For example:

```
<contents id= "toc"></contents>
```

When the processor sees this it will create a flow object, which contains the content of every `<chapter>` element, rendered in a 10 point font.

Note that if we hadn't included:

```
        style*
        {
              display:none;
        }
```

in our mode rule; the whole content of the book would have been displayed in contents!

Another way to do this would be to write a prototype for a flow object called, say, `body`.

```
prototype body extends block
{
      //lay out the table of contents

      with mode toc       //just displays chapter elements.
            {
            processChildren (element,this)
            }

            // Now layout the document proper

            processChildren(element,this)
}
```

Now using the style rule in our above example:

```
        style document
              {
              Display:body;
              }
```

Our document will now be laid out with a table of contents at the top. Note how we don't even have to use the `<contents>` tag. Spice gives us a shorthand way to do this, which will accomplish exactly the same effect.

```
        style document
                    {
                    Display: block with mode toc, block with mode regular
                    }
```

You are directed to the notes and tutorials referenced in Appendix B for further information.

Media Dependent Style Sheets

Spice also allows us to specify separate media to use, for example in a 'show and tell' you may want some of the presentation in sound and some in vision. To accomplish this we use the `media` rule.

```
media aural
{
      style body
      {
            volume: medium;
            voiceFamily: male;
      }
```

```
        style abbr
        {
                volume: medium;
                voiceFamily: female;
        }
```

So, anything in the presentation with a style of `body` applied to it will be rendered aurally in a male voice, anything with a style of `abbr` will be rendered in a female voice. We can now use this statement in our prototypes with `media aural` as follows:

```
with media aural
{
        ProcessChildren(element,this);
}
```

to create auditory flow objects.

Graphics

When we looked at our first attempt at creating a prototype

```
prototype wroxheader extends block
```

we used

```
this.append (new Text("Chapter"));
```

to add text to our flow object. We could also have made reference to a graphic, either by means of a URL or by referring to a standard library. For example:

```
this.append (new Graphic("Wroxlogo"));
```

or

```
this.append (new Graphic("http:/www.wrox.com/graphics/logo.gif"));
```

Linking in Spice Style Sheets

In our original example we saw how we could import a style sheet into another style sheet to take part in the cascade. Here is how you would associate a Spice style sheet with your XML or HTML document.

To specify a style sheet use the standard PI (Processing Instruction) in XML. For example:

```
<?xml-stylesheet href= "docstyle.spi" type= "text/spice"?>
```

In HTML use the `LINK` tag:

```
<LINK REL= "stylesheet" href= "docstyle.spi" type= "text/spice">
```

Summary of Spice

At present Spice is just at the Note stage (submitted 3rd February 1998) and as far as I know there is no W3C activity as of yet. However, a browser is promised in the near future, and as Spice lends itself well to ActiveX controls or to Java Applets, it may well be there with the other style languages that will be used for styling XML documents.

Summary

In this chapter we had a look at the presentation of XML. We saw that as XML elements, unlike HTML elements, have no intrinsic meaning to the browser we have to provide a style sheet.

We saw that there were two ways to display XML, we can either transform it to another format, such as HTML, and then display it or we can display it directly with the use of a style sheet. At the present direct display is not a popular option as the browser support for XML is weak, however this will change with the version 5 browsers.

We then had a look at two of the various styling languages available, namely CSS and Spice. In the next chapter we shall be moving on to have a look at XSL.

Extensible Stylesheet Language (XSL)

Introduction

In this chapter we will have a very brief look at the new XSL specification of 18th August 1998. The old XSL specification was based on a note of October 1997, and the functionality of a simple tool, `msxsl.exe` that had been provided by Microsoft. This tool transformed XML documents, together with an 'old' XSL-type style sheet, into HTML inline styled documents. This has proven to be very popular, and is probably the simplest way to 'display' XML documents available today

> *Full details on how to use this tool are outside the scope of this chapter, but are available in* Professional Style Sheets *(Wrox Press, ISBN 1-861001-65-7) or are available at* `http://www.hypermedic.com/style`.

The `msxsl.exe` tool is still available from Microsoft at `http://www.microsoft.com/xml` and can be used in conjunction with 'old-style' XSL as described in the original note.

This chapter concentrates on 'new style' XSL. Unfortunately there is no tool, comparable to the `msxsl.exe` available for 'new' XSL yet, so this chapter falls into that category only too familiar (and frustrating!) to XML aficionados of "Look at this neat stuff. Won't it be great to use when we have a tool available?" (However, at the time of writing, the latest Beta of Internet Explorer 5 from Microsoft augurs some considerable support for 'new' XSL.)

In addition, we should note that at the time of writing the August Working Draft of the XSL specification was very much a 'work in progress' with many significant gaps in its coverage of certain issues.

The specification also explicitly states that it does not define the mechanism by which XSL style sheets should be associated with XML documents. Although it does suggest that one possible mechanism for doing so might be to indicate a reference to an XSL style sheet using a processing instruction within an XML document in much the same way as for CSS style sheets. So for XSL the processing instruction might read:

```
<?xml:stylesheet href="mystyle.xsl" type="text/xsl"?>
```

However, at the time of writing this is merely informed speculation.

In spite of these caveats, XSL is obviously set to become a major part of the technology centered on XML, and this chapter will provide you with all the essential information you'll need to gain a head start on forthcoming implementations.

What We'll Cover

This chapter is not designed to be exhaustive; all we are aiming at is to provide a working knowledge of the 'new' XSL specification, and to give you enough information to comprehend the specification yourself. Like most documents that are in the process of being compiled, the specification can be rather heavy going. But hopefully the information in this chapter will give you a head start.

In this chapter we will have a look at:

- The general concepts behind XSL
- Constructing Result Trees from Source Trees
- Formatting and styling the Result Tree

We will begin with a quick look at the basics of the process of styling with XSL style sheets.

Brief Overview

An XML document is comprised of a number of objects. This was fully discussed in Chapter 7, but for the moment here we will just concern ourselves with element objects and text objects.

XSL will take these objects and write a separate document tree consisting of flow objects, it will then style these flow objects and output them to the user agent for processing.

Producing styled output is a three-part process:

- A tree of flow objects is built from the Source Tree of the original XML document, which XSL calls the Result Tree
- Style rules are applied to each node of the Result Tree.
- The user-agent displays the Result Tree using the appropriate styling.

The XSL document consists of a number of **template** rules that have two parts, a '**pattern**' part, and an '**action**' part. (Don't worry too much about the terminology here, as all these terms will be explained as we progress through the chapter.)

The pattern part of the rule selects an object in the original source document from which it will create a **flow object** for the result document.

The action part of the rule describes what kind of flow object to make and what styling is to be applied to it.

Once the styled Result Tree is completed, it is passed to the user agent for display.

Here is a very simple example to illustrate the process. Don't worry too much about the syntax for now, just concentrate on the general concepts.

Hello XSL!

Here is our simple well-formed XML file:

```
<greeting>Hello XSL!</greeting>
```

And here is our XSL file (a little over-simplified but we just want to get across the general idea. We have left out the namespace information from the `xsl:stylesheet` start tag (see 'Namespaces and XSL Style Sheets' later) for clarity's sake).

```
<xsl:stylesheet>

            <!--Here is the pattern part.-->

      <xsl:template match="greeting">

            <!--Here is the action part-->

            <fo:block color="red" font-size="16pt">
                  <xsl:apply-templates/>
            </fo:block>
      </xsl:template>
</xsl:stylesheet>
```

Here we see an `xsl:template` element that is matched to an element in our XML file. This is the pattern part of the template rule.

The matching is done by means of the '`match`' attribute, and selects the document object, in this case the `<greeting>` element from our source XML document, from which a flow object is to be constructed and styled.

Once we have selected the document object to match on we go to the action part of the rule.

First we specify the kind of flow object we want to create, which in this case is a '`block`' flow object, by using the element `<fo:block>`. We will say a little about flow objects in the next section, but essentially a block flow object is a flow object with a line break before and after it. (Don't worry about the `fo:` namespace prefix for now, as we'll deal with it a bit later on.)

We apply styling to the flow object by using attributes. Note that these attributes are identical to the CSS properties. In CSS we would put `color:red`, and we convert that to an XSL style attribute by putting `color="red"`.

We now process the children of the greeting element by using the <xsl:apply-templates/> element. The greeting element has just one child, and that is the text node "Hello XSL!" which will be passed to the user agent for display as a block flow object with red text of 16pt.

In summary: The xsl:template element contains the formatting and styling information. The <greeting> element is to be formatted as a 'block' element (which has a line break before and after it), and we specify styling of a 'red' font color of 16 point size.

The formatting element <fo:block> contains the processing information in the form of the element <xsl:apply-templates/>, which instructs the processor to apply the styling and formatting to the children of the <greeting> element, in this case the text-node "Hello XSL!". This simple document only has one child, but if there were more the processing would be passed to all the children (unless these were assigned different styling).

Flow Objects

A flow object is a concept that is used in styling. As a document is printed, or displayed, it 'flows' on to the page or screen. In fact every single character can be considered to be a flow object with its own unique styling. For practical purposes however we usually think in terms of larger flow objects, such as a heading, a paragraph, or a phrase.

The two terms you will hear most often are 'inline' flow object, and 'block' flow object. Essentially an inline flow object is a flow object without a line break before and after it, and a block flow object has a line break before and after it.

In HTML SPAN, I, B, EM, are all examples of in-line flow objects, and P, DIV, H*n*, and PRE, are all examples of block flow objects.

XSL Template Basics

At its simplest an XSL style sheet is an XML document containing 'template' rules.

Like any XML document it must follow the XML rules for well-formed documents. This basically means that there must be a unique opening and closing tag (in practice <xsl:stylesheet></xsl:stylesheet> suffices), and all the other tags must be nested.

The basic XSL building block is the template rule that describes how the original XML element node is converted into an XSL element node that can be formatted, styled, and displayed. As we said earlier, it consists of two parts: a pattern part and an action part.

Patterns select a node (usually an element) from the source document using the following criteria:

- Name
- Element Ancestry
- ID
- Wildcards
- The attributes of the source element
- An element's position relative to its siblings
- An element's uniqueness relative to its siblings

The action part of the template contains:

- An element creating a formatting object in the Result Tree, e.g. <fo:block></fo:block> will create a formatting object of the block type (see note 1 below).
- Styling to be applied to the formatting object in the form of attributes, e.g. <fo:block font-size="16pt"> would indicate that styling in the form of a 16 point font is to be applied to the formatting object (see note 2 below).
- The nature of the processing to be performed in the form of an empty tag. E.g. <xsl:process-children/> would cause the processor to process all the children of the matched element with the styling and formatting detailed in the other parts of the rule (see notes 3 & 4 below).

(1) In 'old' XSL both DSSSL and HTML formatting objects could be used. In 'new' XSL the specification supplies a list of flow objects identified by the 'fo:' *namespace. These are detailed later in the sections on Layout Formatting Objects and Content Flow Objects.*

(2) For the most part the style properties mimic the CSS properties except the syntax is [style property]=["value"].

(3) The WG make it clear that the name 'process-children' may change.

(4) It is by no means certain, but it is likely that in the 'new' XSL, as in CSS, the descendants of the flow object will inherit many of the style properties.

The processing part can also carry out the following operations.

- Generate fresh style objects
- Add literal text
- Duplicate and clone flow objects
- Filter elements
- Re-order elements (Expected to appear in future versions of XSL)

XSL Tree Construction

In a nutshell, an XML/XSL processor will take a source XML document, and construct a 'tree', known as the Source Tree, from the XML document. It will then use the XSL style sheet to construct a separate tree, the Result Tree, from the Source Tree. In the process of doing this it can reorder, and/or duplicate the Source Tree nodes as well as adding new flow objects in the form of elements or text.

If you are unfamiliar with the terms 'tree', node, 'child', 'parent', etc. see Chapter 6 on XML and the DOM.

The nodes of the newly formed Result Tree are the nodes that will have styling applied to them to form 'styled' flow objects.

Note how this is different in concept to CSS-type styling where styling is applied directly to the Source Tree to create a styled flow object. The extra 'tree' in the XSL process means that the eventual output, after the XSL style sheet has been applied, can have a very different structure to the original Source Tree, enhancing the range of things you can do to customize the eventual output.

The following diagrams illustrate the difference.

Here is basic flow of the XSL styling process:

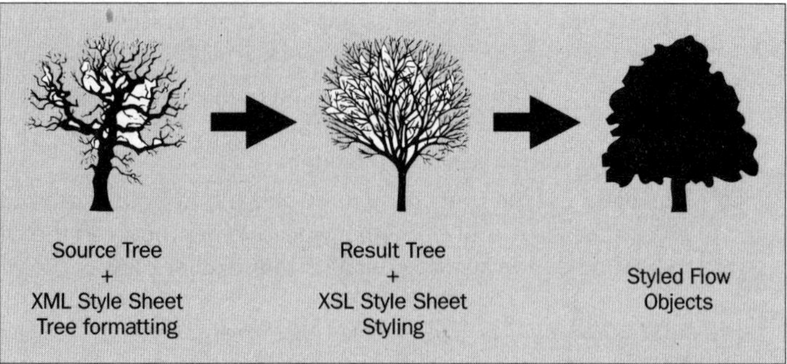

And here is the process in CSS:

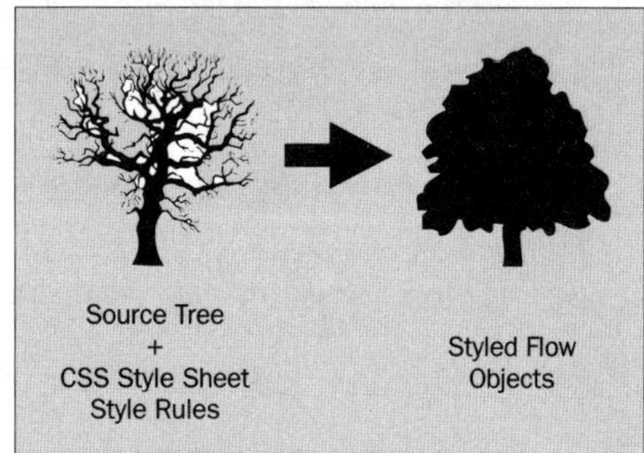

The ability to redraw the Source Tree not only adds tremendously to the functionality, but also makes much richer styling possible in XSL, whereas in XML/CSS we would have to alter the source document if we wanted to add a flow object.

Here is a simple example. Don't worry about the syntax of the style sheet for now, all will be explained later!

Source Document

Here's a well-formed XML document about a famous sheep, `dolly.xml`:

```
<xdoc>
     <greeting>Hello Dolly!</greeting>
     <question>Can you clone me?</question>
     <sheepobject>Dolly</sheepobject>
</xdoc>
```

To display it let's match it with both a CSS- and an XSL-type style sheet in turn. First the CSS-type sheet.

Using CSS

Here's the CSS-type style sheet, `dolly.css`:

```
     xdoc{
           display:block;
           font-family:times new roman,serif;
           font-size:12pt;
```

```
        }
        question{
              display:block;
        }
        sheepobject{
              display:block;
              font-size:16pt;
        }
```

The tree of the document would remain unaltered, i.e. only the Source Tree would be decorated. Here is a representation of the tree:

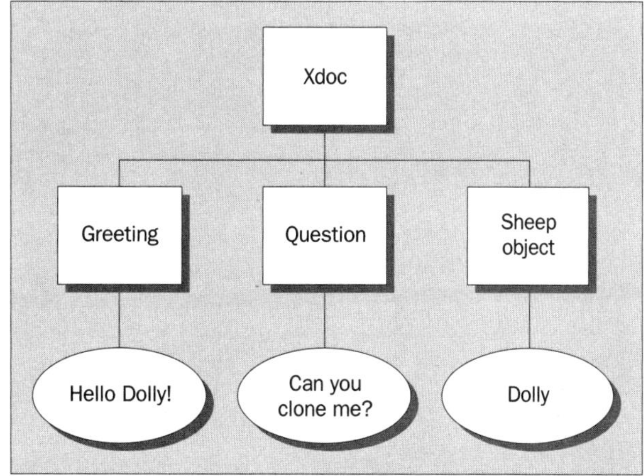

The result, if printed out to a CSS compliant browser, would look like this:

The styling has merely been added directly to the source document elements to create a styled flow object.

Using XSL

Now let's use an XSL-type style sheet.

In the following code we have not only added some text into the Result Tree by using the <xsl:text> element, but we have also processed the <sheepobject> child four times!

Don't worry too much if you can't understand the code, we will be examining it in some detail in the next section. Just note that we have processed the same child four times as well as adding some text (In DOM terminology, we have created a text node). Here's our XSL-type style sheet:

```
<xsl:stylesheet
     xmlns:xsl="http://www.w3.org/TR/WD-xsl"
     xmlns:fo="http://www.w3.org/TR/WD-xsl/FO"
     result-ns="fo">

     <xsl:template match="/">
          <fo:page-sequence
               font-family="times new roman,serif"
               font-size="12pt">
               <xsl:apply-templates/>
          </fo:page-sequence>
     </xsl:template>

     <xsl:template match="*">
          <fo:block
               font-family="times new roman,serif"
               font-size="12pt">
               <xsl:apply-templates/>
          </fo:block>
     </xsl:template>

     <xsl:template match="sheepobject">
          <fo:block
               font-size="16pt">
               <xsl:text>YES I CAN!</xsl:text>
               <xsl:apply-templates/>
               <xsl:apply-templates/>
               <xsl:apply-templates/>
               <xsl:apply-templates/>
          </fo:block>
     </xsl:template>
</xsl:stylesheet>
```

What the XSL document does is use the Source Tree to construct a separate Result Tree, which now looks like this:

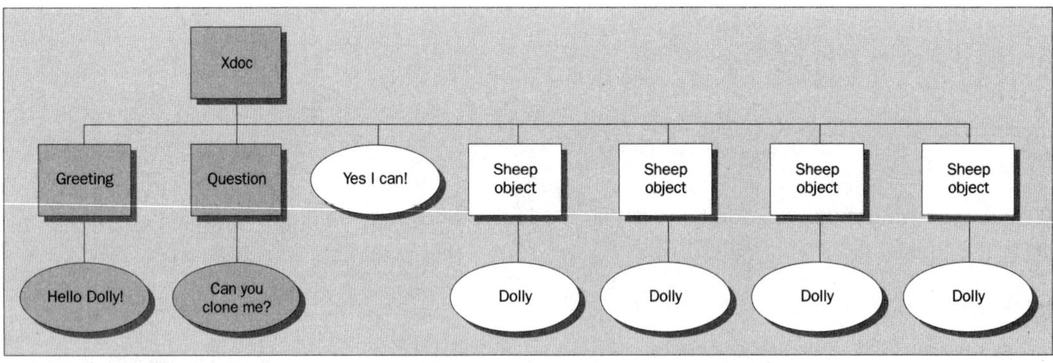

For purpose of clarity, the original nodes have been colored gray.

The result in an XML/XSL compliant browser would look something like this:

Note that both the screenshot in this and the previous section are cheats. We manually converted the XML file to HTML to show how it should display in an XML/style-sheet aware browser.

Building the Result Tree from the Source Tree

Let's just have a quick look at how the XSL processor builds a Result Tree from the Source Tree. It uses a process of recursion.

Recursion is a process whereby a program will carry on repeating itself. Here's how it works in the above example. Here's our simple XML document again:

```
<xdoc>
     <greeting>Hello Dolly!</greeting>
     <question>Can you clone me?</question>
     <sheepobject>Dolly</sheepobject>
</xdoc>
```

The processor goes to the source document and starts off with the element `xdoc`. It sees that it has certain XSL style sheet rules associated with it, and that it also has to process its children. Before applying any style rules it will then go off and look at the children. `xdoc` has three, so it goes to the first, `greeting`, finds the style rule, and sees it has to process `greeting`'s children, which it does. It notes that the text node (of course) does not have any children, so it goes back and starts processing the second child element, `question`. A good example of code that uses recursion can be found in Chapter 6 (XML and the DOM), under the 'Some Simple Implementations' heading.

Let's run through this process in more detail. Here is our style sheet again:

```
<xsl:stylesheet
     xmlns:xsl="http//www.w3.org/TR/WD-xsl"
     xmlns:fo="http//www.w3.org/TR/WD-xsl/FO"
     result-ns="fo">
```

```
        <xsl:template match="/">
              <fo:page-sequence
                    font-family="times new roman,serif"
                    font-size="12pt">
                    <xsl:apply-templates/>
              </fo:page-sequence>
        </xsl:template>

        <xsl:template match="*">
              <fo:block
                    font-family="times new roman,serif"
                    font-size="12pt">
                    <xsl:apply-templates/>
              </fo:block>
        </xsl:template>

        <xsl:template match="sheepobject">
              <fo:block
                    font-size="16pt">
                    <xsl:text>YES I CAN!</xsl:text>
                    <xsl:apply-templates/>
                    <xsl:apply-templates/>
                    <xsl:apply-templates/>
                    <xsl:apply-templates/>
              </fo:block>
        </xsl:template>
  </xsl:stylesheet>
```

For the root node <xdoc>, the best match it can find is in the template rule

```
<xsl:template match="/">
```

"/" is shorthand for the root, and here it means the root element of the source document. (We will look at the syntax in a moment.)

When it finds the match it looks for instructions as to what to do. The first instruction it finds is to make a 'page-sequence'-type flow object:

```
<fo:page-sequence ...
```

(We will explain what a page-sequence flow object is later on.) And it also finds instructions as to how to display the text in the attributes of the `fo:page-sequence` start tag:

```
font-family="times new roman,serif"
font-size="12pt"
```

so that the text will be displayed in a Times New Roman font, or if the processor can't find that font on the host machine it will use a default serif font, of 12 points.

As the processor moves through the rule, it finds an instruction

```
<xsl:apply-templates/>
```

to process all of xdoc's children, so it now does this, and looks for the best match for each of the children.

The first child the processor comes across is the greeting element. It can't find a match for greeting, so it uses our wild card match "*",

```
<xsl:template match="*">
```

which creates a block flow object fo:block,

```
<fo:block
     font-family="times new roman,serif"
     font-size="12pt">
     <xsl:apply-templates/>
</fo:block>
```

and styles greeting and its children with a 12pt Times New Roman font.

The processor then moves on to the next child of greeting, the question element, and, failing to find a specific template rule to match, applies the wildcard template for a second time.

Having finished with the question element the processor then moves on to the sheepobject element, and finds a better match!

```
<xsl:template match="sheepobject">
```

It then creates the fo:block flow object specified that contains an attribute specifying that the flow object should be formatted with 16-point sized text.

```
<fo:block
     font-size="16pt">
```

Within this 'block' the first instruction is

```
<xsl:text>YES I CAN!</xsl:text>
```

Which creates a text flow object with the string value of "YES I CAN!" and inserts it into the Result Tree as the first child of the block flow object.

The next instruction within the block is

```
<xsl:apply-templates/>
```

which creates a text flow object (font-size of 16pt) from the string "Dolly". There are then three more 'xsl:apply-templates' instructions to be dealt with

```
<xsl:apply-templates/>
<xsl:apply-templates/>
<xsl:apply-templates/>
```

Each of these creates a new text flow object from the string "Dolly" to put into the Result Tree. The Result Tree then contains four copies of the "Dolly" flow object.

This process is a form of recursion. The XSL processor will work its way all through the tree creating 'Result' flow objects from the information given to it.

Inheritance

Note that although only the children of a given element are processed, the style applied to the child will flow down to all its descendants, until an alternate styling is indicated. So if I specified 16-point text for the root element, ALL the descendant elements would have 16-point text unless it was otherwise specified for a particular descendant element. The fresh styling would flow down to all the descendants of that element as well.

Default Match

If we omitted to put a process-children instruction on one of the template rules, then obviously none of the descendants of that node would be processed. (This is a good way to intentionally leave out material from the source document; see later.) What would happen though if we just didn't write a template rule?

This would prevent the recursion process from operating, so to prevent this there is an implied built-in rule.

This rule applies to both element nodes and the root node. The following shows the equivalent of the built-in template rule:

```
<xsl:template match="*|/">
  <xsl:apply-templates/>
</xsl:template>
```

This prevents the processing from coming to a halt, since the match is made for the root '/', OR (pipe-stem character '|') any children '*' for which a specific template match can't be found.

Next we will have a look at how XSL makes use of namespaces to define and identify its element before moving on to discuss the template rules in detail.

Namespaces and XSL Style Sheets

The XSL specification makes full use of namespaces. Although it certainly helps to understand namespaces, a deep comprehension is not really necessary to understand how they work in XSL style sheets. We will give a very simplified account, enough for you to understand the meaning of the various parts of the 'style sheet' element.

If however you are the type who really likes to work from the ground up, consult the namespace specification at http://www.w3.org/TR/WD-xml-names.

All style sheets conforming to the XSL specification should be contained in the root element

```
<xsl:stylesheet>
...
</xsl:stylesheet>
```

We have already looked at this in our second style sheet example above. Here is the whole element again. Note that there are three attributes, `xmlns:xsl`, `xmlns:fo`, and `result-ns="fo"`

```
<xsl:stylesheet
     xmlns:xsl="http//www.w3.org/TR/WD-xsl"
     xmlns:fo="http//www.w3.org/TR/WD-xsl/FO"
     result-ns="fo">
     ...
</xsl:stylesheet>
```

All style sheets conforming to the XSL specification must have the first attribute and its value, exactly as stated: `xmlns:xsl="http//www.w3.org/TR/WD-xsl"`.

> *1.Actually the official XML DTD for XSL gives the attribute value of* `xmlns:xsl` *as* `#FIXED`, *so even if you don't put it in its presence is assumed, PROVIDED you reference the DTD (as you would for an ordinary XML document using* `SYSTEM "....dtd"` *in a* `<!DOCTYPE...` *declaration at the top of the style sheet).*

> *2.*`xmlns` *is a reserved XML keyword element. It is always followed by a colon, and then an abbreviation (e.g. in this case* `xsl` *or* `fo`*), then an equal sign, and then a URI address. What it is telling the processor is that if it comes across an element with a prefix of* `xsl:` *it belongs to the* `http//www.w3.org/TR/WD-xsl` *namespace, or with* `fo:` *it belongs to* `the http//www.w3.org/TR/WD-xsl/FO` *namespace.*

What this does is tell the processor that whenever it comes across an element with the prefix '`xsl:`', it should be interpreted according to the XSL specification. In other words all elements like this are in the '`xsl`' namespace.

The second attribute is in theory optional, but in practice it should be there. It tells the processor that elements with the prefix '`fo:`' (short for flow objects) are in the '`fo`' namespace, and the styling to be applied is to use the formatting vocabulary as described in the XSL specification. So when the processor sees `<fo:block font-size="10pt">` it will know that the style sheet is referring to syntax as laid out in the '`fo`' namespace.

> *It would of course be possible to use another kind of styling vocabulary such as that found at* `http://www.mystyle.org`, *and if you want to go to the effort of writing one, AND getting application vendors to support it, best of luck to you!*

The third attribute `result-ns="fo"` merely tells the processor that a Result Tree using the '`fo`' formatting object vocabulary is being constructed.

Other Styling Namespaces

There is a proposal on foot to use the established CSS vocabulary as a namespace. This is discussed later on in the section on the CSS Namespace. The W3C Note can be found at

`http://www.w3.org/TR/NOTE-XSL-and-CSS`

This namespace attribute would be declared in the root `xsl:stylesheet` element as follows:

```
     xmlns:css="http://www.w3.org/TR/NOTE-XSL-and-CSS"
```

Of course the processor would need to be informed that we are building a tree from the css namespace with

```
        result-ns="css"
```

Other xsl:stylesheet Attributes

The attributes that 'xsl:stylesheet' can take are shown below. They are for the most part self-explanatory.

Here is the list of attributes declared in the official DTD:

```
<!ATTLIST xsl:stylesheet
        result-ns NMTOKEN #IMPLIED
        default-space (preserve|strip) "preserve"
        indent-result (yes|no) "no"
        id ID #IMPLIED
        xmlns:xsl CDATA #FIXED "http://www.w3.org/TR/WD-xsl"
>
```

result-ns

As stated above this informs the processor that a tree is going to be constructed, usually using the 'fo' namespace (if we want things to conform to, and be interpretable in terms of, the XSL specification).

default-space

As you are aware, the standard HTML practice is to strip out, or rather collapse the white space. In XML (and XSL) the standard practice is to preserve it.

indent-result

It is not yet clear from the specification what this means. It probably means that all output text should be indented a certain amount.

Now we move on to discuss templates and the syntax of the expressions that can be used to specify which part of an XML document a styling template should be matched with.

XSL Template Rules

The basis of the XSL style sheet is the template rule, which makes a template that allows a user agent to construct a styled Result node from a Source node. We have already seen the <xsl:template> tag in operation.

As we said earlier, the template really has two parts, the 'pattern matching' part, and a 'processing action' part.

The matching part identifies the source (XML) node to which the processing action is to be applied. The matching information is contained in the match attribute.

The processing part defines how the children are to be processed and what styling is to be applied to them. This processing information (elements specifying flow objects and processing) is contained in the template's child elements.

In the following sections we discuss the various methods for specifying the match that the template is to make. After that we discuss the formatting flow objects in more detail.

Simple matches

Here we will have a look at the simpler pattern matches involving matches by name, ancestry, descent, position and ID.

Matching By Name

The simplest match is indeed very simple. The source element is simply identified by its name using the match attribute, as in our earlier example. The value we give to the match attribute is also called the pattern.

So

```
<xsl:template match="greeting">
```

matches that template to all the `<greeting>` elements in our source document.

Matching By Ancestry

Just as in CSS a match can be made by using the element's ancestry.

In CSS the rule

```
P EM {[insert style declarations  here]}
```

would match any `EM` element that has `P` as an ancestor.

In XSL we would have to do the following to mimic this match pattern.

```
<xsl:template match= "P//EM">
```

Note the use of the double forward slash which is required syntax. The double slash indicates that the `EM` element may be one or more levels of nesting below its `P` ancestor. So the above would select to style an `EM` element that had a `P` element somewhere in its ancestry.

For example, it would match the `<EM>` element below:

```
<P>
    <FIRST>
    <SECOND>
         ...
              ...
                 <EM>
                    Text to be styled
                 </EM>
              ...
         ...
    </SECOND>
  </FIRST>
</P>
```

To match an EM that is a child of P we would put:

```
<xsl:template match= "P/EM">
```

Note that here we just use the single forward slash, indicating a strict parent-child relationship with no intervening levels.

```
<xsl:template match= "DIV/P/EM">
```

The above would match an EM that has a DIV as a grandparent, and P as a parent.

Matching Several Names

In CSS we can group several selectors together, e.g.

```
H1, H2, H3 {[insert style declarations here]}
```

will match the H1, H2, and H3 elements.

In XSL we need to separate the source elements by a pipe-stem |, to get the same pattern.

```
<xsl:template match= "H1 | H2 | H3">
```

would achieve the same result.

Matching the Root

It is often useful to put all the basic style properties on the root of a document to enable all the descendant nodes to inherit the properties.

> *Note that the root is not the same as the document's root element, which can be matched by name; it comes before this, and it is the root object of the whole document, and in terms of the DOM is the document node (see Chapter 6). It is really a fiction. The reason for the distinction is that if the document node and the document's root element were the same thing, and we named the root element in our style template, e.g.* <xsl:template match="xdoc">*, then used* <xsl:apply-templates/>*, the root element would not be processed!*

This is achieved by using a single forward slash to represent the root (document node). The match

```
<xsl:template match= "/">
```

would select the root pattern.

Wildcard Matches

If we wanted to make a match to select any elements in the XML document for which we hadn't specified a template, then we would use the wildcard selector '*'. The following template tag

```
<xsl:template match= "*">
```

would match every node in the source document (for which no other rule was specified). Note that

```
<xsl:template match= "/|*">
```

would match the whole document as the forward slash matchs the root, and the asterisk matches all the elements. This can be useful for specifying a rule to apply if no other applies. The XSL compliant user agent is required to assume a built-in rule as follows.

Built-in template rule

As we saw above, the Source document tree is matched to the Result output tree by a process of recursion. To stop this recursive process from halting because no suitable rule is available, the XSL compliant user agent must assume a built-in template rule if it finds no other (as we mentioned earlier in the section 'Default Match'). As you may recall, this rule is of the form:

```
<xsl:template match= "/|*">
     <xsl:apply-templates/>
</xsl:template>
```

There is nothing, of course, to prevent us from writing our own rule. E.g.

```
<xsl:template match= "/|*">
      [censored material]</xsl:template>
```

would stop processing of all nodes for which a style rule was not provided and would substitute the string "`[censored material]`" in the Result Tree.

Matching By ID

The syntax for matching by ID is identical to the XPointer syntax (see Chapter 5), namely:

```
<xsl:template match= "id([id here])">
```

So in the XML document we could have

```
<greeting id="A1">Hello World!</greeting>
```

and the following line in the XSL style sheet would match the template to an element whose ID attribute had the value "`A1`", in this case the `<greeting ...>` element above.

```
<xsl:template match= "id(A1)">
```

Matching By Attribute

The syntax for matching by attribute is:

```
<xsl:template match= "element name[@ attribute-name=attribute-value]">
```

Rather confusingly the specification uses square brackets to hold the attribute name and value. As you are probably aware, square brackets are traditionally used for enclosing a generic term when defining code.

To see how attribute matching works, consider the following XML document that we wish to style:

```
<xdoc>
      <chapter num="ch1">
            <chtitle>first</chtitle>
            <para type="opening">Some text</para>
            <para type="regular">Some <emph>emphasised</emph> text</para>
            <para>A para with no attribute</para>
            <para type="closing">Some more text</para>
      </chapter>

      <chapter num="ch2">
            <chtitle>second</chtitle>
            <para type="opening">Some text</para>
            <para type="regular">Some <emph>emphasised</emph> text</para>
            <para>A para with no attribute</para>
            <para type="closing">Some more text</para>
      </chapter>

      <chapter num="ch3">
            <chtitle>third</chtitle>
            <para type="opening">Some text</para>
            <para type="regular">Some <emph>emphasised</emph> text</para>
            <para>A para with no attribute</para>
            <para type="closing">Some more text</para>
      </chapter>
</xdoc>
```

We could then use the following template matches in our XSL style sheet:

```
<xsl:template match="para">
```

to match all `para` elements;

```
<xsl:template match="para[@type]">
```

would match all `para` elements with a `type` attribute; and

```
<xsl:template match="para[@type='opening']">
```

would match all `para` elements with a `type` attribute that also had a value of `"opening"`.

We could use

```
<xsl:template match="chapter[@num='ch1']/para[attribute(type)=
opening']">
```

which would match all `para` elements with a `type` attribute that also had a value of `"opening"`, that also have a parent of `chapter` with a `num` attribute with a value of `"ch1"` (i.e. the very first `para` in our XML code example).

Matching By Child

Elements can also be matched by a child qualifier.

The general syntax given in the specification for this is:

```
<xsl:template match= "element-name[child-name]">
```

Again note the rather confusing use of square brackets.

In our example above

```
<xsl:template match=  "para[emph]">
```

would match all `para` elements with an `emph` child.

Matching By Position

XSL also allows matching based on a pattern using position qualifiers.

Here are the various position qualifiers as defined in the specification:

`first-of-type().`	The element must be the first sibling of its type.
`not-first-of-type().`	The element must not be the first sibling of its type.
`last-of-type().`	The element must be the last sibling of its type.
`not-last-of-type().`	The element must not be the last sibling of its type.
`first-of-any().`	The element must be the first sibling element of any type
`not-first-of-any().`	The element must not be the first sibling element of any type.
`last-of-any().`	The element must be the last sibling element of any type.
`not-last-of-any().`	The element must not be the last sibling element of any type.
`only-of-type().`	The element must have no element siblings of the same type.
`not-only-of-type().`	The element must have one or more element siblings of the same type.
`only-of-any().`	The element must have no element siblings at all.
`not-only-of-any().`	The element must have one or more element siblings.

The syntax for matching with position qualifiers is:

```
<xsl:template match= "element[ position description ]">
```

Again note the rather confusing use of square brackets.

For the XML example document, we could specify an XSL template match of

```
<xsl:template match= "chapter[first-of-type()]">
```

that would match the first `chapter` element. (The `chapter` element with an `id` of `ch1`.) Or we could use

```
<xsl:template match= "chapter[last-of-type()]">
```

to match the last `chapter` element. (The `chapter` element with an `id` of `ch3`.)

Resolving Match Conflicts

It is likely that there will be more than one template rule applying to the same source element. When this occurs the more specific rule will apply. (Paraphrasing the specification) the rules work as follows.

A match pattern specified that makes reference to the element's specified ID attribute name, is considered to be more specific than one that does not. If two patterns both refer to the element's ID, or if neither pattern does, then the one with more 'components' is the more specific. Where 'components' are element type or attribute type names (and any specific attribute values).

Here are examples from the specification (section 2.6.11) of rules given in decreasing order of specificity.

1. `id(employee-of-the-month)`
2. `employee[attribute(type)='contract',attribute(country)='USA']`
3. `employee[attribute(type)='contract']`
4. `employee`
5. `*`

Note that `id` is always the most specific and a wild card "*" the least.

Layout Formatting Objects

In this section we look at the 'page'-layout formatting objects defined in the latest version of the XSL specification.

Simple Formatting Objects

'Old' XSL used a group of DSSSL and HTML formatting objects. 'New' XSL provides its own list of formatting objects defined in the specification, and referred to using the '**fo:**' namespace. The formatting object is applied to the Result Tree node by being contained in the 'action' part of the template element.

This takes the general syntax:

```
<xsl:template match= "[pattern]">            <!--identifies the match-->

     <fo:[formatting-object] ([style property]= "[value]")*>
```

```
            [processing instructions]*

        </fo:[formatting-object]>

    </xsl:template>
```

Although the specification promises several layout styles in the future, the August 1998 specification details just the page-sequence object, and the simple-page-master object.

The page-sequence object acts as an ancestor to a series of pages, either print-style pages, or Internet-style pages. The specification promises that in the future it will also introduce a flow-map object for other kinds of formatting.

page-sequence

The page-sequence object acts as an ancestor object to contain one to several flow objects or page sequences. It can hold one or more 'single-page-master' children, or up to six child 'queues' (see below).

In practice it acts as a vehicle to contain style rules that can be inherited by the rest of the document. For example in the template rule:

```
<xsl:template match="/">
      <fo:page-sequence
            font-family="times new roman,serif"
            font-size="12pt"
            background-color= "white'
            color= "black">
            <xsl:process-children/>
      </fo:page-sequence>
</xsl:template>
```

the font and color rules will be inherited by the other flow objects in the Result Tree, unless alternates are specified. This is similar to the style rules designated for the <BODY> element in HTML.

simple-page-master

This formatting object is declared using the syntax

```
<fo:simple-page-master  [style properties]>
```

This flow object describes a simple page that can be divided up into six areas. (See the diagram in the section on 'queue' below.)

This model can be used for either print or Internet media.

The element MUST take a 'master-name' attribute, which can have one of the following values:

- first

Formatting for the first page of a series of pages.

- odd

Equivalent of "left-hand page" in print media.

- even

Equivalent of "right-hand page" in print media.

- scrolling

The type of page used in on-screen presentation.

So the code for this formatting object would look like:

```
<fo:simple-page-master  master-name="first"  [other properties] >
```

The specification's editors promise more complex layout objects, such as columns, in forthcoming versions.

Now let's look at the more basic flow objects that will be contained in the pages.

Content Flow Objects

Here are some of the more common content formatting objects with a brief description of each.

queue

This appears in the style sheet as the element

```
<fo:queue…
```

The 'queue' flow object is probably the most obtuse of the flow objects. In fact it is really not a flow object at all but really a place to gather flow objects for assignment to a given area.

This flow object can ONLY be a child of page-sequence. It takes an attribute of 'queue-name' which takes one of six values: title, header, body, footer, start-side, or end-side. The 'body' is where the main content of the document goes.

The diagram shows these six areas on a page.

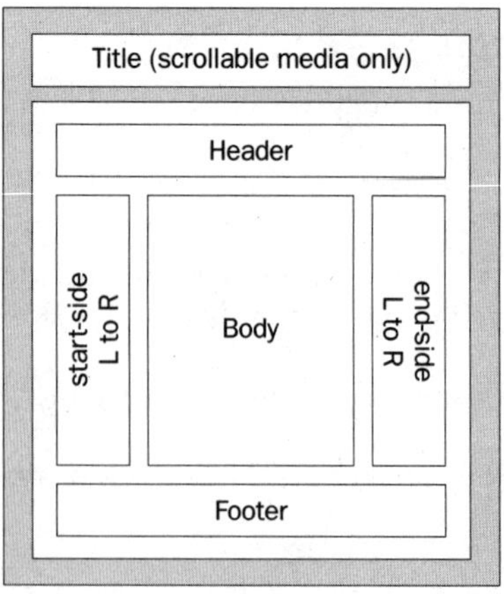

Note that the title queue area only applies to scrollable media.

How flow objects are to be assigned to the flow area is not at all clear from the current specification. But it also makes it clear that subsequent editions will tell us how to use this formatting object to number pages, provide headers and footers dictionary-style, and also provide side and end notes.

sequence

This formatting object is created with the element

```
<fo:sequence...
```

This flow object is used to group flow objects that share an inherited set of properties. Although it is not exactly the same as a CSS 'inline' flow object, it serves much the same purpose.

Consider the following code snippet:

```
<xsl:template match= "emphasis">
      <fo:sequence font-style="italic">
            <xsl:process-children/>
      </fo:sequence>
</xsl:template>
```

This will construct a Result Tree flow object that will style all elements with the name 'emphasis' in italic font. In HTML both the <SPAN> and the <EM> elements are examples of inline flow objects.

block

We seen the syntax for this element earlier

```
<fo:block...
```

This will construct a block type flow object. In practice this means that it will have a line break both before and after it. In HTML both the <P> and <DIV> elements are examples of block flow objects.

list

This flow object is created with

```
<fo:list...
```

The list flow object acts as a container for the list-item, list-item-label, and the list-item-body flow objects. The following diagram shows how they are related.

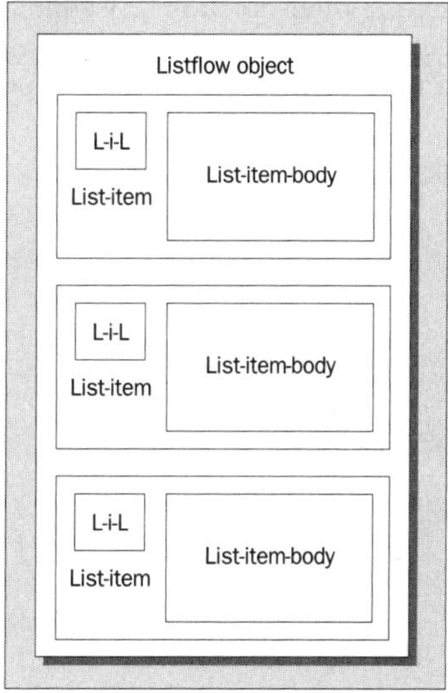

Note that if you wish to nest lists, the second list must be contained as a child of the `list-item-body` flow object.

rule-graphic

A '`rule-graphic`' flow object appears as

```
<fo:rule-graphic...
```

The '`rule-graphic`' flow object corresponds to the horizontal rule of HTML, but with added functionality. It can be either an inline or block flow object.

graphic

```
<fo:graphic...
```

The '`graphic`' flow object corresponds to the `<IMG>` flow object of HTML, but again with added functionality. It can be either an inline or block flow object.

score

```
<fo:score...
```

'`score`' is an inline flow object that can take text-decoration, such as underlines, strike-throughs, overbars, etc.

block-level-box

```
<fo:block-level-box...
```

'`boxes`' offer functionality similar to the CSS boxes. They are used to provide borders, margins and backgrounds and provide spacing between the border of the box and the content. They can be of either the inline or the block type.

inline-box

```
<fo:inline-box...
```

(See `block-level-box`.)

page-number

```
<fo:page-number...
```

This flow object is used to instruct the formatter to construct and present a page number in the style desired. In other words, it tells the user agent to create content.

link

```
<fo:link...
```

This will create an area where one can put `link-end-locator` flow objects. `link-end-locator` flow objects contain information about the destination that the user can link to. If there is more than one `link-end-locator` within the `link` object, the user agent should provide some means, e.g. a drop down list, whereby the user can make a selection.

link-end-locator

```
<fo:link-end-locator...
```

`link-end-locator` flow objects provide information about the destination of a link (equivalent to `HREF= "[URI]"` in HTML).

character

This flow object allows you to treat a single character as a flow object. The syntax is:

```
<fo:character...
```

Now we'll take a look at the styling properties that can be specified as attributes of the flow object elements above.

Simple styling

Each formatting or flow object may take certain style properties. Each formatting or flow object may inherit some styling properties from ancestor nodes. Which properties may be inherited depend on the objects concerned. XSL makes a great effort to be compatible with CSS, and thus many of the styling properties have the same names as the CSS style properties. However there are some additional properties in XSL (one example (chosen at random!) is `char-kern-mode`). An alphabetical list of all possible XSL styling properties can be found in section 3.24 of the August '98 XSL specification. The CSS styling properties are enumerated in Appendices F and G.

If you are familiar with CSS style sheets a quick way to employ this knowledge to produce a simple XSL style sheet is given in the next section.

Converting CSS to XSL

Here is a CSS style rule. It consists of a selector and a declaration. The declaration consists of several property/value pairs separated by semi-colons.

```
[selector]{font-name:times new roman, serif; font-size:14pt; background-
olor:#800000; }
```

To convert a CSS declaration to an XSL style declaration insert the CSS properties/value pairs into the XSL syntax in the following way

```
<fo:[formatting object] [css property-name]= "[css value]">
```

so that the above CSS declaration becomes

```
<fo:[formatting object] font-name=" times new roman, serif"  font-size= "14pt"
     background-color="#800000">
```

There are several other properties unique to the `fo:` namespace. We show an example of a `graphic` flow object that uses quite a few in the section below on More Complex Styling.

Simple Processing

As we have seen earlier the first part of the styling action involves prescribing the flow object to be created and the style properties to be applied. The second part of the action involves processing or building a Result Tree flow object from the Source Tree.

xsl:process-children

The standard instruction to the XSL processor is

```
<xsl:process-children/>
```

This will process all the children of the source element we have matched.

As we saw earlier in the `dolly.xml` example, if we repeat this instruction, we will get another copy of the flow objects.

Adding a Text Flow Object

We can add a text flow object by the simple expedient of including the text in our processing model, so in the following:

```
     <xsl:template match= "emphasis">
           <fo:sequence font-style="italic">
           Note Well!:-
           <xsl:apply-templates/>
           </fo:sequence>
     </xsl:template>
```

The text string "`Note Well!:-`" would be placed before every piece of emphasized text. Note however, that when used this way white space will be collapsed. If it is important to preserve white space put the text in an '`xsl:text`' element as follows.

xsl:text

The `xsl:text` element implicitly contains the `xml:space` (XML reserved) attribute with the default value of '`preserve`'. As a result, white space is preserved inside `xsl:text` elements automatically.

```
<xsl:text>
Can you preserve white space?


YES I CAN!
</xsl:text>
```

xsl:process

If we just want to process certain children, the `xsl:process` element gives us a means to do this. The elements to be processed are selected out by name.

```
<xsl:template match= "book">
     <fo:block font-size= "12pt">
          <apply-templates= "chapter-title"/>
     </fo:block>
</xsl:template>
```

would style all the `chapter-title` children of `book` elements with a 12-point sized font.

Selection patterns can be used in the same manner as for template `match` attributes to specify the `select` value.

Missing formatting objects

Missing from the current specification are some important formatting objects. The authors of the specification promise that this situation will be remedied in forthcoming versions. Here are some of the flow objects that they promise to address.

- Tables
- Multi-column and sophisticated page layout
- Side-by-side and floating objects
- Extracted content, e.g. index, table of contents, endnotes, side notes.
- International objects.
- Additional building blocks apart from page numbering
- Math

Also note that although this is not a formatting object, the current XSL style language does not currently provide support similar to the CSS `@media` rule, which allows you to specify special styling for particular methods of output, e.g. screen, ordinary print, or Braille.

More complex styling

The styling properties we looked at above are for the most part similar to their CSS cousins. The XSL specification also provides some unique properties. You are referred to the specification for a comprehensive list. It is also likely that in future versions of the draft this list will be added to or otherwise modified.

As there are no implementations (except possibly the forthcoming public release of Microsoft's Internet Explorer 5), the list in the specification is just offered as an example of the richness of formatting that should become possible with XSL.

Below is a list for the `graphic` flow object. You will note that some of the properties have comments in brackets beginning with either 'DSSSL:' or 'CSS:'. These indicate whether the name of the property is the '-same-' in DSSSL or CSS, or has another name particular to those specifications. The term `Non-core` indicates that an XSL formatter need not implement this object or property but should include a default fallback action to implement instead to prevent processing errors occurring where a style sheet specifies these properties.

The `graphic` flow object has the following properties:

inline
block-level-alignment
break-after (DSSSL:-same-)
break-before (DSSSL:-same-)
color (DSSSL:-same-)
external-graphic-id
graphic-max-height
graphic-max-width
graphic-scale
indent-end (DSSSL:end-indent, CSS:-object-margin-)
indent-start (DSSSL:start-indent, CSS:-object-margin-)
inhibit-wrap
keep (DSSSL:-same-)
keep-with-previous (DSSSL:-same-)
keep-with-next (DSSSL:-same-)
position-point-x
position-point-y
position-preference (DSSSL:-same-)
space-after-maximum (DSSSL:space-after) **Non-core**
space-after-minimum (DSSSL:space-after) **Non-core**
space-after-optimum (DSSSL:space-after)
space-before-maximum (DSSSL:space-before) **Non-core**
space-before-minimum (DSSSL:space-before) **Non-core**
space-before-optimum (DSSSL:space-before)
writing-mode (DSSSL:-same-)

Treatment of White Space

XSL style sheets are XML documents. The default in XML is to preserve white space. This can be emphasized in individual style sheets by using the `xsl:preserve-space` element in the XSL style sheet, or for individual elements the attribute `xml:space` with a value of '`preserve`' can be used.

Conversely the `xsl:stylesheet` element can take an attribute of `default-space`, which can take the value '`strip`' or the value '`preserve`'. The value '`strip`' which will establish a default of collapsing white space throughout the resulting document. If the attribute is not present in the `xsl:stylesheet` element a default of '`preserve`' is assumed.

When the value for the `default-space` attribute in the `xsl:stylesheet` element is '`preserve`' (explicitly set or by default) then for individual Result elements the `xsl:strip-space` element can be employed to remove them from the list of elements for which white space is preserved.

The CSS Namespace

Other namespaces can provide formatting models as well. An interesting proposal for using CSS properties to build flow objects can be found at:

`http://www.w3.org/TR/NOTE-XSL-and-CSS`

Declaring the result-ns

For just one namespace, i.e. the `fo:`, namespace the Result Tree is declared thus:

```
<xsl:stylesheet
     xmlns:xsl="http//www.w3.org/TR/WD-xsl"
     xmlns:fo="http//www.w3.org/TR/WD-xsl/FO"
     result-ns="fo">
```

It is not immediately clear whether two different formatting namespaces will be allowed in the same style sheet, but there is really no reason why they shouldn't be. Two formatting namespaces would probably be declared as follows.

```
<xsl:stylesheet
xmlns:xsl="http//www.w3.org/TR/WD-xsl"
xmlns:fo="http//www.w3.org/TR/WD-xsl/FO"
xmlns:css="http://www.w3.org/TR/NOTE-XSL-and-CSS"
result-ns="fo"
result-ns="css">
```

Let's take a brief look at how the CSS specification's authors (Hakon Lie and Bert Bos) suggest that CSS formatting objects could be used.

The basic template rule, with its pattern and its action, still applies. Here is a basic template rule that uses the CSS namespace:

```
<template match="partnumber">
  <css:chunk display="block"
             font-weight="bold"
             margin-top="20px">
    <css:chunk display="inline"
               color="red">
      Part number:<css:space/>
    </css:chunk>
    <css:chunk color="green">
      <process-children/>
    </css:chunk>
  </css:chunk> <!-- end of block -->
</template>
```

Notice the use of the element `css:chunk` to create a flow object.

CSS properties are converted to an XSL format (with the simple conversion method we saw earlier in Converting CSS to XSL) and applied as attributes of the `css:chunk`.

This example would produce a string "`Part number:` " in red text followed by the contents of the '`partnumber`' element in green text.

You are referred to the (well written!) W3C Note mentioned at the beginning of this section for further discussion of the CSS namespace.

This namespace is particularly interesting as it will probably be the easiest for the "big two" (Microsoft and Netscape) browsers to implement, since their version 4.x browsers already contain significant support for CSS. We may well see a tool for this namespace before the XSL `fo:` namespace.

The other interesting thing is that there is already a well-educated body of programmers out there who would have little difficulty in using CSS objects in XSL, and existing CSS editing tools could be easily converted to support this format.

The Future of XSL

There are several deficiencies in the XSL specification, probably the most glaring are the lack of support for scripting, the lack of a table flow object, and the lack of support for forms. However it is likely that this will be remedied in forthcoming revisions of the Working Draft.

The final XSL specification will be a monumental effort. The authors have set as a *minimum* goal that it have all the functionality of CSS and DSSSL combined! So what we will end up with is a very powerful and possibly very complex tool.

The problems that will arise are:

- Will there be good cheap software support for the specification?
- Will it be simple enough for the average XML programmer to use in preference to, say, CSS?

If the answer to both of these questions is 'Yes' then look for this specification to be the one for the future.

If the answer to either is 'No' (the questions go hand in hand), then XSL will become just another programming language with a few enthusiasts to keep it going.

However one use for XSL's extra tree manipulation capabilities is mentioned on the W3C's site for XSL-related information (`http://www.w3c.org/Style/xsl`). There they suggest that XSL could be used in combination with CSS to provide a higher degree of control over the output of applications. That is, for some more complex applications it might be a good idea to "use XSL on the server to condense or customize some XML data into a simpler XML document, then use CSS to style it on the client".

Summary

In this chapter we had a look at the basics of the new XSL styling language. We saw how:

- XSL produces a Result Tree from a Source tree.
- the XSL template rule has both a 'pattern' part and an 'action' part.
- we match templates to nodes on the Source Tree.
- we use namespaces to identify our formatting objects
- we define formatting objects, style them, and then process them.

We ended with a brief look at the new CSS formatting paradigm.

Please Note:

You are strongly advised to check our Web site for updates to this chapter before attempting to install and run the sample applications.

We will provide updates to this chapter and to the sample application files on our Web site at `http://webdev.wrox.co.uk/books/1525/`.

XML is a rapidly evolving field, and this was particularly the case when this book was being written. While the theory behind this chapter is perfectly sound, it is likely that the publicly available parser components that we use may have been updated in line with changes to the XML standards. For example, the method and property names are unlikely to remain the same as indicated in this chapter.

Before trying to install and run the application, please check for updates on the Web site to avoid disappointment.

9

XML and the Data Tier

There has been much discussion about XML replacing HTML. While HTML is concerned with displaying data in a consistent manner, XML is concerned with *describing* data. Given that, the power of XML resides in its ability to represent data from the Middle Tier (often referred to as the Business Tier) or Data Tiers of an *n*-tier architecture to external systems without customized software for each disparate client. XML, being a text-based language for describing data, allows communication to occur between computers regardless of their underlying operating system. Using XML as a transparent data translation system makes truly Web-based computing, across heterogeneous platforms, possible.

The delivery of data across the Internet need not only be between Web browsers and Web servers. Business-to-business transactions can occur between two servers that automate order processing, order progress reports, or monetary exchange, delivering an Internet-based promise of what Electronic Data Interchange (EDI) claimed years ago. Because of the ubiquity of the Internet, its cost effectiveness as a communication mechanism, and emerging XML standards, EDI may well be replaced by specific XML applications.

This chapter focuses on delivering data to clients of any type (Web browsers, other servers, etc.) using XML as the generic mechanism, and using the tools and skills that existing Web developers have become accustomed to. The chapter presents the delivery of data to clients using files generated by Microsoft's SQL Server, SQL stored procedures, and Active Server Pages. Heavy emphasis is placed upon SQL Server processing to show that XML processing can be spread across the Client, Middle, and Data Tiers. This spreading of the load is used to maximize the efficiency of the system and improve user response. This chapter also shows how to protect back office computing resources by processing the XML data on a Web server, preventing direct access to a sensitive computing resource and hiding the topology of your Web computing environment.

Methods of Delivering XML

Depending upon the application, there are two methods of using XML data as a communication platform between a client and a server:

- Using the database engine to generate the XML data
- Using middleware systems to convert to/from XML and the legacy infrastructure

Each method has its strengths and weaknesses. Middleware computing can provide a central point of access to many systems, database driven or not. Middleware can also perform rules–based processing on data that is being translated. However, the middleware approach can be expensive to build and may be overkill for a specific application. It can also be slower than database-created XML for seldom–changing data.

Database-created XML, on the other hand, can only incorporate data contained within the database system. It is harder to flexibly represent some data, since it deals with individual rows and not hierarchical data. However, the relational database engine makes the processing of multiple data sources linked throughout the database a snap. For seldom–changing data, it is the fastest choice, as the XML data is generated only upon changes, not every time a client requests it. If data mining is a requirement, the only real solution then becomes generating the XML data from a SQL Server, since there are few, if any, tools for OLAP processing in the middleware realm.

> *NOTE: This chapter focuses on using Microsoft's SQL Server 6.5 as the data repository. Therefore, any references to SQL Server indicate Microsoft's SQL Server and not other SQL Server products such as Sybase's SQL Server or Oracle's database products.*

This chapter shows how to generate XML files using the Web Task feature of SQL Server to generate static files, SQL stored procedures to generate dynamic data snapshots, and some Middle Tier processing to generically return XML data and to receive updates from a client. None of the delivery methods expose the SQL Server directly to the client (see the following diagram). Everything is passed through a Web server. By not granting direct access to the client, you gain security and the flexibility to change your back office systems without having to update the client software or having the client know such changes have occurred. This is a big boon for organizations that are incrementally rolling out features of a system, as all of the software is updated on the Middle or Data Tiers without the client ever knowing. This approach also allows organizations to modify systems based upon demand. For example, if a given XML document is requested only nightly with the same settings each time, the Information Technology (IT) group of the organization may decide to generate the report nightly using a SQL Server Web Task rather than doing a dynamic database query, thus saving processing time.

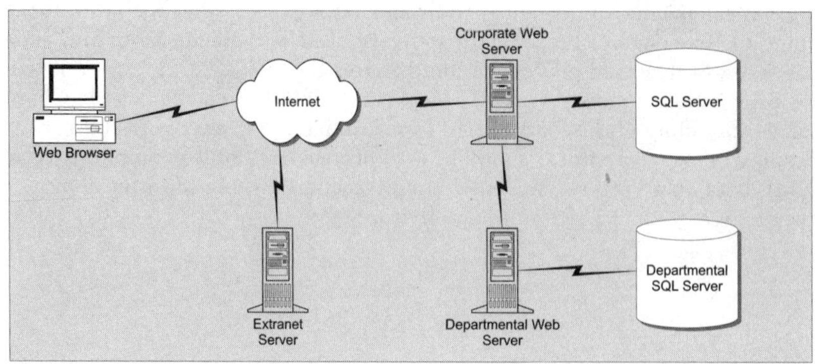

This diagram shows a high level view of clients and servers accessing XML data from a corporate Web server.

As you will see in the coming sections, there are many ways to deliver information from the Data Tier to requesting clients.

The Employee Phone List Application

In a typical corporate environment, each employee receives a list or booklet with each employee's phone numbers listed. As employees leave and come on board, the list must be recreated and reissued to all of the employees, making the old list obsolete. Off to the recycling bin it goes. This chapter's sample application is an electronic version of the employee phone list. The data is housed in a database, and employees view the list from within their Web browsers. The phone list is always up to date and the expense of copying and distributing the phone list is removed. Depending on your point of view, an added benefit is the availability of that list to external parties, such as business partners, other departments, or even customers.

The sample application focuses on just delivering minimal information about an employee. It does not provide a full set of the information you may want to provide. Its basic function is to list the employees in the database, their telephone numbers, and the type of phone(s) they may have (fax, cellular, pager, etc). The data for this employee list is housed in four normalized tables which give a taste of real world conditions (see the following diagram). The data from this application is delivered to the Web browser using XML and HTML. In order to update the list, there is an HTML page with a list of the employees, an HTML form for creating an update request, and an Active Server Page that receives XML `POST`s modifying the data in the tables. Some of the XML data is generated dynamically with each browser request, while other XML data is written to a file to show how to use SQL Server's Web Task feature. This allows the use of off peak time to create XML documents that can be viewed by clients. The next section discusses SQL Server's ability to generate Web type files.

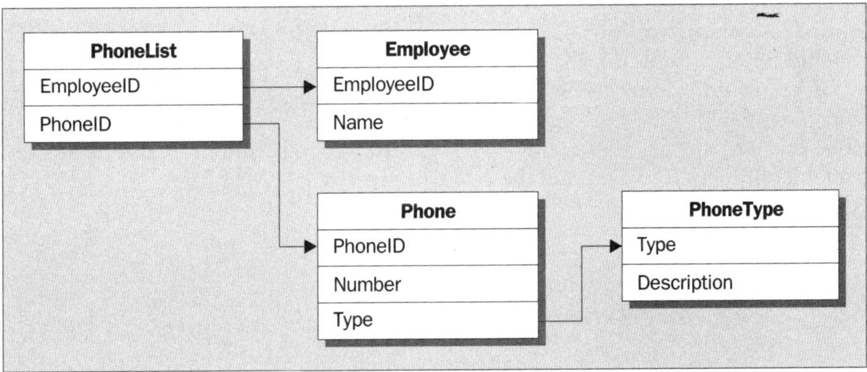

The diagram shows the phone list entity relationship.

SQL Server Generated XML

There are two different methods of generating XML from within SQL Server. You can either use Web Tasks, which are automated tasks that run at specific intervals and generate either HTML or XML files, or you can use stored procedures to return results sets that are formatted into XML. This first section is dedicated to discussing Web Tasks, and is followed by a section discussing the use of stored procedures to return XML result sets.

Web Tasks for Auto-generating XML Files

Microsoft's SQL Server has a feature which is meant to make the generation of HTML files from SQL statements easy. Normally, this is used to create reports that are published on a Web site. Often, this is the foundation of an internal IT reporting system that is egalitarian in access, since the only requirement is a Web browser. Old reporting systems used the paper method and had strict distribution lists due to costs, etc. As network computing has flattened the organizational structure, access to previously 'privileged' information is often just a click away.

Since these types of reports are the same for all people who wish to review them, there is no reason to build custom Web software that interactively queries for the data and builds HTML results. All that really needs to happen is for a single session to be created that generates one or more HTML pages. This is what Web Tasks were designed for. Each task can be performed at a specified interval: daily reports can be generated every night, weekly reports on Monday at five a.m., or reports can be made hourly. These tasks are performed automatically by the SQL Executive and are more efficient in terms of resource usage, since the task involves no network traffic. The tasks can be scheduled to run until a certain date is reached or a specified number of instances have occurred. You can also include links to other reports. It will even automatically generate the HTML code for you in the form of a table. Don't expect any artistic design awards though, for really nice looking HTML pages you need to provide SQL Server with a template file, where it inserts the column data based upon key words that you embed into the HTML source.

All this time we have only been mentioning HTML. That is because the Web Tasks were meant to generate HTML. An XML specification had not been completed when Web Tasks were added to SQL Server. The real flexibility of the template feature of SQL Server is the ability to use it to generate XML. The server does not care whether the file contains anything other than the keywords it uses to insert current row data. In the following template file, there is not one line of HTML. Instead the XML element tags to define a well-formed document can be found with the keywords `<%begindetail%>`, `<%enddetail%>`, and `<%insert_data_here%>`.

`<%begindetail%>` and `<%enddetail%>` are used to mark the area where a given SQL query's results set should be used to fill the `<%insert_data_here%>` statements. `<%insert_data_here%>` indicates where column data should be placed from the results set.

There must be one `<%insert_data_here%>` keyword for each column in the results set. Here's the Web Task template file used to generate the XML phone list:

```
<EmployeeList>
<%begindetail%>
     <Entry>
          <Employee><%insert_data_here%></Employee>
          <Phone><%insert_data_here%></Phone>
          <Type><%insert_data_here%></Type>
     </Entry>
<%enddetail%>
</EmployeeList>
```

Multiple SQL queries can be used to fulfill multiple `<%begindetail%>` and `<%enddetails%>` pairs. This allows for some complex reporting capabilities. One drawback of the Web Task template file approach is that you cannot nest `<%begindetail%>` and `<%enddetail%>` pairs within each other like so:

```
<!— Example of what you can not do with Web Task templates. -->
<EmployeeList>
<%begindetail%>
    <Entry>
         <Employee><%insert_data_here%>
         <%begindetail%>
         <Phone><%insert_data_here%></Phone>
              <Type><%insert_data_here%></Type>
         <%enddetail%>
         </Employee>
    </Entry>
<%enddetail%>
</EmployeeList>
```

which is very frustrating given XML's hierarchical structure. If this feature was present, you could easily build rich XML documents that take advantage of the hierarchical structure to minimize redundant data transmission and build complex object models. However, given the nesting limitation, the output of our XML template contains multiple `<Employee></Employee>` elements for the same employee, when one would have sufficed. Here's the Web Task output from the `Phone List XML Template`:

```
<EmployeeList>
    <Entry>
         <Employee>John Doe</Employee>
         <Phone>555-1212</Phone>
         <Type>Business</Type>
    </Entry>

    <Entry>
         <Employee>John Doe</Employee>
         <Phone>555-1216</Phone>
         <Type>Home FAX</Type>
    </Entry>

    <Entry>
         <Employee>Jane Doe</Employee>
         <Phone>555-1213</Phone>
         <Type>Home</Type>
    </Entry>

    <Entry>
         <Employee>Jim Johnson</Employee>
         <Phone>555-1214</Phone>
         <Type>Cellular</Type>
    </Entry>

    <Entry>
         <Employee>Sally Mae</Employee>
         <Phone>555-1215</Phone>
         <Type>Business FAX</Type>
    </Entry>
</EmployeeList>
```

This, along with the other files for this chapter, can be downloaded from `http://webdev.wrox.co.uk/books/1525`. We've talked about how to create XML using a Web Task template file and some of the features of a Web Task, now it is time to discuss how to create a Web Task.

Using the SQL Server Web Assistant

The easiest way to create an automated Web Task is to use the SQL Server Web Assistant. This feature was new to SQL Server 6.5. It provides a wizard that steps you through the process of creating a Web Task, hiding all of the underlying functionality with the Graphical User Interface (GUI). The first step in creating the Web Task is in identifying the SQL Server that it is to run on. Since this part of the wizard is self-explanatory we aren't going to write about it here. The first step of interest is in setting the SQL query that is to return the XML data.

This can be done graphically, by entering a query in directly, or by using an existing stored procedure, which is the method shown in this screen shot.

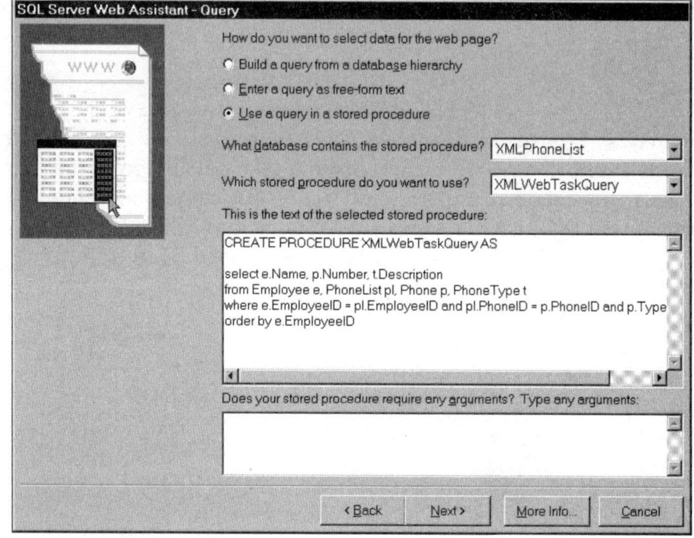

The wizard also allows you to enter any special parameters that the stored procedure might take. Notice that you can select the database and query by using a drop down list. This is a big help in cases where you cannot remember that exact name or syntax of the stored procedure you wish to use.

The next step that the wizard takes you through pertains to scheduling when the task is to be run. It provides a drop down list that reflects the options that are available from within a SQL script, as seen in the next screen shot.

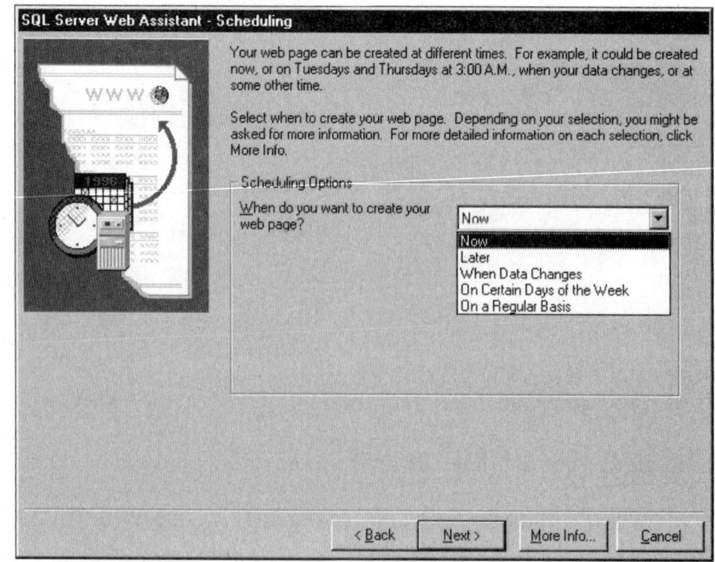

If you choose one of the options other than Now, further dialog children appear that let you configure the days, times, etc. that the task is to be run.

The next step that is presented in this chapter centers around the choosing of the template file and identifying the output file. The template file specified below is the same one that is used throughout this chapter. The output file can have any name but is in this case named consistently with the template file name, as seen in the next screen shot.

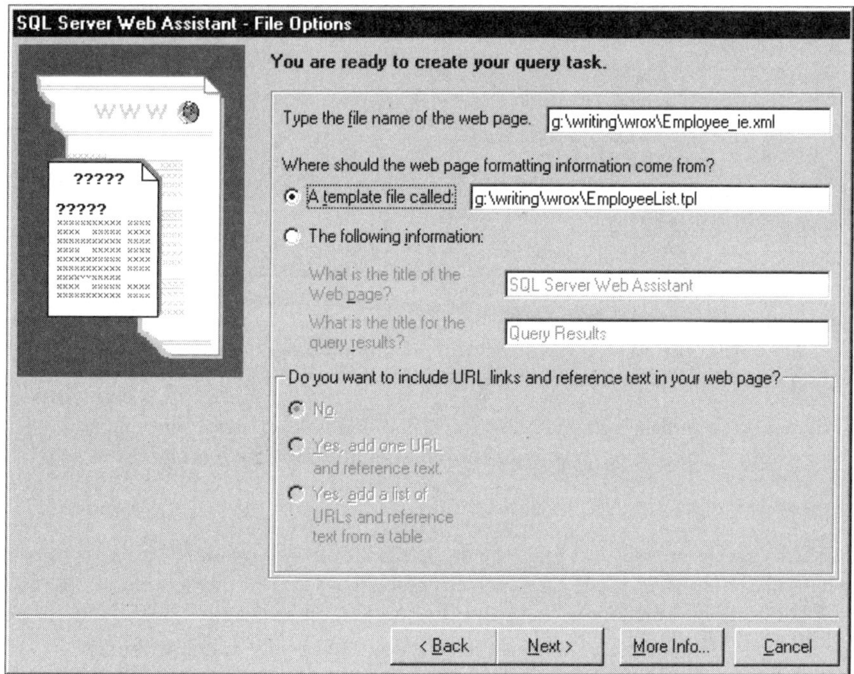

The remaining steps of the wizard are devoted to the customization of the HTML output. Since we are not interested in presenting the data as a pleasing Web page and are creating XML data, these wizard steps are skipped. Because the template file option was chosen, any settings in the presentation of the data are ignored anyway.

The SQL Server Web Assistant is a simple way to quickly generate Web Tasks. However, by hiding everything in the GUI, you do not get to understand the how's and why's of the process. The following sections explain this in detail.

Creating a Web Task using SQL

SQL Server provides a system stored procedure called `sp_makewebtask` to create a Web Task. This stored procedure calls an extended stored procedure which resides in a DLL, although this may be more information than you care to know. If you specify recurring characteristics, a task is added to the system process table and can be viewed using the SQL Enterprise Manager's Server|Scheduled Tasks... menu option. The use of the stored procedure `sp_makewebtask` to create a recurring Web Task can be seen in this screen shot:

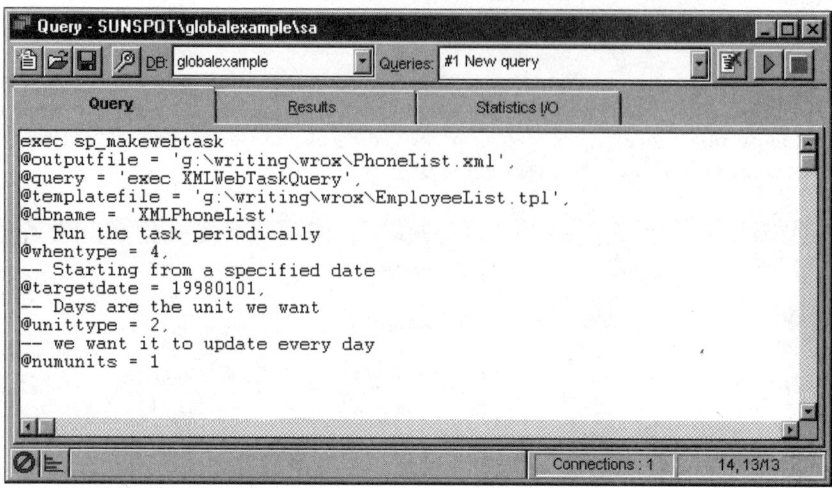

Using the method above, you must specify the query you want to execute, the database name that the tables live in, the output file name, and the template file name. The remaining parameters to the stored procedure are devoted to describing the interval of the scheduled task:

- `@targetdate` indicates the date that the scheduled task is to start running. Note that the date is not a standard `datetime` data type, but rather an integer. The format for the date is `YYYYMMDD`.

The rest of the parameters are used to describe the frequency of the task's execution:

- `@whentype` parameter is set to create the XML file every *n* minutes, hours, days, or weeks depending on the `@unittype` parameter (which is set to 2 for days). Refer to the Transact SQL Help for more information on the `@whentypes` that are available.
- `@unittype` options are: `1` for hours, `2` for days, `3` for weeks, and `4` for minutes.
- `@numunits` is the final parameter that describes the frequency of the task, it designates the number of units to skip before running the task again.

For instance, if `@unittype` is set to `4` and `@numunits` is set to `15`, the Web Task will run every 15 minutes. Using the `sp_makewebtask` allows for a great deal of flexibility. With flexibility, however, comes complexity. An easier method of creating recurring Web Tasks is to use the SQL Enterprise Manager's New Task dialog box accessed via Server|Scheduled Tasks... as shown here:

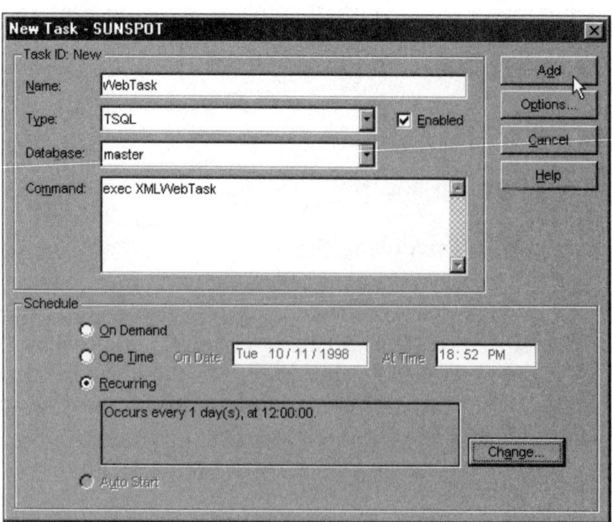

Instead of calling the sp_makewebtask directly, the example above calls a stored procedure that was created for use with triggers. It in turn calls sp_makewebtask telling it to run once and immediately. It can be made recurring using the GUI, which is much easier than trying to remember all of the parameters and their meaning based upon the other parameter's context. The net effect is the same: an XML file is generated automatically using the frequency you specify.

Triggers and Web Tasks

There are times when daily or even hourly reports are not sufficient. The reports need to be current up to the very last data change, yet the users all view the same report with no customization, date ranges, or search criteria. This requirement still does not make it sensible to expend the effort and CPU usage required to build reports dynamically using Active Server Pages and stored procedures. So, how do you capture up to the minute information when the data changes sporadically and inconsistently across time? Triggers are the answer.

Triggers are essentially stored procedures that run on a given table under certain events. The events are either Insert, Update, or Delete. You can execute SQL code for one, two, or all three of the events. You can run different code for each type of event. Triggers are just the right answer whenever you need to do some special processing on a data change event. Here is the PhoneType Web Task trigger.

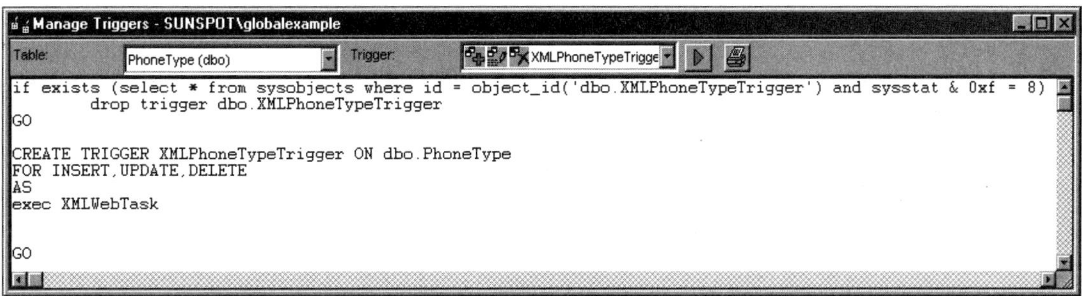

To keep the XML data as fresh as possible, there are a series of triggers that regenerate the file. Since the processing is the same for Inserts, Updates, and Deletes, each trigger handles all three events. The previous screenshot shows the trigger used to watch for changes to the PhoneType table. The triggers presented here call the XMLWebTask stored procedure to regenerate the XML data. It uses the same single-run Web Task discussed earlier in the chapter. Each trigger is uniquely named and is based upon a specific table. As you can see from the following SQL code, the triggers all do the same processing, have the same event mask (Insert, Update, Delete) and are named in a way which identifies the table they are associated with and the fact that they generate XML files. This is to make it easier to understand what they do while looking at them from within SQL Enterprise Manager's Manage|Triggers... GUI. Here's the SQL code to create the triggers, it can be downloaded from our Web site at http://webdev.wrox.co.uk/books/1525:

```
if exists (select * from sysobjects where id = object_id('dbo.XMLEmployeeTrigger')
nd sysstat & 0xf = 8)
     drop trigger dbo.XMLEmployeeTrigger
GO

CREATE TRIGGER XMLEmployeeTrigger ON dbo.Employee
```

```
FOR INSERT,UPDATE,DELETE
AS
exec XMLWebTask
GO

if exists (select * from sysobjects where id = object_id('dbo.XMLPhoneTrigger')
and sysstat & 0xf = 8)
     drop trigger dbo.XMLPhoneTrigger
GO

CREATE TRIGGER XMLPhoneTrigger ON dbo.Phone
FOR INSERT,UPDATE,DELETE
AS

exec XMLWebTask

GO

if exists (select * from sysobjects where id =
object_id('dbo.XMLPhoneListTrigger') and sysstat & 0xf = 8)
     drop trigger dbo.XMLPhoneListTrigger
GO

CREATE TRIGGER XMLPhoneListTrigger ON dbo.PhoneList
FOR INSERT,UPDATE,DELETE
AS

exec XMLWebTask

GO

if exists (select * from sysobjects where id =
object_id('dbo.XMLPhoneTypeTrigger') and sysstat & 0xf = 8)
     drop trigger dbo.XMLPhoneTypeTrigger
GO

CREATE TRIGGER XMLPhoneTypeTrigger ON dbo.PhoneType
FOR INSERT,UPDATE,DELETE
AS

exec XMLWebTask

GO
```

To fully appreciate what happens during a trigger, the stored procedure code should be examined. The following code is used to create an immediate, non-recurring Web Task (the `XMLWebTask` stored procedure) that uses the template file discussed previously in this chapter.

```
if exists (select * from sysobjects where id = object_id('dbo.XMLWebTask') and
ysstat & 0xf = 4)
     drop procedure dbo.XMLWebTask
GO

CREATE PROCEDURE XMLWebTask AS
exec sp_makewebtask @outputfile = 'g:\writing\wrox\PhoneList.xml',
@query = 'exec XMLWebTaskQuery',
@templatefile = 'g:\writing\wrox\EmployeeList.tpl',
@dbname = 'XMLPhoneList'
GO
```

The XMLWebTask stored procedure in turn specifies the XMLWebTaskQuery, which is another stored procedure that returns a subset of all of the tables' columns joined using their respective keys. Here is the code for the XMLWebTaskQuery:

```
if exists (select * from sysobjects where id = object_id('dbo.XMLWebTaskQuery')
nd sysstat & 0xf = 4)
      drop procedure dbo.XMLWebTaskQuery
GO

CREATE PROCEDURE XMLWebTaskQuery AS

select e.Name, p.Number, t.Description
from Employee e, PhoneList pl, Phone p, PhoneType t
where e.EmployeeID = pl.EmployeeID and pl.PhoneID = p.PhoneID and p.Type = t.Type
order by e.EmployeeID
GO
```

By now you may be suspecting that generating the XML files using triggers could be a CPU hog if the tables change often. If the flux of the tables is too great, your system resources will be used for creating hundreds (or thousands) of XML files. If the frequency comes in bursts, then that may not be a problem. But if your application is continuously updating the database, you are probably better off going with Active Server Pages and stored procedures to build the XML data on the fly. Although this is more CPU intensive, the load of the work is spread between two or more machines making the overall impact on your SQL Server lower. Of course, each application may have requirements that make this approach difficult too. In which case, you might go with scheduled Web Tasks recurring on the minute. The trade off between recurring Web Tasks and triggers is one that needs to be evaluated on a per application basis.

All of this chapter thus far has centered around the creation of XML data. Now that the data is sitting on a server somewhere, we need a client to download and display it to the user. The next section details the HTML and JavaScript necessary to display the XML data as a table to the user.

The HTML Page to Display the XML File

Now that we can generate the XML files in a variety of ways, it is time to look at how to get and display that XML file to the user. In previous chapters, Microsoft's XML parser has been discussed. The parser, which takes a URL to an XML source, parses the XML elements into an object model. In the HTML page, the JavaScript code uses the MSXML parser to build an HTML table and assign it to a SPAN element within the HTML page. This all happens in the BODY tag's onLoad event so that the resulting effect has the XML generated table appearing at the same time as the other HTML elements.

The following screen shot displays the PhoneList.xml file generated by a Web Task:

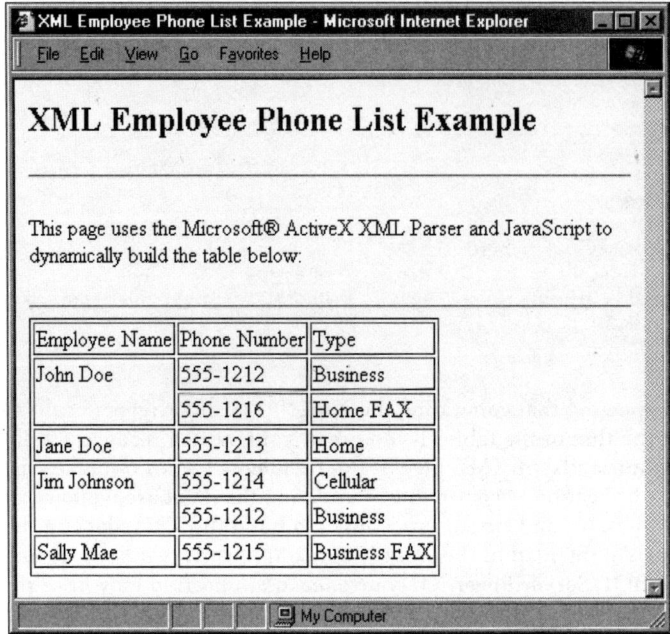

The HTML page is not the fanciest ever created, but that was not its point. The code underneath to generate the table is where the real value lies. The first thing that it does is tell the MSXML parser where to fetch the data from which occurs in OnFetchXmlData() seen below. The URL for the data must come from the same domain and directory that the HTML page came from or the user will see a scripting error. The ResolveURL() method makes sure that the request for XML data comes from the same domain and directory as the HTML page. Here is the code for EmployeePhoneList.htm. The complete file can be downloaded from our Web site at http://webdev.wrox.co.uk/books/1525:

```
<!DOCTYPE HTML PUBLIC "-//W3C//DTD HTML 3.2 Final//EN">

<HTML>
<HEAD>
    <TITLE>XML Employee Phone List Example</TITLE>
</HEAD>

<SCRIPT LANGUAGE="JavaScript">
    //<!--

    // Xml document holder
    var XmlDoc;

    function ResolveURL(url)
    {
        var loc = window.location.toString();
        var i = loc.lastIndexOf("/");
        var result = loc.substring(0,i+1) + url;
        return result
    }
```

```
function OnFetchXmlData()
{
    // Create an instance of the XML parser
    XmlDoc = new ActiveXObject("msxml");
    // Tell the parser to get the data from the server
    XmlDoc.url = ResolveURL("PhoneList.xml");
    // Pause while the fetching & parsing occurs
    window.setTimeout("CheckProgress()",100);
}
```

The code then pauses to let the component read and process the data. The state of the parser is polled until the file has completed parsing, at which point the table building function, `BuildXmlTable()`, is called.

```
function CheckProgress()
{
    var state = XmlDoc.readyState;
    // Check for the parser being done
    if( state == 0 || state == 1 || state == 2 || state == 3)
    {
        // Sleep momentarily and check again
        window.setTimeout("CheckProgress()",100);
    }
    else if( state == 4 )
    {
        // Everything is parsed so now build the HTML code
        // to display the data as a table
        BuildXmlTable();
    }
    else
    {
        alert("Failed to load XML data");
    }
}
```

The next function creates the HTML table definition on the fly, calculating the `ROWSPAN` for each employee. This calculation would not have to occur if we could generate the XML data a little differently. However, as we discussed earlier, there is no way to accomplish this because of the nesting limitation in Web Tasks. Instead the data is examined on the client-side and is effectively converted to the one employee element and many phone elements paradigm shown previously.

```
function BuildXmlTable()
{
    // Start the table
    var tableHTML = "<TABLE BORDER BORDERCOLOR=#000000><tr><td>Employee
    Name</td><td>Phone Number</td><td>Type</td></tr>";
    // Get the root of the XML tree <ITEMLIST>
    var root = XmlDoc.root;
    var nIndex = 0;
    // Get the array of children items
    var arrItems = root.children;
    // This is the current phone list entry
    var entry = null;
```

```
        var nRowSpan = 0;
        // Loop through each <Entry> in the <EmployeeList> and add to the table
        for( nIndex = 0; nIndex < arrItems.length; nIndex++ )
        {
            // Get the <Entry> object at this index
            entry = arrItems.item(nIndex);
            if( nRowSpan == 0 )
            {
         // Calculate the number of rows to span
         nRowSpan = CalcRowSpan(nIndex,arrItems);
         // Now build the html code for this entry
         tableHTML = tableHTML + "<tr><td VALIGN=TOP rowspan=" + nRowSpan + ">";
         tableHTML = tableHTML + entry.children.item("Employee").text + "</td>";
         }
         tableHTML = tableHTML + "<td>" + entry.children.item("Phone").text +
"</td>";
         tableHTML = tableHTML + "<td>" + entry.children.item("Type").text +
"</td>";
            // Close this line of the table
            tableHTML = tableHTML + "</tr>";
            // Decrement the row span so that it will eventually reset itself
            nRowSpan--;
         }
        // Close the table tag
        tableHTML = tableHTML + "</TABLE>"
        // Display the newly created table
        EmployeeListSpan.innerHTML = tableHTML;
    }

    function CalcRowSpan(nStartIndex,arrEntries)
    {
        // Save the employee name
        var strName = arrEntries.item(nStartIndex).children.item("Employee").text;
        // Empty out the holder vars
        var strCurrName = strName;
        var nCount = 0;
        var nIndex = nStartIndex + 1;
        // Loop through array counting the occurances of an employee's name
        while( nIndex < arrEntries.length && strName == strCurrName )
        {
            // Get the next employee name
            strCurrName = arrEntries.item(nIndex).children.item("Employee").text;
            // Increment the index and the rowspan count
            nIndex++;
            nCount++;
        }
        return nCount;
    }

    //-->
</SCRIPT>

<BODY BGPROPERTIES="FIXED" BGCOLOR="#FFFFDD" ONLOAD="OnFetchXmlData()">

<H2>XML Employee Phone List Example</H2>

<HR>

<P>
```

```
This page uses the Microsoft&reg; ActiveX XML Parser and JavaScript to<br>
dynamically build the table below:
</P>

<HR>

<SPAN ID="EmployeeListSpan"></SPAN>

</BODY>
</HTML>
```

Creating XML with Stored Procedures

As stated earlier in this chapter, there are two methods by which SQL Server can generate XML data. The first is using the Web Tasks as we have already discussed. The second is to create a stored procedure that returns the result set as XML data. This is a good method for generating up-to-the-minute XML datasets on the Web server without expensive overheads. The only special processing occurs on the SQL Server, where the SQL stored procedure has already been compiled for efficiency. This saves you, on average, 30% of CPU overhead since the SQL parsing is already performed. All you need is a simple ASP page that passes the XML data straight back to the requesting client.

Using stored procedures in this way is a bit trickier than creating a Web Task. The Web Task operates on the data, using the `<%insert_data_here%>`, on a per row basis, whereas result sets are returned as a complete set of rows, making the processing of each row problematic. Fortunately, cursors, first seen in the ODBC libraries for SQL Server, were added to SQL Server. This allows for row level manipulation of the data, including the ability to modify or delete the rows as they are encountered.

But, even with this feature the creation of XML data is not particularly easy. One of the first problems is the inability to create temporary variables of the `text` type. `chars` and `varchars` have a length limit of 255, which is quickly exceeded when creating XML data. The 255 limitation of `chars` and `varchars` changes to 8192 in SQL Server 7.0, however this will still be too small for many XML applications. So the only solution is to create a temporary table that has a column of type `text`. Temporary tables are often created using the `SELECT...INTO` statement with a query that inserts all of the rows that you want stored in the table; others prefer to use the `CREATE TABLE` followed by an `INSERT`, claiming that it makes more readable stored procedure code. Either method is fine. This makes things interesting when using cursors to selectively insert, or manipulate the data that you are inserting, into the temporary table. For this application, we only want one row of XML data, since the ASP page is to serve as a pass through and should not be asked to perform special processing such as concatenating rows into one string.

To create the temporary table, the `GetXML` stored procedure inserts a `text` version of the opening root tag, `<EmployeeList>`, into the table (see following code). The # symbol tells SQL Server that this table is a local temporary table, which will be dropped when the stored procedure completes. You can also create a global temporary table, which is a table that is dropped when the session is closed as opposed to when the stored procedure ends. Global temporary tables are identified using the ## notation. Once the row is inserted, a local variable is set to the `text` column's pointer, which is a `varbinary(16)`. This pointer is used for all subsequent manipulations of the `text` row.

```
if exists (select * from sysobjects where id = object_id('dbo.GetXML') and sysstat
 0xf = 4)
     drop procedure dbo.GetXML
```

```
GO

CREATE PROCEDURE GetXML AS
BEGIN

       -- Create a temporary table to hold the XML data
       SELECT "XML" = CONVERT(text,'<EmployeeList>')
       INTO #Work

       DECLARE @@ptrval varbinary(16)
       -- Determine the pointer of the XML column in the temp table
       SELECT @@ptrval = TEXTPTR(XML)
       FROM #Work
```

The next step is to create some local variables to hold the rows returned by the cursor's `SELECT` statement. The cursor `WorkCursor` is created to iterate through the result set's rows. Unfortunately, you cannot specify a stored procedure for the result set part of the cursor, so the guts of the `XMLWebTaskQuery` are used instead.

```
DECLARE @Name varchar(255)
DECLARE @Number varchar(32)
DECLARE @Desc varchar(255)

-- Use a cursor to iterate through the rows building XML data
DECLARE WorkCursor CURSOR
FOR SELECT e.Name, p.Number, t.Description
    FROM Employee e, PhoneList pl, Phone p, PhoneType t
    WHERE e.EmployeeID = pl.EmployeeID and pl.PhoneID = p.PhoneID and p.Type =
t.Type
      ORDER BY e.EmployeeID
FOR READ ONLY
```

Just like in recordsets, you must move to the first row in the cursor before you can start looking at the data. This also sets the `@@fetch_status` variable to indicate whether the move to the next row was successful. When you use the `FETCH` statement, the SQL Server copies the `columnar` data into the three local variables in the order that the columns appear in the row set. The code then uses the column data, text pointer variable, and the `UPDATETEXT` command to append the data to the one `text` record in the `#Work` table. In the call to `UPDATETEXT` the `@@ptrval` variable identifies the SQL Server pointer for the text column in the `#Work` table. The two options following the text pointer indicate that the text is to be concatenated to the end of the column data (`NULL`) and that there is to be zero characters replaced (`0`). Notice that the XML elements are wrapped around the column data as it is inserted into the temporary table. This same process occurs until all of the rows in the cursor have been processed, at which point the cursor is released. The final step is to return the data to the caller. Here is the full code for the `GetXML` Stored Procedure that returns XML data, it can be downloaded from our Web site at `http://webdev.wrox.co.uk/books/1525`:

```
       -- Prepare the cursor for work
       OPEN WorkCursor
       -- Get the first row
       FETCH NEXT FROM WorkCursor INTO @Name, @Number, @Desc
       WHILE @@fetch_status = 0
       BEGIN
```

```
            -- Add the XML tags and the column vars to the text field
            UPDATETEXT #Work.XML @@ptrval NULL 0 '<Entry><Employee>'
            UPDATETEXT #Work.XML @@ptrval NULL 0 @Name
            UPDATETEXT #Work.XML @@ptrval NULL 0 '</Employee><Number>'
            UPDATETEXT #Work.XML @@ptrval NULL 0 @Number
            UPDATETEXT #Work.XML @@ptrval NULL 0 '</Number><Type>'
            UPDATETEXT #Work.XML @@ptrval NULL 0 @Desc
            UPDATETEXT #Work.XML @@ptrval NULL 0 '</Type></Entry>'

            -- Move to the next record in the cursor
            FETCH NEXT FROM WorkCursor INTO @Name, @Number, @Desc

      END

      -- Release our cursor
      DEALLOCATE WorkCursor

      -- Add the closing element
      UPDATETEXT #Work.XML @@ptrval NULL 0 '</EmployeeList>'

      -- Return the result set
      SELECT * FROM #Work

   END

   GO
```

Here is the result of the `GetXML` Stored Procedure:

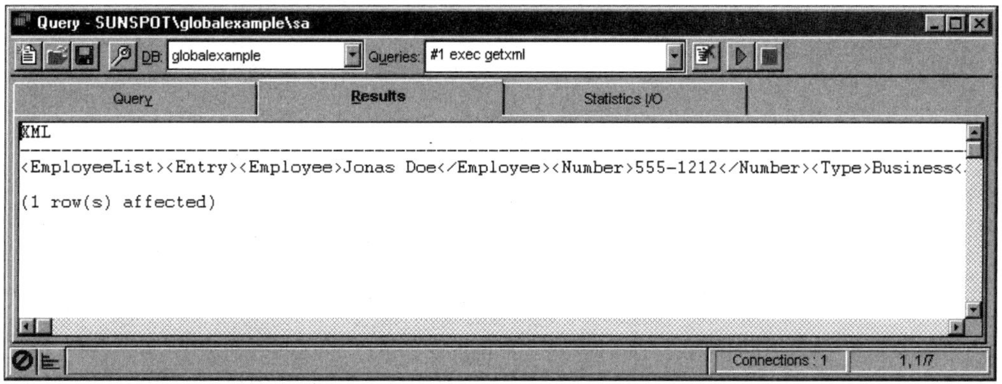

This stored procedure will be revisited when we discuss the ASP page code that returns the results of this query in its raw form. The next section of the chapter covers how to return XML data to requesting clients using the `GetXML` stored procedure and the ADO (ActiveX Data Objects) recordsets from within an Active Server Page. The latter can take any ADO recordset object and return XML data from it.

Middleware Generated XML

To this point we have focussed on generating XML data directly from the SQL Server. The remaining portions of this chapter center around the Middle Tier as a mechanism for returning the XML data and for updating the SQL Server from supplied XML strings.

The following screen shot shows the results of the `MiddleTierViewPhoneList.asp`. Although the file shows two identical tables, they were generated using different methods. The table on top was generated using the `PhoneListUsingGetXML.asp` Active Server Page, which uses the stored procedure discussed in the previous section (`GetXML`) as the XML source. The bottom table was generated using the `PhoneListUsingXmlRecordSet.asp`, which generates the XML from any ADO recordset. Both of the Active Server Pages' processing use the `XmlForAsp` ActiveX component, which is a control that wraps around the MSXML parser. This is used because the MSXML parser only accepts a URL for input (and does security checks) and has no provision for returning a string of the XML data to the caller. The component can be found on Microsoft's site at `http://www.microsoft.com/xml` or at `http://www.15seconds.com`, a resource for Active Server Page developers.

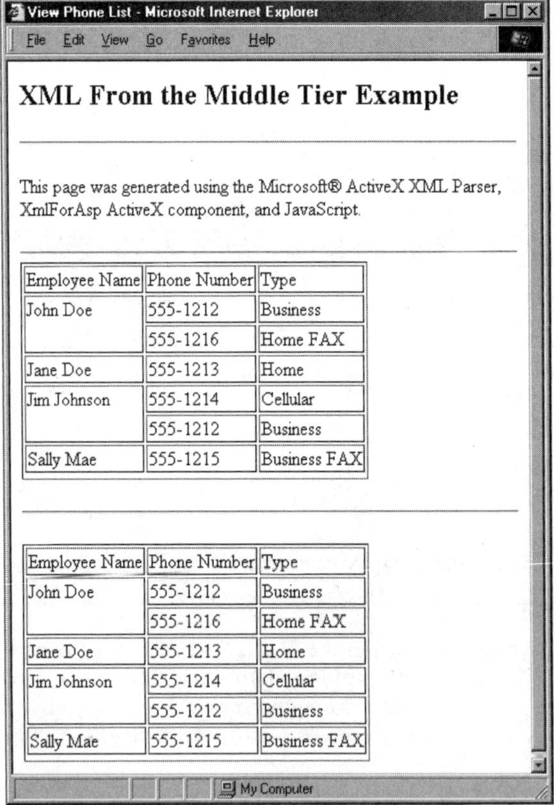

There are three separate pieces of server-side code to build the page seen in this screen shot. Let's first examine the code that returns the XML data for the top table, `PhoneListUsingGetXML.asp`.

PhoneListUsingGetXML.asp

There is not too much to this ASP file. It creates a connection to the database and calls the `GetXML` stored procedure, which was explored previously. It then outputs the XML header, `<?xml version="1.0"?>`, followed by the XML column from the recordset. The only thing this file does is act as a go-between for the client. The data that is returned from this query is processed on the Web server, converting it to the HTML table as you'll see in a later section. Here is the VBScript code for this page, the full code for this page can be downloaded from our Web site at `http://webdev.wrox.co.uk/books/1525`:

```
<!--#include virtual="/XMLPhoneList/Connect.inc"-->

<%
      ' Create a database connection object
      Set Conn = Server.CreateObject("ADODB.Connection")
      ' Tell it which ODBC data source to use
      Conn.Open strConnect
      ' Call the stored procedure
      Set XmlSet = Conn.Execute("{Call GetXML}")
      ' Add the XML header and then the one row/column
%>
<?xml version="1.0"?>
<%=XmlSet("XML")%>
```

PhoneListUsingXmlRecordSet.asp

The bottom table created by `MiddleTierViewPhoneList.asp` is generated from a different XML source. It uses the `PhoneListUsingXmlRecordSet.asp` as its XML data source. This Active Server Page uses a Server-Side Include to include a generic function for returning XML data from a recordset, which we cover in the next section. Just as in the previous Active Server Page, this page's main responsibility is to open a connection to the database and execute a stored procedure. The stored procedure is the same one used by the Web Task code. This simply returns the employee name, number, and the phone type from the database with all of the correct tables joined and ordered by employee ID for consistency of the output. If the order by employee ID was not specified, the two tables created when `MiddleTierViewPhoneList.asp` was run may or may not have been in the same order. Finally, this code returns the XML string that was generated by the `XmlFromRecordSet()` method. Here is the code for `PhoneListUsingXmlRecordSet.asp` which can be downloaded from our Web site at `http//webdev.wrox.co.uk/books/1525`:

```
<!--#include virtual="/XMLPhoneList/Connect.inc"-->
<!--#include virtual="/XMLPhoneList/XMLFromRecordSet.inc"-->

<%
      ' This sample uses the "universal" XML generator from a recordset

      ' Create a database connection object
      Set Conn = Server.CreateObject("ADODB.Connection")
      ' Tell it which ODBC data source to use
      Conn.Open strConnect
      ' Call the stored procedure that the Web Task uses
      Set XmlSet = Conn.Execute("{Call XMLWebTaskQuery}")
      ' Use the XMLFromRecordSet function to return a XML string
```

```
        strXml = XmlFromRecordSet(XmlSet,"Set","Row")
        ' Now output the header and the string
%>
<?xml version="1.0"?>
<%=strXml%>
```

The Universal Function for Generating XML from Recordsets

The `PhoneListUsingXmlRecordSet.asp` uses a Server-Side Include to include this generic function for returning XML data from any recordset object. Given that this is a generic function, it requires two items passed into it: the name to use for the root node and the name to use for each record that is returned. In our example above, the root node is named `Set`, which will appear in the XML data as `<Set>`. The name for the XML wrapper around each record is named `Row`, which will appear in the XML data as `<Row>`. The elements inside of the `<Row>` wrapper are named after each column returned in the recordset, which will change for each different recordset object used.

This function uses a local variable to build the XML data. It starts by building the root element, `<Set>`. It then loops through each of the rows in the recordset, adding the `<Row>` and `</Row>` elements around the field data. Finally, it walks through the field collection creating the data as:

```
<FieldName>FieldValue</FieldName>
```

using the `Field.Name` and `Field.Value`. Notice that the `Field.Value` is trimmed of spaces on the right side. This is done because SQL Server pads `char` datatypes with trailing spaces to the end of the field length. Since this is a generic function that is used with both `varchar` and `char` data types, it is best to be safe and trim the extra data. There is no sense in shipping the extra data around, so it is stripped out. Once all of the rows have been added the closing element, `</Set>`, is appended to the string, which is then returned. Here is the code for the universal function that generates XML from recordsets, it can be downloaded from our Web site at `http://webdev.wrox.co.uk/books/1525`:

```
<%
     ' This function returns an XML string from any recordset
           ' Building the string is done by:
           '    Adding the Set wrapper
           '    Adding a Row wrapper for each Row
           '    Adding a Column open/data/close for each Column in a Row
           '    Adding the Row closing tag
           '    Adding the Set closing tag

     Function XmlFromRecordSet(RecordSet,strSetTag,strRowTag)
           strXml = ""
           ' Now add the Set wrapper
           strXml = strXml & "<" & strSetTag & ">"
           ' Make sure some rows were returned
           If Not RecordSet.EOF And Not RecordSet.BOF Then
                 ' Loop through each row
                 Do While Not RecordSet.EOF
                       ' Add the Row opening tag
                       strXml = strXml & "<" & strRowTag & ">"
                       ' Now iterate through each field using the name of
                       ' the field as the tag name and the value of the
                       ' field as the value of the tag
                       For Each Field In RecordSet.Fields
                             ' Add the opening tag
```

```
                    strXml = strXml & "<" & Field.Name &  ">"
                    ' Add the tag's value. Right trim the value
                    ' since the char() type is padded with spaces
                    strXml = strXml & RTrim(Field.Value)
                    ' Add the closing tag
                    strXml = strXml & "</" & Field.Name &  ">"
                Next
                ' Add the Row closing tag
                strXml = strXml & "</" & strRowTag & ">"
                ' Move to the next row in the recordset
                RecordSet.MoveNext
            Loop
        End If
        ' Now add the Set closing tag
        strXml = strXml + "</" & strSetTag & ">"
        ' Return the string to the caller
        XmlFromRecordSet = strXml
    End Function
%>
```

The following table compares the XML data returned using the two Active Server Pages, so that you can see the differences between the generic method and the `GetXML` stored procedure.

PhoneListUsingGetXML.asp	**PhoneListUsingXmlRecordSet.asp**

`<?xml version="1.0"?>`
`<EmployeeList>`
`    <Entry>`
`        <Employee>Jonathon Doe`
`          </Employee>`
`        <Number>555`
`1212</Number>`
`        <Type>Business</Type>`
`    </Entry>`
`...`
`</EmployeeList>`
	`<?xml version="1.0"?>`
	`<Set>`
	`    <Row>`
	`        <Name>Jonathon Doe`
	`          </Name>`
	`        <Number>555-1212</Number>`
	`        <Description>Business`
	`          </Description>`
	`    </Row>`
	`...`
	`</Set>`

Converting the Data from XML to HTML Tables

At this point the data must be converted from XML to the HTML tables shown in the `MiddleTierViewPhoneList.asp` screen shot (at the start of this section). The code to build the tables is essentially the same as the `EmployeePhoneList.htm`, but was made more generic for this example (see the full code listing for `MiddleTierViewPhoneList.asp`). First the MSXML parser is created, followed by the `XmlForAsp` helper component. Next, the strings used for holding the table definitions are cleared. Then the first XML document is loaded using the `XmlForAsp` helper object's `ReadFromFile()` method, which takes either a URL or a file name, reads the document located there, and inserts the document into the MSXML parser. Though the MSXML parser also takes a URL as a method of loading the data, doing so from within this Active Server Page generates a security error. This error happens because Microsoft designed the XML parser to run on the client not the server; this means that the security guarantees that the data comes from the same 'sandbox' that the page came from. The `XmlForAsp` object works around this security constraint.

```
<!DOCTYPE HTML PUBLIC "-//W3C//DTD HTML 3.2 Final//EN">

<HTML>
<HEAD>
    <TITLE>View Phone List</TITLE>
</HEAD>

<SCRIPT LANGUAGE=JavaScript RUNAT=Server>

    // Create an instance of the XML parser
    var XmlDoc = new ActiveXObject("msxml");
    // XmlForScripting helper
    var objXmlHelp = new ActiveXObject("XmlForAsp.XmlForScripting");
    // Strings to hold the tables that are built
    var strGetXmlTable = "";
    var strRecordSetTable = "";

    // Load the document from the stored procedure url
    objXmlHelp.ReadFromFile("http://" + Request.ServerVariables("SERVER_NAME") +
        "/XMLPhoneList/PhoneListUsingGetXML.asp",XmlDoc);
    // We are using the record set version so build the
    // table accordingly
    strGetXmlTable = BuildXmlTable("Employee","Number","Type");

    // Load the document from the record set url
    objXmlHelp.ReadFromFile("http://" + Request.ServerVariables("SERVER_NAME") +
        "/XMLPhoneList/PhoneListUsingXmlRecordSet.asp",XmlDoc);

    // We are using the record set version so build the
    // table accordingly
    strRecordSetTable = BuildXmlTable("Name","Number","Description");
```

Once the file has loaded, the `BuildXmlTable()` function is called. Note that it now takes three parameters; the names of each element to use to build the HTML table (see the comparisons table). It also returns a string that is outputted later in the code. The same processing is then performed on the second URL, generating a second XML string. Both of these strings are then output where the `<SPAN>` tag was in the previous example, `EmployeePhoneList.htm`.

Here is the full code for `MiddleTierViewPhoneList.asp` the full code for this page can be downloaded from our Web site at `http://webdev.wrox.co.uk/books/1525`:

```
    function BuildXmlTable(strColName1,strColName2,strColName3)
    {
        // Start the table
        var tableHTML = "<TABLE BORDER BORDERCOLOR=#000000><TR><TD>Employee
          _Name</TD><TD>Phone Number</TD><TD>Type</TD></TR>";
        // Get the root of the XML tree
        var root = XmlDoc.root;
        var nIndex = 0;
        // Get the array of children items
        var arrItems = root.children;
        // This is the current phone list entry
        var entry = null;
        var nRowSpan = 0;
        // Loop through each row in the set and add to the table
        for( nIndex = 0; nIndex < arrItems.length; nIndex++ )
```

```
        {
           // Get the row object at this index
           entry = arrItems.item(nIndex);
           if( nRowSpan == 0 )
           {
              // Calculate the number of rows to span
              nRowSpan = CalcRowSpan(nIndex,arrItems,strColName1);
              // Now build the html code for this entry
              tableHTML = tableHTML + "<TR><TD VALIGN=TOP rowspan=" + nRowSpan + _
">";
              tableHTML = tableHTML + entry.children.item(strColName1).text + _
"</TD>";
           }
            tableHTML = tableHTML + "<TD>" + entry.children.item(strColName2).text
+
               _"</TD>";
            tableHTML = tableHTML + "<TD>" + entry.children.item(strColName3).text
+
               _"</TD>";
            // Close this line of the table
            tableHTML = tableHTML + "</TR>";
            // Decrement the row span so that it will eventually reset itself
            nRowSpan--;
        }
        // Close the table tag
        tableHTML = tableHTML + "</TABLE>"
        return tableHTML;
    }

    function CalcRowSpan(nStartIndex,arrEntries,strColName1)
    {
        // Save the employee name
        var strName =
arrEntries.item(nStartIndex).children.item(strColName1).text;
        // Empty out the holder vars
        var strCurrName = strName;
        var nCount = 0;
        var nIndex = nStartIndex + 1;
        // Loop through array counting the occurances of an employee's name
        while( nIndex < arrEntries.length && strName == strCurrName )
        {
            // Get the next employee name
            strCurrName = arrEntries.item(nIndex).children.item(strColName1).text;
            // Increment the index and the rowspan count
            nIndex++;
            nCount++;
        }
        return nCount;
    }

</SCRIPT>

<BODY BGPROPERTIES="FIXED" BGCOLOR="#FFFFFF">

<H2>XML From the Middle Tier Example</H2>

<HR>

<P>
```

```
This page was generated using the Microsoft&reg; ActiveX XML Parser, <BR>
XmlForAsp ActiveX component, and JavaScript.<BR>
</P>

<HR>

<%=strGetXmlTable%>

<BR>
<HR>
<BR>

<%=strRecordSetTable%>

</BODY>
</HTML>
```

So far, we have generated XML using SQL Server, displayed it using HTML and JavaScript on the client, and performed some Middle Tier processing on the data to strip out the necessity of having MSXML on the client computer. The final stop on this journey shows you how to submit XML to a Web server and have that update the back end database.

HTML Form to Update a Phone List Entry

All of the samples to date have been read-only applications, which is fine for reporting. However, most client/server applications have some form of updating, adding to, or modifying the existing data. **Online Trading Protocol** (**OTP**), which is an XML-based business-to-business transaction specification, is a protocol specification that transmits and receives transactional data as XML between two or more servers and possibly a client. Open Financial eXchange (OFX), while not yet an XML-based specification, is moving that way with the convergence of OFX/Gold known as IFX. OFX centers on the delivery of financial transactions from personal financial managers (Quicken, Money) to banks and brokerages. Both of these server implementations of the protocols convert XML requests into back-end legacy system fulfillment.

As an example of how to accept XML requests, the final mini-application of this chapter takes XML commands from the client and updates the database. It is used to update a single name, a single number, a single phone description, or any combination of these. The modifications are done using an HTML form that builds an XML string. This string is `POST`ed to an ASP page, which parses the XML request and updates the database accordingly. Here is the HTML page before an update:

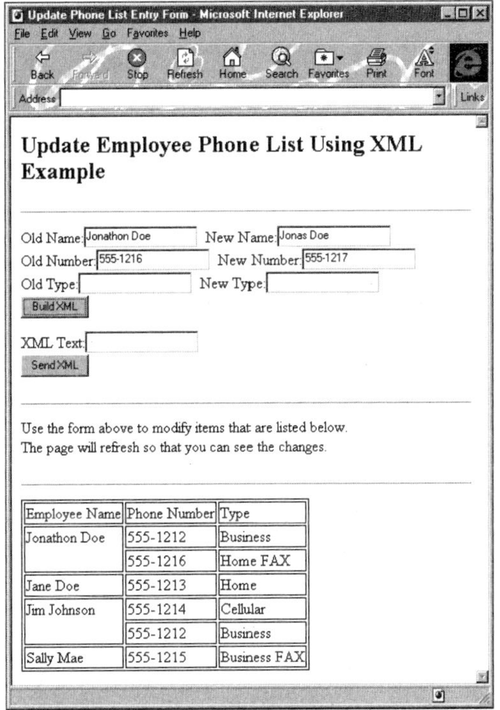

And here is the same page after an update:

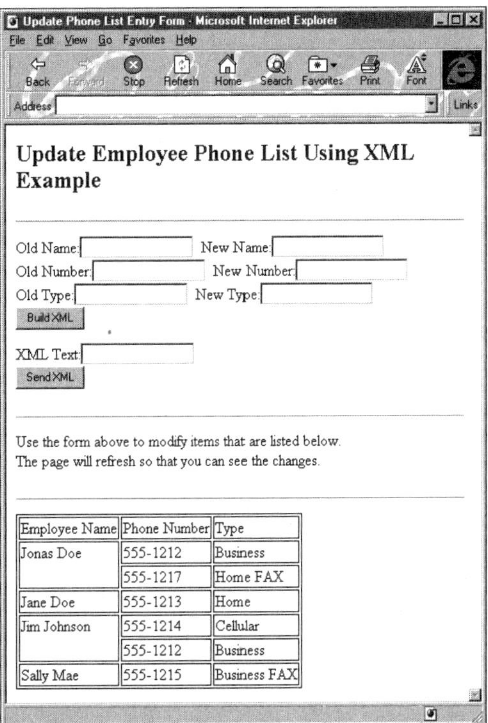

To change an entry, you enter the old name that you want to modify from the table shown at the bottom, followed by the new name as you want it to appear. The same steps are performed for the phone number and the phone type. Once the fields are filled in, click on the **Build XML** button, which creates an XML string from the fields and enters it in the **XML Text:** field.

```
<!DOCTYPE HTML PUBLIC "-//W3C//DTD HTML 3.2 Final//EN">

<HTML>
<HEAD>
    <TITLE>Update Phone List Entry Form</TITLE>
</HEAD>

<SCRIPT LANGUAGE="JavaScript">
    //<!--

    function OnBuildXML()
    {
        // Build a string containing the XML needed to update the DB
        UpdateForm.XmlString.value = "<UpdateList><UpdateEntry><OldName>" +
            BuildForm.OldName.value + "</OldName><NewName>" +
            BuildForm.NewName.value + "</NewName><OldNumber>" +
            BuildForm.OldNumber.value + "</OldNumber><NewNumber>" +
            BuildForm.NewNumber.value + "</NewNumber><OldType>" +
            BuildForm.OldType.value + "</OldType><NewType>" +
            BuildForm.NewType.value + "</NewType></UpdateEntry></UpdateList>";
    }

    //-->
</SCRIPT>
```

To send the XML string to the Web server, click on the **Send XML** button, which `POST`s the data to `UpdatePhoneList.asp`. To see how this is done, let's take a look at the ASP page source that generates the HTML page.

```
<BODY BGPROPERTIES="FIXED" BGCOLOR="#FFFFDD">

<H2>Update Employee Phone List Using XML Example</H2>

<HR>

<FORM METHOD="post" NAME="BuildForm">
Old Name:<input type="Text" name="OldName" value="">
New Name:<input type="Text" name="NewName" value=""><br>
Old Number:<input type="Text" name="OldNumber" value="">
New Number:<input type="Text" name="NewNumber" value=""><br>
Old Type:<input type="Text" name="OldType" value="">
New Type:<input type="Text" name="NewType" value=""><br>
<INPUT TYPE="button" VALUE="Build XML" NAME="BuildXml" ONCLICK="OnBuildXML()">
</FORM>

<form method="post" name="UpdateForm"_
action="<%="http://" & Request.ServerVariables("SERVER_NAME") & _
"/XMLPhoneList/UpdatePhoneList.asp"%>">
XML Text:<input type="Text" name="XmlString" value=""><br>
<input type="submit" value="Send XML" name="Send XML"></p>
</form>
```

```
<HR>

<P>
Use the form above to modify items that are listed below.<br>
The page will refresh so that you can see the changes.
</P>

<HR>
```

The page is a simple piece of HTML coding, created using ASP, consisting of two forms and a table. The table code is built using yet another slight variation of the previous table creation samples. The two forms are passed back to the client (see above): one with a custom `onClick` event method that builds an XML string and copies it into the XML Text: field, and the other with an *action* property pointing to the URL
`http://webdev.wrox.co.uk/books/1525/XMLPhoneList/UpdatePhoneList.asp`.

The real work is done at the Web server. Here is the code for the Active Server Page that generates the Update Phone List Entry HTML page, again the full code can be downloaded from our Web site at `http://webdev.wrox.co.uk/books/1525`:

```
<SCRIPT LANGUAGE=JavaScript RUNAT=Server>

    // This is the ASP code to load the XML data from a file
    // and process the file on the server

    // Xml document holder
    var XmlDoc = new ActiveXObject("msxml");
    // XmlForScripting helper
    var objXmlHelp = new ActiveXObject("XmlForAsp.XmlForScripting");
    // Load from an URL
    objXmlHelp.ReadFromFile("http://" + Request.ServerVariables("SERVER_NAME") +
        "/XMLPhoneList/PhoneListUsingGetXML.asp",XmlDoc);


    function CalcRowSpan(nStartIndex,arrEntries)
    {
        // Save the employee name
        var strName = arrEntries.item(nStartIndex).children.item("Employee").text;
        // Empty out the holder vars
        var strCurrName = strName;
        var nCount = 0;
        var nIndex = nStartIndex + 1;
        // Loop through array counting the occurances of an employee's name
        while( nIndex < arrEntries.length && strName == strCurrName )
        {
            // Get the next employee name
            strCurrName = arrEntries.item(nIndex).children.item("Employee").text;
            // Increment the index and the rowspan count
            nIndex++;
            nCount++;
        }
        return nCount;
    }
```

```
    // Start the table
    var tableHTML = "<TABLE BORDER BORDERCOLOR=#000000><TR><TD>Employee Name
         </TD><TD>Phone Number</TD><TD>Type</TD></TR>";
    // Get the root of the XML tree <ITEMLIST>
        var root = XmlDoc.root;
    var nIndex = 0;
    // Get the array of children items
    var arrItems = root.children;
    // This is the current phone list entry
    var entry = null;
    var nRowSpan = 0;
    // Loop through each <Entry> in the <EmployeeList> and add to the table
    for( nIndex = 0; nIndex < arrItems.length; nIndex++ )
    {
        // Get the <Entry> object at this index
        entry = arrItems.item(nIndex);
        if( nRowSpan == 0 )
        {
            // Calculate the number of rows to span
            nRowSpan = CalcRowSpan(nIndex,arrItems);
            // Now build the html code for this entry
            tableHTML = tableHTML + "<TR><TD VALIGN=TOP ROWSPAN=" + nRowSpan +
">";
            tableHTML = tableHTML + entry.children.item("Employee").text +
"</TD>";
        }
        tableHTML = tableHTML + "<TD>" + entry.children.item("Number").text +
"</TD>";
        tableHTML = tableHTML + "<TD>" + entry.children.item("Type").text +
"</TD>";
        // Close this line of the table
        tableHTML = tableHTML + "</TR>";
        // Decrement the row span so that it will eventually reset itself
        nRowSpan--;
    }
    // Close the table tag
    tableHTML = tableHTML + "</TABLE>"

</SCRIPT>

<%=tableHTML%>

</BODY>
</HTML>
```

And here is the XML string created by `OnBuildXml()`:

```
<UpdateList>
     <UpdateEntry>
            <OldName>John Doe</OldName>
            <NewName>John Doe Sr.</NewName>
            <OldNumber></OldNumber>
            <NewNumber></NewNumber>
            <OldType>Fax machine</OldType>
            <NewType>Dial up modem</NewType>
     </UpdateEntry>
</UpdateList>
```

When the XML data arrives at the Web server (in the form of the data seen in the previous section of code for the XML output), it takes the XML string from the request object and uses the `XmlForAsp` helper ActiveX component to insert the string into the MSXML parser (shown in the next section of code). This has the same effect as if the document was loaded from a URL: the parser converts the XML data into an object hierarchy.

```
<!--#include virtual="/XMLPhoneList/Connect.inc"-->

<%
      ' Updates a phone list entry using XML

      ' Need to create an instance of the XML parser
      Set objXmlDoc = CreateObject("msxml")
      ' Create an instance of the ASP helper for MSXML
      Set objXmlHelp = CreateObject("XmlForAsp.XmlForScripting")
      ' Insert the passed in XML string into the parser
      objXmlHelp.XmlString(objXmlDoc) = Request("XmlString")
```

Once the data is in object form, a connection to the database is created. The code then retrieves the root node and its children, which can be zero or more `<UpdateEntry>...</UpdateEntry>` elements. For each child in the element collection, a series of three SQL statements are created and executed. Each statement updates a given table using the old value as the key to find the record to update to the new value. Here is the code for the Active Server Page to process the update request, the full code for the page can be downloaded from our Web site at `http://webdev.wrox.co.uk/books/1525`:

```
      ' Create a database connection object
      Set Conn = Server.CreateObject("ADODB.Connection")
      ' Tell it which ODBC data source to use
      Conn.Open strConnect

      ' Get the root of the XML tree
      Set root = objXmlDoc.root
      nIndex = 0
      ' Get the array of children items
      Set arrItems = root.children
      ' Loop through each update request and update the database
      For nIndex = 0 To arrItems.length - 1
            ' Get the update object at this index
            Set objUpdate = arrItems.item(nIndex)
            ' Build the SQL string to update the name
            strSql = "UPDATE Employee set Name = '" & _
                  objUpdate.children.item("NewName").text & "' where Name = '" & _
                  objUpdate.children.item("OldName").text & "'"
            ' Now perform the update
            Conn.Execute(strSql)
            ' Build the SQL string to update the Number
            strSql = "UPDATE Phone set Number = '" & _
                  objUpdate.children.item("NewNumber").text & "' where Number =
'"_
                            & objUpdate.children.item("OldNumber").text & "'"
            ' Now perform the update
            Conn.Execute(strSql)
            ' Build the SQL string to update the phone type
            strSql = "UPDATE PhoneType set Description = '" & _
```

```
                    objUpdate.children.item("NewType").text & "' where _
                         Description = '" & objUpdate.children.item("OldType").text &
"'"

              ' Now perform the update
              Conn.Execute(strSql)
       Next
%>
```

This example can be used to process any number of updates. The HTML page shown in our example only sends one `<UpdateEntry>...</UpdateEntry>` element to be processed at a time. A departmental server, however, could batch up changes into a larger file and submit them to the master list once a week. This same approach could be used for any type of batch updating. The concept could be applied to larger applications that talked with a series of back-end hosts to fulfill requests.

Summary

In the course of this chapter, we have shown you:

- How to use SQL Server to generate XML reporting data
- How to display this data in tabular form
- How to turn XML requests into SQL updates

The approaches taken here should provide you with a strong foundation of tools that lend themselves to the construction of large client/server systems. Through the use of stored procedures, Web Tasks, and Middle Tier processing, you should be able to make these large endeavors spread the workload across multiple tiers and computing architectures, yielding responsive, robust systems.

Please Note:

You are strongly advised to check our Web site for updates to this chapter before attempting to install and run the sample applications.

We will provide updates to this chapter and to the sample application files on our Web site at `http://webdev.wrox.co.uk/books/1525/`.

XML is a rapidly evolving field, and this was particularly the case when this book was being written. While the theory behind this chapter is perfectly sound, it is likely that the publicly available parser components that we use may have been updated in line with changes to the XML standards. For example, the method and property names are unlikely to remain the same as indicated in this chapter.

Before trying to install and run the application, please check for updates on the Web site to avoid disappointment.

10

Server-side XML

You may be tempted to think of XML only in terms of marking fixed documents and parsing them for information. But XML can also be thought of as a self-describing data format executed entirely in text. As such, it becomes an ideal mechanism for exchanging information between clients and servers. Any parsing you can do in a stand-alone application or Web browser can also occur on a server. This notion of XML as a common language of the Web opens the door to new opportunities in terms of clients and servers. We will be able to create servers that do not assume the client is a human user waiting to view content.

As soon as we say "server", we also imply a client and a network between them. Internet and intranet applications open up some possibilities for which XML is an ideal choice. Although there are more efficient data representations, XML text permits very loose coupling between clients and servers. It will become possible for future clients to discover a desired exchange format from a server previously unknown to it and conduct a transaction. We'll illustrate the specific challenges using a simple intranet application that allows a user to search for and retrieve technical papers marked up in XML. This will show the basics of composing and parsing XML dynamically on both the client and the server.

In general, a client-server XML application needs to answer some specific challenges:

- Formatting a message for the server
- Transferring XML between the client and server
- Parsing client messages on the server and performing a task
- Dynamically generating an XML document for return to the client

Why Use XML on the Server?

Traditional client-server applications are tightly coupled. They share binary message formats and transmission protocols. Even if the client and server platforms are dissimilar – say, remote procedure calls between a Windows client and a Unix host – a common binary network transmission format is prescribed. Both client and server software tend to come from the same vendor or require development using a common toolkit. This is a good approach for well-defined applications under some central control. Binary formats are much more compact than text, although text compresses well. When a distributed system is organized around rigid adherence to an explicit API or protocol, using binary formats for transferring data is the most efficient option. Unfortunately, such organization is limiting. Custom protocols are generally limited to a small number of development teams, resulting in narrow distribution of the software. Common protocols like HTTP and FTP have achieved extraordinary acceptance, but it is hard to envision hundreds or thousands of protocols reaching the same level of acceptance. The problem is that binary protocols must be followed exactly. There is no tolerance for minor errors and little tolerance for extension without prior coordination.

Consider the World Wide Web. The authors of Web sites are seldom the developers of Web browsers. There is no coordination between authors and Web surfers. Yet the functionality of a server application is available to any browser that possesses the necessary features. Basic, standardized HTML works everywhere, and proprietary extensions tend to degrade rather than break a given page. Everything depends on the HTTP protocol and HTML. So we can author a Web site with nothing more than a text editor if it suits us. We are ready for any client and we speak a language read by all clients. As we build applications on the Internet, we should keep the same degree of freedom. By using XML, we open our servers to any client that shares our understanding of the task at hand. Stores and shoppers, doctors and patients – so long as we share a common interest, we should be able to converse electronically.

XML allows us to write applications that are extremely tolerant of minor imperfections provided we do not insist on strictly validating a document against its schema. If our tags follow the basic rules of XML, we call the document well-formed. A well-formed document that strictly follows an explicit schema is said to be valid. If we assume a document follows a schema but do not require it to be strictly valid, we can adapt to minor errors in obeying the schema. Tagged elements are self-describing – simply look at the tag name and you can see what you must deal with. Tags can be in any order the document schema permits. At worst, a human user can look at raw XML and understand what's there, an important concern during development and debugging. Best of all, XML divorces data and its meaning from its visual presentation. Neither client nor server need be aware of what the other is doing to implement the client-server contract.

Because we are freed from the shackles of a common toolkit, we can expect the nature of clients to expand considerably. Right now, we expect a human sitting in front of a browser on the client end, and an automated process on the server. But what about the future? Clients and servers are going to get much more interesting.

Clients: Agents, Browsers, and More

Typically, client-server Web applications consist of a user interacting with a Web browser on the client side, and some process on the server generating HTML. The exchange is synchronous. In a system like this, there is little motivation to use XML. We're going to be viewing the results of the server process, so we can simply transmit HTML and save some processing on the client. The situation changes, however, if we take the user out of the immediate transaction. We might imagine an automated process on the client – perhaps a supply chain application performing transactions like Electronic Data Interchange (EDI), only with XML in place of binary formats. Not only is XML easier to write to than the proprietary EDI formats, but XML can be transmitted over HTTP. While firewalls require special configuration to enable the passage of EDI data, they are commonly configured to permit HTTP traffic to pass. In general, then, such an application can be implemented with far less effort and bother than a formal EDI implementation. Further information on the use of XML for EDI can be found at `http://www.xmledi.com`. A specification for data exchange in health care, Health Level Seven, uses SGML as one encoding format, but XML might be added in the future. In such cases, we want to maintain the data *as* data, deferring rendering into human-friendly form until final presentation to a user in the future.

The timing of exchanges need not be synchronous. Electronic commerce applications, in particular, would be best implemented using reliable, asynchronous messaging systems. XML would be generated and queued for transmission. Once received, the XML might reside on the server for some time before processing or forwarding to another server for additional processing. The XML exchange may be part of a long transaction in which a programmatic agent expects to be notified when the XML is received and again when the transaction completes. We may not always build server-based applications based on a synchronous model. We've left the browser far behind and introduced new clients like e-mail and automated client processes responding to messages or database operations.

Much has been made of automated agents roving the Internet, performing tasks on behalf of users. XML is an excellent format for agent interactions. It is a simple format, easily implemented on any computing platform. Because XML is tagged, agents expecting only well-formed XML can be extremely fault-tolerant, ignoring tags they do not understand. For example, if the DTD had been extended with new tags since the receiving agent was implemented, or if the implementing programmer had an imperfect understanding of the DTD, the document will be invalid. If the agent detects invalid XML, it can degrade to processing the data as well-formed. When the namespaces specification (which we met in Chapter 4) is finalized, agents will be able to retrieve an up-to-date data schema over the Internet from the DTD's creator.

The current conception of a client is going to undergo expansion as use of wide area networking increases. XML is a simple and easily implemented formatting scheme ideally suited to the loosely coupled, data-driven clients we'll see. Let's take a look at a conventional system that uses XML to enable the server to work with non-traditional clients.

The Technical Papers System

We're going to build a simple system for maintaining technical papers. Each paper resides on the server in XML format using a simple DTD. The papers include a title, the author's autobiographical information, and the body of the paper. The body also includes an abstract.We also have a database that captures key information about each paper, such as title, author, and date of publication. We want the user to be able to specify some search criteria and obtain a table of papers matching the criteria. Selecting one paper retrieves the XML file from the server and presents it in the browser using XSL to provide rich formatting according to style rules found on the server.

You can either run this example from our Web site directly, or download the code and build it yourself. Both are available from `http://webdev.wrox.co.uk/books/1525`

> **This application does not run in Internet Explorer 5. However, it requires the file `msxml.dll` from the IE 5.0 beta (at the time of writing IE5 had not been released). Once you have obtained this and you are running IE4, go to the command line and type `"regsvr32 msxml.dll"`. This will register the new XML parser, replacing your old (IE 4.0) parser. `msxml.dll` is installed in the `Winnt\system32` directory. You may wish to install the new parser in another directory to allow for re-registering the old parser later.**

The Client

So far, this doesn't sound so unusual. We've all seen, or even built, systems that posted data from HTML forms to a server and received dynamically generated HTML in return. Unfortunately, such a scheme limits our clients to Web browsers. It is a view-only representation that excludes data-only clients such as we envision. We're going to use XML to do two things: preserve the distinction between data and presentation, and exchange information with the server in a manner tolerant of changes and errors in the exchanged data format. Our client will generate XML representing search parameters, then parse XML from the server containing the search results. With this exchange of dynamically generated XML in place, our server will be useful for serving many types of clients, not just the graphical one we'll build to illustrate the concept.

Setting Up Queries

We start out in the conventional fashion. Our client's opening page contains HTML form elements for eliciting criteria for searches of the database by author, title, and publication date. Not seen are an XML parser component and an empty `<DIV>` area. The page also has a number of JavaScript functions within it to implement the client-side functionality.

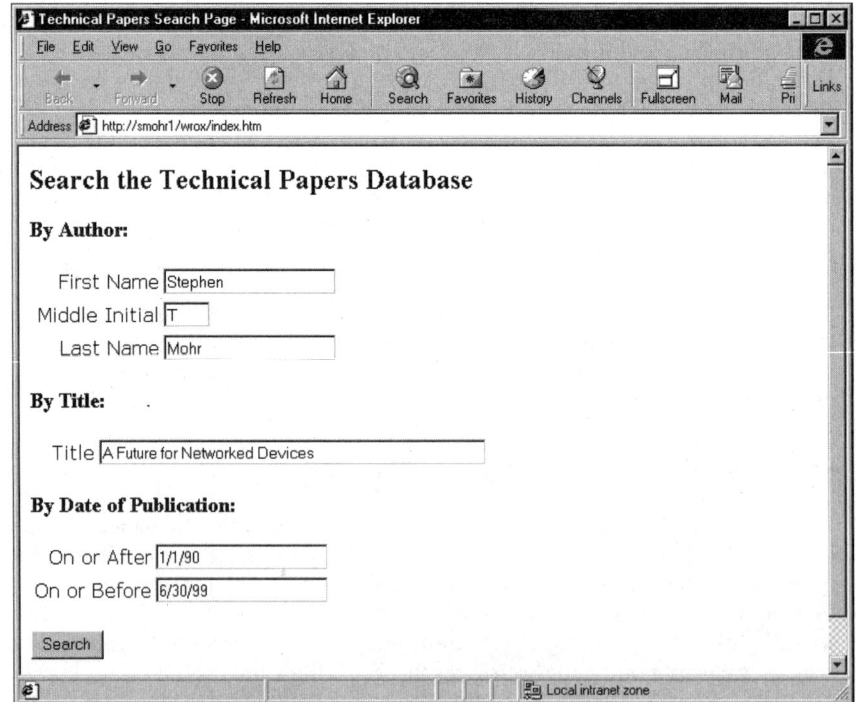

The database used in this example, available with the rest of the code from `http://webdev.wrox.co.uk/books/1525`, *maintains the publication date as a date field. You can input a date for searches in any short-date format.*

We'll use JavaScript functions and DHTML as implemented in Microsoft Internet Explorer version 4.0+ to extract the criteria and format a request as XML for the server. This tool selection is chiefly because we are going to use a script-friendly XML parser written as a COM component. If you wish to try this with Netscape's browser, you will need a plug-in to allow the use of ActiveX components like the parser. Additionally, Netscape's DHTML implementation differs from Microsoft's so you might need to adapt the script code in places. For simplicity, then, we'll stick with Internet Explorer. Most important, the response will be inserted into the `<DIV>` at the bottom of the page – the user will not have to leave the search page to view the results no matter how many searches he performs.

At the time of writing, the ActiveX XML parser provided with Microsoft Internet Explorer was undergoing a dramatic transition. The new version, then in beta testing and slated for delivery with Internet Explorer 5.0, offered a new object model that tracks the evolving W3C XML document object model (DOM). I used this version of the XML parser component rather than Microsoft's earlier COM parser to illustrate the new DOM. Some slight changes may appear in the parser component's interfaces when the DOM is finalized. The major differences in the object models offered by the two versions can be seen by comparing the references at `http://www.microsoft.com/xml`.

I restricted this example to Microsoft DHTML for simplicity and clarity. Certainly, in a production environment you will need to detect the browser type when the request for the search criteria page arrives at the server and return a browser-specific search page.

Getting Lists of Papers

The results of each search appear as an HTML table. The paper's title appears as a hyperlink to the page that returns the selected paper. The search results, however, come back from the server as XML, so we'll have to generate the tables dynamically in the client as we parse the response. The parser in the search page retrieves and parses the XML from the server. Once the search results have been parsed, JavaScript in the search page walks the parse tree and generates HTML that is dynamically inserted into the `<DIV>` at the bottom of the page.

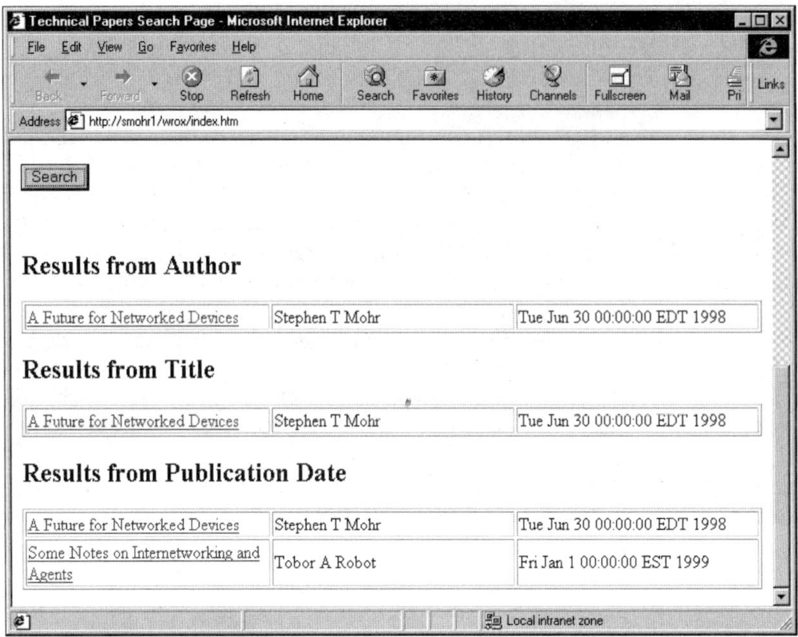

Viewing the Paper

When the user clicks on a hyperlink, the name of the selected paper's XML file is sent as a parameter to an Active Server Page (ASP). A Web page is dynamically generated and sent to the client. This page contains the XSL processor component which provides rich visual formatting to our data. The component retrieves the technical paper and the associated XSL rule sheet from the server. It applies the rules to the XML content to generate HTML for the final, richly formatted page.

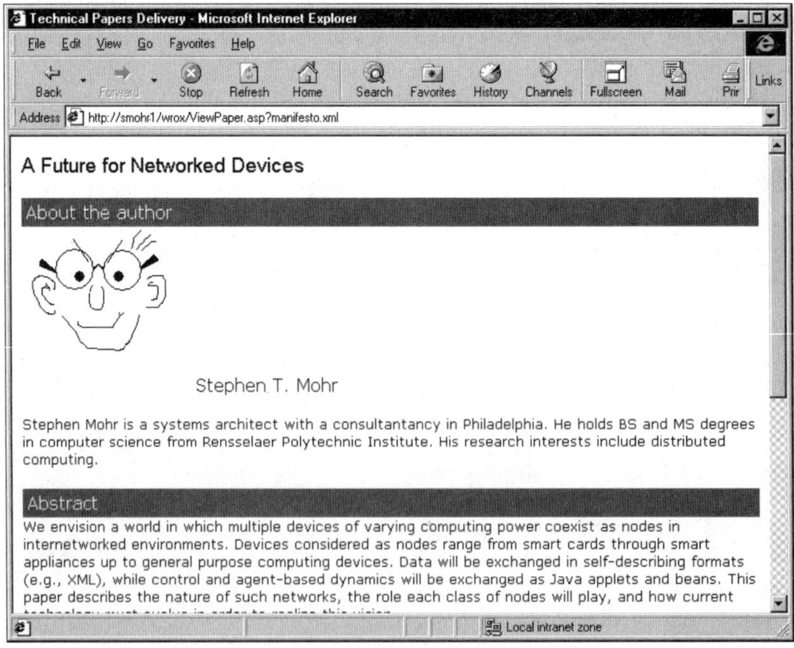

The Server

So far we've skipped over discussing how the server works, yet it is the heart of the system. The key is an ASP combining JavaScript and ActiveX components to parse XML, execute database queries, then generate XML dynamically to send back to the client.

Issuing Queries

The XML sent by the client is parsed at the server by an instance of the same XML parser we used on the client. We will again use JavaScript to walk the tree. This time, however, we will compose a SQL query and execute it for each search requested by the client. As each result set is returned we iterate through the cursor and send XML containing the search results back to the client. We will use ActiveX Data Objects (ADO), a collection of COM components provided by Microsoft, to do the database work, but any database access mechanism that can be run from an ASP would serve. Here is the DTD for paper search queries:

```
<!ELEMENT PaperQuery (BYAUTHOR | BYTITLE | BYDATE)+>

<!ELEMENT BYAUTHOR (FNAME?, MI?, LNAME?)>
<!ELEMENT FNAME (#PCDATA)>
<!ELEMENT MI (#PCDATA)>
<!ELEMENT LNAME (#PCDATA)>

<!ELEMENT BYTITLE TITLE>
<!ELEMENT TITLE (#PCDATA)>

<!ELEMENT BYDATE (AFTER?, BEFORE?)>
<!ELEMENT AFTER (#PCDATA)>
<!ELEMENT BEFORE (#PCDATA)>
```

The `<BYAUTHOR>` tag may appear odd at first glance – we've made everything optional! This is one place where a desirable feature of the client is hard to express precisely in XML. We want our users to be able to search for papers using any combination of the author's name so long as some piece of it appears. This is difficult if not impossible to express in the rigorous syntax of a DTD.

The `<BYTITLE>` tag introduces a bit of indirection that may appear unnecessary at first glance. It contains a `<TITLE>` tag, which contains `#PCDATA`. I elected not to compress this to `<!ELEMENT BYTITLE (#PCDATA)>` to preserve the idea that we contain the search parameters within a tag denoting the search type. We could conceivably expand this type of search to contain a `<SUBTITLE>` tag at some future date. This is purely a conceptual decision and does not reflect general XML practice. Any DTD reflects its author's conception of the problem domain, so there is almost never one "right" answer. In short – feel free to experiment!

Generating Responses

Each SQL query retrieves the name of the author, the name of the XML file containing the paper, the paper's title, and the publication date of the paper from the Access database. We've defined a DTD to represent this, although we won't formally use it in running code. We won't be using the validating feature of our parser, so the DTD never comes into play. In fact, the XML we generate never makes the linkage between the XML and this DTD. Each paper is marked with a `<paper>` tag:

```
<!ELEMENT PaperResponse (BYAUTHOR | BYTITLE | BYDATE | NoResults)*>
<!ELEMENT BYAUTHOR (paper)+>
<!ELEMENT BYTITLE (paper)+>
<!ELEMENT BYDATE (paper)+>
<!ELEMENT NoResults EMPTY>

<!ELEMENT paper (docURL?, title, author, pubdate)>
<!ELEMENT docURL (#PCDATA)>
<!ELEMENT title (#PCDATA)>
<!ELEMENT author (#PCDATA)>
<!ELEMENT pubdate (#PCDATA)>
```

The data returned from our server may contain the results of more than one search. For example, if you provide criteria for each group on our initial page, you will get a `<PaperResponse>` wrapping a `<BYAUTHOR>` tag containing the papers matching the author criteria, a `<BYTITLE>` tag containing the papers matching the title criteria, and a `<BYDATE>` tag containing the papers matching the date criteria. Each search is independent of the others. If no papers are found, a `<NoResults/>` tag is passed.

The XML will be generated by JavaScript functions. The functions write the XML back to the client as it is generated. Since the XML is destined directly for the parser on the client, it is imperative that no HTML tags are transmitted or we will break our client application, because the client is not expecting any HTML tags.

This is a conceptual view of the tasks performed in the search portion of our client-server application. Our JavaScript functions will take the user-provided criteria and compose a well-formed XML string. This is appended to the name of our server-side page, `papersearch.asp`, and given to the embedded XML parser component. The parser requests this page from the server, causing the server to return a stream of XML containing the results of the searches it performs. We walk the parse tree provided by the parser and create HTML tables which we dynamically insert into the search page.

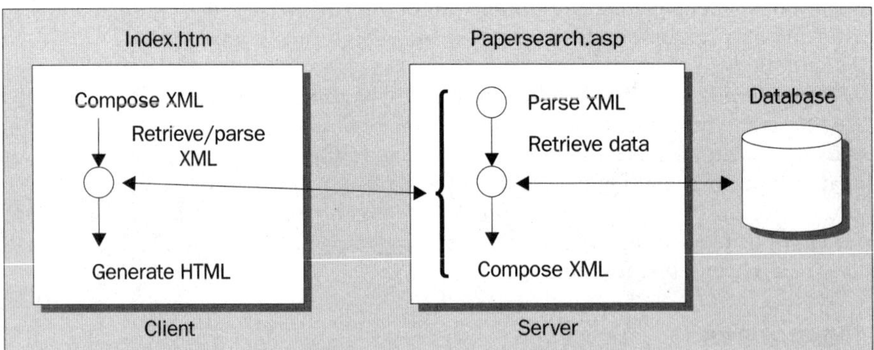

Our simple example does not provide a mechanism for adding new papers to the Web site. If you experiment with the sample code and wish to add to the database found at `http://webdev.wrox.co.uk/books/1525`*, you need to update the database and add some files. Specifically, you will need a graphic (JPEG, GIF, etc.) image for the author, an XML file marked up according to the DTD, and a new row in the papers table of the database* `techpapers.mdb`*. That table has entries for the first, middle, and last names of the author, the title and publication date of the paper, and a URL to locate the XML version of the technical paper.*

Publishing Papers

We'd like the paper to be well-formatted when it is finally presented. We can accomplish this with Dynamic HTML (DHTML). Each paper will consist of the paper's title, followed successively by the author's biographical information, and the body of the paper. The body, in turn, consists of an abstract followed by paragraphs or bulleted lists. There is some standardized text – About the author, for example – that we'd like to avoid repeating in each XML file. We're going to include a picture of the author, but we don't want to include the HTML `<IMG>` tag in the XML so as to avoid information that is relevant solely to visual presentation on the client. Obviously, the XSL rules are going to be doing a little translation for us. Another benefit of using XSL is that we can move elements like the author block without rewriting the XML. Changing the rules in the XSL rule sheet will take care of that for us. We'll use an off-the-shelf ActiveX XSL processor component to implement this. In fact, with a little bit of server-side JavaScript, we can use a single page to present any document in our system.

The following diagram is the flow of tasks for retrieving and displaying a formatted paper using XSL. Clicking on a link in the search results requests `ViewPaper.asp` with the name of the XML file containing the paper appended to it. The JavaScript that executes on the server retrieves this filename and embeds it in the page returned to the client. When the page loads on the client, the XSL processor component retrieves the paper and our XSL style sheet containing the rules which govern our presentation format. It applies the rules to the paper to obtain formatted HTML. At that point, another function retrieves the HTML and inserts it into the page for the user to see.

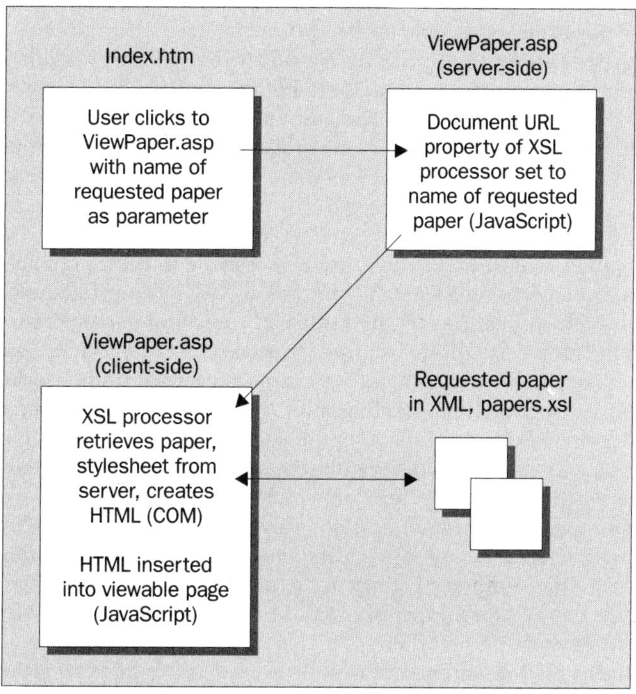

Core Architecture Considerations

This system will work, but is it a good design? Unlike a badly designed stand-alone application, a badly designed distributed system affects all users of the network. Introducing XML processing to the client changes the classic distribution of work between client and server by requiring the client to format the data for presentation. Transmitting potentially lengthy streams of XML from the client to the server raises issues that may not be obvious. Before we start writing the code behind our application, we should pause to consider some wider issues concerning the architecture.

Trade-offs in Client-Server Development

One consideration that is often overlooked when XML is added to the client-server mix is the additional processing that must occur on the client. Traditional applications using a form to obtain fully formatted HTML from the server truly constitute a thin client system. The processing capabilities and configuration of the client are modest. Utilizing XML as an exchange mechanism adds parsing code to both sides, and XML-generating code to the client. The search parameters page the client sees contains fairly extensive code, as we shall see. If we only intend to use the server with this particular client, this additional code is unnecessary. After all, we could have written the server so that it sent us HTML, thereby eliminating the need to parse XML and convert it to HTML. In fact, if we did that, we could dispense with XML entirely, turning our page into a conventional forms-based HTML page. Using XML for data exchange, we've made our server independent of the client. This is obviously important when considering the future breed of automated clients we anticipate. It can also help conventional Web site developers manage differing browser capabilities. Rather than merge all the formatting code for the different platforms into one very long server-side script, we can instead install a gateway page routing clients to the appropriate search page based on their browser class. Pages with browser-specific DHTML can be served to general purpose clients. Very thin client devices without the memory or processing capacity to handle the client side can receive HTML generated by an XSL processor on the server. The amount of work is essentially the same, but we've isolated the core data-handling code. Changes in presentation can be made independently. This eliminates the possibility of maintenance on presentation code having an unintended side effect on the data-handling code.

In our sample case, we've decided to make our system accessible to future clients whose capabilities and purposes we cannot anticipate. This warrants the use of XML as our data exchange format as well as in the markup of the technical papers themselves. Preserving data-specific markup all the way to the client also allows for future use of the intermediate search product. If we were to add a paper's abstract to the other items returned, we could use the same server to produce reading lists and library catalogs. The usual advantage of XML in enabling intelligent searches of documents would hold for such mass listings. How is this better than allowing the user to search the main database? The database server may be heavily loaded. The user may frequently be disconnected from the network, or separated from the server by a low data rate connection. In such cases, the low rate of change in the collection would make local searching of a reasonably up-to-date summary listing an attractive alternative to a live search of the database. Such a scheme would require some mechanism for specifying how long to store the summary listing on the client before requiring an update from the server. An agent acting on behalf of a human user would never translate the XML into HTML, of course, but would instead perform some other action. In each case, the use of XML offers us flexibility in making our distribution choices. Since our server is designed to return XML instead of HTML, we can use it unchanged in these new applications. Because we are building a long-term library capability, XML makes good sense for the data exchange mechanism. It will work with many kinds of client from a human reader to a Web Bot performing automated searches. If we were developing a single use application, we would stick with basic forms and HTML for the search and restrict XML to document markup.

There is no one best answer to the questions of how to distribute processing and how long to preserve the meaning of the data. Project goals and the nature of our computing environment must dictate the technologies selected to implement a distributed system. Even a hot new technology like XML must submit to basic software engineering principles.

Transmission Issues

How do we get XML from the client to the server for processing? HTTP is meant to stream arbitrarily large amounts of data from the server to the client, so we have no concerns there. Clients, however, traditionally transmit much less – just enough to specify what document the user wants. XML is potentially verbose. Are we going to run into difficulties? There are three general techniques we can use, ranging from simple yet limited to complex and powerful:

- HTTP requests
- Asynchronous file transfer
- Stream transfers outside HTTP

HTTP Requests

The simplest technique is to make the XML the single parameter on an HTTP request. A forms-based application would send its parameters in a URL of the form:

```
somepage.asp?Param1=XXX&Param2=YYY.
```

Instead, we will make a URL where a string in XML format takes the place of the form's parameters:

```
papersearch.asp?<PaperQuery><BYAUTHOR>...</PaperQuery>
```

This makes our server-side programming easy. We simply recover the request's parameter and feed it to an XML parser.

There are, however, two drawbacks. First, although HTTP 1.1 places no limits on the length of a URL (for a GET operation), servers and proxies will have varying upper length limits. In that case, you will be limited in how many searches you can define in one exchange. While using a `POST` operation would remove these length restrictions, unfortunately, in our example, the embedded XML parser component is doing the file retrieval, so the choice of `GET` vs. `POST` is out of our hands. We are explicitly trading capability for simplicity. Second, our parser uses standard HTTP encoding for URLs. Thus, all non-alphanumeric characters get converted into the escape character `%` followed by the two-character hexadecimal code for the original character. Spaces in a title we're searching for will be replaced by %20, so Deep Thoughts on Computing becomes Deep%20Thoughts%20on%20Computing. Our server must compensate for this.

File Transfer

Another approach is to transfer a file to the server using FTP, then have the receiving process read it from disk. This is well suited to bulk data transfer, but presents several problems. First, direct synchronous exchanges are out of the question. We must either have some background process scanning the server's disk for the arrival of files, or the client must notify the server after the file has been transferred. Either method involves some complexity when dealing with non-trivial systems. Finally, we have the problem of returning an answer to the client. Typically, the client will poll the server at periodic intervals or the server will e-mail the client. Still, there are many off-the-shelf FTP implementations available to the programmer, so this method should not be dismissed.

Custom Sockets Programming

A final technique is to establish a direct socket connection outside HTTP and perform a transfer between a specialized component on the client and a matching component on the server. This would appear to be ideal, but we shouldn't rush into this without reflection. To begin with, we would need to design and implement our own protocol, never a trivial task. Although FTP could handle the transfer, it possesses the asynchronous difficulties we have just discussed. If we are going to resort to custom programming, we should insist on closer integration between the transfer protocol and our application logic. Next, clients and servers would need to agree on the protocol, virtually eliminating the kind of wide-area, loosely coupled exchanges we envision for the future.

Firewalls would present an additional problem for this technique. Most firewalls are readily configured for common security options dealing with well known Internet protocols and ports. Our protocol would require special configuration in every firewall between our clients and servers. Still, if all the clients that intended to use our server were under our control, this might be a viable approach. We might use a Java Applet in the client's search page to establish the connection with the server. Were we to do this, however, it is unlikely that we would be able to implement our server in a scripting language. We would need a Java component, Unix daemon, or Windows NT service to act as our server.

Our simple system involves relatively small amounts of XML being sent to the server. We'll opt for simplicity, therefore, and get on with the business of composing and parsing XML.

Creating XML on the Client

Our client begins with a default page, `index.htm`. This page provides a user interface backed by JavaScript functions that format the user's search parameters as an XML file for transmission to the server. Other JavaScript functions handle the server's reply.

User Interface

Our search page consists of some rather typical HTML form elements, but no form. We're going to get our user's input directly via Internet Explorer's DHTML object model and JavaScript. This allows us to control how, when, and in what format the search parameters travel to the server. We'll permit searches by author name, paper title, and date of publication, but let's concentrate on the author name search. The three text input elements are placed inside table cells for formatting. This is the HTML for the author search portion. The full code for this page – called `index.htm` – can be downloaded from our Web site at `http://webdev.wrox.co.uk/books/1525`:

```
<h3>By Author:</h3>

<table border="0" width="41%">
  <tr>
    <td width="41%" align="right"><font face="Verdana">First Name</font></td>
    <td width="59%"><input TYPE="text" SIZE="20" NAME="FNAME"></td>
  </tr>
  <tr>
    <td width="41%" align="right"><font face="Verdana">Middle Initial</font></td>
    <td width="59%"><input TYPE="text" SIZE="4" NAME="MI"> </td>
```

```
    </tr>
    <tr>
      <td width="41%" align="right"><font face="Verdana">Last Name</font></td>
      <td width="59%"><input TYPE="text" SIZE="20" NAME="LNAME"></td>
    </tr>
  </table>
```

Note the form element names: FNAME, MI, and LNAME. We'll need these later. The search process is triggered when the user clicks on the Search button. This is also an HTML form element, but it has a small amount of code associated with it:

```
<p align="left"><input TYPE="button" VALUE="Search" ONCLICK="OnSearch()"
AME="SearchBtn">
</p>
```

Packaging Search Parameters as XML

The code ONCLICK="OnSearch()" associates the JavaScript function OnSearch() with the button on our page by invoking it when the user clicks on the button. This is where things start to get interesting. We're going to compose the XML for our different types of searches based on the contents of the form elements.

```
function OnSearch()
{
  var sQueryXML = "";
  var parser = document.all("xmlDOM");

  // See if the user wants a 'by name' search
  if (FNAME.value != "" || MI.value != "" || LNAME.value != "")
   sQueryXML += makeByName(FNAME.value, MI.value, LNAME.value);

  // Check for a 'by title' search
  if (TITLE.value != "")
   sQueryXML += makeByTitle(TITLE.value);

  // Check for a 'publication date' search
  if (AFTER.value != "" || BEFORE.value != "")
   sQueryXML += makeByPubDate(AFTER.value, BEFORE.value);

  // Avoid a network round-trip if you have no search requests
  if (sQueryXML != "")
  {
   // if we have at least one query, wrap it with the root tag
   sQueryXML = "<PaperQuery>" + sQueryXML + "</PaperQuery>";

   // Set the XML parser's doc URL to a request on the server
   parser.asynch = "false";
   parser.load("papersearch.asp?" + sQueryXML);

   HandleResponse(document.all("results"));
  }
}
```

We need to compose some XML to send to the server, and we use the string variable `sQueryXML` for this purpose. We check each form element for search parameters. If any are found, we send them off to a JavaScript function that returns the parameters encoded as XML. If we have at least one query, we want to send it off to the server. To do this we need an instance of the COM XML parser to handle the response, and we've laid one out on the page with the following HTML:

```
<object classid="clsid:E54941B2-7756-11D1-BC2A-00C04FB925F3"
ame="xmlDOM"></object>
```

This is simply a non-visual ActiveX component. The class ID refers to the version 5.0 ActiveX XML parser. This version closely supports the W3C XML DOM, Level 1, as it progressed to version 1.0 recommendation status. The line:

```
var parser = document.all("xmlDOM"); in OnSearch()
```

simply retrieves a reference to the parser object from the current document's collection of page elements.

If a text input element contains any text, we compose XML for a search of the associated type. Thus, if any of the text elements `FNAME`, `MI`, or `LNAME` contain anything, we request a search by author name. The XML for each search type is appended to `sQueryXML`. We've put the author search composition code in its own function:

```
function makeByName(sFirst, sMid, sLast)
{
  // Open the by author tag
  var sQueryString = "<BYAUTHOR>";

  if (sFirst != "")
     sQueryString += "<FNAME>" + sFirst + "</FNAME>";

  if (sMid != "")
     sQueryString += "<MI>" + sMid + "</MI>";

  if (sLast != "")
     sQueryString += "<LNAME>" + sLast + "</LNAME>";

  // Close the author tag
  sQueryString += "</BYAUTHOR>";

  return sQueryString;
}
```

This is reasonably direct. The values of the associated input elements are passed in. Each is checked to see if it contains any text. If it does, it is wrapped in the appropriate tag delimiters and appended to a string that will be passed back as the return value of the function. Everything is contained within the `<BYAUTHOR>` tag, indicating the search type to the server. The functions for the other searches, `makeByTitle()` and `makeByPubDate()`, are similar. When we return to `OnSearch()`, we complete our XML by providing the root tag:

```
if (sQueryXML != "")
{
  sQueryXML = "<PaperQuery>" + sQueryXML + "</PaperQuery>";
  ...
```

The XML assembled for the author search in the sample screenshot now looks like this:

```
<PaperQuery>
   <BYAUTHOR>
      <FNAME>Stephen</FNAME>
      <MI>T</MI>
      <LNAME>Mohr</LNAME>
   </BYAUTHOR>
</PaperQuery>
```

Purists will note we're not using the parser to construct and validate the XML with a DTD. We also aren't performing field validation as you would expect to do in production code to ensure that markup isn't entered by the user. In our sample, we're developing the code for both the client and the server. Consequently, it is easy for us to ensure that our code is generating valid XML for this application. In many cases, the code was developed in parallel. As a result, we opt for this lightweight approach. The parser provided with Internet Explorer 5.0, however, is optionally a validating parser. In the general case of clients and servers written by widely separated or mutually unknown developers, XML validation will be a real concern. In that case, we would have no assurances that the teams worked from the same version of the DTD, so we might want to formally validate the XML as it is exchanged to prevent errors in understanding. We'll take up the issue later in this chapter.

Handling XML Returned from the Server

Returning to `OnSearch()`, we finish the job by obtaining the search results in XML form and converting them to HTML:

```
// Set the XML parser's doc URL to a request on the server

parser.load("papersearch.asp?" + sQueryXML);

HandleResponse(document.all("results"));
```

How did we get from composing a search request to handling a response? The `load()` method of the parser loads the file associated with the passed URL. The ASP `papersearch.asp` on the server will dynamically generate the response XML for the query contained in `sQueryXML`. We compose the URL for our request, hand it to the parser, and the parser makes the request for us. When the `load()` method returns, the parser either has a parse tree for the search results or is in an error state. Let's pause in our client development and follow our query to the server.

Manipulating XML in Active Server Pages

Active Server Pages are Microsoft's answer to CGI scripts. They are scripted pages executing in the server's process, so they make more efficient use of server resources and offer better performance than CGI. The source for Active Server Pages looks somewhat different to that for your typical Web page. ASP source code is usually a mix of HTML and script code freely interwoven. In our case, `papersearch.asp` is generating pure XML, so we have no HTML, not even the `<head>` and `<body>` tags. Before going into detail, consider the beginning of `papersearch.asp`:

```
<%@ LANGUAGE = JavaScript %>

<%

var dbConn, dbRecordSet;

   /* Create a parser object and retrieve the XML search request
    from the server's Request object. */

   var parser = Server.CreateObject("microsoft.xmldom");
   parser.loadXML(Request.ServerVariables("QUERY_STRING"));

   if (parser.readyState == 4 && parser.lastError.reason == "")
   {
    var docroot = parser.documentNode;

    if (docroot.nodeName == "PaperQuery")
    {
      // Establish a global connection
      dbConn = Server.CreateObject("ADODB.Connection");
      dbConn.Open("TechPapers", "server", "");
      dbRecordSet = Server.CreateObject("ADODB.RecordSet");

      // Process the searches requested
      AssembleQueries(docroot);

      // Clean up resources
      dbRecordSet.Close();
      dbConn.Close();
      dbConn = null;
      dbRecordSet = null;
    }
    else
      Response.Write("<InvalidQuery></InvalidQuery>");
   }
   else
    Response.Write("<Error></Error>");
```

This body of JavaScript is analogous to the `main()` function in a traditional C language application. It will be executed as ASP enters the page. The directive `<%@ LANGUAGE=JavaScript %>` establishes the default server-side scripting language for our page. This time, instead of statically placing the parser component on the page, we'll create it in the script. `Server` is a global object offered by Microsoft Internet Information Server's (IIS) ASP implementation to provide ASP code with access to server functions. The `CreateObject()` method tells the server object to instantiate a new ActiveX component.

> *For our purposes,* `new ActiveXObject("microsoft.xmldom")` *would work as well. Involving the server in the creation process, however, is a good habit to get into. If we want to try some optimizations such as saving the object over the lifetime of a user session or ASP application in IIS 4.0, we must let the server create the object instance so that it can handle object lifetime issues properly.*

Global Server Objects

Two other useful objects provided by ASP are Request and Response. Request allows us to obtain information about the request passed to this page. Request.ServerVariables is a collection of variables passed in the request. In our case:

```
Request.ServerVariables("QUERY_STRING")
```

obtains the entire XML string composed on the client to encode our search parameters. Response is an object representing the stream returning to the client. Response.Write() is simply a method allowing us to write a string to the stream. Our server-side XML response could be much longer than the client-side request XML since we are potentially dealing with the information for many titles. We shouldn't keep it all in one string. Consequently, we'll call Response.Write() whenever we have some XML fragment and let the ASP implementation worry about buffering.

Loading an XML String

Our technique for loading the parser with XML is slightly different from the one we used on the client. We needed the client to retrieve a dynamically generated file named by a URL. Here, we have the XML in a string – the query string – and we want to feed it to the parser. We can use the parser's loadXML() method for this. The parser accepts the string as a complete XML file and attempts to parse it.

> *The earlier Microsoft COM parser offered a similar feature through the* IPersistStreamInit *COM interface but did not make it available through the interface accessible from scripts. At that time, you had to write a helper ActiveX component to take the XML string and feed it to the parser. The presence of* loadXML() *is a major improvement for server-side development.*

Getting to the Root of the Parse Tree

We expect to have a parse tree or an error condition when loadXML() returns. When the parser has finished loading the XML, the readyState property will be set to 4. This does not, however, indicate that the XML was parsed successfully. It simply means that no fatal error interfered with loading. For this reason, we also retrieve the lastError object and ensure that the reason property is empty.

```
if (parser.readyState == 4 && parser.lastError.reason == "")
```

When both conditions are satisfied, we may proceed safe in the knowledge that there will be at least a root node. We obtain this node with the parser's documentNode() method call. Node objects have three important properties we'll need throughout our project. These are:

- nodeType – ELEMENTs are type 0
- nodeName – a string with the tag name, e.g., PaperQuery for <PaperQuery>
- nodeValue – the text contained within the tag (including any embedded tags)

We must perform a quick check of the root node's name to ensure that we are receiving XML intended for this server. In our system, the root is `<PaperQuery>`. If we fail this check, we pass back some well-formed XML indicating an error, which the client will process (we will come back to this later). If, however, a client is approaching us with a proper search, we'll prepare to walk the parse tree further and issue database queries.

Setting Up Database Resources

At this point, it is worth setting up our global database connection. This avoids repeating the code in the various functions specific to the search types. It also eliminates the overhead of making and breaking the connection repeatedly. I'm using COM components from Microsoft's ActiveX Data Objects collection, but any database access technique will do here.

```
dbConn = Server.CreateObject("ADODB.Connection");
dbConn.Open("TechPapers", "server", "");
dbRecordSet = Server.CreateObject("ADODB.RecordSet");
```

Our example uses a Microsoft Access database. Readers experienced with Access must note that ADO requires the SQL-92 compliant wildcard character -- % -- for wildcard searches, not the asterisk as is typically used in Access.

Walking the Parse Tree

The function `AssembleQueries()` is the inverse of the `OnSearch()` function in the client page. It walks the immediate child nodes of the parse tree root node and directs detailed processing based on the type of search requested.

```
function AssembleQueries(oRoot)
{

  var childNode;
  var sQueryStem = "SELECT Papers.Title, Papers.PaperURL, Papers.PubDate,
      Papers.AuthorFirst, Papers.AuthorMI, Papers.AuthorLast FROM Papers ";

  Response.Write("<PaperResponse>");  // Establish the XML doc root

  // Each child represents a single database search
  for (var nChild = 0; nChild < oRoot.childNodes.length; nChild++)
  {
   childNode = oRoot.childNodes.item(nChild);
   if (childNode.nodeType == 0)
   {
     if (childNode.nodeName == "BYAUTHOR")
      AssembleAuthor(sQueryStem, childNode);

     if (childNode.nodeName == "BYTITLE")
      AssembleTitle(sQueryStem, childNode);

     if (childNode.nodeName == "BYDATE")
      AssemblePubDate(sQueryStem, childNode);
   }
  }
  Response.Write("</PaperResponse>");
}
```

Each node has a collection, childNodes, containing references to all its immediate children. The number of children is denoted by the property childNodes.length, while any individual child node is retrieved by passing its ordinal index into the childNodes.index() method. Each search requested by the client is represented by an XML element off the root. If the user specified parameters for all three types of searches, the root will have <BYAUTHOR>, <BYTITLE>, and <BYDATE> elements as its children.

Since we're not using the validating features of the parser, we need to account for the fact that the incoming XML might be invalid. We'd also like to provide a measure of forward compatibility. That is, a client written according to a newer DTD than the server is using will transmit some older elements the server can understand and process. This is a distinct possibility in a loosely coupled situation over the Internet. For example, an industry group might publish a DTD for a particular kind of task. Clients and servers might be written by third parties, so we might get into a situation where an up-to-date client requests service from an out-of-date server. We could insist on validation and reject anything that didn't adhere to the server's DTD, but that might screen out requests the server can accommodate to some degree. The server should degrade gracefully. We will simply skip any child node that is not an ELEMENT or is an ELEMENT whose name we do not recognize. For example:

```
if (childNode.nodeType == 0)
{
      if (childNode.nodeName == "BYAUTHOR")
```

As long as the client places all its search requests immediately off the root of the document, our server will respond to the three types of searches it knows about.

> *We could also improve robustness by recursing into any node we do not recognize. This would allow future versions of the DTD to embed searches within a containing tag. That way, our server would locate all searches it recognizes wherever they occur within the request XML and skip any names unknown to it. In the interests of simplicity, we'll forego this additional measure of forward compatibility.*

Continuing the focus on the search by author name, let's assume the server received a <BYAUTHOR> tag. We must parse this tag, extract the search parameters, and compose the appropriate SQL query.

Retrieving the Parameters

The JavaScript function AssembleAuthor() in papersearch.asp is called with a string containing the SELECT clause of our SQL query and the <BYAUTHOR> element node.

```
function AssembleAuthor(sStem, oChild)
{
   var paramNode;
   var sFirst = "", sMI = "", sLast = "";
   var sConstraintClause = "", sQuery="";
   var nParam = 0;

   for (nParam = 0; nParam < oChild.childNodes.length; nParam++)
   {
      // Extract the parameters we understand
      paramNode = oChild.childNodes.item(nParam);
```

```
        if (paramNode.nodeType == 0)
        {
           if (paramNode.nodeName == "FNAME")
              sFirst = "AuthorFirst LIKE '" + paramNode.nodeValue + "'";

           if (paramNode.nodeName == "MI")
              sMI = "AuthorMI LIKE '" + paramNode.nodeValue + "'";

           if (paramNode.nodeName == "LNAME")
              sLast = "AuthorLast LIKE '" + paramNode.nodeValue +"'";
        }
     }

     // Build a SQL WHERE clause from the parameters passed
     sConstraintClause = sFirst;

     if (sConstraintClause != "" && sMI != "")
        sConstraintClause += " AND ";

     sConstraintClause += sMI;

     if (sConstraintClause != "" && sLast != "")
        sConstraintClause += " AND ";

     sConstraintClause += sLast;

     // Complete the constraint clause and execute the query
     if (sConstraintClause != "")
        sConstraintClause = "WHERE " + sConstraintClause;
     sQuery = sStem + sConstraintClause + ';';

     MakeResponse(1, sQuery);
  }
```

Let's take a closer look at this code.

The <BYAUTHOR> element is defined in the server's DTD as:

```
<!ELEMENT BYAUTHOR (FNAME?,MI?,LNAME?)>
```

Thus, we'll check all the children of this node, ensuring each is of type ELEMENT, and check each node's name to ensure they are some tag we recognize.

```
paramNode = oChild.childNodes.item(nParam);

if (paramNode.nodeType == 0)
{
   if (paramNode.nodeName == "FNAME")
```

Here again the focus is on keeping the coupling between the client and server code as loose as possible, rather than ensuring XML validity. This is in keeping with our philosophy of an Internet of interacting agents with imperfect knowledge of one another. Future DTDs for this application might allow searches by the author's age or professional affiliation. Our current server will not recognize those parameters, but it will be able to respond to the simple name parameters.

Since we can have any combination of first and last name and middle initial, we choose to assemble each condition of the `WHERE` clause individually. After we have all the parameters contained in the `<BYAUTHOR>` request, we'll concatenate them to complete the clause. This concatenation occurs after we've emerged from iterating through the child node collection. Care must be taken to ensure we assemble a valid SQL query. Having assembled the query in the variable `sQuery`, we want to execute the query against the database. That code is common to all our searches, so we arbitrarily define a search type enumeration for the first parameter of the function `MakeResponse()`. The enumeration is:

- 1 - BYAUTHOR
- 2 - BYTITLE
- 3 - BYDATE

If the enumeration seems unfamiliar, recall that we are focusing on searches by the name of the author. The full source code, available for download at `http://webdev.wrox.co.uk/books/1525`, contains the searches by paper title or publication date. The second parameter of the function call is the string containing the SQL query.

Getting Answers to the User's Questions

Now that we have a SQL query to ask the question the client wants answered, we need to execute it, iterate through the resulting cursor, and generate the XML to return to the client. We tie the database and XML actions together to avoid keeping too much data around in strings between responses. The idea is to get the parameters for a single search, do a little database work, and send the resultant XML on its way as soon as possible. Whether the XML is transmitted to the client immediately depends on the buffering configuration of the HTTP server; we've done our part and can forget this portion of the response.

Data Retrieval Using ActiveX Data Objects

We've decided to use Microsoft's ActiveX Data Objects (ADO) for our database work. This is a relatively simple and flat object framework that will be Microsoft's future standard for this kind of work under Windows. We'll keep this section brief however, because you could use whatever database API you prefer.

Here are the first few lines of `MakeResponse()`:

```
function MakeResponse(nQueryType, sQuery)
{
  var sTypeEndTag;

  dbRecordSet = dbConn.Execute(sQuery);


if (dbRecordSet.EOF && dbRecordSet.BOF)
   Response.Write("<NoResults></NoResults>");
```

This is simple enough. We ask the global database connection to execute our query, and accept a recordset object in return. This is equivalent to a database cursor in SQL. If the recordset is empty, both the `BOF` and `EOF` (beginning and end of file, respectively) properties are true. If at least one row was returned, the recordset will be positioned to one of the rows, i.e., neither `BOF` nor `EOF` will be true. If the recordset is empty, we write the `<NoResults>` tag to inform the client his search parameters did not match any items in our database.

At this point, we know we have some rows in our recordset. After writing the search-type tag back to the stream, we have to iterate through the recordset writing a <paper> tag for each row. Setting aside the XML writing lines for a moment, this looks like:

```
while (!dbRecordSet.EOF)
   {
    // Some XML-generating code here

    dbRecordSet.MoveNext();
   }
```

Dynamically Generating XML

The interesting part of this application is the XML, so let's take a look at that now. Here's the complete `MakeResponse()` function:

```
function MakeResponse(nQueryType, sQuery)
{
   var sTypeEndTag;

   dbRecordSet = dbConn.Execute(sQuery);

   if (!dbRecordSet.BOF)
      dbRecordSet.MoveFirst();

   if (dbRecordSet.EOF)
      Response.Write("<NoResults></NoResults>");

   // nQueryType is arbitrary and completely internal to this page
   switch (nQueryType)
   {
      case 1:
         Response.Write("<BYAUTHOR>");
         sTypeEndTag = "</BYAUTHOR>";
         break;

      case 2:
         Response.Write("<BYTITLE>");
         sTypeEndTag = "</BYTITLE>";
         break;

      case 3:
         Response.Write("<BYPUBDATE>");
         sTypeEndTag = "</BYPUBDATE>";
         break;
   }

   /* Step through the recordset composing a <Paper> subtree
      for each row returned. */

   while (!dbRecordSet.EOF)
   {
      Response.Write("<Paper>");
      if (dbRecordSet("PaperURL") != "")
         Response.Write("<docURL>" + dbRecordSet("PaperURL") + "</docURL>");

      if (dbRecordSet("Title") != "")
         Response.Write("<title>" + dbRecordSet("Title") + "</title>");
```

```
      // Assemble the complete name from its parts
      sName = dbRecordSet("AuthorFirst") + " " +
         dbRecordSet("AuthorMI") + " " + dbRecordSet("AuthorLast");
      if (sName != "" && sName != "  ")
         Response.Write("<author>" + sName + "</author>");

      if (dbRecordSet("PubDate") != "")
         Response.Write("<pubdate>" + dbRecordSet("PubDate") + "</pubdate>");

      Response.Write("</Paper>");
      dbRecordSet.MoveNext();
    }
    Response.Write(sTypeEndTag);

}
```

First, we write the search type tag, <BYAUTHOR> in our example, and save the end tag for later use. Next, we open the <paper> tag and write tags for any column of the row that is not empty.

```
Response.Write("<Paper>");
if (dbRecordSet("PaperURL") != "")
   Response.Write("<docURL>" + dbRecordSet("PaperURL") + "</docURL>");

if (dbRecordSet("Title") != "")
   Response.Write("<title>" + dbRecordSet("Title") + "</title>");
. . .
```

Since our data is self-describing, we can write to the client in such a way that we don't have to generate placeholders for missing data. We write the </paper> end tag to finish the row. When we finish writing <paper> tags for all the rows in our recordset, we write the end tag for our search type. Walking back up the call stack, we recall that `AssembleQueries()` executes the following line to close the response XML after returning from this function:

```
Response.Write("</PaperResponse>");
```

We've finished generating the XML file we need to satisfy our client's request. The text of the XML generated for the author type search, shown in the screen shot at the beginning of this chapter, is:

```
<PaperResponse>
   <BYAUTHOR>
      <paper>
         <docURL>manifesto.xml</docURL>
         <title>A Future for Networked Devices</title>
         <author>Stephen T Mohr</author>
         <pubdate>Tue Jun 30 00:00:00 EST 1998</pubdate>
      </paper>
   </BYAUTHOR>
</PaperResponse>
```

How the Client Responds

Recall that all the activity on the server side followed from setting the URL property of the client's parser object. The parser requested a file, loaded what was returned from the server, and parsed the file into a tree (assuming the file was well-formed). The last two lines of the client function `OnSearch()` were:

```
parser.load("papersearch.asp?" + sQueryXML);
HandleResponse(document.all("results"));
```

These lines caused the parser component to make a request of the server. The document returned was the XML for our search results, as generated by the Active Server Page. The component loaded the returned document and parsed it. The function `HandleResponse()` is where we will convert the XML into HTML for presentation to the user.

Preparing to Parse XML on the Client

Internet Explorer keeps a collection of objects corresponding to all the HTML elements on the page. By passing in the name of the `<DIV>` where we want to put our results, we obtain a reference to the corresponding object:

```
document.all("results");
```

We pass this reference to the function `HandleResponse()`. By now, the code to check the status of the parser should be familiar:

```
function HandleResponse(oDIV)
{
  var parser = document.all("xmlDOM");
  var docroot;
  var nChildCount;
  var sTable = "";

  // Clear the result area in the page
  oDIV.innerHTML = "";

  /* If the parser is ready, check the root for correct type. */

  if (parser.readyState == 4 && parser.lastError.reason == "")
  {
      docroot = parser.documentNode;

      if (docroot.nodeName == "PaperResponse")
      {
         for (nChild = 0; nChild < docroot.childNodes.length; nChild++)
         {
            sTable = HandleResults(docroot.childNodes.item(nChild));

            /* The string will be empty if the child node is not of a type
               we handle. If we have a table, insert it into the page. */

            if (sTable != "")
               oDIV.insertAdjacentHTML("beforeEnd", sTable);
```

```
            }
        }
        else
            window.alert("Improper response type;" +
                "check with server administrator.");
    }
    else
        window.alert("Parser not ready or response not well-formed." +
            "Ensure you are contacting an appropriate server.");
}
```

After clearing the `results` `<DIV>`, we check to ensure the parser is not in an error state, then we obtain the root node.

```
oDIV.innerHTML = "";

if (parser.readyState == 4 && parser.lastError.reason == "")
{
   docroot = parser.documentNode;
. . .
```

If it is the tag we expect, `<PaperResponse>`, we proceed. We pass each immediate child node to the function `HandleResults()`. If an HTML table is generated in that function, we place it in the results area of our page:

```
if (docroot.nodeName == "PaperResponse")
{
   for (nChild = 0; nChild < docroot.childNodes.length; nChild++)
   {
      sTable = HandleResults(docroot.childNodes.item(nChild));

      if (sTable != "")
         oDIV.insertAdjacentHTML("beforeEnd", sTable);
. . .
```

In our example, the child is the `<BYAUTHOR>` tag. Recall that under our DTD, the immediate children of the root are the search types `BYAUTHOR`, `BYDATE`, and `BYTITLE`. So far, the code is very similar to what we saw on the server, and with good reason. The parsing tasks are mirror images of one another, and the COM parser component behaves the same way in both environments. If you choose another technology to implement the parsing, you may encounter some minor problems depending on the server and the technology chosen. The combination of JavaScript and ActiveX is very friendly to programmers.

One slight difference is how we handle errors. On the server, we had no immediate user, so we had to transmit the error as an XML tag. Since this function is executing in the browser, however, we can take advantage of DHTML to present the user with a dialog box. For example:

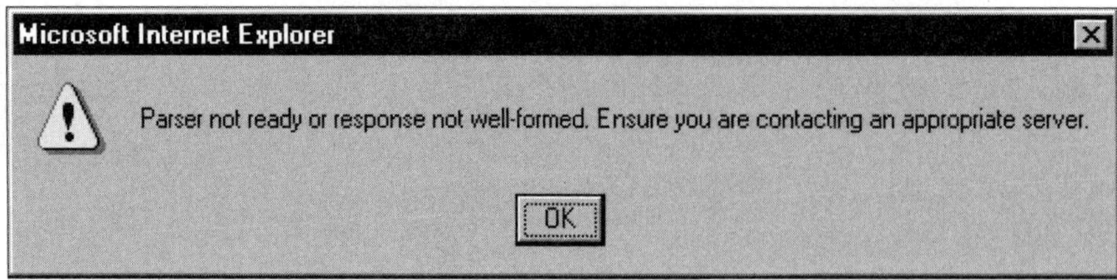

Preparing for Results

It would seem we're ready to do some serious HTML generation at this point, but we have one minor impediment. Our client page permits the user to transmit up to three distinct search requests at a time. It would be nice to check the search type in the XML response and provide a visual cue to the user so he knows what results correspond to which query. This is what we do in `HandleResults()`:

```
function HandleResults(node)
{
  var i;
  var sReply = "";
  var child;

  if (node.nodeType == 0) // an XML ELEMENT
  {
   if (node.nodeName == "BYAUTHOR")
     sReply = '<h2>Results from Author</h2>';

   if (node.nodeName == "BYTITLE")
     sReply = '<h2>Results from Title</h2>';

   if (node.nodeName == "BYPUBDATE")
     sReply = '<h2>Results from Publication Date</h2>';

   if (sReply != "")  // We have a result set we recognize
   {
     sReply = sReply + '<table border="1" width="100%">';

     for (i = 0; i < node.childNodes.length; i++)
     {
      /* Iterate through the children, responding only
        to what we recognize, i.e., papers */

      child = node.childNodes.item(i);
      if (child.nodeType == 0)
      {
        if (child.nodeName == "Paper")
         sReply = sReply + MakeHTMLFromPaper(child);

        if (child.nodeName == "NoResults")
         sReply = sReply + '<tr><td width="100%">No papers
           found</td></tr>';
      }
     }

     // Close out the table
     sReply = sReply + '</table>';
```

```
      }
    }
    return sReply; // may be empty
  }
```

We check the child node type and create a level two heading if we recognize the type. So for an author search, we have:

```
  if (node.nodeType == 0)
     {
     if (node.nodeName == "BYAUTHOR")
        sReply = '<h2>Results from Author</h2>';
  . . .
```

Now we turn our attention to the next level of the tree. This is where we expect to find `<paper>` tags. If we do, we hand control off to `MakeHTMLFromPaper()`. Recall, however, the server sends back `<NoResults></NoResults>` if no rows are returned from the database query. In this case, we write the HTML for a one row (`<tr>`), one cell (`<td>`) HTML table containing the text No papers found:

```
  if (child.nodeName == "Paper")
     sReply = sReply + MakeHTMLFromPaper(child);
  if (child.nodeName == "NoResults")
     sReply = sReply + '<tr><td width="100%">No papers found</td></tr>';
  . . .
```

Listing Summary Information in a Table

At last we've cleared away all the possible problems. By the time we reach `MakeHTMLFromPaper()`, we know we've got results and we know what kind of search generated them. We're ready to present the information to the user. The first part of the function closely resembles what we saw on the server. We look at each node, see what it is, and store it in the appropriate string for assembly into a larger string later. We're taking advantage of the self-describing nature of XML to give us some flexibility. If the tags come in at the right level of the parse tree but in some other order, we'll still be able to get the right information in the right cell of the table. We could have insisted on using the parser with DTD validation, but we want to keep things informal to accommodate minor, non-fatal errors in implementation.

```
  function MakeHTMLFromPaper(paperNode)
  {
    var i;
    var childNode;
    var sRow = "";
    var sPubTitle = "", sPubLink ="", sAuthor, sPubDate;

    for (i = 0; i < paperNode.childNodes.length; i++)
    {
        /* Iterate through the children and obtain the required pieces
           of data in whatever order they appear. */

        childNode = paperNode.childNodes.item(i);
```

```
        if (childNode.nodeType == 0) // check for ELEMENT node
        {
           if (childNode.nodeName == "title")
              sPubTitle = childNode.nodeValue;

           if (childNode.nodeName == "docURL")
              sPubLink = childNode.nodeValue;

           if (childNode.nodeName == "author")
              sAuthor = childNode.nodeValue;

           if (childNode.nodeName == "pubdate")
              sPubDate = childNode.nodeValue;
        }
    }
```

Now we have the pieces we need, so let's write them out as HTML. We want the cells in our table to be nicely aligned, so we include the `width` attribute in the cell (`<td>`) tag. We want each cell to be approximately one third of the width of the table.

```
    /* We have all the data items, so let's format
     a row in an HTML table. */

    sRow += '<tr><td width="34%">';

    /* First cell is a link if a URL was passed, simple
       text otherwise. */

    if (sPubLink != "")
    {
       sRow += '<a href="ViewPaper.asp?' + sPubLink + '">';
       if (sPubTitle != "")
          sRow += sPubTitle + '</a>';
       else
          sRow += 'Untitled paper' + '</a>';
    }
    else
    {
     if (sPubTitle != "")
       sRow += sPubTitle;
    }

    sRow += '</td><td width="33%">';
    if (sAuthor != "")
       sRow += sAuthor;
    sRow += '</td>';

    sRow = sRow + '<td width="33%">';
    if (sPubDate != "")
       sRow += sPubDate;
    sRow += '</td></tr>';

    return sRow;
 }
```

There's a bit of complication in the first cell. If the paper is listed in the database with a URL to the XML file containing the paper, we want a link. This is an anchor tag in HTML - `<a href=ViewPaper.asp?XML_paper>`. `ViewPaper.asp` is another ASP we use on the server to help handle the XML/XSL to HTML conversion. If the paper's title appears without the URL, i.e., we haven't got a copy of the paper, then we want the title to appear as simple text.

```
if (sPubLink != "")
{
   sRow += '<a href="ViewPaper.asp?' + sPubLink + '">';
   if (sPubTitle != "")
      sRow += sPubTitle + '</a>';
   else
      sRow += 'Untitled paper' + '</a>';
}
else
{
   if (sPubTitle != "")
      sRow += sPubTitle;
}
...
```

The last two cells, author and publication date, are straightforward.

Having composed a string containing the HTML for a row in the table, we return the string to the calling function, `HandleResults()`. It appends the result to a string it's been keeping of the HTML for an entire search. This string is returned to `HandleResponse()`, which adds it to the end of whatever content is in the results `<DIV>`:

```
sTable = HandleResults(docroot.childNodes.item(nChild));

if (sTable != "")
   oDIV.insertAdjacentHTML("beforeEnd", sTable);
```

Search by search, this is how the results are presented to the user.

Paper Presentation

Sooner or later, the user will want to see a technical paper. Presenting the raw XML would be something of a disappointment for the user, not to mention being hard to read. We've just gotten through generating a lot of DHTML in our code, and we'd like to have someone else do the work for a change. Fortunately, we were shrewd enough to select the Extensible Stylesheet Language (XSL) as our mode of presentation.

Several methods of associating presentation style with XML data exist. Two major ones are Cascading Style Sheets and the Extensible Stylesheet Language (XSL). The use of Cascading Style Sheets is more mature, although their use with XML is just beginning to be implemented in the major Web browsers. XSL, in turn, is still working its way through the specification process with the W3C. We are on the edge then, making a selection of technology solely on the basis of capability.

Cascading Style Sheets are easy to construct, but they do not permit more than the association of stylistic elements with XML tags. XSL, by contrast, is a rule-driven system based on the context of XML tags. It generates source code based on XML tags in a given context. Since both techniques are covered in Chapters 7 and 8 of this book, we're going to restrict our discussion here to the particular use of XSL in our sample application. For further information on style sheets, check out *Professional Style Sheets for HTML and XML*, from Wrox Press (ISBN 1-1861001-65-7).

XSL permits us to generate text that does not appear in the original XML. We want to present standard headings for the author's information and the abstract. Rather than force authors to include About the author and Abstract in every paper, we let XSL generate this text for us. XSL also permits us to shift the order of presentation of tags. If you examine the raw XML for our papers, you will find that the author's name precedes the picture, yet in our presentation the picture precedes the name. This is a trivial use of XSL, but it illustrates the ability to make significant structural changes in presentation with legacy XML. If we wished to make a major alteration to the presentation, perhaps to push the author's information to the end of the paper, we could simply modify our XSL style rules. The XML would remain unchanged. Indeed, since XSL rules are applied to XML at runtime, we could provide different presentation styles, even suppressing certain tags depending on the context in which the tags are found.

An ASP for Presentation

We again turn to Active Server Pages to implement the presentation of technical papers in our system. The actual generation of DHTML will occur on the client, but we need to take certain actions on the server. The page returned to the client will have an XSL processor component in it. Two properties need to be set: the XSL file to apply and the XML file to which the XSL file must be applied. The XSL file is the same for all papers, but we need a small piece of code in the ASP to retrieve the name of the desired XML file from the request string and insert it into the client page it is generating. Remember that this page, `ViewPaper.asp`, is requested with the URL `ViewPaper.asp?XML_Filename`. Here is the ASP source code:

```
    <script FOR="window" EVENT="onload">
      var xslHTML = XSLControl.htmlText;
      document.all.item("xslTarget").innerHTML = xslHTML;
    </script>

    <body>
      <object ID="XSLControl" CLASSID="CLSID:2BD0D2F2-52EC-11D1-8C69-0E16BC000000"
        CODEBASE="http://www.microsoft.com/xml/xsl/msxsl.cab" STYLE="display:none">
        <param NAME="documentURL"
            VALUE="<%=Request.ServerVariables("QUERY_STRING") %>">
        <param NAME="styleURL" VALUE="papers.xsl">
      </object>

      <div id="xslTarget"></div>

    </body>
  </html>
```

You'll recognize the `<object>` tag from our original client search page:

```
  <object ID="XSLControl" CLASSID="CLSID:2BD0D2F2-52EC-11D1-8C69-0E16BC000000"
        CODEBASE="http://www.microsoft.com/xml/xsl/msxsl.cab" STYLE="display:none">
```

The ID gives the component a name we can use in scripting. The CLASSID identifies the COM control to the operating system, allowing Internet Explorer to find the correct implementation. The CODEBASE attribute simply tells the browser where to go to obtain the control if it is not installed on the client system. The STYLE="display:none" attribute ensures the control remains invisible on the page. The only code executing on the server is the call to Request.ServerVariables() in the line:

```
<param NAME="documentURL" VALUE="<%=Request.ServerVariables("QUERY_STRING") %>">
```

Unlike our prior server-side code, we're using the <% code %> syntax to embed this line in the midst of HTML which should be returned to the client. The equals sign tells ASP to output the return value of the method call to the HTML stream going back to the client. Consequently, if the user requested the XML file robot.xml and subsequently viewed the HTML source in his browser, he would see:

<param NAME="documentURL" VALUE="robot.xml">.

How the XSL Processor Works

The XSL processor is an ActiveX component. It does the majority of the work required to present a paper in human-friendly form. Some idea of its burden can be gained from realizing that it must first perform all the tasks of the XML parser before it can get to the task of matching XSL rules to tags in the parse tree.

The XSL processor component is a technology preview from Microsoft. As such, its stability and compatibility varies with different versions of Internet Explorer. The application depicted used Internet Explorer 4.0 for rendering. At the time of this writing, the first working draft of the XSL specification had just been released. The draft makes substantial changes to the syntax used in this chapter. Reliable indications are that Microsoft will support the new syntax (Seen in Chapter 8) in their XSL processor at some future time, but obviously, I can only provide working style sheet rules in the old syntax. The changes do not effect the nature of XSL – rules applied to XML tags in some context – only the syntax. When and if Microsoft changes their component to reflect the new XSL changes, we would need to replace this component with the updated version.

Placing Formatted HTML into the Page

The interesting activity in this page occurs when it arrives on the client and is loaded. An instance of the XSL processor is created on the page. Its first task is to retrieve from the server the XML and XSL files referenced in its properties. Having done this, it applies the rules in the XSL file to the tags in the XML file to internally generate HTML. All this occurs before the browser finishes loading the page. When the page is fully loaded, the browser triggers the onload event. The following event handler in the page then executes:

```
<script FOR="window" EVENT="onload">
    var xslHTML = XSLControl.htmlText;
    document.all.item("xslTarget").innerHTML = xslHTML;
</script>
```

The processor's htmlText property is a string containing the HTML generated by applying the XSL rules to the XML tags. The next line simply sets the content of the <DIV> on this page named xslTarget equal to this string. Everything the user sees on the page is in this string and was generated by the XSL processor.

Combining XML Tags and XSL Rules

We've said the XSL processor applies style rules to XML tags. What, exactly, does this mean? An XSL file consists of a collection of rules to be matched with tags appearing in the text of the XML document. This matching process permits sophisticated, context-sensitive application of style rules, but our example is fairly simple.

Bear in mind this style sheet rule is written in the old syntax so as to work with the existing XSL processor from Microsoft. My intention here is to provide a feel for the nature of XSL and round out our sample with some simple visual presentation. The new syntax differs dramatically; however, the new approach still follows the same sequence: match some context of XML tags, then provide the specified output. XSL is covered in greater detail in Chapter 8.

One of the rules is designated as the root rule where processing begins:

```
<xsl>
<rule>
      <root/>
      <HTML>
            <SPAN>
                  <select-elements>
                        <target-element type="paper-title"/>
                  </select-elements>
                  <BR/>
                  <select-elements>
                        <target-element type="author"/>
                  </select-elements>
                  <BR/>
                  <select-elements>
                        <target-element type="document-body"/>
                  </select-elements>
            </SPAN>
      </HTML>
</rule>
```

This says we've selected the title, author block, and document body of the paper for display (<select-elements> tag in the rule), in that order. The XML tags to match are indicated as the type attribute of <target-elements> tags in the XSL rules. We earlier suggested moving the author's block to the end of the presented document. If you swap the <target elements> tags for "author" and "document-body", that is exactly what will happen. The <author> tag, however, contains other tags within it, so the processor continues to try to match rules to tags within <author>.

We've decided we want a stock caption, About the author, in white letters on a teal bar. Following that, we want to create the HTML to include the image (with alternate text) of the author followed by the author's name and curriculum vitae. Note that we're reversing the order of appearance for the image and the author's name from how they appear in the XML file.

```
<rule>
      <target-element type="author"/>
      <DIV background-color="teal"
           color="white"
           font-family="Verdana,arial,helvetica,sans-serif"
           font-size="12pt" padding="4px"> About the author </DIV>
      <SPAN font-family="Verdana, arial, helvetica, sans-serif">
```

```
            <select-elements>
                  <target-element type="picture"/>
            </select-elements>

            <select-elements>
                  <target-element type="name"/>
            </select-elements>
            <BR/><BR/>
            <select-elements>
                  <target-element type="cv"/>
            </select-elements>
      </SPAN>
</rule>

<rule>
      <target-element type="picture"/>
      <SPAN>
            <IMG SRC="=text" ALT="Author's likeness"/>
      </SPAN>
</rule>

<rule>
      <target-element type="name"/>
      <SPAN font-size="12pt">
      <children/>
      </SPAN>
</rule>

<rule>
      <target-element type="cv"/>
      <DIV background-color="#EEEEEE" color="black" font-size="10pt">
            <children/>
      </DIV>
</rule>
```

Everything inside the <select-elements> tag and following the <target-element/> tag is HTML we want written. In the "`picture`" element, we use the "`=text`" directive to write out the value of the tag:

```
<rule>
      <target-element type="picture"/>
      <SPAN>
            <IMG SRC="=text" ALT="Author's likeness"/>
      </SPAN>
</rule>
```

We perform similar formatting for the paper's title and abstract before going on to the document body.

```
<rule>
      <target-element type="paper-title"/>
      <SPAN font-family="Arial, helvetica, sans-serif" font-size="14pt"
      _align="left">
            <children/>
      </SPAN>
```

```
        <BR/>
    </rule>

    <rule>
        <target-element type="document-body"/>
            <select-elements>
                <target-element type="abstract"/>
            </select-elements>
            <BR/><BR/>
            <select-elements>
                <target-element type="paper-text"/>
            </select-elements>
    </rule>

    <rule>
        <target-element type="abstract"/>
        <DIV background-color="teal" color="white" font
        _family="Verdana,arial,helvetica,sans-serif" font-size="12pt" padding="4px">
        _Abstract </DIV>
        <DIV id="abstract" font-family="Verdana, arial, helvetica, sans-serif"
        _font-size="10pt" color="black" background-color="#EEEEEE">
            <children/>
        </DIV>
    </rule>

    <rule>
```

Namespaces, Metadata, and Future Applications

Back when we were generating well-formed XML on the client, we noted that it might be desirable to be able to obtain a DTD for validating the XML. But we've used XML in the hope of facilitating interactions between clients and servers with no prior coordination. How can we discover the proper application semantics at the time of the transaction? Two ongoing experiments in the XML community called **namespaces** and **XML-Data** may provide the answer.

XML Namespaces

It became clear to XML architects that documents might be composed using schemas from several sources. Common tag names could then conflict. We use the common term `paper`. It is extremely unlikely that we are the first, nor even the last, people on the Web to decide to use this name for an XML tag. Clients need to know which element definition to use. Namespaces are a means of noting the source of the definition that applies to a particular tag. You insert an element into your document which establishes a name for your namespace. An attribute of the element provides the URL for the source of the schema. Tags whose names may conflict with others are given the URL's name as a prefix. At present, this is the syntax we might use in a future implementation of our system:

```
<PaperResponse xmlns:TechPapers="http://www.mypapers.org/schema/>
...
</PaperResponse>
```

Namespaces are still a working draft at the W3C. Syntax and capabilities of namespaces may surely change as this concept evolves. We are presenting this strictly as an illustration of what might be available to programmers in the near future.

Clearly, this is a step in the right direction. Namespaces would let us interrogate the authoritative source of application semantics for some body of XML tags. Our hypothetical software agent could "learn" about the information conveyed in a set of XML tags identified by a namespace. Unfortunately, there is one little problem. DTDs are written in a different syntax to XML. Does this mean every client, be it agent, browser, or middleware facilitator, must support two parsers – one for XML syntax and one for DTD syntax? Another initiative, XML-Data, at an even earlier stage of the standardization process, may answer this problem and add a new opportunity of its own.

XML-Data

XML-Data is an XML vocabulary for defining metadata schemas. Schemas can be syntactic, as in XML itself, or conceptual, as in object models and relational databases. XML-Data, therefore, provides a way of defining an arbitrary construct for our application semantics in XML format. We're back to supporting a single parser, providing we require all XML validating parsers to have implicit knowledge of XML-Data.

> *XML-Data is a note submitted to the W3C. This means the organization acknowledges receipt of the submission but neither endorses it nor promises to commit resources to evaluating it. While some sort of metadata description syntax expressed in XML is likely to become part of the XML family, do not expect to be able to base actual programs on XML-Data features for some time.*

If XML-Data becomes part of the toolset of the server application developer, we have another opportunity. In our system, we had two types of data the user could obtain: paper summary information and complete technical papers. The data contained in our database was hidden from the user. Although this encapsulation is good programming practice, it is desirable to be able to describe additional information the user could obtain. Thus, we might use XML-Data to describe some further subset of the database schema. A client could be told that additional information is available regarding the author, for example.

The last vestiges of rigid coupling between implementing code and data semantics are crumbling. Our automated clients of the future will communicate with servers unknown to them by obtaining the schema of the XML vocabularies they speak. They will discover what information they contain. If these suit their capabilities and search goals, they will compose valid XML transactions and process XML-encoded responses.

Summary

We've seen how XML can be used to facilitate client-server transactions using XML. Specifically, we've explored the fundamentals of the following tasks:

- ❑ Programmatically generating well-formed XML
- ❑ Transferring XML from the client to the server by one of several means
- ❑ Parsing XML using Microsoft's ActiveX implementation of the XML DOM
- ❑ Turning XML into DHTML elements for display
- ❑ Rendering XML using the ActiveX XSL processor technology preview component

We've also established a motivation for using XML in preference to more traditional techniques. In contrast to older methods, XML is an open, self-describing format rendered in a data type – text – supported by every conceivable platform. At present, this allows us to be tolerant of small errors in the implementation of our DTD, provided we use well-formed XML rather than formal, DTD-validated XML. In the course of this exploration, we created a server which, although demonstrated with a human user in mind, could be used by programmatic agents without any change to the server-side code. This is a complete departure from most server applications written with some methods commonly in use.

Finally, we looked to the future and saw the promise XML brings to distributed applications over the Internet. The strengths of XML, if combined with several new initiatives, will give us the ability to create powerful applications of unconventional agents cooperating with client-neutral servers. These ad hoc collaborations will use "just in time" discovery of server capabilities to accomplish the goals of the user. XML, a humble text-driven format, promises to be powerful indeed.

11

Case Study 1 - The Travel Broker

This chapter illustrates an XML application architecture. First, we review some key reasons as to why XML enables the production of applications never before possible. A specific problem is then outlined and the architecture for solving the problem is discussed. Finally, each component is detailed with code examples. Specifically, we start by covering the following topics:

- Key features of XML
- How XML is used in a 3-tier architecture
- Steps in designing an XML DTD
- Mapping a database to an XML document
- Implementation of an XML server with Microsoft tools

The architecture of the application is based on a three-tier architecture including Data Services, Business Services and User Services. Business Services act as an agent to fetch data from various sources according to a user's request and consolidate it into a single source. User Services take the information from the Business Services and format it for presentation to the user. We finish by covering:

- How to use the Document Object Model (DOM) to process an XML document
- How to create a new XML document from a collection of other XML documents
- How to use the Microsoft MSXSL processor from VBScript within an Active Server Page
- How to write an XSL Style Sheet to format an XML document on the server

This case study requires knowledge of VBScript in Active Server Pages (ASP), and also some familiarity with databases, specifically SQL. The database is accessed with ActiveX Data Objects (ADO) so an understanding of ADO helps. Finally the transport for the application is HTTP so an understanding of URLs is also important.

The Travel Broker

Here is the scenario. You want to find a resort to go to for a holiday. You have constraints such as the following:

- Amount of money you want to spend
- The day you leave
- Country to visit
- Amenities of the resort

Not only do you have these constraints but you also want to try and ensure that the weather is going to be nice. Arriving in the middle of the stormy season would not be enjoyable! You decide to try to find a holiday destination using the World Wide Web. You access a search engine and then start browsing Web sites. You realize you have to get out your pencil and paper and draw up a matrix to do comparisons. After a couple of hours you think – there has to be a better way.

The Solution

Then you find the answer to your prayers – The Travel Broker! The Travel Broker is a Web site (sorry, it is a mythical Web site at this point) that will automatically find a holiday package for you based on your criteria. You specify what you want in a holiday and the type of weather you hope to have and voilà! – You get a prioritized listing of holiday packages from different travel package vendors.

Of course, there are broker Web sites like this that already exist on the World Wide Web. The problem is that most broker Web sites require a lot of maintenance to keep data from different sources up to date. A broker Web site does not sell anything itself, it just collects the information from many vendors and collates them together. The collation process is manual. The broker Webmaster has to get information from each vendor and assemble it together. A better way is for vendors to publish their information in a well-known format so brokers can automatically obtain it. This eliminates the manual data acquisition and collating step and ensures the data is up to date. The automated web sites that do exist typically use technologies that are difficult to use (e.g. LDAP and EDI). Fortunately, XML ensures a common data schema while having a low barrier to authorship. Let us look at the architecture to implement this solution.

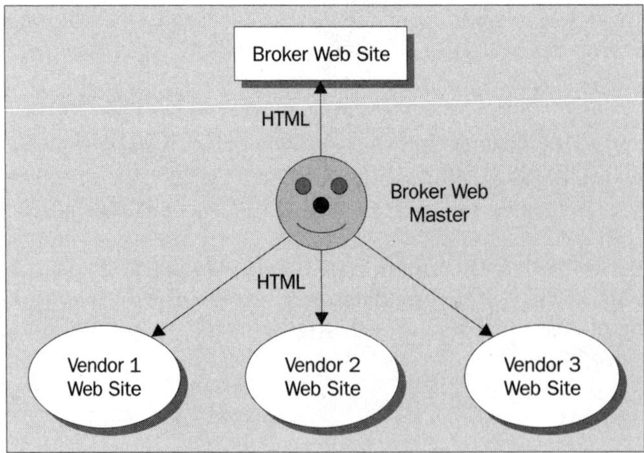

Our XML-based alternative would have a similar structure, but with an application replacing the task of manual integration.

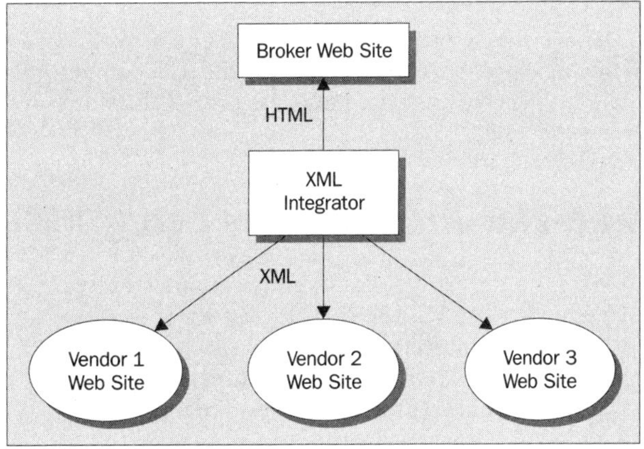

The Architecture

Many enterprises are moving towards business solutions constructed from a logical network of services. Each service both supplies and consumes data and functionality from other services. These services may be distributed across both physical distance and different operating systems. Often the logical network is implemented with a three-tier architecture. This model fits very well with a Web-based application using XML. A generic three-tier architecture will be discussed and then we will see how it fits in with our web-based application.

Three-Tier Architecture

A three-tier architecture is logically divided into three distinct areas: data services, business services and user services. Each tier has its own responsibilities. Together they form a cohesive, flexible and scalable application. Note that the application may use all of the services or just some of them. For example, user services for a banking application may use two different data services: one data service for bill payment and one data service for bank account activity. Note the designer of such a system would have to consider a transaction mechanism to ensure consistency between data services.

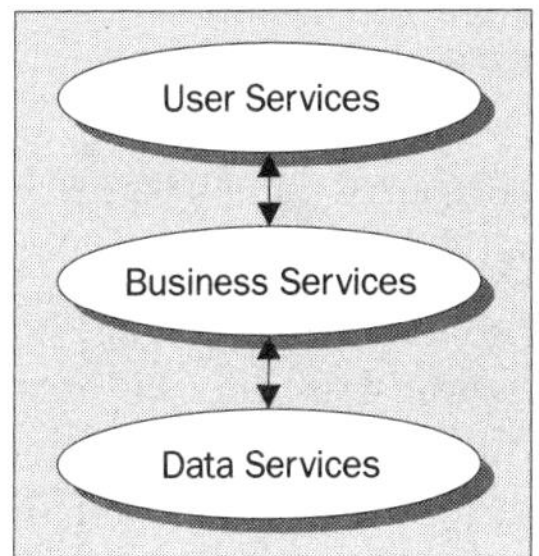

Data Services

Data services are responsible for locating and storing data. Data services provide an abstraction for the business services so the business services need not know where the data is located, how it is implemented or how it is accessed. Data services should provide mechanisms for keeping data integrity such as transaction management.

Business Services

Business services are responsible for implementing business specific rules. They interact with data services by requesting and storing data. Operations, calculations and validation may be applied to retrieved data. Business services transform data into information by the application of rules. Business services are non-visual.

User Services

User services are the visual portion of an information application. They format and display the data. They also provide mechanisms for the user to manipulate the data. Properly defined user services take into account the activities the users will be involved with and the style of interaction the users are expecting.

Three-Tier Architecture using XML

XML fits very well into a three-tier architecture. XML is the glue between service layers. It enables different user interfaces to be used for the same application and it enables applications to transparently use different sources of data.

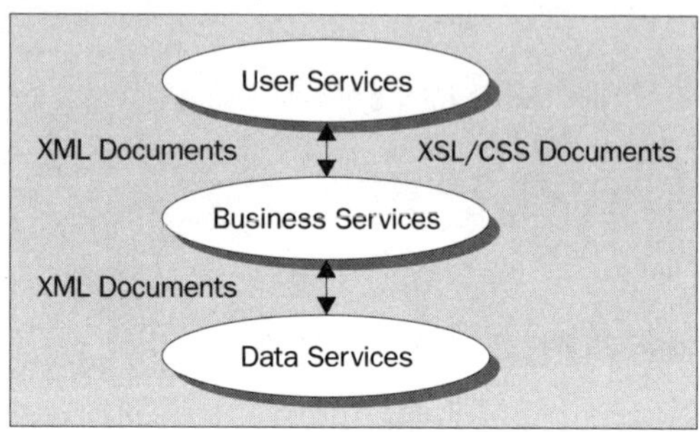

Data Services – XML Document Generation

The source of data for an application resides with the data services. The user of the data services does not care how the data is stored. XML is an ideal format for data services since it acts as a common format for different data stores. It opens up the data services tier enabling data to be published in a well-known format. Anyone can now use the data without having to use specialized APIs for each type of data source. The data services implement the publishing of structured data, in XML. An example of data services implemented with XML is a library exposing their database of books through XML documents.

Business Services – Data Integration

Business services in an XML application acts like an agent on behalf of the user. It takes the user's request, decides what information is required and how to get it. After receiving the information it synthesizes it into a form usable by the user. For example a user's request may generate a request of 10 XML documents from different data sources. The business services tier processes the documents, resulting in a single XML document to present to the user. Business services provides automated searching and filtering as well as integrating diverse information in XML.

User Services – HTML Presentation

User services prepare the data for human use. The advantage of using XML is that the presentation can easily be changed without affecting the data itself. To render (present) the information, HTML is an ideal choice since HTML is the rendering language for all current Web browsers. There are various choices of converting the data from XML to HTML. The document can be formatted on the web server and sent to the client as HTML or the XML document can be sent directly to the client browser with formatting instructions. Theoretically, formatting instructions can be either a CSS or XSL style sheet. Let us look at the issues in more detail.

Formatting on the Server

The advantage of formatting the document for presentation on the server is the protection obtained from different browser implementations of XSL or Cascading Style Sheets (CSS). The disadvantage is that the server now has additional work to do, delaying the response to the client. This is unfortunate because offloading work to the client is an important goal. In this case, the web server has an XSL or CSS processor built-in to create the HTML document sent to the client.

Formatting on the Client

Sending an XML document with formatting instructions to the browser offloads work from the server to the client. This results in better overall system performance. However, since each browser works from a different code-base for processing XSL and CSS (if they even support XSL or CSS) results are unpredictable. Doing formatting on the client works well in an Intranet situation because the type and version of the browser can be ensured across the users.

Formatting Using CSS

CSS 1 has been around since December 1996 and has thus had a chance to make it into the development community. Portions of CSS 1 already work with HTML in IE 3.0, IE 4.0 and Navigator 4.0. CSS does not work with XML on any current web browsers. IE 5 will have some support for using CSS and XML. For more information on Style Sheets see Professional Style Sheets for HTML and XML (ISBN 1-861001-657), from Wrox Press.

Formatting Using XSL

XSL is currently under development. The first working draft was released on the 18th of August '98. This means that presently it is not a good idea to design a production system using XSL since the specifications may change. As well, there is no native support for XSL in mainstream browsers yet. The advantage of a three-tier XML architecture is you can implement user services using CSS 1 initially and switch over to XSL when it is more robust without impacting the rest of the system.

Using Multiple Solutions

In a production system, one solution is to implement multiple solutions. This type of solution is seen now where people create different versions of their web-site for different browsers. In addition, some people also have Java version and non-Java versions as well as a Frames version and a non-Frames version of their web site. Either the user is given the choice of which type of web site to use or the web server determines which browser is making the request and automatically serves the correct documents. It sounds like a lot more work but the advantage is that you can use the advanced features of the browsers to off-load some of the work to the client and also have more exciting web pages.

For example in an XML situation, you can set up the application with the following rules:

- If the browser is IE4, return an XML document with a CSS
- Otherwise, format the document as HTML using an XSL processor on the server and return it to the client OR
- Format the document as HTML using a CSS on the server and return it to the client

From a development point of view, the content (the XML document) stays the same no matter the type of browser. The choice is then up to the developer to either maintain both a CSS and an XSL document for styling or just use CSS for styling.

We are about to move into the detailed implementation of the Travel Broker. The following diagram shows the relationship of the conceptual three-tier architecture to the actual implemented components. The name of the zip file containing all the required source code for a component is also given.

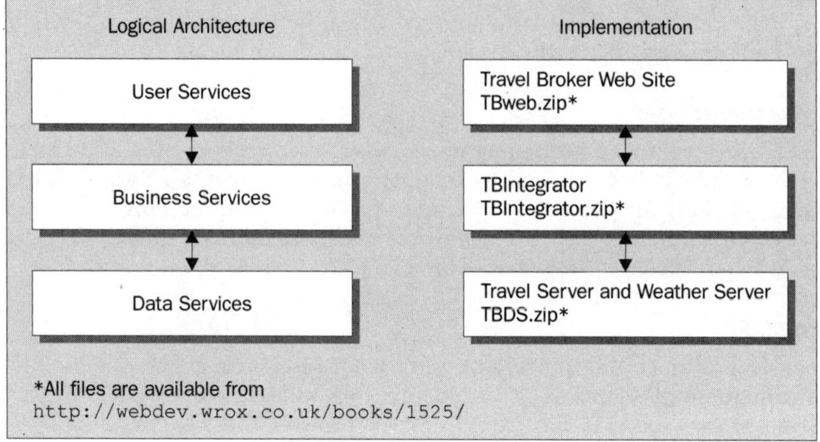

Travel Broker Data Services

The Travel Broker XML Server is the data services portion of the Travel Broker application. It is responsible for maintaining the data required for the Travel Broker application. As well, it is responsible for publishing the data in a well defined format, that is, as an XML document.

The travel package data includes what packages are available, when they are available and how much they cost. We also need weather information so the data services have support for providing weather conditions for different locations at different times of the year.

For our Travel Broker application we are only performing an inquiry for available travel packages to the data services. In a real system other applications, for example a booking application, would also use the data services. Weather information might be passed to other independent applications as well: those relating to farming or air traffic, for instance. As you may be aware, such data is usually stored in databases.

Databases

There are two databases that our application will need to use.

Travel Package Database

The travel package database holds all the package information a travel vendor has available. Vendors, or agencies, would have their own database. The information stored includes a description of the holiday, when the holiday is available and how many places are left for a particular departure time.

Structure

The travel package database is divided into three tables. The tables are `Packages`, `Price` and `Availability`. The schema is depicted in the following diagram:

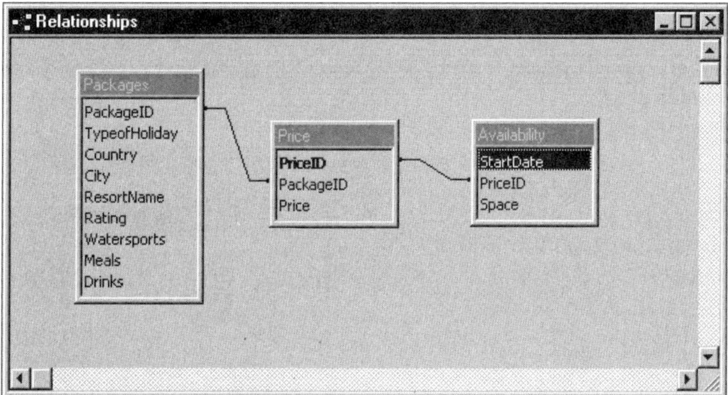

The Packages table describes a holiday a person could take. Country, City and ResortName indicate the location of the holiday. Samples of the resort qualities represented in the database are TypeofHoliday, Rating, Watersports, Meals and Drinks. Depending on the time of year, the prices for a resort holiday vary, so the price is stored in a separate table called Price. Finally, the actually allocated departure time and the number of places available for that time are stored in another table called Availability.

Implementation

For our example we have generated a Microsoft Access database. We will be accessing the database via **ODBC** so if you want you can use the defined schema and build your own database. ODBC is an acronym for **Open Database Connectivity** and provides a common API regardless of the database management system (DBMS). The database is available at

```
http://webdev.wrox.co.uk/books/1525/
```

You can request the database with your browser and then save it to disk when the dialog pops up. Once you have done that we have to hook it up to ODBC.

In the Windows Control panel, double-click on the ODBC icon. Then click on the System DSN property page tab. Since the web server will access the database it has to be a system DSN. Then click Add and then select Microsoft Access Driver. Finally, fill out the dialog as in the following screen shot. Note that when you select the database you put the path of where you saved the database.

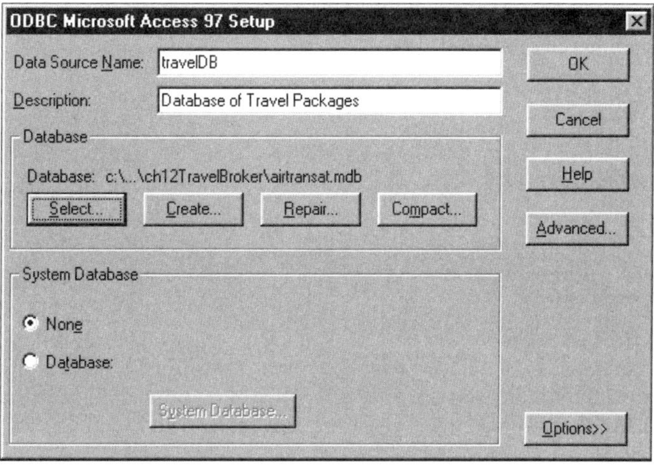

There, now we can easily access the database via ODBC.

Weather Database

The weather database holds seasonal weather information for various cities around the world. It represents typical weather for a given month. Temperature ranges, average wind and average precipitation is included.

Structure

The weather database has two tables: `Location` and `Weather`. The database structure is depicted in the following diagram.

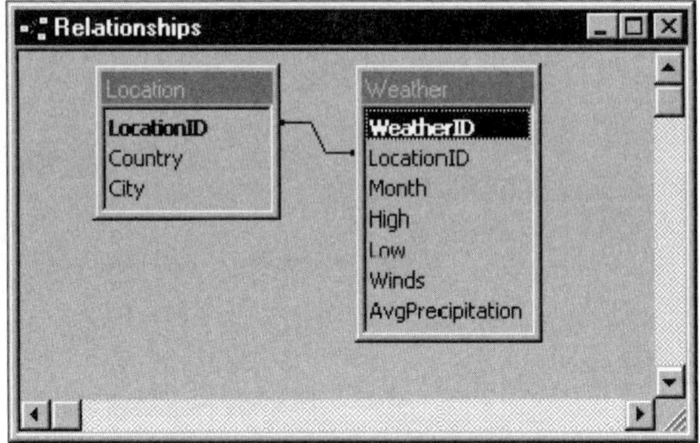

The `Location` table holds the city and country for which weather records are stored. The `Weather` table links into the `Location` table and has the weather details for each month of the year. Weather details that are recorded are the high and low (in Celsius), the wind speeds (in km/h) and the average precipitation for that month.

Database Implementation

A sample Microsoft Access database is available at: `http://webdev.wrox.co.uk/books/1525/`
Again, this database needs to be hooked up to ODBC. Follow the same steps as implementing the travel database but change the final dialog box to look like the following diagram.

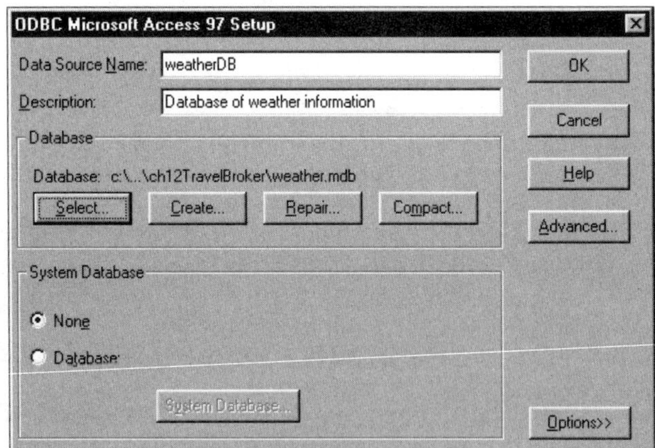

XML DTDs

In order to achieve the goal of "Publishing of well-formed data", we need to publish the rules for organizing the data. The organizational rules for the data are published with a DTD. The DTD many be used by many people and is the basis for the way in which they interpret the data. For these reasons it is important to put time and effort into creating a DTD.

Attributes vs. Elements

One of the big discussions about DTD designs is whether to use elements or attributes to represent information. There is no one correct way to design a DTD. Since I come from an object-oriented background, I used object-oriented ideas to guide my XML design. Basically, if some information is a "has-a" relationship I code it with an element. If information is an "is-a" relationship, I use an attribute. For example, if I was describing a car, the doors, windows and engine would all be elements because a car has all those objects. However, color, brand and year would all be attributes of a car.

Travel Broker DTD

In order that developers know how to conform to a travel package document, they need some rules. Following is the travel package DTD outlining those rules.

```
<!-- DTD for a travel packages document -->

<!-- Start of element declarations -->
<!ELEMENT travelpackages (country*)>
<!ELEMENT country (city+)>
<!ELEMENT city (resort+)>
<!ELEMENT resort (package+)>
<!ELEMENT package EMPTY>
<!-- End of element declarations -->

<!-- Start of attribute declarations -->
<!ATTLIST country name CDATA #REQUIRED>
<!ATTLIST city name CDATA #REQUIRED>
<!ATTLIST resort
    name CDATA #REQUIRED
    rating (1|2|3|4|5) #IMPLIED
    typeofholiday (Beach|Touring) #IMPLIED
    watersports (True|False) #IMPLIED
    meals (True|False) #IMPLIED
    drinks (True|False) #IMPLIED>
<!ATTLIST package
    dateofdep CDATA #REQUIRED
    price CDATA #REQUIRED>
<!-- End of attribute declarations -->
```

We see the root element of the document is `travelpackages`. The root element can contain zero or more `country` elements. If the travel server queried returns a document with no `country` elements this means that no records were found. A `country` element must contain one or more `city` elements. We are enforcing the rule that if a country is returned it must contain additional information in its child nodes. A `city` element must contain one or more `resort` elements. A resort is the specific place we would actually go for the holiday. Finally, a `resort` element must contain one or more `package` elements. A package is when we would depart for the resort and how much it would cost. A `package` element cannot contain any child elements.

`country` and `city` each have one attribute: `name`. The name attribute identifies the country or city and thus is required.

A `resort` also requires a `name` attribute. In addition to the `name` attribute, a `resort` element has implied attributes describing it. Since the attributes are implied, they may or may not be listed. The optional attributes are listed below.

- `rating` – The rating of the resort on a scale from 1 to 5.
- `typeofholiday` – A categorization of the holiday. It can be a `Beach` or `Touring` holiday.
- `watersports` – Values: `True` or `False`. If this attribute is `True`, the resort has watersports.
- `meals` – If this attribute is `True`, the resort has meals included.
- `drinks` – If this attribute is `True`, the resort has drinks include.

Note that for the attributes taking a value of true or false, an absence of the attribute does not mean that the resort does not have that feature. Rather, its absence means it cannot be determined if the resort has that particular feature. Another way to accomplish this would be to have a required tri-state attribute of `True`, `False` and `Unknown`.

A `package` has two required attributes `dateofdep` and `price`. The date the holiday begins is represented by the `dateofdep` element. The price for one person is represented by the `price` element.

Here is a sample document generated according to the DTD:

```
<?xml version="1.0"?>
<!DOCTYPE travelpackages SYSTEM "travel.dtd">
<travelpackages>
    <country name="Cuba">
        <city name="Cayo Coco">
            <resort name="Club Tryp Cayo Coco" rating ="4" typeofholiday ="Beach"
                              watersports ="True" meals ="True" drinks ="True">
                <package dateofdep="5/8/98" price="879"/>
                <package dateofdep="5/1/98" price="879"/>
            </resort>
        </city>
        <city name="Varadero">
            <resort name="Sol Club Palmeras" rating ="3" typeofholiday ="Beach"
                           watersports ="False" meals ="True" drinks ="False">
                <package dateofdep="5/30/98" price="799"/>
                <package dateofdep="5/23/98" price="889"/>
                <package dateofdep="5/16/98" price="889"/>
            </resort>
        </city>
    </country>
</travelpackages>
```

Here we see two resorts are available according to our query. Both are in Cuba, one in Cayo Coco and one in Varadero. Both are Beach holidays, one has watersports and the other does not. Both have meals included and one has drinks included. Finally, there are a variety of departure dates available.

Weather DTD

In order that developers know how to conform to a weather document, they need some rules. Following is the weather package DTD outlining those rules.

```
<!-- DTD for a weather document -->

<!-- Start of element declarations -->
<!ELEMENT weather (country*)>
```

```
<!ELEMENT country (city+)>
<!ELEMENT city (month+)>
<!ELEMENT month (avgprecipitation? | winds? | high | low)>
<!ELEMENT avgprecipitation EMPTY>
<!ELEMENT winds EMPTY>
<!ELEMENT high EMPTY>
<!ELEMENT low EMPTY>
<!-- End of element declarations -->

<!-- Start of attribute declarations -->

<!ATTLIST country name CDATA #REQUIRED>
<!ATTLIST city name CDATA #REQUIRED>
<!ATTLIST month
     name (january|february|march|april|may|
           june|july|august|september|october|november|december) #REQUIRED>
<!ATTLIST avgprecipitation
    cm CDATA #REQUIRED
    in CDATA #IMPLIED>
<!ATTLIST winds
    km/h CDATA #REQUIRED
    mph CDATA #IMPLIED>
<!ATTLIST high
            c CDATA #REQUIRED
            f CDATA #IMPLIED>
<!ATTLIST low percent
            c CDATA #REQUIRED
            f CDATA #IMPLIED>
<!-- End of attribute declarations -->
```

The root element of the document is `weather`. Similar to the travel DTD, the root element can have zero or more `country` elements. If a `country` element exists, it must have child elements. The child of a `country` element is `city`. The child of a `city` element is `month`. A `month` element must have a temperature range so the `high` and `low` elements are required. There can be zero or one `avgprecipitation` elements and zero or one `winds` elements. Note that measurements can be listed both in metric and imperial. Since one can be derived from another, metric is required and imperial is optional.

Again, `country` and `city` elements must be identified so they have a required `name` attribute. The `month` element also has a required `name` attribute. For the description of the weather we allow different measurement units by using the attributes. Metric is required and imperial is optional.

Here is a sample document generated according to the DTD:

```
<?xml version="1.0"?>
<!DOCTYPE weather SYSTEM "weather.dtd">
<weather>
    <country name="United States">
        <city name="Fort Lauderdale">
            <month name="April">
                <avgprecipitation CM="8"/>
                <winds kph="40"/>
                <high c="28"/>
                <low c="21"/>
            </month>
```

```
            <month name="May">
                <avgprecipitation CM="6"/>
                <winds kph="45"/>
                <high c="30"/>
                <low c="22"/>
            </month>
        </city>
    </country>
</weather>
```

This document shows the weather for Fort Lauderdale in the United States for April and May. Details for the weather include the average precipitation in centimeters, the wind speed in kilometers per hour and the temperature high and low in Celsius.

Implementation with ASP and ADO

The data services transport interface is implemented via HTTP. HTTP has been chosen as the communication protocol between tiers, over others such as DCOM and CORBA, for a few reasons. HTTP is probably the most widely known protocol so it is good for teaching examples such as this one. It is also lightweight, has support on various operating systems and is cheap. One disadvantage is that unless precautions are taken it is not very secure.

For this demonstration we will be using Microsoft IIS4 with Active Server Pages (ASP), VBScript and ActiveX Data Objects (ADO). Other systems could be used provided the interfaces stay the same. In fact, the idea behind XML and three-tier architecture is to allow different systems to cooperate and create an integrated, but diverse, system.

This implementation was chosen for a few reasons. XML documents can be generated without any specialized components with this system. VBScript is easy to follow so it is good for demonstration purposes. As well, many people are familiar with the ASP/VBScript/ADO setup. A disadvantage is you would not get the same performance as a solution that is compiled to native executable code. As well, there is no validation performed against the generated XML document.

If you want to see a demonstration without waiting, go to `http://webdev.wrox.co.uk/books/1525/`.

Travel Server

The travel server is implemented as an Active Server Page using IIS4. Travel vendors would each have their own travel server. A client prepares an HTTP request as a URL, makes the request and receives a response via HTTP. Let us look at the process in detail.

Input

The request is made up of the web server name, the active server page name and the parameters for the query. The parameters are contained in the URL as name-value pairs in the query string. Specifically, the request is of the form:

```
http://server/travelds.asp?Country=VAL1&City=VAL2&Month=VAL3&Watersports=V
AL4&Price=VAL5&Space=VAL6
```

server	the domain name of the travel server
Country (optional)	the country that travel packages are requested for
City (optional)	the city that travel packages area requested for
Month (optional)	the month that a travel package is requested
Watersports (optional)	True if the travel package has watersports
Price (optional)	the maximum price for the travel package
Space (optional)	the number of people for the travel package
VAL(1-6)	are the values to constrain the match

Optional means that name-value pair does not need to be included in the URL.

Output

The output generated is an XML document that adheres to our travel package DTD. It contains the results according to the details of the request passed in. If none of the parameters are specified all the records are returned. Let us look at an example:
`http://server/travelds.asp?Country=Canada&Month=January`.

In this case, all the available travel records for Canada in January are returned. Most likely these are all ski holidays considering the country and time of year. If you weren't aware of the weather conditions for a Canadian winter and were hoping for a beach holiday you would be in for a surprise. This is where selection by using a weather server comes in!

Implementation

Following is the ASP code for the file `travelds.asp`. It does all the work required from receiving the request to returning the resulting XML document.

```
<%@ LANGUAGE=VBSCRIPT%>
<% Response.ContentType = "text/plain" %>
<%

' Build the SQL query from the form variables passed in the URL.
Dim curCountry
Dim firstCountry
Dim curCity
Dim firstCity
Dim resort
Dim firstResort
Dim doEndTags

firstCountry = True
firstCity = True
firstResort = True
doEndTags = False

SQLStatement = "SELECT * FROM Price tPrice, Packages tPkg, Availability tAvail
WHERE tPkg.PackageId = tPrice.PackageId AND tPrice.PriceID = tAvail.PriceID"
```

```
If Len( Request.QueryString( "Month" ) ) > 0 Then
    SQLStatement = SQLStatement + " AND Month( tAvail.StartDate ) = '" +
Request.QueryString( "Month" ) + "'"
End If
If (Len( Request.QueryString( "Country" ) ) > 0) AND Request.QueryString(
"Country" ) <> "Any" Then
    SQLStatement = SQLStatement + " AND tPkg.Country = '" + Request.QueryString(
"Country" ) + "'"
End If
If Len( Request.QueryString( "City" ) ) > 0 Then
    SQLStatement = SQLStatement + " AND tPkg.City = '" + Request.QueryString(
"City" ) + "'"
End If
If Len( Request.QueryString( "Watersports" ) ) > 0 Then
    SQLStatement = SQLStatement + " AND tPkg.Watersports = " +
Request.QueryString( "Watersports" )
End If
If Len( Request.QueryString( "Price" ) ) > 0 Then
    SQLStatement = SQLStatement + " AND tPrice.Price <= " + Request.QueryString(
"Price" )
End If
If Len( Request.QueryString( "Space" ) ) > 0 Then
    SQLStatement = SQLStatement + " AND tAvail.Space >= " + Request.QueryString(
"Space" )
End If

SQLStatement = SQLStatement + " ORDER BY tPkg.Country, tPkg.City, tPkg.ResortName"
%>

<?xml version="1.0"?>
<!DOCTYPE travelpackages SYSTEM "travel.dtd">
<travelpackages>
<%
    Set Conn = Server.CreateObject("ADODB.Connection")
    Conn.Open "travelDB"
    Set travelRecs = Conn.Execute(SQLStatement)

    ' Loop through the records creating XML elements.
    Do While Not travelRecs.EOF

        doEndTags = True

        ' Start a new COUNTRY element if we are into a new one.
        If curCountry <> travelRecs( "COUNTRY" ) Then
            If firstCountry = False Then
                Response.Write( vbTab + vbTab + vbTab + "</resort>" + vbNewLine )
                Response.Write( vbTab + vbTab + "</city>" + vbNewLine )
                Response.Write( vbTab + "</country>" + vbNewLine )
                firstResort = True
                firstCity = True
            End If
            curCountry = travelRecs( "COUNTRY" )
            Response.Write( vbTab + "<country name=" + Chr(34) + curCountry +
Chr(34)
                        + ">" + vbNewLine )
            firstCountry = False
        End If
```

```
    ' Start a new CITY element if we are into a new one.
    If curCity <> travelRecs( "CITY" ) Then
        If firstCity = False Then
            Response.Write( vbTab + vbTab + vbTab + "</resort>" + vbNewLine )
            Response.Write( vbTab + vbTab + "</city>" + vbNewLine )
            firstResort = True
        End If
        curCity = travelRecs( "CITY" )
        Response.Write( vbTab + vbTab + "<city name=" + Chr(34) + curCity +
                        Chr(34) + ">" + vbNewLine )
        firstCity = False
    End If

    ' Start a new RESORT element if we are into a new one.
    If curResort <> travelRecs( "RESORTNAME" ) Then
        If firstResort = False Then
            Response.Write( vbTab + vbTab + "</resort>" + vbNewLine )
        End If
        curResort = travelRecs( "RESORTNAME" )
        Response.Write( vbTab + vbTab + vbTab + "<resort name=" + Chr(34) +
                        curResort + Chr(34) )
        Response.Write( " vendor =" + Chr(34) + "Sunquest" + Chr(34) )
        Response.Write( " rating =" + Chr(34) + CStr(travelRecs( "RATING" )) +
                        Chr(34) )
        Response.Write( " typeofholiday =" + Chr(34) + CStr(travelRecs(
                          "TYPEOFHOLIDAY" )) + Chr(34) )
        Response.Write( " watersports =" + Chr(34) + CStr(travelRecs(
                          "WATERSPORTS" )) + Chr(34) )
        Response.Write( " meals =" + Chr(34) + CStr(travelRecs( "MEALS" )) +
                        Chr(34) )
        Response.Write( " drinks =" + Chr(34) + CStr(travelRecs( "DRINKS" )) +
                        Chr(34) + ">" + vbNewLine )
        firstResort = False
    End If

  %>
              <package dateofdep="<%=travelRecs( "STARTDATE" )%>"
                       price="<%=travelRecs( "PRICE" )%>"/>
<%
  travelRecs.MoveNext
  Loop

  ' Only add end tags if we actually have elements.
  If doEndTags = True Then
      Response.Write( vbTab + vbTab + vbTab + "</resort>" + vbNewLine )
      Response.Write( vbTab + vbTab + "</city>" + vbNewLine )
      Response.Write( vbTab + "</country>" + vbNewLine )
  End If
%>
</travelpackages>
```

Let us have a closer look at the code. A SQL statement is formed, ADO is used to query the database and the XML document is pieced together with VBScript.

All fields from all the tables in the travel database are returned from the SQL query. A join is performed on all the tables. The query is constrained by what the user, which is the HTTP client, specifies in the HTTP request. If a field is not specified in the query string of the HTTP request, it is not included in the SQL query. Any value passed in the query string is put into the SQL query. For example, consider the following HTTP request.

```
http://server/travelds.asp?Country=Mexico&Month=May&Price=900
```

It becomes the following SQL query.

```
SELECT * FROM Price tPrice, Packages tPkg, Availability tAvail
WHERE tPkg.PackageId = tPrice.PackageId AND tPrice.PriceID = tAvail.PriceID AND
Month( tAvail.StartDate ) = 'May' AND tPkg.Country = 'Mexico' AND tPrice.Price <=
900
ORDER BY tPkg.Country, tPkg.City, tPkg.ResortName
```

Note that we cheat a little for the month. The date of departure is stored in the database as a specific date, yet the query is based on a month. The `Month()` function is used, which may not work with databases other than Microsoft Access, to extract the month from the database field.

As well, for clarity, no data input validation is performed. This is a particular problem because any text could be put into the form variables and this text would get inserted into the 'where' clause of the SQL statement. The important point to realize is that you can design a solution that will get the job done, but, because it is exposed on the Internet, you have to consider the implications of your design if someone decides to use your application for uses other than was intended.

After the SQL query is created, it is executed on the database with ADO. A recordset containing the result is returned. The records are iterated over and the XML document is built by pasting in the record information in the right places.

Since the XML elements `country`, `city` and `resort` are container elements they are treated specially. We need to order them in the returned records and handle the start and end tags.

One difficulty is that some of the information may be repeated in the returned records, specifically the `Country` and `City` fields. In the XML document we only want it listed once. So we set up a flag to tell us when the country or city has changed and only then is the country or city start tag inserted into the XML stream. Another difficulty is getting the end tags in the correct position. Again we use a flag to help get this right. The end tags are actually inserted before the start tags of the next record except in the case of the first record. Also, end tags are tacked on the end of the document if there were records returned.

Weather Server

The weather server works by sending an HTTP `GET` request. The Web server queries the database according to the request and returns an XML weather document.

Input

The request is of the form:

```
http://server/weatherds.asp?Country=VAL1&City=VAL2&Month=VAL3
```

server	The domain name of the weather server
`Country` (optional)	The country that weather is being queried for
`City` (optional)	The city that weather is being queried for
`Month` (optional)	The month that weather is being queried for
`VAL`(1-3)	The values to constrain the match.

Output

The output generated is an XML document that adheres to our weather report DTD. It contains the results according to our request passed in. If none of the parameters are specified all the records are returned. Let us look at an example:

```
http://server/weatherds.asp?Country=Australia
```

In this case weather records for all cities in Australia and for all months in the year will be returned.

Implementation

Following is the ASP code for the file `weatherds.asp`. It does all the work required from receiving the request to returning the resulting XML document.

```
<%@ LANGUAGE=VBSCRIPT%>
<% Response.ContentType = "text/plain" %>
<%

' Build the SQL query from the form variables passed in the URL.
Dim curCountry
Dim firstCountry
Dim curCity
Dim firstCity
Dim doEndTags

firstCountry = True
firstCity = True
doEndTags = False

SQLStatement = "SELECT * FROM weather tW, location tLoc WHERE tW.LocationId =
                                                            tLoc.LocationId"
If Request.QueryString( "Country" ) <> "Any" Then
    SQLStatement = SQLStatement + " AND tLoc.Country = '" + Request.QueryString(
          "Country" ) + "'"
End If
If Len( Request.QueryString( "City" ) ) > 0 Then
    SQLStatement = SQLStatement + " AND tLoc.City = '" + Request.QueryString(
          "City" ) + "'"
End If
If Len( Request.QueryString( "Month" ) ) > 0 Then
    SQLStatement = SQLStatement + " AND tW.Month = " + Request.QueryString(
"Month" )
End If
```

```
SQLStatement = SQLStatement + " ORDER BY tLoc.Country, tLoc.City"
%>

<?xml version="1.0"?>
<!DOCTYPE weather SYSTEM "weather.dtd">
<weather>
<%
    Set Conn = Server.CreateObject("ADODB.Connection")
    Conn.Open "weatherDB"
    Set weatherRec = Conn.Execute(SQLStatement)

    ' Loop through the records creating XML elements.
    Do While Not weatherRec.EOF

        doEndTags = True

        ' Start a new COUNTRY element if we are into a new one.
        If curCountry <> weatherRec( "COUNTRY" ) Then
            If firstCountry = False Then
                Response.Write( vbTab + "</country>" + vbNewLine )
            End If
            curCountry = weatherRec( "COUNTRY" )
            Response.Write( vbTab + "<country name=" + Chr(34) + curCountry +
                                    Chr(34) + ">" + vbNewLine )
            firstCountry = False
        End If

        ' Start a new CITY element if we are into a new one.
        If curCity <> weatherRec( "CITY" ) Then
            If firstCity = False Then
                Response.Write( vbTab + vbTab + "</city>" + vbNewLine )
            End If
            curCity = weatherRec( "CITY" )
            Response.Write( vbTab + vbTab + "<city name=" + Chr(34) + curCity +
                                    Chr(34) + ">" + vbNewLine )
            firstCity = False
        End If

%>
            <month name="<%=weatherRec("MONTH")%>">
                <precipitation cm="<%=weatherRec("AVGPRECIPITATION")%>"/>
                <winds speed="<%=weatherRec("WINDS")%>"/>
                <high c="<%=weatherRec("HIGH")%>"/>
                <low c="<%=weatherRec("LOW")%>"/>
            </month>
<%
    weatherRec.MoveNext
    Loop

    ' Only add end tags if we actually have elements.
    If doEndTags = True Then
        Response.Write( vbTab + vbTab + "</city>" + vbNewLine )
        Response.Write( vbTab + "</country>" + vbNewLine )
    End If
%>
</weather>
```

The approach is similar to the generation of the travel XML document. One of the first operations is preparing the SQL statement to execute. Since `country` and `city` will be the outer elements in the XML document, we order the SQL by them so that records of the same country and city will be grouped together. We are using ADO to execute the SQL command and return a Recordset. We then iterate through the records pulling out the information we want.

As with the travel XML document, flags are used to tell us when the country or city has changed and only then is the country or city start tag inserted into the XML stream. As well, end tags are inserted before the start tags of the next record except in the case of the first record. Also, end tags are tacked on the end of the document if there were records returned.

What's Next

The data services portion of the application is finished. Now we need to build the business services and user services. The business services will be responsible for taking the client's request, fetching the appropriate XML documents and processing them into a single XML response document. The user services will take the XML response document and format it for presentation to the user. We do the formatting with XSL on the server since CSS and XML do not work on the client yet.

Business Services

Business services implement rules on behalf of the user to create information from data. Note that user in the context of business services is most likely another application. The business rules filter, search and integrate data to synthesize the information the user is looking for. In this way, business services can be thought of as an agent for the user. The business services implement the XML features of automated searching and filtering and integrating diverse information.

The business services for the Travel Broker does the following:

- Takes the user's request for a travel package and weather conditions
- Fetches the travel package data from different sources
- Filters the travel data
- Fetches the weather data
- Filters the travel data depending on the weather data results
- Creates an XML document representing the results
- Sends the synthesized XML document back to the user

We will look at these points in more detail. First we will dive right in and try out the application then we will look at the implementation.

Example

Go to your browser and visit the page `http://webdev.wrox.co.uk/books/1525/`
Click on the business services demo. Fill out the form presented to you and click OK.

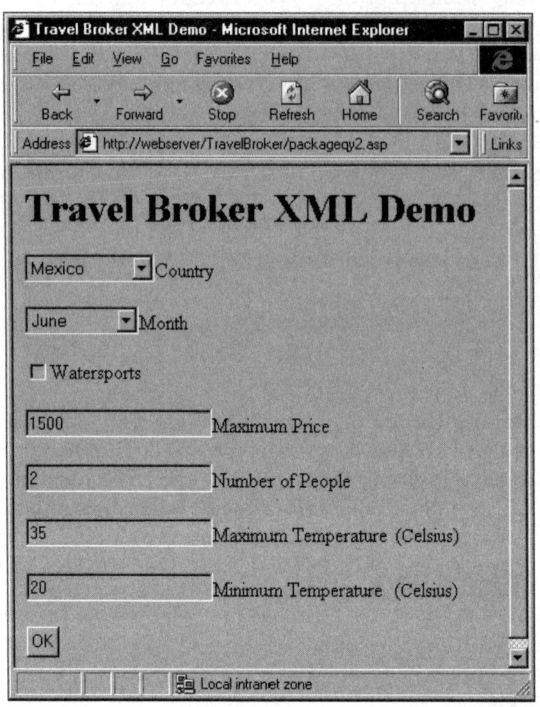

Returned to you is the raw XML document as seen below. I have added some carriage returns in to make the file easier to read. The document has the combined results of all the travel servers and is pruned according to the weather information.

```
<?xml version="1.0"?>
<travelpackages>
    <country name="Mexico">
        <city name="Cancun">
            <resort name="Crown Paradise Club Cancun" rating="4"
                typeofholiday="Beach"
                watersports="True" meals="True" drinks="True">
                <package dateofdep="6/28/98" price="1339"/>
                <package dateofdep="6/21/98" price="1319"/>
                <package dateofdep="6/14/98" price="1319"/>
                <package dateofdep="6/7/98" price="1319"/>
            </resort>
        </city>
        <city name="Puerto Vallarta">
            <resort name="Qualton Club and Spa" rating="4" typeofholiday="Beach"
                watersports="True" meals="True" drinks="False">
                <package dateofdep="6/26/98" price="1219"/>
                <package dateofdep="6/19/98" price="1089"/>
                <package dateofdep="6/12/98" price="1089"/>
                <package dateofdep="6/5/98" price="1089"/>
            </resort>
        </city>
    </country>
</travelpackages>
```

This document is very similar to the sample XML document shown in the data services section of the previous chapter, and in fact is valid according to the travel package Document Type Definition (DTD). The difference is that this document was formed as a composition of a number of XML documents and then was pruned according to some business rules. The business rules use data from other XML documents (produced by the weather server) and input from the user.

Implementation

The tools used for the implementation are Microsoft Internet Information Server 4 with Active Server Pages. VBScript is used for scripting the Active Server Pages. HTTP is the transport used for moving the XML document between the business services and its user as well as between business services and the data services.

Following is a diagram depicting the data flow:

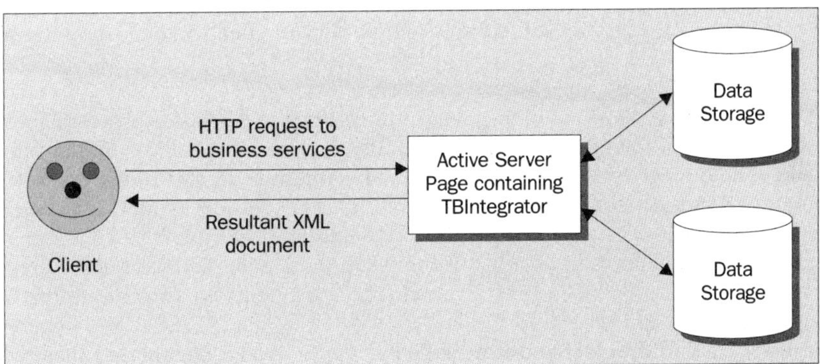

In the example, the user fills out the HTML form and presses OK. An HTTP request is created with the URL of the Active Server Page that implements business services and the form variables. The Active Server Pages instantiate a COM component, `TBIntegrator`, which has all the business services functionality. The form variables are assigned to properties of the COM component and the business rules are executed. An XML document with the results is returned from the COM component.

TBIntegrator

In our example the business services are implemented with a COM component named `TBIntegrator`. Since it is a COM server it can be used in any COM client such as Visual Basic or an Active Server Page. We will be using it in an Active Server Page. The client of `TBIntegrator`, which for us is the user services, sets various properties of `TBIntegrator`. These properties represent the request for the server. Specifically, they are constraints the end-user wants to apply for finding a holiday. Then a method is called to obtain the information from various data services, filter it and integrate it into an XML document that is returned to the client.

The project for building `TBIntegrator` can be obtained from
`http://webdev.wrox.co.uk/books/1525/`
and is called `TBIntergrator.zip`. It is a Visual C++ 6.0 project built with the ATL COM AppWizard. Download the file, unzip it into a directory and you should be able to load the project into Visual C++ 6.0. The project should also load into and build in Visual C++ 5.0.

When we built data services in the first part of the chapter we were able to use just the standard components to easily create an XML document. `TBIntegrator` actually needs to fetch and parse XML documents so we are going to get some help from Microsoft's `msxsl.dll` that has an `XMLDocument` COM component that we can use for parsing and manipulating an XML document.

MSXSL.DLL

Microsoft provides an XML parser as part of one of IE4's dynamic link libraries, specifically, `MSXML.DLL`. Unfortunately this implementation contains all the system headers when it is imported with `#import`, resulting in name collisions. There is also a parser in Microsoft's XSL processing component, `MSXSL.DLL`. It imports without any problem.

The code uses the Microsoft parser in the `MSXSL.DLL` component. The easiest way to install it is by trying a Microsoft demo. Go to `http://www.microsoft.com/xml/xsl/XSLControlDemo/XSLControl.htm` with Internet Explorer (Navigator generates an error). You will be asked if you want to install a component from Microsoft. When you say yes, the MSXSL control will be downloaded to your computer and installed.

The parser in `MSXSL.DLL` is a non-validating parser in contrast to Microsoft's Java parser, which is a validating parser. A non-validating parser checks that the document is well formed but it does not check if it is valid. The document is well formed if the document conforms to the syntactical rules of XML. A document is valid if it conforms to the rules of its DTD. A non-validating parser is faster than a validating parser because a lot less operations have to be performed. Since a non-validating parser is used, we are relying on the producer of the XML documents to ensure they are valid. These business rules applied within `TBIntegrator` rely on the documents conforming to the DTD.

`MSXSL.DLL` is used as a COM object and is accessed using the **Active Template Library** (ATL). Putting the following line at the beginning of the `TBIntegrator.cpp` file implements the component:

```
#import <msxsl.dll>
```

This command incorporates information from the MSXSL type library into the code making it easier to access individual interfaces. Details of MSXSL are not covered in this chapter.

Note that if you want to include information from `msxml.h` you require the following lines. These defines prevent information generated from the type library from colliding with the header file.

```
#define __IXMLElementCollection_INTERFACE_DEFINED__
#define __IXMLDocument_INTERFACE_DEFINED__
#define __IXMLElement_INTERFACE_DEFINED__

#include "msxml.h"
```

Code Details

The following diagram shows the classes of `TBIntegrator`.

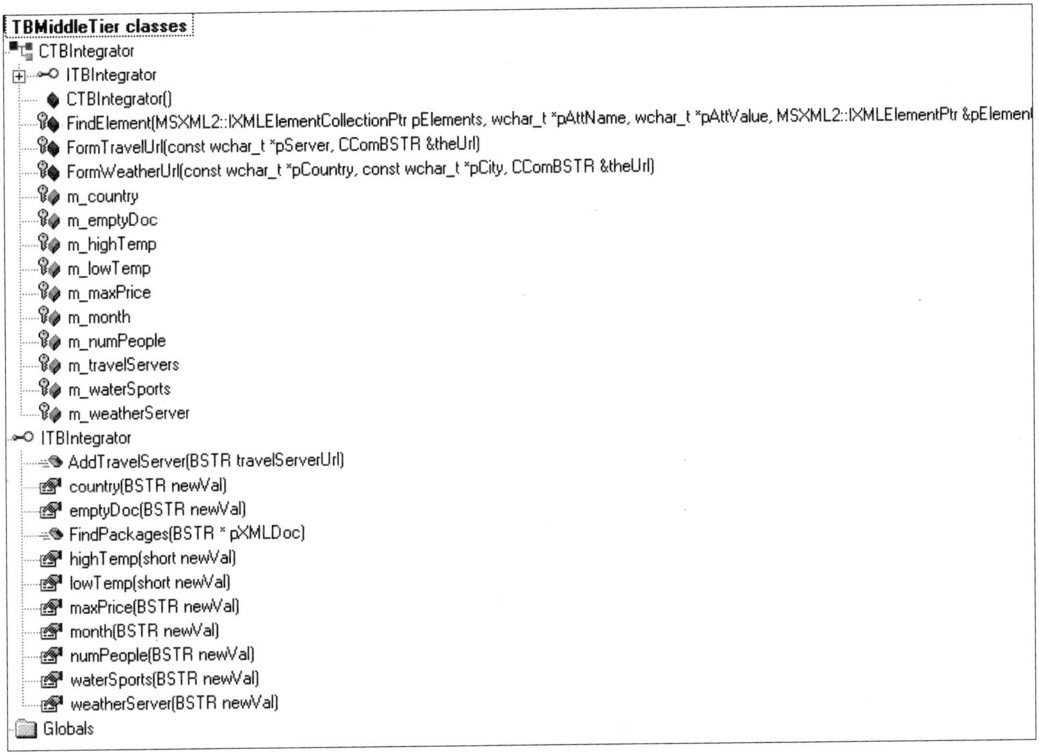

```
TBMiddleTier classes
CTBIntegrator
    ITBIntegrator
    CTBIntegrator()
    FindElement(MSXML2::IXMLElementCollectionPtr pElements, wchar_t *pAttName, wchar_t *pAttValue, MSXML2::IXMLElementPtr &pElement
    FormTravelUrl(const wchar_t *pServer, CComBSTR &theUrl)
    FormWeatherUrl(const wchar_t *pCountry, const wchar_t *pCity, CComBSTR &theUrl)
    m_country
    m_emptyDoc
    m_highTemp
    m_lowTemp
    m_maxPrice
    m_month
    m_numPeople
    m_travelServers
    m_waterSports
    m_weatherServer
ITBIntegrator
    AddTravelServer(BSTR travelServerUrl)
    country(BSTR newVal)
    emptyDoc(BSTR newVal)
    FindPackages(BSTR * pXMLDoc)
    highTemp(short newVal)
    lowTemp(short newVal)
    maxPrice(BSTR newVal)
    month(BSTR newVal)
    numPeople(BSTR newVal)
    waterSports(BSTR newVal)
    weatherServer(BSTR newVal)
Globals
```

The `TBIntegrator` component works by setting up the information and then calling the method `FindPackages()`. Let us first look at the only interface of the component, `ITBIntegrator`. This interface exposes the properties and methods to the COM container, which in this case is an Active Server Page. The interface has a number of `put` methods to set up the query. There is no provision for `get` methods because in our application we don't have any requirements to return the information. As well, the component does not modify the information that is `put`. The following is a description of the information that is set.

Property	Description	Required
`EmptyDoc`	The URL of an XML document that server uses as the template for the XML that will be constructed	Yes
`Weather Server`	The URL of a Web server that serves weather information as an XML document. The weather XML server was discussed in the previous weather server section.	Yes
`Country`	The country to search for resorts	No
`MaxPrice`	The maximum price for a travel package	No
`Month`	The month for the travel package	Yes

Table Continued on Following Page

Property	Description	Required
NumPeople	The number of people going on holiday	No
Watersports	Whether or not the resort has watersports	No
Hightemp	The maximum temperature for the month	Yes
LowTemp	The minimum temperature for the month	Yes

Additionally, the method, AddTravelServer, adds a travel web server that conforms to the travel server requirements discussed in the previous travel server section. Internally, the TBIntegrator component builds a list of these servers and will obtain travel packages from each one. Each travel server represents a travel vendor.

The method that does all the work is FindPackages. It uses all the properties that TBIntegrator was configured with and creates an XML document according to its built in rules. We will see these rules when we walk through the code.

The following diagram shows how the Active Server Page, the TBIntegrator COM component and MSXSL.DLL are related. The ASP instantiates TBIntegrator and sets various properties on it. When TBIntegrator is asked to FindPackages() it uses MSXSL.DLL to create an XML document using IXMLDocument2. It accesses various parts of the document using the interfaces IXMLElementCollection and IXMLElement.

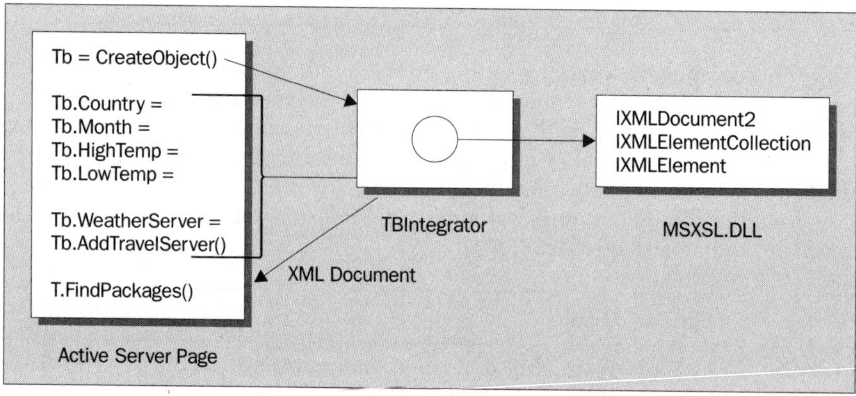

From a C++ point of view, all the properties are implemented with member variables. When a put is called, the member variable is set to the new value. The travel servers are represented by a **Standard Template Library** (STL) list. When AddTravelServer() is called, the passed in value is added to the list.

There are three protected C++ member functions used to help in the code.

```
void CTBIntegrator::FormWeatherUrl( const wchar_t *pCountry, const wchar_t *pCity,
                                    CComBSTR &theUrl ) const
```

This method generates a URL for requesting an XML document from the weather server. It takes the base URL set as the weather server property and adds country, city and month as query parameters.

```
void CTBIntegrator::FormTravelUrl( const wchar_t *pServer, CComBSTR &theUrl )
const
```

This method generates a URL for requesting an XML document from a travel server. It takes the base URL that is passed in and adds the component properties: country, month, watersports, maxprice and numPeople as query parameters if they have been provided.

```
bool CTBIntegrator::FindElement( MSXML2::IXMLElementCollectionPtr pElements,
wchar_t
            *pAttName, wchar_t *pAttValue, MSXML2::IXMLElementPtr &pElement )
const
```

This method is a helper method for finding an element based upon an attribute value. A collection of XML elements is passed in along with an attribute name and attribute value. The first XML element in the collection that has the attribute value passed in is assigned to the IXMLElementPtr. True is returned if an element with that attribute value is found in the collection and False otherwise. Hopefully, helper methods like this will be provided in future releases of the XML parser.

Now for the method that implements the logic of TBIntegrator, FindPackages().

- Obtain a template document to be the returned document
- For each travel server set with AddTravelServer,

    Form a travel server request URL
    Obtain the XML document resulting from the query
    Merge the XML document into the returned document

- For each Country and City in the returned XML document

    Form a weather server request URL
    Obtain the XML document resulting from the query
    Prune the returned XML document based upon the weather data

- Return the XML document

We'll look at the code a few lines at a time so it doesn't get too confusing. Note that we are using COM pointers. They throw exceptions when an error occurs so all the parsing work is done within a try block.

```
STDMETHODIMP CTBIntegrator::FindPackages(BSTR * pXMLOut)
{
    HRESULT    answer = S_OK;
    USES_CONVERSION;

    try
    {
        MSXML2::IXMLDocument2Ptr      pReturnedDoc( __uuidof(
MSXML2::XMLDocument2 ) );
        MSXML2::IXMLDocument2Ptr      pWeatherDoc( __uuidof( MSXML2::XMLDocument2
) );
        MSXML2::IXMLDocument2Ptr      pTravelDoc( __uuidof( MSXML2::XMLDocument2
) );
```

```
        MSXML2::IXMLElementCollectionPtr   pTravelCountries( NULL );
        MSXML2::IXMLElementCollectionPtr   pReturnedCountries( NULL );
        MSXML2::IXMLElementPtr      pReturnedRoot( NULL );
        MSXML2::IXMLElementPtr      pTravelRoot( NULL );
        MSXML2::IXMLElementPtr      pTCountryElement( NULL );
        MSXML2::IXMLElementPtr      pRCountryElement( NULL );

    CComBSTR              theUrl;
    const CComVariant     countryTagName( "COUNTRY" );
    const CComVariant     cityTagName( "CITY" );
    const CComVariant     resortTagName( "RESORT" );
    VARIANT                 varEmpty;

    // Initialize some variables;
    varEmpty.vt = VT_EMPTY;
```

To start, some ATL smart pointers are declared. There are three XML documents that will be active at one time - the document to be returned, the current weather document and the current travel document. We also need some collections of XML elements. We keep a pointer to the root element of the returned document and the root element of the current travel document. Tag names for `country`, `city` and `name` are initialized as `const` variant variables. We also need an empty variant so that is initialized as well.

```
    // Initialize the document being created.
    pReturnedDoc->URL = m_emptyDoc.m_str;
    pReturnedRoot = pReturnedDoc->root;
```

A template XML document that has generated elements but no specific data elements is used as the starting point of the returned document. It looks like the following:

```
<?xml version="1.0"?>
<travelpackages>

</travelpackages>
```

To obtain the template, the URL for the returned XML document is set as a property. The root element of the returned document is obtained from the fetched document.

```
    // Build the XML document by querying all the travel servers.
    SERVER_LIST::const_iterator    travelIter;

    for ( travelIter = m_travelServers.begin(); travelIter !=
        m_travelServers.end(); travelIter++ )
    {
        FormTravelUrl( (*travelIter).c_str(), theUrl );

        // Fetch the travel document.
        pTravelDoc->URL = theUrl.m_str;

        pTravelRoot = pTravelDoc->root;
        pTravelCountries =
            pTravelRoot->Getchildren( )->item( countryTagName, varEmpty );
```

The next step is to iterate through all the travel servers and query them for travel packages. The base URL is obtained from the travel server list, the request URL is formed and the XML document is fetched. The root of the current travel document is assigned as well as the collection of countries.

```
for ( int i = 0; i < pTravelCountries->length; i++ )
{
    pTCountryElement = pTravelCountries->item( CComVariant( i ), varEmpty );

    // See if we already have the country.
    if ( FindElement( pReturnedCountries, L"Name",
        _bstr_t(pTCountryElement->getAttribute( L"Name" )), pRCountryElement )
)
    {
      MSXML2::IXMLElementCollectionPtr    pTravelCities;
      MSXML2::IXMLElementCollectionPtr    pReturnedCities;
      MSXML2::IXMLElementPtr              pTCityElement;
      MSXML2::IXMLElementPtr              pRCityElement;

        pReturnedCities = pRCountryElement->Getchildren()->item(
                    cityTagName, varEmpty );
        pTravelCities = pTCountryElement->Getchildren()->item(
                    cityTagName, varEmpty );
```

For each `country` element in the collection of `country` elements, we check if the country is already contained in the returned document. It will be if a previous travel server had travel packages for that particular country. If it is in the returned document we then need to check the cities.

```
        for ( int j = 0; j < pTravelCities->length; j++ )
        {
            pTCityElement = pTravelCities->item( CComVariant( j ), varEmpty );
            // See if we already have the city.
            if ( FindElement( pReturnedCities, L"Name",
                _bstr_t(pTCityElement->getAttribute( L"Name" )),
                pRCityElement ) )
            {
                MSXML2::IXMLElementCollectionPtr  pResorts;
                MSXML2::IXMLElementPtr            pResortElement;

                pResorts = pTCityElement->Getchildren()->item(
                            resortTagName, varEmpty );
                for ( int k = 0; k < pResorts->length; k++ )
                {
                    pResortElement = pResorts->item(CComVariant( j ),
                                varEmpty );
                    pRCityElement->addChild( pResortElement, -1, -1 );
                }
            }
```

For each `city` element in the collection of `city` elements we need to check if the city is already contained in the returned document. Again, it will be if a previous travel server had travel packages for that particular city. If it is in the returned document we add each resort to the city element in the returned document.

```
            else
            {
                answer = pRCountryElement->addChild( pTCityElement, -1, -1 );
            }
```

If the city is not already in the returned document we add the `city` element, which includes all its children, to the returned document's `country` element.

```
        else
        {
            answer = pReturnedRoot->addChild( pTCountryElement, -1, -1 );
        }
```

Similarly, if the country was not found in the returned document, the current travel document's country is added to the returned document.

After iterating through all the travel servers, the returned document has all the travel packages appropriate to what the user requested. `TBIntegrator` has integrated the travel information from different sources, but the weather information has not been checked yet. What happens next is the returned XML document is used as the data source to drive what information is required by the weather server.

```
    pReturnedCountries =
        pReturnedRoot->Getchildren()->item( countryTagName, varEmpty );

    if ( pReturnedCountries != NULL )
    {
        // Prune the XML document with the weather data.
    MSXML2::IXMLDocument2Ptr    weatherDoc( __uuidof( MSXML2::XMLDocument2 ) );
    MSXML2::IXMLElementCollectionPtr      pReturnedCities( NULL );
    MSXML2::IXMLElementPtr                pRCityElement( NULL );
    MSXML2::IXMLElementPtr                pWCountryElement( NULL );
    MSXML2::IXMLElementPtr                pWCityElement( NULL );
    MSXML2::IXMLElementPtr                pWMonthElement( NULL );
    MSXML2::IXMLElementPtr                pWLowElement( NULL );
    MSXML2::IXMLElementPtr                pWHighElement( NULL );
    MSXML2::IXMLElementPtr                pWeatherRoot( NULL );
    MSXML2::IXMLElementCollectionPtr      pLowCollection( NULL );
    MSXML2::IXMLElementCollectionPtr      pHighCollection( NULL );
        CComVariant                     firstRec( 0 );
        CComVariant                     lowVal;
        const CComVariant              lowTagName( "LOW" );
        CComVariant                     highVal;
        const CComVariant              highTagName( "HIGH" );
```

If we have some countries in the returned document, we set up to prune them according to the weather information. Again, variables are set up for use. For variable naming, a `W` represents items in the weather document and an `R` represents items in the returned document. For example, `pWCityElement` is a pointer to a city element in the weather XML document.

```
    for ( int i = 0; i < pReturnedCountries->length; i++ )
    {
        pRCountryElement = pReturnedCountries->item( CComVariant( i ),
                                                      varEmpty );
        pReturnedCities = pRCountryElement->Getchildren()->item( cityTagName,
                                                           varEmpty );

        for ( int j = 0; j < pReturnedCities->length; j++ )
        {
```

```
            pRCityElement = pReturnedCities->item( CComVariant( j ), varEmpty );

            FormWeatherUrl( _bstr_t(pRCountryElement->getAttribute( L"Name" )),
               _bstr_t(pRCityElement->getAttribute( L"Name" )), theUrl );
```

To prune the returned document we need to get the weather for each city.

```
               weatherDoc->URL = theUrl.m_str;
               pWeatherRoot = weatherDoc->root;

               pWCountryElement = pWeatherRoot->Getchildren()->item( firstRec,
                                                                    varEmpty );

               pWCityElement = pWCountryElement->Getchildren()->item(
                   firstRec, varEmpty );
               pWMonthElement = pWCityElement->Getchildren()->item(
                   firstRec, varEmpty );

               pLowCollection = pWMonthElement->Getchildren()->item(
                   lowTagName, varEmpty );
               pWLowElement = pLowCollection->item( firstRec, varEmpty );

               lowVal = pWLowElement->getAttribute( L"C" );
               lowVal.ChangeType( VT_I2 );

               pHighCollection = pWMonthElement->Getchildren()->item(
                   highTagName, varEmpty );
               pWHighElement = pHighCollection->item( firstRec, varEmpty );

               highVal = pWHighElement->getAttribute( L"C" );
               highVal.ChangeType( VT_I2 );
```

The weather document is fetched, and the information required for pruning the travel package document tree is obtained by traversing the document tree. Specifically, we traverse down to the month element. The weather details are child elements of the month element. For example, the DTD says only one LOW element exists as a child of the month element. Therefore, we can safely ask for the first element of the collection of LOW elements that are children of the month element. Once we have the LOW element, we get the actual low temperature in degrees Celsius by asking for the C attribute. It is returned as a variant string so we change the type to an integer to do easier comparison later.

```
               if ( (m_lowTemp > lowVal.iVal) || (m_highTemp < highVal.iVal) )
               {
                   answer = pRCountryElement->removeChild( pRCityElement );
               }
```

If the weather conditions are not satisfied, the city element is removed from the document. Note: this means the children of the city are also removed from the document.

```
    // The country element has no children left, remove it.
    if ( pRCountryElement->Getchildren()->length == 0 )
    {
        pReturnedRoot->removeChild( pRCountryElement );
    }
```

If all the cities were removed from the document because they do not have the right weather conditions, the `country` element is left with no children. If this is the case, the `country` element is removed.

```
    // Get the string representation of the document.
    CComQIPtr< IPersistStreamInit, &IID_IPersistStreamInit >    pPSI;
    IStream                     *pStream = NULL;
    char                         *pStr;
    HGLOBAL                     hGlobal = NULL;

    answer = pReturnedDoc->QueryInterface(IID_IPersistStreamInit,(void **)&pPSI );

    answer = CreateStreamOnHGlobal( NULL, TRUE, &pStream );
    answer = pPSI->Save( pStream, TRUE );
    answer = GetHGlobalFromStream( pStream, &hGlobal );
    pStr = (char *)GlobalLock( hGlobal );
    DWORD dwSize = GlobalSize( hGlobal );

    CComBSTR     tempBStr( dwSize, pStr );

    *pXMLOut = tempBStr.Detach();

    GlobalUnlock( hGlobal );
```

At this point, the XML document has been fully processed. We need to return it as a string to the caller rather than the binary structure that it is in at this point. `XMLDocument` supports `IpersistStreamInit` so we get a string representation of the XML document by using this interface.

```
    catch ( const _com_error &comErr )
    {
        ATLTRACE( "Error: 0x%x - %s\n", comErr.Error(), comErr.Description() );
        answer = comErr.Error();
    }
```

Finally, we have a catch block which will receive any errors that occur during the processing. Note that this demonstration program does not really handle errors at all. A production system would need much stronger error handling and recovery.

Now, the `TBIntegrator` is complete and ready to be used. Later in this chapter we will be putting the component in an Active Server Page that ties together business services and user services.

User Services

User services prepare information for delivery to the end user. User services apply formatting rules to render information. The needs of the user are taken into account for the rendering. Two examples of different rendering are: someone with limited vision that requires a large font rendering, and someone accessing information by phone who requires an aural rendering. In both cases the source information is the same.

User services depend on XML's feature of separating information and presentation. The source information is available as an XML document. User services determine the needs of the user and pick the appropriate rendering for the XML document. The rendering of the XML document can be through using CSS or XSL.

Example

Again, let's jump in with a demo and then go through the implementation. Go to your browser and visit the page `http://webdev.wrox.co.uk/books/1525/`. Click on the user services demo.

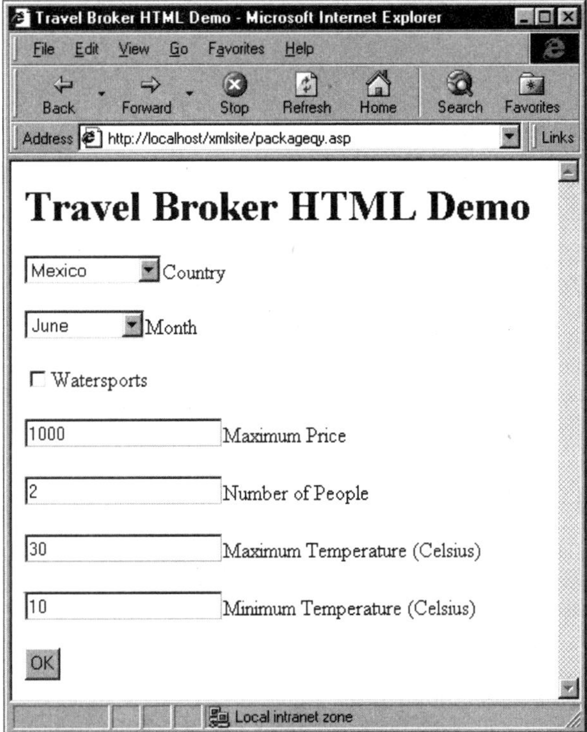

You see a form that is exactly the same as presented in data services. What is different this time is an HTML document will be returned instead of an XML document. Fill out the form presented to you and click OK. Returned to you are the HTML formatted results.

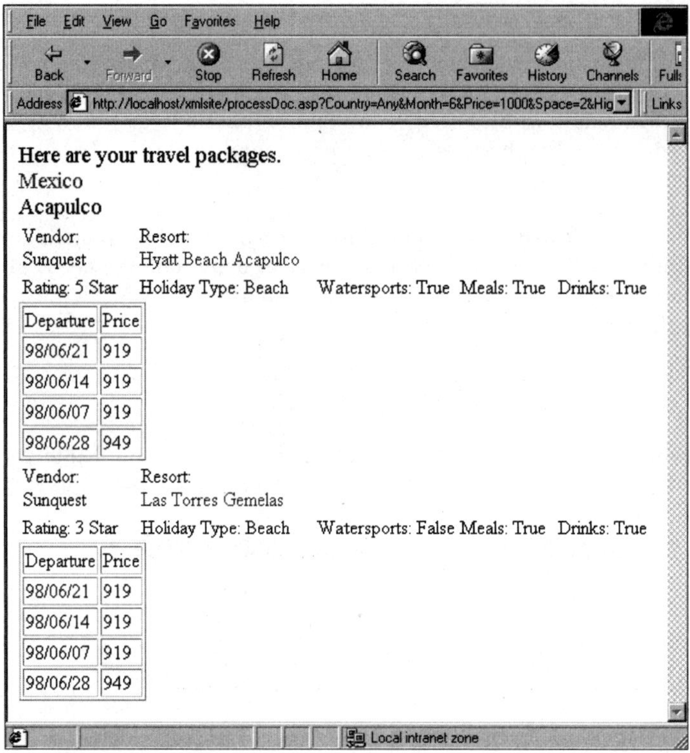

Formatting on the Client with CSS

Formatting an XML document on the client with CSS offers the benefit of off-loading work from the server to the client. This results in better overall system performance. Currently, IE5 is the only browser offering some support of this option. Since it is in Beta at the time of writing an example is not included.

Formatting on the Server with XSL

Formatting an XML document on the server offers protection from differences between browsers. The server is in control of exactly what HTML will be produced and then sent to the browser to be rendered. However, since the web server is doing more work performance is reduced.

The Microsoft `XSLControl` enables formatting of an XML document with XSL. The result is an HTML document. For our implementation we are going to instantiate an `XSLControl` in an Active Server Page on the web server. It will take the resultant XML document from the business services, apply an XSL document for styling and return the resultant HTML document to the Active Server Page. The Active Server Page then returns the HTML document to the client.

The generation of HTML on the web server is similar to the Limon example in the next chapter, in that the browser has no idea how the document was formed; it just receives the HTML document. The two applications differ in that the Travel Broker generates the document dynamically when the request is made whereas Limon has generated the completed HTML document beforehand. The advantage of dynamically generating the document is that data returned is up to date with the back-end database, which is what you want for a travel query/reservation system. The disadvantage is a lot of processing has to be done to finally return the HTML document.

If you have been following the steps for installing `msxsl.dll` in the business services section you will already have the `XSLControl` installed.

XSL Document

The XSL document controls the rendering of our document. Let us look at each of the rules.

```
<xsl>
    <rule>
        <root/>
        <HTML>
            <TITLE>Travel Package Results</TITLE>
            <BODY color="black" background-color="white" font-size="14pt">
                <H2>Here are your travel packages.</H2><BR/>
                <children/>
            </BODY>
        </HTML>
    </rule>
...
```

The `root` rule sets the context for the entire document. It identifies the root of the source document tree setting the tags that we want to wrap around the document.

```
...
    <rule>
        <target-element type="country"/>
        <DIV color="red">
            <eval>this.getAttribute("name")</eval>
        </DIV>
        <children/>
    </rule>
...
```

This rule finds the `country` element and defines the rendering of the value of the `name` attribute in red.

```
...
    <rule>
        <target-element type="city"/>
        <DIV color="blue">
            <eval>this.getAttribute("name")</eval>
        </DIV>
        <children/>
    </rule>
...
```

This rule finds the `city` element and defines the rendering of the value of the `name` attribute in blue.

```
...
<rule>
    <target-element type="resort"/>
        <TABLE>
            <TR>
                <TD WIDTH="120">Vendor:
                <eval>this.getAttribute("vendor")</eval></TD>
                <TD WIDTH="200">Resort:
                    <DIV color="purple">
                        <eval>this.getAttribute("name")</eval>
                    </DIV>
                </TD>
            </TR>
            <TR>
                <TD WIDTH="120">Rating: <eval>this.getAttribute("rating")</eval>
                        Star</TD>
                <TD WIDTH="200">Holiday Type:
                        <eval>this.getAttribute("typeofholiday")</eval></TD>
                <TD WIDTH="135">Watersports:
                         <eval>this.getAttribute("watersports")</eval></TD>
                <TD WIDTH="100">Meals:
                <eval>this.getAttribute("meals")</eval></TD>
                <TD WIDTH="100">Drinks:
                <eval>this.getAttribute("drinks")</eval></TD>
            </TR>
        </TABLE>
        <TABLE BORDER="1">
            <children/>
        </TABLE>
</rule>
...
```

This rule finds the `resort` element and renders its attribute values. The values are placed in a table for better formatting. The children of `resort` are the various travel packages available for that resort. We want to put each package in a table row so a `<TABLE>` element is wrapped around the `<children/>`.

```
...
<rule>
    <target-element type="package" position="first-of-type"/>
        <TR>
            <TD>Departure</TD><TD>Price</TD>
        </TR>
        <TR>
            <TD><eval>this.getAttribute("dateofdep")</eval></TD>
            <TD><eval>this.getAttribute("price")</eval></TD>
        </TR>
</rule>
...
```

As mentioned, each package is a table row. We want to put a heading on the table so the first row has to be treated as a special case. This rule accomplishes this with the pattern,
`<target-element type="package" position="first-of-type"/>`
This pattern identifies the first `package` element in the XML document being rendered.

```
...
<rule>
    <target-element type="package"/>
        <TR>
            <TD><eval>this.getAttribute("dateofdep")</eval></TD>
            <TD><eval>this.getAttribute("price")</eval></TD>
        </TR>
</rule>

</xsl>
```

The final rule renders all of the `package` elements except for the first one. The `package` elements are put into a table row.

Implementation

An Active Server Page hosts the document integration component, `TBIntegrator` and the formatting component, `XSLControl`. It also coordinates the information passed between them. The page takes the request in the form:

```
http://server/processDoc.asp?Country=VAL1&
Month=VAL2&Watersports=VAL3&Price=VAL4&Space=VAL5&HighTemp=VAL6&LowTemp=VA
L7
```

`server`	The domain name of the travel server
`Country` (optional)	The destination country
`Month` (required)	The desired travel month
`Watersports` (optional)	True if the travel package has watersports
`Price` (optional)	The maximum price for the travel package
`Space` (optional)	The number of people going on the holiday
`HighTemp` (optional)	The maximum temperature during the holiday
`LowTemp` (optional)	The minimum temperature during the holiday
`VAL(1-7)`	Are the values to constrain the match. If an optional value is not provided, that attribute is unconstrained

Let's walk through the code in the page itself.

```
<SCRIPT LANGUAGE=VBScript RUNAT=server>

' Create the integrated document.
Set tbInt = Server.CreateObject( "WROX.TBIntegrator.1" )

If Request.QueryString( "Country" ) <> "Any" Then
    tbInt.Country = Request.QueryString( "Country" )
End If
```

```
tbInt.month = Request.QueryString( "Month" )
tbInt.waterSports = Request.QueryString( "WaterSports" )
tbInt.maxPrice = Request.QueryString( "Price" )
tbInt.numPeople = Request.QueryString( "Space" )

If Len( Request.QueryString( "HighTemp" ) ) <> 0 Then
    tbInt.highTemp = Request.QueryString( "HighTemp" )
End If

If Len( Request.QueryString( "LowTemp" ) ) <> 0 Then
    tbInt.lowTemp = Request.QueryString( "LowTemp" )
End If

tbInt.emptyDoc = "http://localhost/xmlsite/empty.xml"
tbInt.weatherServer = "http://sageconsultants.com/TravelBroker/weatherds.asp"
tbInt.AddTravelServer ("http://sageconsultants.com/TravelBroker/travelds.asp")
tbInt.AddTravelServer ("http://localhost/xmlsite/travelds.asp")

xmlDoc = tbInt.FindPackages()

Set tbInt = Nothing
...
```

This section does the XML document integration. A `TBIntegrator` object is created and its properties are set from the `QueryString` values. The template for the final XML document, the weather server URL, and a list of travel server URLs are hard-coded into the ASP. Finally, `FindPackages` is called to do all the work by implementing the business rules. We saw earlier in the chapter how `FindPackages` works. If successful, it returns the resultant XML document that has all the travel packages according to the criteria set by the user. Finally, we get rid of the `TBIntegrator` object by setting it to nothing. Releasing resources as soon as possible enhances the performance of the application.

```
...
' Write the result XML document to a file.
Set fs = CreateObject( "Scripting.FileSystemObject" )
Set aFile = fs.CreateTextFile( "pkData.xml", True )
aFile.Write( xmlDoc )
aFile.Close

Set fs = Nothing
...
```

Unfortunately, this code is a bit of patchwork that is required between the components `TBIntegrator` and `XSLControl`. The XML document is returned as a string from `TBIntegrator`. The other component, `XSLControl`, will only accept a source XML document as a URL. Therefore, we write the XML string to a file and pass this file name to `XSLControl`. Hopefully future versions of `XSLControl` will take input as a string.

```
...
' Format the XML document
Set    xslProc = Server.CreateObject( "XSLControl.XSLControl.1" )

xslProc.documentURL = "pkData.xml"
xslProc.styleURL = "http://localhost/xmlsite/render1.xsl"
Response.Write( xslProc.htmlText )
```

```
Set xslProc = Nothing

</SCRIPT>
```

The final step formats the resultant XML document as an HTML document. An `XSLControl` object is created. The source XML document URL is set, as is the style URL. The resulting HTML document is available as a string property of the control. It is written to the client and we get rid of `XSLControl` by setting it to nothing.

Hopefully, if all has gone well, the user will see the results of the query in the browser and a holiday could now be booked!

Summary

The first part of the Travel Broker application, data services, was detailed. We saw how a back end database can be encapsulated with an XML document. We saw how XML makes publishing the information to the Internet via HTTP possible. Data services accomplish the XML goal of publishing well-formed data.

To implement the data services tier we learned how to do the following:

- Design two XML DTDs
- Convert an HTTP request to a SQL query
- How to map a database response to an XML document
- How to create an XML document with Active Server Pages

Travel Broker is built upon a three-tier architecture including data services, business services and user services. Each service can be located on different physical machines. XML is used as the glue between the tiers. XML enables the application to publish structured data, and to automate the searching, filtering, and integration of information from diverse sources. It also permits the separation of data from its presentation.

Various Microsoft technologies were used to demonstrate XML technology: VBScript within an Active Server Page accessing a database with ADO enabled data services. Business services were implemented with Microsoft's C++ parser used within a COM component created with ATL and C++. Finally, User Services were implemented with VBScript in an Active Server Page, and Microsoft's `XSLControl`.

Further References

Files for this chapter: `http://webdev.wrox.co.uk/books/1525/`

W3C CSS discussion is at: `http://www.w3.org/Style/CSS/`

W3C XSL discussion is at: `http://www.w3.org/Style/XSL/`

Elements vs. Attributes Discussion: `http://www.sil.org/sgml/elementsandAttrs.html`

Microsoft's XSL information: `http://www.microsoft.com/xml/xsl/`

12

The Weeds of El Limon: A Customized XML Based Web Publishing System

In this chapter we will present a Web project which we accomplished by building a simple publishing system: a Java application which turns a collection of XML files and images into a set of Web pages. In our case we made a flora of weeds and other small plants we observed in a village in the Dominican Republic. We had to make many Web pages that were nearly identical – a challenge very similar to building an online catalog. If you're facing a similar challenge, you can copy the design of our program to get a running start. I found this project particularly interesting because I grew as a Webmaster from being able to make individual Web pages into building comprehensive and consistent sites.

How We Got Into This Predicament

In January 1998, Olivia and I took a trip to the village of El Limon in the Dominican Republic, which is the centre of a remarkable development project. We thought that we were going to help string wires from their new micro-hydroelectric powerplant to the village, but the materials had not yet arrived, so we had to find something else to do.

We quickly took an interest in the plants growing in the village, particularly the weeds, and realized that one of the most critical things lacking from the village was agricultural knowledge and record-keeping. So we decided to get the ball rolling by creating a flora for the village with a focus towards small weedy plants. The villagers in Limon already had a laptop computer at this point and they were planning to get Internet access through cellular telephone as soon as the telephone company brought cellular telephone services into the area. We decided that our flora could be best delivered as a set of Web pages. Not only could we distribute it online via the Web to anyone who wanted to see them, but we could also distribute it to the villagers on a removable disk until they obtained an Internet connection.

Why Plain Web Pages Weren't Good Enough

I was worrying about the Web form the weeds would eventually assume even before leaving Limon, though at first, the only thing I was certain of was that writing the HTML for them by hand would be a mistake. You can write 30-some Web pages individually, but someday you'll decide that you want all the headers blue instead of green, or you'll discover that some part of your HTML causes someone's Web browser to self-destruct. Then, you'll have lots of fun changing every one of those 30-some files individually, consistently, every time the site needs maintenance.

Every Web site is a combination of two things: style and content. Style is the choice of color, layout and presentation while, in our case, the content is the descriptions and images of the weeds. To make a product that looks professional, it's important to maintain stylistic consistency from one page to the next. On a small project, it's possible to attain consistency through superhuman discipline, but this becomes more difficult as a project gets larger and involves more people.

Web pages are also expected to evolve. It takes many phases of revision, based on other people's feedback and your own rethinking, to make a product which is "just right", and, well, individually writing a pile of HTML documents is about the most unmaintainable way to build a Web site that you could think of. It would make changing the site's style so difficult that I'd probably decide that it was a waste of time. Similarly, having to alter the content of the pages, say, by identifying more plants or finding that my previous identifications were incorrect, would mean changing the page for the affected plants, the indexes, and any other pages dependent on the new information – without introducing more errors.

A Web creator should expect to evolve too. At first I just made Web pages because I could, without regard to their sustainability. Eventually I realized that to graduate to more complex Web projects, I'd have to learn how to automate the process of adding style to content.

Why XML?

The first step after deciding that you want to automatically add style to content is to get your content, in our case, the images and descriptions of the weeds, into a form that the style adding program can manipulate. Several solutions are possible:

One would be to write the weed descriptions in a language similar to the C preprocessor, which allows inserting macros and conditionally including materials. Although this sort of solution is simple, it is limited, because all you can do is fill in slots in a template. As a result, it is difficult or impossible to change the order in which information is presented.

A comma-separated file of the descriptions would be easy to make. The problem with it and other primitive data formats is that Weeds is too complex to be practical for them. A comma-separated file is good for simple data, such as a list of stars and their positions in the sky. For the weeds, different types of information are available for different weeds. Some aren't identified at all, and the number of common names can vary. Each weed contains a large block of text in which I'd like to be able to use commas and other punctuation freely, and also mark up with hyperlinks. If I was very clever I might be able to make this work, but the solution would be fragile and create more work in the end.

Another solution would be to use a database. However, the advantages of a database pay off if the database is large (hundreds or thousands of items) and if you want to search it in a complex way. If I were making a Web site with hundreds of weeds, and if I wanted to make the site dynamic and searchable by complex queries, then a database would be advantageous. But for 32 weeds, installing a database, learning how to program it, and getting it to work wouldn't be worth the effort. Past that, the design of my program, which separates the interpretation of XML, the representation of data, and the generation of HTML, would make it possible for me to use a database in the future if I want. Also, XML can work with databases. XML text can be stored inside a field in a database, or XML can be used as a format for importing and exporting data from databases.

Other possibilities, including XML, involve storing the information in a structured form similar to a database. This way, processing software can identify and process each part of the description of a weed flexibly and independently. XML provided me with a simple framework to write a structured language for describing the weeds.

A structured language lets software understand what the parts of a document mean. I think of an analogy as I look at a CD jewel case sitting next to my computer. If I were making a Web page about the album, I could scan in the back cover and turn it into a JPEG file - the image could be inserted in a page by those people able to view it. On the other hand, a computer program couldn't do much with the image; it certainly couldn't determine the name of the band or the titles of the songs. Alternately, I could use HTML to make a Web page that looks like the album cover, avoiding the use of images for fonts. Somebody could then use a search engine to find the page by, say, typing in the title of one of the songs, and a Web browser could read the page to a blind person. (Accessability for people with disabilities is a major issue in HTML 4.) Even so, the search engine could only see the page as a vast expanse of text. It can't tell which words are the title of the album, the name of the artist, or the copyright notice. XML allows highly structured markup, allowing you to tag every part of the document, making it accessable to sophisticated processing. Specifically, we can select certain pieces of information from diverse sources, and merge this to be presented in a particular style.

Although I could develop my own system for structured markup, using XML has many benefits. Since there are many XML parsers already available, I am saved the bother of writing my own. Because many people and institutions will be using XML in the years to come, many tools, both free and commercial, will be created for editing and processing XML – some of which I may be able to use. Also, if I can convince people that my DTD is a good format for exchanging descriptions of plants, it would be a great way for me to share them with other people.

Why Static Web Pages?

Having decided that I wanted to store the descriptions of the weeds in XML, I had to choose between a Java Applet, pages generated generated dynamically on the server, or static Web pages for presenting the information to the user.

An Applet makes possible application-like graphical interaction, but I had no vision of what to do with that flexibility. I'd have to invent a new user interface that viewers would have to learn (or more likely not learn). Download time would also be a problem. Since a typical XML parser weighs in at 100k in `.jar` form, users with a slow connection (most of them) would, on a good day, spend a minute looking at a grey box while the Applet loads. Most would hit the back button long before it was done. Once current XML parsers are included in Web browsers, along with richer Java API's, it's likely that you'll be able to write smaller Applets that use XML. Today this approach is viable only if your users will tolerate the wait. (MSIE 4.0 does contain MSXML version 1.0, but MSXML 1.0 is compatible with neither the final XML specification, nor the current MSXML 1.8.) Another problem is that with any client-side executable, you have to draw a line as to which browsers to support. The more neat features you want to use, the smaller the audience you can reach.

Another exciting application of XML would be to generate Web pages dynamically on the server. This could make it possible for a user to see a personalized view of the weeds, or to create highly interactive applications that would allow users to add comments about the weeds or even add their own weeds. Dynamic generation of pages would also be advantageous if the number of weeds were so large (thousands) that it would be inconvenient to store and maintain thousands of static pages on the server. Because the software runs on the server, users don't need to be running a specific browser and no time is spent sending software across the wire. A dynamic approach has a lot of potential, but I chose not to do it because it would make things unjustifyably complex for the level of functionality I needed.

In the end, I decided to use static Web pages. Although static Web pages aren't the fanciest thing going, they are simple and mature. A Web server that serves static pages can take many more hits than a dynamic server and has far fewer things that can go wrong. Since static pages don't need special software on the server anyone can have a mirror site, and the pages can be stored on a floppy, hard drive or CD-ROM. Finally, because I wanted to make a site that looks and works like a printed document, a set of static Web pages has the right look and feel. It's important to remember that this decision isn't permanent. With all of my data in structured form, I can always write new programs to present it in new ways.

Why Java?

I wrote the software that converts the XML weed descriptions into HTML in Java, because I'm comfortable with it and I've used it for many other projects. Java is simple and strongly typed, it makes object-oriented design fun and easy. Also, because Java is a child of the Internet, it can play many roles in a Web project. Everyone has heard of the Java Applet, but it's also possible to write ordinary applications in Java, such as my program, and Java Servlets, which run on Web servers as efficient replacements for CGI scripts.

In summary, I knew that this project would be too hard to do if we had to edit individual HTML pages. Therefore, I had to build a publishing system to automate the task of adding style to content. I chose to write the descriptions of our weeds in XML and write a Java program to compile those XML descriptions into a set of static Web pages.

Writing XML

Choosing an XML Parser

Although I could have written my own XML parser, I wanted to use an existing one, so first I considered the biggest division: a validating vs. non-validating parser. A validating parser checks your documents against the DTD and will refuse to parse invalid ones. The disadvantage is that a validating parser is larger and consumes more memory, which is important if it has to be downloaded by a viewer. A validating parser is also slower. However, because I was planning to write my XML documents by hand (and making mistakes), and because memory and speed weren't issues, I decided to use a validating parser. If I were writing an Applet, it would be best to test documents during development using a validating parser but use a non-validating parser in the Applet so as to save memory, bandwidth and time without the risk of invalid documents gumming up the works. A number of free XML parsers in Java were available in early February, but Microsoft's parser, MSXML in Java version 1.8, stood out from the rest because it was well documented. Because the XML draft specification changed after the release of MSIE 4.0, the MSXML/Java version 1.0 built into MSIE 4.0 is incompatible with version 1.8. (MSXML/Java can be downloaded from
`http://www.microsoft.com/xml/parser/jparser.asp`
where additional information about it can be found.)

A major factor in my decision was that source code was available for MSXML. Even though MSXML is well documented, even the best documentation has mistakes and omissions and taking a quick look at the source can provide a final answer to most questions. All software has bugs, particularly software that is in beta or using cutting edge technologies. If you've got the source often you can fix little bugs by yourself in minutes. When I discovered that MSXML out of the box wouldn't read external entities in a DTD, making it hard for me to import a list of foreign accent characters into my document, I poked around with the source quickly and changed one line of code to fix the problem.

An Example Document

XML programmers who will be processing files based on a standard DTD, such as MathML, CDF or RDF, or an existing DTD someone else wrote, won't have to write one.

I wrote my DTD based on a vision of what I wanted my final XML files to look like. I knew I needed tags for family, Latin, and common names, as well as a way to tag the plant descriptions for language and source. This idea was close to what the XML looks like today:

```
<?xml version="1.0"?>
<!DOCTYPE plantdata system "limon.dtd">
<plantdata>
 <species id="6">
<family>Cucurbitacea</family>
<latin>Momordica charantia L.</latin>
<common>balsam pear</common>
<common>balsam apple</common>
<common>cerasee bush</common>
<common xml:lang="es">archucha</common>
<common xml:lang="es">balsamina</common>
<common xml:lang="es">achochilla</common>
<common xml:lang="es">pepinillo</common>
<common xml:lang="es">cunde amor</common>
```

```
<common xml:lang="es">melao de Sao Caetano</common>
<common xml:lang="es">carcilla</common>

<text type="description" source="Direnzo98">
Vine, climbs by tendrils. Leaves are alternate, soft and lightly
hairy. Leaves are deeply lobed with five lobes. (Length about <cm>3</cm>)
Yellow flowers arise from leaf axils as do tendrils. Flower has five
petals, bright orange small clusters of pistils and stamen at center.
(Diameter about <cm>1.5</cm>) Pods are oval tapering to a point with rows of
 little spikes, green turning orange as they mature. Exploded
pods show bright orange peels and four red seeds. Inside is sticky.
Pod length (about <cm>2.5</cm>) Stem is hairy, very hairy at terminal
end. Found growing on fence along main road in full sun.
</text>
</species>
</plantdata>
```

The DTD

The document type description is a precise format definition of a class of XML documents. Because I was starting from scratch, instead of writing a program to work with somebody else's file format, I had to write my own DTD. Since I started with no experience with XML or with MSXML, I wrote the DTD one tag at a time. Each time I added a new feature to the DTD, I also added a few lines of code to the Java class MSXMLSpeciesFactory, the part of my program responsible for understanding the parse tree output of MSXML. This was a good way to learn XML one step at a time while always having a working program to experiment with. After I had a working prototype, I made small changes to make my DTD more consistent with the XML and XML-Linking standards. The current DTD is:

```
<!ELEMENT plantdata ( species )+>
<!ELEMENT species ( family?,latin*,common*,text*,cite*) >
<!ATTLIST species id CDATA #REQUIRED>

<!ELEMENT family ( #PCDATA ) >
<!ELEMENT latin ( #PCDATA ) >
<!ELEMENT common ( #PCDATA ) >
<!ATTLIST common  xml:lang CDATA "en">

<!ELEMENT text ( #PCDATA | a | cm | ref )* >
<!ATTLIST text type CDATA #REQUIRED>
<!ATTLIST text source CDATA #REQUIRED>
<!ATTLIST text xml:lang CDATA "en">

<!ELEMENT a (#PCDATA)>
<!ATTLIST a href CDATA #REQUIRED>
<!ATTLIST a xml:link CDATA #FIXED "simple">

<!ELEMENT cm (#PCDATA)>

<!ELEMENT ref EMPTY>
<!ATTLIST ref id CDATA #REQUIRED>


<!ELEMENT cite EMPTY >
<!ATTLIST cite source CDATA #REQUIRED>
<!ATTLIST cite page CDATA "">
```

```
<!ENTITY % ISOlat1 PUBLIC
  "ISO 8879-1986//ENTITIES Added Latin 1//EN//XML"
  "ISOlat1.pen" >
%ISOlat1;
```

Big Decisions

The XML specification contains the potential to create a vast range of document types. For instance, XML allows a DTD to contain recursive element definitions. This would be excellent for XML documents that have to represent tree-like data structures, but I decided early on that I wanted to avoid recursion because it would be complex and I didn't need it. I decided that the overall structure of my document would be much like an entry in a database. There would be several fields that I could fill in, with properties such as the family of a plant, the Latin name, and the common name.

I decided that it would be adequate to make the contents of a `<species>` tag, the element that defines a plant, have a very rigid structure. The family name is specified first, then the Latin name, then the common names, then blocks of texts describing the plants, and then a list of bibliographic citations – everything is always in the same order. I decided to make the content of a `<text>` tag less structured. Much like HTML, the contents of a `<text>` tag are ordinary text interspersed with a small set of tags for adding references to other plants, hyperlinks to arbitrary URLs, and for marking the units of numerical quantities.

Defining Elements

New elements are defined with the `<!ELEMENT>` tag. The relationship between tags is defined with a syntax similar to regular expression; for example, the element definition

```
<!ELEMENT species ( family?,latin*,common*,text*,cite*)>
```

means that the `species` element is allowed to contain, in order, one or zero (`?`) `<family>` elements, and zero or more (`*`) `<latin>`, `<common>`, `<text>` or `<cite>` elements. I also defined the attribute,

```
<!ATTLIST species id CDATA #REQUIRED>
```

which tells the XML parser that every `<species>` element must have an ID attribute specified, such as `<species id="6">`. One decision that I had to make was what information should go in attributes and what information should go in child elements. Both child elements and attributes can be made mandatory, so it would be reasonable, for instance, to make the species `ID` be an attribute or to make a new `<id>` element for containing the species ID. I decided it would save a few keystrokes to make it an attribute, so I did. Attributes have two big limitations compared to child elements, which led me to put the rest of the `<species>` element information in child elements. First, an attribute can hold only one value, but you can include a variable number of child elements in an element. Plants can have more than one Latin or common name, so I decided that those qualities should be specified in child elements. Although a plant can only have one family name, I decided to put it in a child element along with the Latin and common names for consistency. It would be possible to put multiple names in a single attribute string separated with commas, but I felt that this would be awkward and error prone.

The <family>, <latin> and <common> elements all wrap up a bit of text, like <family>Cucurbitacea</family>, so we tell the XML parser that the <family> element contains plain ordinary text, which XML calls #PCDATA. We define those elements as:

```
<!ELEMENT family  ( #PCDATA )>
```

From our reference books, we had the common names of some plants in English, Spanish and Portuguese. To specify the language of each common name, we used the standard "xml:lang" attribute. I made the language tagging decision based on conformity to standards. What I win is a design that was thought through by experts, and the knowledge that other people's XML processing software will be able to automatically understand my language tags. The "xml:lang" attribute is built into XML. XML parsers that comply with the standard will allow any tag in a document to contain the "xml:lang" attribute even if you do not define it explictly, but by defining it explictly I get to set a default, improve compatibilty with older parsers which do not implement the "xml:lang" feature (which was added at the last minute), and warn humans reading the DTD that I intend to use this feature. In early versions of my DTD, I tagged <common> and <text> for language using the 'LANG' attribute which I defined myself, following the language tagging convention for HTML 4.0. I changed this when I learned about "xml:lang".

The values that the xml:lang *attribute can hold are defined in the Internet Engineering Task Force's RFC1776 (RFC documents can be obtained from* http://www.ietf.org/*) which in turn is based on the ISO 639 standard. A list of language names can be found at* http://www.sil.org/sgml/iso639a.html.

The <text> element is more complex than the other child elements of <species> because, like <species>, it too contains child elements. Unlike <species>, however, <text> does not contain child elements in a rigid order, but instead allows a fluid mixture of child elements and text, much like HTML. It is defined,

```
<!ELEMENT text ( #PCDATA | a | cm | ref )*>
```

where (#PCDATA | a | cm | ref) means "#PCDATA or any element of the types <a>, <cm> or <ref/>" and * means zero or more of the same. Therefore, a <text> contains a mix of #PCDATA and those three elements. The <a> tag provides a hyperlinking capability, like the <A> tag in HTML that allows linking to any URL. The syntax of the <a> tag is designed to conform to the XML-linking proposal (see http://www.w3.org/TR/1998/WD-xlink-19980303). Because I use the standard syntax for hyperlinks, other XML applications such as Webcrawlers should be able to detect and follow hyperlinks in my documents.

The purpose of the <ref/> tag is to make an internal hyperlink from one plant to another keyed by the ID number of the referenced plant. Unlike the <a> tag, I wanted the text of the hyperlink – either the first Latin name of the plant, or the ID number if the plant is not identified – to be fixed. Therefore I decided to make <ref/> an empty tag which contains nothing and has only the ID attribute to specify the plant that it links to. I also provided the <cm> tag to mark numerical quantities measured in centimeters, so instead of writing 5 cm, I could write <cm>5</cm>. This would make it possible for a program to identitify the units of numerical quantities and convert them, for instance, from centimeters to inches.

The <text> element also contains several attributes. Although I haven't taken advantage of the capability yet, I wanted to be able to have more than one block of text per plant. For instance, we've found books that describe some of the plants in both English and Spanish, and we might want to incorporate the Spanish definitions into our site if we get permission from the publishers. We also have entries in our notebooks about our experiences with the plants that are interesting but don't belong in the descriptions, that may someday be added. Also, in the future, we might get somebody to help translate our descriptions into Spanish. If any such additional text gets entered into our system, we'd like to be able to tell our software to, for instance, put only English or only Spanish text into a set of Web pages, so we could make different versions for different languages, or to only include the descriptions that we wrote of plants. To deal with this, I added the `source` and `type` attributes and made the "`xml:lang`" attribute for marking language explicit. As in the case of the `id` attribute of <species>, I probably could have put this information in child elements of <text>. However, I felt that the right solution was to cleanly separate the text itself, contained inside the <text> element, and the information about the text (meta-information) which is contained in the attributes of <text>.

Like the attributes of <text>, the <cite> tag is also built for the future. My current Web page generation program does not process the <cite> tag; however, the default behavior of XML processing software is to ignore tags that it does not understand. The <cite> tag is specified in the DTD, so MSXML will validate it. MSXML also provides Element objects in the document tree it hands to my program, but when my program traverses the document tree, it never asks for <cite> elements, so they are ignored. Even so, the <cite> tag has the useful feature of providing a place to keep track of bibliographic citations inside the Weeds. Even now, I can read it when I look at my XML files with a text editor, and in the future I may upgrade my software to automatically add hyperlinks to a bibliography.

The last two lines in the DTD declare a parameter entity:

```
<!ENTITY % ISOlat1 PUBLIC
 "ISO 8879-1986//ENTITIES Added Latin 1//EN//XML"
 "ISOlat1.pen" >
%ISOlat1;
```

to import a list of entity declarations from an external file, a piece of which looks like

```
...
 <!ENTITY Agrave "&#192;" >     <!-- capital A, grave accent -->
 <!ENTITY Aacute "&#193;" >     <!-- capital A, acute accent -->
 <!ENTITY Acirc  "&#194;" >     <!-- capital A, circumflex accent -->
 <!ENTITY Atilde "&#195;" >     <!-- capital A, tilde -->
...
```

The purpose of this file is to import the definitions of accented characters used in European languages such as Spanish. These are the standard entity definitions used in HTML, so the effect is to make my XML document transparent to these characters.

I got the file ISOlat1.pen from Rick Jelliffe who sent me an e-mail after seeing an early version of my DTD, which included just a few character entity declarations that I had added by hand for the two accented characters that appeared in the Spanish common names of my weeds. By simply including this file in my DTD, I made my document transparent to the entities used for accented characters in HTML 4.0, making it easy to add international text. ISOLat1.pen, together with several similar files such as ISOLat2.pen and ISOtech.pen, which make available other parts of the HTML 4.0 entity set, are available with the XML files available on the (Wrox/Honeylocust) Web site. (See the section "Building the Weeds..." at the end of the chapter.)

A minor problem I encountered in developing this DTD was that MSXML version 1.8 did not support external parameter entities inside a DTD. Since Microsoft was so kind as to provide the source code, I fixed this problem by making a one-line change the source and recompiling. This is discussed later in the Section, "MSXML: Hacking the Source".

Evolution

Because I started out with no experience in XML, I built this DTD one line at a time. I started with a single XML file and the early draft of the Java class that is the interface between MSXML and the rest of my program, MSXMLSpeciesFactory, and slowly added elements to the DTD, the XML file, and to the code. This was a good way to get my hands dirty and learn XML fast while building some working code.

After you have a small collection of XML files, you may still want to make changes in your DTD. The problem with this is that you then need to change your software and your XML files to match. It was easy for me to change my software, since I made the decision to put all of the XML dependence in my program in a single Java class. A tool that I found useful when I changed my DTD was a global search and replace program. For instance, in the first draft of my DTD I used an attribute titled "LANG" to tag languages instead of the standard "xml:lang" attribute and had already written 32 XML files using the old attribute. With a combination of UNIX shell scripts and the sed command I was able to replace every occurrence of "LANG" with "xml:lang" in just a minute. It's easy to change your DTD when your project is confined to your desktop, rather than when it involves multiple people, files and applications, so you should refine your DTD in the early stages of your project while you still can.

In summary, if you are defining your own file format using XML, you will have to write your own DTD. I started with a picture in my mind of what my XML files would look like, using a rigid database-like format for the family, Latin and common names of plants, and a free-flowing HTML-like format for text descriptions of the plants. I wrote my DTD incrementally, adding elements, attributes, and entities one at a time along with the software for interpreting them since this made it easy to learn XML.

Processing XML

A Three-Layer Architecture

Something I enjoy about starting a new programming project is the chance to try out new ideas while building it. After all, if you always do everything the same way, you never get the chance to learn and become a better programmer. Before writing a single line of code, I sat down and made a few decisions about the broad strokes of the design, and about the discipline I would apply to myself in little matters.

My major architectural decision before I started coding was that the program would be roughly organized in three layers: input, data, and output.

The data layer is a set of Java classes, program objects designed to hold the descriptions of plants, that stand between the input and output layers. The job of the input layer is to convert the XML element output of MSXML into the format of the data layer. The output layer converts the information in the data layer into HTML documents.

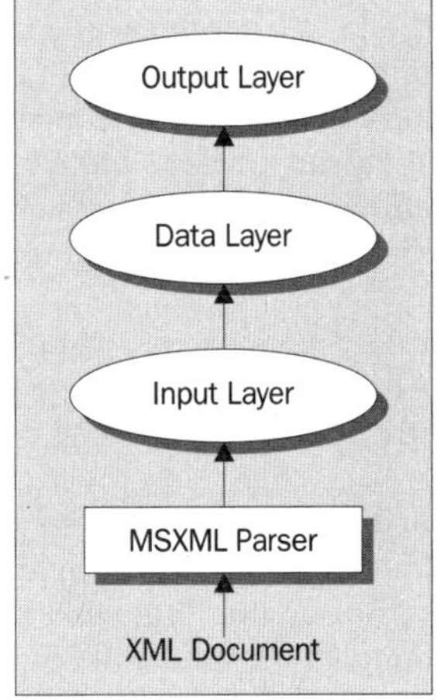

The main reason that I decided to build three layers was that XML is a rapidly evolving technology that I didn't fully understand. If I built my whole program around MSXML, the designer of MSXML would have made many of the design decisions of my program for me. Without experience in MSXML, I would have bought into a set of decisions I didn't understand. So, I designed my program so that only one class depended on MSXML, so if I wanted to use another XML parser or if I wanted to abandon XML for another system such as a database, it would be straightforward. Writing the output layer is easier, because it only sees special-purpose objects from the data layer which have exactly the methods I want to manipulate, rather than a collection of Element, Attribute and Entity objects which are complex and general. Finally, if I wanted to produce output that isn't HTML, say I wanted to make a printed flora using LaTeX, I could keep my input and data layers and just write a new output layer.

Another way in which a data layer is helpful has to do with the strongly typed nature of the Java language. It is possible to turn the Elements returned by MSXML into HTML directly; for example, I could get the language of a `text` element by doing

```
msxmlElement.getAttribute("xml:lang");
```

rather than

```
myTextObject.getLanguage().
```

But suppose I misspelled the name of the attribute. If I typed

```
msxmlElement.getAttribute("xml:fang");
```

the program would compile just fine and MSXML would simply return a null reference when this method was called. Unless I was careful to add code to detect this null reference, this incorrect result could propagate into my program and cause unpredictable problems, including ones that might not be obvious until an end user starts using the program. On the other hand, if I type:

```
myTextObject.getFangluage()
```

the Java compiler will complain immediately. By putting all of my XML-specific code in one place, I minimize the number of times that I need to access attributes by name, and the risk of making this kind of mistake. The most important principle in the design was simplicity. I wanted to make my Web site quickly, while retaining the potential for expansion. I didn't want to put a lot of time and effort into developing features that I didn't need. In the end, the simpler you can make your program, the less code you need to write and the faster you can get the job done.

I used Java's access control and packaging mechanisms to help enforce the three-layer architecture. Although you can dream up a design and back it up with superhuman discipline, a good thing about strongly typed languages is that you can get the compiler to enforce your design decisions for you.

A downside is that you can spend a lot of time fighting the compiler, but when you work with the language rather than against it, you'll find that strong typing is a great way to help strengthen your self-discipline. But what kind of discipline do you want? First, I had a good understanding of how to connect the data and output layers, so I was ready to formalize the relationship between them. On the other hand, I wasn't so sure what the best relationship between the input and data layers would be, so I wanted to be able to change it easily.

My solution to this was to break the program into two different Java packages: one called `honeylocust.limon`, which contains the output layer, and one called `honeylocust.limon.representation`, which contains the input and data layers. This way Java enforces strict control over the data/output layer interface and looser control over the input/data layer interface. It's not that I don't want to have a good design for the input/data layer interface, but that I'd rather experiment with different ideas and gain some perspective before strengthening that aspect of the design if I need to in the future.

The Data Layer

Species.java

The object used to represent a plant is Species. Because I'd like to have the option of substituting different implementations of Species (so we can renumber the plants) I decided to write both an interface and an implementation for Species. The interface contains all of the methods that I'd like to be accessible to the output layer. This interface's notable omissions are methods for setting or changing the state of Species. The output layer cannot change a Species object, so the Species object is *immutable* with respect to the output layer.

When I started building object-oriented systems, I felt that I needed to build the maximum level of functionality into every class I designed, so I always build methods into my objects which would allow other objects to change them. Later, I learned that by writing only the methods I needed, I could write less code and gain many advantages. For instance, objects that live in a multithreaded environment, such as GUI systems (the Java AWT and Microsoft Windows are threaded, for example) and server platforms, can be damaged when two threads try to change them simultaneously. An immutable object is immune to these problems, known as "race conditions", since it cannot be changed at all. If we wish to "change" an immutable object, we simply create a new object with the change we desire. Since the old object is still available, it's easy to back the change out if we'd like to implement features such as multi-level undo or transactions.

Besides, the smaller and simpler an interface is, the less code there is to write and maintain.

```
package honeylocust.limon.representation;

import java.io.File;

public interface Species {

 public String getId();
 public LanguageString getFamily();
 public LanguageString[] getLatin();
 public LanguageString[] getCommon();
 public Text[] getTexts();
 public boolean identified();
 public File getBigImage();
 public File getSmallImage();
};
```

SpeciesImpl.java

SpeciesImpl is an implementation of Species. Because SpeciesImpl is not a public class, it can't be instantiated by code in packages other than `honeylocust.limon.representation`, and because it implements the Species interface, the methods that are defined in Species can be accessed from the output layer, but nothing else. Note that this object is not immutable as seen by the input layer. If I wanted it to be, I could provide a constructor containing all the data in this object and make all the fields private. However, such a constructor would be complex and require frequent modification during the early stages of coding, so I decide to allow the input layer's only class, `MSXMLSpeciesFactory`, to create a Species object and initialize it by writing into the fields of the Species object directly.

One of my coding conventions shows up in this class. It's easy to get confused about which variables are local and which ones are class fields when programming Java. To put an end to this problem, I've gotten into the habit of prefacing all my data field variable names with "d_". I also make static variables (which are shared by all instances of a class) start with "s_" and configurable parameters start with "p_". This isn't required, but I've spared myself a lot of trouble ever since I started doing this.

```
package honeylocust.limon.representation;

import java.util.Vector;
import java.io.File;

class SpeciesImpl implements Species {

 String d_id;
 LanguageString d_family;
 LanguageString d_latin[];
 LanguageString d_common[];
 Text d_texts[];
 File d_bigImage;
 File d_smallImage;

 public String getId() {
 return d_id;
 };
```

```
    public LanguageString getFamily() {
    return d_family;
    };

    public LanguageString[] getLatin() {
    return (LanguageString[]) d_latin.clone();
    };

    public LanguageString[] getCommon() {
    return (LanguageString[]) d_common.clone();
    };

    public Text[] getTexts() {
    return (Text[]) d_texts.clone();
    };

    public boolean identified() {
    if (d_latin==null)
     return false;

    if (d_latin.length==0)
     return false;

    return true;
    };

    public File getBigImage() {
    return d_bigImage;
    };

    public File getSmallImage() {
    return d_smallImage;
    };

};
```

LanguageString.java

LanguageString is a class that represents a string and the language the string is written in. LanguageString is an example of a completely immutable class. An obscure Java feature that gets used in LanguageString, among other places, is string interning. I first learned about interning at

`http://developer.netscape.com/docs/technote/simple/Internment.html`

The `String` class in Java has a method called `String.intern()` which returns a reference to the string you call it on. Each reference is unique, but refers to the same string. That is, every interned string with the same value is the same string. Consider the following code snippet:

```
String a="Hello";
String b="Hello";

String c=a.intern();
String d="Hello".intern();

if (a==b)
 System.out.println("a==b");
```

```
if (c==d)
 System.out.println("c==d");
```

The output of the above is

```
<output>
c==d
</output>
```

This works because `String` is just like any other object. "a" and "b" are really references to two different, independently created `String` objects. The equality operator for objects compares object references – two objects are equal if they are the exact same object, not if the *value* of those objects is the same. Because `a` and `b` point to two different strings, `a==b` is false.

Sure, you can always compare their values using `String.compareTo()` or `String.equals()`, but sometimes it's more convenient to compare strings with the `==` operator. This is where interning comes in. The `String.intern()` method uses a hash table to keep track of every string it creates, so that it returns only one string with any particular value. Since `c` and `d` both have the value "Hello" and were created by intern, `c` and `d` are the same object, and `c==d` is true.

By using string interning, I made a tradeoff. It takes time to intern a string, but afterwards string comparisons are faster and simpler to code. Each unique string you `intern()` costs memory in the internal hashtable which will never be garbage collected, which is a potential memory leak. Interning is good for strings which are symbols, strings that often have the same value (such as keywords), and variable names in a programming language. For instance, it's worth interning the strings which represent the names of (human) languages (ISO 639 strings to be precise) since many different LanguageStrings will be written in just the same few languages. In this case, my program doesn't consume an excessive amount of time or memory, so I used interning to make the many string comparisons in my program simpler to code, since development time often costs more than computer time.

Interning isn't just something Java does for Strings, it's something that you can do for your own classes. LanguageString itself provides an interning facility. I built it in because many plants share the same family name, and it makes it convenient to check that two plants are in the same family. The author of MSXML also decided interning is a good idea for Name objects. Since there is no public constructor for Name objects, every instance is created through the `Name.create()` function so that all Names are interned.

Another JDK 1.1 feature used in LanguageString is Blank **Finals**. When you write something like:

```
private final String d_string;
```

you are declaring a variable `final` (and therefore immutable). In JDK 1.0.2, `final` worked like **`const`** in C, and the value of the variable must be specified when it is declared, like

```
private final String d_string="foo";
```

In JDK 1.1 you're not required to specify the value of a `final` variable where it is declared, providing you do specify its value in the static initializer and all of the constructors and never change it after that.

```
package honeylocust.limon.representation;

import com.sun.java.util.collections.Comparable;
import java.util.Hashtable;

public class LanguageString implements Comparable {

 private final String d_string;
 private final String d_language;

 private static String s_defaultLanguage="en".intern();
 private static final Hashtable s_symbols=new Hashtable();
                                                // used for intern() facility

 public LanguageString(String s) {
  d_string=s;
  d_language=s_defaultLanguage;
 };

 public LanguageString(String s,String lang) {
  d_string=s;
  if (lang==null)
  lang=s_defaultLanguage;

  d_language=lang.intern();
 };

 public String toString() {
  return d_string;
 };

 public String getLanguage() {
 return d_language;
 };

 public int compareTo(Object o) throws ClassCastException {
 if (!(o instanceof LanguageString))
  throw new ClassCastException();

 LanguageString other=(LanguageString) o;

 // the following could become a performance bottleneck but it works

 return (d_string.toUpperCase()).compareTo(other.d_string.toUpperCase());
 };

// this does the same thing for LanguageString that String.intern()
// does for String.

 public LanguageString intern() {
 String uniqname=d_string+"&"+d_language;
 synchronized(s_symbols) {
  LanguageString interned=(LanguageString) s_symbols.get(uniqname);
  if(interned==null) {
  interned=this;
     s_symbols.put(uniqname,this);
  }
  return interned;
 }
 }
};
```

Text.java and TextImpl.java

A **Text** is a piece of text, tagged as to its origin and language. It corresponds to the `<text>` element in `limon.dtd`. A Text is a collection of TextChunks. Because I'm immediately interested in providing an alternate implementation of Text, I've made it an interface and provided `TextImpl.java`, an implementation of Text.

```
package honeylocust.limon.representation;

public interface Text {

 public String getType();
 public TextChunk[] getChunks();
 public String getSource();

 public String getLanguage();
 public String getText();
};

package honeylocust.limon.representation;

class TextImpl implements Text {

 TextChunk[] d_chunks;

 String d_type;
 String d_source;
 String d_language;

 public TextImpl() {
 };

 public TextImpl(Text t) {
 d_type=t.getText();
 d_source=t.getSource();
 d_language=t.getLanguage();
 d_chunks=t.getChunks();
 };

 public String getType() {
 return d_type;
 }

 public TextChunk[] getChunks() {
 return ((TextChunk[]) d_chunks.clone());
 }

 public String getSource() {
 return d_source;
 }

 public String getLanguage() {
 if (d_language==null)
  return "en".intern();

 return d_language;
 }

 public String getText() {
 StringBuffer sb=new StringBuffer();
```

```
  for(int i=0;i<d_chunks.length;i++)
   sb.append(d_chunks[i].getText());

  return sb.toString();
  };
 e
 };
```

TextChunk.java

TextChunk is itself an interface. The only thing it needs to do is return a default representation of itself as a string. This ensures that we can print out a Text simply by chaining these strings together. A smarter program for outputting texts could supply its own code for doing something special with RefChunks, AnchorChunks and other special chunk types. Because I didn't want to build any HTML dependence into this code, fancy chunk types simply return information about themselves rather than returning the HTML it would take to render them.

```
package honeylocust.limon.representation;

import java.util.Vector;

public interface TextChunk {
 abstract public String getText();
};
```

PlainChunk.java

```
package honeylocust.limon.representation;

public class PlainChunk implements TextChunk {

 private final String d_text;

 public PlainChunk(String text) {
 d_text=text;
 };

 public String getText() {
 return d_text;
 };

};
```

AnchorChunk.java

```
package honeylocust.limon.representation;

public class AnchorChunk implements TextChunk {

 String d_text;
 String d_href;

 public AnchorChunk(String text,String href) {
 d_text=text;
 d_href=href;
 };
```

```
 public String getText() {
 return d_text;
 };

 public String getHref() {
 return d_href;
 };

};
```

CMChunk.java

```
package honeylocust.limon.representation;

public class CMChunk implements TextChunk {

 String d_text;

 public CMChunk(String text) {
 d_text=text;
 };

 public String getText() {
 return d_text+" cm";
 };

};
```

RefChunk.java

```
package honeylocust.limon.representation;

public interface RefChunk extends TextChunk {

 public String getId();

};
```

RefChunkImpl.java

```
package honeylocust.limon.representation;

public class RefChunkImpl implements RefChunk {

 private final String d_id;

 public RefChunkImpl(String id) {
 d_id=id;
 };

 public String getText() {
 return "Plant "+d_id;
 };

 public String getId() {
 return d_id;
 };

};
```

Summary

Since both XML and HTML are rapidly evolving, I didn't want the design of my XML reader and my HTML generator to be tied together, therefore I built a data layer to provide a representation of the plants independent of the details of XML reading and HTML generation. The structure of the data layer is parallel to the structure of my XML files. For instance, the Species object corresponds to the `<species>` tag, and the Text object corresponds to the `<text>` tag. Attributes and simpler child elements are now accessed through methods. For instance, common names are accessed through the **`getCommon()`** method of Species. They are represented by LanguageString objects which hold both a string and a letter code (e.g."**en**" for English) designating the language the string is written in.

The Input Layer

MSXML: Hacking the Source

According to the XML specification, a document type description (DTD) can include text from another file through an external entity, much as a C program can include text with the `#include` directive. I found that MSXML in Java version 1.8 did not support this feature, so I made a small change in the source code to add it. Before doing so I checked the license for restrictions on derivative works, and happily, Microsoft's main concern was that I not attempt to foist my modified version of MSXML as a genuine Microsoft product. To avoid confusion for both humans and programs that might want to use the original version of MSXML, I renamed MSXML's Java packages. This was accomplished by running an automatic search and replace on all of MSXML's files replacing the string "`com.ms.xml`" with "`honeylocust.msxml`".

Often a bug or shortcoming in a program can be repaired by changing a single line. The challenge is finding which line to change in an 11,080 line program written and designed by somebody else. Looking at somebody else's code is like looking through a keyhole – from looking at just one part of the program at a time, you have to understand enough about the program to find the part responsible.

The first sign of trouble was the error message

<output>
Missing entity 'aacute'.
Location: file:/afs/msc.cornell.edu/home/henley/houle/media/limon/plantxml/10.xml(13,38)
Context: <PLANTDATA><SPECIES><COMMON>
</output>

When I copied the internal entity declarations directly into my DTD it worked correctly, so I concluded that external entities were not being loaded into DTD's. After looking at the documentation, I noticed that the Document object had a "`setLoadExternal()`" method which controlled the loading of external entitites. I looked at the source code for that method:

```
public void setLoadExternal(boolean yes) {
 loadExternal = yes;
}
```

which made me realize that the Document object has a field called `loadExternal`. I used the UNIX `grep` command to find any instances of the word "`loadExternal`" in the entire source and found

```
<output>
om/Document.java:  loadExternal = true;
om/Document.java:  loadExternal = true;
om/Document.java:  loadExternal = yes;
om/Document.java: public boolean loadExternal()
om/Document.java:  return loadExternal;
om/Document.java:  parser.parse(url,this,dtd,this,caseInsensitive,loadExternal);
om/Document.java:  parser.parse(in,this,dtd,this,caseInsensitive,loadExternal);
om/Document.java: boolean loadExternal;

</output>
```

The only references to `loadExternal` were in the `Document` method, but the value of `loadExternal` gets passed into the parse method of the parser

```
public void load(URL url) throws ParseException {
 clear();
 URLdoc = url;
 parser = new Parser();
 parser.parse(url,this,dtd,this,caseInsensitive,loadExternal);
}
```

This made me focus my attention on the `Parser` object in the `com.ms.xml`.parser package. I took a look at the `parse` method

```
public final void parse(URL url, ElementFactory factory, DTD dtd, Element root,
                  boolean caseInsensitive, boolean loadExt) throws ParseException
{
 this.dtd = dtd;
 this.root = root;
 this.loadexternal = loadExt;
 setURL(url);
 setFactory(factory);
 this.caseInsensitive = caseInsensitive;
 safeParse();
}
```

and found that the parser has its own field labeled "`loadexternal`" that controls whether external entities will be loaded. I went looking for uses of this variable and found

```
if (loadexternal)
 loadDTD(en.getURL(), current.defaultNameSpace);
```

This led me to the problem. It turned out that in the `loadDTD` method, MSXML creates a new parser to parse the DTD. The only trouble is that it doesn't tell the new parser that it too should load external entities. Adding this feature took just one line.

```
public final void loadDTD(String urlStr, Atom nameSpace) throws ParseException {
 try {
  URL u = new URL(url, urlStr);
  Parser parser = new Parser();
  parser.dtd = this.dtd;
  parser.setURL(u);
  parser.setFactory(factory);
```

```
    parser.caseInsensitive = this.caseInsensitive;
    parser.loadexternal=this.loadexternal; // Added by Paul Houle 1998
    Element root = factory.createElement(null,Element.ELEMENT, nameDOCTY
  PE,null);
    parser.newContext(root, null, Element.ELEMENT, false, nameSpace,
                                               current.spaceTable);
    parser.parseInternalSubset();
   } catch (IOException e) {
    error("Couldn't find external DTD '" + urlStr + "'");
   }
  }
```

which makes the new parser inherit the same value of `loadExternal` as the current parser. Now external entities can be used inside a DTD.

The Input Layer: Turning XML into Species

For sanity preservation, I decided to put all of the dependence on MSXML into one class. This means I can switch to another parser or data format just by changing this class. It also means that when I change my DTD or if I have to make changes in the code that are specific to XML, there is only one place to look.

MSXMLSpeciesFactory

MSXMLSpeciesFactory is a factory class, and all of its methods are static. Its job is to create and fully initialize new instances of Species as defined in an XML document. First, we import all of the classes that we need from MSXML and from the standard Java libraries. Although I could import whole packages at a time, like

```
import honeylocust.msxml.om.*;
```

by importing individual classes I keep myself concious of exactly what my code depends on. This is also a big help for people who read your code and have to figure out what is connected to what.

```
package honeylocust.limon.representation;

import honeylocust.msxml.om.Document;
import honeylocust.msxml.om.Element;
import honeylocust.msxml.om.ElementCollection;
import honeylocust.msxml.parser.ParseException;
import honeylocust.msxml.util.Name;

import java.io.File;
import java.net.MalformedURLException;
import java.net.URL;
import java.util.Vector;
```

Next I create a number of static fields that let us refer, in a compact manner, to names that are going to occur again and again. It's easier to write `n_SPECIES` rather than `Name.create("species")`. This style also enlists the compiler in spell-checking your Names. Much like the use of the "d_" prefix to mark data fields, I marked the beginning of all my names with "n_" to keep track of them.

```
public class MSXMLSpeciesFactory {

  static final Name n_SPECIES=Name.create("species");
  static final Name n_FAMILY=Name.create("family");
  static final Name n_LATIN=Name.create("latin");
  static final Name n_COMMON=Name.create("common");
  static final Name n_TEXT=Name.create("text");
  static final Name n_A=Name.create("a");
  static final Name n_CM=Name.create("cm");
  static final Name n_REF=Name.create("ref");
...
```

MSXMLSpeciesFactory has two public methods. One takes a File and an argument, the other takes a URL. Both read any `<species>` tags and their child elements out of XML and add them to a Vector. MSXML can load XML from one of two sources, an InputStream or a URL. Although it is possible to pass a FileInputStream into MSXML, then MSXML wouldn't be aware of what directory the file is in. This is important because I'd like MSXML to find a DTD stored in the same directory as the XML file. Referencing the DTD with a relative URL solves the problem. The version of parseLimon which takes a file does nothing more than convert the File object (which actually represents a file name in a cross-platform manner) into a "file:" URL and then call the version of parseLimon which takes a URL.

The version which takes a URL creates a new XML document object, configures the parser to allow loading external objects such as DTD's, and uses the `Document.load()` method to load the document.

A document conforming to the `limon.dtd` contains a single `<plantdata>` element, which contains a list of `<species>` elements. We get the root element, `<plantdata>`, and then use `root.getChildren()` to get an ElementCollection of SpeciesElements which we hand off to our own parseSpecies for handling.

```
public static void parseLimon(Vector v,File f) throws Exception {
parseLimon(v,new URL("file:"+f.getAbsolutePath()));
};

public static void parseLimon(Vector v,URL u) throws Exception {
Document d=new Document();
d.setLoadExternal(true);
try {
 d.load(u);
} catch(ParseException e) {
 d.reportError(e,System.out);
 System.exit(-1);
};

Element root=d.getRoot();
ElementCollection plants=root.getChildren();

for(int i=0;i<plants.getLength();i++) {
 Element plantElement=plants.getChild(i);
 if (plantElement.getTagName()==n_SPECIES) {
    Species species=MSXMLSpeciesFactory.parseSpecies(plantElement);
    v.addElement(species);
 };
};
};
```

As a simple way to organize the class, I decided to write a method for parsing each kind of element, parseSpecies, to take an Element object as a parameter and return a Species object. I have to make it check whether the Element passed in is really a Species element. Since MSXML returns NULL when you try to access a nonexistent element or attribute, it's a good idea to practice defensive programming.

Here we create a SpeciesImpl, which gets downcasted to Species after it leaves this method. Since a method which only knows an object is of type Species can't mess with its default fields, this reinforces access control. This isn't a bulletproof use of access protection against a programmer determined to abuse it, but a disciplined use appropriate within a package.

Then we go through the attributes and subelements of the `<species>` element to parse it. First we grab the ID attribute using `Element.getAttribute()`. Since the family element is simple, we include the code to parse it within the method. Note that we `intern()` the LanguageString because many plants are in the same family and it's convenient to be able to compare the objects directly.

It's also nice to write convenience methods for functions that are reusable. For instance, the `getSingleChild()` method makes it easy to handle cases when, like `<family>` inside of `<species>`, there is at most one instance of a subelement in an element and you don't want to mess with ElementCollections.

```
static Species parseSpecies(Element e) throws Exception {
if (e.getTagName()!=n_SPECIES)
 throw new Exception("Element must be a SPECIES Element for second-stage
parse!");

SpeciesImpl species=new SpeciesImpl();

species.d_id=(String) e.getAttribute("id");
Element familyElement=getSingleChild(e,n_FAMILY);
if (familyElement!=null)
 species.d_family=new LanguageString(familyElement.getText(),"la").intern();

species.d_latin=convertToLanguageStringArray(e,n_LATIN,"la");
species.d_common=convertToLanguageStringArray(e,n_COMMON);

ElementCollection textElements=new ElementCollection(e,n_TEXT,-1);
Text[] texts=new Text[textElements.getLength()];

for(int i=0;i<textElements.getLength();i++) {
 texts[i]=parseText(textElements.getChild(i));
};

species.d_texts=texts;

return species;
};

// Convenience method:
// If there is only one child of a certain type, this method gets it
// without the bother of fussing with a Collection

static Element getSingleChild(Element e,Name kind) throws Exception {
ElementCollection ec=new ElementCollection(e,kind,-1);
if (ec.getLength()>1)
 throw new Exception("I'm only supposed to get a single child!");
```

```
  if (ec.getLength()==0)
   return null;
  else
   return ec.getChild(0);
  };

  /* In this case there isn't any language data in the XML and all of */
  /* the strings will be in the same language */

  static LanguageString[] convertToLanguageStringArray(Element e,Name kind,String
lang) throws Exception {
  ElementCollection ec=new ElementCollection(e,kind,-1);

  LanguageString[] sarray=new LanguageString[ec.getLength()];

  for(int i=0;i<ec.getLength();i++) {
   sarray[i]=new LanguageString(ec.getChild(i).getText().trim(),lang);
  };

  return sarray;
  };
```

convertToLanguageStringArray also works around a bug in MSXML v 1.8. MSXML doesn't appear to automatically keep track of the default values of attributes, so we have to fill them in ourselves.

```
  static LanguageString[] convertToLanguageStringArray(Element e,Name kind) throws
xception {
  ElementCollection ec=new ElementCollection(e,kind,-1);

  LanguageString[] sarray=new LanguageString[ec.getLength()];

  for(int i=0;i<ec.getLength();i++) {
   Element child=ec.getChild(i);
   String lang=(String) child.getAttribute("xml:lang");
   if (lang==null)
    lang="en";

   sarray[i]=new LanguageString(ec.getChild(i).getText().trim(),lang);
  };

  return sarray;
  };
```

Just as `<species>` is parsed by `parseSpecies`, `parseText()` handles the `<text>` tag.

```
  static Text parseText(Element e) {
  TextImpl text=new TextImpl();

  text.d_type=(String) e.getAttribute("type");
  text.d_source=(String) e.getAttribute("source");
  text.d_language=(String) e.getAttribute("xml:lang");

  ElementCollection chunkElements=new ElementCollection(e,null,-1);
  text.d_chunks=new TextChunk[chunkElements.getLength()];

  for(int i=0;i<chunkElements.getLength();i++) {
   Element f=chunkElements.getChild(i);
```

```
    if (f.getTagName()==n_A) {
        text.d_chunks[i]=parseAnchorChunk(f);
    } else if (f.getTagName()==n_CM) {
        text.d_chunks[i]=parseCMChunk(f);
    } else if (f.getTagName()==n_REF) {
        text.d_chunks[i]=parseRefChunk(f);
    } else
        text.d_chunks[i]=parsePlainChunk(f);

  };
  return text;
  };
```

Finally, each kind of text chunk is parsed by its own method.

```
  static PlainChunk parsePlainChunk(Element e) {
  return new PlainChunk(e.getText());
  };

  static CMChunk parseCMChunk(Element e) {
  return new CMChunk(e.getText());
  };

  static RefChunk parseRefChunk(Element e) {
  return new RefChunkImpl((String) e.getAttribute("ID"));
  };

  static AnchorChunk parseAnchorChunk(Element e) {
  return new AnchorChunk(e.getText(),(String) e.getAttribute("href"));
  };
};
```

Attaching Images

An important pair of attributes of Species that aren't set by MSXMLSpeciesFactory are the filenames of the large and small images that go with each plant. Because this information isn't currently stored in the XML files and has nothing to do with the XML parser, I decided to give this function its own class, ImageAttach. An instance of ImageAttach is passed a File object, which holds the directory where images are stored. ImageAttach assumes that there will be two files, a bigImage with the name `[species id].gif` and a smallImage with the name `[species id]half.gif`. This class performs an important service by ensuring that all of the images are in place – the `attachImages()` method throws a FileNotFoundException if the image files are not found, causing the program to abort.

This isn't the most beautiful part of the program – currently two methods need to be called to initialize a Species. First, it is created by MSXMLSpeciesFactory, then the images need to be filled in by ImageAttach. This poses the risk that a programmer could do the first but not the second. In a large project this would be dangerous, but here it is only a minor blemish.

```
package honeylocust.limon.representation;

import java.io.File;
import java.io.FileNotFoundException;
import java.util.Enumeration;
import java.util.Vector;
```

```
public class ImageAttach {

  final File d_path;

  public ImageAttach(File path) {
  d_path=path;
  };

  public void attachImages(Vector v) throws FileNotFoundException {
  for(Enumeration e=v.elements();e.hasMoreElements();) {
   SpeciesImpl s=(SpeciesImpl) e.nextElement();
   attachImages(s);
  };

  };

  void attachImages(SpeciesImpl s) throws FileNotFoundException {
  s.d_bigImage=safeFile(s.getId()+".gif");
  s.d_smallImage=safeFile(s.getId()+"half.gif");
  };

  File safeFile(String s) throws FileNotFoundException {
  File f=new File(d_path,s);
  if (!f.exists())
   throw new FileNotFoundException(s);

  return f;
  };

};
```

Summary

The input layer consists of just two classes. One of them is MSXMLSpeciesFactory, which is responsible for using MSXML to parse XML files and converting that information into Species objects. The other is ImageAttach which locates the files that contain images, ensures that they exist, and completes the creation of the data layer by attaching the images to the Species objects.

The Output Layer

Designing the HTML

The purpose of the output layer is to turn Species objects into styled Web pages. Although I thought it was important to make the pages have a distinctive and consistent look, my expectation that the people of Limon and others might want to view the pages using automatic language translation software was a strong constraint. (At

`http://babelfish.altavista.digital.com/`

there is an impressive demonstration which automatically translates Web pages between English and several European languages.) Although `.gif` files of 'fontified' text can greatly improve the look of Web pages, I decided not to do this because such text cannot be automatically translated.

Information architecture

I started by designing the structure of the site as a whole, whose final design essentially mirrors that of a print flora. I decided to have one Web page for each plant, as well as index pages by Latin name, common name, and family name. There would also be a top "cover" page that would orient new users to the Weeds and several appendices containing an essay about the project and information about the authors. Although much of the structure of the site is visible to the users, I also had to decide where to put all of the hidden files that the HTML files depend on, such as image files and style sheets. In an early draft of the project, the directory organization was:

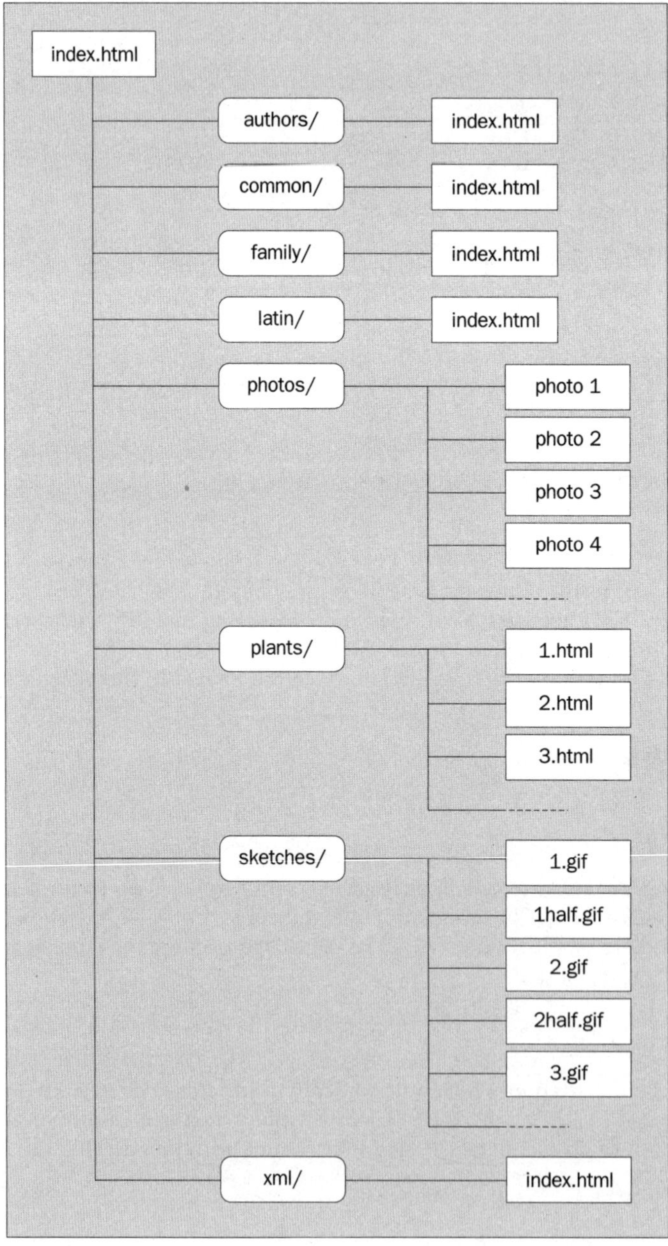

Because I built a publishing system that automatically generates the site, I had an easy time changing the layout of the site to one that is more flexible.

There were three pressures driving me to change the file organization of the site. One of them was realizing that the numbering of our weeds didn't convey any information other than the order in which we found the plants. Perhaps the first plants we found were the most common, but that isn't very scientific. All print floras sort plants by family, then by genus and species. This way you can flip through the pages and find plants that are similar to each other, making the navigational system even more useful. If the plants are renumbered, then either the plant images would have to be renumbered or the HTML files would have to have links to plants with different numbers. At the time, I had just copied all of the plant images into the sketches directory by hand and the XML processor didn't touch them – it just assumed that they were there to make hyperlinks to. Any quick solution to this problem would be error prone – if the numbers of the plant Web pages were different than the numbers of the weeds, the pages would be confusing to a human maintaining the Web site. If the numbers of the plant images were to be changed, this process would have to be automated, since as we identify more plants, the order of the plants (and their images) would change.

A second pressure was that Olivia and I had recently read the notorious "Killer Web Sites" by Dave Seigel

```
http://www.killersites.com/
```

which taught us that by putting extra attention into compressing image files, you can make a big difference in how fast a site loads without seriously compromising quality. We were able to cut the size of the images nearly in half with little reduction in quality by reducing the number of colors to 32 with ImageMagick

```
http://www.wizards.dupont.com/cristy/ImageMagick.html
```

By going even further, we were able to make an edition that, although it didn't look quite as good as the original, would fit on a single floppy, a big plus for a product to be distributed in low-tech parts of the world. So, we also wanted a way to choose between different sets of images to let us produce both a standard edition with flawless images and a slightly compromised edition that would fit on a floppy.

The third problem was the one that really forced the change, though. On a Unix system, it is customary to do all of the development for a site on a working Web server since a Unix server simply makes all the files underneath a specified directory available to the world. Often there are two Web servers, one used for testing and one used for production, and password protection can be used to ensure that the public doesn't see anything that you don't want to make available. Editing a site on a working Web server avoids the problems that arise from differences between the environment on the server and a local machine. There is no risk of files being lost, overwritten, or garbled when they are moved, and all of the CGI scripts and other server facilities are always available.

However, when it came time to make a ZIP disk edition of "Weeds" to send to Limon, I made the dismaying discovery that "Weeds" didn't work correctly on a local file system. The problem was my reliance on the behavior of a Web server, which serves the page "index.html" in a directory when the browser asks for "/", so I'd have to change all my links that end in "/" to end in "/index.html". Even though I think the Web looks nicer when all the ugly mechanics aren't sticking out, being able to run Weeds off a local file system, instead of off a Web server, is essential for a product of interest to people who have a computer but no network connection, as is the case with Limon. Although it would be possible to install a Web server on the user's computer, it's much simpler to modify our file layout so the pages work correctly off the local file system.

Since this third problem had to be solved, forcing me to rewrite the parts that makes hyperlinks, I decided this would be a good chance to change the file organization. To keep information together and make the layout comprehensible to a human who has to work on the Web site, now it looks like this:

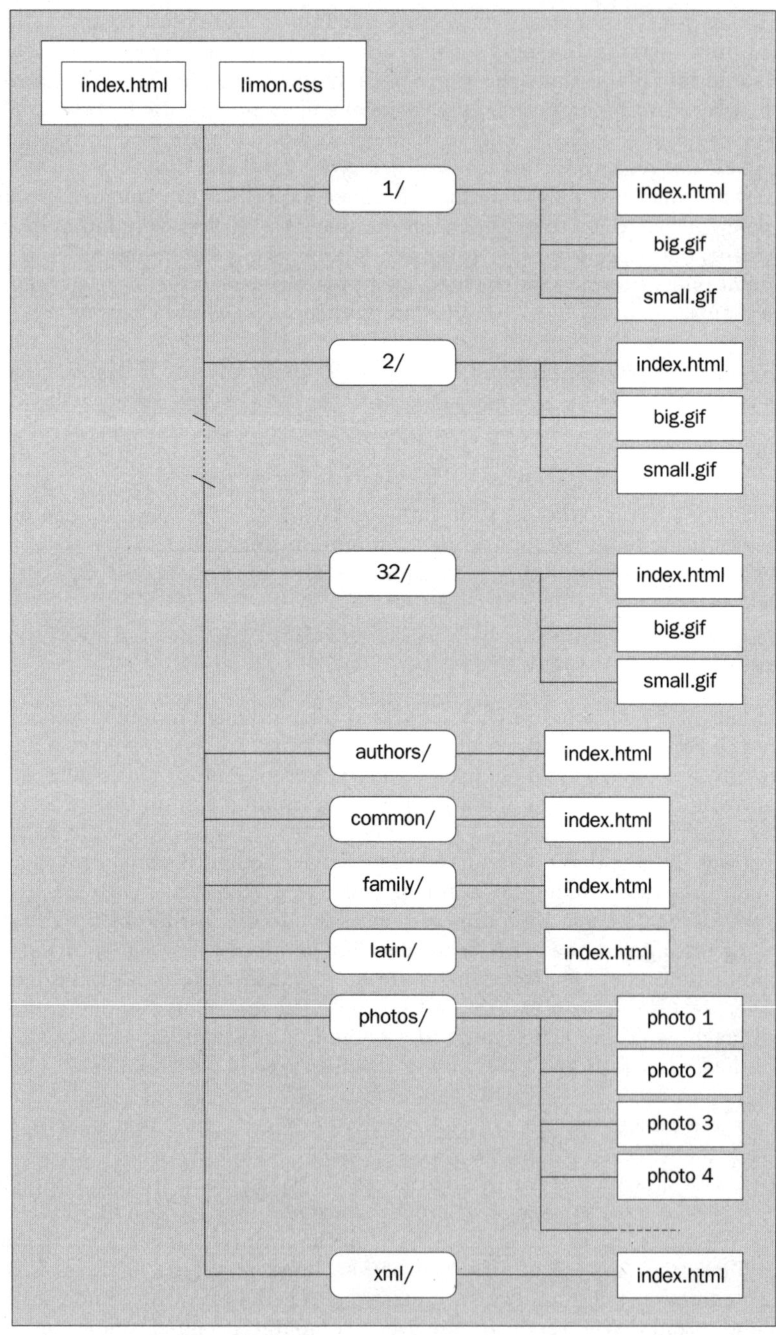

The Look

I decided to make the prototype of the style for my site be the Web page for a single plant. At the top there is a colored bar giving the number and Latin name of a plant, and at the bottom a similar looking colored bar with navigational links. A small image of the plant floats on the right hand side of the page: this image is a hyperlink to a large image of the plant. On the left is the description of the plant along with its family name, Latin name and a list of common names.

```
<IMG SRC="screen/plant6.gif">
```

Here is the HTML for Plant 6. The `<HEAD>` of the document is stuffed full of `<META>` tags designed to tell search engines about the document. The `<LINK>` tag is used to provide navigational hints to search engines and user agents as well as to tell browsers where to find the style sheet for the site. By using the "LANG" attribute on the `<HTML>` tag we tell search engines, translators and browsers that the default language of the document is English.

6/index.html

```
<HTML LANG="en">
<HEAD><TITLE>6 Momordica charantia L.</TITLE>
<META NAME="ROBOTS" CONTENT="ALL" LANG="en">
<META NAME="Author" CONTENT="Olivia S. Direnzo and Paul A. Houle" LANG="en">
<META NAME="Date" CONTENT="14 Jun 1998 18:31:55 GMT" LANG="en">
<META NAME="Copyright" CONTENT="&copy; 1998 Honeylocust Media Systems
(http://www.honeylocust.com/)" LANG="en">
<META NAME="Keywords" CONTENT="El Limon,Weeds,Botany,xml,Cucurbitacea,Momordica
charantia L.,balsam pear,balsam apple,cerasee bush,archucha,balsamina,
achochilla,pepinillo,cunde amor,melao de Sao Caetano,carcilla" LANG="en">
<META NAME="Description" CONTENT="A collection of descriptions and illustrations
of weeds observed in El Limon, a small village in the Dominican Republic during
January 1998. " LANG="en">
<LINK REL="Index" HREF="../common/index.html">
<LINK REL="Index" HREF="../family/index.html">
<LINK REL="Index" HREF="../latin/index.html">
<LINK REL="Begin" HREF="../1/index.html">
<LINK REL="Top" HREF="..">
<LINK REL="Contents" HREF="..">
<LINK REL="Start" HREF="..">
<LINK REL="Prev" HREF="../5/index.html">
<LINK REL="Next" HREF="../7/index.html">
<LINK REL="STYLESHEET" HREF="../limon.css" TYPE="text/css">
</HEAD>
```

In the body of the document, we first create the title bar at the top of the page. We're using Cascading Style Sheets, so the `CLASS` attribute in `<TD CLASS=navbar>` sets the table cell background color as well as the text foreground color and text size in the cell; this will be discussed in more detail later.

```
<BODY BGCOLOR=#FFFFFF>
<TABLE CELLSPACING=0 WIDTH=100%>
<TR><TD CLASS=navbar>6 Momordica charantia L.</TD></TR>
</TABLE>
<A HREF="big.gif">
<IMG SRC="small.gif" HEIGHT=396 WIDTH=278 ALIGN=RIGHT ALT="[Momordica charantia L.
illustration]" BORDER=0>
</A>
```

Next comes the text description of the plants. Here we use the HTML 4.0 <SPAN> tag to mark the language of the names of plants. By itself, the <SPAN> tag has no effect on how a browser displays text, but it does allow one to mark off sections of the text for style sheets to work on.

```
<B>Family Cucurbitacea</B>
<BR>Latin name: <I><SPAN LANG="la">Momordica charantia L.</SPAN></I>
<BR>Common names: <I> balsam pear, balsam apple, cerasee bush,
<SPAN LANG="es">archucha</SPAN>, <SPAN LANG="es">balsamina</SPAN>, <SPAN
LANG="es">achochilla</SPAN>, <SPAN LANG="es">pepinillo</SPAN>, <SPAN
LANG="es">cunde amor</SPAN>, <SPAN LANG="es">melao de Sao Caetano</SPAN>, <SPAN
LANG="es">carcilla</SPAN></I>
<P>

 Vine, climbs by tendrils. Leaves are alternate, soft and lightly hairy. Leaves
are deeply lobed with five lobes. (Length about 3 cm ) Yellow flowers arise from
leaf axils as do tendrils. Flower has five petals, bright orange small clusters of
pistils and stamen at center. (Diameter about 1.5 cm ) Pods are oval tapering to a
point with rows of little spikes, green turning orange as they
mature. Exploded pods show bright orange peels and four red seeds. Inside is
sticky. Pod length (about 2.5 cm ) Stem is hairy, very hairy at terminal end.
Found growing on fence along main road in full sun.

<P><B>Additional resources:</B>

<UL>

<LI><A HREF="big.gif">Large botanical illustration</A>

</UL>
```

In the end, we create the navigation bar and add a copyright notice. I found that to control the color of anchors, I had to put a style on the anchor tags themselves.

```
<BR CLEAR=ALL>
<TABLE CELLSPACING=0 WIDTH=100%><TR><TD CLASS=navbar>
<A CLASS=navlink HREF="../5/index.html">PREVIOUS</A>
<A CLASS=navlink HREF="../index.html">TOP</A>
<A CLASS=navlink HREF="../7/index.html">NEXT</A>
<A CLASS=navlink HREF="../family/index.html">FAMILY</A>
<A CLASS=navlink HREF="../latin/index.html">LATIN</A>
<A CLASS=navlink HREF="../common/index.html">COMMON</A>
</TD></TR></TABLE>
<BR CLEAR=all><HR>
<I>Version 0.94a &copy; 1998 <A HREF="http://www.honeylocust.com/">Honeylocust
Media Systems.</A>
 Contact: <A HREF="mailto:houle@msc.cornell.edu">houle@msc.cornell.edu</A>
</BODY></HTML>
```

Style sheets

The first draft of Weeds did not use Cascading Style Sheets, and as a result, was seriously incompatible with older browsers, particularly with Netscape 2. The trouble was that Netscape 2 recognizes the <FONT COLOR> tag but doesn't know about the <TD BGCOLOR> attribute for setting table cell background colors, resulting in the navigation and title bars reducing to invisible, white text on a white background.

```
<IMG SRC="screen/plant6ns2old.gif">
<CAPTION>Plant 6, before stylesheets, on Netscape 2</CAPTION>
```

The first version of "Weeds" was released after we tested on Netscape 4 on Unix and Windows and on IE 4 on Windows and Mac. The first batch of people who visited the site were the kind of people who are into cutting edge Web technologies, about 80% of whom were running a 4.0 browser. We discovered the `<FONT COLOR>` problem when showing the page to a person whose computer was running Netscape 2.

Living with multiple platforms, browsers and versions of browsers is a fact of life on the Web, and things are only going to get worse in the near future, with people going online with their televisions, cellular phones, and even from street corner Web browsers. We could limit ourselves to one version, one browser, or one platform, but this would lock viewers out, and any such decision would look particularly silly in the future when today's latest version becomes a relic of the past.

It's important to have a policy about compatibility. First I decided that I was going to maintain one and only one version of Weeds. One of the most common questions people ask about CGI scripts is "How do I serve a different page to viewers using different browsers?" My answer is that you don't want to do that. Maintaining multiple versions of the page is likely to become a nightmare. Not only will there be different versions to maintain, but the code that detects browsers would itself be a place where the system can fail. Since an increasing number of people are surfing the Web through proxy servers, it's getting harder to know what browser people are using. Drawing the line on what browsers to support would be difficult, given the hundreds of major and minor ones out there, and of course, what happens when the version 5.0 browsers appear? The multiplier effect that would occur if I wanted to specialize the product in other ways, for instance, if I wanted versions for three different browsers and in two different languages with two choices of image quality, would mean too many different combinations to maintain.

Knowing that I was only going to make a single version, I decided to design the site for the version 4.0 major browsers (Netscape and Microsoft), with the requirement that the site be legible on others. Style sheets provided the ideal solution. Instead of using the `<FONT>` tag, which can wreak havoc when a browser partially understands it, I decided to let the text look plain in old browsers and spice it up with style sheets for new ones. Although the 4.0 browsers support CSS-Positioning, which in principle allows style sheets to exert precise control on the positioning of text, I decided to stick with tables for formatting, because both of the major browsers implement their own different subsets of the CSS-P standard and because the tables didn't seem to be causing problems.

Since style sheets are still evolving, it's a good idea to test style sheet pages with both major browsers. There are many minor problems with their implementations, for instance, Netscape doesn't appear to be able to set the `font-size` property of text unless the `font-family` property is also specified. Even so, it took very little work to make CSS replace `<FONT COLOR>` and table backgrounds consistently in both Netscape and IE 4, even though the browsers do seem to diverge in their support for CSS-Positioning.

> *An excellent tutorial and reference on stylesheets can be found in **Professional Stylesheets for HTML and XML** by Frank Boumphrey (1998 Wrox Press, ISBN 1-861001-65-7)*

Because I was new to style sheets, and because the style of the top page is deliberately similar to the others, I decided to start out by adapting the top page to style sheets. Once that was done, I could change my site compiler to start emitting the HTML for style sheets. The style sheet for Weeds is `limon.css`

limon.css

```
/* styles that are used across the site */

.navbar { background-color:green;
          color:white;
          font-family:sans-serif;
          font-size:large; }

.navlink {  color:white;
            text-decoration:none; }

.unknown{   color:red;
            font-weight:bold;   }

BODY { background-color:white;
       font-family:times,serif; }

/* styles used for the top page */

.menubox { background-color:green;
           background-image:url(leaves.jpg);
           color:white;
           font-family:times,serif;
          font-size:large;}

.menulink { color:white; }

/* styles used for the xml writeup */

.codebar { background-color:blue;
           color:white; }

.codebody { background-color:yellow;
            color:black; }

/* styles for the "about the authors" section */

DIV.head { font-family:helvetica,sans-serif; font-size: 48px ; color: #f800f8;}
DIV.titles {font-family:helvetica,sans-serif; font-size: 30px ; color: teal;}
#oliviahead {position: absolute ; top: 50 px ; left: 130 px;}
#oliviatitles {position: absolute ; top: 100 px ; left: 150 px;}
#paulhead {position: relative; top: -100px ; left: -130px;}
#paultitles {position: relative; top: -100 px ; left: -100 px;}
#blurb {position: relative; top: -78px;}
```

All of the pages that make up the site use the same style sheet. They link to it by containing a

```
<LINK REL="STYLESHEET" HREF="../limon.css" TYPE="text/css">
```

tag in the <HEAD> of the document. Since all the style information is in one place, now I can play with the whole site's background and link colors and such just by editing the style sheet.

An important decision I made was to adapt my program permanently to use style sheets. I thought about adding a switch to the code to emit the old-fashioned HTML but decided that it wouldn't be worth the bother.

Not only is the style sheet version of the document more compatible, but it's simpler too. In the old version, the HTML for the title bar looked like

```
<TD BGCOLOR=#000000>
 <FONT COLOR=#FFFFFF>
 <FONT SIZE=+2>
 <FONT FACE='sans-serif'>6 Momordica charantia L.</FONT>
 </FONT>
 </FONT>
</TD>
```

and in the new version, it's just

```
<TD CLASS=navbar>6 Momordica charantia L.</TD>
```

A big improvement. Another benefit of style sheets is that the look of the site can be changed without recompiling. One day I decided I wanted the title and navigation bars to be green instead of black and made the change by one quick edit to the style sheet.

Finally, here is how the new page looks in Netscape 2. It looks a little bit plain, but nothing is missing.

```
<IMG SRC="screen/plant6ns2.gif">
<CAPTION>Plant 6 in the style-sheet version seen with Netscape 2</CAPTION>

<H4>Index pages</H4>

<IMG SRC="screen/latin.gif">
<CAPTION>index by latin name</CAPTION>

<IMG SRC="screen/common.gif">
<CAPTION>index by latin name</CAPTION>
```

Having decided what the individual plants' Web pages would look like, next I had to design the index pages. The title bar and navigation bar are essentially the same. Because a single-column index would waste a lot of valuable screen space, I made the indexes double-columned by using tables. The HTML code for table looks like

```
<TABLE WIDTH=100% COLS=2>
 <TR>
 <TD WIDTH=50% VALIGN=top>
  .. left hand column ..
 </TD>
 <TD WIDTH=50% VALIGN=top>
  .. right hand column ..
 </TD>
 </TR>
</TABLE>
```

By specifying the width of all the table cells and the number of columns, Netscape 4.0 and Internet Explorer 4.0 can correctly display the table when only part of it has been downloaded. Both the Latin and common name indices are produced by essentially the same code – the Java classes that make the indices inherit most of their intelligence from a common class. In the index-making code, I added an option that adds large capital letters at the beginning of each alphabetical section. Because there are many common names, I enabled this option for the common names, but disabled it for the Latin names since the large capital letters looked silly when there was only one item under them.

```
<IMG SRC="screen/family.gif">
```

The index by family is similar to the other two indices, but is organized using HTML lists to group together plants in the same family.

Metainformation

I made some design decisions that were invisible to the user, taking advantage of new features in HTML 4.0 for adding meta-information to documents which are described in depth in the official specification at

```
http://www.w3.org/TR/REC-html40/
```

One important new feature is the ability to specify the language of a document, as well as parts of a document when a document is composed of more than one language. By using language marking, language translation software can avoid the mistake of trying to translate text that should not be translated. This is important for the Weeds of El Limon, because the Latin names of plants are written in Latin and we include common names in both English and Spanish. To take an example,

```
<HTML LANG="en">
```

tells any browser, search engine or other program that the default language of the page is English. Any section of text can be marked as being in a different language by using the SPAN tag, for instance

```
<SPAN LANG="es">Loco Cabayo</SPAN>
```

is marked as being in Spanish. Many other tags also can contain the `LANG` attribute, such as

```
<META NAME="keywords" LANG="en" CONTENT="Weeds,Botany,XML">
```

HTML 4.0 also adds new features that let you tell browsers and search engines about the structure of your documents. This interested me because I get very frustrated when a search engine gives me the URL of a page that is part of a large collection and I can't find the top page of the site. This inconvenience can be prevented by adding a `<LINK>` tag in the `<HEAD>` of the document,

```
<LINK REL=TOP HREF="http://www.honeylocust.com/limon/">
```

Other kinds of document relationships can be specified in the `REL` attribute, such as `INDEX`, `APPENDIX`, `NEXT` and `PREV`. In addition to these new features, there are many `<META>` tags that are recognized inside the `<HEAD>` of documents by major search engines, such as

```
<META NAME=AUTHOR CONTENT="Paul Houle (paul@honeylocust.com)">
<META NAME=DATE CONTENT="31 May 1998">
<META NAME=COPYRIGHT CONTENT="&copy; 1998 Honeylocust Media Systems">
<META NAME=KEYWORDS CONTENT="El Limon,Weeds, Botany,XML">
<META NAME=DESCRIPTION CONTENT="A collection of descriptions and
illustrations...">
```

In the description of the code that generates HTML, namely `GenerateHtml.java`, you will find the code that adds this meta-information.

The Top Page and Appendices

"Weeds of El Limon" needed a top page; to keep a consistent look it had to be designed to look much like the other pages. It's possible that I could have made it automatically generated as well, which could have helped enforce a consistent look. I decided it would be easier to write the page by hand, using Cascading Style Sheets. It was obvious that I'd have to keep the title bar, but I decided to lose the navigation bar since the top page would already have navigational links. I decided to include both a simple menu and a small bit of text with hyperlinks. Putting an image in the table cell is an easy way to spice it up.

```
<IMG SRC="screen/top.gif">
<CAPTION>Top page</CAPTION>
```

Currently, "Weeds" has two appendices that I also generated by hand. Both use `limon.css` as a stylesheet. One of them is a brief technical essay about the page (a very short version of this write-up) and another is a blurb about the authors that uses CSS-Positioning to overlay words on top of pictures and attain a fancy effect on 4.0 browsers. In writing this page I was disappointed in the compatibility of the 4.0 browsers with each other and with the W3 Consortium's specification in the area of CSS-Positioning. Neither browser appears to implement the right and bottom attributes that would make it easy to position elements with respect to the right edge of page. In the end I had to fight a number of quirks of both Netscape and IE that I still don't clearly understand, and the page still doesn't look so great on older browsers. But the page is frivolous so it's a good place to show off a trick that isn't ready for prime time.

A Hidden, Embarrassing Problem

Another problem lurked in the HTML design of Weeds that made me very glad I had a publishing system that made it easy to correct. One night Olivia and I went to a public computer lab at a local college where a bunch of old Macs were running Netscape 1.1. Viewing our page there, we discovered that Netscape 1.1 does not understand single quotes as in `<A HREF='url'>`, so all of our link and image tags using them were broken. This also prevented `pavuk`, a Web mirroring tool that we like,

```
http://www.idata.sk/%7Eondrej/pavuk/
```

from following many of the links. Since newer browsers let us use either single or double quotes, we never realized that single quotes don't work with older browsers. Sure, Netscape 1.1 is really old, but using single quotes is a silly reason to lock people out – particularly for a product intended for use by people in the third world who don't have the latest hardware and software. Since all of our pages are generated by a program, this problem was easy to fix by simply changing our software and recompiling the pages. If I'd written the HTML by hand, I could have spent a lot of time tracking down every instance of single quotes. My global search and replace script would help, but the process would be less than fun.

Note that we had to discover these problems for ourselves. Even though our server logs proved that some people had viewed our pages with Netscape 2 and even with Netscape 1.1, Web viewers are notorious for not reporting problems they have with your pages. Once I wrote a page with Javascript in it that crashed hundreds of older browsers before I met somebody in person who informed me of the problem. If you want to find problems with your Web pages, you really have to test them yourself.

Summary

The design of our HTML was seriously constrained since we wanted to create a unique look without depending on text in images because some of our viewers would be relying on language translation software. Over time, we changed our HTML design as we discovered incompatibilities with older browsers and problems when viewing our pages from a local file system. We settled on using Cascading Style Sheets as a way of setting style that creates a minimum of problems for old browsers and found that it greatly simplified our HTML.

Generating HTML

Generator.java

`Generator.java` is the mainline of our HTML generator. `Generator.java` uses objects from the input and and data layer to read the contents of the XML files into memory, and then uses other objects from the output layers to create Web pages. `Generator.java` provides a simple command line interface, since the program isn't complex enough to justify a graphical user interface. If you did want to write a GUI, this is the class you would modify.

We start with the basics...

```
package honeylocust.limon;

import honeylocust.limon.representation.ImageAttach;
import honeylocust.limon.representation.MSXMLSpeciesFactory;
import honeylocust.limon.representation.Species;

import java.io.File;
import java.util.Vector;
import java.util.Enumeration;
```

The only method in Generator is a single `static main` method, much like a C program that begins with `main()`. This is a good time to mention my coding policy on exceptions. Because the Java language is very restrictive about the use of exceptions, when you first start programming Java you are going to get into terrible fights with the compiler over them – it took me about a year to make peace with them. Your first impulse is to catch exceptions close to the places where they are thrown. This is a mistake, because Java's exception handling is a good way to organize the global handling of errors. To work with that system, it's important to realize you should only catch an exception if you need to. As a result, I write my whole `main()` method so that it catches any exceptions thrown underneath it and prints a stack trace. (That's the purpose of the `try` and `catch`.)

The first part of this program is responsible for turning XML files into Species objects. The command line contains a list of filenames, each of which is an XML document containing weed descriptions. The program iterates over the command line arguments and parses each file. An ImageAttach object is used to locate the image files that belong to each plant. Then a PlantIndex object is created and used to maintain a simple database of the weeds allowing us to search for plants by name.

Once the plants are ready and stored in our simple database, the program is ready to generate the Web pages for each plant as well as the Latin, common and family name indices.

```
public class Generator {

 public static void main(String argv[]) {
 try {
  Vector v=new Vector();
  for(int i=0;i<argv.length;i++)
     MSXMLSpeciesFactory.parseLimon(v,new File(argv[i]));

  ImageAttach ia=new ImageAttach(new File("32colors"));
  ia.attachImages(v);

  PlantIndex pi=new PlantIndex();
  pi.addPlants(v);

  File basePath=new File("output");
  GenerateHtml.setHtmlPath(basePath);
  GenerateHtml.setCSSPath("../limon.css");

  for(Enumeration e=v.elements();e.hasMoreElements();) {
     Species s=(Species) e.nextElement();
     System.out.println("Generating "+s.getId());
     (new GeneratePlant(pi,s)).generate();
  };

  GenerateLatin glatin=new GenerateLatin(pi);
  glatin.generate();

  GenerateCommon gcommon=new GenerateCommon(pi);
  gcommon.setAddLetters(true);
  gcommon.generate();

  GenerateFamily gfamily=new GenerateFamily(pi);
  gfamily.generate();

 } catch(Exception e) {
  e.printStackTrace();
 }

 System.exit(0);
}

}
```

The next four classes are utility classes that provide functions that will be used by a number of other classes. The PlantIndex class is a simple database which makes it possible to look up plants by name, and the MultiHashtable class is used by PlantIndex to link a single Family name to more than one plant in a Family. WebImage automates the process of creating an `<IMG>` tag, by providing an interface to the complex syntax of the `<IMG>` tag, and automatically finding the height and width of an image and putting that in the tag. To find the size of an image, WebImage depends on the GifInfo class.

PlantIndex.java

To help generate the HTML indexes of the plants, I realized that I'd need to make a simple database that makes it possible to look up plants by their Latin, common and family name as well as by their ID. Because this is a neat package of functionality, I decided to put all indexing functions in a single class, PlantIndex. For ID, Latin, and common, PlantIndex uses the `java.util.Hashtable` to link keys to plants. Because more than one plant can be in the same family and because Hashtable can link only one value to any key, I had to invent my own class, MultiHashtable, (which is described after PlantIndex) that allows a key to point to more than one plant. We start by initializing the Hashtables:

```
package honeylocust.limon;

import honeylocust.limon.representation.LanguageString;
import honeylocust.limon.representation.Species;


import java.util.Vector;
import java.util.Enumeration;
import java.util.Hashtable;

public class PlantIndex {

 Integer d_maxPlantNumber;
 Integer d_minPlantNumber;

 Hashtable d_plantsById;
 Hashtable d_plantsByLatin;
 Hashtable d_plantsByCommon;
 MultiHashtable d_plantsByFamily;

 Hashtable d_languageCommon;

 public PlantIndex() {
 d_minPlantNumber=null;
 d_maxPlantNumber=null;

 d_plantsById=new Hashtable();
 d_plantsByLatin=new Hashtable();
 d_plantsByCommon=new Hashtable();
 d_plantsByFamily=new MultiHashtable();
 };
```

With the PlantIndex initialized, the next step is to fill up the Hashtables with plants and their keys,

```
 public synchronized void addPlants(Vector v) {
 for(Enumeration e=v.elements();e.hasMoreElements();)
  addPlant((Species) e.nextElement());
 };

 public synchronized void addPlant(Species s) {
 d_plantsById.put(s.getId(),s);

 try {
  int plantNumber=Integer.parseInt(s.getId());
  if (d_maxPlantNumber==null || d_maxPlantNumber.intValue() < plantNumber)
     d_maxPlantNumber=new Integer(plantNumber);
```

```
     if (d_minPlantNumber==null || d_minPlantNumber.intValue() > plantNumber)
        d_minPlantNumber=new Integer(plantNumber);

    } catch(NumberFormatException e) {
    };


    if (s.getFamily()!=null)
     d_plantsByFamily.put(s.getFamily(),s);
    else
     d_plantsByFamily.put(new LanguageString("Unknown").intern(),s);

    if (s.identified()) {
     LanguageString latin[]=s.getLatin();
     for(int i=0;i<latin.length;i++) {
     LanguageString lname=latin[i];
        if (d_plantsByLatin.get(lname)!=null)
         System.err.println("Warning: duplicate latin name -> "+lname.toString());

        d_plantsByLatin.put(lname,s);
     };

     LanguageString common[]=s.getCommon();
     for(int i=0;i<common.length;i++) {
     LanguageString cname=common[i];
        if (d_plantsByCommon.get(cname)!=null)
         System.err.println("Warning: duplicate commmon name -> "+cname);

        d_plantsByCommon.put(cname,s);
     };
    };
    };
```

Then we provide a number of functions for accessing the indices.

```
    public Species getById(String key) {
    return (Species) d_plantsById.get(key);
    };

    public synchronized LanguageString[] getLatinNames() {
    return getKeyArray(d_plantsByLatin);
    };

    LanguageString[] getKeyArray(Hashtable h) {
    LanguageString s[]=new LanguageString[h.size()];
    int i=0;
    for(Enumeration e=h.keys();e.hasMoreElements();)
     s[i++]=(LanguageString) e.nextElement();

    return s;
    };

    public Species getByLatin(LanguageString key) {
    return (Species) d_plantsByLatin.get(key);
    };

    public synchronized LanguageString[] getCommonNames() {
    return getKeyArray(d_plantsByCommon);
    };
```

```
  public Species getByCommon(LanguageString key) {
  return (Species) d_plantsByCommon.get(key);
  };

  public synchronized LanguageString[] getFamilies() {
  return (LanguageString[]) d_plantsByFamily.keyArray();
  };

  public Species[] getByFamily(LanguageString key) {
  return (Species[]) d_plantsByFamily.get(key);
  };

  public LanguageString speciesName(Species s) {
  if (!s.identified())
   return new LanguageString("Plant "+s.getId());

  return((s.getLatin())[0]);
  };
```

And some functions for accessing plant `id`'s as numbers.

```
  public int getMaxPlantNumber() {
  return d_maxPlantNumber.intValue();
  };

  public int getMinPlantNumber() {
  return d_minPlantNumber.intValue();
  };

  public boolean isNumericId() {
  return (d_maxPlantNumber!=null);
  };

  public Integer plantNumber(Species s) {

  boolean numeric=true;
  int myNumber=0;

 try {
   myNumber=Integer.parseInt(s.getId());
  } catch(NumberFormatException e) {
   numeric=false;
  };

  if (!numeric)
   return null;

  return new Integer(myNumber);
  };

 };
```

MultiHashtable.java

MultiHashtable is a very simple class that is much like a Hashtable except that each key can have multiple values. Rather than invent my own data structures (which might be a good idea if they had to be very fast or scale to extreme sizes), I decide to save work by using a Hashtable. It maps keys to `java.util.Vectors`, each of which is an expandable array that keeps track of the multiple values.

```
package honeylocust.limon;

import honeylocust.limon.representation.LanguageString;
import honeylocust.limon.representation.Species;

import java.util.Vector;
import java.util.Hashtable;
import java.util.Enumeration;

public class MultiHashtable {

 Hashtable p_ht;

 public MultiHashtable() {
 p_ht=new Hashtable();
 };

 public synchronized void put(Object key,Object value) {

 Vector v=(Vector) p_ht.get(key);
 if (v==null) {
  v=new Vector();
  p_ht.put(key,v);
 };

 if(!v.contains(value)) {
  v.addElement(value);
 };
 };

 public synchronized Species[] get(Object key) {
 Vector v=(Vector) p_ht.get(key);
 if (v==null)
  return new Species[0];

 Species o[]=new Species[v.size()];
 v.copyInto(o);
 return o;
 };

 public Enumeration keys() {
 return p_ht.keys();
 };

 public LanguageString[] keyArray() {
 LanguageString o[]=new LanguageString[p_ht.size()];
 int i=0;
 for(Enumeration e=keys();e.hasMoreElements();)
  o[i++]=(LanguageString) e.nextElement();

 return o;
 };

};
```

WebImage.java and GifIno.java

The HTML <IMG> tag is complex since it has many attributes such as SRC, ALT and ALIGN. It's particularly bothersome that we have to specify the HEIGHT and WIDTH attributes of each image. To simplify this task, I created a WebImage object that represents a single <IMG> tag, lets us manipulate its attributes through methods, and that automatically sizes images. WebImage depends on another class, GifInfo.java which I'll discuss next, to measure the size of images. If we tell WebImage the path of an image and its other attributes, it automatically generates an <IMG> tag. The first half of WebImage is responsible for collecting information about an image:

```
package honeylocust.limon;

import java.io.PrintWriter;
import java.io.File;
import java.io.FileNotFoundException;

public class WebImage {

 static GifInfo d_gifinfo=new GifInfo();

 public String d_src;
 public String d_alt;
 public String d_align;
 public String d_webpath;
 public boolean d_border;

 int d_width,d_height;

 public WebImage(File dir,String src) throws
InterruptedException,FileNotFoundException {
 d_src=src;
 File f=new File(dir,src);

 if (!(f.exists()))
      throw new FileNotFoundException(f.getAbsolutePath());

 int z[]=d_gifinfo.getDimensions(f);
 d_width=z[0];
 d_height=z[1];
 d_webpath="";
 d_border=true;
 };

 public void setWebpath(String s) {
 d_webpath=s;
 };

 public void setAlign(String s) {
 d_align=s;
 };

 public void setAlt(String s) {
 d_alt=s;
 };

 public void setBorder(boolean b) {
 d_border=b;
 };
...
```

The second part of WebImage inserts the image in the page.

```
...
 public void insert(PrintWriter w) {
 w.print("<IMG SRC=\""+d_webpath+d_src+"\" HEIGHT="+d_height+" WIDTH="+d_width);
 if(d_align!=null)
  w.print(" ALIGN="+d_align);

 if(d_align!=null)
  w.print(" ALT=\""+d_alt+"\"");

 if(!d_border)
  w.print(" BORDER=0");

 w.println(">");
 };

};
```

`GifInfo.java` is a utility class that makes it easy to measure the size of an image in a non-graphical program. The Java AWT has very powerful facilities for manipulating images, however, they are more than what we need. I'd really like to call a method that takes the filename of an image and just returns the size of the image. The AWT doesn't provide this. Instead, it provides a system for incrementally loading images over the web. You can start this process by calling the `prepareImage()` method of any AWT component or of `java.awt.Toolkit`, however, the method call returns before it's done loading the image. This is called asynchronous behavior. On the Web, it's a good thing, because it can take a long time to load an image and it would be a shame if your program locked up when it was loading an image. On the other hand, my program runs from the command line and will just take a second to load an image from a disk, so I don't need all this power. The job of GifInfo is twofold. First, it creates a `java.awt.ToolKit` object that makes it possible to access AWT functions in a non-graphical program, and secondly it provides a method for getting the size of an image that is synchronous. That is, the method does not return until it is done running. The first part of the program gets an instance of Toolkit to access AWT functions,

```
package honeylocust.limon;

import java.awt.Panel;
import java.awt.Toolkit;
import java.awt.Image;
import java.awt.image.ImageObserver;
import java.io.File;

public class GifInfo {

 Toolkit d_tool;

 public GifInfo() {
 d_tool=(new Panel()).getToolkit();
 };
...
```

The `getDimensions()` method does most of the work. It uses the `getImage()` and `prepareImage()` methods of Toolkit to start the image loading process. It creates an instance of GifInfoObserver, which is an inner class of GifInfo, to be notified when information is available about the image. To convert the asynchronous behavior of prepareImage to the synchronous behavior of `getDimensions()` I have to understand Java's threading system. In short, once the image loading is started, the `getDimensions()` method calls the `wait()` method on the GifInfoObserver. This makes the thread that called getDimensions stop. When the AWT is finished loading the image, one of the AWT threads will call the `imageUpdate()` method of GifInfoObserver which uses the `notify()` method to "wake up" the thread which was waiting on it. Then, `getDimensions()` can read the height and width of the image and return that information to the method that called it.

```
...
 public int[] getDimensions(File f) throws InterruptedException {
 return getDimensions(f.getAbsolutePath());
 };

 public int[] getDimensions(String s) throws InterruptedException {
 Image i=d_tool.getImage(s);
 int x[]=new int[2];

 GifInfoObserver o=new GifInfoObserver(ImageObserver.ALLBITS);
 synchronized(o) {
  d_tool.prepareImage(i,-1,-1,o);
  o.wait();
 }

 x[1]=i.getHeight(null);
 x[0]=i.getWidth(null);

 i.flush();
 return x;
 };

 class GifInfoObserver implements ImageObserver {
 int d_waitFor;

 public GifInfoObserver(int waitFor) {
  d_waitFor=waitFor;
 };

 public synchronized boolean imageUpdate(Image i,int flags,int x,int y,int
width,int height) {

  if ((flags&ImageObserver.ERROR)!=0) {
      System.out.println("Error in imageUpdate.");
      notify();
      return false;
  };

  if ((flags&d_waitFor)!=0)
      return true;

  notify();
  return false;
 };
 };
};
```

GenerateHtml.java

I was faced with an interesting challenge in designing the code that generates HTML. My program was going to write a number of very similar looking Web pages, so it would be very desirable to use the same code for making navigation bars, headers, footers and navigation links. I wanted to be able to reuse the same code as much as possible and have a simple design, so I decided to use inheritance.

Using inheritance is a serious decision in Java because Java doesn't support multiple inheritance. Some people think of this as a serious limitation, but Java wins some benefits by having only single inheritance. Java's inheritance mechanism is much simpler than C++, meaning it's easier for a programmer to use, and much easier to write compilers for. People starting out in Java tend to use inheritance too much. It isn't the only code reuse tool in our bag of tricks – besides, since you can only inherit from one class it's a scarce resource.

So I decided to create an abstract base class for coding the Weeds, `GenerateHtml.java`, and build a hierarchy in which I add features selectively to create different kind of pages. The pages for individual plants are generated by GeneratePlant, which is a subclass of GenerateHtml. GenerateIndex contains the brains for generating the indexes by Latin and common names. GenerateIndex itself is an abstract class, since most of the logic for the Latin and common name pages is the same. GenerateLatin and GenerateCommon subclass GenerateIndex, adding just the methods necessary to get a list of keys in the index and to get the ID of a plant given a key – they call PlantIndex to do this work. Finally, GenerateFamily has to make a very different kind of index, since more than one plant can have the same family name, so instead of being part of the GenerateIndex hierarchy, it just subclasses from GenerateHtml.

GenerateHtml provides many of the services needed to generate a Web page. It generates the `<HEAD>` of the page, `<META>` and `<LINK>` tags for the good of search engines, as well as the title bar at the top of the page and the navigation bar at the bottom of the page. It also provides a method for outputting two column text which is used in the index pages, a method for converting LanguageStrings into language-marked HTML, and some rudimentary functions for manipulating files: these are used to copy image files from their original location into the Web page directories. The first part looks like this:

```
package honeylocust.limon;

import honeylocust.limon.representation.LanguageString;
import java.io.PrintWriter;
import java.io.FileWriter;
import java.io.IOException;
import java.io.File;
import java.io.FileInputStream;
import java.io.FileNotFoundException;
import java.io.FileOutputStream;
import java.util.Vector;
import java.util.Date;


public abstract class GenerateHtml {

 private static File s_htmlPath;
 private static String s_cssPath;

 PrintWriter d_out;
 File d_dir;
```

```
GenerateHtml(File dir,String s) throws IOException {
ensureDirectory(dir);
d_out=new PrintWriter(new FileWriter(new File(dir,s)));
d_dir=dir;
};

static File toHtmlPath(String s) {
return new File(s_htmlPath,s);
};

static void setHtmlPath(File s) {
s_htmlPath=s;
};

static void setCSSPath(String s) {
s_cssPath=s;
};
...
```

This class doesn't have a constructor because it has no data fields to be initialized. There are two parameters, `s_htmlPath` and `c_cssPath`, that are declared static because they're shared by all instances of `GeneratHtml.java`. This way one can call

```
GenerateHtml.setCSSPath(String s)
```

to set the location of the shared cascading style sheet. The risk is that a programmer could accidentally mess up the configuration for some of the pages by changing the CSSPath at the wrong time, or worse, in a multithreaded environment, it could be messed up by another thread. However, the alternative of configuring each instance individually is even more error prone. More complex solutions exist, but they'd take time to design and implement and are just as likely to screw up in ways that are even more complicated and inscrutable.

In the next section, we define methods that contain the basic properties of a page that we'd like the option of overriding in the future in a subclass. By default we'd like the language of each document to be English, and it would be awful to have to specify this each time. However, by simply subclassing it in a class, we can change it to something else with no trouble. (I should probably say first that these are all used to fill out `<META>` tags in the top of the page.)

Another feature of this bit of code is an abstract method that defines another property that goes into the head: the title. Here the second part:

```
...
public abstract String computeTitle();

public String getLanguage() {
return "en".intern();
};

public String getRobotInfo() {
return "ALL";
};

public String getAuthor() {
return "Olivia S. Direnzo and Paul A. Houle";
};
```

```
    public Date getDate() {
    return new Date();
    };

    public String getCopyright() {
    return "&copy; 1998 Honeylocust Media Systems (http://www.honeylocust.com/)";
    };

    public String getKeywords() {
    return "El Limon,Weeds,Botany,xml";
    };

    public String getDescription() {
    return "A collection of descriptions and illustrations of weeds observed in El
   Limon, a small village in the Dominican Republic during January 1998. ";
    };

    public String getVersion() {
    return "0.95a";
    };
   ...
```

Another important set of methods are the ones that generate the <HEAD> of the document. The design pattern for HTML generation is clear. A series of methods called `generateX()` generate various parts of the document. Anything repetitive is delegated to a submethod to save work. Also attached in this section is the code that generates the tail:

```
   ...
    public void generateHead() {
    d_out.println("<HTML LANG=\""+getLanguage()+"\">");
    d_out.println("<HEAD><TITLE>"+computeTitle()+"</TITLE>");
    generateMetaInformation();
    generateCSSInsert();
    d_out.println("</HEAD>");
    d_out.println("<BODY BGCOLOR=#FFFFFF>");
    };

    public void generateMeta(String name,String content) {
    if (content==null || content.length()==0)
     return;

    d_out.println("<META NAME=\""+name+"\" CONTENT=\""+content+"\"
   lang=\""+getLanguage()+"\">");
    };

    public void generateCSSInsert() {
    if (s_cssPath!=null)
         generateLink("STYLESHEET",s_cssPath,"text/css");
    };

    public void generateLink(String rel,String href ) {
    if (href==null || href.length()==0)
     return;

    d_out.println("<LINK REL=\""+rel+"\" HREF=\""+href+"\">");
    };
```

```
public void generateLink(String rel,String href,String type ) {
if (href==null || href.length()==0)
 return;

d_out.println("<LINK REL=\""+rel+"\" HREF=\""+href+"\" TYPE=\""+type+"\">");
};

public void generateMetaInformation() {
generateMeta("ROBOTS",getRobotInfo());
generateMeta("Author",getAuthor());
generateMeta("Date",getDate().toGMTString());
generateMeta("Copyright",getCopyright());
generateMeta("Keywords",getKeywords());
generateMeta("Description",getDescription());
generateLink("Index","../common/index.html");
generateLink("Index","../family/index.html");
generateLink("Index","../latin/index.html");
generateLink("Begin","../1/index.html");
generateLink("Top","..");
generateLink("Contents","..");
generateLink("Start","..");
};

void generateTail() {
d_out.println("<BR CLEAR=all><HR>");
d_out.print("<I>Version "+getVersion()+" ");
d_out.println("&copy; 1998 <A HREF=\"http://www.honeylocust.com/\">Honeylocust
Media Systems.</A>");
d_out.println(" Contact:
<A HREF=\"mailto:paul@honeylocust.com\">paul@honeylocust.com </A>");
d_out.println("</BODY></HTML>");
};
...
```

Another segment of the code generates the bar at the top of the page, and the navigational bar at the bottom. Again I try to write small methods. One method, `generateNavInsert()`, is deliberately designed to be overridden. It can be replaced by a method that also adds PREV and NEXT buttons next to the TOP button.

```
...
void generateNavLink(String text,String url) {
d_out.print("<A CLASS=navlink HREF=\""+url+"\">"+text+"</A>");
};

void generateNavSpacer() {
d_out.print(" | ");
};

public void generateNavInsert() {
generateNavLink("TOP","../index.html");
generateNavSpacer();
};

public void generateNavBar() {
d_out.println("<BR CLEAR=ALL>");

d_out.println("<TABLE CELLSPACING=0 WIDTH=100%><TR><TD CLASS=navbar>");
generateNavInsert();
```

```
    generateNavLink("FAMILY","../family/index.html");
    generateNavSpacer();
    generateNavLink("LATIN","../latin/index.html");
    generateNavSpacer();
    generateNavLink("COMMON","../common/index.html");
    d_out.println("</TD></TR></TABLE>");

    };
...
```

The rest of the program is a set of utility functions that exist to be exploited by the children of GenerateHTML. `outputTwoCol()` takes a vector of strings in HTML format and converts them into two column output. It's very simple and assumes that the vertical height is proportional to the number of lines, which is only approximately true. Even so, it is adequate for the job and can be replaced with something better (the change being inherited by all the children) if the need arises. `ensureDirectory()` and `copyFiles()` are some utility functions for manipulating files that the children will need, they are candidates to put in a separate utilities class. `copyFiles()`, again, is a compromise between perfect functionality and the need to code simply and fast – because it loads a file into memory in one shot it wouldn't scale up to copying, say, a 40 megabyte file on my laptop. On the other hand, if it only has to copy a 100k `.gif` file, it's just fine. If scalability becomes a problem, it can be replaced.

```
...
    public void outputTwoCol(Vector v) {
    int half=v.size()/2;
    d_out.println("<TABLE WIDTH=100% COLS=2>");
    d_out.println("<TR><TD WIDTH=50% VALIGN=top>");
    for(int i=0;i<half;i++)
        d_out.println(v.elementAt(i).toString());

    d_out.println("</TD><TD WIDTH=50% VALIGN=top>");
    for(int i=half;i<v.size();i++)
        d_out.println(v.elementAt(i).toString());

    d_out.println("</TD></TR></TABLE>");

    };

    public String toHtml(LanguageString l) {
    if (l.getLanguage()==getLanguage()) {
     return l.toString();
    } else {
     return "<SPAN LANG=\""+l.getLanguage()+"\">"+l.toString()+"</SPAN>";
    };
    };

    public static File ensureDirectory(File dir,String s) throws IOException{
    return ensureDirectory(new File(dir,s));
    };

    public static File ensureDirectory(File f) throws IOException{
    if (f.exists()) {
     if (!f.isDirectory())
        throw new IOException("File "+f.toString()+" already exists and is not a
directory.");
```

```
    return f;
   }

   f.mkdirs();
   return f;
   };

   public static void copyFile(File from,File to) throws IOException {
   FileInputStream inStream=new FileInputStream(from);
   FileOutputStream outStream=new FileOutputStream(to);
   byte buff[]=new byte[inStream.available()];
   inStream.read(buff);
   outStream.write(buff);
   inStream.close();
   outStream.close();
   };

  };
```

GeneratePlant.java

With this infrastructure to build on, we can start writing the code that writes the plants. This is `GeneratePlant.java`:

```
package honeylocust.limon;

import honeylocust.limon.representation.AnchorChunk;
import honeylocust.limon.representation.LanguageString;
import honeylocust.limon.representation.Species;
import honeylocust.limon.representation.RefChunk;
import honeylocust.limon.representation.Text;
import honeylocust.limon.representation.TextChunk;


import java.io.PrintWriter;
import java.io.File;
import java.io.FileWriter;
import java.io.IOException;
import java.io.FileNotFoundException;

public class GeneratePlant extends GenerateHtml {

 PlantIndex d_index;
 Species d_species;
 File d_dir;

 public GeneratePlant(PlantIndex index,Species s) throws IOException {
 super(toHtmlPath(s.getId()),"index.html");
 d_dir=ensureDirectory(toHtmlPath(s.getId()));
 d_species=s;
 d_index=index;
 };
...
```

Because GeneratePlant is going to have to refer to the index, it gets passed the index in the constructor.

Now I override some methods to provide the correct meta-information for the weeds. Even the generateMetaInformation method is overridden to provide two additional `<META>` tags (PREV and NEXT) that won't be relevant for all documents.

```
...
public String computeTitle() {
return computeTitle(d_species);
};

private String computeTitle(Species s) {
if (!s.identified()) {
 return (s.getId()+" Not Identified");
};

String latin=s.getLatin()[0].toString();
Integer myNumber=d_index.plantNumber(s);
String number=(myNumber!=null) ? myNumber.toString()+" " : "";

return number+latin;
};

public String getKeywords() {
StringBuffer sb=new StringBuffer(super.getKeywords());
LanguageString family=d_species.getFamily();
if (family!=null) {
 sb.append(',');
 sb.append(family.toString());
};

if (d_species.identified()) {
 LanguageString latin[]=d_species.getLatin();
 for(int i=0;i<latin.length;i++) {
     sb.append(',');
     sb.append(latin[i].toString());
 };

 LanguageString common[]=d_species.getCommon();
 for(int i=0;i<common.length;i++) {
     sb.append(',');
     sb.append(common[i].toString());
 };

};

return sb.toString();
};

public void generateMetaInformation() {
super.generateMetaInformation();

Integer myNumber=d_index.plantNumber(d_species);

boolean numeric=((myNumber!=null) && d_index.isNumericId());

if (numeric && myNumber.intValue() > d_index.getMinPlantNumber()) {
 generateLink("Prev","../"+(myNumber.intValue()-1)+"/index.html");
};
```

```
 if (numeric && myNumber.intValue() < d_index.getMaxPlantNumber()) {
  generateLink("Next","../"+(myNumber.intValue()+1)+"/index.html");
 };
 };
...
```

Here we override `generateNavInsert()` so that it also includes links to the previous and next pages if they exist

```
...
 public void generateNavInsert() {

 Integer myNumber=d_index.plantNumber(d_species);

 boolean numeric=((myNumber!=null) && d_index.isNumericId());

 if (numeric && myNumber.intValue() > d_index.getMinPlantNumber()) {
  generateNavLink("PREVIOUS","../"+(myNumber.intValue()-1)+"/index.html");
  generateNavSpacer();
 };

 super.generateNavInsert();

 if (numeric && myNumber.intValue() < d_index.getMaxPlantNumber()) {
  generateNavLink("NEXT","../"+(myNumber.intValue()+1)+"/index.html");
  generateNavSpacer();
 };
 };
...
```

and calls the code that generates the weeds

```
...
 public synchronized void generate(Species s) throws
IOException,InterruptedException {

 File dir=ensureDirectory(toHtmlPath(s.getId()));

 PrintWriter w=new PrintWriter(new FileWriter(new File(dir,"index.html")));
 setSpecies(s);

 copyImages(dir,s);

 try {
  generateHead(w);
  generateTopBar(w);
  generateInline(w,s,dir);
  generateFamily(w,s);
  generateLatin(w,s);
  generateCommon(w,s);
  generateDescriptions(w,s);
  generateAdditional(w);

  generateNavBar(w);
  generateTail(w);
 }
 catch(GenerateHtmlException e) {
```

```
   System.err.println(">> Error Generating HTML for Species "+s.getId());
   System.err.println(">> "+e.toString());
   System.err.println();

  };

 w.close();

};

 public void generateInline(PrintWriter w,Species s,File dir) throws
InterruptedException,FileNotFoundException {
 WebImage wi=new WebImage(dir,"small.gif");
 w.println("<A HREF=\"big.gif\">");
 wi.setAlign("RIGHT");
 wi.setAlt('['+d_index.speciesName(s).toString()+" illustration]");
 wi.setBorder(false);
 wi.insert(w);
 w.println("</A>");
 };

 public void generateFamily(PrintWriter w,Species s) {
 if (s.getFamily()==null) {
  w.println("<SPAN CLASS=unknown>Family Unknown</SPAN>");
 }
 else {
  w.println("<B>Family "+s.getFamily()+"</B>");
 };
 };

 public void generateLatin(PrintWriter w,Species s) {
 LanguageString latin[]=s.getLatin();
 if (latin.length==0) {
  w.println("<BR><SPAN CLASS=unknown>Species not identified</SPAN>");
 } else {
  w.println("<BR>Latin name: <I>"+toHtml(latin[0])+"</I>");
 }
 };

 public void generateCommon(PrintWriter w,Species s) {
 LanguageString common[]=s.getCommon();
 if (common.length==0)
  return;

 if (common.length==1) {
  w.println("<BR>Common name: <I>");
 } else
  w.println("<BR>Common names: <I>");

 for(int i=0;i<common.length;i++) {
  w.print(toHtml(common[i]));
  if (i<common.length-1)
     w.print(", ");
 }

 w.println("</I>");
 };

 public void generateDescriptions(PrintWriter w,Species s) throws
GenerateHtmlException {
```

```
Text texts[]=s.getTexts();
for(int i=0;i<texts.length;i++)
 if(selectText(texts[i]))
    generateText(w,texts[i]);
};

boolean selectText(Text t) {
return true;
};

void generateText(PrintWriter w,Text t) throws GenerateHtmlException {
w.println("<P>");
TextChunk[] chunks=t.getChunks();
for(int i=0;i<chunks.length;i++) {
 generateChunk(w,chunks[i]);
};
};

void generateChunk(PrintWriter w,TextChunk c) throws GenerateHtmlException {
if (c instanceof AnchorChunk) {
 generateAnchorChunk(w,(AnchorChunk) c);
} else if (c instanceof RefChunk) {
 generateRefChunk(w,(RefChunk) c);
} else
 w.println(c.getText());
};

void generateAnchorChunk(PrintWriter w,AnchorChunk ac) {
w.println("<A HREF=\""+ac.getHref()+"\">"+ac.getText()+"</A>");
};

void generateRefChunk(PrintWriter w,RefChunk ac) throws GenerateHtmlException {
Species target=d_index.getById(ac.getId());
if (target==null)
 throw new GenerateHtmlException("Invalid ref id.");

w.println("<A
HREF=\"../"+ac.getId()+"/index.html\">"+d_index.speciesName(target)+"</A>");
};

public void generateAdditional(PrintWriter w) {
Species s=d_species;
w.println("<P><B>Additional resources:</B>\n");
w.println("<UL>\n");
w.println("<LI><A HREF=\"big.gif\">Large botanical illustration</A>\n");
w.println("</UL>\n");

};


public void copyImages(File dir,Species s) throws IOException {
File bigImg=new File(dir,"big.gif");
File smallImg=new File(dir,"small.gif");
copyFile(s.getBigImage(),bigImg);
copyFile(s.getSmallImage(),smallImg);
};
...
```

Here I use a new feature of JDK 1.1 that makes it much easier to make up your own exceptions. GenerateHtmlException is an **inner class**, which is a new feature in JDK 1.1. An inner class is a class that is defined inside of another class and is visible only within a class. Java encourages programmers to make new classes often, for instance, each time you want to define a new kind of Exception, or when you want to write an event handler under the JDK 1.1 event model. If you define an entirely new class and make a new `.java` file for each one, this can create a lot of clutter which can be eliminated by using inner classes. The official specification for inner classes is at

`http://java.sun.com/products/jdk/1.1/docs/guide/innerclasses/spec/innerclasses.doc.html/`

```
...
 class GenerateHtmlException extends Exception {
 public GenerateHtmlException(String s) {
  super(s);
 };
 };
};
```

GenerateIndex.java

Just as GenerateHtml provides a framework for building general Web pages on, GenerateIndex provides a framework for building index pages on. By overriding just a few key methods, I can create two kinds of indexes, one for family names and one for common names

```
package honeylocust.limon;

import honeylocust.limon.representation.LanguageString;
import honeylocust.limon.representation.Species;

import java.io.IOException;
import java.io.File;
import java.util.Vector;
import netscape.util.Sort;

public abstract class GenerateIndex extends GenerateHtml {

 PlantIndex d_index;
 boolean p_addLetters;

 public GenerateIndex(PlantIndex index,File dir) throws IOException {
 super(dir,"index.html");
 d_index=index;
 p_addLetters=false;
 };
...
```

The next two methods use the design pattern for accessors in the Java Beans framework. This makes it easy for other objects to configure the behavior of this object. Specifically, the setAddLetters option provides the possibility of making tall initial capital letters at the start of alphabetical sections in the index.

```
...
 public void setAddLetters(boolean addLetters) {
 p_addLetters=addLetters;
 };
```

```
 public boolean getAddLetters() {
 return p_addLetters;
 };
...
```

The next two methods get overridden to decide what sort of index to make. `getKeys()` is a list of items in the index and `getSpecies()` gets the species that goes with a particular key.

```
 abstract LanguageString[] getKeys();

 abstract Species getSpecies(LanguageString key);

 public synchronized void generate() throws IOException,InterruptedException {

 generateHead();
 generateTopBar();
 generateIndex();
 generateNavBar();
 generateTail();

 d_out.close();
 };

 public void generateIndex() {
 LanguageString keys[]=getKeys();
 Sort.sort(keys,null,0,keys.length,true);
 Vector entries=new Vector();
 char letter=' ';
 for(int i=0;i<keys.length;i++) {
  Species s=getSpecies(keys[i]);
  char nextLetter=Character.toUpperCase(keys[i].toString().charAt(0));
  String prefixString="";

  if (p_addLetters && nextLetter>letter)
     prefixString="<BIG>"+nextLetter+"</BIG><BR>";

  letter=nextLetter;

  entries.addElement(prefixString+"
          <A HREF=\"../"+s.getId()+"/index.html\">"+toHtml(keys[i])+"</A><BR>")

 };
 outputTwoCol(entries);
 };

};
```

GenerateLatin/Common.java

At this point making a specific index is just filling in the blanks.

```
package honeylocust.limon;

import honeylocust.limon.representation.LanguageString;
import honeylocust.limon.representation.Species;

import java.io.IOException;
```

```
public class GenerateLatin extends GenerateIndex {

 public GenerateLatin(PlantIndex index) throws IOException {
 super(index,toHtmlPath("latin"));
 };

 public String computeTitle() {
 return "Index by Latin Name";
 };

 LanguageString[] getKeys() {
 return d_index.getLatinNames();
 };

 Species getSpecies(LanguageString k) {
 return d_index.getByLatin(k);
 };

};
```

and

```
package honeylocust.limon;

import honeylocust.limon.representation.LanguageString;
import honeylocust.limon.representation.Species;

import java.io.IOException;

public class GenerateCommon extends GenerateIndex {

 public GenerateCommon(PlantIndex index) throws IOException {
 super(index,toHtmlPath("common"));
 };

 public String computeTitle() {
 return "Index by Common Name";
 };

 LanguageString[] getKeys() {
 return d_index.getCommonNames();
 };

 Species getSpecies(LanguageString k) {
 return d_index.getByCommon(k);
 };
};
```

GenerateFamily.java

The index by family is radically different from the other two, because it is a two-level hierarchy. A family can contain more than one species. We want to print all the plants in a particular family together, sorted first by family and then by species. This is done by

```
package honeylocust.limon;

import honeylocust.limon.representation.LanguageString;
import honeylocust.limon.representation.Species;
```

```
import com.sun.java.util.collections.Arrays;
import java.io.IOException;
import java.util.Vector;
//import netscape.util.Sort;

public class GenerateFamily extends GenerateHtml {

 PlantIndex d_index;

 public GenerateFamily(PlantIndex index) throws IOException {
 super(toHtmlPath("family"),"index.html");
 d_index=index;
 };

 public String computeTitle() {
 return "Index by Family";
 };

 public synchronized void generate() throws IOException,InterruptedException {

 generateHead();
 generateTopBar();
 generateIndex();
 generateNavBar();
 generateTail();

 d_out.close();

 };

 public void generateIndex() {
 LanguageString keys[]=d_index.getFamilies();
 Sort.sortStrings(keys,0,keys.length,true,true);
 Vector entries=new Vector();

 for(int i=0;i<keys.length;i++) {
  StringBuffer sb=new StringBuffer();
  sb.append("<B>"+toHtml(keys[i])+"</B>\n");
  sb.append("<UL TYPE=\"square\">\n");
  Species s[]=d_index.getByFamily(keys[i]);
  for(int j=0;j<s.length;j++) {
  sb.append("<LI><A
HREF=\"../"+s[j].getId()+"/index.html\">"+toHtml(d_index.speciesName(s[j]))+"</A>
n");
  };
  sb.append("</UL>");

  entries.addElement(sb);

 };
 outputTwoCol(entries);
 };
};
```

Building the Weeds of El Limon for yourself

The following sets of instructions are for setup on Windows or Unix platforms only.

Building the Weeds on Windows

First you need to download the relevant .zip code files for the Weeds project from either of the following Web sites:

```
http://www.honeylocust.com/limon/xml/index.html
http://webdev.wrox.co.uk/books/1525/
```

Then you also need a copy of the Sun Java 1.1.7 JDK for Windows, which can be obtained free from:

```
http://java.sun.com/products/jdk/
```

Install the JDK as instructed, including

```
C:\JDK1.1.7\BIN
```

in your PATH statement in the autoexec.bat file in the root directory of your hard drive, e.g. as follows:

```
PATH C:\;C:\WINDOWS;C:\WINDOWS\COMMAND;C:\DOS;C:\JDK1.1.7\BIN;
```

and, if it doesn't already have a classes folder in the directory structure, create a classes folder off the main JDK 1.1.7 folder.

Unzip the Weeds Java class files from ifcUtil.jar, hnyMSXML.jar, and limon.jar to the classes directory that you made within the JDK 1.1.7 folder. Then unzip the plantxml.zip and images.zip to the same classes directory. When you've finished you should have a directory structure that looks like this:

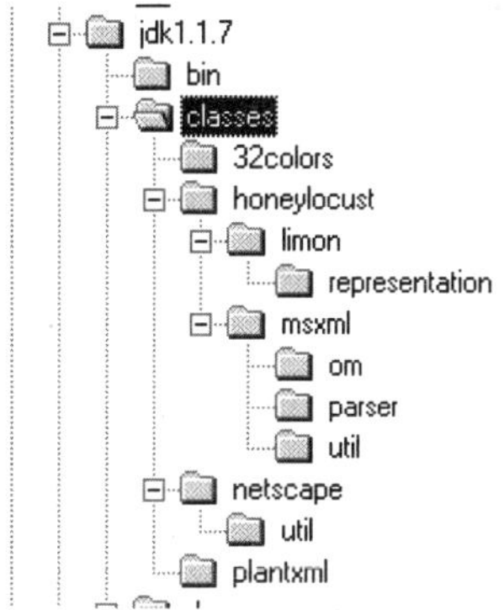

You can then either edit your autoexec.bat file to set the CLASSPATH environment variable by putting in a line as follows:

```
Set CLASSPATH=%CLASSPATH%;C:\JDK1.1.7\CLASSES;
```

or you can type it in at the DOS prompt in the DOS window. If you edit your autoexec.bat file you may need to reboot your machine for it to take effect. If you type it in at the DOS prompt the CLASSPATH variable will only remain set with that value for as long as the DOS window is open.

In the DOS window go to the C:\JDK1.1.7\classes directory and type in at the prompt,

```
java  honeylocust.limon.Generator  plantxml\*.xml
```

The basic set of Web pages should then be constructed by the application and placed in a folder called `output` within the `C:\JDK1.1.7\classes` folder.

In order to get the full effect you then need to unzip the contents of `output.zip` to the `output` folder. If you then start your Windows Explorer and double-click on the file called `index.html` in the `output` folder, your browser should start up and display the main index of the Weeds project. Or alternatively, start up your browser and **File-Open** `index.html`.

Building the Weeds on Unix

First you need to download the relevant `.zip` code files from either of the following Web sites:

```
http://www.honeylocust.com/limon/xml/index.html
http://webdev.wrox.co.uk/books/1525/
```

Then you also need a copy of most recent version of the Java 1.1.x Development Kit (JDK) available for your platform. This is available from your Unix vendor's website. For some popular versions of Unix this will be:

Operating System	Website for the JDK
Solaris	http://java.sun.com/products/jdk/
Linux	http://www.blackdown.org/java-linux.html
Digital	http://www.digital.com/java/
AIX	http://www.ibm.com/java/tools/jdk.html

Install the JDK as instructed. Next, unpack the `limon.zip` file in your home directory. You can do this by typing:

```
% cd $HOME
% unzip limon.zip
```

Then you need to set the `CLASSPATH` so that Java can find the `.class` files that make up the '`limon`' package. To do so with `csh` or a compatible shell, type:

```
% setenv LIMON ~/limon
% setenv CLASSPATH
$LIMON/ifcUtil.jar:$LIMON/hnyMSXML.jar:$LIMON/limon.jar:$CLASSPATH
```

If you're using a shell descended from the Bourne shell such as `sh` or `bash`, type:

```
$ export LIMON=$HOME/limon
$ export
CLASSPATH=$LIMON/ifcUtil.jar:$LIMON/hnyMSXML.jar:$LIMON/limon.jar:$CLASSPATH
```

If you'd rather unpack the `limon.zip` into another directory, be sure to update the `$LIMON` environment variable to reflect this. You may wish to put the above lines in your `~/.login` so that they will run automatically whenever you log in.

Next type:

```
% cd $LIMON
% unzip plantxml.zip
% unzip images.zip
% unzip output.zip
```

to unpack the supporting files. Finally, type:

```
% java honeylocust.limon.Generator  plantxml\*.xml
```

to generate the Web pages and place them in the directory `$LIMON/output`.

Summary

XML can be used to separate style and content, and make it possible to build larger Web projects than could be managed by hand. We used XML to compose a flora by writing descriptions of plants in XML and using a Java application to turn the descriptions into HTML. Since style and content can be manipulated separately, we've been able to improve the pages' looks and compatibility with older and minor Web browsers. Having taken care designing our software, we quickly produced a working product that will be adaptable to future demands.

13

Channel Definition Format (CDF)

An area of Web development where Extensible Markup Language has made a big impact is in Active Channels for Internet Explorer 4+ (CDF technology isn't supported by Netscape Communicator 4). It is XML that lies behind the command center of channels - the Channel Definition Format (CDF) file. As such CDF is an application of XML.

An Active Channel, in its most basic incarnation, is a set of Web pages and associated files (such as images and sound files) and a CDF file. The Web pages form the information part of the channel while the CDF file provides the channel builder with a flexible and easy to use methods for the visitors to gain access to that information. With just one click the visitors (or subscribers as they are called) can download all the information and store it locally in the IE4 cache and have a navigation hierarchy created on the Channel Pane of the browser. The subscriber can then view all the information whilst offline with greater speed and less cost than if connected to the Internet.

The CDF file that is created for the channel content is, in effect, metadata. That is, data about data. A CDF file contains no content as such; it is a 'site map' that you create in order to make viewing and navigation quicker and easier for the subscriber. The CDF file uses XML to control the key areas of Active Channel deployment and the subsequent refreshing of the information:

- What makes up the channel's content; this can be regular HTML pages, screensavers, Active Desktop Components.
- How IE4 should use those pages (there are four modes: normal display, full screen theatre mode, as screensavers, or as a desktop component)
- Whether all of the channel content should be downloaded for offline viewing, or just have the navigation hierarchy created for ease of navigation while online
- The formation of the Channel Pane navigation hierarchy on IE4
- Channel personalization in the form of logos, icons, titles and abstracts
- The subsequent download schedule that the channel should use for updating the content

Is it really possible to include all this information in one small CDF file? (Generally in the region of 1 – 2 kb for a 10 – 15 document channel, although as you will see later, the more items you have in the CDF file, the larger it will get.) Thanks to the versatility of the XML that is used to create the CDF files for Active Channels the answer is yes! CDF files are small and easy to create requiring nothing more complex than your favorite text editor (the humble Windows Notepad is ideal for CDF file creation). Before we take a look at how this is possible, let's look at a scenario where CDF technology can be used to boost the performance and usability of an existing Web site without having to alter any of the existing pages.

> **It is important to bear in mind at this point that Active Channels are designed to be viewed offline. The technique of adding a CDF file to an existing website will work fine as long as there is no use of server-side components such as CGIs, ASP or Microsoft FrontPage extensions. If you want to create a channel from a site which uses these types of components you will either need to make your channel operate online or alter the code of the pages to make use of client-side technologies such as scripting (VBScript and JavaScript) and databinding.**

CDF Case Study – XYZ Corp

We're going to take a look at a fictitious company, XYZ Corp, and look at how they could benefit by taking advantage of CDF technology to create an Active Channel.

Background

XYZ Corp specialize in producing custom widgets for the ever-growing widget market (good old widgets!). XYZ Corp already have their own Web site that they use to serve a dual purpose:

- The online catalog allows customers to have instant access to the entire range of widgets available along with current prices. This reduces their printing and distribution costs and allows their customers quicker access to their range of products.
- The online catalog with special offers is also used by the travelling salespeople at XYZ Corp who have instant access to information on the whole range of products and prices. The salespeople use laptops and cellular phones to connect to the Web site as required.

XYZ Corp updates their main online catalog and special offers pages every Friday afternoon. They also have a What's New page listing new products and special offers and a What's Happening at XYZ page which provides both customers and staff with information about the company's activities and news. The site also has a few other pages containing information on the terms and conditions for customers, and product and services warranty statements.

At present, in order to receive the updated catalog produced on a weekly basis, customers need to remember to visit the appropriate page (either by using a bookmark they had created or relying on memory, a jotted note, or receiving an e-mail notification when the page changes, to find the relevant URL). Customers have to visit the catalog each and every time they want to refer to it, which costs them in connection time, their own time and bandwidth.

XYZ Corp would like to make their online services more appealing to their customers by improving them in the following ways:

- Give users easy access to their Web site without the need to remember URLs or create bookmarks, thus increasing customer usage of the online service
- Improve the 'time to screen' speed at which customers can view and use their extensive online catalog, since customers will be viewing the data from their hard drive cache rather than 'live' from the Internet
- Ensure that customers have all the latest information on products, services and pricing close at hand

Let's move on to find out how we can leverage CDF technology to help solve these issues.

How Using CDF Technology Can Help

By using CDF technology to create an Active Channel we can address these three issues all at once, without having to spend any time, effort, or money in actually changing the layout of the Web site in any way. That is not to say that XYZ couldn't create a dedicated set of pages purely for use in the channel where they could leverage other benefits that IE4 has to offer such as DHTML and databinding! Here is how CDF could be used to help XYZ Corp achieve its vision:

- Customers will no longer need to remember the URL of the pages they want to visit. They will have easy one-click assess to the site via the Channel Bar on their desktops or the IE4 Channel Pane.

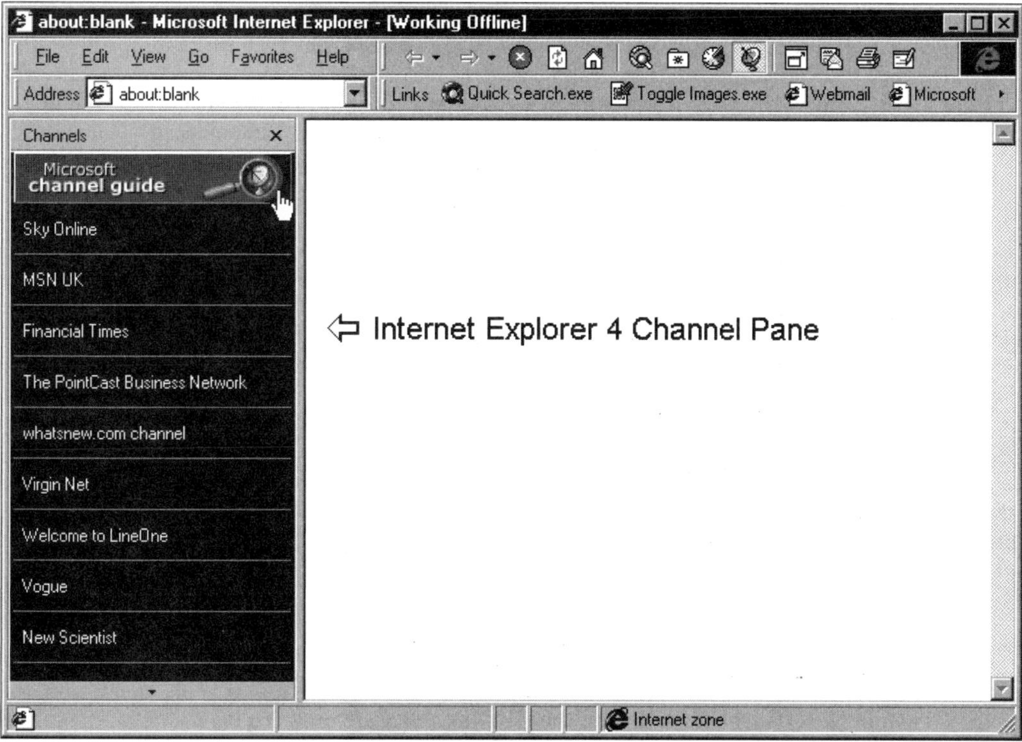

The CDF file can be set so that the catalog and other relevant documents are downloaded and stored locally in the subscriber's browser cache, making them immediately accessible without needing to go online to retrieve the documents again. This will reduce both the load on the server and help to replace a paper version of their catalog for customers using IE4. Reductions in printing and distribution costs are savings that can be passed on to the customers in the form of competitive pricing.

If the update schedule for the channel is set to coincide with the time and day that the catalog is updated, then this will mean that IE4 will download the channel content automatically so that the customers will have the latest catalog waiting for them on their computers. This guarantees that they have the latest information and prices on ranges of products.

Creation of an Active Channel will also be of enormous benefit to the travelling salespeople of XYZ Corp who need access to the information in the catalog. The CDF file will allow IE4 to refresh the channel information once weekly and store the data locally in the temporary internet files cache on their laptops, obviating the need to connect to the Internet in the interim to gain access to the catalog. This will save considerably on their cellular phone connection costs and also dramatically increase the speed of display of the information (the speed of connection via cellular phones is normally 9600 kbps on GSM 900 and 1800 networks, although higher speeds are possible on GSM 1900 systems).

The actual method IE4 uses to update the content is dependant on the type of connection the user has to the Internet. Users with a permanent Internet connection (via a leased line say) will find that the content is updated at regular intervals while they are not using their PCs (IE4 does this to reduce the load on system resources). Those with dial-up access to the Internet have two options:

- They can choose to have IE4 automatically dial-up and activate their Internet connection and check for changes to the channel content (this only applies to users who connect to the Internet using Microsoft Windows Dial-Up Networking).
- They can have IE4 check for content changes whilst they are browsing other sites on the Internet. This happens invisibly and the user is not notified that the update is being carried out.

Creating the CDF File

If a simple CDF file is all that is needed to give dramatic improvements to the existing Web site then let's see how we go about making one.

Before we start to open up Notepad and get on with making our CDF files we need to take a few minutes to look at the pages XYZ Corp want to include in their channel. Here is a listing of the pages they want to include, along with their URLs:

Page	URL
Main Page	http://www.xyzcorp.com/index.htm
Product Catalog	http://www.xyzcorp.com/catalog.htm
Special Offers	http://www.xyzcorp.com/special.htm
What's New	http://www.xyzcorp.com/new.htm
What's Happening at XYZ	http://www.xyzcorp.com/happening.htm
Terms and Conditions	http://www.xyzcorp.com/terms.htm
Warranty	http://www.xyzcorp.com/warranty.htm

Now we are in a position to start to create the CDF file for the XYZ Corp Active Channel. It is time to open Notepad and start inputting some XML! The file should be saved with a **.CDF** extension. To override the natural tendency that Notepad has to save with a .txt extension you should enclose the whole file name in quotes.

We can start off by putting in some of the skeleton of the CDF file:

```
<?xml version="1.0" encoding="UTF-8"?>
<CHANNEL>

</CHANNEL>
```

Here we have the two basic elements that make a CDF file. The first element declares that the document is an XML document and declares the XML version used along with the encoding character set. It is worth noting that this is the only CDF element to use the question mark (?) in the delimiter – all others use the forward slash (/). The second element is the CHANNEL element, within which we'll be declaring the channel and sub-channel information.

At this point we have introduced two of the three types of elements that we will encounter during the creation of CDF files.

Element Type	Example
Empty element with attributes	<ELEMENT ATTR1="value" ATTR2="value"/>
Element with content and end tag	<ELEMENT>Element Content Here </ELEMENT>

Table Continued on Following Page

Element Type	Example

Parent element with attributes and child elements	`<PARENT ATTR1="value">`
	`<CHILD1>`
	`Content`
	`</CHILD1>`
	`<CHILD2 ATTR1="value"/>`
	`</PARENT>`

Avoiding CDF File Errors

So far we've seen examples of an empty element with attributes (`<?xml version="1.0" encoding="UTF-8"?>`) and as we'll see in a moment the `<CHANNEL>` element is an example of a parent element with attributes and child elements. Elements without end tags might be difficult for people familiar with HTML to get used to, but the key is to remember that this is XML and not HTML. Remember that it is important to follow the correct syntax with regard to end tags, as closing elements incorrectly will result in errors being generated when the channel is subscribed to.

Errors in your CDF file can show up at various stages during and after the subscription to the channel. This dialog box displays an error message during the content updating process:

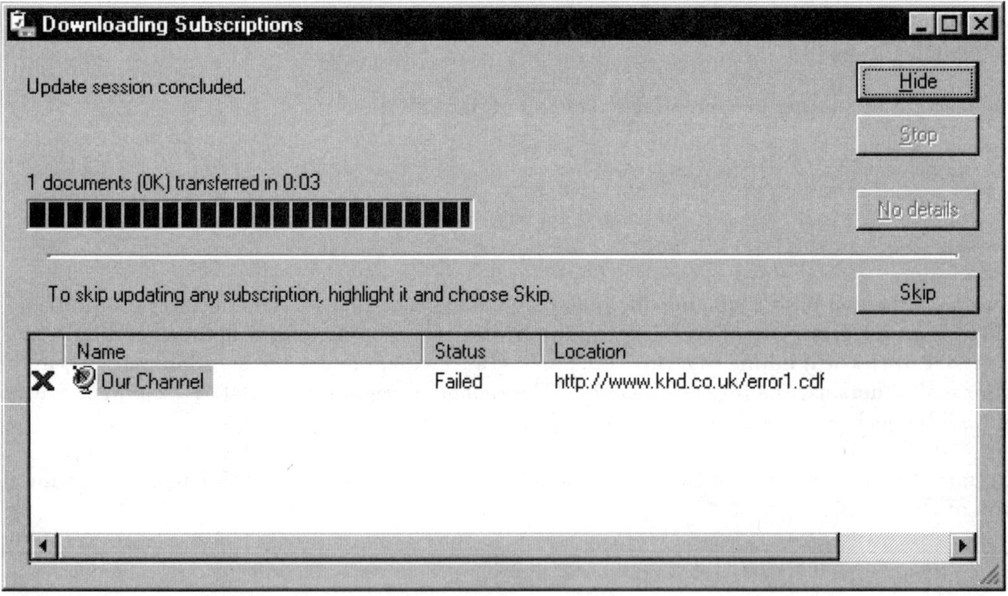

The next screen shot is the IE4 Manage Subscriptions dialog box (accessible by clicking Favorites | Manage Subscriptions) showing that an error occurred during channel update:

C:\WINNT\Subscriptions
File Edit View Go Favorites Help
Address C:\WINNT\Subscriptions
Links
Name
Last update
Status
Next update
Location
Our Channel
01/04/98 20...
Error: Unrecoverable update e...
02/04/98 00...
http://www.khd.co.uk/error1.cdf
1 object(s)

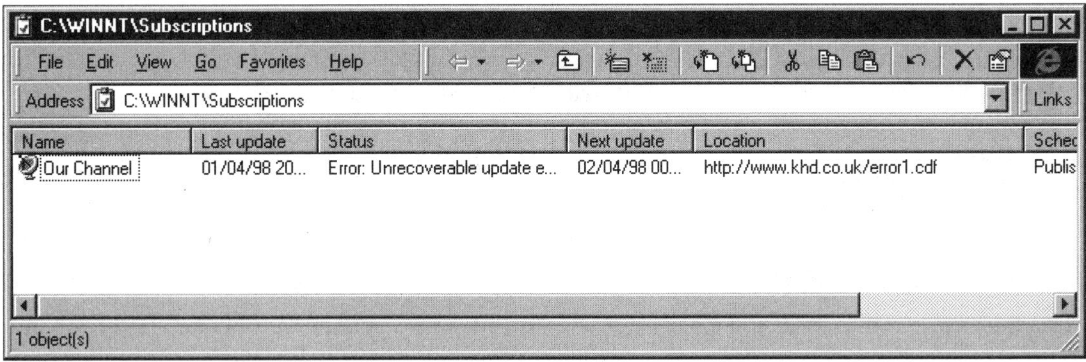

And the next one is really horrible! When the user tries to view a channel with a faulty CDF file this is what they are faced with – a dialog box informing them that there was a problem with the way the channel is authored! Aaaaarrrgh! At least this error message does give you information about where the CDF parser encountered the error in the CDF file.

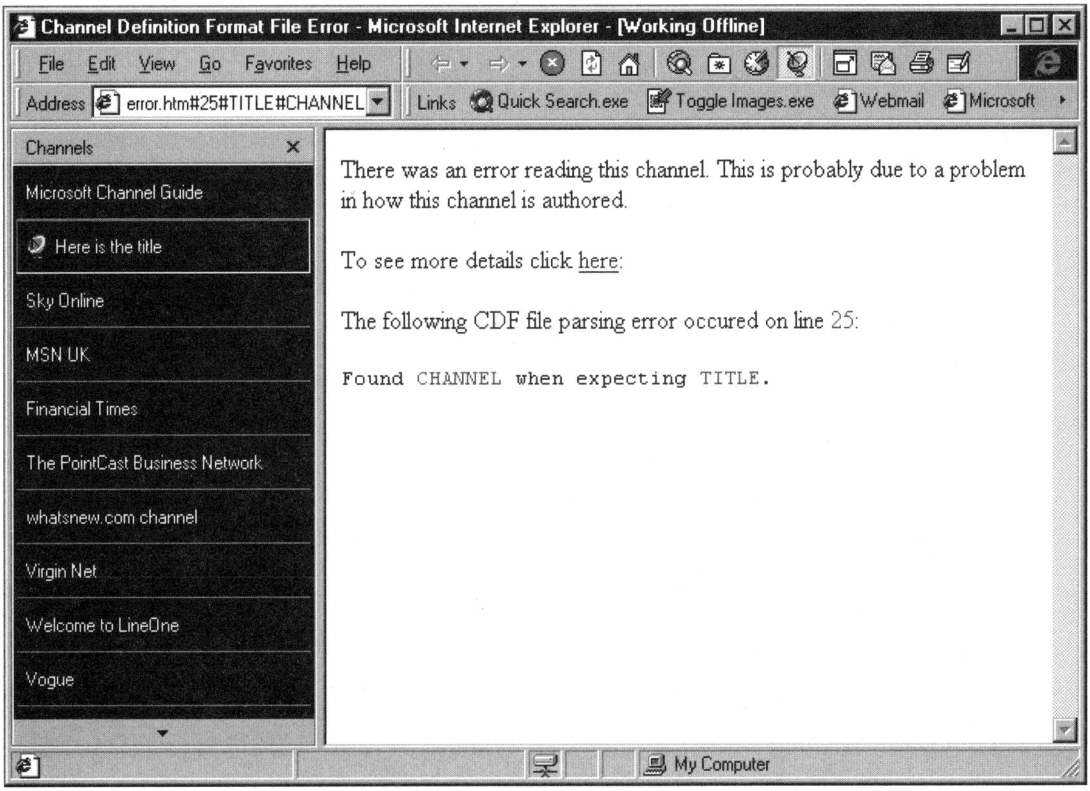

Channel Definition Format File Error - Microsoft Internet Explorer - [Working Offline]
File Edit View Go Favorites Help
Address error.htm#25#TITLE#CHANNEL
Links Quick Search.exe Toggle Images.exe Webmail Microsoft
Channels
Microsoft Channel Guide
Here is the title
Sky Online
MSN UK
Financial Times
The PointCast Business Network
whatsnew.com channel
Virgin Net
Welcome to LineOne
Vogue
There was an error reading this channel. This is probably due to a problem in how this channel is authored.
To see more details click here:
The following CDF file parsing error occured on line 25:
Found CHANNEL when expecting TITLE.
My Computer

If you are building this example, depending upon which build of IE4 you have, it may be necessary to delete your existing version of the XYZ Corp Channel before trying your next version, otherwise it may not update properly. The easiest way to do this is to right click on your mouse over the channel in the channel pane in IE and selecting delete. Then you can reload the channel with its new features.

Back to the CDF File Creation

If we look again at the URLs of the pages we want to add to the channel we find that they are all in the root of `www.xyzcorp.com`. Armed with this information, we can make our life easier straight from the start by adding an attribute to the `CHANNEL` element to declare a base URL from which all relative URLs within the CDF file are resolved. This is not required but it does make authoring the CDF file easier, since you don't have to keep typing in the whole URL. This attribute is `BASE` (surprise, surprise!).

```
<?xml version="1.0" encoding="UTF-8"?>
<CHANNEL BASE="http://www.xyzcorp.com/">

</CHANNEL>
```

The next attribute we can add is the `HREF` attribute. This attribute declares the page to which IE4 first navigates when the subscriber opens the channel. We can look at this as the main page of the channel. In this example it is `INDEX.HTM`.

```
<?xml version="1.0" encoding="UTF-8"?>
<CHANNEL BASE="http://www.xyzcorp.com/" HREF="index.htm">

</CHANNEL>
```

There are three more attributes we can add to the `CHANNEL` element. These are `PRECACHE`, `LEVEL` and `LASTMOD`. Let's look at `PRECACHE` first.

`PRECACHE` specifies whether the content should be downloaded and stored in the `Temporary Internet Files` folder of the Windows operating system. If `PRECACHE` is set to `"YES"` or omitted (which has the same effect as setting it to `"YES"` as this is the default) the content will only be downloaded if the subscriber chooses to download the content during the initial subscription routine. If `PRECACHE` is set to `"NO"` then content will not be downloaded.

`LEVEL` is used in conjunction with `PRECACHE` to specify how many links deep IE4 will **link crawl** in order to cache pages. Link crawl is the term used to describe the feature of IE4 where it automatically follows each of the hyperlinks on the page and caches the content (HTML documents, images, sound files and all frame content if the link is to a frameset) it finds for offline viewing. The default is `"0"` which precaches only the URL specified by the `HREF` attribute. The value of this attribute can be set to either `"0"`, `"1"`, `"2"` or `"3"`.

LEVEL=1

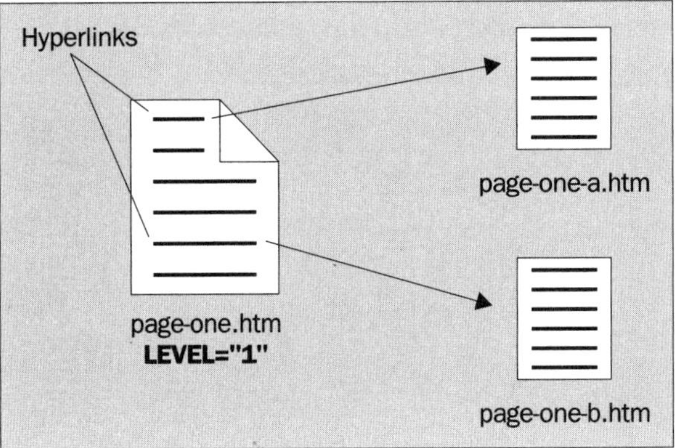

LEVEL=2

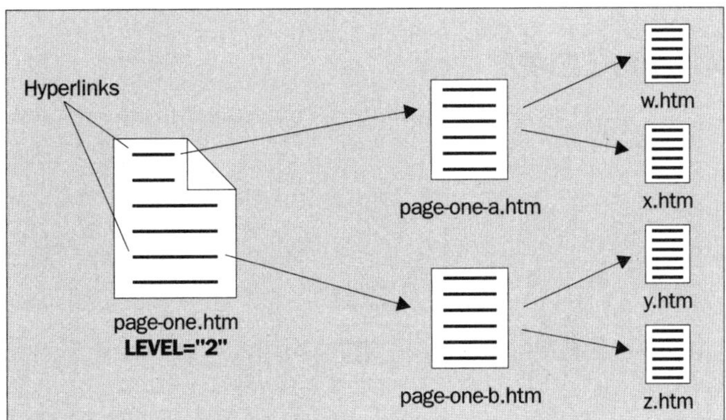

LEVEL=3

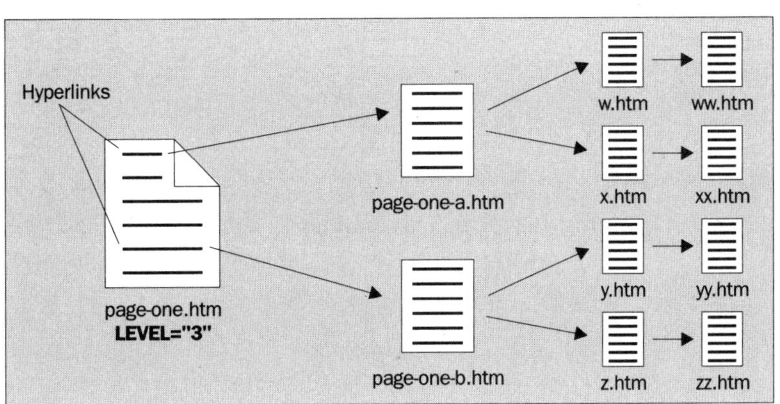

LEVEL=4

If you set the value of `LEVEL` to something which is invalid (`"4"` for example) then IE4 will link crawl down three levels and cache the pages (and their contents) but won't go any further.

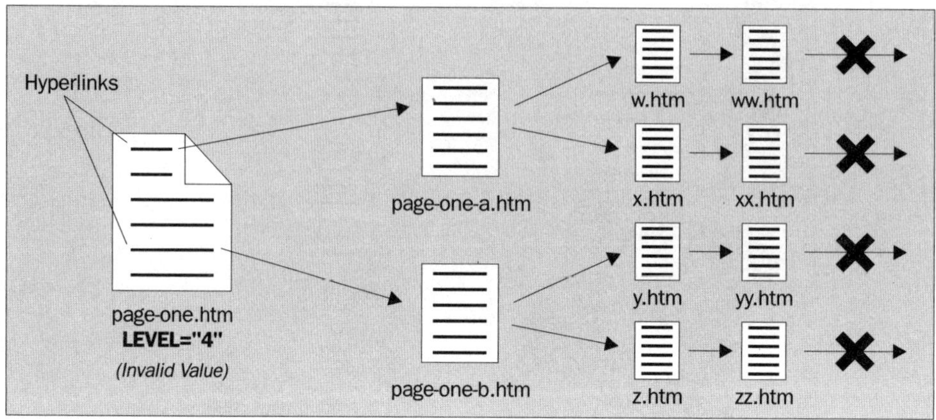

How PRECACHE Affects LEVEL

If `PRECACHE` is set to `"NO"` then the `LEVEL` attribute is ignored irrespective of the value it has been given.

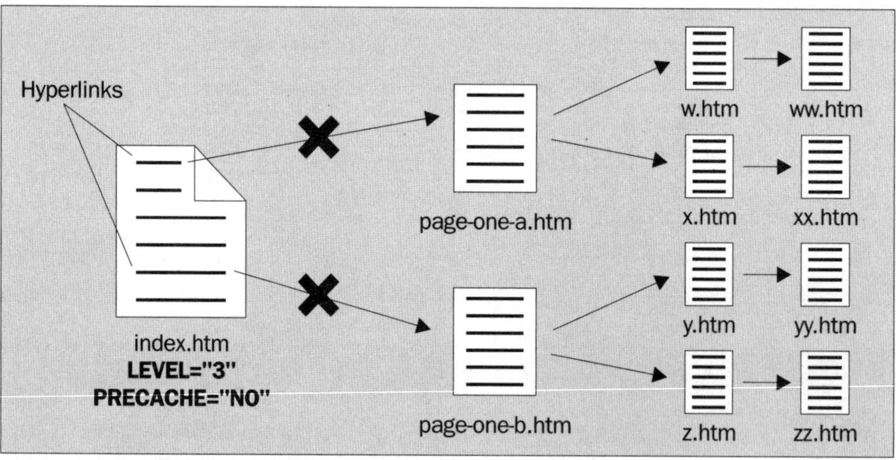

Using LASTMOD

The third attribute we can look at is `LASTMOD`. This attribute specifies the date and time (GMT) when the page indexed by the `HREF` attribute was last updated. It takes the following form, `yyyy-mm-ddThh:mm` where:

yyyy	Specifies the year
mm	Specifies the month (01 – 12)
dd	Specifies the day (01 – 31)
hh	Specifies the hour (00 – 23)
mm	Specifies the minutes (00 – 59)

This attribute allows IE4 to determine whether the content has changed since the last time it was downloaded. The item is downloaded only if the date associated with the cached item is older than the LASTMOD value declared in the CDF file. This reduces load on the server and online time for subscribers, and it is recommended that this attribute be used.

What does XYZ Corp want to do with their page? They want it cached and LASTMOD attributes added but do not want any links on the pages to be crawled. The attributes we need for this are as follows:

```
<?xml version="1.0" encoding="UTF-8"?>
<CHANNEL BASE="http://www.xyzcorp.com/" HREF="index.htm" PRECACHE="YES" LEVEL="0"
LASTMOD="1998-06-01T12:00">
</CHANNEL>
```

The LASTMOD attribute declares that the page was last updated on the 1st of June 1998 at noon.

More ABSTRACTs and TITLEs

We mentioned earlier the ability to declare titles and abstracts. These serve a particular purpose and are worth including if only for completeness. Both TITLE and ABSTRACT are child elements of CHANNEL. TITLE is used as the default title name for the Channel Bar (this can be changed during subscription) while ABSTRACT is displayed as a ToolTip when the user hovers the cursor over the channel button in the Channel Pane or channel bar.

```
<?xml version="1.0" encoding="UTF-8"?>
<CHANNEL BASE="http://www.xyzcorp.com/" HREF="index.htm" PRECACHE="YES" LEVEL="0"
 _LASTMOD="1998-06-01T12:00">

 <TITLE>Here is the title</TITLE>
 <ABSTRACT>And here is the abstract!</ABSTRACT>

</CHANNEL>
```

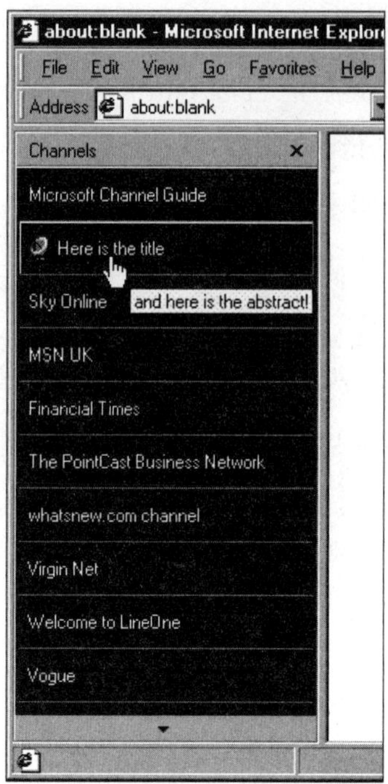

Testing the CDF File

So far we've created a CDF file that, if XYZ Corp were to upload it to their server, would work. Where the CDF file is uploaded to is primarily up to the channel builder. If a `BASE` has been set for the `CHANNEL` element then it can simply be uploaded to this location and made available to subscribers via a normal hyperlink. The only requirement is that the CDF file is uploaded to the same domain as the channel content since, for security reasons, IE4 cannot access channel content not residing at the same domain as the CDF file.

Loading the CDF file into the browser would download and cache the main front page of the channel and add the channel to the Channel Bar and Channel Pane. Let's build on this by adding the other pages to the CDF file.

Adding Content to the CDF File

Adding pages to the CDF file requires another child element of `CHANNEL`, the `ITEM` element. An item is a unit of information that usually corresponds to a Web page. In an Active Channel, items appear in the navigation hierarchy exposed in the Channel Pane. We've already come across the four attributes of `ITEM` when we looked at `CHANNEL`. These are `HREF`, `LASTMOD`, `PRECACHE` and `LEVEL`.

Let's add the first `ITEM` to the CDF file. We'll add the page for the catalog first.

```
<?xml version="1.0" encoding="UTF-8"?>
<CHANNEL BASE="http://www.xyzcorp.com/" HREF="index.htm" PRECACHE="YES" LEVEL="0"
_LASTMOD="1998-06-01T12:00">
```

```
 <TITLE>Here is the title</TITLE>
 <ABSTRACT>And here is the abstract!</ABSTRACT>

   <ITEM HREF="catalog.htm" PRECACHE="YES" LEVEL="0" LASTMOD="1998-06-01T12:00">

   </ITEM>

</CHANNEL>
```

We can also add `TITLE` and `ABSTRACT` to our `ITEM` just as we did for the `CHANNEL` element.

```
<?xml version="1.0" encoding="UTF-8"?>
<CHANNEL BASE="http://www.xyzcorp.com/" HREF="index.htm" PRECACHE="YES" LEVEL="0"
_LASTMOD="1998-06-01T12:00">

 <TITLE>Here is the title</TITLE>
 <ABSTRACT>And here is the abstract!</ABSTRACT>

   <ITEM HREF="catalog.htm" PRECACHE="YES" LEVEL="0" LASTMOD="1998-06-01T12:00">
    <TITLE>XYZ Catalog</TITLE>
    <ABSTRACT>Browse the latest widget catalog</ABSTRACT>
   </ITEM>

</CHANNEL>
```

If we load the CDF file up onto the server and take a look at it we can see that IE4 has added the first `ITEM` to the hierarchy automatically.

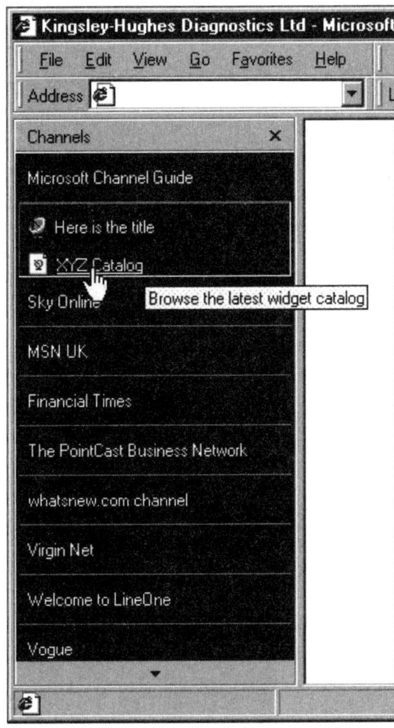

We now need to include the Special Offers page. But there is a catch. We don't want it to be visible on the Channel Pane, as is the catalog, we want to access it via a hyperlink off the catalog page. How can we do this? Since there are some links on the catalog page that we don't want downloaded, we've prevented them being crawled to by setting `level` to `"0"` in the CDF file. So, what can we do? Well, first of all we can add this page to the CDF file just as we did with the catalog (only this time we can omit the `TITLE` and `ABSTRACT` elements since we won't want or need these displayed on the Channel Pane), as follows:

```
<?xml version="1.0" encoding="UTF-8"?>
<CHANNEL BASE="http://www.xyzcorp.com/" HREF="index.htm" PRECACHE="YES" LEVEL="0"
_LASTMOD="1998-06-01T12:00">

 <TITLE>Here is the title</TITLE>
 <ABSTRACT>And here is the abstract!</ABSTRACT>

   <ITEM HREF="catalog.htm" PRECACHE="YES" LEVEL="0" LASTMOD="1998-06-01T12:00">
    <TITLE>XYZ Catalog</TITLE>
    <ABSTRACT>Browse the latest widget catalog</ABSTRACT>
   </ITEM>

   <ITEM HREF="special.htm" PRECACHE="YES" LEVEL="0" LASTMOD="1998-06-01T12:00">
   </ITEM>

</CHANNEL>
```

If we load this page into the browser we will see that the page we have just added to the CDF file will be visible on the Channel Pane.

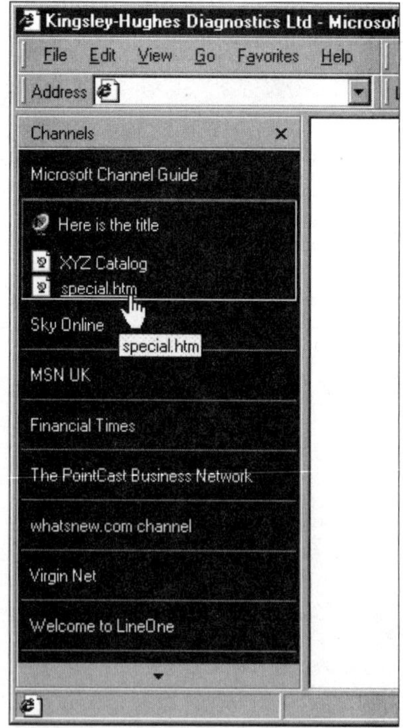

Note that since we didn't add a `TITLE` or `ABSTRACT`, the filename is used for both. How do we hide this `ITEM`? For this we need a new child element of the `ITEM` element. This child element is `USAGE`. The `USAGE` element has six possible values:

Value	Description
"Channel"	These appear in the browser channel pane. This is the default behavior when no USAGE element appears under an ITEM.
"Email"	This one item is e-mailed to the subscriber when the channel content is updated (only one USAGE element with a value set to "Email" is allowed per CDF). Delivery to the user's mailbox is handled by IE4.
"NONE"	If "NONE" is used as the only USAGE element in an ITEM, the item will not appear in the Channel Pane.
"ScreenSaver" (Or "SmartScreen" a trademark of PointCast Inc.)	This one item is displayed as a screen saver (one Screensaver per CDF).
"DesktopComponent"	These items are displayed in a frame located on the Active Desktop. A CDF item with this usage value can only be used in the context of an Active Desktop item. An Active Channel requires a separate CDF file.
"SoftwareUpdate"	This indicates the CDF file is being used for a Software Distribution Channel to automatically update software over the Web. An Open Software Description (OSD) file is also required for Software Distribution Channels.

To serve our purpose here we need to set the value of USAGE to "NONE".

```
<?xml version="1.0" encoding="UTF-8"?>
<CHANNEL BASE="http://www.xyzcorp.com/" HREF="index.htm" PRECACHE="YES" LEVEL="0"
_LASTMOD="1998-06-01T12:00">
 <TITLE>Here is the title</TITLE>
 <ABSTRACT>and here is the abstract!</ABSTRACT>

   <ITEM HREF="catalog.htm" PRECACHE="YES" LEVEL="0">
    <TITLE>XYZ Catalog</TITLE>
    <ABSTRACT>Browse the latest widget catalog</ABSTRACT>
   </ITEM>

   <ITEM HREF="special.htm" PRECACHE="YES" LEVEL="0" LASTMOD="1998-06-01T12:00">
    <USAGE VALUE="NONE"></USAGE>
   </ITEM>
</CHANNEL>
```

Note that the closing </USAGE> is required for this element. And just to prove it works, let's load it into IE4!

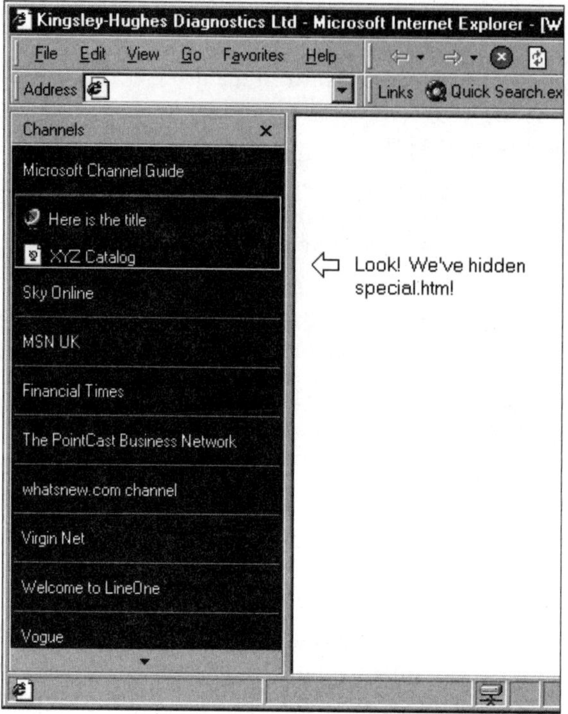

The next two pages we want to add to our CDF file are the Terms and Conditions page and the Warranty page. We could simply add these as two more items, but we want to be a little more sophisticated than that! We want to add them in a sub-channel on the Channel Pane. Sub-channels can be thought of as Windows folders, inside which are files. This is a great way to organize the layout of information on the Channel Pane and also categorize topics under subject headings so as to make things easier to find. Just as you wouldn't put all your files on your computer into one super folder, because of the nightmare that would be generated when you wanted to find anything, you don't need to do that when organizing the Channel Pane navigation hierarchy.

Note that using sub-channels just forms a 'virtual' folder list on the Channel Pane and does not in any way bear any resemblance to the layout you have for the content on the server. Sub-channels are created by nesting CHANNEL elements inside the initial CHANNEL element. Here's how we start:

```
<?xml version="1.0" encoding="UTF-8"?>
<CHANNEL BASE="http://www.xyzcorp.com/" HREF="index.htm" PRECACHE="YES" LEVEL="0"
_LASTMOD="1998-06-01T12:00">

 <TITLE>Here is the title</TITLE>
 <ABSTRACT>and here is the abstract!</ABSTRACT>

   <ITEM HREF="catalog.htm" PRECACHE="YES" LEVEL="0" LASTMOD="1998-06-01T12:00">
    <TITLE>XYZ Catalog</TITLE>
    <ABSTRACT>Browse the latest widget catalog</ABSTRACT>
   </ITEM>
```

```
    <ITEM HREF="special.htm" PRECACHE="YES" LEVEL="0" LASTMOD="1998-06-01T12:00">
     <USAGE VALUE="NONE"></USAGE>
    </ITEM>

    <CHANNEL>

    </CHANNEL>
</CHANNEL>
```

We can now give this sub-channel 'folder' a `TITLE` and `ABSTRACT` of its own to make it stand out on the Channel Pane.

```
<?xml version="1.0" ENCODING="UTF-8"?>
<CHANNEL BASE="http://www.xyzcorp.com/" HREF="index.htm" PRECACHE="YES" LEVEL="0"
 _LASTMOD="1998-06-01T12:00">
.
...
.
   <ITEM HREF="special.htm" PRECACHE="YES" LEVEL="0" LASTMOD="1998-06-01T12:00">
    <USAGE VALUE="NONE"></USAGE>
   </ITEM>

   <CHANNEL>
    <TITLE>The Small Print!</TITLE>
    <ABSTRACT>Check out the XYZ Corp small print here!</ABSTRACT>
   </CHANNEL>
</CHANNEL>
```

Finally, we can add the `ITEM`s to the sub channel:

```
<?xml version="1.0" encoding="UTF-8"?>
<CHANNEL BASE="http://www.xyzcorp.com/" HREF="index.htm" PRECACHE="YES" LEVEL="0"
 _LASTMOD="1998-06-01T12:00">

...

   <CHANNEL>
    <TITLE>The Small Print<TITLE>
    <ABSTRACT>Check out the Small Print here!</ABSTRACT>
       <ITEM HREF="terms.htm" PRECACHE="YES" LEVEL="0" LASTMOD="1998-06-01T12:00">
        <TITLE>XYZ Corp Terms and Conditions</TITLE>
        <ABSTRACT>All the small print on Terms and Conditions</ABSTRACT>
       </ITEM>
       <ITEM HREF="warranty.htm" PRECACHE="YES" LEVEL="0" LASTMOD="1998-06
01T12:00">
        <TITLE>XYZ Corp Warranty</TITLE>
        <ABSTRACT>The warranty statement on our widgets</ABSTRACT>
       </ITEM>
   </CHANNEL>
</CHANNEL>
```

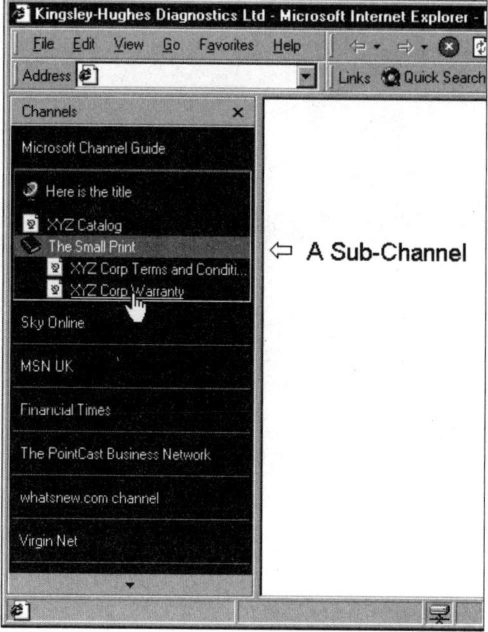

Encoding Characters for CDF

Note that Terms and Conditions was written exactly like that and not Terms & Conditions. As with XML, certain characters need to be encoded in CDF files when placed between an element start and end tag. These characters are:

Character	Encoded value
<	`<`
>	`>`
'	`'`
"	`"`
&	`&`

If we had wanted to include the text as Terms & Conditions we would have written it as:

```
Terms &amp; Conditions
```

Failure to observe this convention will result in parsing errors during the subscription or update process.

Adding Further Pages to the CDF File

Without further ado we can add the remaining two pages into another sub-channel we want to create on the Channel Pane.

```
<?xml version="1.0" encoding="UTF-8"?>
<CHANNEL BASE="http://www.xyzcorp.com/" HREF="index.htm" PRECACHE="YES" LEVEL="0"
_LASTMOD="1998-06-01T12:00">
 <TITLE>Here is the title</TITLE>
 <ABSTRACT>And here is the abstract!</ABSTRACT>
.
   <CHANNEL>
    <TITLE>The Small Print</TITLE>
    <ABSTRACT>Check out the Small Print here!</ABSTRACT>
       <ITEM HREF="terms.htm" PRECACHE="YES" LEVEL="0" LASTMOD="1998-06-01T12:00">
        <TITLE>XYZ Corp Terms and Conditions</TITLE>
        <ABSTRACT>All the small print on Terms and Conditions</ABSTRACT>
       </ITEM>
       <ITEM HREF="warranty.htm" PRECACHE="YES" LEVEL="0" LASTMOD="1998-06-
        _01T12:00">
        <TITLE>XYZ Corp Warranty</TITLE>
        <ABSTRACT>The warranty statement on our widgets</ABSTRACT>
       </ITEM>
   </CHANNEL>

   <CHANNEL>
    <TITLE>At XYZ Corp</TITLE>
    <ABSTRACT>Find out what's going on at XYZ Corp</ABSTRACT>
       <ITEM HREF="new.htm" PRECACHE="YES" LEVEL="0" LASTMOD="1998-06-01T12:00">
        <TITLE>What's New at XYZ Corp</TITLE>
        <ABSTRACT>Discover what's new at XYZ Corp here</ABSTRACT>
       </ITEM>
       <ITEM HREF="happening.htm" PRECACHE="YES" LEVEL="0" LASTMOD="1998-06-
        _01T12:00">
        <TITLE>What's happening at XYZ Corp</TITLE>
        <ABSTRACT>Keep up with all that's going on at XYZ Corp here</ABSTRACT>
       </ITEM>
   </CHANNEL>

</CHANNEL>
```

We now have a fully functioning CDF file. XYZ Corp can upload it to their server, add a prominent link to it and let clients and customers subscribe to their brand new Active Channel. (OK, they might need to tidy up the `TITLE`s and `ABSTRACT`s we've put on their channel!) But this is just the beginning. We can use XML in the form of CDF to get much more leverage on IE4. Here are just some of the things we can do with CDF:

Add an Active Screensaver to the channel content

Add a `SCHEDULE` to automate updating

Add logos and icons to the Channel Bar and Channel Pane to personalize the channel

Let's take a look at these in turn, starting with the benefits of including an Active Screensaver.

Adding an Active Screensaver

An Active Screensaver is a new concept made possible by IE4. Put simply, an Active Screensaver is an ordinary HTML page displayed by IE4 as a screensaver. Anyone with knowledge of HTML (or better still, DHTML – as it is this which makes it '*Active*') and the ability to make a CDF file can create an Active Screensaver.

Let's assume that someone at XYZ Corp has created a great DHTML Active Screensaver and they want to include it in with the other channel content. The screensaver is called `ssaver.htm` and has been uploaded to the root of the XYZ Corp Web site. We have one question to answer – how do we add it to the CDF file? Remember back to when we introduced the `USAGE` element. One of the possible values for this child element of `ITEM` was `"ScreenSaver"`.

All we need to do to add a screensaver to the CDF file is add the page in as an `ITEM` and assign it a `USAGE` element with the value set to `"ScreenSaver"`.

```
<?xml version="1.0" encoding="UTF-8"?>
<CHANNEL BASE="http://www.xyzcorp.com/" HREF="index.htm" PRECACHE="YES" LEVEL="0"
_LASTMOD="1998-06-01T12:00">
.
   <ITEM HREF="special.htm" PRECACHE="YES" LEVEL="0" LASTMOD="1998-06-01T12:00">
    <USAGE VALUE="NONE"></USAGE>
   </ITEM>

   <ITEM HREF="ssaver.htm" PRECACHE="YES" LEVEL="0" LASTMOD="1998-06-01T12:00">
    <USAGE VALUE="ScreenSaver"></USAGE>
   </ITEM>

   <CHANNEL>
    <TITLE>The Small Print</TITLE>
    <ABSTRACT>Check out the Small Print here!</ABSTRACT>
       <ITEM HREF="terms.htm" PRECACHE="YES" LEVEL="0" LASTMOD="1998-06-01T12:00">
        <TITLE>XYZ Corp Terms and Conditions</TITLE>
        <ABSTRACT>All the small print on Terms and Conditions</ABSTRACT>
       </ITEM>
.
   </CHANNEL>

</CHANNEL>
```

At present you can only add one Active Screensaver per CDF file. If more than one is present then the first one will be used.

When subscribers bring down a screensaver they will be presented with this dialog box (unless they've seen it before and checked the 'don't ask me again' checkbox):

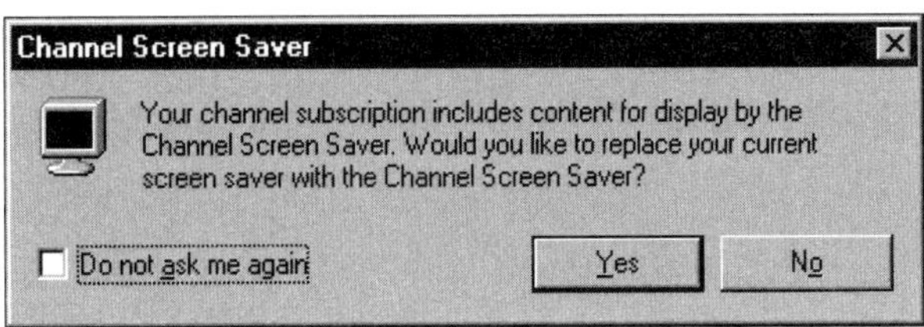

If the subscriber already has another Active Screensaver installed then the new one and old one will simply alternate at a set interval (default interval is 30 seconds). There are no set limits to the number of Active Screensavers that a user can have installed at any one time.

Automating Channel Update

One of the powerful features available to the channel builder is to **push** the new content out to existing subscribers on a regular basis. Don't let the word push bring up visions of having to have some sophisticated server or some new kind of server extension running. The word push is in fact rather inaccurate - **managed pull** might be a much better word since all the work (other than creating the CDF file) is done on the client side by IE4 (the only common example of push at work is email!). All the channel builder needs to do is tell the browser that they want it to do this for them. This request is done utilizing XML in the CDF file.

We tell IE4 that we need this function using the element `SCHEDULE`, which is a child element of `CHANNEL`.

We begin by adding this element to the CDF file we created earlier.

```
<?xml version="1.0" encoding="UTF-8"?>
<CHANNEL BASE="http://www.xyzcorp.com/" HREF="index.htm" PRECACHE="YES" LEVEL="0"
_LASTMOD="1998-06-01T12:00">

 <TITLE>The XYZ Corp Active Channel</TITLE>
 <ABSTRACT>Welcome to the XYZ Corp Channel - Home of the Widget!</ABSTRACT>

   <SCHEDULE>
...
   </SCHEDULE>

   <ITEM HREF="catalog.htm" PRECACHE="YES" LEVEL="0" LASTMOD="1998-06-01T12:00">
    <TITLE>XYZ Catalog</TITLE>
    <ABSTRACT>Browse the latest widget catalog</ABSTRACT>
   </ITEM>

   <CHANNEL>
  ...
   </CHANNEL>

</CHANNEL>
```

There can only be a maximum of one `SCHEDULE` per CDF file and that must appear in the top-level channel.

At the beginning we said that the XYZ Corp catalog would be updated weekly, on a Friday, so we would like to set a schedule that reflected this. To do this we need to use an empty child element of SCHEDULE, called INTERVALTIME.

INTERVALTIME specifies how often the channel should attempt to update. Since we want to update our channel weekly we can set a value to INTERVALTIME of DAY="7" (other possibilities being HOUR and MIN).

```
<?xml version="1.0" encoding="UTF-8"?>
<CHANNEL BASE="http://www.xyzcorp.com/" HREF="index.htm" PRECACHE="YES" LEVEL="0"
_LASTMOD="1998-06-01T12:00">

  <TITLE>The XYZ Corp Active Channel</TITLE>
  <ABSTRACT>Welcome to the XYZ Corp Channel - Home of the Widget!</ABSTRACT>

    <SCHEDULE>
     <INTERVALTIME DAY="7"/>
    </SCHEDULE>

...
```

Note that this element doesn't need a closing tag because it is an empty element, although a forward slash in the closing delimiter is required.

This has achieved part of what we wanted to – get the channel to update weekly. The problem is, it hasn't given us any control over when updates cycles should start. Using the CDF file we've created, if someone subscribes on a Monday, then barring IE4 being unable to get online, the next update should occur the following Monday. Similarly, if someone subscribes on a Thursday then the next update would be the following Thursday. This would mean that the catalog these subscribers received would almost be obsolete before they got it. We need a method to control when the schedule starts. What we are looking for is an attribute of SCHEDULE called STARTDATE.

If we want the schedule to start on a Friday, the trick is to choose a date from the past that corresponded to a Friday, which we can then add to the SCHEDULE.

```
<?xml version="1.0" encoding="UTF-8"?>
<CHANNEL BASE="http://www.xyzcorp.com/" HREF="index.htm" PRECACHE="YES" LEVEL="0"
_LASTMOD="1998-06-01T12:00">

  <TITLE>The XYZ Corp Active Channel</TITLE>
  <ABSTRACT>Welcome to the XYZ Corp Channel - Home of the Widget!</ABSTRACT>

    <SCHEDULE STARTDATE="1998-05-29">
     <INTERVALTIME DAY="7"/>
    </SCHEDULE>

...
```

Now we've set a day on which the SCHEDULE starts, we want to force updates to occur as close to the catalog update day as possible. We need to turn to another empty child element of SCHEDULE called LATESTTIME. This specifies the latest time during the interval stated that the SCHEDULE will be updated. If the catalog is updated Friday afternoon then you might want to give subscribers until Tuesday to update. In that case you would add the following to the CDF file:

```
<?xml version="1.0" encoding="UTF-8"?>
<CHANNEL BASE="http://www.xyzcorp.com/" HREF="index.htm" PRECACHE="YES" LEVEL="0"
_LASTMOD="1998-06-01T12:00">

 <TITLE>The XYZ Corp Active Channel</TITLE>
 <ABSTRACT>Welcome to the XYZ Corp Channel - Home of the Widget!</ABSTRACT>

   <SCHEDULE STARTDATE="1998-05-29">
    <INTERVALTIME DAY="7"/>
    <LATESTTIME DAY="4"/>
   </SCHEDULE>

...
```

Changing `<LATESTTIME DAY="4" />` to `<LATESTTIME DAY="2" />` would allow updates to occur until Sunday. If IE4 fails to update the content within these allocated periods then no further attempts are made until the start of the next cycle.

Now we have set up the CDF file schedule in such a way that subscribers get the latest information, reducing the possibility that they are looking at old information.

Once we have a SCHEDULE in place the reason for using LASTMOD becomes clear. It prevents users downloading content that they already had since only content with a newer LASTMOD date than that in the cache is downloaded. This saves on download times, bandwidth and online charges for users connecting via a modem. It also reduces load on the server that hosts the site, which is never a bad thing to try to achieve. Remember to change the LASTMOD dates for new content in the CDF file though, otherwise none of your new content will ever get seen by subscribers!

Customizing the Channel with Personalized Logos and Icons

How many companies in the past wished they could get a link to their Web site onto the Windows desktops of their clients and customers? And what if you could customize that link with a special icon or logo? It would certainly be too good an opportunity to pass, wouldn't it? Well, if you wanted another reason why your company or organization should have an Active Channel then this is it. As a channel builder you have the opportunity to use four different kinds of image to personalize the channel. These are:

- A logo for display on the Channel Bar. This is 32 pixels high and 80 pixels wide.
- A logo for display on the Channel Pane. This is 32 pixels high and 194 pixels wide.
- An icon for items on the Channel Pane. This is 16 pixels high and 16 pixels wide.
- An icon for sub-channels (size as above).

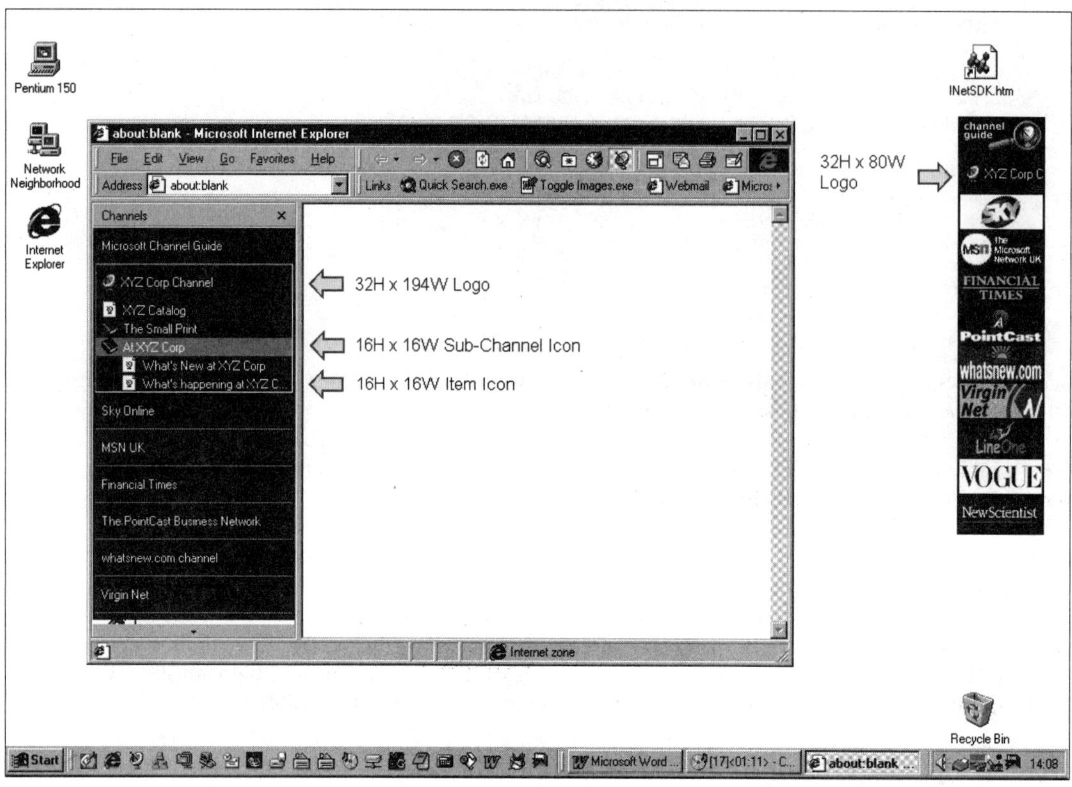

Let's take a closer look at how we can add these images to the channel. We'll look at the Channel Bar and Channel Pane logos first. To add these logos we use, not surprisingly, an empty element called LOGO. LOGO has two attributes, HREF and STYLE. HREF specifies the URL of the image to be used (.GIF, .JPG/JPEG and other IE4 supported file formats can be used although animated GIF files are not supported). STYLE specifies how the image should be used and can take one of three possible values:

Value	Description
IMAGE	Channel Bar logo
IMAGE-WIDE	Channel Pane logo
ICON	Icon for items on Channel Pane or sub-channels. Each ITEM can have a different icon (the LOGO tag then becomes a child element of ITEM) or all be the same (LOGO is then a child element of CHANNEL).

Let's add the LOGO element to our CDF file to add the Channel Bar and Channel Pane logos.

```
<?xml version="1.0" encoding="UTF-8"?>
<CHANNEL BASE="http://www.xyzcorp.com/" HREF="index.htm" PRECACHE="YES" LEVEL="0"
_LASTMOD="1998-06-01T12:00">
```

```
<TITLE>The XYZ Corp Active Channel</TITLE>
<ABSTRACT>Welcome to the XYZ Corp Channel - Home of the Widget!</ABSTRACT>

  <LOGO HREF="button.gif" STYLE="IMAGE"/>
  <LOGO HREF="button_w.gif" STYLE="IMAGE-WIDE"/>

  <SCHEDULE STARTDATE="1998-05-29">
   <INTERVALTIME DAY="7"/>
   <LATESTTIME DAY="4"/>
  </SCHEDULE>

...
```

These two lines add the logos to the Channel Bar and Channel Pane.

On the left we have the logo inserted into the Channel bar.

On the right, here is the image in the Channel guide.

We can now finish off personalizing the channel by adding the icons for the ITEM and sub-channels. Here is how we add the icons for the sub-channels:

```
<?xml version="1.0" encoding="UTF-8"?>
<CHANNEL BASE="http://www.xyzcorp.com/" HREF="index.htm" PRECACHE="YES" LEVEL="0"
_LASTMOD="1998-06-01T12:00">

...
  <ITEM HREF="ssaver.htm" PRECACHE="YES" LEVEL="0" LASTMOD="1998-06-01T12:00">
   <USAGE VALUE="ScreenSaver"></USAGE>
  </ITEM>
```

```
   <CHANNEL>
    <LOGO HREF="http://www.xyzcorp.com /icon_s.gif" STYLE="ICON"/>
    <TITLE>The Small Print</TITLE>
    <ABSTRACT>Check out the Small Print here!</ABSTRACT>
       <ITEM HREF="terms.htm" PRECACHE="YES" LEVEL="0" LASTMOD="1998-06-01T12:00">
        <TITLE>XYZ Corp Terms and Conditions</TITLE>
        <ABSTRACT>All the small print on Terms and Conditions</ABSTRACT>
       </ITEM>
...
   <CHANNEL>
    <LOGO HREF="http://www.xyzcorp.com /icon_s.gif" STYLE="ICON"/>
    <TITLE>At XYZ Corp</TITLE>
    <ABSTRACT>Find out what's going on at XYZ Corp</ABSTRACT>
       <ITEM HREF="new.htm" PRECACHE="YES" LEVEL="0" LASTMOD="1998-06-01T12:00">
        <TITLE>What's New at XYZ Corp</TITLE>
        <ABSTRACT>Discover what's new at XYZ Corp here</ABSTRACT>
       </ITEM>
...
   </CHANNEL>

</CHANNEL>
```

And now we can add the icons for the ITEMs in the CDF file:

```
<?xml version="1.0" encoding="UTF-8"?>
<CHANNEL BASE="http://www.xyzcorp.com/" HREF="index.htm" PRECACHE="YES" LEVEL="0"
_LASTMOD="1998-06-01T12:00">

...
   <ITEM HREF="catalog.htm" PRECACHE="YES" LEVEL="0" LASTMOD="1998-06-01T12:00">
    <LOGO HREF="http://www.xyzcorp.com /icon.gif" STYLE="ICON"/>
    <TITLE>XYZ Catalog</TITLE>
    <ABSTRACT>Browse the latest widget catalog</ABSTRACT>
   </ITEM>
...
   <CHANNEL>
    <LOGO HREF="http://www.xyzcorp.com /icon_s.gif" STYLE="ICON"/>
    <TITLE>The Small Print</TITLE>
    <ABSTRACT>Check out the Small Print here!</ABSTRACT>
       <ITEM HREF="terms.htm" PRECACHE="YES" LEVEL="0" LASTMOD="1998-06-01T12:00">
        <LOGO HREF="http://www.xyzcorp.com /icon.gif" STYLE="ICON"/>
        <TITLE>XYZ Corp Terms and Conditions</TITLE>
        <ABSTRACT>All the small print on Terms and Conditions</ABSTRACT>
       </ITEM>
       <ITEM HREF="warrenty.htm" PRECACHE="YES" LEVEL="0" LASTMOD="1998-06-
       _01T12:00">
        <LOGO HREF="http://www.xyzcorp.com /icon.gif" STYLE="ICON"/>
         <TITLE>XYZ Corp Warranty</TITLE>
         <ABSTRACT>The warranty statement on our widgets</ABSTRACT>
       </ITEM>
   </CHANNEL>

   <CHANNEL>
    <LOGO HREF="http://www.xyzcorp.com /icon_s.gif" STYLE="ICON"/>
    <TITLE>At XYZ Corp</TITLE>
    <ABSTRACT>Find out what's going on at XYZ Corp</ABSTRACT>
       <ITEM HREF="new.htm" PRECACHE="YES" LEVEL="0" LASTMOD="1998-06-01T12:00">
        <LOGO HREF="http://www.xyzcorp.com /icon.gif" STYLE="ICON"/>
        <TITLE>What's New at XYZ Corp</TITLE>
```

```
        <ABSTRACT>Discover what's new at XYZ Corp here</ABSTRACT>
       </ITEM>
       <ITEM HREF="happening.htm" PRECACHE="YES" LEVEL="0" LASTMOD="1998-06-
        _01T12:00">
        <LOGO HREF="http://www.xyzcorp.com /icon.gif" STYLE="ICON"/>
         <TITLE>What's happening at XYZ Corp</TITLE>
         <ABSTRACT>Keep up with all that's going on at XYZ Corp here</ABSTRACT>
       </ITEM>
   </CHANNEL>

</CHANNEL>
```

And there you go! All done. This is what the end result looks like:

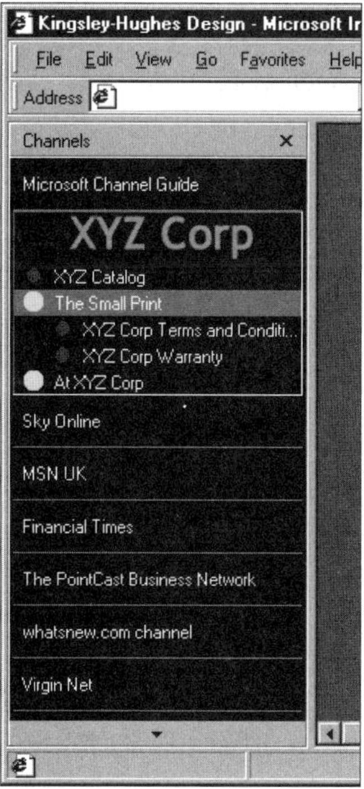

All XYZ Corp has to do now is sit back and wait for the subscribers to come flocking to their channel!

Summary

In this case study we've covered the basics of channel creation. We've not examined all the elements or attributes and their associated impact on how the channel behaves – these matters are beyond the scope of this case study. What we covered here was how we can use XML, in the form of a CDF file, to make an existing Web site more functional, improve site navigation, and make it easier for the end user to manage in terms of updates, by creating an Active Channel.

Why did Microsoft choose to use XML as the language for CDF? They certainly could have chosen to create a new format (as Netscape did with their format that uses JavaScript). One reason must be that XML has already gained popularity among the developer community. Another compelling reason is the fact that the syntax is straightforward and easy to learn – speeding the uptake of the new technology by the Web developer community.

We've looked at how to use XML to leverage IE4 in order to:

- Create a skeleton CDF file and add the basic components that make up a channel
- Control how the channel is cached for viewing
- Create and control the layout of the navigation hierarchy on the Channel Pane
- Add a screensaver to the channel content
- Control the updating of the channel using a `SCHEDULE`
- Personalize the channel with logos and icons for display on the Channel Bar and Channel Pane

We also looked at how to avoid some of the common problems that plague channel builders. Happy channel building!

Languages and Notations

The following appendix explains the form EBNF syntax used in the various specifications. Although you should have a general understanding of the syntax, a detailed understanding (or reference to a guide such as this) is only necessary for detailed perusal of the Specifications.

Extended Backus-Naur Form (EBNF) Notation

The formal grammar of XML is given using a simple Extended Backus-Naur Form (EBNF) notation. EBNF is designed primarily to be read by machines but is also designed to be human readable. (I suppose that depends on your definition of human readable!)

EBNF or a modified form of it is used in several other W3C specs as well as having widespread use throughout the computing world. A modified form is used in DTD's. We highlight the terms and their definitions in boxes, then give detailed examples of their use.

#xN

`#xN` This represents a hexadecimal integer `N` as defined in ISO/IEC 10646.

For example in the XML document white space is defined as follows:

```
White Space
_ S ::=  (#x20 |_#x9 |_#xD |_#xA)+
```

Which means that white space is one or more (that's what the `+` means) combination in any order (that's what the `pipestem (|)` means) of the ISO/IEC 10646 characters.

Hexadecimal number 20 (=ASCII decimal32, a space),
Hexadecimal number 9 (=ASCII decimal9, a tab),
Hexadecimal number D (=ASCII decimal 13, a new line),
Hexadecimal number A (=ASCII decimal 10, a line feed).

[a-zA-Z], [#xN-#xN]

`[a-zA-Z], [#xN-#xN]` Matches any character with a value in the range(s) indicated (inclusive).

For example in the XML spec a permitted character (`char`) is defined as follows:

```
Char ::=  #x9 |_#xA |_#xD |_[#x20-#xD7FF] |_[#xE000-#xFFFD] |_[#x10000-#x10FFFF]
```

`[#x20-#xD7FF]` means that any character in the range `#x20` to `#xD7FF` can be used as a legal character. (This includes all the ASCII characters.) `#x9`, `#xA`, `#xD` means that white space can be included.

Again note the pipestem which indicates alternatives.

[^abc], [^#xN#xN#xN]

`[^abc], [^#xN#xN#xN]` The ^ symbol means 'excluding'

```
AttValue ::=  '"' ([^<&"] |_Reference)* '"'   |_ "'" ([^<&'] |_Reference)* "'"
```

In the above reference for `AttValue` the `[^<&]` means that Reference (defined else where in the spec) can be any value as long as it does not include the character's `&` or `<`.

[^a-z] [^#xN-#xN]

`[^a-z] [^#xN-#xN]` This refers to a range of values.

I couldn't find a reference in the XML spec but here's an example:

```
FirstHalfAlphabet::=([n-z] | alphabet)
```

This means that `FirstHalfAlphabet` can be any letter in alphabet (presumably defined else where as the characters a-z) except in those in the range n-z.

"string" 'string'

`"string" 'string'` Both refer to a literal string.

In the XML spec we have the following:

```
DefaultDecl ::=  '#REQUIRED' |_'#IMPLIED'
```

Which means that the default declaration can take one of two string values `'#REQUIRED'` or `'#DEFAULT'`.

(expression)

`(expression)` expression is treated as a unit and may be combined as described in this list. This form of notation is very common in all the W3 specs.

A?

`A?` matches `A` or nothing; optional `A`.

This means that the inclusion of `A` is optional. In the XML spec we have this definition of a general entity declaration, where `S` stands for white space.

```
GEDecl ::=  '<!ENTITY' S Name S EntityDef S? '>'
```

The first two white spaces are compulsory, but the last one is optional.

A B

`A B` matches `A` followed by `B`.

For example in the following definition of a public ID:

```
PublicID ::=  'PUBLIC' S PubidLiteral
```

We are told that a `PublicID` must take the form of the string `'PUBLIC'`, followed by white space, followed by `PubidLiteral` (which is defined else where in the spec.)

A | B

`A | B` matches `A` or `B` but not both.

We have already seen examples of this above, but to recap, in the following definition of `PEDef`, its value can be `EntityValue` or `_ExternalID` but not both.

```
PEDef ::=  EntityValue |_ExternalID
```

A - B

`A - B` matches any string that matches `A` but does not match `B`.

For example in the XML declaration the following example is given:

```
PITarget ::=  Name - (('X' |_'x') ('M' |_'m') ('L' |_'l'))
```

This means that a `PITarget` can have any name value (which is defined elsewhere) as long as the sequence XML or any combination in upper or lower case is excluded)

A+

A+ matches one or more occurrences of A.

```
CharRef ::=  '&#' [0-9]+ ';'  |_'&#x' [0-9a-fA-F]+ ';'
```

The above means that a character reference must consist of the beginning string '&#' plus one or more numeric characters (1 through 9) or one or more numeric characters or the letters A through F, terminated by a semi-colon.

A*

A* matches zero or more occurrences of A.

```
EncName ::=  [A-Za-z] ([A-Za-z0-9._] |_'-')*
```

Which means that an encoding character must have one character in the range a-z (upper or lower case) plus an optional additional number of characters which can be in the range a-z, 0-9 numeric, a period or an underscore, or can be a hyphen.

The XML Specification

The XML spec uses EBNF as defined above.

The XML 1.0 specification can be found at:

http://www.w3.org/TR/REC-xml

The CSS1 Specification

The CSS1 specification uses a modified (and more human readable!) EBNS syntax. It can be found at:

http://www.w3.org/TR/REC-CSS1

Example Syntax	Explanation
<Fish>	All values are enclosed in angle brackets.
Fish	This represents a keyword that must appear literally (case immaterial). Commas and slashes should also appear literally.
A B C	A must occur, then B, then C, in that order.
A | B	Expresses alternatives. A or B must occur.
A || B	Note this syntax is not really EBNF. A or B or both must occur, but in any order.
[Fish]	Brackets are used to group items together.
Fish*	Fish is repeated zero or more times. (Pure EBNF)

Example Syntax	Explanation
`Fish+`	`Fish` is repeated one or more times. (Pure EBNF)
`Fish?`	`Fish` is optional. (Pure EBNF)
`Fish{A,B}`	Note this syntax is not really EBNF. `Fish` must occur at least `A` times and at most `B` times.

The CSS2 Specification

The CSS2 specification uses a modified EBNS syntax. The specification can be found at:

```
http://www.w3.org/TR/PR-CSS2/
```

The Grammar can be found at:

```
http://www.w3.org/TR/PR-CSS2/grammar.html
```

If yo understand EBNF you should have no difficulty reading the specifications or understanding the Gr

XML Resources and References

There are many useful XML resources available on the Internet. This appendix lists several of them, first are a number of general sites, these are followed by specific chapter references.

The W3C site is the home of all the XML specifications, as well as a number of other useful resources.
`http://www.w3.org`

Microsoft has a rapidly expanding range of XML resources on their SiteBuilder site. You can also download a number of XML parsers from this site.
`http://www.microsoft.xml`

Tim Brays site hosts a number of resources and links to useful information. This is where you can download Tim's Lark and Larval parsers.
`http://www.textuality.com/XML/`

Peter Flynn's maintains an extensive FAQ list at:
`http://www.ucc.ie/xml/`

James Tauber hosts three sites on XML:
`http://www.xmlinfo.com` for general XML information
`http://www.schema.net` for DTD's and other schemata and
`http://www.xmlsoftware.com` for XML-related software

ArborText are heavily involved in the production of XML specifications, their site covers XML news, resources and links, and can be found at:
`http://www.arbortext.com/xml.html`

XML.com is an impressive collection of XML resources including a very useful version of the annotated XML spec (created by Tim Bray) at:
`http://www.xml.com/`

Lisa Rein runs a comprehensive site with lots of XML resources including a FAQ, links to several parsers, and other XML resources at:
`http://www.finetuning.com/`

WebDeveloper.Com host The XML Files, with tutorials, links and discussion, they can be found at:
`http://webdeveloper.com/xml/`

Café Con Leche is a large source of XML related news and information it can be found at:
`http://sunsite.unc.edu/xml/`

CommerceNet's XML Exchange is a resource for sharing DTDs and other Schemas. You can find these at:
`http://www.xmlx.com/`

Poet Software maintain a site that has several useful links to papers on XML. See:
`http://www.poet.com/xml/`

Robin Cover has a list of resources on XML at:
http://www.oasis-open.org/cover/xml.html

The XML/EDI group promotes EDI as an XML application, their site is hosted at:
http://www.xmledi.com/

Find out all about Llamas, the wonderful creatures featured in Chapter 2 and on the chapter dividers at:
`http://www.llamaweb.com`
`http://www.frolic.org`

Chapter 3 XML Schemas

XML-Data Note
`http://www.w3.org/TR/1998/NOTE-XML-data/`

Document Content Definition Note
`http://www.w3.org/TR/NOTE-dcd/`

Schema for Object-Oriented XML Note
`http://www.w3.org/TR/NOTE-SOX`

Chapter 4 Namespaces

The working document for Namespaces. This chapter is based on the September 16th 1998 version:
`http://www.w3.org/TR/WD-xml-names`

The Federal Aviation Agency's Web page. Some really interesting (but not XML related) information:
`http://www.faa.gov`

If you are a closet snob, or just want to find out more about the British system of Aristocracy, this page is invaluable!
`http://www.baronage.co.uk`

The Working Draft document for Resource Description Framework (RDF):
`http://www.w3.org/TR/WD-rdf-syntax`

The Working Draft document for XSL:
`http://www.w3.org/TR/WD-xsl`

Chapter 5 Linking in XML

The design principles of XLL:
`http://www.w3.org/TR/NOTE-xlink-principles`

The XLink specification:
`http://www.w3.org/TR/WD-xlink`

The XPointer specification:
`http://www.w3.org/TR/WD-xptr`

Note that the above URLs are to the latest version of the specifications. This chapter was based on the March specification, which was the latest at time of writing (October 1998).

Robin Cover's XML pages. Links to everywhere.
`http://www.oasis-open.org/cover/`

An interesting 176 slide talk by Eve Mahler, the co-editor of the XLL specification
`http://www.oasis-open.org/cover/xlink9805/index.htm`

How Can the XML Pointer Language (XLink and XPointer) Help Solve the Problem of Broken Links on the Net?- Posting from Eve Maler.
`http://www.oasis-open.org/cover/maler980331.html`

Chapter 6 XML and the DOM

The W3 DOM Recommendation can be found at:
`http://www.w3.org/TR/REC-DOM-Level-1`

Chapter 7 Displaying XML

CSS

The CSS1 specification can be found at:
`http://www.w3.org/TR/REC-CSS1`

The CSS2 specification can be found at:
`http://www.w3.org/TR/REC-CSS2`

Linking an XML document to a style sheet is discussed in a note found at:
`http://www.w3.org/TR/NOTE-xml-stylesheet`

Spice

A brief overview of the subject, read this before reading the note:
http://www.w3.org/People/Raggett/spice

The original note on spice presented to W3:
http://www.w3.org/TR/1998/NOTE-spice-19980123.html_

A comparison of XSL and Spice:
http://www.sil.org/sgml/spice-XSL980224.html

DSSSL-Online or XS

References and a tutorial on DSSSL by the author of this chapter, including notes on how to use JADE:
http://www.hypermedic.com/style

Paul Prescod's tutorial on DSSSL. Well worth a read even if you don't want to learn about the subject:
http://itrc.uwaterloo.ca/~papresco/dsssl/tutorial.html

Daniel M. Germán tutorial, goes into slightly more detail than Paul Prescod. Another excellent tutorial:
http://www.sil.org/sgml/dssslGerman.html

James Clark's home page with numerous DSSSL references:
http://www.jclark.com/dsssl

The DSSSL-Online spec can be found at:
http://sunsite.unc.edu/pub/sun-info/standards/dsssl/dssslo/do960816.htm

All the references on Schemas that you could possibly want are at:
http://www-swiss.ai.mit.edu/scheme-home.html

Chapter 9 XSL

These pages contain the latest news on the XSL front:
http://www.w3.org/Style/XSL/

A list of the requirements for XSL can be found here:
http://www.w3.org/TR/WD-XSLReq

Here is the Working Draft of the XSL specification:
http://www.w3.org/TR/WD-xsl

And a note on the CSS namespace can be found at this site:
http://www.w3.org/TR/NOTE-XSL-and-CSS

Chapter 13 Channel Definition Format

Microsoft SiteBuilder Network.
`http://www.microsoft.com/sitebuilder`

The Microsoft Online Internet Client SDK:
`http://www.microsoft.com/msdn/sdk/inetsdk/help/default.htm`

Extensible Markup Language (XML) 1.0 Specification

This appendix is taken from the W3C Recommendation 10-February-1998 available at:

http://www.w3.org/TR/REC-xml

Editors:

Tim Bray (Textuality and Netscape) tbray@textuality.com
Jean Paoli (Microsoft) jeanpa@microsoft.com
C. M. Sperberg-McQueen (University of Illinois at Chicago) cmsmcq@uic.edu

Abstract

The Extensible Markup Language (XML) is a subset of SGML that is completely described in this document. Its goal is to enable generic SGML to be served, received, and processed on the Web in the way that is now possible with HTML. XML has been designed for ease of implementation and for interoperability with both SGML and HTML.

Status of this document

This document has been reviewed by W3C Members and other interested parties and has been endorsed by the Director as a W3C Recommendation. It is a stable document and may be used as reference material or cited as a normative reference from another document. W3C's role in making the Recommendation is to draw attention to the specification and to promote its widespread deployment. This enhances the functionality and interoperability of the Web.

This document specifies a syntax created by subsetting an existing, widely used international text processing standard (Standard Generalized Markup Language, ISO 8879:1986(E) as amended and corrected) for use on the World Wide Web. It is a product of the W3C XML Activity, details of which can be found at `http://www.w3.org/XML`. A list of current W3C Recommendations and other technical documents can be found at `http://www.w3.org/TR`.

This specification uses the term URI, which is defined by [Berners-Lee et al.], a work in progress expected to update [IETF RFC1738] and [IETF RFC1808].

The list of known errors in this specification is available at `http://www.w3.org/XML/xml-19980210-errata`.

Please report errors in this document to `xml-editor@w3.org`.

Extensible Markup Language (XML) 1.0

Table of Contents

Appendices

1. Introduction

Extensible Markup Language, abbreviated XML, describes a class of data objects called XML documents and partially describes the behavior of computer programs which process them. XML is an application profile or restricted form of SGML, the Standard Generalized Markup Language [ISO 8879]. By construction, XML documents are conforming SGML documents.

XML documents are made up of storage units called entities, which contain either parsed or unparsed data. Parsed data is made up of characters, some of which form character data, and some of which form markup. Markup encodes a description of the document's storage layout and logical structure. XML provides a mechanism to impose constraints on the storage layout and logical structure.

A software module called an **XML processor** is used to read XML documents and provide access to their content and structure. It is assumed that an XML processor is doing its work on behalf of another module, called the **application**. This specification describes the required behavior of an XML processor in terms of how it must read XML data and the information it must provide to the application.

1.1 Origin and Goals

XML was developed by an XML Working Group (originally known as the SGML Editorial Review Board) formed under the auspices of the World Wide Web Consortium (W3C) in 1996. It was chaired by Jon Bosak of Sun Microsystems with the active participation of an XML Special Interest Group (previously known as the SGML Working Group) also organized by the W3C. The membership of the XML Working Group is given in an appendix. Dan Connolly served as the WG's contact with the W3C.
The design goals for XML are:

1. XML shall be straightforwardly usable over the Internet.
2. XML shall support a wide variety of applications.
3. XML shall be compatible with SGML.
4. It shall be easy to write programs which process XML documents.
5. The number of optional features in XML is to be kept to the absolute minimum, ideally zero.
6. XML documents should be human-legible and reasonably clear.
7. The XML design should be prepared quickly.
8. The design of XML shall be formal and concise.
9. XML documents shall be easy to create.
10. Terseness in XML markup is of minimal importance.

This specification, together with associated standards (Unicode and ISO/IEC 10646 for characters, Internet RFC 1766 for language identification tags, ISO 639 for language name codes, and ISO 3166 for country name codes), provides all the information necessary to understand XML Version 1.0 and construct computer programs to process it.

This version of the XML specification may be distributed freely, as long as all text and legal notices remain intact.

1.2 Terminology

The terminology used to describe XML documents is defined in the body of this specification. The terms defined in the following list are used in building those definitions and in describing the actions of an XML processor:

may

Conforming documents and XML processors are permitted to but need not behave as described.

must

Conforming documents and XML processors are required to behave as described; otherwise they are in error.

error

A violation of the rules of this specification; results are undefined. Conforming software may detect and report an error and may recover from it.

fatal error

An error which a conforming XML processor must detect and report to the application. After encountering a fatal error, the processor may continue processing the data to search for further errors and may report such errors to the application. In order to support correction of errors, the processor may make unprocessed data from the document (with intermingled character data and markup) available to the application. Once a fatal error is detected, however, the processor must not continue normal processing (i.e., it must not continue to pass character data and information about the document's logical structure to the application in the normal way).

at user option

Conforming software may or must (depending on the modal verb in the sentence) behave as described; if it does, it must provide users a means to enable or disable the behavior described.

validity constraint

A rule which applies to all valid XML documents. Violations of validity constraints are errors; they must, at user option, be reported by validating XML processors.

well-formedness constraint

A rule which applies to all well-formed XML documents. Violations of well-formedness constraints are fatal errors.

match

(Of strings or names:) Two strings or names being compared must be identical. Characters with multiple possible representations in ISO/IEC 10646 (e.g. characters with both precomposed and base+diacritic forms) match only if they have the same representation in both strings. At user option, processors may normalize such characters to some canonical form. No case folding is performed.

(Of strings and rules in the grammar:) A string matches a grammatical production if it belongs to the language generated by that production. (Of content and content models:) An element matches its declaration when it conforms in the fashion described in the constraint "Element Valid".

for compatibility

A feature of XML included solely to ensure that XML remains compatible with SGML.

for interoperability

A non-binding recommendation included to increase the chances that XML documents can be processed by the existing installed base of SGML processors which predate the WebSGML Adaptations Annex to ISO 8879.

2. Documents

A data object is an **XML document** if it is well-formed, as defined in this specification. A well-formed XML document may in addition be valid if it meets certain further constraints.

Each XML document has both a logical and a physical structure. Physically, the document is composed of units called entities. An entity may refer to other entities to cause their inclusion in the document. A document begins in a "root" or document entity. Logically, the document is composed of declarations, elements, comments, character references, and processing instructions, all of which are indicated in the document by explicit markup. The logical and physical structures must nest properly, as described in "4.3.2 Well-Formed Parsed Entities".

2.1 Well-Formed XML Documents

A textual object is a well-formed XML document if:

1. Taken as a whole, it matches the production labeled `document`.
2. It meets all the well-formedness constraints given in this specification.
3. Each of the parsed entities which is referenced directly or indirectly within the document is well-formed.

Document			
[1]	document	::=	prolog element Misc*

Matching the `document` production implies that:

1. It contains one or more elements.
2. There is exactly one element, called the **root**, or document element, no part of which appears in the content of any other element. For all other elements, if the start-tag is in the content of another element, the end-tag is in the content of the same element. More simply stated, the elements, delimited by start- and end-tags, nest properly within each other.

As a consequence of this, for each non-root element `C` in the document, there is one other element `P` in the document such that `C` is in the content of `P`, but is not in the content of any other element that is in the content of `P`. `P` is referred to as the **parent** of `C`, and `C` as a **child** of `P`.

2.2 Characters

A parsed entity contains **text**, a sequence of characters, which may represent markup or character data. A **character** is an atomic unit of text as specified by ISO/IEC 10646 [ISO/IEC 10646]. Legal characters are tab, carriage return, line feed, and the legal graphic characters of Unicode and ISO/IEC 10646. The use of "compatibility characters", as defined in section 6.8 of [Unicode], is discouraged.

Character Range				
[2]	`Char`	`::=`	`#x9 | #xA | #xD | [#x20-#xD7FF] | [#xE000-#xFFFD] | [#x10000-#x10FFFF]`	`/*any Unicode character, excluding the surrogate blocks, FFFE, and FFFF. */`

The mechanism for encoding character code points into bit patterns may vary from entity to entity. All XML processors must accept the UTF-8 and UTF-16 encodings of 10646; the mechanisms for signaling which of the two is in use, or for bringing other encodings into play, are discussed later, in "4.3.3 Character Encoding in Entities".

2.3 Common Syntactic Constructs

This section defines some symbols used widely in the grammar.

`S` (white space) consists of one or more space (#x20) characters, carriage returns, line feeds, or tabs.

White Space		
[3]	`S::=`	`(#x20 | #x9 | #xD | #xA)+`

Characters are classified for convenience as letters, digits, or other characters. Letters consist of an alphabetic or syllabic base character possibly followed by one or more combining characters, or of an ideographic character. Full definitions of the specific characters in each class are given in "B. Character Classes".

A **Name** is a token beginning with a letter or one of a few punctuation characters, and continuing with letters, digits, hyphens, underscores, colons, or full stops, together known as name characters. Names beginning with the string "`xml`", or any string which would match `(('X'|'x') ('M'|'m') ('L'|'l'))`, are reserved for standardization in this or future versions of this specification.

Note: The colon character within XML names is reserved for experimentation with name spaces. Its meaning is expected to be standardized at some future point, at which point those documents using the colon for experimental purposes may need to be updated. (There is no guarantee that any name-space mechanism adopted for XML will in fact use the colon as a name-space delimiter.)

In practice, this means that authors should not use the colon in XML names except as part of name-space experiments, but that XML processors should accept the colon as a name character.

An `Nmtoken` (name token) is any mixture of name characters.

<table>
<tr><th colspan="4">Names and Tokens</th></tr>
<tr><td>[4]</td><td>NameChar</td><td>::=</td><td>Letter | Digit | '.' | '-' | '_' | ':'
| CombiningChar | Extender</td></tr>
<tr><td>[5]</td><td>Name</td><td>::=</td><td>(Letter | '_' | ':') (NameChar)*</td></tr>
<tr><td>[6]</td><td>Names</td><td>::=</td><td>Name (S Name)*</td></tr>
<tr><td>[7]</td><td>Nmtoken</td><td>::=</td><td>(NameChar)+</td></tr>
<tr><td>[8]</td><td>Nmtokens</td><td>::=</td><td>Nmtoken (S Nmtoken)*</td></tr>
</table>

Literal data is any quoted string not containing the quotation mark used as a delimiter for that string. Literals are used for specifying the content of internal entities (`EntityValue`), the values of attributes (`AttValue`), and external identifiers (`SystemLiteral`). Note that a `SystemLiteral` can be parsed without scanning for markup.

<table>
<tr><th colspan="4">Literals</th></tr>
<tr><td>[9]</td><td>EntityValue</td><td>::=</td><td>'"' ([^%&"] | PEReference | Reference)* '"'</td></tr>
<tr><td></td><td></td><td></td><td>| "'" ([^%&'] | PEReference | Reference)* "'"</td></tr>
<tr><td>[10]</td><td>AttValue</td><td>::=</td><td>'"' ([^<&"] | Reference)* '"'</td></tr>
<tr><td></td><td></td><td></td><td>| "'" ([^<&'] | Reference)* "'"</td></tr>
<tr><td>[11]</td><td>SystemLiteral</td><td>::=</td><td>('"' [^"]* '"') | ("'" [^']* "'")</td></tr>
<tr><td>[12]</td><td>PubidLiteral</td><td>::=</td><td>'"' PubidChar* '"' | "'" (PubidChar - "'")* "'"</td></tr>
<tr><td>[13]</td><td>PubidChar</td><td>::=</td><td>#x20 | #xD | #xA | [a-zA-Z0-9] |
[-'()+,./:=?;!*#@$_%]</td></tr>
</table>

2.4 Character Data and Markup

Text consists of intermingled character data and markup. **Markup** takes the form of start-tags, end-tags, empty-element tags, entity references, character references, comments, CDATA section delimiters, document type declarations, and processing instructions.

All text that is not markup constitutes the **character data** of the document.

The ampersand character (&) and the left angle bracket (<) may appear in their literal form *only* when used as markup delimiters, or within a comment, a processing instruction, or a CDATA section. They are also legal within the literal entity value of an internal entity declaration; see "4.3.2 Well-Formed Parsed Entities". If they are needed elsewhere, they must be escaped using either numeric character references or the strings "`&`" and "`<`" respectively.

The right angle bracket (>) may be represented using the string "`>`", and must, for compatibility, be escaped using "`>`" or a character reference when it appears in the string "`]]>`" in content, when that string is not marking the end of a CDATA section.

In the content of elements, character data is any string of characters which does not contain the start-delimiter of any markup. In a CDATA section, character data is any string of characters not including the CDATA-section-close delimiter, "`]]>`".

To allow attribute values to contain both single and double quotes, the apostrophe or single-quote character (') may be represented as "`'`", and the double-quote character (") as "`"`".

Character Data			
[14]	`CharData`	`::=`	`[^<&]* - ([^<&]* ']]>' [^<&]*)`

2.5 Comments

Comments may appear anywhere in a document outside other markup; in addition, they may appear within the document type declaration at places allowed by the grammar. They are not part of the document's character data; an XML processor may, but need not, make it possible for an application to retrieve the text of comments. For compatibility, the string "`--`" (double-hyphen) must not occur within comments.

Comments			
[15]	`Comment`	`::=`	`'<!--' ((Char - '-') | ('-' (Char - '-')))* '-->'`

An example of a comment:

```
<!-- declarations for <head> & <body> -->
```

2.6 Processing Instructions

Processing instructions (PIs) allow documents to contain instructions for applications.

Processing Instructions			
[16]	`PI`	`::=`	`'<?' PITarget (S (Char* - (Char* '?>' Char*)))? '?>'`
[17]	`PITarget`	`::=`	`Name - (('X' | 'x') ('M' | 'm') ('L' | 'l'))`

PIs are not part of the document's character data, but must be passed through to the application. The PI begins with a target (`PITarget`) used to identify the application to which the instruction is directed. The target names "`XML`", "`xml`", and so on are reserved for standardization in this or future versions of this specification. The XML Notation mechanism may be used for formal declaration of PI targets.

2.7 CDATA Sections

CDATA sections may occur anywhere character data may occur; they are used to escape blocks of text containing characters which would otherwise be recognized as markup. CDATA sections begin with the string "`<![CDATA[`" and end with the string "`]]>`":

CDATA Sections			
[18]	CDSect	::=	CDStart CData CDEnd
[19]	CDStart	::=	'<![CDATA['
[20]	CData	::=	(Char* - (Char* ']]>' Char*))
[21]	CDEnd	::=	']]>'

Within a CDATA section, only the CDEnd string is recognized as markup, so that left angle brackets and ampersands may occur in their literal form; they need not (and cannot) be escaped using "`<`" and "`&`". CDATA sections cannot nest.

An example of a CDATA section, in which "`<greeting>`" and "`</greeting>`" are recognized as character data, not markup:

```
<![CDATA[<greeting>Hello, world!</greeting>]]>
```

2.8 Prolog and Document Type Declaration

XML documents may, and should, begin with an **XML declaration** which specifies the version of XML being used. For example, the following is a complete XML document, well-formed but not valid:

```
<?xml version="1.0"?>
<greeting>Hello, world!</greeting>
```

and so is this:

```
<greeting>Hello, world!</greeting>
```

The version number "`1.0`" should be used to indicate conformance to this version of this specification; it is an error for a document to use the value "`1.0`" if it does not conform to this version of this specification. It is the intent of the XML working group to give later versions of this specification numbers other than "`1.0`", but this intent does not indicate a commitment to produce any future versions of XML, nor if any are produced, to use any particular numbering scheme. Since future versions are not ruled out, this construct is provided as a means to allow the possibility of automatic version recognition, should it become necessary. Processors may signal an error if they receive documents labeled with versions they do not support.

The function of the markup in an XML document is to describe its storage and logical structure and to associate attribute-value pairs with its logical structures. XML provides a mechanism, the document type declaration, to define constraints on the logical structure and to support the use of predefined storage units. An XML document is **valid** if it has an associated document type declaration and if the document complies with the constraints expressed in it.

The document type declaration must appear before the first element in the document.

Prolog			
[22]	prolog	::=	XMLDecl? Misc* (doctypedecl Misc*)?
[23]	XMLDecl	::=	'<?xml' VersionInfo EncodingDecl? SDDecl? S? '?>'
[24]	VersionInfo	::=	S 'version' Eq (' VersionNum ' | " VersionNum ")
[25]	Eq	::=	S? '=' S?
[26]	VersionNum	::=	([a-zA-Z0-9_.:] | '-')+
[27]	Misc	::=	Comment | PI | S

The XML **document type declaration** contains or points to markup declarations that provide a grammar for a class of documents. This grammar is known as a document type definition, or **DTD**. The document type declaration can point to an external subset (a special kind of external entity) containing markup declarations, or can contain the markup declarations directly in an internal subset, or can do both. The DTD for a document consists of both subsets taken together.

A **markup declaration** is an element type declaration, an attribute-list declaration, an entity declaration, or a notation declaration. These declarations may be contained in whole or in part within parameter entities, as described in the well-formedness and validity constraints below. For fuller information, see "4. Physical Structures".

Document Type Definition				
[28]	doctypedecl	::=	'<!DOCTYPE' S Name (S ExternalID)? S? ('[' (markupdecl | PEReference | S)* ']' S?)? '>'	[VC: Root Element Type]
[29]	markupdecl	::=	elementdecl | AttlistDecl | EntityDecl | NotationDecl | PI | Comment	[VC: Proper Declaration/PE Nesting]
				[WFC: PEs in Internal Subset]

The markup declarations may be made up in whole or in part of the replacement text of parameter entities. The productions later in this specification for individual nonterminals (`elementdecl`, `AttlistDecl`, and so on) describe the declarations *after* all the parameter entities have been included.

Validity Constraint: Root Element Type

The `Name` in the document type declaration must match the element type of the root element.

Validity Constraint: Proper Declaration/PE Nesting

Parameter-entity replacement text must be properly nested with markup declarations. That is to say, if either the first character or the last character of a markup declaration (`markupdecl` above) is contained in the replacement text for a parameter-entity reference, both must be contained in the same replacement text.

Well-Formedness Constraint: PEs in Internal Subset

In the internal DTD subset, parameter-entity references can occur only where markup declarations can occur, not within markup declarations. (This does not apply to references that occur in external parameter entities or to the external subset.)

Like the internal subset, the external subset and any external parameter entities referred to in the DTD must consist of a series of complete markup declarations of the types allowed by the non-terminal symbol `markupdecl`, interspersed with white space or parameter-entity references. However, portions of the contents of the external subset or of external parameter entities may conditionally be ignored by using the conditional section construct; this is not allowed in the internal subset.

External Subset			
[30]	extSubset	::=	TextDecl? extSubsetDecl
[31]	extSubsetDecl	::=	(markupdecl | conditionalSect | PEReference | S)*

The external subset and external parameter entities also differ from the internal subset in that in them, parameter-entity references are permitted *within* markup declarations, not only *between* markup declarations.

An example of an XML document with a document type declaration:

```
<?xml version="1.0"?>
<!DOCTYPE greeting SYSTEM "hello.dtd">
<greeting>Hello, world!</greeting>
```

The system identifier "`hello.dtd`" gives the URI of a DTD for the document.

The declarations can also be given locally, as in this example:

```
<?xml version="1.0" encoding="UTF-8" ?>
<!DOCTYPE greeting [
  <!ELEMENT greeting (#PCDATA)>
]>
<greeting>Hello, world!</greeting>
```

If both the external and internal subsets are used, the internal subset is considered to occur before the external subset. This has the effect that entity and attribute-list declarations in the internal subset take precedence over those in the external subset.

2.9 Standalone Document Declaration

Markup declarations can affect the content of the document, as passed from an XML processor to an application; examples are attribute defaults and entity declarations. The standalone document declaration, which may appear as a component of the XML declaration, signals whether or not there are such declarations which appear external to the document entity.

Standalone Document Declaration				
[32]	SDDecl	::=	S 'standalone' Eq (("'" ('yes' | 'no') "'") | ('"' ('yes' | 'no') '"'))	[VC: Standalone Document Declaration]

In a standalone document declaration, the value "yes" indicates that there are no markup declarations external to the document entity (either in the DTD external subset, or in an external parameter entity referenced from the internal subset) which affect the information passed from the XML processor to the application. The value "no" indicates that there are or may be such external markup declarations. Note that the standalone document declaration only denotes the presence of external *declarations*; the presence, in a document, of references to external *entities*, when those entities are internally declared, does not change its standalone status.

If there are no external markup declarations, the standalone document declaration has no meaning. If there are external markup declarations but there is no standalone document declaration, the value "no" is assumed.

Any XML document for which `standalone="no"` holds can be converted algorithmically to a standalone document, which may be desirable for some network delivery applications.

Validity Constraint: Standalone Document Declaration

The standalone document declaration must have the value "no" if any external markup declarations contain declarations of:

- attributes with default values, if elements to which these attributes apply appear in the document without specifications of values for these attributes, or
- entities (other than `amp`, `lt`, `gt`, `apos`, `quot`), if references to those entities appear in the document, or

- attributes with values subject to normalization, where the attribute appears in the document with a value which will change as a result of normalization, or
- element types with element content, if white space occurs directly within any instance of those types.

An example XML declaration with a standalone document declaration:

```
<?xml version="1.0" standalone='yes'?>
```

2.10 White Space Handling

In editing XML documents, it is often convenient to use "white space" (spaces, tabs, and blank lines, denoted by the nonterminal `S` in this specification) to set apart the markup for greater readability. Such white space is typically not intended for inclusion in the delivered version of the document. On the other hand, "significant" white space that should be preserved in the delivered version is common, for example in poetry and source code.

An XML processor must always pass all characters in a document that are not markup through to the application. A validating XML processor must also inform the application which of these characters constitute white space appearing in element content.

A special attribute named `xml:space` may be attached to an element to signal an intention that in that element, white space should be preserved by applications. In valid documents, this attribute, like any other, must be declared if it is used. When declared, it must be given as an enumerated type whose only possible values are "`default`" and "`preserve`". For example:

```
    <!ATTLIST poem   xml:space (default|preserve) 'preserve'>
```

The value "`default`" signals that applications' default white-space processing modes are acceptable for this element; the value "`preserve`" indicates the intent that applications preserve all the white space. This declared intent is considered to apply to all elements within the content of the element where it is specified, unless overriden with another instance of the `xml:space` attribute.

The root element of any document is considered to have signaled no intentions as regards application space handling, unless it provides a value for this attribute or the attribute is declared with a default value.

2.11 End-of-Line Handling

XML parsed entities are often stored in computer files which, for editing convenience, are organized into lines. These lines are typically separated by some combination of the characters carriage-return (#xD) and line-feed (#xA).

To simplify the tasks of applications, wherever an external parsed entity or the literal entity value of an internal parsed entity contains either the literal two-character sequence "#xD#xA" or a standalone literal #xD, an XML processor must pass to the application the single character #xA. (This behavior can conveniently be produced by normalizing all line breaks to #xA on input, before parsing.)

2.12 Language Identification

In document processing, it is often useful to identify the natural or formal language in which the content is written. A special attribute named `xml:lang` may be inserted in documents to specify the language used in the contents and attribute values of any element in an XML document. In valid documents, this attribute, like any other, must be declared if it is used. The values of the attribute are language identifiers as defined by [IETF RFC 1766], "Tags for the Identification of Languages":

Language Identification			
[33]	LanguageID	::=	Langcode ('-' Subcode)*
[34]	Langcode	::=	ISO639Code | IanaCode | UserCode
[35]	ISO639Code	::=	([a-z] | [A-Z]) ([a-z] | [A-Z])
[36]	IanaCode	::=	('i' | 'I') '-' ([a-z] | [A-Z])+
[37]	UserCode	::=	('x' | 'X') '-' ([a-z] | [A-Z])+
[38]	Subcode	::=	([a-z] | [A-Z])+

The Langcode may be any of the following:

- a two-letter language code as defined by [ISO 639], "Codes for the representation of names of languages"
- a language identifier registered with the Internet Assigned Numbers Authority [IANA]; these begin with the prefix "`i-`" (or "`I-`")
- a language identifier assigned by the user, or agreed on between parties in private use; these must begin with the prefix "`x-`" or "`X-`" in order to ensure that they do not conflict with names later standardized or registered with IANA

There may be any number of `Subcode` segments; if the first subcode segment exists and the Subcode consists of two letters, then it must be a country code from [ISO 3166], "Codes for the representation of names of countries." If the first subcode consists of more than two letters, it must be a subcode for the language in question registered with IANA, unless the `Langcode` begins with the prefix "`x-`" or "`X-`".

It is customary to give the language code in lower case, and the country code (if any) in upper case. Note that these values, unlike other names in XML documents, are case insensitive.

For example:

```
<p xml:lang="en">The quick brown fox jumps over the lazy dog.</p>
<p xml:lang="en-GB">What colour is it?</p>
<p xml:lang="en-US">What color is it?</p>
<sp who="Faust" desc='leise' xml:lang="de">
  <l>Habe nun, ach! Philosophie,</l>
```

```
<l>Juristerei, und Medizin</l>
<l>und leider auch Theologie</l>
<l>durchaus studiert mit heißem Bemüh'n.</l>
</sp>
```

The intent declared with xml:lang is considered to apply to all attributes and content of the element where it is specified, unless overridden with an instance of xml:lang on another element within that content.

A simple declaration for xml:lang might take the form

```
xml:lang  NMTOKEN  #IMPLIED
```

but specific default values may also be given, if appropriate. In a collection of French poems for English students, with glosses and notes in English, the xml:lang attribute might be declared this way:

```
<!ATTLIST poem   xml:lang NMTOKEN 'fr'>
<!ATTLIST gloss  xml:lang NMTOKEN 'en'>
<!ATTLIST note   xml:lang NMTOKEN 'en'>
```

3. Logical Structures

Each XML document contains one or more **elements**, the boundaries of which are either delimited by start-tags and end-tags, or, for empty elements, by an empty-element tag. Each element has a type, identified by name, sometimes called its "generic identifier" (GI), and may have a set of attribute specifications. Each attribute specification has a name and a value.

Element				
[39]	element	::=	EmptyElemTag	
			| STag content ETag	[WFC: Element Type Match]
				[VC: Element Valid]

This specification does not constrain the semantics, use, or (beyond syntax) names of the element types and attributes, except that names beginning with a match to (('X'|'x')('M'|'m')('L'|'l')) are reserved for standardization in this or future versions of this specification.

Well-Formedness Constraint: Element Type Match

The Name in an element's end-tag must match the element type in the start-tag.

Validity Constraint: Element Valid

An element is valid if there is a declaration matching elementdecl where the Name matches the element type, and one of the following holds:

1. The declaration matches `EMPTY` and the element has no content.
2. The declaration matches `children` and the sequence of child elements belongs to the language generated by the regular expression in the content model, with optional white space (characters matching the nonterminal `S`) between each pair of child elements.
3. The declaration matches `Mixed` and the content consists of character data and child elements whose types match names in the content model.
4. The declaration matches `ANY`, and the types of any child elements have been declared.

3.1 Start-Tags, End-Tags, and Empty-Element Tags

The beginning of every non-empty XML element is marked by a **start-tag**.

Start-tag				
[40]	`STag`	`::=`	`'<' Name (S Attribute)* S? '>'`	`[WFC: Unique Att Spec ]`
[41]	`Attribute`	`::=`	`Name Eq AttValue`	`[VC: Attribute Value Type ]`
				`[WFC: No External Entity References ]`
				`[WFC: No < in Attribute Values ]`

The `Name` in the start- and end-tags gives the element's **type**. The `Name-AttValue` pairs are referred to as the **attribute specifications** of the element, with the `Name` in each pair referred to as the **attribute name** and the content of the `AttValue` (the text between the `'` or `"` delimiters) as the **attribute value**.

Well-Formedness Constraint: Unique Att Spec

No attribute name may appear more than once in the same start-tag or empty-element tag.

Validity Constraint: Attribute Value Type

The attribute must have been declared; the value must be of the type declared for it. (For attribute types, see "3.3 Attribute-List Declarations".)

Well-Formedness Constraint: No External Entity References

Attribute values cannot contain direct or indirect entity references to external entities.

Well-Formedness Constraint: No < in Attribute Values

The replacement text of any entity referred to directly or indirectly in an attribute value (other than "`<`") must not contain a <.

An example of a start-tag:

```
<termdef id="dt-dog" term="dog">
```

The end of every element that begins with a start-tag must be marked by an **end-tag** containing a name that echoes the element's type as given in the start-tag:

End-tag			
[42]	ETag	::=	'</' Name S? '>'

An example of an end-tag:

```
</termdef>
```

The text between the start-tag and end-tag is called the element's **content**:

Content of Elements			
[43]	content	::=	(element | CharData | Reference | CDSect | PI | Comment)*

If an element is **empty**, it must be represented either by a start-tag immediately followed by an end-tag or by an empty-element tag. An **empty-element tag** takes a special form:

Tags for Empty Elements				
[44]	EmptyElemTag	::=	'<' Name (S Attribute)* S? '/>'	[WFC: Unique Att Spec]

Empty-element tags may be used for any element which has no content, whether or not it is declared using the keyword EMPTY. For interoperability, the empty-element tag must be used, and can only be used, for elements which are declared EMPTY.

Examples of empty elements:

```
<IMG align="left"
 src="http://www.w3.org/Icons/WWW/w3c_home" />
<br></br>
<br/>
```

3.2 Element Type Declarations

The element structure of an XML document may, for validation purposes, be constrained using element type and attribute-list declarations. An element type declaration constrains the element's content.

Element type declarations often constrain which element types can appear as children of the element. At user option, an XML processor may issue a warning when a declaration mentions an element type for which no declaration is provided, but this is not an error.

An **element type declaration** takes the form:

Element Type Declaration				
[45]	elementdecl	::=	'<!ELEMENT' S Name S contentspec S? '>'	[VC: Unique Element Type Declaration]
[46]	contentspec	::=	'EMPTY' | 'ANY' | Mixed | children	

where the Name gives the element type being declared.

Validity Constraint: Unique Element Type Declaration

No element type may be declared more than once.

Examples of element type declarations:

```
<!ELEMENT br EMPTY>
<!ELEMENT p (#PCDATA|emph)* >
<!ELEMENT %name.para; %content.para; >
<!ELEMENT container ANY>
```

3.2.1 Element Content

An element type has **element content** when elements of that type must contain only child elements (no character data), optionally separated by white space (characters matching the nonterminal S). In this case, the constraint includes a content model, a simple grammar governing the allowed types of the child elements and the order in which they are allowed to appear. The grammar is built on content particles (cps), which consist of names, choice lists of content particles, or sequence lists of content particles:

Element-content Models				
[47]	children	::=	(choice | seq) ('?' | '*' | '+')?	
[48]	cp	::=	(Name | choice | seq) ('?' | '*' | '+')?	
[49]	choice	::=	'(' S? cp (S? '|' S? cp)* S? ')'	[VC: Proper Group/PE Nesting]
[50]	seq	::=	'(' S? cp (S? ',' S? cp)* S? ')'	[VC: Proper Group/PE Nesting]

where each Name is the type of an element which may appear as a child. Any content particle in a choice list may appear in the element content at the location where the choice list appears in the grammar; content particles occurring in a sequence list must each appear in the element content in the order given in the list. The optional character following a name or list governs whether the element or the content particles in the list may occur one or more (+), zero or more (*), or zero or one times (?).

The absence of such an operator means that the element or content particle must appear exactly once. This syntax and meaning are identical to those used in the productions in this specification.

The content of an element matches a content model if and only if it is possible to trace out a path through the content model, obeying the sequence, choice, and repetition operators and matching each element in the content against an element type in the content model. For compatibility, it is an error if an element in the document can match more than one occurrence of an element type in the content model. For more information, see "E. Deterministic Content Models".

Validity Constraint: Proper Group/PE Nesting
Parameter-entity replacement text must be properly nested with parenthetized groups. That is to say, if either of the opening or closing parentheses in a `choice`, `seq`, or `Mixed` construct is contained in the replacement text for a parameter entity, both must be contained in the same replacement text. For interoperability, if a parameter-entity reference appears in a `choice`, `seq`, or `Mixed` construct, its replacement text should not be empty, and neither the first nor last non-blank character of the replacement text should be a connector (`|` or `,`).

Examples of element-content models:

```
<!ELEMENT spec (front, body, back?)>
<!ELEMENT div1 (head, (p | list | note)*, div2*)>
<!ELEMENT dictionary-body (%div.mix; | %dict.mix;)*>
```

3.2.2 Mixed Content

An element type has **mixed content** when elements of that type may contain character data, optionally interspersed with child elements. In this case, the types of the child elements may be constrained, but not their order or their number of occurrences:

Mixed-content Declaration			
[51]	Mixed	::= '(' S? '#PCDATA' (S? '|' S? Name)* S? ')*'	
		| '(' S? '#PCDATA' S? ')'	[VC: Proper Group/PE Nesting]
			[VC: No Duplicate Types]

where the Names give the types of elements that may appear as children.

Validity Constraint: No Duplicate Types

The same name must not appear more than once in a single mixed-content declaration.

Examples of mixed content declarations:

```
<!ELEMENT p (#PCDATA|a|ul|b|i|em)*>
<!ELEMENT p (#PCDATA | %font; | %phrase; | %special; | %form;)* >
<!ELEMENT b (#PCDATA)>
```

3.3 Attribute-List Declarations

Attributes are used to associate name-value pairs with elements. Attribute specifications may appear only within start-tags and empty-element tags; thus, the productions used to recognize them appear in "3.1 Start-Tags, End-Tags, and Empty-Element Tags". Attribute-list declarations may be used:

- To define the set of attributes pertaining to a given element type.
- To establish type constraints for these attributes.
- To provide default values for attributes.

Attribute-list declarations specify the name, data type, and default value (if any) of each attribute associated with a given element type:

Attribute-list Declaration			
[52]	AttlistDecl	::=	'<!ATTLIST' S Name AttDef* S? '>'
[53]	AttDef	::=	S Name S AttType S DefaultDecl

The Name in the AttlistDecl rule is the type of an element. At user option, an XML processor may issue a warning if attributes are declared for an element type not itself declared, but this is not an error. The Name in the AttDef rule is the name of the attribute.

When more than one AttlistDecl is provided for a given element type, the contents of all those provided are merged. When more than one definition is provided for the same attribute of a given element type, the first declaration is binding and later declarations are ignored. For interoperability, writers of DTDs may choose to provide at most one attribute-list declaration for a given element type, at most one attribute definition for a given attribute name, and at least one attribute definition in each attribute-list declaration. For interoperability, an XML processor may at user option issue a warning when more than one attribute-list declaration is provided for a given element type, or more than one attribute definition is provided for a given attribute, but this is not an error.

3.3.1 Attribute Types

XML attribute types are of three kinds: a string type, a set of tokenized types, and enumerated types. The string type may take any literal string as a value; the tokenized types have varying lexical and semantic constraints, as noted:

Attribute Types				
[54]	AttType	::=	StringType | TokenizedType | EnumeratedType	
[55]	StringType	::=	'CDATA'	
[56]	TokenizedType	::=	'ID'	[VC: ID]

Attribute Types		
		[VC: One ID per Element Type]
		[VC: ID Attribute Default]
	| 'IDREF'	[VC: IDREF]
	| 'IDREFS'	[VC: IDREF]
	| 'ENTITY'	[VC: Entity Name]
	| 'ENTITIES'	[VC: Entity Name]
	| 'NMTOKEN'	[VC: Name Token]
	| 'NMTOKENS'	[VC: Name Token]

Validity Constraint: ID

Values of type `ID` must match the `Name` production. A name must not appear more than once in an XML document as a value of this type; i.e., ID values must uniquely identify the elements which bear them.

Validity Constraint: One ID per Element Type

No element type may have more than one ID attribute specified.

Validity Constraint: ID Attribute Default

An ID attribute must have a declared default of `#IMPLIED` or `#REQUIRED`.

Validity Constraint: IDREF

Values of type `IDREF` must match the `Name` production, and values of type `IDREFS` must match `Names`; each `Name` must match the value of an ID attribute on some element in the XML document; i.e. `IDREF` values must match the value of some ID attribute.

Validity Constraint: Entity Name

Values of type `ENTITY` must match the `Name` production, values of type `ENTITIES` must match `Names`; each `Name` must match the name of an unparsed entity declared in the DTD.

Validity Constraint: Name Token

Values of type `NMTOKEN` must match the `Nmtoken` production; values of type `NMTOKENS` must match `Nmtokens`.

Enumerated attributes can take one of a list of values provided in the declaration. There are two kinds of enumerated types:

Enumerated Attribute Types				
[57]	EnumeratedType	::=	NotationType | Enumeration	
[58]	NotationType	::=	'NOTATION' S '(' S? Name (S? '|' S? Name)* S? ')'	[VC: Notation Attributes]
[59]	Enumeration	::=	'(' S? Nmtoken (S? '|' S? Nmtoken)* S? ')'	[VC: Enumeration]

A NOTATION attribute identifies a notation, declared in the DTD with associated system and/or public identifiers, to be used in interpreting the element to which the attribute is attached.

Validity Constraint: Notation Attributes

Values of this type must match one of the notation names included in the declaration; all notation names in the declaration must be declared.

Validity Constraint: Enumeration

Values of this type must match one of the Nmtoken tokens in the declaration.

For interoperability, the same Nmtoken should not occur more than once in the enumerated attribute types of a single element type.

3.3.2 Attribute Defaults

An attribute declaration provides information on whether the attribute's presence is required, and if not, how an XML processor should react if a declared attribute is absent in a document.

Attribute Defaults				
[60]	DefaultDecl	::=	'#REQUIRED' | '#IMPLIED'	
			| (('#FIXED' S)? AttValue)	[VC: Required Attribute]
				[VC: Attribute Default Legal]
				[WFC: No < in Attribute Values]
				[VC: Fixed Attribute Default]

In an attribute declaration, #REQUIRED means that the attribute must always be provided, #IMPLIED that no default value is provided. If the declaration is neither #REQUIRED nor #IMPLIED, then the AttValue value contains the declared **default** value; the #FIXED keyword states that the attribute must always have the default value. If a default value is declared, when an XML processor encounters an omitted attribute, it is to behave as though the attribute were present with the declared default value.

Validity Constraint: Required Attribute

If the default declaration is the keyword #REQUIRED, then the attribute must be specified for all elements of the type in the attribute-list declaration.

Validity Constraint: Attribute Default Legal

The declared default value must meet the lexical constraints of the declared attribute type.

Validity Constraint: Fixed Attribute Default

If an attribute has a default value declared with the #FIXED keyword, instances of that attribute must match the default value.

Examples of attribute-list declarations:

```
<!ATTLIST termdef
          id      ID      #REQUIRED
          name    CDATA   #IMPLIED>
<!ATTLIST list
          type    (bullets|ordered|glossary)  "ordered">
<!ATTLIST form
          method  CDATA   #FIXED "POST">
```

3.3.3 Attribute-Value Normalization

Before the value of an attribute is passed to the application or checked for validity, the XML processor must normalize it as follows:

- a character reference is processed by appending the referenced character to the attribute value
- an entity reference is processed by recursively processing the replacement text of the entity
- a whitespace character (#x20, #xD, #xA, #x9) is processed by appending #x20 to the normalized value, except that only a single #x20 is appended for a "#xD#xA" sequence that is part of an external parsed entity or the literal entity value of an internal parsed entity
- other characters are processed by appending them to the normalized value

If the declared value is not CDATA, then the XML processor must further process the normalized attribute value by discarding any leading and trailing space (#x20) characters, and by replacing sequences of space (#x20) characters by a single space (#x20) character.

All attributes for which no declaration has been read should be treated by a non-validating parser as if declared CDATA.

3.4 Conditional Sections

Conditional sections are portions of the document type declaration external subset which are included in, or excluded from, the logical structure of the DTD based on the keyword which governs them.

Conditional Section			
[61]	conditionalSect	::=	includeSect | ignoreSect
[62]	includeSect	::=	'<![' S? 'INCLUDE' S? '[' extSubsetDecl ']]>'
[63]	ignoreSect	::=	'<![' S? 'IGNORE' S? '[' ignoreSectContents* ']]>'
[64]	ignoreSectContents	::=	Ignore ('<![' ignoreSectContents ']]>' Ignore)*
[65]	Ignore	::=	Char* - (Char* ('<![' | ']]>') Char*)

Like the internal and external DTD subsets, a conditional section may contain one or more complete declarations, comments, processing instructions, or nested conditional sections, intermingled with white space.

If the keyword of the conditional section is `INCLUDE`, then the contents of the conditional section are part of the DTD. If the keyword of the conditional section is `IGNORE`, then the contents of the conditional section are not logically part of the DTD. Note that for reliable parsing, the contents of even ignored conditional sections must be read in order to detect nested conditional sections and ensure that the end of the outermost (ignored) conditional section is properly detected. If a conditional section with a keyword of `INCLUDE` occurs within a larger conditional section with a keyword of `IGNORE`, both the outer and the inner conditional sections are ignored.

If the keyword of the conditional section is a parameter-entity reference, the parameter entity must be replaced by its content before the processor decides whether to include or ignore the conditional section.

An example:

```
<!ENTITY % draft 'INCLUDE' >
<!ENTITY % final 'IGNORE' >

<![%draft;[
<!ELEMENT book (comments*, title, body, supplements?)>
]]>
<![%final;[
<!ELEMENT book (title, body, supplements?)>
]]>
```

4. Physical Structures

An XML document may consist of one or many storage units. These are called **entities**; they all have **content** and are all (except for the document entity, see below, and the external DTD subset) identified by **name**. Each XML document has one entity called the document entity, which serves as the starting point for the XML processor and may contain the whole document.

Entities may be either parsed or unparsed. A **parsed entity's** contents are referred to as its replacement text; this text is considered an integral part of the document.

An **unparsed entity** is a resource whose contents may or may not be text, and if text, may not be XML. Each unparsed entity has an associated notation, identified by name. Beyond a requirement that an XML processor make the identifiers for the entity and notation available to the application, XML places no constraints on the contents of unparsed entities.

Parsed entities are invoked by name using entity references; unparsed entities by name, given in the value of `ENTITY` or `ENTITIES` attributes.

General entities are entities for use within the document content. In this specification, general entities are sometimes referred to with the unqualified term *entity* when this leads to no ambiguity. Parameter entities are parsed entities for use within the DTD. These two types of entities use different forms of reference and are recognized in different contexts. Furthermore, they occupy different namespaces; a parameter entity and a general entity with the same name are two distinct entities.

4.1 Character and Entity References

A **character reference** refers to a specific character in the ISO/IEC 10646 character set, for example one not directly accessible from available input devices.

Character Reference				
[66]	`CharRef`	`::=`	`'&#' [0-9]+ ';'`	
			`| '&#x' [0-9a-fA-F]+ ';'`	`[WFC:` Legal Character `]`

Well-Formedness Constraint: Legal Character

Characters referred to using character references must match the production for Char.

If the character reference begins with "`&#x`", the digits and letters up to the terminating `;` provide a hexadecimal representation of the character's code point in ISO/IEC 10646. If it begins just with "`&#`", the digits up to the terminating `;` provide a decimal representation of the character's code point.

An **entity reference** refers to the content of a named entity. References to parsed general entities use ampersand (`&`) and semicolon (`;`) as delimiters. **Parameter-entity references** use percent-sign (`%`) and semicolon (`;`) as delimiters.

Entity Reference				
[67]	`Reference`	`::=`	`EntityRef | CharRef`	
[68]	`EntityRef`	`::=`	`'&' Name ';'`	`[WFC:` Entity Declared `]`
				`[VC:` Entity Declared `]`
				`[WFC:` Parsed Entity `]`

Entity Reference		
		[WFC: No Recursion]
[69]	PEReference ::= '%' Name ';'	[VC: Entity Declared]
		[WFC: No Recursion]
		[WFC: In DTD]

Well-Formedness Constraint: Entity Declared

In a document without any DTD, a document with only an internal DTD subset which contains no parameter entity references, or a document with "standalone='yes'", the Name given in the entity reference must match that in an entity declaration, except that well-formed documents need not declare any of the following entities: amp, lt, gt, apos, quot. The declaration of a parameter entity must precede any reference to it. Similarly, the declaration of a general entity must precede any reference to it which appears in a default value in an attribute-list declaration. Note that if entities are declared in the external subset or in external parameter entities, a non-validating processor is not obligated to read and process their declarations; for such documents, the rule that an entity must be declared is a well-formedness constraint only if standalone='yes'.

Validity Constraint: Entity Declared

In a document with an external subset or external parameter entities with "standalone='no'", the Name given in the entity reference must match that in an entity declaration. For interoperability, valid documents should declare the entities amp, lt, gt, apos, quot, in the form specified in "4.6 Predefined Entities". The declaration of a parameter entity must precede any reference to it. Similarly, the declaration of a general entity must precede any reference to it which appears in a default value in an attribute-list declaration.

Well-Formedness Constraint: Parsed Entity

An entity reference must not contain the name of an unparsed entity. Unparsed entities may be referred to only in attribute values declared to be of type ENTITY or ENTITIES.

Well-Formedness Constraint: No Recursion

A parsed entity must not contain a recursive reference to itself, either directly or indirectly.

Well-Formedness Constraint: In DTD

Parameter-entity references may only appear in the DTD.

Examples of character and entity references:

```
Type <key>less-than</key> (&#x3C;) to save options.
This document was prepared on &docdate; and
is classified &security-level;.
```

Example of a parameter-entity reference:

```
<!-- declare the parameter entity "ISOLat2"... -->
<!ENTITY % ISOLat2
        SYSTEM "http://www.xml.com/iso/isolat2-xml.entities" >
<!-- ... now reference it. -->
%ISOLat2;
```

4.2 Entity Declarations

Entities are declared thus:

Entity Declaration			
[70]	EntityDecl	::=	GEDecl | PEDecl
[71]	GEDecl	::=	'<!ENTITY' S Name S EntityDef S? '>'
[72]	PEDecl	::=	'<!ENTITY' S '%' S Name S PEDef S? '>'
[73]	EntityDef	::=	EntityValue | (ExternalID NDataDecl?)
[74]	PEDef	::=	EntityValue | ExternalID

The `Name` identifies the entity in an entity reference or, in the case of an unparsed entity, in the value of an `ENTITY` or `ENTITIES` attribute. If the same entity is declared more than once, the first declaration encountered is binding; at user option, an XML processor may issue a warning if entities are declared multiple times.

4.2.1 Internal Entities

If the entity definition is an `EntityValue`, the defined entity is called an **internal entity**. There is no separate physical storage object, and the content of the entity is given in the declaration. Note that some processing of entity and character references in the literal entity value may be required to produce the correct replacement text: see "4.5 Construction of Internal Entity Replacement Text".

An internal entity is a parsed entity.

Example of an internal entity declaration:

```
<!ENTITY Pub-Status "This is a pre-release of the
  specification.">
```

4.2.2 External Entities

If the entity is not internal, it is an **external entity**, declared as follows:

External Entity Declaration			
[75]	ExternalID	::=	'SYSTEM' S SystemLiteral

External Entity Declaration				
			| 'PUBLIC' S PubidLiteral S SystemLiteral	
[76]	NDataDecl	::=	S 'NDATA' S Name	[VC: Notation Declared]

If the NDataDecl is present, this is a general unparsed entity; otherwise it is a parsed entity.

Validity Constraint: Notation Declared

The Name must match the declared name of a notation.

The SystemLiteral is called the entity's **system identifier**. It is a URI, which may be used to retrieve the entity. Note that the hash mark (#) and fragment identifier frequently used with URIs are not, formally, part of the URI itself; an XML processor may signal an error if a fragment identifier is given as part of a system identifier. Unless otherwise provided by information outside the scope of this specification (e.g. a special XML element type defined by a particular DTD, or a processing instruction defined by a particular application specification), relative URIs are relative to the location of the resource within which the entity declaration occurs. A URI might thus be relative to the document entity, to the entity containing the external DTD subset, or to some other external parameter entity.

An XML processor should handle a non-ASCII character in a URI by representing the character in UTF-8 as one or more bytes, and then escaping these bytes with the URI escaping mechanism (i.e., by converting each byte to %HH, where HH is the hexadecimal notation of the byte value).

In addition to a system identifier, an external identifier may include a **public identifier**. An XML processor attempting to retrieve the entity's content may use the public identifier to try to generate an alternative URI. If the processor is unable to do so, it must use the URI specified in the system literal. Before a match is attempted, all strings of white space in the public identifier must be normalized to single space characters (#x20), and leading and trailing white space must be removed.

Examples of external entity declarations:

```
<!ENTITY open-hatch
         SYSTEM "http://www.textuality.com/boilerplate/OpenHatch.xml">
<!ENTITY open-hatch
         PUBLIC "-//Textuality//TEXT Standard open-hatch boilerplate//EN"
         "http://www.textuality.com/boilerplate/OpenHatch.xml">
<!ENTITY hatch-pic
         SYSTEM "../grafix/OpenHatch.gif"
         NDATA gif >
```

4.3 Parsed Entities

4.3.1 The Text Declaration

External parsed entities may each begin with a **text declaration**.

Text Declaration			
[77]	TextDecl	::=	'<?xml' VersionInfo? EncodingDecl S? '?>'

The text declaration must be provided literally, not by reference to a parsed entity. No text declaration may appear at any position other than the beginning of an external parsed entity.

4.3.2 Well-Formed Parsed Entities

The document entity is well-formed if it matches the production labeled `document`. An external general parsed entity is well-formed if it matches the production labeled `extParsedEnt`. An external parameter entity is well-formed if it matches the production labeled `extPE`.

Well-Formed External Parsed Entity			
[78]	extParsedEnt	::=	TextDecl? content
[79]	extPE	::=	TextDecl? extSubsetDecl

An internal general parsed entity is well-formed if its replacement text matches the production labeled `content`. All internal parameter entities are well-formed by definition.

A consequence of well-formedness in entities is that the logical and physical structures in an XML document are properly nested; no start-tag, end-tag, empty-element tag, element, comment, processing instruction, character reference, or entity reference can begin in one entity and end in another.

4.3.3 Character Encoding in Entities

Each external parsed entity in an XML document may use a different encoding for its characters. All XML processors must be able to read entities in either UTF-8 or UTF-16.

Entities encoded in UTF-16 must begin with the Byte Order Mark described by ISO/IEC 10646 Annex E and Unicode Appendix B (the ZERO WIDTH NO-BREAK SPACE character, #xFEFF). This is an encoding signature, not part of either the markup or the character data of the XML document. XML processors must be able to use this character to differentiate between UTF-8 and UTF-16 encoded documents.

Although an XML processor is required to read only entities in the UTF-8 and UTF-16 encodings, it is recognized that other encodings are used around the world, and it may be desired for XML processors to read entities that use them. Parsed entities which are stored in an encoding other than UTF-8 or UTF-16 must begin with a text declaration containing an encoding declaration:

Encoding Declaration			
[80]	EncodingDecl	::=	S 'encoding' Eq ('"' EncName '"' | "'" EncName "'")

Encoding Declaration				
[81]	EncName	::=	[A-Za-z] ([A-Za-z0-9._] | '-')*	/*Encoding name contains only Latin characters */

In the document entity, the encoding declaration is part of the XML declaration. The `EncName` is the name of the encoding used.

In an encoding declaration, the values "`UTF-8`", "`UTF-16`", "`ISO-10646-UCS-2`", and "`ISO-10646-UCS-4`" should be used for the various encodings and transformations of Unicode / ISO/IEC 10646, the values "`ISO-8859-1`", "`ISO-8859-2`", ... "`ISO-8859-9`" should be used for the parts of ISO 8859, and the values "`ISO-2022-JP`", "`Shift_JIS`", and "`EUC-JP`" should be used for the various encoded forms of JIS X-0208-1997. XML processors may recognize other encodings; it is recommended that character encodings registered (as *charsets*) with the Internet Assigned Numbers Authority [IANA], other than those just listed, should be referred to using their registered names. Note that these registered names are defined to be case-insensitive, so processors wishing to match against them should do so in a case-insensitive way.

In the absence of information provided by an external transport protocol (e.g. HTTP or MIME), it is an error for an entity including an encoding declaration to be presented to the XML processor in an encoding other than that named in the declaration, for an encoding declaration to occur other than at the beginning of an external entity, or for an entity which begins with neither a Byte Order Mark nor an encoding declaration to use an encoding other than UTF-8. Note that since ASCII is a subset of UTF-8, ordinary ASCII entities do not strictly need an encoding declaration.

It is a fatal error when an XML processor encounters an entity with an encoding that it is unable to process.

Examples of encoding declarations:

```
<?xml encoding='UTF-8'?>
<?xml encoding='EUC-JP'?>
```

4.4 XML Processor Treatment of Entities and References

The table below summarizes the contexts in which character references, entity references, and invocations of unparsed entities might appear and the required behavior of an XML processor in each case. The labels in the leftmost column describe the recognition context:

Reference in Content

as a reference anywhere after the start-tag and before the end-tag of an element; corresponds to the nonterminal `content`.

Reference in Attribute Value

as a reference within either the value of an attribute in a start-tag, or a default value in an attribute declaration; corresponds to the nonterminal `AttValue`.

Occurs as Attribute Value

as a `Name`, not a reference, appearing either as the value of an attribute which has been declared as type `ENTITY`, or as one of the space-separated tokens in the value of an attribute which has been declared as type `ENTITIES`.

Reference in Entity Value

as a reference within a parameter or internal entity's literal entity value in the entity's declaration; corresponds to the nonterminal `EntityValue`.

Reference in DTD

as a reference within either the internal or external subsets of the DTD, but outside of an `EntityValue` or `AttValue`.

	Entity Type				Character
	Parameter	Internal General	External Parsed General	Unparsed	
Reference in Content	Not recognized	Included	Included if validating	Forbidden	Included
Reference in Attribute Value	Not recognized	Included in literal	Forbidden	Forbidden	Included
Occurs as Attribute Value	Not recognized	Forbidden	Forbidden	Notify	Not recognized
Reference in EntityValue	Included in literal	Bypassed	Bypassed	Forbidden	Included
Reference in DTD	Included as PE	Forbidden	Forbidden	Forbidden	Forbidden

4.4.1 Not Recognized

Outside the DTD, the `%` character has no special significance; thus, what would be parameter entity references in the DTD are not recognized as markup in `content`. Similarly, the names of unparsed entities are not recognized except when they appear in the value of an appropriately declared attribute.

4.4.2 Included

An entity is **included** when its replacement text is retrieved and processed, in place of the reference itself, as though it were part of the document at the location the reference was recognized. The replacement text may contain both character data and (except for parameter entities) markup, which must be recognized in the usual way, except that the replacement text of entities used to escape markup delimiters (the entities `amp`, `lt`, `gt`, `apos`, `quot`) is always treated as data. (The string

"AT&T;" expands to "AT&T;" and the remaining ampersand is not recognized as an entity-reference delimiter.) A character reference is **included** when the indicated character is processed in place of the reference itself.

4.4.3 Included If Validating

When an XML processor recognizes a reference to a parsed entity, in order to validate the document, the processor must include its replacement text. If the entity is external, and the processor is not attempting to validate the XML document, the processor may, but need not, include the entity's replacement text. If a non-validating parser does not include the replacement text, it must inform the application that it recognized, but did not read, the entity.

This rule is based on the recognition that the automatic inclusion provided by the SGML and XML entity mechanism, primarily designed to support modularity in authoring, is not necessarily appropriate for other applications, in particular document browsing. Browsers, for example, when encountering an external parsed entity reference, might choose to provide a visual indication of the entity's presence and retrieve it for display only on demand.

4.4.4 Forbidden

The following are forbidden, and constitute fatal errors:

- the appearance of a reference to an unparsed entity.
- the appearance of any character or general-entity reference in the DTD except within an `EntityValue` or `AttValue`.
- a reference to an external entity in an attribute value.

4.4.5 Included in Literal

When an entity reference appears in an attribute value, or a parameter entity reference appears in a literal entity value, its replacement text is processed in place of the reference itself as though it were part of the document at the location the reference was recognized, except that a single or double quote character in the replacement text is always treated as a normal data character and will not terminate the literal. For example, this is well-formed:

```
<!ENTITY % YN '"Yes"' >
<!ENTITY WhatHeSaid "He said &YN;" >
```

while this is not:

```
<!ENTITY EndAttr "27'" >
<element attribute='a-&EndAttr;>
```

4.4.6 Notify

When the name of an unparsed entity appears as a token in the value of an attribute of declared type `ENTITY` or `ENTITIES`, a validating processor must inform the application of the system and public (if any) identifiers for both the entity and its associated notation.

4.4.7 Bypassed

When a general entity reference appears in the `EntityValue` in an entity declaration, it is bypassed and left as is.

4.4.8 Included as PE

Just as with external parsed entities, parameter entities need only be included if validating. When a parameter-entity reference is recognized in the DTD and included, its replacement text is enlarged by the attachment of one leading and one following space (#x20) character; the intent is to constrain the replacement text of parameter entities to contain an integral number of grammatical tokens in the DTD.

4.5 Construction of Internal Entity Replacement Text

In discussing the treatment of internal entities, it is useful to distinguish two forms of the entity's value. The **literal entity value** is the quoted string actually present in the entity declaration, corresponding to the non-terminal `EntityValue`. The **replacement text** is the content of the entity, after replacement of character references and parameter-entity references.

The literal entity value as given in an internal entity declaration (`EntityValue`) may contain character, parameter-entity, and general-entity references. Such references must be contained entirely within the literal entity value. The actual replacement text that is included as described above must contain the *replacement text* of any parameter entities referred to, and must contain the character referred to, in place of any character references in the literal entity value; however, general-entity references must be left as-is, unexpanded. For example, given the following declarations:

```
<!ENTITY % pub    "&#xc9;ditions Gallimard" >
<!ENTITY   rights "All rights reserved" >
<!ENTITY   book   "La Peste: Albert Camus,
&#xA9; 1947 %pub;. &rights;" >
```

then the replacement text for the entity "`book`" is:

```
La Peste: Albert Camus,
© 1947 Éditions Gallimard. &rights;
```

The general-entity reference "`&rights;`" would be expanded should the reference "`&book;`" appear in the document's content or an attribute value.

These simple rules may have complex interactions; for a detailed discussion of a difficult example, see "D. Expansion of Entity and Character References".

4.6 Predefined Entities

Entity and character references can both be used to **escape** the left angle bracket, ampersand, and other delimiters. A set of general entities (`amp`, `lt`, `gt`, `apos`, `quot`) is specified for this purpose. Numeric character references may also be used; they are expanded immediately when recognized and must be treated as character data, so the numeric character references "`<`" and "`&`" may be used to escape `<` and `&` when they occur in character data.

All XML processors must recognize these entities whether they are declared or not. For interoperability, valid XML documents should declare these entities, like any others, before using them. If the entities in question are declared, they must be declared as internal entities whose replacement text is the single character being escaped or a character reference to that character, as shown below.

```
<!ENTITY lt     "&#38;#60;">
<!ENTITY gt     "&#62;">
<!ENTITY amp    "&#38;#38;">
<!ENTITY apos   "&#39;">
<!ENTITY quot   "&#34;">
```

Note that the < and & characters in the declarations of "lt" and "amp" are doubly escaped to meet the requirement that entity replacement be well-formed.

4.7 Notation Declarations

Notations identify by name the format of unparsed entities, the format of elements which bear a notation attribute, or the application to which a processing instruction is addressed.

Notation declarations provide a name for the notation, for use in entity and attribute-list declarations and in attribute specifications, and an external identifier for the notation which may allow an XML processor or its client application to locate a helper application capable of processing data in the given notation.

<table>
<tr><th colspan="3">Notation Declarations</th></tr>
<tr><td>[82] NotationDecl</td><td>::=</td><td>'<!NOTATION' S Name S (ExternalID | PublicID) S? '>'</td></tr>
<tr><td>[83] PublicID</td><td>::=</td><td>'PUBLIC' S PubidLiteral</td></tr>
</table>

XML processors must provide applications with the name and external identifier(s) of any notation declared and referred to in an attribute value, attribute definition, or entity declaration. They may additionally resolve the external identifier into the system identifier, file name, or other information needed to allow the application to call a processor for data in the notation described. (It is not an error, however, for XML documents to declare and refer to notations for which notation-specific applications are not available on the system where the XML processor or application is running.)

4.8 Document Entity

The **document entity** serves as the root of the entity tree and a starting-point for an XML processor. This specification does not specify how the document entity is to be located by an XML processor; unlike other entities, the document entity has no name and might well appear on a processor input stream without any identification at all.

5. Conformance

5.1 Validating and Non-Validating Processors

Conforming XML processors fall into two classes: validating and non-validating.

Validating and non-validating processors alike must report violations of this specification's well-formedness constraints in the content of the document entity and any other parsed entities that they read.

Validating processors must report violations of the constraints expressed by the declarations in the DTD, and failures to fulfill the validity constraints given in this specification. To accomplish this, validating XML processors must read and process the entire DTD and all external parsed entities referenced in the document.

Non-validating processors are required to check only the document entity, including the entire internal DTD subset, for well-formedness. While they are not required to check the document for validity, they are required to **process** all the declarations they read in the internal DTD subset and in any parameter entity that they read, up to the first reference to a parameter entity that they do *not* read; that is to say, they must use the information in those declarations to normalize attribute values, include the replacement text of internal entities, and supply default attribute values. They must not process entity declarations or attribute-list declarations encountered after a reference to a parameter entity that is not read, since the entity may have contained overriding declarations.

5.2 Using XML Processors

The behavior of a validating XML processor is highly predictable; it must read every piece of a document and report all well-formedness and validity violations. Less is required of a non-validating processor; it need not read any part of the document other than the document entity. This has two effects that may be important to users of XML processors:

- Certain well-formedness errors, specifically those that require reading external entities, may not be detected by a non-validating processor. Examples include the constraints entitled Entity Declared, Parsed Entity, and No Recursion, as well as some of the cases described as forbidden in "4.4 XML Processor Treatment of Entities and References".
- The information passed from the processor to the application may vary, depending on whether the processor reads parameter and external entities. For example, a non-validating processor may not normalize attribute values, include the replacement text of internal entities, or supply default attribute values, where doing so depends on having read declarations in external or parameter entities.

For maximum reliability in interoperating between different XML processors, applications which use non-validating processors should not rely on any behaviors not required of such processors. Applications which require facilities such as the use of default attributes or internal entities which are declared in external entities should use validating XML processors.

6. Notation

The formal grammar of XML is given in this specification using a simple Extended Backus-Naur Form (EBNF) notation. Each rule in the grammar defines one symbol, in the form

```
symbol ::= expression
```

Symbols are written with an initial capital letter if they are defined by a regular expression, or with an initial lower case letter otherwise. Literal strings are quoted.

Within the expression on the right-hand side of a rule, the following expressions are used to match strings of one or more characters:

`#xN`

where `N` is a hexadecimal integer, the expression matches the character in ISO/IEC 10646 whose canonical (UCS-4) code value, when interpreted as an unsigned binary number, has the value indicated. The number of leading zeros in the `#xN` form is insignificant; the number of leading zeros in the corresponding code value is governed by the character encoding in use and is not significant for XML.

`[a-zA-Z]`, `[#xN-#xN]`

matches any character with a value in the range(s) indicated (inclusive).

`[^a-z]`, `[^#xN-#xN]`

matches any character with a value *outside* the range indicated.

`[^abc]`, `[^#xN#xN#xN]`

matches any character with a value not among the characters given.

`"string"`

matches a literal string matching that given inside the double quotes.

`'string'`

matches a literal string matching that given inside the single quotes.

These symbols may be combined to match more complex patterns as follows, where `A` and `B` represent simple expressions:

`(expression)`

`expression` is treated as a unit and may be combined as described in this list.

`A?`

matches `A` or nothing; optional `A`.

`A B`

matches `A` followed by `B`.

`A | B`

matches `A` or `B` but not both.

`A - B`

matches any string that matches `A` but does not match `B`.

`A+`

matches one or more occurrences of `A`.

`A*`

matches zero or more occurrences of `A`.

Other notations used in the productions are:

`/* ... */`

comment.

`[ wfc: ... ]`

well-formedness constraint; this identifies by name a constraint on well-formed documents associated with a production.

`[ vc: ... ]`

validity constraint; this identifies by name a constraint on valid documents associated with a production.

Appendices

A. References

A.1 Normative References

IANA

(Internet Assigned Numbers Authority) *Official Names for Character Sets*, ed. Keld Simonsen et al. See ftp://ftp.isi.edu/in-notes/iana/assignments/character-sets.

IETF RFC 1766

IETF (Internet Engineering Task Force). *RFC 1766: Tags for the Identification of Languages*, ed. H. Alvestrand. 1995.

ISO 639

(International Organization for Standardization). *ISO 639:1988 (E). Code for the representation of names of languages.* [Geneva]: International Organization for Standardization, 1988.

ISO 3166

(International Organization for Standardization). *ISO 3166-1:1997 (E). Codes for the representation of names of countries and their subdivisions -- Part 1: Country codes* [Geneva]: International Organization for Standardization, 1997.

ISO/IEC 10646

ISO (International Organization for Standardization). *ISO/IEC 10646-1993 (E). Information technology -- Universal Multiple-Octet Coded Character Set (UCS) -- Part 1: Architecture and Basic Multilingual Plane.* [Geneva]: International Organization for Standardization, 1993 (plus amendments AM 1 through AM 7).

Unicode

The Unicode Consortium. *The Unicode Standard, Version 2.0.* Reading, Mass.: Addison-Wesley Developers Press, 1996.

A.2 Other References

Aho/Ullman

Aho, Alfred V., Ravi Sethi, and Jeffrey D. Ullman. *Compilers: Principles, Techniques, and Tools.* Reading: Addison-Wesley, 1986, rpt. corr. 1988.

Berners-Lee et al.

Berners-Lee, T., R. Fielding, and L. Masinter. *Uniform Resource Identifiers (URI): Generic Syntax and Semantics.* 1997. (Work in progress; see updates to RFC1738.)

Brüggemann-Klein

Brüggemann-Klein, Anne. *Regular Expressions into Finite Automata.* Extended abstract in I. Simon, Hrsg., LATIN 1992, S. 97-98. Springer-Verlag, Berlin 1992. Full Version in Theoretical Computer Science 120: 197-213, 1993.

Brüggemann-Klein and Wood

Brüggemann-Klein, Anne, and Derick Wood. *Deterministic Regular Languages.* Universität Freiburg, Institut für Informatik, Bericht 38, Oktober 1991.

Clark

James Clark. Comparison of SGML and XML. See `http://www.w3.org/TR/NOTE-sgml-xml-971215`.

IETF RFC1738

IETF (Internet Engineering Task Force). *RFC 1738: Uniform Resource Locators (URL)*, ed. T. Berners-Lee, L. Masinter, M. McCahill. 1994.

IETF RFC1808

IETF (Internet Engineering Task Force). *RFC 1808: Relative Uniform Resource Locators*, ed. R. Fielding. 1995.

IETF RFC2141

IETF (Internet Engineering Task Force). *RFC 2141: URN Syntax*, ed. R. Moats. 1997.

ISO 8879

ISO (International Organization for Standardization). *ISO 8879:1986(E). Information processing -- Text and Office Systems -- Standard Generalized Markup Language (SGML).* First edition -- 1986-10-15. [Geneva]: International Organization for Standardization, 1986.

ISO/IEC 10744

ISO (International Organization for Standardization). *ISO/IEC 10744-1992 (E). Information technology -- Hypermedia/Time-based Structuring Language (HyTime).* [Geneva]: International Organization for Standardization, 1992. *Extended Facilities Annexe.* [Geneva]: International Organization for Standardization, 1996.

B. Character Classes

Following the characteristics defined in the Unicode standard, characters are classed as base characters (among others, these contain the alphabetic characters of the Latin alphabet, without diacritics), ideographic characters, and combining characters (among others, this class contains most diacritics); these classes combine to form the class of letters. Digits and extenders are also distinguished.

Characters			
[84]	Letter	::=	BaseChar | Ideographic
[85]	BaseChar	::=	[#x0041-#x005A] | [#x0061-#x007A] | [#x00C0-#x00D6] | [#x00D8-#x00F6] | [#x00F8-#x00FF] | [#x0100-#x0131] | [#x0134-#x013E] | [#x0141-#x0148] | [#x014A-#x017E] | [#x0180-#x01C3] | [#x01CD-#x01F0] | [#x01F4-#x01F5] | [#x01FA-#x0217] | [#x0250-#x02A8] | [#x02BB-#x02C1] | #x0386 | [#x0388-#x038A] | #x038C | [#x038E-#x03A1] | [#x03A3-#x03CE] | [#x03D0-#x03D6] | #x03DA | #x03DC | #x03DE | #x03E0 | [#x03E2-#x03F3] | [#x0401-#x040C] | [#x040E-#x044F] | [#x0451-#x045C] | [#x045E-#x0481] | [#x0490-#x04C4] | [#x04C7-#x04C8] | [#x04CB-#x04CC] | [#x04D0-#x04EB] | [#x04EE-#x04F5] | [#x04F8-#x04F9] | [#x0531-#x0556] | #x0559 | [#x0561-#x0586] | [#x05D0-#x05EA] | [#x05F0-#x05F2] | [#x0621-#x063A] | [#x0641-#x064A] | [#x0671-#x06B7] | [#x06BA-#x06BE] | [#x06C0-#x06CE] | [#x06D0-#x06D3] | #x06D5 | [#x06E5-#x06E6] | [#x0905-#x0939] | #x093D | [#x0958-#x0961] | [#x0985-#x098C] | [#x098F-#x0990] | [#x0993-#x09A8] | [#x09AA-#x09B0] | #x09B2 | [#x09B6-#x09B9] | [#x09DC-#x09DD] | [#x09DF-#x09E1] | [#x09F0-#x09F1] | [#x0A05-#x0A0A] | [#x0A0F-#x0A10] | [#x0A13-#x0A28] | [#x0A2A-#x0A30] | [#x0A32-#x0A33] | [#x0A35-#x0A36] | [#x0A38-#x0A39] | [#x0A59-#x0A5C] | #x0A5E | [#x0A72-#x0A74] | [#x0A85-#x0A8B] | #x0A8D | [#x0A8F-#x0A91] | [#x0A93-#x0AA8] | [#x0AAA-#x0AB0] | [#x0AB2-#x0AB3] | [#x0AB5-#x0AB9] | #x0ABD | #x0AE0 | [#x0B05-#x0B0C] | [#x0B0F-#x0B10] | [#x0B13-#x0B28] | [#x0B2A-#x0B30] | [#x0B32-#x0B33] | [#x0B36-#x0B39] | #x0B3D | [#x0B5C-#x0B5D] | [#x0B5F-#x0B61] | [#x0B85-#x0B8A] | [#x0B8E-#x0B90] | [#x0B92-#x0B95] | [#x0B99-#x0B9A] | #x0B9C | [#x0B9E-#x0B9F] | [#x0BA3-#x0BA4] | [#x0BA8-#x0BAA] | [#x0BAE-#x0BB5] | [#x0BB7-#x0BB9] | [#x0C05-#x0C0C] | [#x0C0E-#x0C10] | [#x0C12-#x0C28] | [#x0C2A-#x0C33] | [#x0C35-#x0C39] | [#x0C60-#x0C61] | [#x0C85-#x0C8C] | [#x0C8E-#x0C90] | [#x0C92-#x0CA8] | [#x0CAA-#x0CB3] | [#x0CB5-#x0CB9] | #x0CDE | [#x0CE0-#x0CE1] | [#x0D05-#x0D0C] | [#x0D0E-#x0D10]

<table>
<tr><td></td><td></td><td></td><td>| [#x0D12-#x0D28] | [#x0D2A-#x0D39] | [#x0D60-#x0D61] | [#x0E01-#x0E2E] | #x0E30 | [#x0E32-#x0E33] | [#x0E40-#x0E45] | [#x0E81-#x0E82] | #x0E84 | [#x0E87-#x0E88] | #x0E8A | #x0E8D | [#x0E94-#x0E97] | [#x0E99-#x0E9F] | [#x0EA1-#x0EA3] | #x0EA5 | #x0EA7 | [#x0EAA-#x0EAB] | [#x0EAD-#x0EAE] | #x0EB0 | [#x0EB2-#x0EB3] | #x0EBD | [#x0EC0-#x0EC4] | [#x0F40-#x0F47] | [#x0F49-#x0F69] | [#x10A0-#x10C5] | [#x10D0-#x10F6] | #x1100 | [#x1102-#x1103] | [#x1105-#x1107] | #x1109 | [#x110B-#x110C] | [#x110E-#x1112] | #x113C | #x113E | #x1140 | #x114C | #x114E | #x1150 | [#x1154-#x1155] | #x1159 | [#x115F-#x1161] | #x1163 | #x1165 | #x1167 | #x1169 | [#x116D-#x116E] | [#x1172-#x1173] | #x1175 | #x119E | #x11A8 | #x11AB | [#x11AE-#x11AF] | [#x11B7-#x11B8] | #x11BA | [#x11BC-#x11C2] | #x11EB | #x11F0 | #x11F9 | [#x1E00-#x1E9B] | [#x1EA0-#x1EF9] | [#x1F00-#x1F15] | [#x1F18-#x1F1D] | [#x1F20-#x1F45] | [#x1F48-#x1F4D] | [#x1F50-#x1F57] | #x1F59 | #x1F5B | #x1F5D | [#x1F5F-#x1F7D] | [#x1F80-#x1FB4] | [#x1FB6-#x1FBC] | #x1FBE | [#x1FC2-#x1FC4] | [#x1FC6-#x1FCC] | [#x1FD0-#x1FD3] | [#x1FD6-#x1FDB] | [#x1FE0-#x1FEC] | [#x1FF2-#x1FF4] | [#x1FF6-#x1FFC] | #x2126 | [#x212A-#x212B] | #x212E | [#x2180-#x2182] | [#x3041-#x3094] | [#x30A1-#x30FA] | [#x3105-#x312C] | [#xAC00-#xD7A3]</td></tr>
<tr><td>[86]</td><td>Ideographic</td><td>::=</td><td>[#x4E00-#x9FA5] | #x3007 | [#x3021-#x3029]</td></tr>
<tr><td>[87]</td><td>CombiningChar</td><td>::=</td><td>[#x0300-#x0345] | [#x0360-#x0361] | [#x0483-#x0486] | [#x0591-#x05A1] | [#x05A3-#x05B9] | [#x05BB-#x05BD] | #x05BF | [#x05C1-#x05C2] | #x05C4 | [#x064B-#x0652] | #x0670 | [#x06D6-#x06DC] | [#x06DD-#x06DF] | [#x06E0-#x06E4] | [#x06E7-#x06E8] | [#x06EA-#x06ED] | [#x0901-#x0903] | #x093C | [#x093E-#x094C] | #x094D | [#x0951-#x0954] | [#x0962-#x0963] | [#x0981-#x0983] | #x09BC | #x09BE | #x09BF | [#x09C0-#x09C4] | [#x09C7-#x09C8] | [#x09CB-#x09CD] | #x09D7 | [#x09E2-#x09E3] | #x0A02 | #x0A3C | #x0A3E | #x0A3F | [#x0A40-#x0A42] | [#x0A47-#x0A48] | [#x0A4B-#x0A4D] | [#x0A70-#x0A71] | [#x0A81-#x0A83] | #x0ABC | [#x0ABE-#x0AC5] | [#x0AC7-#x0AC9] | [#x0ACB-#x0ACD] | [#x0B01-#x0B03] | #x0B3C | [#x0B3E-#x0B43] | [#x0B47-#x0B48] | [#x0B4B-#x0B4D] | [#x0B56-#x0B57] | [#x0B82-#x0B83] | [#x0BBE-#x0BC2] | [#x0BC6-#x0BC8] | [#x0BCA-#x0BCD] | #x0BD7 | [#x0C01-#x0C03] | [#x0C3E-#x0C44] | [#x0C46-#x0C48] | [#x0C4A-#x0C4D] | [#x0C55-#x0C56] | [#x0C82-#x0C83] | [#x0CBE-#x0CC4] | [#x0CC6-#x0CC8] | [#x0CCA-#x0CCD] | [#x0CD5-#x0CD6] | [#x0D02-#x0D03] | [#x0D3E-#x0D43] | [#x0D46-#x0D48] | [#x0D4A-#x0D4D] | #x0D57 | #x0E31 | [#x0E34-#x0E3A]</td></tr>
</table>

			| [#x0E47-#x0E4E] | #x0EB1 | [#x0EB4-#x0EB9] | [#x0EBB-#x0EBC] | [#x0EC8-#x0ECD] | [#x0F18-#x0F19] | #x0F35 | #x0F37 | #x0F39 | #x0F3E | #x0F3F | [#x0F71-#x0F84] | [#x0F86-#x0F8B] | [#x0F90-#x0F95] | #x0F97 | [#x0F99-#x0FAD] | [#x0FB1-#x0FB7] | #x0FB9 | [#x20D0-#x20DC] | #x20E1 | [#x302A-#x302F] | #x3099 | #x309A
[88]	Digit	::=	[#x0030-#x0039] | [#x0660-#x0669] | [#x06F0-#x06F9] | [#x0966-#x096F] | [#x09E6-#x09EF] | [#x0A66-#x0A6F] | [#x0AE6-#x0AEF] | [#x0B66-#x0B6F] | [#x0BE7-#x0BEF] | [#x0C66-#x0C6F] | [#x0CE6-#x0CEF] | [#x0D66-#x0D6F] | [#x0E50-#x0E59] | [#x0ED0-#x0ED9] | [#x0F20-#x0F29]
[89]	Extender	::=	#x00B7 | #x02D0 | #x02D1 | #x0387 | #x0640 | #x0E46 | #x0EC6 | #x3005 | [#x3031-#x3035] | [#x309D-#x309E] | [#x30FC-#x30FE]

The character classes defined here can be derived from the Unicode character database as follows:

- Name start characters must have one of the categories Ll, Lu, Lo, Lt, Nl.
- Name characters other than Name-start characters must have one of the categories Mc, Me, Mn, Lm, or Nd.
- Characters in the compatibility area (i.e. with character code greater than #xF900 and less than #xFFFE) are not allowed in XML names.
- Characters which have a font or compatibility decomposition (i.e. those with a "compatibility formatting tag" in field 5 of the database -- marked by field 5 beginning with a "<") are not allowed.
- The following characters are treated as name-start characters rather than name characters, because the property file classifies them as Alphabetic: [#x02BB-#x02C1], #x0559, #x06E5, #x06E6.
- Characters #x20DD-#x20E0 are excluded (in accordance with Unicode, section 5.14).
- Character #x00B7 is classified as an extender, because the property list so identifies it.
- Character #x0387 is added as a name character, because #x00B7 is its canonical equivalent.
- Characters ':' and '_' are allowed as name-start characters.
- Characters '-' and '.' are allowed as name characters.

C. XML and SGML (Non-Normative)

XML is designed to be a subset of SGML, in that every valid XML document should also be a conformant SGML document. For a detailed comparison of the additional restrictions that XML places on documents beyond those of SGML, see Clark.

D. Expansion of Entity and Character References (Non-Normative)

This appendix contains some examples illustrating the sequence of entity- and character-reference recognition and expansion, as specified in "4.4 XML Processor Treatment of Entities and References".

If the DTD contains the declaration

```
<!ENTITY example "<p>An ampersand (&#38;#38;) may be escaped
numerically (&#38;#38;#38;) or with a general entity
```

then the XML processor will recognize the character references when it parses the entity declaration, and resolve them before storing the following string as the value of the entity "`example`":

```
<p>An ampersand (&#38;) may be escaped
numerically (&#38;#38;) or with a general entity
(&amp;amp;).</p>
```

A reference in the document to "`&example;`" will cause the text to be reparsed, at which time the start- and end-tags of the "`p`" element will be recognized and the three references will be recognized and expanded, resulting in a "`p`" element with the following content (all data, no delimiters or markup):

```
An ampersand (&) may be escaped
numerically (&#38;) or with a general entity
(&amp;).
```

A more complex example will illustrate the rules and their effects fully. In the following example, the line numbers are solely for reference.

```
1 <?xml version='1.0'?>
2 <!DOCTYPE test [
3 <!ELEMENT test (#PCDATA) >
4 <!ENTITY % xx '&#37;zz;'>
5 <!ENTITY % zz '&#60;!ENTITY tricky "error-prone" >' >
6 %xx;
7 ]>
8 <test>This sample shows a &tricky; method.</test>
```

This produces the following:

- in line 4, the reference to character 37 is expanded immediately, and the parameter entity "`xx`" is stored in the symbol table with the value "`%zz;`". Since the replacement text is not rescanned, the reference to parameter entity "`zz`" is not recognized. (And it would be an error if it were, since "`zz`" is not yet declared.)
- in line 5, the character reference "`<`" is expanded immediately and the parameter entity "`zz`" is stored with the replacement text "`<!ENTITY tricky "error-prone" >`", which is a well-formed entity declaration.

- in line 6, the reference to "`xx`" is recognized, and the replacement text of "`xx`" (namely "`%zz;`") is parsed. The reference to "`zz`" is recognized in its turn, and its replacement text ("`<!ENTITY tricky "error-prone" >`") is parsed. The general entity "`tricky`" has now been declared, with the replacement text "`error-prone`".
- in line 8, the reference to the general entity "`tricky`" is recognized, and it is expanded, so the full content of the "`test`" element is the self-describing (and ungrammatical) string *This sample shows a error-prone method.*

E. Deterministic Content Models (Non-Normative)

For compatibility, it is required that content models in element type declarations be deterministic. SGML requires deterministic content models (it calls them "unambiguous"); XML processors built using SGML systems may flag non-deterministic content models as errors.

For example, the content model `((b, c) | (b, d))` is non-deterministic, because given an initial `b` the parser cannot know which `b` in the model is being matched without looking ahead to see which element follows the `b`. In this case, the two references to `b` can be collapsed into a single reference, making the model read `(b, (c | d))`. An initial `b` now clearly matches only a single name in the content model. The parser doesn't need to look ahead to see what follows; either `c` or `d` would be accepted.

More formally: a finite state automaton may be constructed from the content model using the standard algorithms, e.g. algorithm 3.5 in section 3.9 of Aho, Sethi, and Ullman [Aho/Ullman]. In many such algorithms, a follow set is constructed for each position in the regular expression (i.e., each leaf node in the syntax tree for the regular expression); if any position has a follow set in which more than one following position is labeled with the same element type name, then the content model is in error and may be reported as an error.

Algorithms exist which allow many but not all non-deterministic content models to be reduced automatically to equivalent deterministic models; see Brüggemann-Klein 1991 [Brüggemann-Klein].

F. Autodetection of Character Encodings (Non-Normative)

The XML encoding declaration functions as an internal label on each entity, indicating which character encoding is in use. Before an XML processor can read the internal label, however, it apparently has to know what character encoding is in use--which is what the internal label is trying to indicate. In the general case, this is a hopeless situation. It is not entirely hopeless in XML, however, because XML limits the general case in two ways: each implementation is assumed to support only a finite set of character encodings, and the XML encoding declaration is restricted in position and content in order to make it feasible to autodetect the character encoding in use in each entity in normal cases. Also, in many cases other sources of information are available in addition to the XML data stream itself. Two cases may be distinguished, depending on whether the XML entity is presented to the processor without, or with, any accompanying (external) information. We consider the first case first.

Because each XML entity not in UTF-8 or UTF-16 format *must* begin with an XML encoding declaration, in which the first characters must be '<?xml', any conforming processor can detect, after two to four octets of input, which of the following cases apply. In reading this list, it may help to know that in UCS-4, '<' is "#x0000003C" and '?' is "#x0000003F", and the Byte Order Mark required of UTF-16 data streams is "#xFEFF".

- `00 00 00 3C`: UCS-4, big-endian machine (1234 order)
- `3C 00 00 00`: UCS-4, little-endian machine (4321 order)
- `00 00 3C 00`: UCS-4, unusual octet order (2143)
- `00 3C 00 00`: UCS-4, unusual octet order (3412)
- `FE FF`: UTF-16, big-endian
- `FF FE`: UTF-16, little-endian
- `00 3C 00 3F`: UTF-16, big-endian, no Byte Order Mark (and thus, strictly speaking, in error)
- `3C 00 3F 00`: UTF-16, little-endian, no Byte Order Mark (and thus, strictly speaking, in error)
- `3C 3F 78 6D`: UTF-8, ISO 646, ASCII, some part of ISO 8859, Shift-JIS, EUC, or any other 7-bit, 8-bit, or mixed-width encoding which ensures that the characters of ASCII have their normal positions, width, and values; the actual encoding declaration must be read to detect which of these applies, but since all of these encodings use the same bit patterns for the ASCII characters, the encoding declaration itself may be read reliably
- `4C 6F A7 94`: EBCDIC (in some flavor; the full encoding declaration must be read to tell which code page is in use)
- other: UTF-8 without an encoding declaration, or else the data stream is corrupt, fragmentary, or enclosed in a wrapper of some kind

This level of autodetection is enough to read the XML encoding declaration and parse the character-encoding identifier, which is still necessary to distinguish the individual members of each family of encodings (e.g. to tell UTF-8 from 8859, and the parts of 8859 from each other, or to distinguish the specific EBCDIC code page in use, and so on).

Because the contents of the encoding declaration are restricted to ASCII characters, a processor can reliably read the entire encoding declaration as soon as it has detected which family of encodings is in use. Since in practice, all widely used character encodings fall into one of the categories above, the XML encoding declaration allows reasonably reliable in-band labeling of character encodings, even when external sources of information at the operating-system or transport-protocol level are unreliable.

Once the processor has detected the character encoding in use, it can act appropriately, whether by invoking a separate input routine for each case, or by calling the proper conversion function on each character of input.

Like any self-labeling system, the XML encoding declaration will not work if any software changes the entity's character set or encoding without updating the encoding declaration. Implementors of character-encoding routines should be careful to ensure the accuracy of the internal and external information used to label the entity.

The second possible case occurs when the XML entity is accompanied by encoding information, as in some file systems and some network protocols. When multiple sources of information are available, their relative priority and the preferred method of handling conflict should be specified as part of the higher-level protocol used to deliver XML. Rules for the relative priority of the internal label and the MIME-type label in an external header, for example, should be part of the RFC document defining the text/xml and application/xml MIME types. In the interests of interoperability, however, the following rules are recommended.

- If an XML entity is in a file, the Byte-Order Mark and encoding-declaration PI are used (if present) to determine the character encoding. All other heuristics and sources of information are solely for error recovery.
- If an XML entity is delivered with a MIME type of text/xml, then the `charset` parameter on the MIME type determines the character encoding method; all other heuristics and sources of information are solely for error recovery.
- If an XML entity is delivered with a MIME type of application/xml, then the Byte-Order Mark and encoding-declaration PI are used (if present) to determine the character encoding. All other heuristics and sources of information are solely for error recovery.

These rules apply only in the absence of protocol-level documentation; in particular, when the MIME types text/xml and application/xml are defined, the recommendations of the relevant RFC will supersede these rules.

G. W3C XML Working Group (Non-Normative)

This specification was prepared and approved for publication by the W3C XML Working Group (WG). WG approval of this specification does not necessarily imply that all WG members voted for its approval. The current and former members of the XML WG are:

Jon Bosak, Sun (Chair); James Clark (Technical Lead); Tim Bray, Textuality and Netscape (XML Co-editor); Jean Paoli, Microsoft (XML Co-editor); C. M. Sperberg-McQueen, U. of Ill. (XML Co-editor); Dan Connolly, W3C (W3C Liaison); Paula Angerstein, Texcel; Steve DeRose, INSO; Dave Hollander, HP; Eliot Kimber, ISOGEN; Eve Maler, ArborText; Tom Magliery, NCSA; Murray Maloney, Muzmo and Grif; Makoto Murata, Fuji Xerox Information Systems; Joel Nava, Adobe; Conleth O'Connell, Vignette; Peter Sharpe, SoftQuad; John Tigue, DataChannel

XML-Data & DCD Datatypes

This table is copied from the W3 note at:

`http://www.w3.org/TR/1998/NOTE-XML-data/`

Specific Datatypes

This includes all highly popular types and all the built-in types of popular database and programming languages and systems such as SQL, Visual Basic, C, C++ and Java(tm).

Name	Parse type	Storage type	Examples
`string`	`pcdata`	string (Unicode)	Ομωνυμα λεγαται ων ονομα μονον κοινον, ο δε κατα τουνομα λογοσ της ουσιας ετεροσ, οιον ζυον ο τε ανθροπος και το γεγραμμενον.
`number`	A number, with no limit on digits, may potentially have a leading sign, fractional digits, and optionally an exponent. Punctuation as in US English.	string	15, 3.14, -123.456E+10
`int`	A number, with optional sign, no fractions, no exponent.	32-bit signed binary	1, 58502, -13

Table Continued on Following Page

Name	Parse type	Storage type	Examples
float	Same as for number	64-bit IEEE 488	.314159265358979E+1
fixed.14.4	Same as number but no more than 14 digits to the left of the decimal point, and no more than 4 to the right.	64-bit signed binary	12.0044
boolean	"1" or "0"	bit	0, 1 (1=="true")
dateTime.iso8601	A date in ISO 8601 format, with optional time and no optional zone. Fractional seconds may be as precise as nanoseconds.	Structure or object containing year, month, hour, minute, second, nanosecond.	19941105T08:15:00301
dateTime.iso8601tz	A date in ISO 8601 format, with optional time and optional zone. Fractional seconds may be as precise as nanoseconds.	Structure or object containing year, month, hour, minute, second, nanosecond, zone.	19941105T08:15:5+03
date.iso8601	A date in ISO 8601 format. (no time)	Structure or object containing year, month, day.	19541022
time.iso8601	A time in ISO 8601 format, with no date and no time zone.	Structure or object exposing day, hour, minute	
time.iso8601.tz	A time in ISO 8601 format, with no date but optional time zone.	Structure or object containing day, hour, minute, zonehours, zoneminutes.	08:15-05:00

Name	Parse type	Storage type	Examples
`i1`	A number, with optional sign, no fractions, no exponent.	8-bit binary	1, 255
`i2`	"	16-bit binary	1, 703, -32768
`i4`	"	32-bit binary	
`i8`	"	64-bit binary	
`ui1`	A number, unsigned, no fractions, no exponent.	8-bit unsigned binary	1, 255
`ui2`	"	16-bit unsigned binary	1, 703, -32768
`ui4`	"	32-bit unsigned binary	
`ui8`	"	64-bit unsigned binary	
`r4`	Same as `number`	IEEE 488 4-byte float	
`r8`	"	IEEE 488 8-byte float	
`float.IEEE.754.32`	"	IEEE 754 4-byte float	
`float.IEEE.754.64`	"	IEEE 754 8-byte float	
`uuid`	Hexidecimal digits representing octets, optional embedded hyphens which should be ignored.	128-bytes Unix UUID structure	F04DA480-65B9-11d1-A29F-00AA00C14882

`uri`	Universal Resource Identifier	Per W3C spec	`http://www.ics.uci.edu/pub/ietf/uri/draft-fielding-uri-syntax-00.txt`
			`http://www.ics.uci.edu/pub/ietf/uri/`
			`http://www.ietf.org/html.charters/urn-charter.html`

Table Continued on Following Page

Name	Parse type	Storage type	Examples
bin.hex	Hexidecimal digits representing octets	no specified size	
char	string	1 Unicode character (16 bits)	
string.ansi	string containing only ascii characters <= 0xFF.	Unicode or single-byte string.	This does not look Greek to me.

All of the dates and times above reading "iso8601.." actually use a restricted subset of the formats defined by ISO 8601. Years, if specified, must have four digits. Ordinal dates are not used. Of formats employing week numbers, only those that truncate year and month are allowed (5.2.3.3 d, e and f).

XML DTD for XML-Data

This DTD for Schema is taken from the W3 note at:

`http://www.w3.org/TR/1998/NOTE-XML-data/`

```
<!ENTITY % nodeattrs 'id ID #IMPLIED'>

<!-- href is as per XML-LINK, but is not required unless there is
      no content -->

<!ENTITY % linkattrs
                    'id ID #IMPLIED
                     href CDATA #IMPLIED'>

<!ENTITY % typelinkattrs
                    'id ID #IMPLIED
                     type CDATA #IMPLIED'>

<!ENTITY % exattrs
                    'name CDATA #IMPLIED
                     content (OPEN|CLOSED) "OPEN" >

<!ENTITY % elementTypeElements1
                    'genus? correlative? superType*'>

<!ENTITY % elementTypeElements2
                    'description,
                     (min|minExclusive)?,
                     (max | maxInclusive)?,
                     domain*,
                     key*,
                     foreignKey*,
```

```
                    (datatype | ( syntax?, objecttype+ ) )?
                    mapsTo?'>

<!ENTITY % elementConstraints
                    'min? max? default?'>

<!ENTITY % elementAttrs
                    'occurs (REQUIRED|OPTIONAL|ONEORMORE|ZEROORMORE) "REQUIRED"
'>

<!ENTITY % rangeAttribute
                    'range CDATA #IMPLIED'  >

<!-- The top-level container -->
<!element schema     ((elementType|linkType|
                      extendType|
                      intEntityDcl|extEntityDcl|
                      notationDcl|extDcls)*)>
<!attlist schema %nodeattrs;>

<!-- Element Type Declarations -->

<!element elementType (%elementTypeElements1;,
                      ((element|group)*|empty|any|string|mixed)?,
                       attribute*
                       %elementTypeElements2 )>

<!attlist elementType %nodeattrs;
                     %exattrs >

<!-- Element types allowed in content model -->

<!-- Note this is just short for a model group with only one element in it -->
<!element element  (%elementConstraints;) >

<!-- The type is required -->
<!attlist element   %typelinkattrs;
                   %elementAttrs;
                   presence (FIXED) #IMPLIED >

<!-- A group in a content model: and, sequential or disjunctive -->
<!element group     ((group|element)+)>
<!attlist group     %nodeattrs;
                   %elementattrs;
                   presence (FIXED) #IMPLIED
                   groupOrder (AND|SEQ|OR) 'SEQ'>

<!element any       EMPTY>
<!element empty     EMPTY>
<!element string    EMPTY>

<!-- mixed content is just a flat, non-empty list of elements -->
<!-- We don't need to say anything about <string/> (CDATA), it's implied -->

<!element mixed        (element+)>
<!attlist mixed        %nodeattrs;>

<!element superType  EMPTY>
<!attlist superType %linkattrs;>
```

```
<!element genus  EMPTY>
<!attlist genus %typelinkattrs;>

<!element description  MIXED>
<!attlist description %nodeattrs;>

<!element domain  EMPTY>
<!attlist domain %typelinkattrs;>

<!element default MIXED>
<!attlist default %nodeattrs;>

<!element min MIXED>
<!attlist min %nodeattrs; >

<!element max MIXED>
<!attlist max %nodeattrs; >

<!element maxInclusive MIXED>
<!attlist maxInclusive %nodeattrs; >

<!element minExclusive MIXED>
<!attlist minExclusive %nodeattrs; >

<!element key (keyPart+)>
<!attlist key %nodeattrs;>

<!element keyPart EMPTY>
<!attlist keyPart %linkattrs;>

<!element foreignKey foreignKeyPart* >
<!attlist foreignKey %nodeattrs;
                     %rangeAttribute;
                     key CDATA #IMPLIED >

<!element foreignKeyPart EMPTY>
<!attlist foreignKeyPart %linkattrs;>

<!-- Datatype support -->

<!element datatype (elementType?) >
<!attlist datatype %typelinkattrs;
       presence (IMPLIED|SPECIFIED|REQUIRED|FIXED) #IMPLIED >

<!element syntax >
<!attlist syntax %linkattrs; >

<!element objecttype >
<!attlist objecttype %linkattrs; >


<!-- Mapping support -->

<!element mapsTo (implies?)>
<!attlist mapsTo %typelinkattrs;>

<!element implies (implies?)>
<!attlist implies %typelinkattrs;>

<!-- Alias support -->
```

```
<!element elementTypeEquivalent EMPTY>
<!attlist elementTypeEquivalent %typelinkattrs; >

<!element correlative EMPTY>
<!attlist correlative %linkattrs;>


<! Subtype of ElementType that is explicitly a relation. -->

<!element relationType (%elementTypeElements1;,
                        ((element|group)*|empty|any|string|mixed)?,
                        attribute*
                        %elementTypeElements2)>
<!attlist relationType %nodeattrs;
                   %exattrs; >



<!-- Attributes -->
<!-- default value must be present if presence is specified or fixed -->
<!-- presence defaults to specified if default is present, else implied -->

<!element attribute  (%PropertyElements1,
                      %PropertyElements2,
                      %elementConstraints)>
<!attlist attribute  %typelinkattrs;
                     name CDATA #IMPLIED
                     %elementAttrs
                     dt          CDATA #IMPLIED
                     atttype    (URIREF|
                                 ID|IDREF|IDREFS|ENTITY|ENTITIES|
                                 NMTOKEN|NMTOKENS|
                                 ENUMERATION|NOTATION|CDATA) CDATA
                     %rangeAttribute;
                     default CDATA #IMPLIED
                     values NMTOKENS #IMPLIED
                     presence (IMPLIED|SPECIFIED|REQUIRED|FIXED) #IMPLIED >

<!-- Notation and Entity Declarations -->
<!-- Note: as this is written, only external entities
      can have structure without escaping it -->
<!-- 'par' is TRUE iff parameter entity. -->
<!-- systemID and publicId (if present) must have the required syntax -->

<!ENTITY % notationattrs '%nodeattrs
                          systemID CDATA #IMPLIED
                          publicID CDATA #IMPLIED'>

<!ENTITY % entityattrs   '%notationattrs
                          name CDATA #IMPLIED
                          par     (TRUE | FALSE) "FALSE">


<!-- Notation Declarations -->

<!element notationDcl        EMPTY>
<!attlist notationDcl        %notationattrs>

<!element intEntityDcl       PCDATA>
<!attlist intEntityDcl       %entityattrs; >
```

```
<!-- The entity will be treated as binary if a notation is present -->
<!element extEntityDcl        EMPTY>
<!attlist extEntityDcl        %entityattrs;
                              notation CDATA #IMPLIED>

<!-- External entity with declarations to be included -->
<!element extDcls             EMPTY>
<!attlist extDcls             %entityattrs;>
```

CSS1 Properties

We have deliberately separated CSS1 and CSS2 properties, because CSS1 properties are almost completely implemented by the two main browsers, whereas CSS2 properties, (with the exception of some of the position properties), are not. If you find a property in this appendix you can be reasonably sure that it will cause an appropriate display in the two mainstream browsers.

We have noted where the properties are not well applied in Communicator 4 or IE4, but as implementation of CSS is being upgraded all the time, this may be moot information.

The following is a list of properties from the CSS1 Recommendation. We follow the section division of the Recommendation, so you will find the properties divided into the following types:

- Font Properties
- Color and Background Properties
- Text Properties
- Box Properties
- Classification Properties

The proposal can be found at:

`http://www.w3.org/TR/REC-CSS1`

We will point to the appropriate part of the specification for each set of properties as we go through them. You will find more details on each property in the specification.

Font Properties

These are covered in Section 5.2 of the CSS1 specification.

Property Name	Property Syntax	Possible Values	Initial Value	Applies to	In-herited
font-family	font-family:[[<family-name> | <generic-name>],]*[<family-name> | <generic-name>]	Use any font family name. <generic-family> values are: serif sans-serif *cursive* *fantasy* monospace	Browser determines initial value	All	Yes
font-style	font-style: *<value>*	normal | italic | oblique	normal	All	Yes
font-variant	font-variant: *<value>*	normal| SMALLCAPS	normal	All	Yes
font-weight	font-weight: *<value>*	normal |bold | bolder | lighter | 100 | 200 | 300 | 400 | 500 | 600 | 700 | 800 | 900	normal	All	Yes

Property Name	Property Syntax	Possible Values	Initial Value	Applies to	In-herited
'font-size'	font-size: <*value*> *value*= <absolute-size> | <relative-size> | <length> | <percen_tage>	<absolute-size> xx-small | x-small | small | medium | large | x-large | xx-large <relative-size>:- larger | smaller <*length*> | <*percentage*>:- In relation to parent element	medium	All	Yes
font	font: <*value*>	[<font-style> || <font-variant> || <font-weight>]? <font-size> [/<line-height>] <font-family>	Undefined	All	Yes

Color and Background Properties

These are covered in section 5.3 of the CSS1 specification.

Property Name	Property Syntax	Possible Values	Initial Value	Applies to	In-herited
color	color: <*value*>	keyword | numerical RGB specification			

Table Continued on Following Page

<table>
<tr><th>Property Name</th><th>Property Syntax</th><th>Possible Values</th><th>Initial Value</th><th>Applies to</th><th>In-herited</th></tr>
<tr><td>background-color</td><td>back_ground-color: <value></td><td><color> | transparent</td><td>transparent</td><td>All</td><td>No</td></tr>
<tr><td>background-image</td><td>back_ground-image: <value></td><td><url> | none</td><td>none</td><td>All</td><td>No</td></tr>
<tr><td>background-repeat
(Buggy in Communicator 4)</td><td>back_ground-repeat: <value></td><td>repeat | repeat-x | repeat-y | no-repeat</td><td>repeat</td><td>All</td><td>No</td></tr>
<tr><td>background-attachment
(not supported in Communicator 4)</td><td>back_ground-attach_ment: <value></td><td>scroll | fixed</td><td>scroll</td><td>All</td><td>No</td></tr>
<tr><td>background-position
(Buggy in Communicator 4)</td><td>back_ground-position: <value></td><td>[<length> | <percentage>]{1,2} | [top | center | bottom] || [left | center | right]</td><td>0%,0%</td><td>Block and replaced elements</td><td>No</td></tr>
<tr><td>background</td><td>back_ground: <value></td><td><background-color> || <background-image> || <background-repeat> || <background-attachment> || <background-position></td><td>Undefined</td><td>All</td><td>No</td></tr>
</table>

Text Properties

These are covered in section 5.4 of the CSS1 specification.

<table>
<tr><th>Property Name</th><th>Property Syntax</th><th>Possible Values</th><th>Initial Value</th><th>Applies to</th><th>In-herited</th></tr>
<tr><td>letter-spacing

(not supported in Communicator 4)</td><td>letter-spacing: <value></td><td>normal | <length></td><td>normal</td><td>All</td><td>Yes</td></tr>
<tr><td>text-decoration</td><td>text-decoration:<value></td><td>none | [underline || overline || line-through || blink]</td><td>none</td><td>All</td><td>No</td></tr>
<tr><td>vertical-align

(Implementation partial and buggy)</td><td>vertical-align: <value></td><td>baseline | sub | super | top | text-top | middle | bottom | text-bottom | <percentage>

<percentage> is relative to elements line-height property</td><td>base_line</td><td>Inline Elements</td><td>No</td></tr>
<tr><td>text-transform</td><td>text-trans_form: <value></td><td>none | Capitalize | UPPER_CASE | lower_case</td><td>none</td><td>All</td><td>Yes</td></tr>
</table>

Table Continued on Following Page

Property Name	Property Syntax	Possible Values	Initial Value	Applies to	In-herited
text-align	text-align: <*value*>	left | right | center | justify (justify not supported in Communicator 4)	left	Block elements	Yes
text-indent	text-indent: <*value*>	<*length*> | <*percentage*>	0	Block elements	Yes
line-height	line-height: <*value*>	normal | <*number*> | <*length*> | <*percentage*> <*number*>: - line-height=font-size **x** num. <*percentage*>:- relative to font-size.	normal	All	Yes

Box Properties

These are covered in section 5.5 of the CSS1 specification.

Property Name	Property Syntax	Possible Values	Initial Value	Applies to	Inherited
margin-top	margin-top: *<value>*	*<length>* | *<percentage>* | auto *<percentage>* :- refers to the **parent** elements **width**. Negative values are permitted	0	All	No
margin-right	margin-right: *<value>*	-:ditto:-	0	All	No
margin-bottom	margin-bottom: *<value>*	-:ditto:-	0	All	No
margin-left	margin-left: *<value>*	-:ditto:-	0	All	No

Table Continued on Following Page

Property Name	Property Syntax	Possible Values	Initial Value	Applies to	In-herited
margin	margin: *<value>*	[*<length>* | *<percentage>* | auto]{1,4} If 4 values are given they apply to top, right, bottom, left, in that order. 1 value applies to all 4 If 2, or 3 values are given, the missing value is taken from the opposite side. *<percentage>*:- refers to the **parent** elements **width**. Negative values are permitted	Undefined	All	No
padding-top	padding-top: *<value>*	*<length>* | *<percentage>* <percentage> :- refers to the **parent** elements **width**. Negative values are **NOT** permitted	0	All	No
padding-right	padding-right:*<value>*	-:ditto:-	0	All	No
padding-bottom	padding-bottom:*<value>*	-:ditto:-	0	All	No

Property Name	Property Syntax	Possible Values	Initial Value	Applies to	In-herited
padding-left	padding-left: *<value>*	-:ditto:-	0	All	No
padding	padding: *<value>*	[*<length>* | *<percentage>* | auto]{1,4} If 4 values are given they apply to top, right, bottom, left, in that order. 1 value applies to all 4 If 2, or 3 values are given, the missing value is taken from the opposite side. *<percentage>*: - refers to the **parent** elements **width**. Negative values are **NOT** permitted	0	All	No
border-top-width	border-top-width: *<value>*	thin | medium | thick | *<length>*	medium	All	No
border-right-width	border-right-width: *<value>*	thin | medium | thick | *<length>*	medium	All	No
border-bottom-width	border-bottom-width: *<value>*	thin | medium | thick | *<length>*	medium	All	No

Table Continued on Following Page

Property Name	Property Syntax	Possible Values	Initial Value	Applies to	In-herited
border-left-width	border-left-width: *<value>*	thin | medium | thick | *<length>*	medium	All	No
border-width	border-width: *<value>*	[thin | medium | thick | *<length>*]{1,4} If 4 values are given they apply to top, right, bottom, left, in that order. 1 value applies to all 4 if 2, or 3 values are given, the missing value is taken from the opposite side.	Undefined	All	No
border-color	border-color: *<value>*	*<color>*{1,4} (see Appendix E) If 4 values are given they apply to top, right, bottom, left, in that order. 1 value applies to all 4 if 2, or 3 values are given, the missing value is taken from the opposite side.	The element color property	All	No

Property Name	Property Syntax	Possible Values	Initial Value	Applies to	In-herited
border-style	border-style: <*value*>	[none | dotted | dashed | solid | double | groove | ridge | inset | outset]{1,4}	none	All	No
border-top	border-top: <*value*>	<border-top-width> || <border-style> || <*color*>	Undefined	All	No
border-right	border-right: <*value*>	<border-right-width> || <border-style> || <*color*>	Undefined	All	No
border-bottom	border-bottom: <*value*>	<border-bottom-width> || <border-style> || < *color* >	Undefined	All	No
border-left	border-left: <*value*>	<border-left-width> || <border-style> || < *color* >	Undefined	All	No
border	border: <*value*>	<border-width> || <border-style> || < *color* >	Undefined	All	No

Table Continued on Following Page

Property Name	Property Syntax	Possible Values	Initial Value	Applies to	In-herited
width	width: <*value*>	<*length*> | <*percentage*> | auto % refers to parent elements width. A replaced element is an element such as IMG or OBJECT in HTML.	auto	Block and replaced elements	No
height	height: <*value*>	<*length*> | auto	auto	Block and replaced elements	No
float	float: <*value*>	left | right | none note:-float removes inline elements from the line.	none	All	No
clear	clear: <*value*>	block | inline | list-item | none	none	All	No

Classification properties

These are covered in section 5.6 of the CSS1 specification.

Property Name	Property Syntax	Possible Values	Initial Value	Applies to	In-herited
display	display: <*value*>	block | inline | list-item | none	Dependant on browser. If tag is unknown as in the case of XML, default is usually inline, although CSS1 default specifies block	All	No
white-space	white-space: <*value*>	normal | pre | nowrap	normal	Block Elements	No
list-style-type	list-style-type: <*value*>	disc | circle | square | decimal | lower-roman | upper-roman | lower-alpha | upper-alpha | none	disc	List-items	Yes
list-style-image	list-style-image: <*value*>	<url> | none	none	List-items	Yes
list-style-position	list-style-position : <*value*>	inside | outside	outside	List-items	Yes
list-style	list-style	<list-style-type> || list-style-position || <*url*>	Undefined	List-items	Yes

CSS2 Properties

CSS2 includes all of the CSS1 properties, although in many cases new values have been added. Most of the new CSS2 properties are not implemented in the current browsers, with the exception of most of the position properties. The absolute position properties are, however, not implemented in Communicator 4.

We cover the properties under the same headings as the specification:

- Box Model
- Visual Rendering Model
- Visual Rendering Model Details
- Visual Effects
- Generated Content and Automatic Numbering
- Paged Media
- Colors and Backgrounds
- Font Properties
- Text Properties
- Lists Tables
- User Interface
- Aural Style Sheets

Where there have been no changes since CSS1, we state this and refer you to Appendix F.

We refer you to the section of the specification which gives you more detail on each section of properties. The specification can be found at:

`http://www.w3.org/TR/PR-CSS2/`

As ever, to see if a property works, just try it.

The only way CSS2 alters CSS1 is in cascade order. In CSS1, an `!important` in an author's style sheet took precedence over an `!important` in an user's style sheet. This has been (correctly) reversed in CSS2.

Box Model

The box properties are essentially unmodified from CSS1, see Appendix F for details of the property names and values.

Visual Rendering Model

This is a new category of property in CSS2, made up as follows:

Two existing CSS1 properties, `float` and `clear`, which are unchanged from CSS1 and are fully detailed in Appendix F.

The CSS1 `display` property adds the following values in CSS2. Otherwise it is unchanged.

```
| run-in | compact | marker | table | inline-table | table-row-group | table-
column-group | table-header-group | table-footer-group | table-row | table-
cell | table-caption
```

Two new properties, `position` and `z-index`, are detailed below. There is variable support for them in IE4 and Communicator 4. (Netscape does not support the `absolute` value for the position property. Use their `<LAYER>` tag instead.) Both the makers promise that their version 5 releases will give full support.

These are covered in section 9 of the CSS2 specification.

Property Name	Property Syntax	Possible Values	Initial Value	Applies to	In-herited
position	position :<*value*>	static | relative | absolute | fixed	static	All	No
box offsets	box offsets: [top | left | bottom | right]	<*length*> | <*percentage*> | auto <*length*> : -The offset is a fixed distance from the reference edge. <*percentage*> : -The offset is a percentage of the containing block's width (for left or right) or height (for top and bottom). **auto**:-The value depends on which of the other properties are auto as well.	auto	All	No
z-index	auto | <*integer*>		auto	Elements that produce absolutely and relatively positioned boxes	No

Visual Rendering Model Details

This is another new section in CSS2. It is made up of the CSS1 `width`, `height`, `line-height` and `vertical-align` properties, which remain unchanged and are detailed in Appendix F, plus four new properties, `min-height`, `max-height`, `min-width` and `max-width`, details of which are set out below.

These are covered in section 10 of the CSS2 specification.

Property Name	Property Syntax	Possible Values	Initial Value	Applies to	Inherited
min-width	min-width:<*value*>	<*length*> | <*percentage*>	0	All	No
max-width	max-width:<*value*>	<*length*> | <*percentage*>	100%	All	No
min-height	min-height:<*value*>	<*length*> | <*percentage*>	0	All	No
max-height	max-height:<*value*>	<*length*> | <*percentage*>	100%	All	No

Visual Effects

This is a new category of property in CSS2. It is covered in section 11 of the specification.

Property Name	Property Syntax	Possible Values	Initial Value	Applies to	Inherited
overflow	see spec	visible | hidden | scroll | auto	visible	Block level and replaced elements	No
clip	see spec	<*shape*> | auto	auto	Block level and replaced elements	No
visibility	visibility:<*value*>	visible | hidden | collapse | inherit	inherit	All	No

Generated Content and Automatic Numbering

Again, this is a new category of property in CSS2 covered in section 12 of the specification. In CSS2 it is possible to generate content in several ways:

- Using the `content` property in conjunction with the `:before` and `:after` psuedo elements.
- In conjunction with the `cue-before` and `cue-after` aural properties.
- Elements with a value of `list-item` for the `display` property.

The style and location of generated content is specified with the `:before` and `:after` psuedo elements. These are used in conjunction with the `content` property, which specifies what is inserted. Unsurprisingly, `:before` and `:after` psuedo elements specify content before and after an element's document tree content. See the specification (section 12) for further details.

Property Name	Property Syntax	Possible Values	Initial Value	Applies to	In-herited
content	see spec	[<*string*> | <*uri*> | <*counter*> | attr(X) | open-quote | close-quote | no-open-quote | no-close-quote]+	empty string	:before and :after pseudo elements	No
quotes	see spec for specifying the `quotes` property and inserting quotes with the `content` property	[<*string*>.,<*string*>.]+ | none | inherit	Depends on user agent	All	Yes

Paged Media

All the following paged media properties are new to CSS2 and are covered in section 13 of the specification.

Property Name	Property Syntax	Possible Values	Initial Value	Applies to	Inherited
size	size: <*value*>	<*length*>{1,2} | auto | portrait | landscape	auto	Page context	N/A
marks (crop marks)	marks: <*value*>	[crop || cross] | none	none	Page context	N/A
page (for using named pages)	page: <*identifier*> <*value*>	[left | right]? | auto	auto	Block level elements	Yes
page-break-before	page-break-before: <*value*>	auto | always | avoid | left | right | inherit	auto	Block-level elements	No
page-break-after	page-break-after: <*value*>	auto | always | avoid | left | right | inherit	auto	Block-level elements	No
page-break-inside	page-break-inside: <*value*>	avoid | auto	auto	Block-level elements	Yes
orphans	orphans: <*integer*>		2	Block-level elements	Yes
widows	widows: <*integer*>		2	Block-level elements	Yes

Colors and Backgrounds

These properties are unchanged from CSS1, to read about them in the CSS2 specification check out Section 14, to see the property listing and values in this book, turn to Appendix F.

Font Properties

The CSS1 properties are unchanged in CSS2, and are listed in Appendix F. There are two new CSS2 font properties, Font Properties are covered in section 15 of the CSS2 specification.

Property Name	Property Syntax	Possible Values	Initial Value	Applies to	Inherited
font-stretch unsupported	font-stretch: <*value*>	normal | wider | narrower | ultra-condensed | extra-condensed | condensed | semi-condensed | semi-expanded | expanded | extra-expanded | ultra-expanded	normal	All	Yes
font-size-adjust	font-size-adjust: <*value*>	<*number*> | none	none	All	Yes

Text Properties

The CSS1 properties are unchanged in CSS2, and are listed in Appendix F. There is one new CSS2 text property. The text properties are covered in section 16 of the CSS2 specification.

Property Name	Property Syntax	Possible Values	Initial Value	Applies to	Inherited
text-shadow	text-shadow:<*value*>	none | [<*color*> || <*length*> <*length*> <*length*>? ,]* [<*color*> || <*length*> <*length*> <*length*>?] | inherit	none	All	No

Lists

The list properties remain unchanged from CSS1, apart from **list-style-type** which has the following new values. They are all covered in section 17 of the specification.

Property Name	Property Syntax	Possible Values	Initial Value	Applies to	Inherited
list-style-type	list-style-type: <*value*>	leading-zero | western-decimal | lower-latin | upper-latin | hebrew | armenian | georgian | cjk-ideographic | hiragana | katakana | hiragana-iroha | katakana-iroha	disc	Elements with the display property set to list-item	Yes

Tables

All the table properties are new to CSS2 and can be found in section 18 of the specification.

Property Name	Property Syntax	Possible Values	Initial Value	Applies to	Inherited
column-span	column-span:<*integer*>		1	table-cell, table-column and table-column-group elements	No
row-span	row-span:<*integer*>		1	table-cell elements	No
table-layout	table-layout: <*value*>	fixed | auto	auto	table and inline-table elements	No

Property Name	Property Syntax	Possible Values	Initial Value	Applies to	Inherited
empty-cells	empty-cells: <*value*>	borders | no-borders	borders	table-cell elements	Yes
speak-header	speak-header: <*value*>	once | always	once	Elements that have header information	Yes

User Interface

The user interface properties are new to CSS2 and can be found in section 19 of the specification.

Property Name	Property Syntax	Possible Values	Initial Value	Applies to	Inherited
cursor	cursor: <*uri*> <*value*>	[[<*uri*>,]* [auto | crosshair | default | pointer | move | e-resize | ne-resize | nw-resize | n-resize | se-resize | sw-resize | s-resize | w-resize| text | wait | help]]	auto	All	Yes
outline	outline: [<outline-color> || <outline-style> || <outline-width>]	<outline-color> || <outline-style> || <outline-width>	See individual properties	All	No

Table Continued on Following Page

Property Name	Property Syntax	Possible Values	Initial Value	Applies to	Inherited
outline-width	outline-width: <*value*>	border-width	medium	All	N/A
outline-style	outline-style: <*value*>	border-style	none	All	N/A
outline-color	outline-color: <*value*>	border-color | invert	invert	All	N/A

Aural Style Sheets

These are a new addition in CSS2 and can be seen in further detail in section 20 of the specification.

Property Name	Property Syntax	Possible Values	Initial Value	Applies to	Inherited
volume	volume: <*value*>	<*number*> | <*percentage*> | silent | x-soft | soft | medium | loud | x-loud	medium	All	Yes
speak	speak: <*value*>	normal | none | spell-out	normal	All	Yes
pause-before	pause-before: <value>	<*time*> | <*percentage*>	Depends on user agent	All	No
pause-after	pause-after: <*value*>	<*time*> | <*percentage*>	Depends on user agent	All	No
pause (shorthand)	pause: <*value*>	[[<*time*> | <*percentage*>]{1, 2}]	Depends on user agent	All	No
cue-before	cue-before: <*value*>	<*uri*> | none	none	All	No
cue-after	cue-after: <*value*>	<*uri*> | none	none	All	No

<table>
<tr><th>Property Name</th><th>Property Syntax</th><th>Possible Values</th><th>Initial Value</th><th>Applies to</th><th>Inherited</th></tr>
<tr><td><b>cue (shorthand)</b></td><td>cue: <<i>value</i>></td><td>[<cue-before> || <cue-after>]</td><td>Not defined for shorthand properties</td><td>All</td><td>No</td></tr>
<tr><td><b>play-during</b></td><td>play-during: <<i>uri</i>> <<i>value</i>></td><td><<i>uri</i>> mix? repeat? | auto | none | inherit</td><td>auto</td><td>All</td><td>No</td></tr>
<tr><td><b>azimuth</b></td><td>azimuth: <<i>value</i>></td><td><<i>angle</i>> | [[left-side | far-left | left | center-left | center | center-right | right | far-right | right-side] || behind] | leftwards | rightwards</td><td>center</td><td>All</td><td>Yes</td></tr>
<tr><td><b>elevation</b></td><td>elevation:<<i>value</i>></td><td><<i>angle</i>> | below | level | above | higher | lower</td><td>level</td><td>All</td><td>Yes</td></tr>
<tr><td><b>speech-rate</b></td><td>speech-rate: <<i>value</i>></td><td><<i>number</i>> | x-slow | slow | medium | fast | x-fast | faster | slower</td><td>medium</td><td>All</td><td>Yes</td></tr>
</table>

Table Continued on Following Page

Property Name	Property Syntax	Possible Values	Initial Value	Applies to	Inherited
voice-family	voice-family: <*value*> <*value*>	[[<specific-voice> | <generic-voice>],]* [<specific-voice> | <generic-voice>]	Depends on user agent	All	Yes
pitch	pitch: <*value*>	<frequency> | x-low | low | medium | high | x-high	medium	All	Yes
pitch-range	pitch-range: <*value*>	<*number*>	50	All	Yes
stress	stress: <*value*>	<*number*>	50	All	Yes
richness	richness :<*value*>	<*number*>	50	All	Yes
speak-punctuation	speak-punctuation: <*value*>	code | none	none	All	Yes
speak-numeral	speak-numeral: <*value*>	digits | continuous	continuous	All	Yes

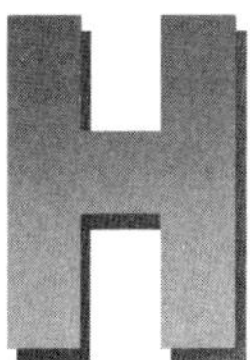

Support and Errata

One of the most irritating things about any programming book can be when you find that bit of code you've just spent an hour typing in simply doesn't work. You check it a hundred times to see if you've set it up correctly and then you notice the spelling mistake in the variable name on the book page. Grrr! Of course, you can blame the authors for not taking enough care and testing the code, the editors for not doing their job properly, or the proofreaders for not being eagle-eyed enough, but this doesn't get around the fact that mistakes do happen.

We try hard to ensure no mistakes sneak out into the real world, but we can't promise that this book is 100% error free. What we can do is offer the next best thing by providing you with immediate support and feedback from experts who have worked on the book and try to ensure that future editions eliminate these gremlins. The following section will take you step by step through the process of posting errata to our web site to get that help. The sections that follow, therefore, are:

- Wrox Developers Membership
- Finding a list of existing errata on the web site
- Adding your own errata to the existing list
- What happens to your errata once you've posted it (why doesn't it appear immediately?)

There is also a section covering how to e-mail a question for technical support. This comprises:

- What your e-mail should include
- What happens to your e-mail once it has been received by us

So that you only need view information relevant to yourself, we ask that you register as a Wrox Developer Member. This is a quick and easy process, that will save you time in the long-run. If you are already a member, just update your membership to include this book.

Wrox Developer's Membership

To get your FREE Wrox Developer's Membership click on Membership in the navigation bar of our home site

`www.wrox.com.`

This is shown in the following screen shot:

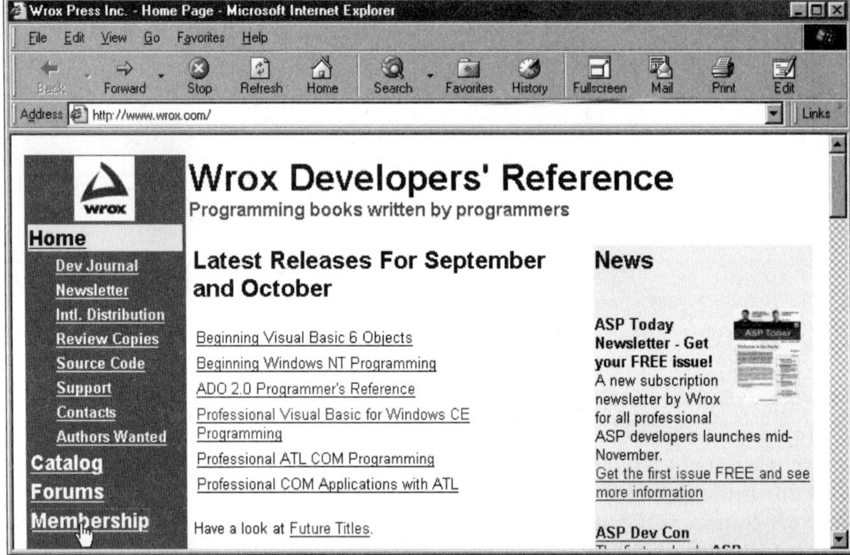

Then, on the next screen (not shown), click on New User. This will display a form. Fill in the details on the form and submit the details using the submit button at the bottom. Before you can say 'The best read books come in Wrox Red' you will get this screen:

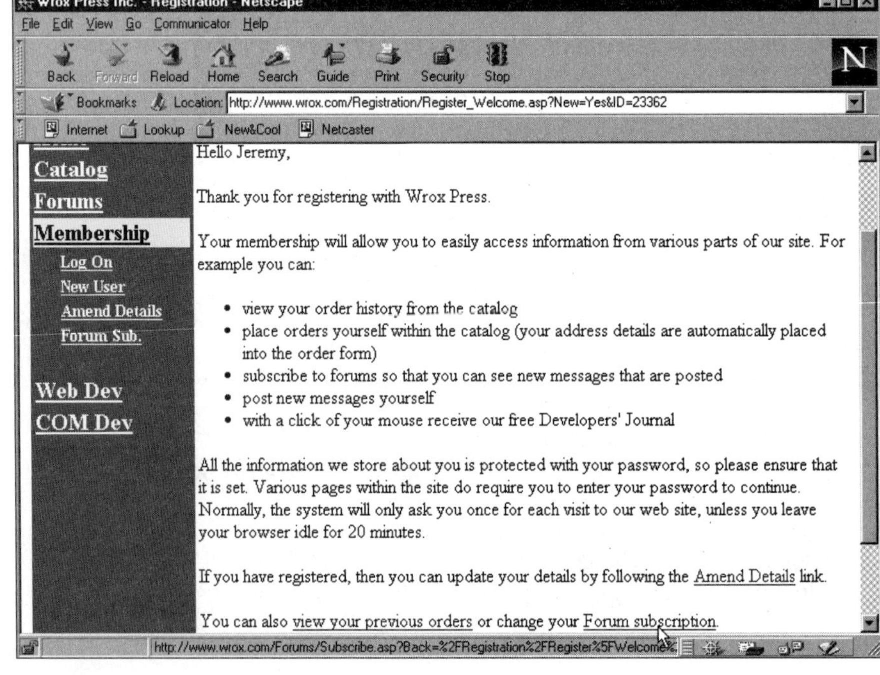

Finding an Errata on the Web Site

Before you send in a query, you might be able to save time by finding the answer to your problem on our web site: `http:\\www.wrox.com`.

Each book we publish has its own page and its own errata sheet. You can get to any book's page by clicking on support from the left hand side navigation bar.

From this page you can locate any books errata page on our site. Select your book from the pop-up menu and click on it.

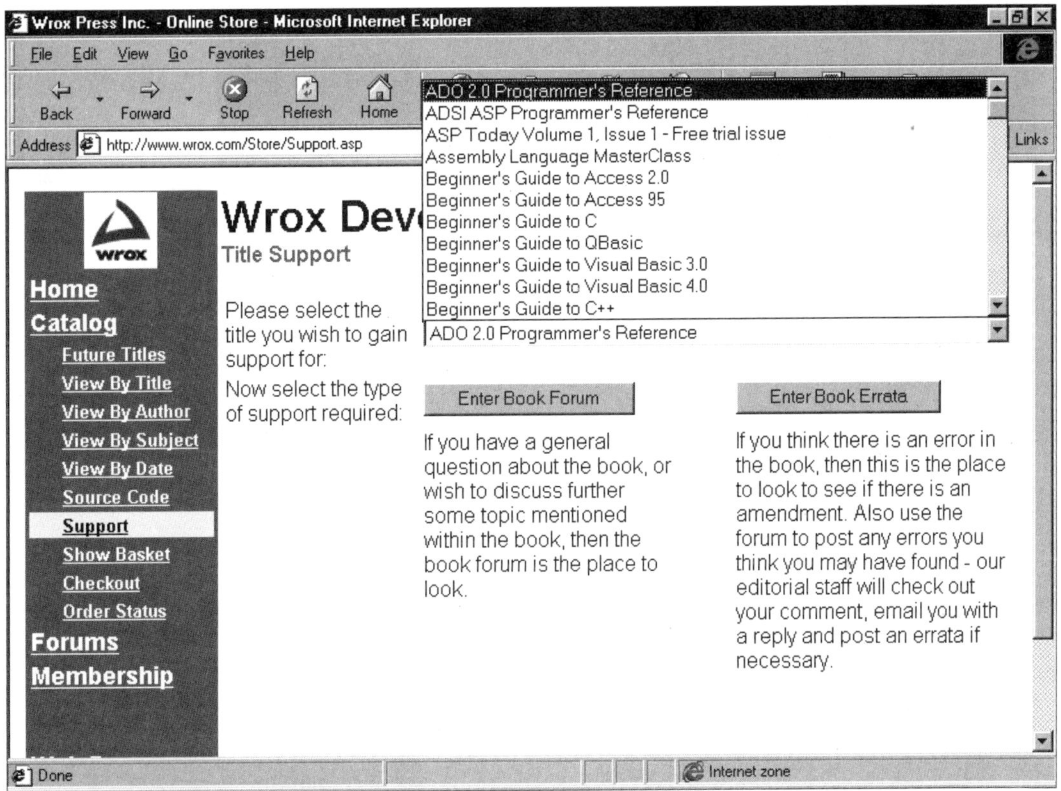

Then click on Enter Book Errata. This will take you to the errata page for the book. Select the criteria by which you want to view the errata, and click the apply criteria button. This will provide you with links to specific errata. For an initial search, you are advised to view the errata by page numbers. If you have looked for an error previously, then you may wish to limit your search using dates. We update these pages daily to ensure that you have the latest information on bugs and errors.

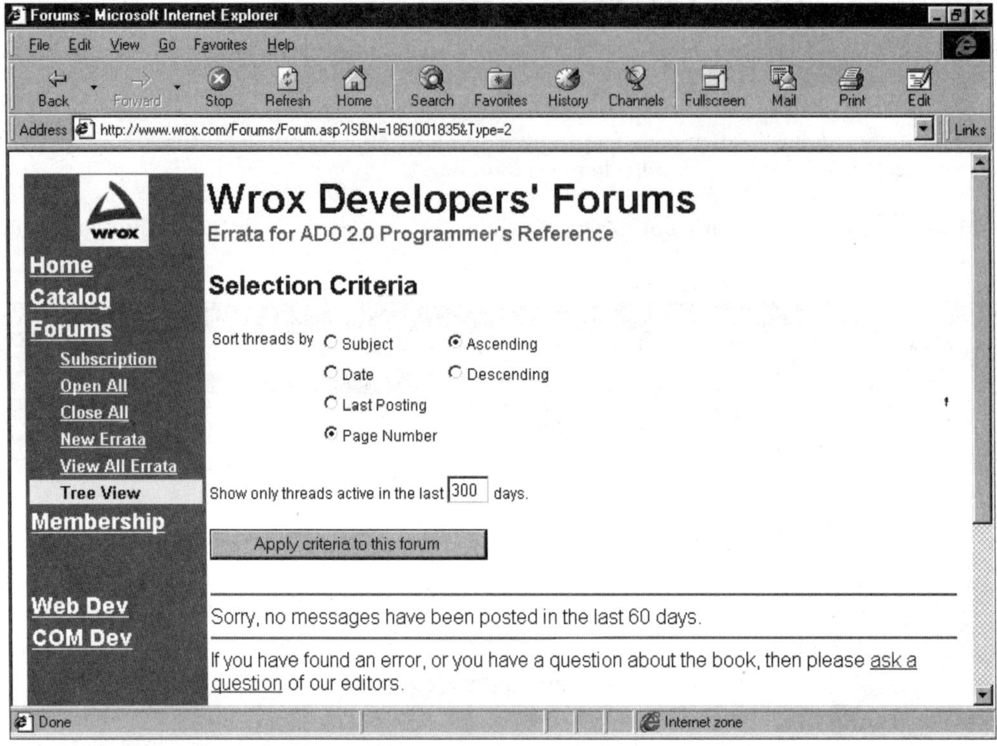

Adding an Errata to the Sheet Yourself

It's always possible that you may find that your error is not listed, in which case you can enter details of the fault yourself. It might be anything from a spelling mistake to a faulty piece of code in the book. Sometimes you'll find useful hints that aren't really errors on the listing. By entering errata you may save another reader hours of frustration, and of course, you will be helping us provide even higher quality information. We're very grateful for this sort of advice and feedback. You can enter errata using the 'ask a question' of our editors link at the bottom of the errata page. Click on this link and you will get a form on which to post your message.

Fill in the subject box, and then type your message in the space provided on the form. Once you have done this, click on the Post Now button at the bottom of the page. The message will be forwarded to our editors. They'll then test your submission and check that the error exists, and that the suggestions you make are valid. Then your submission, together with a solution, is posted on the site for public consumption. Obviously this stage of the process can take a day or two, but we will endeavor to get a fix up sooner than that.

E-mail Support

If you wish to directly query a problem in the book with an expert who knows the book in detail then e-mail `support@wrox.com`, with the title of the book and the last four numbers of the ISBN in the subject field of the e-mail. Your e-mail **MUST** include the title of the book the problem relates to, otherwise we won't be able to help you. The diagram below shows what else your e-mail should include:

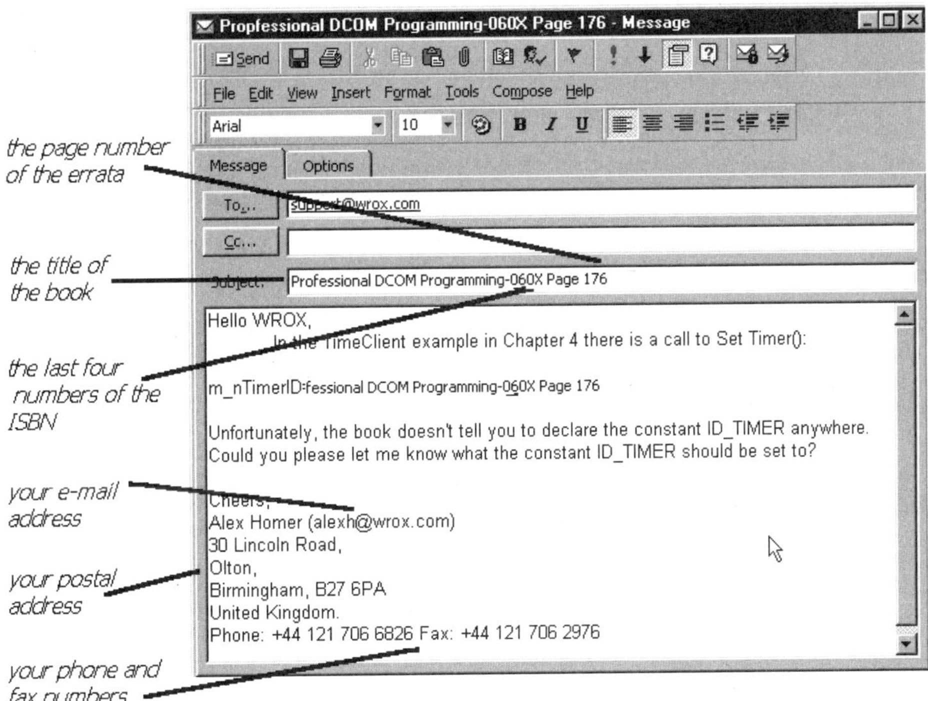

We won't send you junk mail. We need the details to save your time and ours. If we need to replace a disk or CD we'll be able to get it to you straight away. When you send an e-mail it will go through the following chain of support:

Customer Support

Your message is delivered to one of our customer support staff who are the first people to read it. They have files on most frequently asked questions and will answer anything general immediately. They answer general questions about the book and the web site.

Editorial

Deeper queries are forwarded to the technical editor responsible for that book. They have experience with the programming language or particular product and are able to answer detailed technical questions on the subject. Once an issue has been resolved, the editor can post the errata to the web site.

The Authors

Finally, in the unlikely event that the editor can't answer your problem, s/he will forward the request to the author. We try to protect the author from any distractions from writing. However, we are quite happy to forward specific requests to them. All Wrox authors help with the support on their books. They'll mail the customer and the editor with their response, and again all readers should benefit.

What we can't answer

Obviously with an ever growing range of books and an ever-changing technology base, there is an increasing volume of data requiring support. While we endeavor to answer all questions about the book, we can't answer bugs in your own programs that you've adapted from our code. So, while you might have loved the help desk systems in our Active Server Pages book, don't expect too much sympathy if you cripple your company with a live adaptation you customized from Chapter 12. But do tell us if you're especially pleased with the routine you developed with our help.

How to tell us exactly what you think

We understand that errors can destroy the enjoyment of a book and can cause many wasted and frustrated hours, so we seek to minimize the distress that they can cause.

You might just wish to tell us how much you liked or loathed the book in question. Or you might have ideas about how this whole process could be improved. In which case you should e-mail `feedback@wrox.com`. You'll always find a sympathetic ear, no matter what the problem is. Above all you should remember that we do care about what you have to say and we will do our utmost to act upon it.

Index

Symbols

A

D

E

F

G

H

I

J

N

O

T

U

V